A HISTORY
OF
THE SOCIETY OF GRAPHICAL
AND
ALLIED TRADES

A HISTORY
OF
THE SOCIETY OF
GRAPHICAL AND
ALLIED TRADES

JOHN GENNARD

Professor of Human Resource Management
Strathclyde Business School
and

PETER BAIN

Lecturer in Human Resource Management
Strathclyde Business School

First published 1995
by Routledge
11 New Fetter Lane, London EC4P 4EE

Simultaneously published in the USA and Canada
by Routledge
29 West 35th Street, New York, NY 10001

Typeset in 11/13 Times Ten by Florencetype Ltd, Stoodleigh, Devon
Printed and bound in Great Britain by Redwood Books

Printed on acid free paper

British Library Cataloguing in Publication Data

A catalogue record for this book is available from the British Library

Library of Congress Cataloging in Publication Data

A catalogue record for this book has been requested

ISBN 0–415–13076-X (hbk)
ISBN 0–415–13077–8 (pbk)

CONTENTS

CONTENTS

CHAPTER 11   THE FINANCIAL STRUCTURE DEVELOPMENTS

PART III: THE WIDER TRADE UNION AND LABOUR MOVEMENT

CHAPTER 12   RELATIONS WITH WIDER PRINT UNION BODIES

CONTENTS

CONTENTS

CONTENTS

CONTENTS

LIST OF FIGURES AND TABLES

FIGURES AND TABLES

PREFACE

In November 1990 I was approached by the National Executive Council of the Society of Graphical and Allied Trades (1982) with an invitation to write a history of the Society. In May of that year its Biennial Delegate Council had voted overwhelmingly to accept the package for an amalgamation with the National Graphical Association (1982) to form in July 1991 the Graphical, Paper and Media Union. The Society of Graphical and Allied Trades (SOGAT) with a history going back to the 1760s would cease to be an independent trade union. The National Executive Council considered the time was right to commission their union's official history. I was pleased to accept the National Executive Council's invitation.

My objective has been to update Bundock's official history of the National Union of Printing, Bookbinding and Paperworkers and then to describe and analyse the evolution and development of SOGAT over the period 1966 to 1991. The Society has given me open access to all its records and an entirely free hand to write the history as I found it. Any views expressed in this history are entirely my own, without any influence or censorship by the Society.

I have arranged the history in four parts. The first deals with the NUPB&PW/SOGAT relationship with other printing unions and the formation of SOGAT in 1966, its break-up in 1972 and the formation of SOGAT (75) and then SOGAT (82). It concludes with an analysis of the factors leading SOGAT (82) and NGA (82) to form the Graphical, Paper and Media Union. The second part deals with the decision-making and financial structure of NUPB&PW and SOGAT whilst the third part describes and analyses their relationship with the Printing and Kindred Trades Federation, the International Graphical Federation, the International Chemical, Energy and General Workers' Union, the International Federation of Commercial, Clerical, Professional and Technical Employees, the Trades Union Congress, the Scottish Trades Union Congress and the Labour Party. The final part deals with relationships with employers in the general printing industry, provincial newspapers, papermaking and paper conversion, national newspapers and ink manufacturing and covers, *inter alia*, wages, hours of work, holidays, pensions and equality issues. This approach, however, is not without its limitations in that it involves overlapping and any division into separate compartments is unreal.

The history has been written from NUPB&PW/SOGAT official records – National Executive Council minutes, delegate meeting reports, branch circulars, rule books and monthly journals – and interviews with past leading national and branch officials. In addition, the annual reports of the Printing and Kindred Trades Federation, the Trades Union Congress and the Labour Party have provided a great deal of information. The reports of the three post Second World War Royal Commissions on the Press, Courts of Inquiry into printing industry disputes and government and quasi-government bodies, including these covering papermaking, have also been important sources of information. C.J. Bundock's history of the National Union of Printing, Bookbinding and Paperworkers has been a rich and indispensable source of reference as has J. Moran's history of the first 75 years of existence of the National Society of Operative Printers and Assistants.

I wish to express my great appreciation of the kindness and constant helpfulness of Brenda Dean (General Secretary), Danny Sargeant (President), Ted Chard, Bob Gillespie and Teddy O'Brien (National Officers).

A huge debt of gratitude is owed to Mrs Deborah Cadenhead who diligently and cheerfully word processed numerous drafts of the manuscript.

Lastly, research work inevitably impinges upon family life, and thanks for understanding in this matter are due to Anne, John and Julie Gennard.

JOHN GENNARD

FOREWORD

Benjamin Franklin writing in the mid-eighteenth century said,

> Historians relate not so much what is done as what they would
> have believed.

In this rich and informative study, Professor John Gennard has conscientiously borne Franklin's implicit warning in mind and confined
himself to writing a factual and analytical account of events based on
the hard evidence which explains the growth and development of one
of the oldest and proudest trade unions within the British Trade Union
and Labour movement.

When SOGAT and the NGA finally reached agreement to merge
to create a single trade union for the paper, printing and media industries in the UK in 1990, an important chapter in the history of print
trade unionism in Britain came to an end, and the Executive Council
of SOGAT thought it appropriate to invite Professor Gennard to
produce a history of SOGAT for the period 1955 – the date that
Bundock used to conclude his detailed study of the National Union
of Printing, Bookbinding and Paperworkers – to 1991, when SOGAT's
period as an independent trade union ended and it amalgamated with
its sister union, the National Graphical Association, to form the
Graphical, Paper, and Media Union.

SOGAT's National Executive wanted something more than a mere
internal commemorative history, indeed they took the view that the
experiences of the men and women who made up SOGAT's membership during the period deserved a serious piece of scholarship which
would be of interest not only to SOGAT members but to students
and scholars of industrial relations and labour history who wished to
understand how our industry and its system of industrial relations
underwent a dramatic transformation during the second half of the
twentieth century – fuelled by those great motors of change, politics,
economics and technological innovation.

The National Executive therefore in November 1990, approached
Professor John Gennard from the Strathclyde Business School at the

FOREWORD

University of Strathclyde – who has spent over a quarter of a century analysing industrial relations within the UK printing, packaging, and papermaking industries, with an invitation to produce SOGAT's official history. Over the last four years, Professor Gennard has worked diligently, combining the more traditional approaches to historical research with oral history techniques, which has resulted in this remarkable volume. Professor Gennard has exercised great discipline in confining his methodology to an examination and analysis of the voluminous written sources which he has compared in an easy symbiosis with the many oral accounts that he was able to elicit from officers and members who took part in the great events that are related in his book.

Professor Gennard's technique, therefore, has resulted in a delightful and remarkable book, which examines both critically and sympathetically, not just the history of a movement and a union – but of two industries – printing and paper and board – both of which have played, and continue to play, a major contribution to the British economy. It is also a tribute to the many men and women who throughout the history of the union, by their major contribution and commitment to build an association of workers to hand on to future generations, have left their mark, not for their own self-satisfaction but for the improvement of conditions for their colleagues.

SOGAT has given every assistance to Professor Gennard in the compilation of the book, and our vast archives were made freely available to him. One of the conditions on which Professor Gennard accepted his mammoth task was an understanding that we could not seek to interfere, edit or influence the content or analysis contained in the final manuscript. We agreed willingly, and are proud to be associated with a well-written and meticulously researched piece of work, which we have no doubt will stand the test of time and become an obligatory text on the reading lists of students engaged within the field of industrial relations or labour history for many years to come.

National Executive Council

MAIN ABBREVIATIONS USED AND NOTES ON THE TEXT

ABBREVIATIONS

The acronyms in this list cover all the key unions, other organisations and establishments relevant to the text. Individual union branches and divisions, however, are not included here.

ANMW	Association of Newspaper and Magazine Wholesalers
ASLP	Amalgamated Society of Lithographic Printers and Auxiliaries
ATFEF	Advertising, Typesetting and Foundry Employers' Federation
BBF	British Bag Federation
BBPA	British Box and Packaging Association
BCA	British Carton Association
BFMP	British Federation of Master Printers
BFPA	British Fibreboard and Packaging Association
BPBA	British Paper Box Association
BPCC	British Printing Communications Corporation
CAWU	Clerical and Administrative Workers' Union
EETPU	Electrical, Electronic, Telecommunications/Plumbing Union
EFCGU	European Federation of Chemical and General Workers
EFTA	European Free Trade Area
EGF	European Graphical Federation
FIET	International Federation of Commercial, Clerical, Professional and Technical Employees
FLWND	Federation of London Wholesale Newspaper Distributors
FPCA	Fibreboard Packing Case Association

GMBATU	General Municipal Boilermakers' and Allied Trades' Union
GPMU	Graphical, Paper and Media Union
ICEF	International Federation of Chemical, Energy and General Workers
ICF	International Federation of Chemical and General Workers
IGF	International Graphical Federation
IPC	International Publishing Corporation
IPL	International Printers Ltd
LSC	London Society of Compositors
LTS	London Typographical Society
MCC	Maxwell Communications Corporation
MCTS	Monotype Casters and Typefounders' Society
MSMEA	Multi-wall Sack Manufacturers Employers' Association
NALGO	National and Local Government Officers' Association
NATSOPA	National Society of Operative Printers and Assistants
NBPI	National Board for Prices and Incomes
NGA	National Graphical Association
NPA	Newspaper Proprietors' Association
NPIPFS	Newspaper and Printing Industries' Pension Fund Scheme
NS	Newspaper Society
NSPWSND	National Society of Provincial Wholesale Sunday Newspaper Distributors
NUJ	National Union of Journalists
NUM	National Union of Mineworkers
NUPATW	National Union of Printing and Allied Trade Workers
NUPB&PW	National Union of Printing, Bookbinding and Paperworkers
NUPE	National Union of Public Employees
NUWDAT	National Union of Wallcoverings, Decorative and Allied Trades
P&KTF	Printing and Kindred Trades' Federation
PEC	Packaging Employers' Federation
PMMTS	Printing Machine Managers' Trade Society
PWNDA	Provincial Wholesale Newspaper Distributors' Association
RAGA	Reproductive and Graphics Association
SBPIM	Society of British Printing Ink Manufacturers

SDNS	Scottish Daily Newspaper Society
SGA	Scottish Graphical Association
SLADE	Society of Lithographic Artists, Designers, Engravers and Process Workers
SOGAT	Society of Graphical and Allied Trades
SMPS	Society of Master Printers of Scotland
SPEF	Scottish Printing Employers' Federation
STA	Scottish Typographical Association
STUC	Scottish Trades Union Congress
TA	Typographical Association
T&GWU	Transport and General Workers' Union
TEC	Training and Enterprise Council
TUC	Trades Union Congress
USDAW	Union of Shop, Distributive and Allied Workers
YOPS	Youth Opportunities Scheme
YTS	Youth Training Scheme

NOTES ON THE TEXT

(1) Any money referred to pre-decimalisation (February 1971) has been converted from pounds, shillings and pence into decimal pounds and pence.

(2) Imperial tons and metric tonnes have been reported faithfully as they appear in individual sources. No attempt has been made to convert from imperial to metric measure or vice versa.

(3) When SOGAT and the Scottish Graphical Association amalgamated in 1975 they formed SOGAT (75). When NATSOPA and SOGAT (75) amalgamated in 1982 they formed SOGAT (82). When the NGA and SLADE amalgamated in 1982 they formed NGA (82). These legal titles – SOGAT (75), SOGAT (82) and NGA (82) – have been used only where they are essential to understanding. In general the dates have been omitted as the unions were always referred to by members and officials as SOGAT and the NGA respectively.

The publisher has been assured that all quoted material, unless otherwise indicated, has come from the SOGAT archive housed at the modern records library at the University of Warwick and can be accessed there for further reference.

CHAPTER 1

THE PRINTING AND PAPERMAKING INDUSTRIES IN 1955 AND 1991

The Society of Graphical and Allied Trades (SOGAT) was formed on 1 February 1966 with the amalgamation of the National Union of Printing, Bookbinding and Paperworkers (NUPB&PW)[1] and the National Society of Operative Printers and Assistants (NATSOPA). The former, created in 1921, was a merger of the National Union of Bookbinders and Machine Rulers[2] and the National Union of Printing and Paperworkers. This latter union had been formed in 1914 by a marriage of the National Union of Paper Mill Workers and the National Amalgamated Society of Printer's Warehousemen and Cutters.[3] The National Society of Operative Printers and Assistants had been formed in London in 1889 as the Printers' Labourers' Union for assistants in the machine rooms.[4]

The problems of devising a constitution for SOGAT proved insurmountable (see Chapter 5) and in 1972 the amalgamation was dissolved. The NUPB&PW retained the title, SOGAT, but NATSOPA adopted the title the National Society of Operative Printers, Graphical and Media Personnel.[5] On 1 October 1975 SOGAT amalgamated with the Scottish Graphical Association[6] to form SOGAT (75). In 1981 SOGAT (75) began amalgamation talks with NATSOPA which resulted in the formation of SOGAT (82) on 5 July 1982. In 1984 SOGAT (82) began amalgamation talks with the National Graphical Association (82)[7] which led on 30 September 1991 to the formation of the Graphical, Paper and Media Union (the GPMU).

This history examines the development of the Society of Graphical and Allied Trades and its constituent unions over the period 1 January

1955 to 30 September 1991. Its starting point is that at which Bundock concluded his History of the National Union of Printing, Bookbinding and Paperworkers, the bulk of whose membership was employed in the general printing trade followed by papermaking and newspapers. Today these industries are very different to the mid-1950s in terms of their production techniques, their product markets and their skills structures. To understand the development of the NUPB&PW/ SOGAT over the past 36 years a comparison of the environment in which the NUPB&PW operated in 1955 with that of SOGAT (82) in 1991 is the starting point.

THE INDUSTRIES IN 1955

Product Sectors, Processes and Tasks

The Printing Industry

Product Sectors

In 1955 the printing industry divided into a number of subsectors in all of which the NUPB&PW had members. First there was the 'general print' sector which employed the majority (60 per cent) of NUPB&PW members. This sector included firms specialising in security printing, packaging and stationery, catalogues, banknotes, maps, cards, tickets, books, magazines and periodicals. In 1955 over 3,500 periodicals were published in the United Kingdom. A second sector was the provincial press in which were to be found 10 per cent of NUPB&PW members and which consisted of companies producing daily morning and evening papers, and bi-weekly and tri-weekly newspapers. There were in Great Britain 25 daily morning newspapers with a total circulation of three million copies and 75 daily evening newspapers selling in total over seven million copies. The provincial press was dominated by four national chains – Lord Rothermere, Lord Thomson,[8] Cowdry[9] and Drayton.[10] A third sector was national newspapers which produced ten national daily morning newspapers with a total circulation of 16.2 million and ten national Sunday newspapers with a total circulation of 15.3 million.[11] Ten per cent of NUPB&PW members were employed in this sector. The national morning press was dominated by Beaverbrook Newspapers, the Rothermere Group and the Mirror–Pictorial–Odhams Group. National Sunday press ownership was also

2

concentrated into three groups – Beaverbook, the Mirror–Pictorial and News of the World Ltd – who between them owned seven of the ten national Sundays. In addition three London evening newspapers had a total circulation of 3.2 million.

A fourth sector was the wholesale distribution of the printed products which NUPB&PW members had helped produce. Some 4 per cent of NUPB&PW members were to be found in this sector. National newspapers were distributed throughout the UK (except for London) by rail to appropriate points where they were collected and distributed to retail newsagents. In 1955 there were 25 wholesale distributors of daily national newspapers in London and over 200 in England and Wales. In both the provinces and London there were many independent wholesalers coexisting with large wholesale companies such as WH Smith Ltd, Wyman & Sons Ltd and Surridge Dawsons.[12] In London each national newspaper delivered its papers directly to the wholesalers. In Scotland, wholesale distribution was dominated by John Menzies & Co. However, D.C. Thomson and John Leng who published morning, evening, Sunday and weekly newspapers in Dundee and Glasgow, handled their own distribution to retailers.

The distribution of national Sunday newspapers was largely carried out by different wholesalers than for national dailies. Sunday national newspaper wholesalers, were mainly small family owned businesses many of which operated only one day per week. The Sunday wholesale national newspapers trade was always regarded as a separate trade from that of national daily newspaper wholesaling.

Printing Processes and Stages

In 1955 of the three main printing processes – letterpress, lithography and gravure – letterpress dominated. Of the 144,000 NUPB&PW members, 75 per cent were employed in printing firms which used the letterpress process. This used type or blocks to produce the printing image which stood out on a raised surface. Letterpress required print origination based on composing machines that manipulated hot metal or work based on metal but produced by hand. Lithographic printing used a plate on which the printing and non-printing parts were on the same level but the latter were kept damp and free from ink. Litho machines required print origination based on machines that processed film. Photogravure printing used cylinders on which the image was etched. Letterpress and lithographic printing were carried out either on flat bed machines, in which the type or plate remained stationary, or rotary machines, in which the type was attached to revolving cylinders. Gravure printing was predominantly by rotary machines. Printing machines were fed by single sheets of paper or by a web of paper which, after printing, could be cut into individual sheets or folded into sections of a book or periodical, etc.

(i) Typesetting and plate-making   The main stages of production in a printing and publishing house were typesetting, plate-making, printing, finishing, warehousing and despatching, all of which were supported by management, administrative, technical and clerical functions. Some typesetters arranged separate letters to form words and lines of text whilst others used keyboards which operated a casting machine which either produced each line of type in a metal slug or produced paper type which operated a caster which in turn outputted lines made up of separate letters. The typesetters' work was checked and corrected by a reader. In newspapers, page make-up was also done by the typesetters. Copy holders read copy prepared by typesetters whilst revisers corrected proofs for final errors. The plate-making departments produced the printing surfaces. A plate was required for all litho work but for much letterpress work the assembled metal type provided the printing surface. Most large letterpress printers and newspapers made their own blocks and plates but for smaller companies this work was often contracted out to specialist trade houses.

(ii) Printing   The actual printing took place in the press department. In the printing industry some 85 per cent of machine managers and assistants were working letterpress machines. In newspapers the proportion was as high as 90 per cent. Litho machines were mainly confined to the general printing sector. Letterpress and litho printing machines were controlled by machine managers some of whom were members of the NUPB&PW and who were responsible for the quality of the job. They worked with a number of assistants who were either members of the NUPB&PW or NATSOPA (see Chapter 2). The brake-hand was the most senior assistant with responsibility for the speed, tension and braking of the press. Oilers lubricated the machines, fitted and removed metal plates and assisted webbing and rewebbing in the case of web-fed presses. General assistants cleaned the presses, removed copies and waste emerging from the machines and in some national newspaper offices transported the reel of paper to the press. On average, letterpress rotary machines required four times as many assistants as litho presses.

(iii) Finishing, warehousing and despatch   Before printing, the tasks undertaken by NUPB&PW members in the general printing trade sector included finishing, warehousing, despatching, stitching and cutting of paper. After the printing process tasks included folding, counting, collating, gathering, stitching, binding, trimming, packing and despatch. A high proportion of this work was done by hand by semi-skilled or unskilled workers, most of whom were women. However, automatic folders were in use whilst collating/gathering, stitching, wire stapling, trimming and binding were becoming automated.

In 1955 hand binding craft skills of NUPB&PW members were found only in establishments catering for high-quality, special presentation books. The vast majority of books were bound by machine. The first stage in bookbinding was the mechanical folding of large paper sheets into sections. However, this work was done by hand if it was unusually difficult or if the number of sheets to be bound was small. In the second stage the book was gathered together in the proper order and then sewn mechanically. The book was then sent for 'forwarding' which included smoothing its edge, coating glue on its backs and, in the case of quality books, glueing a strip of strong paper to it to make it more rigid. Meanwhile a case which was to cover the book was produced manually. The lettering of the case was done in a blocking press and the book's binding completed by a casing-in machine which brought together the book and its case.

Binding of stationery and machine ruling was used, for example, in the production of school exercise books and ledgers used in banks and offices. The buyers of ledgers required them to last for a long time and the strongest materials, such as leather, webbing tape and thread were used in their production which was predominantly by hand. Machine ruling, in which accuracy was important, was done either by pens or discs. On a pen-ruling machine, paper was fed onto a blanket which carried it under the press which ruled the paper as it travelled along. On a disc-ruling machine, paper was carried by a cylinder and was ruled by discs pressing against its surface.

Printing firms kept large stocks of paper cared for by warehousemen who knew all the papers' different sizes and qualities, how the papers could be matched for a job and how to cut the paper to the right sizes. Warehousemen counted the correct amounts of paper required for a job and then delivered it to the printing department. There were also printed-sheet warehouses where sheets sent from the machine room were checked and stored after printing until required for a further operation, such as bookbinding, for example. The printed sheets, which were cut on a guillotine machine, were stored away and their number, description and position recorded in a stock book. Work in despatching in the general print sector involved the receipt, wrapping, labelling and despatch of the printed product. The bulk of these tasks were done mechanically. However, in national newspapers despatching included hand loading of bundles of newspapers onto vans and lorries for transportation to railway terminals or for collection by wholesalers.

(iv) Wholesaling In 1955 in the wholesale distribution of newspapers, periodicals, magazines and trade publications, two main tasks carried out by NUPB&PW members were packing and driving. Packing was labour-intensive, and with almost everything done by hand the pace of work was intense. Wholesale distribution involved a large permanent work-force supplemented by casual labour as and when required. The publishers' drivers took the newspapers, magazines, periodicals, etc. from the publishers to the wholesalers' warehouses where packers made up parcels to be delivered to each individual retail newsagent. In the wholesale distribution of national newspapers time was of the essence as the product was highly perishable. In London the national morning and Sunday newspapers were collected by 22 wholesalers from the printing works and taken to warehouses where they were sorted into parcels and then delivered to some 7,000 retail newsagents. Wholesalers sought to complete their packaging by 5.00 a.m., but if one of the national papers was late this delayed all London morning papers as they had to go all together in one parcel.

National newspapers printed in London to be sold in the rest of the UK were delivered by the publishers to the appropriate rail terminal. In some cases the newspapers were then taken by train, unpacked to another rail head where they were collected by the wholesalers' drivers and taken to a warehouse, packed into individual parcels and then delivered to each retail newsagent. In other cases wholesale distribution was based on a system of train packers. National newspapers were driven from Fleet Street to a main rail station then loaded into special newspaper packing vans for delivery to the provinces. These vans were fitted with tables and fluorescent lighting. As the train travelled along the track, packers employed by member firms of the Provincial Wholesale Newspaper Distributors' Association broke down the bundles and remade them into parcels for each individual retail newsagent to be dropped off at the appropriate railway station.

Papermaking and Paper Conversion

Product Sectors

A second major industry in which the NUPB&PW had members was papermaking and paper conversion, in which there were a number of subsectors. First, NUPB&PW members were involved in the manufacture of newsprint, writing and printing paper, tissues, industrial and special purpose papers. There were 200 mills producing paper and board in an industry characterised by a small number of large companies operating big mills alongside a number of small firms. In 1955 over half of the UK paper and board output was produced by five large groups – the Bowater Paper Corporation, the Reed Paper Group, the Wiggins Teape Group, Thames Board Mills and the Inversk Group. Bowater was the largest producer of newsprint in the world whilst the Reed Paper Group was the largest UK producer of paper and board. UK production of paper and board at 4 million tons per annum made the UK was the largest paper producer in Europe and the fourth largest in the world.

A second sector in which NUPB&PW members were to be found was the production of rigid boxes and cartons. Rigid boxes were despatched, made up and ready for use with their corners stitched or glued to form a rigid, upright box with a separate hinged lid, as seen, for example, in pill boxes. Cartons differed in that they did not have a separate lid and were erected by the customer. Rigid box production was dominated by small firms and was concentrated in London and the Midlands. Carton firms were usually located close to their main customers, e.g. the tobacco industry.

A third sector employing NUPB&PW members was fibreboard packaging. This was produced from sheets of board or from a layer of corrugated paper between outside layers of board. The edges were glued, taped or stitched together to form a rigid structure but the cases were normally produced and delivered flat. Fibreboard cases were stronger than cartons and thus were used for transporting bulky items. Fibreboard packaging enabled the product inside to remain identifiable, protected from hazards and deliverable in factory-fresh form. The sector was dominated by large firms e.g. Reed Corrugated, Bowater and Thames Board Mills.

A fourth sector containing NUPB&PW members was paper bag and multi-wall sack manufacture. The Trade Boards/Paper Bag Order (1919) defined this sector as the manufacture from paper of any bag or container without a gummed flap, including any printing carried out in the course of the production process. Paper bags in 1955 were produced mainly for use in the retail distribution sector. The stronger multi-wall sacks introduced in the 1920s were used for carrying cement, fertilisers and animal feedstuffs. Paper bag and multi-wall sack manufacturing was dominated by small firms.

Production Processes and Stages

There were seven steps in the papermaking process. The first stage was pulping. Wood pulp was produced mechanically or chemically or by a combination of both depending on the type of pulp required. The second stage was stock preparation during which the fibres were dispersed in water. Mechanical treatment then modified the physical characteristics of the fibres. The third stage was sheet formation, during which the fibres were diluted further and then filtered through a screen or sieve to make a uniform layer or sheet of wet paper.

The fourth stage was couching, whereby the wet sheet of paper was separated from the screen to leave an unwrinkled wet sheet of paper. The fifth stage in the process was pressing, during which the couched paper was placed in contact with a woven cloth and pressed to remove excess water. The sixth stage was the drying process, whereby the moist paper was removed from the felt and dried. In the final stage the dried paper was appropriately treated to produce the required quality of paper which was then cut or slit to the required dimensions, inspected, packed, labelled and finally despatched.

Pulp-making and papermaking were separate processes in the UK but in Canada and the Scandinavian countries they were integrated in large combined plants. The UK papermaking industry needed to consume annually over 2 million tons of wood pulp, nearly all of which was imported, and one million tons of home-produced paper. In paper and board production NUPB&PW members were employed on direct manufacture from the arrival of the raw materials to the despatch of the finished paper and board. In addition to these process tasks, there were those concerned with the repair and maintenance of machinery, equipment, power and buildings. A third group of tasks were performed by staff employees involved in management, research, development, administration, sales and clerical work. The process manual worker jobs were graded into four categories according to skill. Around a quarter of the tasks associated with papermaking were carried out by skilled male workers and their assistants.

Carton-making involved large-scale production with mechanical cutting, creasing and folding and the carton board being printed on directly. The cutting and creasing of the carton sheets was carried out by 'formes' press machines. By 1955 the box carton sector was becoming automated and more employees were undertaking either machine minder or machine assistant tasks. Those NUPB&PW members engaged in forme-making and setting, cutting and creasing, rotary cutting, fancy box making, bending machines and guillotines claimed they were as skilled as printers.

Paper bags and sacks were produced from sheets or from reels of paper. A bag-making machine applied adhesive to form an endless tube which was then cut to the required length with an adhesive base being added. Multi-wall sacks were sealed, stitched, sewn and glued by automatic bottoming machines. Other important tasks in producing multi-wall sacks included cutting and slitting, hydraulic pressing, stock keeping, packaging and despatching.

Employment, Trade Unions and Employers' Organisations

The Printing Industry

Employment

In 1955 the printing industry was dominated by small firms, many of which were family owned. The majority of firms in membership of the British Federation of Master Printers employed under 25 people. Less than 3 per cent employed 300 or more. Newspaper firms were larger and over two-thirds of these employed more than 25. London, with over 1,000 firms engaged in the general print trade, was the dominant centre. Of the 144,000 members of the NUPB&PW, 65,000 were members of its four main London branches.

By 1955 there were 375,000 employees in the printing industry, of which 35 per cent were employed in the printing and publishing of newspapers and periodicals. Some 80 per cent of men and 87 per cent of women in the craft and non-craft categories of cutters, binders and warehouse workers – all NUPB&PW areas – were employed in the general printing and book sections. Of male packaging and despatch workers (NUPB&PW members) 40 per cent were in the newspaper and periodical sectors. The remaining craft and non-craft cutters, binders and warehouse workers were employed in the periodical and stationery sectors. The general printing and stationery sectors employed over 22,000 women, most of them NUPB&PW members, with few skills on hand finishing work. In the general print sector, NUPB&PW organised skilled, semi-skilled and women workers and had to balance the interests of each group which, in a number of ways, but especially in wage bargaining, were in conflict with each other.

Trade Unions

In 1955 there were 12 major trade unions in the printing industry with a total membership of 319,000. The demarcation of jobs between them was clear. In letterpress the craft typesetting functions involved five unions of which two were confined to London and one to Scotland.[13] The Monotype Casters and Typefounders' Society (MCTS) catered for monotype caster attendants in London and part of the English and Welsh provinces.[14] Monotype operators were members of the London Typographical Society (LTS), the Typographical Association (TA) and the Scottish Typographical Association (STA). The largest craft union in the industry was the Typographical Association which organised 62,000 compositors, caster attendants, readers and machine managers in the English provinces, Wales, Northern Ireland and the Irish Republic other than Dublin. In composing rooms, linotype assistants, copy holders and revisers were organised by NATSOPA and proof pullers by the NUPB&PW. The transmission and receiving of text and pictures by electronic means for inclusion in newspapers and journals was the preserve of the National Union of Press Telegraphists[15] whilst the production of information in written form for inclusion in newspapers, journals and periodicals was undertaken by members of the National Union of Journalists. In lithography origination was controlled by the Society of Lithographic Artists, Designers, Engravers and Process Workers (SLADE).

The production of plates for letterpress printing was undertaken by members of the National Society of Electrotypers and Stereotypers. Provers in the process and foundry departments of national newspapers were organised by either the Printing Machine Branch (PMB) of the NUPB&PW or SLADE. Letterpress machine managers in London were organised by the LTS, in Scotland by the STA and in the rest of the UK by the TA. The LTS did not control all the machine rooms in London and in some houses, for example in the *News of the World*, control lay with NATSOPA, and in others the PMB had a presence. These situations had arisen because the London machine managers originally regarded rotary and platen machines as not being within their jurisdiction. By the time the London machine managers realised the situation, NATSOPA in the case of rotary presses and the NUPB&PW in the case of platen presses, had gained control in some houses and were not then prepared to give it up.[16] In lithography, plate making and printing was controlled by the Amalgamated Society of Lithographic Printers (ASLP).

Assistants in the machine room in both the letterpress and litho printing process were organised in some towns by NATSOPA and in others by the NUPB&PW. In the general print sectors and in newspapers in the bindery, warehouse and despatch departments the same situation prevailed. For many years the custom had operated of referring to 'NATSOPA' and 'Paperworker' towns. In a Paperworker town those employed in the bindery, warehouse, despatch and white-paper departments, in addition to men and women in the machine room, were NUPB&PW members. In NATSOPA towns men and women employed in the warehouse, despatch and white-paper departments and those in the printing machine room were NATSOPA members. However, there were certain exceptions to these generalisations. For instance, motor drivers in general printing houses, employees working under the bindery and stationery agreements and employees in box-making were members of the NUPB&PW irrespective of whether employed in a NATSOPA or Paperworker town. On the other hand, in Paperworker towns all those employed in newspaper machine rooms were members of NATSOPA. In addition, there was 'the London set-up' under which all employees in the bindery and the warehouse were NUPB&PW members whilst assistants in the printing machine rooms were NATSOPA members. These complex spheres of influence between the Paperworkers and NATSOPA did not apply in Scotland and Northern Ireland.

The individual printing unions jealously guarded their autonomy but realised the need to speak collectively on many matters and to have a means of resolving their inter-union difficulties. In 1901 the printing unions formed the Printing and Kindred Trades' Federation (P&KTF) to co-ordinate their activities.[17] In 1955 the Federation had 16 affiliated unions with a total membership of 320,525.[18] Its objectives included the establishment of uniform working conditions in different branches of the industry, the co-ordination of union policies, the prevention and settlement of disputes and securing unity of action amongst affiliated unions. It acted for the printing unions on matters of common interest and spoke collectively on their behalf to the TUC and the central government and conducted research and inquiry work for its affiliated unions either collectively or individually. However, the Federation's constitution stated that 'the Federation shall not interfere in the internal management of any union, nor its rules and customs'. Nevertheless, it had been given powers to settle demarcation disputes between affiliated unions via an arbitration board.

Employers' Associations

In 1955, the major employers' organisation in the UK in the general printing sector was the British Federation of Master Printers (BFMP). Founded in 1900, its members were engaged in general printing, periodicals, magazines, books, etc. It comprised 12 regional bodies, known as 'Alliances' which varied greatly in the number of associations and firms they represented. The Federation had in excess of 4,000 member firms which employed over 85 per cent of the total employees engaged in the general printing industry. It negotiated on employment terms and conditions.

The Newspaper Society (NS), founded in 1895, represented the proprietors of the provincial morning, evening and weekly newspapers in England, Wales and Northern Ireland, as well as weekly newspapers published in London. The Society had some 350 members who had 290 newspaper plants. Some Newspaper Society members undertook general printing and were also members of the BFMP. In 1955 member firms of the NS employed 20,000 production employees. In Scotland the Scottish Daily Newspaper Society, established in 1915, represented the interests of publishers of daily newspapers in Scotland, whilst the Scottish Newspaper Proprietors' Association conducted the same functions as the NS with respect to Scottish weekly and bi-weekly newspaper publishers.

The Newspaper Proprietors' Association (NPA), formed in 1906, represented the national newspapers published in London and Manchester. Its member firms employed some 18,000 regular operative staff. Although on labour matters the NPA maintained informal contact with the BFMP and NS it conducted separate negotiations with the unions. NPA members considered their product so specialised they could not be associated with other branches of the industry. They considered themselves vulnerable to union action in a way that did not apply to the provincial press and the general print trade in that they produced a highly perishable product.

The Provincial Wholesale Newspaper Distributors' Association represented the interests of wholesale daily newspaper distributors in England (other than London) and Wales. Its member firms employed 4,350 regular operative staff for whom it negotiated terms and conditions of employment. The Federation of London Wholesale Newspaper Distributors represented the interests of daily newspaper wholesalers in London. Its member firms employed 1,000 regular staff supplemented by a significant number of casual staff recruited from the call system operated by the London Central Branch of the NUPB&PW. The Federation negotiated wages and other employment conditions. The Sunday Newspaper Distributing Association represented the interests of London Sunday national newspaper wholesalers. Its affiliated companies employed a regular staff of 1,000. It negotiated employment conditions. The National Society of Provincial Wholesale Sunday Newspaper Distributors represented the interests of Sunday national newspaper wholesalers in England (other than London), Scotland and Wales. Its member firms employed a regular manual work-force of 1,000. The Society negotiated wages and conditions of employment.

Papermaking and Paper Conversion

Employment

In 1955, the papermaking industry was dominated by eight large groups which controlled between them 62 mills. Coexisting with these firms were 125 small companies which owned 150 mills in total. The large groups accounted for 83 per cent of the market with the remainder divided between the small companies. Half the firms in the paper-making industry accounted for only 6 per cent of the total market.

In 1955 the papermaking industry employed 100,000 people. Supplies of clear water were essential to production and therefore mills tended to be located on or near rivers. In some places the mill dominated the village. The largest group of mills employing 16,100 of the industry's 71,000 manual workers was in the Thames estuary and the Medway with a second concentration of 4,000 manual workers in North West England and North Wales. There were 22,000 women employed in the papermaking industry.

In paper box the occupational structure was highly segregated between men and women whilst in rigid box it was a predominantly female work force which made up boxes on hand-fed machines. Men were employed as skilled machine minders, guillotine operators, dye or sample makers or unskilled labourers. In paper bag manufacture the majority of the 1,000 employees were women but the 3,000-strong work-force in multi-wall sack production was comprised roughly equal numbers of males and females. The skilled tasks were a male preserve whilst part-time working was common amongst female employees. The fibreboard packaging case industry, dominated by large firms, employed 11,000 people in 45 establishments. The average-sized enterprise employed 240 employees but even in the mid-1950s outworkers existed in this sector.

Trade Unions

In paper and board manufacturing the main process unions were the NUPB&PW, the Transport and General Workers' Union and the General and Municipal Workers' Union. Nearly 90 per cent of process manual workers were unionised and of these 80 per cent were members of the NUPB&PW. The main craft unions were the Amalgamated Union of Engineering Workers and the Electrical Trades Union. In 1948, the General and Municipal Workers conceded sole organising rights in papermaking to the NUPB&PW except for the few mills where it had had a long connection. In the rigid box sector unionisation was low although in the early 1950s NUPB&PW branches in several cities had established advisory committees aimed at improving the wages of box-making workers. Union density in the fibreboard packaging sector was high, with the NUPB&PW the dominant union. NATSOPA had members in this sector. Both the NUPB&PW and

NATSOPA had members in paper bag and multi-wall sack manufacture. The level of unionisation was highest amongst manual workers in the multi-wall sack sector.

Employers' Associations

In papermaking the main employers' association was the Employers' Federation of Papermakers and Boardmakers whose member firms employed 100,000 workers. It was responsible for co-ordinating the wages and conditions of work within the industry and conducting national negotiations with the main trade unions on behalf of its member companies.

The Fibreboard Packing Case Manufacturers' Association, founded in 1919, was dominated by large companies. The British Paper Box Association, formed in 1910, provided the employers' representatives to the Paper Box Wages Council established in 1910. As cartons and fibreboard packing cases increased in importance, separate employers' associations emerged for these trades, viz., the Fibreboard Packing Cases Manufacturers' Association in 1919 and the British Carton Association in 1935. It was mainly the large companies which joined these two organisations and small companies remained with the British Paper Box Association.[19] The British Paper Bag Federation provided the employer's representatives to the Paper Bag Wages Council established in 1919.

Industrial Relations Machinery and Procedures

The Printing Industry

General Print Sector and Provincial Newspapers

In 1955 there was no formal national negotiating machinery. *Ad hoc* arrangements existed whereby if one side wished to change the agreement it approached the other and if they were agreeable negotiations to amend the existing agreement took place. The BFMP and the Newspaper Society negotiated jointly with the print unions, including the NUPB&PW, on all matters except for pay. The P&KTF negotiated on behalf of its affiliates with the BFMP and NS on issues such as hours of work and holidays. In 1955 the working week in the general printing trade and the provincial newspaper industry was 43½ hours over five days and paid annual holidays were two weeks. This had been achieved in 1946 following a dispute between the P&KTF and the BFMP.[20]

In the general printing trade and provincial newspapers, individual unions negotiated national minimum wages agreements with the BMPF and the NS. Between 1947 and 1951 the BFMP and the NS unsuccessfully attempted to persuade the unions to co-ordinate their wages claims through the P&KTF rather than submit separate and unrelated claims. In this way it was hoped to achieve a stable wage structure. The print unions, including the NUPB&PW, favoured a stable wage structure but were unable to agree amongst themselves. They were divided over provincial craft parity, the London/provincial craft differential, provincial grading, the craft/non-craft differential, the male/female differential and the system of voting within the P&KTF to determine any co-ordinated wage claim. However, by early 1951 the general printing trade and provincial newspapers had arrived, via a tortuous path and a major industrial dispute between the London Society of Compositors[21] and the London Master Printers' Association, at an agreed wage structure to remain in being until November 1955. The 1951 Agreements with the separate unions all provided, in addition to the five-year stabilisation period, for house rates and merit money to be consolidated for a cost of living bonus and for the following basic weekly rates:

London craft	£7.75
Provincial craft	£7.17½
Provincial non-craft	£5.67½
Women	£3.80

Over the stabilisation period, the cost of living bonus added £1.65 to these rates to give by November 1955 a London craft rate of £9.40, a provincial craft rate of £8.82½, a provincial non-craft rate of £7.32½ and women's rate of £5.45.

In 1919, a Joint Industrial Council for the Printing Industry was established. It consisted of 40 members elected by the BFMP and the NS and 40 members elected by the P&KTF. The Council had no authority to negotiate wage agreements but it provided machinery for settling disputes via conciliation committees, for the selection and training of apprentices and learners and for provision of health and safety.

National Newspapers

In national newspapers there was no formal machinery for negotiating national agreements. *Ad hoc* arrangements existed. The P&KTF often co-ordinated claims by the separate print unions to the NPA on wages. However, on all other issues e.g. hours of work and holidays P&KTF negotiated on behalf of its affiliated unions. However, in collective approaches to the NPA each print union retained its autonomy and any wage agreement reached from such an approach had to be submitted by each union to its members for approval. Chapels also negotiated their own 'house' agreements with the result that actual earnings in Fleet Street bore little relationship to the National Agreement. In 1954 the NPA and the NUPB&PW, signed an Agreement, to terminate on 30 November 1957, which provided for the absorption of a cost of living bonus of £1.05 into basic rates, a cost of living bonus based on movements in the Index of Retail Prices and the addition of 12.5 per cent on the consolidated basic rate to provide a basic weekly rate of £12.01.

There was as yet no Joint Industrial Council (JIC) for national newspapers. In 1919 the NPA opposed the establishment of a JIC for the printing industry, arguing that its interests were distinct from those of general printers and that unlike provincial newspaper owners they had no commercial printing interests. In 1949, consideration had been given to the establishment of a JIC for National Newspapers following a dispute in 1948 in Manchester over a disturbance in the differentials between rates received by TA members employed in NPA offices and its members employed in NS offices. It was felt that if conciliation machinery, as operated by the JIC for the printing industry had existed, the dispute might have been avoided. Following discussions between the NPA and the unions a draft constitution was submitted envisaging dealing on a regular basis with health, welfare and conciliation in industrial disputes. The JIC would have no right to negotiate wages and employment conditions. The NUPB&PW, supported the formation of the JIC but three unions, including NATSOPA, were against. Since these three unions represented the majority of employees in national newspapers steps to establish a JIC ended.

Wholesale Distribution

In 1955 in newspaper and periodicals wholesale distribution there was only *ad hoc* machinery for negotiating collective agreements. The

NUPB&PW negotiated directly with the Provincial Wholesale Newspaper Distributors' Association (PWNDA) and the National Society of Provincial Wholesale Sunday Distributors. It held agreements with each of these Associations covering manual employees' basic pay, holidays, overtime and disputes procedures. In Scotland in the daily newspaper trade there was no industry-wide collective bargaining but the larger firms operated to the PWNDA/NUPB&PW agreement. Throughout provincial wholesale newspaper distribution, company-level bargaining was also well developed in 1955. There was little collective bargaining for white-collar employees.

In the early 1950s, the PWNDA had granted wage increases on condition that the NUPB&PW did not press its claim for both the five-day and five-night week. However, in 1955 an arbitrator awarded a five-shift week, not only for the full night workers but for those NUPB&PW members who commenced work between 4.00 a.m. and 6.00 a.m.[22] In 1955 PWNDA's members of the NUPB&PW on Grade I terms were receiving a weekly basic rate of £10.05 for indoor night workers and drivers and £9.82½ for indoor day workers and drivers.

In London there were two collective agreements covering wholesale distribution. One covered daily national newspapers and the other Sunday national newspapers. These agreements were negotiated between the NUPB&PW London Central Branch and the Federation of London Wholesale Newspaper Distributors and the London Central Branch and the Sunday Newspaper Distributing Association. The London Central Branch jealously guarded these agreements which covered, for manual employees, basic pay, holidays, overtime and disputes procedures. As in the provinces, these collective agreements were supplemented by company-level bargaining. In London there were few collective bargaining arrangements for non-manual employees employed in national newspaper wholesale distribution. In mid-1955, the London Central Branch and the Federation of London Wholesale Newspaper Distributors concluded an Agreement with retrospective effect from 29 November 1954 which provided a basic weekly rate for indoor day workers and drivers of £9.20 and for indoor night workers and drivers of £9.55. The Agreement was the first occasion on which the London Central Branch established a night-work differential.

Papermaking and Paper Conversion

Paper and Board

In 1955 there was no formal machinery for negotiating changes in National Agreements covering wages and other employment conditions. *Ad hoc* arrangements operated. A nation-wide collective Agreement (known as the No. 10 Agreement) covering manual workers existed between the Employers' Federation of Papermakers and Boardmakers and the NUPB&PW, TGWU and NUGMU. The agreement covered, *inter alia*, pay, holidays, overtime rates and consolidation of wartime bonuses into hourly basic rates. In 1954 standard weekly hours for day workers were reduced from 48 to 45 spread over a five-and-a-half-day working week whilst the hours of double day shift workers were reduced from 46 to 44. Annual holiday entitlement was two weeks. In 1955 the hourly rates were for adult males 22p for shift workers, 18p for day workers and 11p per hour for females.

A Joint Industrial Council for Paper and Boardmaking had existed since 1919. In 1943 a recognition and disputes procedure agreement provided a three-stage procedure for dealing with disputes. If matters could not be resolved at the mill level, then a 'district' conference took place involving local officers of the employers' federation and the unions. The final stage was an executive conference attended by national officials of the employers' organisation and the relevant trade unions.

Paper Box

In the paper box industry, terms and conditions of employment were determined by the Paper Box Wages Council established in 1910, which consisted of representatives of employers, the employees and three independent members nominated by government. Its function was to set minimum wage rates and conditions for the industry by majority decision of the council members. Most of the representatives came from the British Paper Box Association and the NUPB&PW. Only the employers' or the workers' side could initiate change in Wages Regulation Orders and the independent members acted as conciliators whose votes were cast in support of one side if no compromise solution could be found. The Minister of Labour approved settlements and had authority to refer issues back to the Wages Council. The Paper Box Wages Council had been established originally as a trade board and covered three types of packaging from paper and cardboard, viz, rigid boxes, cartons and fibreboard cases.[23] In the mid-1950s the minimum rates established by the Paper Box Wages Council were the highest of any wages council. In October 1955 the Minister of Labour approved minimum weekly wage rates of £8.50 for adult male workers and of £4.87½ for adult females.

Paper Bag

In paper bag manufacture, terms and conditions of employment were determined by the Paper Bag Wages Council established in 1919. It was still in existence in 1955 despite mounting pressure from the NUPB&PW for its abolition and replacement by voluntary negotiating machinery. The paper bag employers, like those in paper box manufacturing, opposed the abolition of the Wages Council, arguing that it provided stability in the industry. The NUPB&PW policy of wage parity between the paper bag industry and the printing industry achieved some success in 1955 when three large paper bag firms agreed to pay print wage rates. In the mid-1950s in the paper bag industry, as in paper box, the standard working week was 45 hours and employees were entitled to two weeks' paid holiday after one year's service. Wage rates in the paper bag industry tended in the 1950s to follow those in paper box making and at the end of 1955 weekly wage rates were £8.72½ for skilled workers, £7.15 for unskilled and £5.05 for women.

The Economic Environment

In 1955 the main priority of macro-economic policy was the maintenance of full-time employment. If this caused inflation, then governments regarded the appropriate economic policy response to be the introduction of wage restraints. There was also a consensus existing amongst the main political parties that collective bargaining was a desirable activity, that legal regulation of the industrial relations system be kept to a minimum and that the existing level of immunity for trade unions from legal action by employers when they called their members out on strike was balanced.

The Printing Industry

The 1950s saw rising production and employment in the printing industry. In the mid-1950s a major problem for the industry was an acute shortage of skilled labour. The craft unions resisted demands from the NUPB&PW and NATSOPA that this problem be tackled by permitting new methods of entry, including the upgrading of assistants, into the skilled occupations of the industry. Both the NUPB&PW and NATSOPA favoured a system of adult promotion whereby if assistants, particularly in the machine room, proved their suitability for upgrading they be eligible for training to become craft employees. In the face of craft opposition to the upgrading of assistants, the employers sought to overcome the skill shortage by trading increases in the pay and conditions of craft employees for increases in the number of apprentices permitted to enter the industry and by using existing craft employees more effectively.

However, the increased demand for print work in the 1950s brought problems to the printing unions. The labour supply problems in the industry often resulted in long delays in the completion of printing orders with the result that more work was sent abroad and many firms outside the industry established their own in-plant printing arrangements. By 1955 the share of the UK printing and publishing market accounted for by imports was just under 5 per cent. Newspaper production, however, remained sheltered from the pressures of foreign competition. Its main threat was the introduction of commercial television which was expected to make inroads into the amount of advertising material carried by newspapers.

Even in 1955 the growth in the use of miniature printing processes (for example multigraph and varitypers) by employers in local authorities, nationalised industries, banks and insurance companies posed a threat to the general printing trade. The printing unions, including the NUPB&PW, attempted to organise people engaged on miniature printing machines but they had little success. In 1955, where organisation of employees working miniature printing machines had been achieved, it had invariably been done by non-print unions. A problem in organising these workers was that they were receiving pay and conditions superior to those in the general printing industry. The problem of small office printing machines was to increase in future years but it remained somewhat hidden in 1955 whilst the conventional printing industry experienced full employment.

Papermaking and Paper Conversion

In the 1950s the UK papermaking industry faced increasing competition from imports, considerable surplus capacity, and a falling rate of return on capital. Rationalisation was taking place and employment security was falling. Import penetration was 30 per cent of total UK consumption of paper and board. The industry was disadvantaged relative to its international competitors. Papermaking and pulp-making were separate processes. In Canada and Scandinavia they were integrated, enabling these nations to produce at a cost of about 10 per cent less than was possible in the UK. The UK newsprint industry was also at a competitive disadvantage from the opening of new mills in Scandinavia which were partly financed by inter-governmental funds. However, these competitive handicaps were to some extent offset by an import tariff of 14 to 16.6 per cent on Scandinavian and other foreign paper imports.

The paper and board industry, with the exception of newsprint, had been protected since 1932. The early 1950s witnessed the reduction of this protection and the exposure of an industry whose efficiency had degenerated because of tariff barriers to increased international competitiveness. Many firms had failed to plough sufficient capital back into their businesses, whilst smaller plants operated obsolete plants. The lack of competition had kept production fragmented into small inefficient businesses. The exposing of the industry to international competition meant that by 1955 unemployment amongst NUPB&PW members in the papermaking industry was rising.

The mid-1950s also witnessed the implementation of new production techniques into the industry. Technological developments were to improve the quality of the product and enabled papermaking machines to run at more than twice their present speed and output. By 1955 the market for rigid boxes was already in decline due to increased competition from the emergence of new packaging materials such as plastics and foil.

THE INDUSTRIES IN 1991

Product Sectors, Processes and Tasks

The Printing Industry

The General Print Sector

The general printing sector still covered a wide range of products – packaging, advertising materials, security printing, business forms, books, periodicals, magazines, stationery and catalogues. There were 20,000 printing and publishing businesses – a large number of small, family-owned firms, a number of medium-sized printers and a small number of very large firms employing 1,000 or more. In 1990, printing and publishing, with a turnover of £18 billion was the sixth largest UK manufacturing industry. However, in 1991, unlike 1955, the printing industry operated in an increasingly international market. Limitations on the import or export of print work which existed 35 years previously had been removed bringing increased competition from foreign printers in both the UK and the export market. Despite this, in 1991 the UK printing and publishing industry had a positive foreign trade balance.

A few large companies in the industry were multi-plant, multi-media in terms of product, and multinational, with printing, publishing and electronic media activities across national boundaries. In 1991 relative to 1955 production was concentrated in fewer hands. The 25 largest UK printing and publishing companies accounted for 14 per cent of the industry's total turnover and the top four UK magazine publishers for two-thirds of sales in that sector. In 1991 there were 13,000 book publishers who varied considerably in size and structure, but less than 50 printing firms owned more than 90 per cent of book printing capacity.

National Newspapers

In 1991 in the national newspaper industry, 90 per cent of sales were accounted for by four publishers – News International, the Mirror Group, United Newspapers and the Daily Mail Trust. The total sales of 11 national daily and 10 national Sunday titles amounted to 33 million. Since 1955 the *Daily Herald*, the *Daily Despatch*, *News Chronicle* and the *Daily Sketch* had ceased production. Of the Sunday titles the *Sunday Despatch*, the *Sunday Graphic*, the *Sunday Empire News* and the *Sunday Chronicle* had closed. The *Reynolds News* changed its name to the *Sunday Citizen* and the *Sunday Pictorial* to the *Sunday Mirror*.[24] In the 1980s, new daily morning newspapers appeared, for example, the *Independent*, the *Star* and *Today*, as did a new Sunday newspaper the *Sunday Correspondent*. In mid-1991, the *Sun* was the biggest selling daily newspaper, with a circulation of over 5m whilst the *Evening Standard* was the only London evening newspaper. The 'Press Lords' no longer dominated national newspapers.

Entrepreneurs like Rupert Murdoch and Robert Maxwell were now the dominant figures[25] and both had developed interests in newspaper distribution. In 1955 all national newspapers were printed in 'Fleet Street' and Manchester, but by 1991 all had left these locations. The printing of the *Sun*, *The Times*, *Sunday Times* and the *News of the World* moved to Wapping in 1986 and in the following year the *Daily Telegraph* and the *Daily Mail* moved to the London Docklands.

Another marked change in 1991 relative to 1955 was national newspapers separating their editorial and origination departments from the actual printing process and separating newspaper production into separate companies run by the publishers of the same papers. The most noticeable example of such arrangements was the publishing side of Mirror Group Newspapers being owned by the Maxwell Foundation whilst production facilities were owned by the Maxwell Communications Corporation (MCC). The sale of most MCC's printing interests to a management buy-out did not include the newspaper interests which were sold back early in 1989 to the Mirror Group Newspapers but which remained a separate company.

The provincial press

As in 1955, the provincial press consisted of companies in England, Wales and Northern Ireland printing and publishing morning, evening, Sunday, weekly and bi-weekly newspapers which were not distributed nationally. In 1991 there were 1,300 separate newspaper titles with a total circulation of 16 million. The industry consisted of a large number of companies varying in terms of ownership, control, size, organisation and products. There were companies owned and controlled by one family or by an individual proprietor; others were owned by one family but with a number of minority shareholders and controlled by a board of directors with a family member as chairman. Yet others were controlled directly by a board of directors. Small independently owned newspapers were declining as publishing groups such as the Westminster Press, Thomson Regional News and United Newspapers acquired them. A further complication was that new national titles were printed on a subcontract basis thus blurring the demarcation between the production of regional and national titles. Portsmouth and Sunderland Newspapers and United Newspapers, for example, produced both regional and national newspapers in the same plant.

The late 1970s saw the rise of freesheet newspapers which depended solely on advertising revenue to meet their production costs. Such newspapers had the advantage of the customer receiving a copy free of charge, with no large-scale distribution operation being required as young people simply walked up streets delivering copies to every household. The entrepreneurs behind these 'freesheets' had backgrounds in information, sales and general business. The paid papers responded to this competition by launching their own freesheets and in mid-1990 there were over 600 freesheets throughout the country. In 1984 the value of advertising in weekly freesheets overtook that of 'weekly paid newspapers'. In 1990 the same 20 companies controlled over 50 per cent of weekly freesheets as controlled 50 per cent of the weekly paid-for circulation. Freesheet newspapers businesses tended to contract out their printing and to employ few journalists.

By 1991 newspaper owners were experiencing improved financial performance due to increased circulation, improved advertising revenue, increased output per head and reduced labour costs. However, the same bright picture was not true of the work-force. As the SOGAT Report on National/Regional Newspapers and Distribution to its 1990 Biennial Delegate Council remarked

> for us the past few years have been characterised by takeovers, redundancies, derecognition and other attacks on trade union organisation, reduced pay and worsened conditions.[26]

Wholesale distribution

The dominant change relative to 1955 in wholesale distribution was it was now done by road haulage and not by British Rail. This change began in 1986 when News International, during the Wapping Dispute bypassed the British Rail system by using the TNT road haulage company to deliver directly to retail newsagents. News International were soon followed by the Maxwell empire which established its own road haulage operation called Newsflow. The use of road haulage to deliver directly to the retail newsagents was then adopted by nearly all other national newspaper publishers. On Saturday morning 9 July 1988 weekday newspapers were carried by rail for the last time. In the early hours of Sunday 10 July 1988 Sunday newspapers were carried by rail for the last time. Associated with this change were large-scale redundancies amongst drivers, train packers and station personnel of wholesale newspaper distribution firms.

By 1990 the number of retail wholesalers with whom News International and the Maxwell empire dealt had fallen sharply as they were forced to bid for the franchise to distribute their titles to the retail newsagents. Under these franchising arrangements for wholesalers only one company was responsible for a defined geographical area instead of the previous network of 1,000 wholesalers, some of whom had only a few bundles. News International now used only 182 wholesalers compared with 1,000 in 1980. The Mirror Group had reduced the number of wholesalers it used from over 2,000 in 1980 to 230 in mid-1991. Although established large wholesalers like John Menzies, WH Smith and Surridge Dawson weathered this tendering process, many small wholesalers simply went to the wall or were taken over by the larger companies.

Screen printing and ink manufacture

Although the general print sector, newspapers and paper conversion were SOGAT's big industrial battalions, in 1991 the union also had members in a highly specialised section – silk screen printing. This industry escaped the gaze of publicity but its work was highly visible. From posters on city hoardings and supermarket advertising displays to illuminated vehicle dashboards and computer control panels, high-quality screen printing formed a background to people's everyday lives. Screen printers had been members of the Sign and Display Union which merged in 1973 with NATSOPA and by that route eventually became part of SOGAT. SOGAT's merger with NATSOPA in 1982 took SOGAT into the printing ink manufacturing industry which in 1991 spanned a range of companies from small firms to multinational corporations.

Printing processes and stages

In 1991 relative to 1955 there had been a dramatic change in the use of the main printing processes. Letterpress, which dominated in 1955, had ceased to be the most significant printing process. The main use of letterpress machines, using flexible and flexographic plates was in paperback book production. Gravure now had a larger share of the total print market arising from the use of improved reproduction systems. The dominant printing process in 1991 was lithography. All major national and provincial newspapers were produced by web-offset machines in complete contrast to 1955. The growth of litho mirrored the changes of the late 1960s and early 1970s when hot metal systems were replaced by photocomposition as the dominant mode of print origination. Litho advantages over letterpress included a higher quality of printing, particularly colour. In the late 1960s, the introduction of litho machines into letterpress houses led to disputes between the letterpress and litho craft unions on the one hand and between NATSOPA and the NUPB&PW on the other.[27] In the binding and warehousing departments the production process was more mechanised compared to 1955. Book jacketing machines were common and were capable of binding a book using automatic feeds, full automatic book sewers and casing machines. Computer controlled stock keeping was common and in the machine rooms mechanisation, using robotic technology, for example, had resulted in the introduction of automatic reel feeding. Wholesale distribution had been transformed from a labour-intensive, low-mechanisation industry to a much more capital-intensive industry with little handling work.

(i) Typesetting and plate-making By 1991 hand and mechanical type-setters including monotype casters and filmsetters were few in number. Metal-based typesetting systems had been replaced first by photo-composition and then in the 1970s by computerised composition which in 1991 dominated, particularly in newspapers, where it enabled the combination of three previously separated tasks – editorial, advertising (where SOGAT had members) and composition. The journalist and advertising employees were able to typeset, correct and make up pages, all of which had previously been the preserve of typesetters in the composing department. In magazine and periodical production comput-erised composition had the same effect. Employment opportunities increased in editorial and advertising (a SOGAT area) but fell dramat-ically amongst the typesetters and SOGAT areas of linotype assistants, copy holders and revisers. The expansion of litho also impacted on jobs in the plate-making department with a sharp fall in letterpress plate-makers, photo-engravers and PMB provers. On the other hand, the employment of litho plate-makers had increased relative to 1955.

(ii) Print machine rooms In 1991 the dominance of litho in machine rooms meant more single and multicolour printing machines. One effect of these changes was the almost complete demise of the machine managers in charge of platen machines. By 1991 technological changes in the machine room had reduced the need for semi-skilled labour, since robots now fitted the reels of paper to the machines, and had also resulted in deskilling the machine manager's job with the introduction of computer-aided control mechanisms. Machine managers were responding by undertaking tasks which they had previously regarded as the preserve of SOGAT members.

(iii) The finishing trades   In the binding, finishing, warehousing and despatch areas increased mechanisation had brought a decline in employment as jobs which had previously required manual handling were eliminated. Longer runs made it economical to introduce automation in these departments. However, in 1991 there were still many firms where customer demand meant dealing with one-off jobs and continuing to employ labour-intensive techniques. The growth of freesheet newspapers and the transfer of wholesale distribution from rail to road had meant substantial employment losses in traditional wholesale newspaper houses.

Papermaking and Paper Conversion

Paper and Board

In 1991 firms in paper and board manufacture were producing newsprint, writing and printing paper, industrial and special purpose papers, packaging and other boards. Total output stood at 4.7m tons compared to 3.3m tons in 1955. The markets for paper and board products were international and the industry was now a high-tech, capital-intensive operation requiring maximum utilisation of plant and rapid response to change. In 1991 firms operating either continuous or semi-continuous production systems covered 99.7 per cent of the industry's capacity.

Box and Cartons

In 1991, the paper box and carton sectors faced intensive international competition, particularly from other European Community states. The decline in demand for paper boxes had resulted from cartons and fibreboard case capturing larger shares of the market throughout the 1960s and from the appearance of new packaging materials such as plastics. Rigid box firms had responded by specialising in high-quality work such as presentation boxes. Carton manufacturing was still dominated by big firms dependent upon large volume orders. The four largest carton manufacturers accounted for 25 per cent of the total market and the largest 19 for over 50 per cent. Just over half of carton production was for food use and 17 per cent for soap, detergents, cosmetics and pharmaceuticals.

Small firms still dominated the rigid box sector. Investments had been made in machines for automatic glueing in order to produce collapsible rigid boxes and to satisfy volume orders of standard boxes. However, as in 1955, many companies concentrated on one-off or short-run orders and on speciality box lines, and consequently there had been few changes in production methods since 1955. In contrast, in carton production the introduction of new machinery in the 1970s had increased output on a significant scale and enabled the production of more complex shapes as well as combining previously separate tasks, for example, varnish, cut and strip, or cut and crease. In 1991 laser cutting techniques were used in the industry whilst market requirements for small runs and faster turn rounds had seen the adoption of 'just-in-time' production systems. In 1991, relative to 1955, the production process was more sophisticated, utilising faster, more complex computer controlled machines. Fibreboard production systems were dominated by machines capable of multicoloured work and by faster corrugators with splicing and stacking capabilities.

Paper Bags

In 1991 paper bag manufacture was suffering increased competition from the expanding use of plastic bag and carriers. However, some competitive advantage was being restored as environmental concerns led to renewed interest in the use of paper. The largest market for paper bags was the food and drink industry. The UK paper bag industry remained fragmented with no supplier holding more than a 10 per cent market share. Multi-wall sack manufacture had expanded into printing containers for food, chemicals and refuse. However, the increasing use of plastics threatened these markets despite the development in mid-1991 of a new market for pet foods and freezer bags. Four companies accounted for 60 per cent of the multi-wall sack market at this time. Multi-wall sack manufacture was now a highly mechanised industry employing high-speed machines, electronic scanners, automatic feeders and stackers on sewing lines.

The Work-force

In 1991, the paper and board industry required a work-force capable of adjusting to a continuous process of change and of acquiring new and different skills. SOGAT argued that the industry's multi-skilled employees be reclassified as 'super technicians'. However, at the same time some occupations, such as machine minding, were being reduced to 'button pushing'. There were strong pressures for the national grading structure to be renegotiated. In the late 1980s women were employed for the first time as machine crew members in paper mills.

In 1991, in carton production an increasing proportion of the work-force was employed as machine minders or assistants. Tasks such as waste stripping, banding, packing and glueing were carried out by machines which had displaced female workers. A further change in this sector relative to 1955 was a significant increase in the number of shift workers. The production process required workers with enhanced skills and responsibility as the range of carton styles continued to increase. In fibreboard the proportion of workers employed as machine managers or assistants had increased since 1955, shift working had increased and the number of women employed had fallen. In paper bag manufacturing manual inspection and many mid 1950s' manual jobs had been eliminated but some highly skilled jobs such as colour flexographic printers had increased.

Employment, Trade Unions and Employers' Organisations

The Printing Industry

Employment

In 1991 the general printing trade was still dominated by small firms. Approximately 90 per cent of establishments employed under 50 people whilst only 1 per cent employed 500 or more. The majority of firms, including some of the largest, remained family businesses. Nevertheless, there were some large groups. For example, the British Printing Communications Corporation (BPCC) and the Dickinson Robinson Group. Such groups had been absent in 1955 from the general printing sector. Newspaper firms remained larger than general print trade firms and by 1991 multinational companies such as News International were a significant presence in national newspapers.

In 1991 the total number of employees in printing and newspapers was 340,000. In national newspapers, 41 per cent of employees were non-craft workers whilst in provincial newspapers the proportion was 16 per cent. In national newspapers some 30 per cent of employees were craft manuals whilst in the regional press the percentage was almost 50. A major difference in the work-force relative to 1955 was the number of female employees. In 1991 some 10,000 women were employed in areas that in 1955 would have been traditionally associated with journeymen. There was also a greater proportion of non-manual employees, such as administrators, supervisors, scientists and technicians, in the industry's work-force. In 1971 the proportion of white-collar workers in printing and publishing was about 18 per cent. By 1991 this figure exceeded 25 per cent. In 1991 London was no longer the dominant printing centre in the UK. The London membership of SOGAT totalled 19,000 which was 10 per cent of the total membership. The London Master Printers' Association, which in 1955 conducted independent negotiations with the London-based unions, ceased to exist in 1985 when it merged into the South East Alliance of the BPIF.

Trade Unions

In 1991 the three main unions in the printing industry were the Society of Graphical and Allied Trades (82), the NGA (82) and the NUJ. Their total membership was 320,000. In 1966 the NUPB&PW and NATSOPA amalgamated to form the Society of Graphical and Allied Trades (SOGAT).[28] Attempts after the merger to devise a common Rule Book failed and in 1972 the marriage was dissolved (see Chapter 5). The former NUPB&PW retained the title 'SOGAT' and in 1975 amalgamated with the Scottish Graphical Association[29] to form SOGAT (75). In 1982 SOGAT (75) and NATSOPA[30] amalgamated to form SOGAT (82).

The NGA (82) was the result of the merger of ten previously separate societies. In 1955 the London Society of Compositors (LSC) and the PMMTS had amalgamated to form the LTS which, in 1964 merged with the TA to create the NGA. In 1965 the ACP and the NUPT transferred their engagements to the NGA as, in 1967 did the NSES. In 1969 the ASLP merged with the NGA and 10 years later the National Union of Wallcoverings, Decorative and Allied Trades (NUWDAT) took the same step. NGA (82) came into being in 1982 when the NGA and SLADE amalgamated.

31

The P&KTF had been dissolved in April 1974. Mergers amongst printing unions had reduced the need for a body to co-ordinate common policy. However, the print unions established the TUC Printing Industries Committee (PIC) whose membership also included the AEU and the Electrical, Electronic, Telecommunications/Plumbing Union (EETPU) which organised maintenance workers in the industry. These two unions had been excluded from the P&KTF. The PIC was not an authoritative body and, apart from the limited services of the TUC, had few resources. It was a forum for information exchange but its activities included health and safety, industrial training and monitoring developments affecting the industry. It provided a body for the print unions collectively to consider common problems.

Employers' Organisations

In 1991 the major employers' organisation in the industry was the British Printing Industries Federation which came into being in April 1974 when the BFMP changed its name. It was felt that in the 1970s the words 'Federation of Master Printers' presented an inaccurate description of the organisation. The title did not reflect the fact that the industry had changed from one of master and servant relationship to one of management and employee.

The Newspaper Society was still the organisation representing provincial newspaper employers' interests. The NPA, which changed its name in 1968 to the Newspaper Publishers Association, had dismantled its involvement in industrial relations matters since its members' firm withdrawal from it for industrial relations purposes. In Scotland the main employers' organisation was the Scottish Printing Employers' Federation which was the changed name of the Society of Master Printers of Scotland which had established itself in the early 1980s as an independent body from BPIF. It also represented the interests of the Scottish weekly and bi-weekly newspaper publishers. The Scottish Newspaper Proprietors' Association had disbanded in 1982.

Nineteen seventy-two had seen the emergence of another employers' organisation, namely the Reproduction and Graphics Association (RAGA) which represented the interests of those employers in the ad-setting industry who were not in membership of the Advertising, Typesetting and Foundry Employers' Federation (ATFEF). The screen printers' employers' interests were represented by the Display Producers' and Screen Printers' Association. The printing ink manufacturers' collective interests were represented by the Society of the British Printing Ink Manufacturers.

In 1991 in wholesale newspaper and periodical distribution, the main employers' organisation was the Association of Newspapers and Magazine Wholesalers (ANMW) formed in 1988. In the following year the Federation of London Wholesale Newspaper Distributors merged with the ANMW to become its London Section. The introduction of tendering for franchises to distribute national newspapers led to the collapse in 1988 of the Sunday Newspaper Distributing Association and the National Society of Provincial Wholesale Sunday Newspaper Distributors. Newspaper publishers had insisted as a condition of bidding for a franchise that companies must handle their titles on a seven-day week basis.

Papermaking and Paper Conversion

Employment

In 1991 there were 31,000 employees in paper and board manufacture, a fall of 45 per cent since 1980 and less than a third of the number employed in the 1950s. Following take-over and mergers, particularly in the 1980s, there remained 71 companies running some 109 mills, giving an average work-force size of 300. The industry still remained heavily concentrated in Kent, Scotland and Lancashire/North Wales. The capital intensity of the industry in 1991 relative to 1955 was reflected in the fact that over 20 per cent of the manual work-force was employed in maintenance compared to less than 10 per cent in the mid-1950s. By 1991 carton manufacture too was much more capital-intensive and by the late 1970s almost 40 per cent of carton manufacturers employed more than 100 people, accounting for nearly 90 per cent of the 22,000 jobs in the industry. In 1991 employment in fibreboard packing case was concentrated in a small number of large establishments. Just over half of all establishments employed more than 100 people and over 90 per cent of all employees worked in such establishments. The industry was much more capital-intensive than in the 1950s and, as a consequence, there had been steady decline in numbers employed.

In 1991 the average number of production workers covered by national negotiations and employed in paper box manufacturing companies was 80, a figure that reflected the continuing preponderance of small firms in the sector. Relative to 1955, box manufacture was characterised by a decline in both the number of establishments and of employees. In 1991, most multi-wall sack manufacturers were located close to rural areas, cement plants or grain mills and there were a greater number of multinational companies, mainly from Scandinavia, in the industry than in the mid-1950s.

Trade Unions

In the manufacture of paper, rigid box and carton, fibreboard packing case, paper bag and multi-wall sacks the main trade unions for process and general workers remained SOGAT, T&GWU and the General Municipal Boilermakers' and Allied Trades' Union (GMBATU). The main union for non-manual employees was SOGAT's white-collar branch – Clerical, Managerial and Sales (CMS). In 1991, manual worker unionisation stood at 87 per cent in paper and board, at 40–50 per cent in rigid box and at 90 per cent in cartons, fibreboard packing case and multi-wall sack manufacture. Union density was lower amongst non-manuals where it was mainly confined to clerical grades. Efforts by SOGAT to recruit in small firms in the rigid box sector following the abolition of the Wages Council in 1975 had been largely unsuccessful as many companies, aided by the British Box and Packaging Association, actively resisted unionisation.

Employers' Associations

In paper and board manufacture the main employers' association was the British Paper and Board Industry Federation which claimed its member companies employed almost 90 per cent of manual workers and staff in the industry. In 1989, the Federation altered its rules to allow membership to companies not party to the National Agreement, but in 1990 there were only 10 companies, representing 12 mills, in this membership category. Employers in box and carton manufacture still retained their separate organisations, namely the British Box and Packaging Association (BBPA) and the British Carton Association (BCA). The same was true of employers in fibreboard packaging, although in 1983 Reeds Corrugated Case, one of the largest companies in the sector, had withdrawn from the British Fibreboard Packaging Association (BFPA). In paper bag and multi-wall sack manufacture the employers' organisations had followed different paths. The British

Paper Bag Federation disbanded in the 1980s and became the British Bag Federation (BBF) but the Multi-wall Sack Manufacturers' Association still existed in 1991.

Industrial Relations Machinery and Procedures

The Printing Industry

General Print Sector and Provincial Newspapers

In 1991, no formal machinery for negotiating national agreements existed in general printing, newspaper production or wholesale newspaper distribution sectors and the *ad hoc* arrangements still prevailed. However, the BPIF and the Newspaper Society no longer negotiated jointly with the printing unions. Since 1981 the two organisations had negotiated separately with each of the main printing unions. However, unlike in the 1950s, the basic wage agreements were no longer characterised by stabilisation, cost of living bonuses and wage increases for manpower concessions. A system of annual negotiations with the BPIF and the NS had existed since 1919 but in 1991 the latter terminated national bargaining and the National Agreements it held with SOGAT and the NGA.

In 1991 the standard working week in the general printing trade and provincial newspapers was 37½ hours, which had been achieved following a major industrial stoppage in 1980. Three weeks' annual paid holidays had been achieved in the mid-1960s, four weeks in the early 1970s and five weeks in 1989. In 1991 the basic minimum rate for craft grades in the UK was £165.02 per week and for non-craft grades was £148.88 in the provinces and £149.74 in London. Provincial grade rates for both craft and non-craft employees had been terminated in the 1960s. In 1986, the Printing Industry Pension Scheme (PIPS) negotiated between NGA, SOGAT and the BPIF, provided a voluntary industry-wide, transferable money-purchase pension scheme for print workers. A significant change in 1991 relative to 1955 was that in the general print sector the apprenticeship system no longer existed. This had ended in SOGAT craft areas in 1985 when the BPIF and SOGAT signed the Recruitment, Training and Retraining Agreement. The main principles underlying this agreement were training to standards, joint management chapel manpower planning, comprehensive coverage of all skilled production workers with open age entry to skilled occupations and national certification.

In provincial newspapers a major difference in 1991 relative to 1955 was the decline in the bargaining power of the unions brought about by economic, political and technological developments of the late 1980s in newspaper production. In 1991 the provincial newspaper industry was considerably less unionised than in 1955 because of Newspaper Society member firms' policy of refusing to grant union recognition and of derecognition, especially in clerical areas. Provincial newspaper employers were imposing low pay settlements and increasingly putting employees on individual contracts.

National Newspapers

This aggressive attitude also existed amongst the national newspaper employers who introduced individual contracts for non-manual employees, derecognised SOGAT, the NGA and the NUJ, imposed unilateral changes in wages and employment conditions and introduced more bank holiday working. National newspaper employers were applying downward pressures on employment conditions. In 1990 the *Guardian* imposed a wage freeze whilst the *Financial Times* introduced wage cuts. The *Daily Telegraph* conceded an increase of 5 per cent funded by redundancies and changes in working practices.

Wholesale Distribution

The introduction of tendering for franchises within wholesale newspaper distribution had resulted by 1991 in the total demise of the independent Sunday wholesaler. In the 1989 pay negotiations, Sunday working became an integral part of the Association of Newspaper and Magazine Wholesalers' Agreement and thousands of SOGAT members lost their jobs. Yet, despite this, trade unionism had survived in the industry. However, employers were still attempting to weaken union organisation by policies of derecognition and dismissals.

Papermaking and Paper Conversion

Paper and Board

In 1991 the National Agreement between the BPBIF and SOGAT, GMBATU and T&GWU remained. It was a testimony to the industry's system of industrial relations that radical change had been achieved without industrial conflict. Nevertheless, by 1991 there were disturbing developments. Two US-based papermaking companies (Kimberly-Clark and Scott Ltd) withdrew from the National Agreement whilst some other US companies were undermining existing working conditions. Three new paper mills – Bridgewater, Shotton and Caledonian – decided not to participate in the National Agreement and only one was organised by SOGAT. In 1990, under the National Agreement, the minimum hourly rates for adult day workers ranged from £2.71 to £3.20 for a 40-hour week and from £3.38 to £4.02 for four-shift workers. Paid holiday entitlement was five weeks. In 1982 an enabling agreement, reached at national level, permitted individual mills to negotiate working time on an annual basis. By 1991 one-third of manual employees were working on an annualised hours basis.

Cartons, Paper Box and Paper Bag

In carton manufacturing, since 1976, wages and condition had been covered by the SOGAT/BPIF agreement. After the Wages Council for Box Making was abolished in 1974 pay and conditions of employment were determined by annual negotiations between the BBPA, representing about 100 companies, and SOGAT and the GMBATU. Fibreboard packing case manufacture was removed from the Wages Council for Box Making in 1965 by a joint BFPA/SOGAT application reflecting the growing willingness of the big companies in the sector to negotiate with the unions at national and local level. In 1991 however, only 4,500 production workers were covered by the national agreement. In 1990 adult day-work rates for a 37½-hour week ranged from £122.14 to £152.02, with the national minimum earnings guarantee set at £136.48.

Following the abolition of the Paper Bag Wages Council in 1969 the BPBF negotiated collectively at the national level with SOGAT. However, in 1982 these arrangements were terminated in favour of local-level negotiations. In 1991 in the multi-wall sack industry annual national negotiations between the Multi-wall Sack Manufacturers Employers' Association (MSMEA) and SOGAT, the T&GWU and GMBATU were the order of the day. In 1991 adult day work rates of pay in the industry varied from £125.16 to £139.71 per week, for adult double day shift workers from £150.91 to £167.65 per week and for adult night shift with double day shift workers from £167.68 to £186.28.

37

The Economic Environment

By 1991, the major priority of government in managing the economy was control of inflation by use of interest rate changes, reduction in public expenditure and changes in indirect taxes to prevent spending power outstripping the supply of goods and services in the economy. The level of employment was not the responsibility of government but that of the buyers and sellers of labour services. If employees demanded too high a wage then unemployment would result. Unemployment was prevented by wage rates falling. For the British government, trade unions, by setting minimum standards, prevented unemployment from being reduced. The British government, therefore, saw that its contribution to achieving full employment was to deregulate the labour market. The government's anti-trade-union legislation over the period 1980–91 (see Chapter 13) was seen as contributing to creating employment opportunities.

The Printing Industry

General Print

The 1980s saw a sharp increase in unemployment. In 1982 SOGAT had a membership of 236,660; in 1991 it stood at 157,218. Over the period 1982 to 1991 SOGAT's membership had declined by some 34 per cent. In 1991 the printing and publishing industry faced intensified competition from foreign imports, the growth of in-plant printing departments in many companies across a wide spectrum of industries, the growth of instant print shops and the expansion of advertising and art studios. The industry faced a big threat from the growth of an alternative communications industry based on electronic devices. Electronic information systems, such as Oracle, Ceefax and Prestel, offered an alternative way of communicating information, whilst audio-visual discs and cassettes offered mail order companies and travel companies the means of reaching their customers via their TV screens. New cable methods giving households direct access to information and entertainment also competed with traditional printing methods. Publishers of books and magazines were attracted to these new systems and, in particular, to desk-top publishing.

Papermaking and Paper Conversion

The papermaking industry was usually the first to feel the slump and the first to recover. When economic activity declines, companies do not order paper or packaging materials and that then knocks on to the paper mills. The converse is true. In the mid-1970s and early 1980s the industry suffered badly from the recession. There were many, at this time, who believed papermaking was in terminal decline. It suffered from high interest rates, high inflation and high energy costs coupled with low prices and falling demand. The industry began to recover in 1982 and by 1991 the economic environment was optimistic. British mills had increased output by 7 per cent, imports had fallen by 5 per cent whilst exports had increased by 37 per cent to 1.25 million tonnes. UK mills had found a specialist niche market in quality products. The creation of the Single European Market on 1 January 1993 resulted in a rush of mergers and take-overs as companies sought to obtain a foothold or establish leadership in markets. By 1991 over 60 per cent of the UK paper and board-making industry's capacity was foreign-owned.

The paper conversion industry was also optimistic in 1991. Although plastics had impacted seriously on the demand for paper boxes and bags, the industry had survived. A new demand for paper products had emerged. Plastic sacking had never been successful for cement. The sacks tended to sweat and the cement 'went off' before it could be used. By comparison paper 'breathed' and kept the contents fresh. Similarly, milk products tended to solidify in plastic boxes. However, the paper box and carton industry optimism was not based solely on the spread of 'green' ideas but also on improvement in design and quality and an expectation that localised or specialist markets could be captured whilst the multinational companies concentrated upon pan-European competition. The share of the board 'paper box' sector captured by fibreboard case manufacturers had increased from 38 per cent in 1954 to 52 per cent in 1990.

Over the period 1955 to 1991 the general printing sector and newspaper industries underwent a major industrial revolution which is not yet finished. The origination areas were affected by the rise of photocomposition and then computer-based composition, when for 50 years mechanical composition had been the dominant mode of production. The machine departments had been dramatically affected by the decline of letterpress, the rapid rise of lithography and the slow but steady increase in gravure. The finishing, binding and warehousing departments had been affected by increased automation and mechanisation which eliminated a great deal of handling work and integrated the production, finishing, binding and warehousing functions. In newspaper distribution the dramatic change had been the switch from rail to road haulage where SOGAT had no presence.

In paper and paper conversion over the period 1955 to 1991 the industry also underwent significant change. Protection from foreign competition via import tariffs had been removed, production techniques had become more capital intensive, the presence of multinational companies had increased, and alternative products (notable plastics) to those based on paper had established themselves in the market place.

The creation of SOGAT in 1966 and its development over the next 25 years, at which point it amalgamated with the NGA to form the Graphical, Paper and Media Union (GPMU), can only be explained against this industrial revolution in printing, newspaper production and distribution and in the paper and paper conversion industries.

NOTES

1. The union was originally known when formed in 1921 as the National Union of Printing, Bookbinding, Machine Ruling and Paperworkers. The shortened title was adopted in 1928. For a discussion of the reasons for the creation of the NUPB & PW see C.J. Bundock *The Story of the National Union of Printing, Bookbinding and Paperworkers*, Oxford, 1958, pp. 199–213.
2. The National Union of Bookbinders and Machine Rulers had been formed in 1911 by a merger of the London Consolidated Lodge of Journeymen Bookbinders which had been formed in 1840, and the Bookbinders and Machine Rulers' Consolidated Union, which had been formed in 1872. The creation of the National Union of Bookbinders and Machine Rulers was the merger of the London and Provincial Bookbinders and Machine Rulers. For a fuller discussion see C.J. Bundock *The Story of the National Union of Printing, Bookbinding and Paperworkers*, Oxford, 1958, pp. 1–110 and *SOGAT Journal*, September 1991, pp. 8–11.
3. For a discussion of this merger see C.J. Bundock *The Story of the National Union of Printing, Bookbinding and Paperworkers*, Oxford, 1958, pp. 111–98 and 370–9 and *SOGAT Journal*, September 1991, pp. 12–13.
4. The members objected that they were not labourers so the name was changed to the Operative Printers' Assistants' Society in 1898. When the union recruited outside London the word 'National' was added in 1904 to its title. In 1912 after the union recruited some machine managers the word 'and' was inserted between the words 'Printers' and 'Assistants'. See J. Moran *NATSOPA: 75 Years*, Heinemann, London, 1964, Chapters 2, 3, 4 and 6 and *SOGAT Journal*, September 1991, pp. 16–17.

5. However, it retained the acronym NATSOPA.
6. For a detailed history of the first 100 years of this union (1848–1948) see S.C. Gillespie *The Scottish Typographical Association*, Maclehose, 1953.
7. For a history of the National Graphical Association and its constituent societies over the period 1950–90 see J. Gennard *A History of the National Graphical Association*, Unwin Hyman, 1990.
8. The Thomson organisation controlled leading daily newspapers in Scotland, South Wales and Northern Ireland as well as Sheffield, Manchester and Aberdeen.
9. Its provincial newspapers were all owned by Westminster Press Provincial Newspapers Ltd whose titles included the *Northern Echo* and the *Northern Despatch*.
10. The Drayton Chain owned Provincial Newspapers Ltd which published *inter alia*, the Edinburgh Evening News, the *Yorkshire Post* and the *Blackburn Times*.
11. See 'Balance Sheet of the Press' *Planning*, Vol. 21, No. 384, August 1955.
12. In London other leading wholesalers included Boon, Bulles, Holdens, Dumcumbs, Myours Bros, Marlborough, Martins and Pauls.
13. These were the London Typographical Society, the Association of Correctors of the Press, the Scottish Typographical Association and the Monotype Casters and Typefounders' Society.
14. For a detailed account of the history of this union which merged in 1962 with NUPB&PW see *Monotype Casters and Typefounders' Society, Diamond Jubilee, 1989–1949*, Sixteenth Annual Report, 1949.
15. Its members were employed in national newspapers, provincial newspapers and news agencies.
16. For fuller accounts of these events see C.J. Bundock *The National Union of Printing, Bookbinding and Paperworkers*, Oxford, 1958, Chapters 25, 26, 27 and 30, especially pp. 246–9, pp. 255–7 and pp. 282–90, and J. Moran *NATSOPA: 75 Years*, Heinemann, London, 1964, pp. 51–6.
17. For a description of the events surrounding the formation of the P&KTF see J. Child *Industrial Relations in the British Printing Industry*, Allen & Unwin, 1967, Chapter 12, pp. 194–7 and *Sixty Years of Service, 1901–1961*, Printing and Kindred Trades' Federation, 1961.
18. In addition to the main printing unions the other members were the Pattern Card Makers' Society (334 members) which joined the NUPB&PW in 1963; the Sign and Display Trades Union (449 members) which joined NATSOPA in 1972; the London Society of Music Engravers (40 members) and the Map and Chart Engineers' Association (32 members).
19. In 1960 the Fibreboard Packing Cases Manufacturers' Association, the British Carton Association and the British Paper Box Association came together with other packaging employers' associations to form an umbrella organisation, the Packaging Employers' Confederation (PEC) to provide a joint secretariat for all its constituent employers.
20. See *Report of the Court of Inquiry into the Nature and Circumstances of a Dispute between the British Federation of Master Printers and the Printing and Kindred Trades' Federation*, Cmnd 6912, HMSO, London, 1946, and J. Child *Industrial Relations in the British Printing Industry* Allen & Unwin, 1967, Chapter 18, pp. 299–303.

21. For details of the dispute between the London Society of Compositors and the London Master Printers' Association see *Report of the Court of Inquiry into the Causes of a Dispute between the London Master Printers' Association and the London Society of Compositors*, Cmnd 8074, HMSO, London, 1950.

22. For the details of the arbitrator's decision see *The Paperworker*, Vol. 15, No. 12, April 1955.

23. In the 1960s voluntary collective bargaining agreements were negotiated to cover the large firms in the carton and fibreboard sectors. Firms producing mainly fibreboard were removed from the Council's scope in 1965 but because of the difficulty of finding a definition to distinguish clearly between boxes and cartons, both rigid box and carton production remained within its jurisdiction.

24. Public concern about the state of the national press was brought home by two events – the death in 1960 of the *News Chronicle* and the *Star*, and the acquisition by Daily Mirror Newspapers Ltd of Odhams Press Ltd which published the *Daily Herald* and the *People* as well as a large number of periodicals. Against this background a Royal Commission on the Press was appointed in 1961 to enquire into the economic factors affecting the press generally. See *Report of the Royal Commission on the Press, 1961–1962*, CMND 1811, HMSO, London, 1962. By the mid-1970s concern that economic difficulties facing national newspapers were lowering editorial standards in pursuit of increased circulation and that the solution to the industry's economic difficulties might require government action led in 1974 to the establishment of a third post-second-world-war Royal Commission on the Press which produced an *Interim Report* (Cmnd 6433, HMSO) in 1976 and a *Final Report*, (Cmnd 6810, HMSO) in 1977.

25. In 1991 Rupert Murdoch owned *The Times*, the *Sunday Times*, the *Sun*, the *News of the World* and *Today*.

26. See *Report on National/Regional Newspapers and Distribution*, presented to the SOGAT Biennial Delegate Council, 1990, p. 1.

27. See *Report of the Court of Inquiry into the problems caused by the introduction of Web-offset machines in the printing industry and the problems arising from the introduction of other modern printing techniques and the arrangements which should be adopted within the industry for dealing with them*, Cmnd 3184, HMSO, London, 1967.

28. In 1961 the Book Edge Gilders' Society had joined the NUPB&PW. In 1962 the Monotype Casters and Typefounders' Society and the Papermould and Dandy Roll Society had joined the NUPB&PW. In 1963 the Pattern Card Makers' Society had transferred its engagements into the NUPB&PW.

29. The Scottish Typographical Association had changed its name to the Scottish Graphical Association in 1974.

30. In 1972, the Sign and Display Trades Union had merged with NATSOPA.

PART I

INTER-UNION
RELATIONSHIPS

CHAPTER 2

THE FORMATION OF SOGAT: ITS CAUSES

In 1955, the NUPB&PW organised across all the main printing processes of letterpress, lithography and photogravure. The craft unions organised around particular jobs between and within the main printing techniques. The demarcation between the job boundaries of the unions was relatively unchallenged, but where they were contentious the P&KTF resolved the demarcation and/or organisational problems that arose between its affiliates.

However, by 1955 there were signs that things were changing and there were also predictions that anticipated technological developments would blur the existing job boundaries. In response to these changes the craft unions began in 1956 unsuccessful amalgamation talks designed to achieve one craft union for the industry. The NUPB&PW responded to the proposed craft union amalgamation by starting merger talks with NATSOPA but these broke down in 1958. The NUPB&PW had also reviewed its existing relationships with the craft unions. In April 1955 its Reciprocity Agreement with the TA was widened to allow the latter's Printing Machine Branch members to operate vertical Miehle machines as well as platen machines. In London the PMB had agreement with the London Master Printers for the operation of vertical Miehle machines and small cylinders up to demi-size and for platens and pressmen.

Attempts to rationalise the printing industry's trade union structure continued in the early 1960s. The NUPB&PW was involved in unsuccessful merger attempts with the LTS (1962) and then for technical reasons (see Chapter 3) the ASLP (1963). However, in 1964 the London and the English, Welsh and Irish provincial compositors and machine managers amalgamated into one union to form the National

Graphical Association. Two years later the NUPB&PW and NATSOPA, the two predominantly non-craft unions in the industry, merged to form the Society of Graphical and Allied Trades (SOGAT).[1]

A number of factors explain why SOGAT came into being. First, there were organisational anomalies between NATSOPA and the NUPB&PW. For many years the 'custom of the house' had been established whereby reference was made to 'Paperworker towns' and 'NATSOPA towns'[2] The same grades/groups of workers carrying out the same tasks in the machine rooms, warehouses, despatch and bindery departments were organised in a different union depending on which town they worked in. The situation had little logic. A merger of the two unions would remove these organisational anomalies and eliminate the possibility of disputes between NATSOPA and NUPB&PW over the interpretation and application of the 'custom of the house' arrangements.

Second, in the 1950s and early 1960s in the printing industry the implementation of technological developments blurred, or threatened to blur, the clear demarcation between jobs within and between the main printing processes. These developments involved new production techniques based on lithographic web-fed printing machines and film replacing type. The changes presented a challenge to inter-craft, and more importantly for NATSOPA and the NUPB&PW, to craft/non-craft union job control in machine rooms. Important technical changes were implemented in the binding, finishing and warehousing areas. These involved integration of these departments with the production departments thereby blurring demarcation between the jobs of production areas and those of finishing. The technical developments of the 1950s and early 1960s in the papermaking industry challenged traditional working methods and threatened to substitute unionised labour with new machines.

Third, the 1950s and 1960s saw the growth of substitute print and papermaking and paper conversion products. These years witnessed the continued growth of miniature printing machines in local authorities, nationalised industries, the civil service and the financial sector. They were also years of expansion in the import of printed matter and in alternative outlets to newspapers and magazines for advertising, a major source of revenue from which newspapers covered their costs. This was a period when the UK papermaking industry became exposed to international competition with the ending of tariff barriers with Britain's entry into the European Free Trade Area (EFTA).

Fourth the late 1950s and early 1960s saw a relative decline in

London as a printing centre and the growth of large-scale companies created by mergers and take-overs. Work was lost from London as a result of the closure of printing establishments as well as the merging and take-over of printing firms in London, particularly the Mirror Group take-over of Odhams, Cornwall Press and Amalgamated Press. Work was also lost in that printing firms relocated outside of London in response to financial incentives from central government.

Fifth, the 1955/6 wage negotiations between the printing unions and the BFMP and the NS brought sharp conflict and dissension between craft and the non-craft unions. The negotiations demonstrated that no one union could successfully achieve an advancement in wages and conditions in isolation from the demands of other print unions. Since the end of the Second World War, the general print and provincial newspaper employers had shown a reluctance to conduct separate negotiations with 12 different unions. They had resisted conceding to one union more than they were prepared to grant to other unions. It was 1959 before the printing unions presented a collective claim for an increase in wages and a reduction in hours of work. Such collective approaches continued until 1969. However, the unions realised that collective approaches were a short term measure until the print union structure was rationalised by mergers and the achievement of one union for the industry.

As a result of the five factors outlined above, NUPB&PW and NATSOPA were fearful of redundancy and of increasing employment insecurity, whilst the introduction of litho printing machines and cold composition led them to believe the letterpress and litho craft unions might combine to deny them 'a stake' in the litho revolution. If the NUPB&PW and NATSOPA remained separate unions and a single craft union emerged then there was the possibility they would have little influence over improvements in their members' terms and conditions of employment and would merely have to accept such improvements as the amalgamated craft union would permit. If the two unions were to influence future developments in the industry and not merely receive 'crumbs' from the craft union they required an amalgamation.

ORGANISATIONAL TIDINESS

The spheres of influence arrangements between NUPB&PW and NATSOPA were described in Chapter 1. There were exceptions to the general demarcation lines and even in London there were printing houses where NATSOPA members worked in the warehouse and NUPB&PW members worked in the machine rooms. In Manchester newspaper publishing rooms were staffed by NATSOPA members. In some parts of England bookbinders were NATSOPA members rather than NUPB&PW. In reality in some parts of England NATSOPA organised particular workers whilst in other parts the same workers were organised by NUPB&PW.

Both the NUPB&PW and NATSOPA organised specialist groups. The Paperworkers organised the circulation representatives for magazines and provincial and national newspapers whilst NATSOPA represented the interests of newspaper advertising employees. Although the sphere of influence arrangements represented organisational anomalies, they provided the basis of a friendly relationship between the two unions. One union gained a footing here, the other there, but a 'good neighbourly' policy recognised the established position. In 1960/1 a number of complaints arose over local interpretations of the arrangements and by autumn 1964 some 30 to 40 cases still remained unresolved. When the NUPB&PW and NATSOPA Joint Committee met to resolve these problems the Paperworkers' General Secretary argued the only permanent solution was for the two unions to amalgamate and this task should start immediately. When NATSOPA agreed to amalgamation talks the jurisdictional problems between the two unions were put on hold.

The merger would tidy up these organisational anomalies. No longer in publishing rooms, warehouses or newspapers in London would the NUPB&PW be the appropriate union whilst in Manchester, all other provincial cities and towns and in Scotland, NATSOPA was the appropriate union. Merger would eliminate the situation that in some locations all machine assistants and operatives were members of the Paperworkers whereas in others the same workers were members of NATSOPA. It would also overcome the anomaly of Aylesbury where there were no NATSOPA employees except amongst clerical and administrative grades and of Exeter where there were no Paperworker members and bookbinders, guillotine operators, bookfolders and machine room hands were all in NATSOPA. Although the overlapping interests between the two unions were resolved by 'custom and practice' the organisational anomalies occasionally undermined the two unions' bargaining positions with employers. A merger would eliminate this problem.

TECHNOLOGICAL CHANGE AND DEVELOPMENTS OF THE LATE 1950s AND EARLY 1960s

The mid-1950s and the early 1960s saw technological developments which involved not only new machines but also new production techniques which were based on lithographic web-fed printing machines and film replacing. These changes threatened the dominance of the letterpress craft unions and posed a threat to NUPB&PW and NATSOPA assistants in the machine room as well as NATSOPA assistants, copy holders and revisers. In the bindery and the warehouse the challenge to the NUPB&PW was posed by the developments in mechanical binding, for example, book jacketing machines with automatic feeds, fully automatic book sewers and casing machines. The implications of these changes for the bookbinders were well expressed by a delegate from Manchester to the NUPB&PW 1958 Biennial Delegate Council when moving the following motion:

> That in view of the rapid technological change taking place in the industry this Conference instructs the NEC to send a national officer and/or members of the NEC to the various printing trade fairs held in Europe with the object of reporting on technical advances to the NEC and as necessary to the membership either through the columns of the Paperworker or in a separate report.[3]

It was argued the technical advances on the bindery side would be catastrophic, the attitude of traditional bookbinders towards mechanical binding techniques would have to change and officials of the union go round the Printing Trade Exhibitions obtaining information about different binding machines from which the National Executive Council could determine an appropriate rate for the machine.

The NUPB&PW had two major fears about these technological developments. First, that they would cause redundancies and reduce the general level of employment in the industry. Second, they feared that the craft unions would use the changes to combine and then isolate them with a view to undermining the craft/non-craft differential, to prevent non-skilled employees gaining access to skilled jobs, to invade non-craft job territories, to continue with apprenticeships and to oppose adult promotion to craft jobs and continue the stratification of workers in the industry. These were fears heightened in September 1956 when nine craft unions met to consider the formation of an all-embracing craft union. Neither the NUPB&PW nor NATSOPA was invited to this conference, and they saw the real motive of the craft unions to create a two-union structure based on the 'in' union (the all-embracing craft union) and the 'out' unions (the NUPB&PW and NATSOPA). The NUPB&PW and NATSOPA responded to this threat by entering into amalgamation talks in 1956 but these broke down two years later. By that time however, the possibility of a single craft union had been reduced considerably[4] and the print unions saw the main priority as the achievement of a 40-hour working week rather than rationalising their structures.

The NUPB&PW accepted that technological change would be beneficial in the longer run but was aware that in the interim its members were likely to suffer redundancy. It believed that before automation could be acceptable to its members there must be closer working between the printing unions and that the NUPB&PW should be proactive in initiating such moves. This thinking lay behind at the 1956 Biennial Delegate Council Meeting the Liverpool Branch's successful motion:

> This conference views with grave concern the introduction of automatic and electronic processes into the industry and being mindful of the implications of 'automation', direct the NEC to work in closer co-operation with the demarcation committees of other unions within the industry for the purpose of controlling the manning and remuneration of these methods for the best of our members prior to any agreement being made.[5]

The 1964 Biennial Delegate Council Meeting also urged the NUPB&PW to counter the adverse effects of monopoly and automation by determined efforts to achieve printing trade union unity by amalgamation, by strengthening the P&KTF and by pursuing a policy of further reduction in the working week and longer holidays.

The NUPB&PW feared the letterpress and litho unions would combine to push them out of 'a stake' in the litho revolution, particularly in newspapers, and would begin to organise in NATSOPA and NUPB&PW areas. Given that the formation of the NGA in 1964 was seen as a prelude to a single craft union for the industry, the NUPB&PW and NATSOPA recognised that in these circumstances to remain separate unions was likely to leave them isolated and played off by the craft unions and the employers. These fears were expressed at the 1965 NATSOPA Governing Council in the following terms:

> In this situation obviously if NATSOPA stands still, we shall be isolated, not over a long period of years, but rapidly reduced over a fairly short period of years. If we are reduced then our bargaining power, both with the employers and other unions will consequently be reduced in my opinion to the disadvantage of the people we represent, so the generalship and the policy immediately comes into this.[6]

Both the NUPB&PW and NATSOPA feared that the NGA, professing to be the graphical union, would feel free to take anyone into its membership or to train anyone for membership who found themselves in a 'dead-end' job. They envisaged a powerful and developing NGA could take over jobs that were currently under the jurisdiction of the NUPB&PW and NATSOPA. Both unions realised that unless they merged, their interests and influence in the industry might be lost to the NGA, whose formation was viewed as a means to retain 'new litho jobs' exclusively for craft unions members and to prevent those in predominantly non-craft jobs gaining upgrading to craft status in the printing industry of the future. If NUPB&PW and NATSOPA remained separate unions it would be easier for the craft unions to exercise control over the new jobs and to continue the traditional system of training for access to the higher-paid jobs and thereby excluding adult non-craft employees.

However, in amalgamating, the NUPB&PW and NATSOPA were not motivated solely by defensive reasons. An amalgamation would enable co-ordination of a counter-attack on the craft unions' attempts to maintain a craft dominance over the 'litho revolution'. As a single union they would be better able to challenge the apprenticeship system as the only access to craft occupations and to adopt an aggressive attitude towards the rights of their members to have control over web-offset presses, especially where they were introduced into former letterpress houses. For both the NUPB&PW and NATSOPA the inclusion of the word 'Graphical' in the title of any merged union they might form was an important marker that they were entitled to have members in any part of the industry. The growth of lithography offered NUPB&PW and NATSOPA an excellent opportunity to challenge the craft unions' claim to all skilled jobs and to control the expansion of litho jobs to the exclusion of existing non-craft employees.

A merged NUPB&PW/NATSOPA union would reinforce their view that web-fed litho printing was a new process and the traditional demarcation lines between craft employers and non-craft workers were irrelevant. As one union NUPB&PW and NATSOPA would be in a stronger position to argue that all workers (craft and non-craft) in the industry would need some retraining to be competent to run web-offset machine rooms. A single non-craft union would carry weight confident in seeking equal access to the retraining necessary to enable its members to work the new litho processes. To remain separate unions carried the risk that expanding employment opportunities would be restricted to the craft unions who would resist the upgrading of non-craft employees to skilled status leaving them in 'dead-end' jobs. An 'aggressive' attitude towards retraining and a reform of the apprenticeship system was essential for non-craft employees if they were to have a stake in the 'new litho world'; a single predominantly non-craft union was a necessary condition of this approach.

THE GROWTH OF AN ALTERNATIVE PRINTING INDUSTRY AND PAPERMAKING INDUSTRY

Printing

By the mid-1960s, printing ceased to be a 'sheltered' industry. In the ten-year period from 1955–65, greater product market competition came from three sources – increased imports, expansion of in-plant printing and additional outlets to newspapers and magazines for advertising. The first two threatened the general printing trade whilst the third challenged newspapers and periodicals. Although this alternative printing industry produced lower-quality, lower-price products than the conventional industry, the quality was adequate for most customers' needs. The increased competition arose because the industry could not meet all the demands for print products. Delays in the completion of orders caused customers to place their orders abroad and/or set up their own printing capacity.

However, NUPB&PW and NATSOPA members viewed this product market competition as a potential rather than a real threat to their employment security. Although it represented a loss of work from the industry, there was still much work available and there was an acute shortage of labour in the industry. NUPB&PW and NATSOPA members did not consider that these emerging alternative printing products would ever be a real threat to their employment security.

Import Penetration

By the mid-1960s the printing industry faced increased competition from imported print matter on a larger scale than in the mid-1950s. The competition came from Holland, France, Germany, Japan, Poland and Finland. Increased foreign competition was particularly acute for UK book printers who lost out on price and who were forced to reduce costs and employment levels.

The early 1960s saw the growth of magazines, traditionally printed in the UK, printed on the Continent as publishers claimed they could not find UK printers who were capable of meeting their requirements. They could now have work printed overseas and transported back into the UK and charge the customer a lower price than if the work had been done in the UK. The growth of printing overseas led to redundancies amongst NUPB&PW members. Given that import penetration was likely to continue, the NUPB&PW saw a merger with another print union as a constructive way of increasing its voice in political circles for import protection.

Alternative Outlets for Advertising

Advertising receipts were an important source of revenue for newspapers, magazines and periodicals. The rate charged to advertisers was related to circulation. The higher the circulation the higher the rate that could be charged and vice versa. In the mid-1950s there were few alternative outlets for advertisers to newspapers and magazines. The advent of commercial television in 1956 led to less advertising in printed matter and national newspapers in particular began to lose to this medium.

Given the importance of advertising revenue to newspapers in covering their costs, the rise of alternative outlets for advertisers meant production costs had to be contained. Newspapers and magazines could no longer automatically increase advertising rates to cover increased production costs. At the same time, newspapers and magazines had to offset lost advertising revenues by increasing their cover prices. This carried the danger of lost circulation which in turn made the paper less attractive to advertisers.

By the late 1950s the loss of advertising revenue was a factor in the closure of some periodicals and newspapers and/or their amalgamation. The trend accelerated in the early 1960s with the closure, amongst others, of the *News Chronicle*, the *Empire News*, the *Sunday Despatch*, the *British Evening World* and the *Birmingham Evening Despatch*. By 1963 Glasgow was the only city outside London with two evening newspapers. These closures and mergers contributed to a loss of work in newspapers and magazines with adverse consequences for NUPB& PW and NATSOPA members. Increases in costs would intensify this closure trend. To re-establish the competitiveness of newspapers, employers were considering ways in which production costs might be reduced. The introduction of new production techniques based on lithographic processes was one means of doing this.

Office Printing Machinery

Multigraph, Rotaprint and Multilith machines enabled organisations outside the conventional printing industry to establish their own printing capacity and avoid their printing work being done in the trade. From the end of the Second World War there was a steady increase in the introduction of miniature printing machines into the offices of local authorities, atomic energy establishments, nationalised industries, central government, banks, insurance companies and other private firms. Only a small number of miniature printing machines were installed by conventional printers. A problem for the print unions was reaching agreement for staff on those machines installed outside of the printing industry.

The print unions agreed, in principle, that office printing machines, being litho offset, should be under the control of the ASLP. However, this union could not exercise control over the numbers of machines that existed outside the industry. NATSOPA took the view that they came in on the machine side and were entitled to operate these small litho machines. The PMB of the NUPB&PW claimed the right to operate office printing machines because they involved platen work which was traditionally that of their members.

During 1953 the ASLP concluded agreements with the NUPB&PW, NATSOPA and the TA for the staffing of small litho office machines installed within conventional printing firms. Three principles underlying these were: first, workers in charge of one or more office machines were to be members of the appropriate craft union and assistants were to be members of the appropriate assistant's union; second, small litho office machines were the preserve of the ASLP which had responsibility for negotiating staffing levels and wage agreements; and third, where the ASLP could not supply labour those operating miniature machines would become associate members of the ASLP. These agreements helped control miniature office printing machines inside the printing industry but did little towards gaining influence over those existing outside the industry. The print unions, throughout the 1950s and the early 1960s, continually sought, but with little success, to bring small litho machines outside the printing industry within their jurisdiction.

The problems of controlling miniature printing machines outside the industry were numerous. First, there was no connection between the printing unions and the industries in which these machines were installed. Second, non-print unions recruited workers operating small litho machines outside the printing industry. NALGO organised such workers in local government whilst the Civil Service Union and the Institute of Professional Civil Servants did so in central government. The Transport and General Workers' Union (T&GWU), the General and Municipal Workers' Union (GMB) and the Clerical and Administrative Workers' Union (CAWU) attempted to recruit employees operating office printing machinery in banks, insurance and other private companies. The National Union of Public Employers (NUPE), the T&GWU and the GMB also recruited those working small litho machines in public bodies. Attempts by the print unions to persuade these unions to accept such machines as printing machines and therefore those operating them be organised by print unions made little headway.

Third, the only weapon the print unions had in their armoury was persuasion. Little progress was likely to be made unless pressure could be brought to bear on employers and non-print unions. The print unions turned to the TUC which in 1960 called a meeting of all unions involved to discuss the organisation of office printing machines. Following considerable discussion, the view was expressed that 'the printing unions had a strong moral claim to these machines' and they should make separate approaches to unions in the civil service, local government and the nationalised industries.[7] The print unions asked the other unions involved to transfer their members working on small litho machines to the appropriate print union and to agree in future that any such workers be recruited into the appropriate printing trade union. The request was effectively ignored by the non-print unions[8] and no progress stemmed from the TUC initiative.

Fourth, in central and local government, workers operating minia-ture office printing machines enjoyed better terms and conditions of employment than those applied in the general printing industry. Both the NUPB&PW and NATSOPA recognised that if they obtained recog-nition from central and local government employers they had nothing to offer workers operating small litho machines in these organisations as far as wages and conditions of employment were concerned. Indeed, they would be doing them a disservice since their transfer into a printing union would reduce their employment status from non-manual employees to manual employment and result in the loss of better pensions, hours of work, holiday and sick pay conditions and pay. The NUPB&PW and NATSOPA accepted reluctantly that they were unlikely to make progress in organising the operators of small litho machines outside the conventional printing industry.

The introduction of miniature printing machines into and outside the industry in the late 1950s and early 1960s removed work from the letterpress side of the industry. These developments represented a challenge to the traditional relationships of the printing industry. Both the NUPB&PW and NATSOPA claimed the right to work on these machines and, as one union, they would be better able to challenge the ASLP claim to sole jurisdiction and also better able to use the power of numbers within the TUC to call on its assistance to help with organisational rights on small litho machines outside the conven-tional printing industry.

Papermaking and Board-making

In the 1950s and the 1960s the British papermaking industry faced increasing competition from imports with the result surplus capacity developed and the rate of return on capital fell. The UK paper industry was not a large exporter, and it drew 6 per cent of its raw materials from local forests and imported three tons of pulp a year from sources which were the industry's main competitors. In 1930 imports accounted for 40 per cent of the consumption of paper and board in the UK. By 1939, tariff protection imposed in 1932 had reduced this figure to 30 per cent. However, post-1950, imports increased again and by 1967 had reached 33 per cent.

In the late 1950s and early 1960s the UK newsprint industry suffered from world-wide over-capacity caused by the opening of new mills in Scandinavia which were subsidised by central government funds. Until the early 1960s the competitive deficit of the UK papermaking industry was reduced by an import tariff of 14 to 16.6 per cent on Scandinavian and other foreign imports. This protection was removed in the 1960s. In 1958 the UK joined EFTA where seven member countries agreed over a period of time to remove all trading tariffs between themselves. By 1964 UK tariffs against imported paper had been halved and they were completely removed on 1 January 1967. The effect was to increase the competitive advantage of Scandinavian producers in the UK market to which UK producers reacted by taking on work at prices which were cut to the bone.

The creation of the European Economic Community (EEC) in 1957 presented further problems for British paper manufacturers. The movement in the Community towards a common external tariff raised the duty on paper imports into West Germany which was Europe's largest market for paper and board. The Scandinavian exporters, as non-members of the Community were now excluded from the concentrated efforts on the UK market which as members of EFTA they had been able to access. The UK paper and board manufacturers' efforts to counter the Scandinavians by boosting sales to Europe were not helped by EEC tariffs.

The difficulties facing the industry in the early 1960s were aggravated by the UK government's attitude towards EFTA and the EEC. Membership of EFTA meant the protection needed against Scandinavian competition could not continue. UK non-membership of the EEC meant the industry faced import tariffs of 15–20 per cent in the lucrative markets of West Germany and France. On the other hand, if the UK and Scandinavian countries were admitted to the EEC, the industry's problem would ease. The pressure of Scandinavian producers to sell more in the UK would be reduced as markets would open up in West Germany, France, Italy and the Benelux countries. The same would be true for the UK. It was for these reasons that the NUPB&PW supported UK membership of the EEC and was doubtful of the advantages of EFTA membership.

The 1950s and early 1960s saw import tariff protection for papermaking firms reduced, exposing an industry whose general level of efficiency had degenerated behind tariff barriers. Many firms needed to re-invest and re-equip their capital stock as they operated old plants. Only large companies had taken the necessary economic measures. The tariff barriers had kept inefficient firms in business. Exposing the industry to international competition drove out the marginal firms with a consequent increase in unemployment amongst NUPB&PW members. The Britton Mill closed in 1961 whilst 1963 witnessed the closure of the Tovil and Bridge Mill and the Olive and Partington Mill at Glossip. Mill closures in 1964 included two in Scotland and the Bowater's Sittingbourne Mill. The imposition in 1964 of an import surcharge by the incoming Labour government came too late to prevent further mill closures in 1965. The government withdrew its import surcharge in 1966 and announced the elimination from 1 January 1967 of the remaining EFTA import tariffs. This had a serious impact on the industry. Many mills went on short time, some paper-making machines closed and two more mills closed completely. The only 'good' news was the opening of two integrated (pulp- and paper-making) mills – one by Wiggins Teape at Fort William and the other by Thames Case Board Group at Workington.

The NUPB&PW reacted to the employment effects of the removal of tariff protection and of the implementation of new production techniques by intensifying political lobbying and by seeking links with another trade union in industries that used paper as a raw material. To link with another printing union which organised membership similar grades of employment in terms of skill levels was a natural step. A merger with NATSOPA would create a union with members in paper, printing and ink manufacture. A link-up with NATSOPA would increase influence in the TUC and the Labour Party and assist in gaining wider support for 'political' solutions to the economic problems of the paper- and board-making industry.

THE GROWTH OF LARGE-SCALE COMPANIES AND LOSS OF WORK FROM LONDON

75,000 members of NUPB&PW and NATSOPA worked in London. The late 1950s and early 1960s saw increased redundancy amongst these members due to mergers and take-overs between firms in London, the closure of national newspapers and London based firms relocating their production capacity to the English provinces. NUPB&PW and NATSOPA recognised that as one union it would be easier to cope with these problems. Remaining separate unions would lead to increasing inter-union conflict between the Paperworkers and NATSOPA as the employment opportunities for their members in London declined. In the background was the threat that the craft unions would exploit such conflict to take over NUPB&PW and NATSOPA job territories.

Towards the end of the 1960s a merger between Thomson Allied

Newspapers and Odham Press seemed certain. The NUPB&PW expressed concern at the likely effect on employment of the proposed merger. It was assured by the management of the two groups that the proposed merger would not affect job security or the conditions of employment of its members. Matters became complicated when, in addition to the proposed merger between Thomson Allied Newspapers and Odham Press, there were firm indications of a take-over bid by the Mirror Group. The NUPB&PW feared if the Mirror Group gained control of Odham there would be closures since, when the Mirror Group took over Amalgamated Press in 1959, eight weeklies, four monthlies and seven annual publications folded. The Paperworkers and NATSOPA were also concerned about potential detrimental effects of the take-over of Odhams by the Mirror Group on the *Daily Herald* and the *Sunday People*, since a successful bid would bring eight newspapers under the control of that organisation.

The print unions adopted a unified approach to avoid redundancy resulting from proposed company mergers. If, however, in spite of all efforts redundancy could not be avoided then heavy compensation should be sought for those affected. There remained the problem, however, that minimising the effects of mergers on employment security would be more difficult to achieve if the print unions were forced to react separately to each merger and take-over. Following the Mirror Group take-over of Odhams, four magazines merged into two, causing NUPB&PW redundancies. Given the importance of the London membership to both NUPB&PW and NATSOPA, they recognised as one union they would be better able to minimise the employment insecurity of their London members. However, if this could not be achieved they would each protect the interests of their members as best they could, irrespective of each others common interests.

In October 1960 the closure was announced of the *News Chronicle* and the *Star*. This affected over 3,000 men and women and the print unions were faced with the formidable task of placing these individuals in other suitable employment. The *News Chronicle* merged with the *Daily Mail* and the *Star* with the *Evening News*. However, the *News Chronicle* and *Star* closure was quickly followed by that of the *Empire News*, whilst the end of 1960 saw the cessation of publication of the *Sunday Graphic*. The threat of further national newspaper closures led the government to establish a Royal Commission on the Press in February 1961 to examine the economic and financial factors affecting the production and sales of newspapers, magazines and other periodicals in the UK. In 1963 the NPA presented the P&KTF with a memorandum entitled *'Efficiency in Production'*, setting out how it envisaged employment security in national newspapers in London could be improved. It proposed, *inter alia*, a smaller work-force, lower staffing, less casual working and a redundancy compensation scheme. Its implementation would have meant further losses of work to NUPB&PW members. Nevertheless, the closure of the *News Chronicle* and *Star*, came as a great shock to the London printing unions and was a significant factor in the print unions acknowledging that mergers were necessary if the employment security of their London workers was to be maximised.

Pressures for a merger between NUPB&PW and NATSOPA also came from employers relocating to new locations outside London, moves which were justified on the grounds of excessive staffing levels in London relative to the provinces, a fall-off in magazines readership, a decline in advertising revenue and production costs which were at least 40 per cent lower in the provinces. In February 1963 the International Publishing Corporation produced a memorandum entitled 'Factors Contributing to High London Printing Costs' in which they argued that excessive over-time, staffing and uneconomic work practices were driving work away from London. The company stressed its wish to agree on economies so that London could survive as a print centre. Although as a condition of entering talks the print unions gained assurance of 'no redundancies', they were unable to achieve guarantees that no further work would be transferred from London during the talks.

In August 1963 the IPC's overall plans for London included a smaller work-force. The negotiations became complicated when the IPC in late 1963 transferred the printing of two of its periodicals (*Melody Maker* and *Amateur Gardening*) from London to the provinces. In early 1964 the Paperworkers' Union found itself in dispute with the IPC over inadequate assurances about the transfer of work from London. A policy of non-co-operation in IPC's periodical and general printing houses was introduced and the London Central Branch operated a similar unofficial policy in Mirror Group offices producing the *Sunday Mirror, People, Daily Mirror, Daily Herald* and *Sporting Life*. Discussions between the IPC and NUPB&PW resulted in the calling off of both the official and unofficial action and a resumption of normal working.

In the negotiations on high London printing costs, NATSOPA and the NUPB&PW were prepared to make concessions but not in isolation from those of other print unions. Both NUPB&PW and NATSOPA recognised that as one union it would be easier 'to follow the work into the provinces' and and would also offer greater protection from attempts by letterpress and lithographic craft unions to restrict NATSOPA/NUPB&PW advances both in the provinces and London.

INABILITY OF PRINT UNIONS TO ACT IN ISOLATION

Since 1945 the BFMP and the NS had urged unions to approach them on a collective basis with wage claims rather than each submitting unrelated claims, which tended to result in a settlement with one union on the basis of a claim by another. By the mid-1950s the employers were adamant they would concede to one union only what they would concede to all. All printing unions accepted the desirability for the industry of a wage structure covering London/provincial craft differential and craft/non-craft relativities, but they could not agree how this could be achieved in practice.

During 1919 negotiations between the NS and the BFMP and the print unions produced a comprehensive set of national agreements covering all groups of employees, including women, bindery workers, warehousemen and cutters and machine assistants and which fixed differentials between different classes of workers in the same town and differentials between the same class of workers in different towns. A series of wage cuts in 1921 and 1922[9] disturbed craft parity, reduced the skilled bookbinders' rate below the basic rate for other London craftsmen and widened the London/provincial craft differential, the craft/non-craft differential in London and the craft/non-craft differential in the provinces. In 1947 the TA, the NUPB&PW and NATSOPA submitted claims to the BFMP and the NS to remove 'this 25 years injustice' and re-establish the differentials of the 1919 agreements. The other print unions were reluctant to participate in a collective wages movement and by October 1947 the employers faced 13 unco-ordinated wage claims, the granting of one of which would have altered pay relativities and precipitated an avalanche of leapfrogging claims.

In November 1947 the employers proposed a wage structure which proved to be unacceptable to the print unions. The unions each went their own way and in February 1948 the NUPB&PW and NATSOPA accepted weekly increases varying from 75p to 25p, with a 45p per week increase for women with more than five years' service. Between September 1948 and February 1949 there were further attempts by the

BFMP and then NS and the P&KTF to devise a wage structure. The employers expressed concern at leapfrogging claims and proposed there be craft parity, with semi-skilled and unskilled workers receiving a percentage of the craft rate. When talks broke down in March 1949 the individual unions again went their own separate ways. However, the TA, the ASLP, NATSOPA and the NUPB&PW, who sought to re-establish craft parity for its London bookbinders employed in publishing houses, acted collectively on their separate claims.

The four unions sought to redress the effects on differentials of the wage cuts of 1921 and 1922. However, the BFMP and the NS thought it unwise to make an agreement with the four unions unless the others gave assurance that any settlement would not be the basis for a further round of leapfrogging claims. The employers sought to achieve a wage structure in two stages. First, they would settle the craft rates and then go on to settle the non-craft and the women's rates. However, the other print unions would not give the guarantee the employers sought, whereupon the four unions again went separate ways. In December 1949 the NUPB&PW and NATSOPA made an agreement with BFMP and the NS which increased bookbinders' rates to £6.72 per week in London and to £6.10 per week in Grade 4 towns, increased rates for women ranging from £3.85 per week in London to £3.35 per week in Grade 4 towns. Women with five years' experience received increased weekly rates varying from £3.72½ to £4.22½.

By the end of 1949 the employers had half a wage structure. Craft litho rates and London craft rates remained to be settled. In 1950 the LSC entered into dispute with the London printing employers as it sought to re-establish the 1948 London/provincial craft differential in the light of a TA settlement of November 1949. The dispute was referred to a Court of Inquiry whose report[10] formed the basis of a settlement providing for a London craft rate of £7.50 per week, a cost of living bonus and a stabilisation of the agreement for five years. This London settlement had again disturbed differentials and the employers met with the TA, NUPB&PW, NATSOPA and other print unions to adjust their pay rates in the light of the London settlement. These negotiations provided for an increase in the weekly provincial craft rate of 62½p, of non-craft male rates of 50p and of a 40p per week for women. The NUPB&PW negotiations were more protracted than those with the other unions because of its insistence on improving the pay of its female members. The employers' original offer was an increase of 30p per week, which was increased to 37½p and finally to 40p per week.

There still remained the issue of lack of parity between bookbinders' rates in London publishing houses and LSC members. This had been a sore point for NUPB&PW London bookbinder members for over 30 years. In 1951, the matter was referred to the National Arbitration Tribunal which awarded the London bookbinders parity with LSC rates. By 1951 the printing and provincial newspaper industry had stumbled to an acceptable wage structure. The BFMP and the NS had demonstrated their unwillingness to make settlements with one union or group of unions in isolation from the rest. The ability of one union to improve, and sustain, the relative advantage in terms of its members' wages and conditions in isolation from other print unions had been shown to be limited. The employers' message was clear and was repeated in the 1955/6 negotiations to revise the 1950/1 wage agreements.

In March 1955, in anticipation of the termination of these agreements in November 1955, the P&KTF sought to ascertain if a collective approach on new wage agreements was possible. The LSC and the ACP said they preferred to act unilaterally. However, six unions (NUPB&PW, NATSOPA, TA, STA, NSES and MCTF) agreed to make a collective approach to the BFMP and the NS. Towards the end of November 1955 the unions acting collectively indicated to the BFMP and the NS that they were prepared to settle for weekly increases of 92½p for craftsman, 77½p for semi-skilled adult male workers and 60p for women. However, during the final stages of the negotiations, the TA had withdrawn from the collective movement to act unilaterally. The new agreements for the members of NUPB&PW, NATSOPA, NSES, STA and MCTF came into operation in January 1956.

The LTS and the ACP each pursued their claim independently to the London Master Printers' Association for a new basic rate of £12. When the employers refused to concede the claim the LTS and the ACP instructed their members to 'work to rule', a move the employers countered by dismissing LTS and ACP members. The Ministry of Labour established a Court of Inquiry in response to which the TA, the BFMP and the NS agreed to suspend their differences pending the publication of the Court's report on the London disputes. The Court recommended further efforts be made to establish comprehensive national machinery on a two-tier basis for the negotiation of wages and conditions in the industry.[11]

Following the Court's report, four craft unions (LTS, ACP, TA and the ASLP) came together and negotiated collectively in May 1956 on new agreements which disturbed relativities with the 'January unions'.

The employers agreed to achieve uniformity between the 'two groups of unions'. The five 'January' unions said they expected adjustments to bring craft rates up to those for the 'May' unions, while they expected 87½ per cent of the craft rate for non-craft members, 85 per cent for general assistants and 75 per cent of the Class 3 rate for women. In July 1956 the employers offered to adjust the craft rates of the 'January' unions to the comparative position of the four 'May' unions, but for the non-craft and women they offered 30p, 21p, and 19p (women) which amounted to new money of 5p for men and 2½p for women. The NUPB&PW and NATSOPA successfully sought an improvement of this offer. In September 1956 the five 'January' unions accepted the employers' proposals which brought them into line with the settlement made by the 'May' unions.

The NUPB&PW had easily obtained revised rates for its craft members but had experienced considerable difficulties in gaining further increases for its non-craft and women members. The four 'May' unions (all craft) had stated early during their negotiations with the BFMP and the NS that in their view the craft rate they were seeking to establish was the appropriate wage differential between craft and non-craft employees. They also made it clear that any subsequent increases granted to non-craft employees could result in an application for a further increase in craft rates. With regards to the NUPB&PW women members' rate, the two employers' organisations were adamant that those established in the January 1956 settlements were adequate if not generous. The NUPB&PW had remained determined that its non-craft and female members should have appropriate increases in wages to bring them into line with the May 1956 agreements.

The 1955/6 wage negotiations had brought sharp conflict and dissension between the craft and non-craft unions. The craft unions had sought to widen the craft/non-craft differential and to pursue their own interests regardless of those of the non-craft production employees. Relationships had been soured and the NUPB&PW and NATSOPA recognised the dangers of remaining separate unions, especially if the proposed craft union amalgamation talks, which began in 1956, were successful. In any future attempt to devise a rational wage structure their influence could be diminished, making them less effective too in negotiating for improvements in the terms and conditions of employment of their members. They might have to accept such employment conditions changes as the amalgamated craft union would permit. NUPB&PW and NATSOPA feared there would be no meaningful voice for non-craft employees in wage negotiations. In addition, NUPB&PW and NATSOPA both had craft members and were concerned that as separate unions they would be left to negotiate for these members outside the craft union grouping. Two pockets of craftsmen in two separate largely non-craft unions were threatened with isolation in the face of an all-embracing craft union.

The wage negotiations had confirmed that the BFMP and the NS would not concede to one union anything other than what they were prepared to concede to all. NUPB&PW and NATSOPA accepted that independently of each other and of the craft unions that they were unlikely to gain permanent advances in the wages and conditions of their members. They had come to recognise that the prospect of achieving an individual increase for a particular section of the work-force was determined by the employers' knowledge that any such increase would be quoted by every other union in support of its own claims. Situations in which unions could act in the best interests of their members irrespective of the effects of their actions on other unions were over. It was unrealistic to think in the future in terms of each union acting for itself. The NUPB&PW and NATSOPA saw there was little justification for the print unions continuing to act independently in wage negotiations.

The lack of unity between the printing unions during the 1955/6 wages negotiations led the NUPB&PW to take an initiative at the 1956 P&KTF Administrative Council designed to establish greater unity between the print unions in future wages negotiations. It successfully moved the following motion:

> That, in the opinion of this conference, recent events have demonstrated a serious lack of unity between the unions affiliated to our Federation. As a means towards restoring this unity, this conference instructs the General Secretary to call a meeting of two or three representatives from each union in the Federation, such meeting to endeavour to devise a basic wages structure for the industry.[12]

In subsequent discussions the print unions accepted the idea of a two-tier wage negotiating structure for the industry. There was one tier for craftsmen and one for non-craft employees. Those 'non-craft' unions with craft members put the case for those members at the craft group conference. Unions with both craft and non-craft members put their case to both sections.

Suspicion of the motives of the craft unions by the NUPB&PW and NATSOPA surfaced again when in 1958, in anticipation of the start of negotiations with the BFMP and the NS for new agreements to replace those due to terminate in 1959, separate meetings were called to determine the claims of the craft workers and the non-craft workers. Although the craft unions accepted that the NUPB&PW, ASLP and STA should legitimately be represented at both meetings, when NATSOPA turned up to the craft union meeting they were asked to leave on the grounds they were not considered to be a print craft union. NATSOPA argued to the contrary, stating that unions could not decide into what categories other unions fell. However, in response to the craft unions' insistence that it had no place at the craft union conference, NATSOPA resigned from the P&KTF.

Nevertheless, in 1958 nine printing unions including the NUPB&PW submitted a collective claim to the BFMP and the NS. In reality it was three separate but related claims existing side by side. First there was the craft workers' wages claim and second there was the non-craft workers' claim. Third was a demand for a 40-hour week, an issue that was the negotiating responsibility of the P&KTF. Subsequently NATSOPA rejoined the P&KTF and the collective approach which after a six-week strike in 1959 produced an agreement to operate until 1962 providing wages and hours advances. A collective approach in 1962 resulted in a three-year agreement to operate until 1965.

The general trends and developments in the printing and paper- and board-making industries in the late 1950s and early 1960s that led to the merger of NUPB&PW and NATSOPA to form SOGAT have been reviewed. The two unions feared that technological developments would increase unemployment amongst their members and the implementation of the litho printing revolution would cause the craft unions to exclude the non-craft unions and their members from a 'stake' in this revolution and to continue to prevent non-craft workers from being upgraded to craft employees. However, the NUPB&PW and NATSOPA were not motivated solely by defensive considerations. They acknowledged that an amalgamation would enable an effective counter-attack on the letterpress and litho craft union attempts to maintain a craft dominance over the distribution of the benefits of the 'litho' revolution. The non-craft unions also feared that the loss of work from London and the growth of large-scale firms as a result of mergers and take-overs would undermine job opportunities and the employment security of its members. The organisational anomalies that existed between the two main non-craft unions in the provinces would make it more difficult to 'follow work into the provinces' if they remained separate unions.

All the general developments reviewed in this chapter demonstrate the trade union structure of the printing industry of the mid-1950s was irrelevant. All print unions realised that reform would best be achieved through amalgamation. The craft unions believed first, that there should be the creation of a single craft union for the industry and a single union for non-craft employees, and second, that these two unions should come together to form one union for the industry. The NUPB&PW and NATSOPA believed there should be one union for the industry and that any merger should be welcomed as it would reduce the number of print unions. In 1956 the craft unions attempted to form one letterpress craft union as a prelude to forming one craft union via mergers with the litho craft unions. The letterpress craft unions' merger talks collapsed in 1961 but the LTS and the TA came together to form the NGA on 1 January 1964. It was envisaged that other letterpress craft unions would quickly join them, followed by the litho unions. The NUPB&PW and NATSOPA could not stand by and do nothing. Merger attempts with two craft unions – the LTS in 1962 and ASLP in 1963 – had failed. NUPB&PW and NATSOPA realised they needed to create a single non-craft union to counter-balance the creation of one craft union. The NUPB&PW and NATSOPA had reacted to the 1956 craft union merger talks by entering merger talks themselves. These had failed in 1958. The creation of the NGA in 1964 was seen as the catalyst for the emergence of a single craft union. The NUPB&PW and NATSOPA needed to come together quickly, not only to counter-balance the formation of the NGA but to try to attract some craft unions to join them rather than the NGA. The NUPB&PW and NATSOPA could not to fail in their attempt to bring about a successful amalgamation. They achieved their aim with the creation of the Society of Graphical and Allied Trades in February 1966.

NOTES

1. For NATSOPA this was first time in its history it merged with another major printing trade union. However, from its earliest days it sought amalgamations with other print unions. As early as 1902 it entered into correspondence with several organisations including the Platen Printing Machine Minders, who joined the NUPB&PW in 1924. See J. Moran *NATSOPA: 75 Years*, Heinemann, London, 1964, p. 114.

2. The 'Paperworker'/NATSOPA town situation arose from the overlapping interests of NATSOPA and the former Warehousemen's and Cutters' Union (a constituent society of the NUPB&PW). Many jobs of the members of these two unions were the same. Though relations between the two unions were always friendly there was, at times, conflict over demarcation. In 1906 the two unions decided on amalgamation. Unfortunately, the proposed amalgamation was rejected by NATSOPA members by 14 votes only (in favour 1,280, against 1,294). Another effort was made in 1909 but at that point NATSOPA had internal problems and the matter was dropped.

3. See National Union of Printing, Bookbinding and Paperworkers *Report of the Biennial Delegate Council Meeting, 1958*, pp. 224–6.

4. See J. Gennard *A History of the National Graphical Association*, Unwin Hyman, 1990, Chapter 4, pp. 83–8.

5. See National Union of Printing, Bookbinding and Paperworkers *Report of the Biennial Delegate Council Meeting, 1956*, pp. 260–3.

6. See 'NUPB&PW and NATSOPA – Amalgamation', supplementary report to the *Annual Report of the Governing Council of 1965*, National Society of Operative Printers and Assistants, p. 22.

7. See Printing and Kindred Trades Federation, *Annual Report, 1959–60*, p. 21.

8. Except by the Clerical and Administrative Workers' Union (CAWU) who were prepared to reconsider their position on three conditions – the print unions provide a definition of the circumstances in which small litho machines be regarded as office work and the circumstances when they be recognised as print work; the P&KTF reconsider its decision to refuse affiliation to CAWU, and NATSOPA cease to organise clerical workers in the printing industry. The NUPB&PW and NATSOPA could not accept these conditions.

9. In 1921 the NUPB&PW and NATSOPA accepted reduction of wages by 37½p per week for men and 15p for women. In 1922 the NUPB&PW and NATSOPA accepted weekly wage reductions of 75p for men and 37½p for women applied in instalments between May 1922 and January 1923. In 1921 the LSC and the NSES suffered cuts of 25p per week whilst in 1922 the TA experienced a cut of 62½p per week and the London craft unions one of 30p per week.

10. See *Report of a Court of Inquiry into the Causes and Circumstances of a Dispute between the London Master Printers' Association and the London Society of Compositors*, Cmnd 8074, HMSO, London, 1950.

11. See *Report of a Court of Inquiry into the Causes and Circumstances of Disputes between the London Master Printers' Association and the London Typographical Society and the Association of the Correctors of the Press*, Cmnd 9717, HMSO, London, 1956.

12. See Printing and Kindred Trades Federation *Annual Report 1955* and *Report of Administrative Council, May 1956*, 1956, pp. 36–41.

CHAPTER 3

RELATIONS BETWEEN NUPB&PW AND OTHER PRINTING AND PAPERMAKING UNIONS

THE LETTERPRESS CRAFT UNIONS

The Typographical Association (TA)[1]

Relationships between the NUPB&PW and the TA, governed by a Reciprocity Agreement, were good. For many years the Printing Machine Branch (PMB) of NUPB&PW sought to include vertical Miehle machines in the Reciprocity Agreement to bring it into line with that between itself and the LTS. Until the 1950s the TA opposed any extension of the scope of the agreement and insisted it be confined to platen machines. However, in the mid-1950s, the TA concluded that little would be lost by allowing vertical Miehle machines to be included in the Reciprocity Agreement. In April 1955, the agreement was widened to effect this.

Under the Agreement, the TA recognised the PMB jurisdiction as a radius of 15 miles from the General Post Office in London. Outside this area the PMB accepted that platen and vertical Miehle machines were staffed by TA members. A member of either of the two unions, seeking or obtaining employment within the area of other, had to present his or her card to the secretary of the branch in which employment was taken. If all was in order the individual was admitted to the union as an associate member.

Associate membership applied to TA members employed in London on platen and vertical Miehle machines controlled by the PMB and to

PMB members employed on the same machines in TA areas. Associate members of either union paid a weekly contribution of 1p and a full contribution to their parent society. For industrial purposes, associate members were under the control of their adopted society, but they were not ineligible for office in that society. Associate members could become full members of their adopted society. Any disagreements over the operation of the Reciprocity Agreement were settled by the P&KTF.

In September 1959 the NUPB&PW, in response to a PMB letter which drew attention to its close co-operation with the letterpress craft unions, invited LTS and the TA to discuss amalgamation.[2] When representatives of the NUPB&PW and the TA met in February 1960 the exchanges were friendly and it was agreed, given the similarities in the organisational structures of the two unions, that a merger was feasible. However, the TA was already in amalgamation talks with four other unions – the NUPT, MCTFS, ASLP and the ACP – and needed to consult with them about the NUPB&PW's invitation. Subsequently the TA wrote to the NUPB&PW stating that they regarded the merger invitation as 'a most friendly and statesmanlike one' to which, had the circumstances not been otherwise, they would have been happy to respond positively. The five-union amalgamation initiative had made good progress in drafting a constitution and the TA considered it unwise to break off negotiations in order to start again, almost from the beginning, on drafting a new Rule Book with the NUPB&PW.[3] It was not practical for the NUPB&PW to join these union talks. The TA had no disagreement in principle with the NUPB&PW. Had the five-union amalgamation already been achieved, the practical difficulties associated with the NUPB&PW joining a larger grouping would have been manageable. However, circumstances had conspired otherwise. The NUPB&PW regretted, but understood, the TA's decision, and its friendly relationship with the TA continued.

The London Typographical Society (LTS)

Small Cylinder Machines

The PMB members had operated vertical Miehle machines in London since their introduction from the USA in the late 1920s and early 1930s. Nevertheless, in London machine rooms, the PMB and the LTS operated a Reciprocity Agreement which provided for 'associate membership' and a mechanism whereby members of either union could be employed on printing machines claimed by each Society subject to the operating Society having no members available for such work at the particular time. In 1957, the PMB requested changes to the agreement to give both unions equal control over small cylinder machines up to demy size. They feared their members would be adversely affected by the growing tendency of employers to replace platen machines with small cylinder machines. The LTS objected to encroachment by another union on a field traditionally covered by its members. When an accommodation could not be reached the PMB gave notice to terminate the Reciprocity Agreement.

The minding of horizontal as opposed to vertical cylinder machines had been an old sore between the PMB and the former Printing Machine Managers' Trade Society (PMMTS). In 1931 a P&KTF Arbitration Board had awarded the minding of small horizontal cylinder machines to the PMMTS. Soon after the 1955 PMMTS' amalgamation with the LSC to form the LTS, disputes between the PMB and the LTS resurfaced. Following many unsuccessful attempts to settle the problem on a permanent basis, the NUPB&PW decided, in 1960, to refer the matter of minding horizontal cylinder machines back to the P&KTF for the 1931 decision to be reviewed. The issue was put on ice when the NUPB&PW and the LTS began amalgamation discussions later that year.

However, the break-down of these merger talks in the spring of 1961, resurrected the differences between the two unions over the control of small cylinder machines. Trouble arose at McCorquodale's in London when the company replaced two vertical Miehle machines operated by PMB members by two small heidelberg cylinders slightly over Demy size. The LTS, in the absence of a Reciprocity Agreement, refused to allow PMB members to follow their jobs and operate the cylinder machines. This action annoyed the PMB as it was only seeking a right that the LTS always insisted on for its own membership. When the NUPB&PW cut off supplies of paper to McCorquodales, P&KTF senior officers agreed to meet informally with both sides to explore a possible solution to the differences. A voluntary agreement could not be made. The NUPB&PW referred the matter to a P&KTF Board of Arbitration for a review of its 1931 decision.[4] The NUPB's two nominees were Mr Alf Buckle, General Secretary of the National NSES and Mr Ron Emerick, General Secretary of the ASLP.

In its award, announced on 12 December 1962, the P&KTF stated that it could find no valid grounds for varying its 1931 award, the conditions of which had been:

(i) Cylinder machines be under the control of machine managers and all platen machines be operated by platen minders.

(ii) The above award not to interfere with the employment of members of either union upon the machines on which they were presently engaged. Future vacancies be allocated according to the award.

(iii) The unions make arrangements as to their respective work and devise provisions to harmonise interests.

The P&KTF had ruled in favour of the LTS despite the 1931 Agreement having not been enforced by that union such that several PMB members were working machines which, under the Agreement, belonged to the LTS. The award recommended the two unions devise a new agreement to provide associate membership of the LTS for PMB members, who at the date of the 1962 award were employed on machines that under the 1931 award belonged to the LTS. It also recommended PMB members currently operating these machines, conditional on associate membership of the LTS, be allowed to continue to do so and that if any machines currently staffed by the PMB were replaced by small cylinder machines then PMB members, subject to taking out LTS associate membership, be allowed to operate them. However, when these PMB members ceased employment the staffing was to revert back to the LTS. The P&KTF recognised that the award meant a gradual reduction in the PMB membership but in the short run unemployment amongst its members would be minimised. The P&KTF recommended its award be implemented so as to minimise the hardship of the employees concerned and urged both unions to show the fullest understanding and accommodation in problems which may arise.

The NUPB&PW decided, at a special meeting held on 5 January 1963, that the P&KTF Arbitration Board's finding was unacceptable and they gave the P&KTF six months' notice of termination of their membership. The NUPB&PW was the largest numerical affiliate accounting for about half of the P&KTF membership. It argued the Board's decision ultimately meant the elimination of the PMB which, with over 4,000 members, was larger than some P&KTF affiliates. It could see no justification for the elimination of one of its long-standing branches when all it had sought was a peaceful accommodation with the LTS. The NUPB&PW also considered the Arbitration Board's decision to be unrealistic, since there were many PMB members whom the former PMMTS would not take into membership as a matter of policy and who, as a consequence, had had to join the PMB. Given that the longer-term effect of the Board's decision was the demise of one of its London branches, the NUPB&PW felt resignation from the P&KTF to be the only course open to them.

Following the NUPB&PW's rejection of the P&KTF award, the TUC intervened into the dispute. After long discussions, the LTS agreed to amend the P&KTF award so that, in circumstances where platen machines were replaced by cylinder machines PMB members could work on small cylinder machines controlled by the LTS, on certain conditions. The most significant of these were:

(i) Where PMB members were currently operating cylinder machines they would apply for LTS associate membership, which would be granted. The associate card would then permit the individual to operate cylinder machines at their current place of employment or elsewhere in areas controlled by the LTS.

(ii) Where machines which were within the jurisdiction of the PMB were replaced by machines within the control of the LTS, the PMB members whose machines were being replaced would be allowed to operate the replacement machines subject to gaining LTS associate membership. Applications for LTS associate membership would be approved. PMB members, granted associate cards in these circumstances could seek employment on cylinder machines of demy size and under anywhere in the London area, provided LTS associate membership was maintained.

(iii) When a vacancy occurred on a machine operated by an associate member, the prior right of the operating society to fill that vacancy had to be accepted.

This agreement represented some improvement on the P&KTF award and, after consultation with its PMB members, the NUPB&PW accepted it.

The proposed NUPB&PW/LTS merger 1960–1[5]

In September 1959 the NUPB&PW invited the LTS to discuss the amalgamation of the two unions. Following explanatory talks the LTS announced that there was indeed a basis for merger and submitted to a special delegate conference, held on 11 March 1960, the possible amalgamation with the NUPB&PW. The special conference was attended by almost 3,000 members but the proposal the LTS continue merger talks with the NUPB&PW was rejected by 901 votes to 862. In the light of this decision there little purpose in the NUPB&PW holding a delegate meeting to approve merger talks with the LTS.

The 1960 LTS Annual Conference referred back to the Executive the decision of the March Special Delegate Meeting. On 30 August 1960 the NUPB&PW was notified that the 'reference back' had been considered by the LTS Executive Council but under its rules no action regarding a membership ballot on an amalgamation with the NUPB&PW could be held again before March 1961. Nevertheless, the LTS Executive Council gave authority to proceed with preparation for such a ballot, to appoint a sub-committee of seven and to approach the NUPB&PW to ask whether they would be prepared to meet the LTS for further talks. The June 1960 NUPB&PW Biennial Delegate Council had overwhelmingly carried a resolution instructing its Executive Council

> to move immediately, in any positive way, to make or accept any request that will bring about the amalgamation of unions to the final attainment of one print union to meet the spreading monopolisation of the print industry.[6]

In the light of this motion the NUPB&PW Executive unanimously authorised a meeting with the LTS sub-committee.

A special LTS conference, held in March 1961, agreed by 289 votes to 168 to restart merger talks with the NUPB&PW. In the new union the LTS would maintain its autonomy within the NUPB&PW by becoming its London Typographical Division. The manner in which the Division conducted its business would be a matter for itself within the constraints of the NUPB&PW General Rules. As a division it would have four representatives (2 compositors and 2 machine managers) on the NUPB&PW National Executive Committee and the LTS General Secretary, Mr Bob Wills, would become Joint General Secretary, with Mr Morrison, of the National Union.

However, the negotiations ran into difficulties over the issues of super-annuation and a per capita payment to be made by the LTS into the General Fund of the NUPB&PW. It was eventually agreed LTS members would not contribute to the NUPB&PW's Superannuation Fund, the LTS would contribute up to £30,000 into the NUPB&PW Officers and Staff Pension Fund and pay a £68,000 lump sum into its General Fund to cover the obligations the merged union would inherit from former LTS members. These generous terms were a mark of how anxious the NUPB&PW was to secure an amalgamation with a craft union. The divisional structure was an incentive to the LTS to join the NUPB&PW as it would allow them to retain autonomy and identity in a larger union. In this way it was hoped LTS fears about their interests being swamped by the non-craft and women's interests of the NUPB&PW would be allayed. The attraction of a merger with the NUPB&PW for the LTS was the possibility of gaining a foothold in the provinces and an easier pathway for their members to 'follow their work' as it left London. A merged LTS/NUPB&PW would relay to the TA that, as worked flowed from London into its provinces, the LTS had other options than merely to join with the TA from a perceived position of weakness.

A 'straw ballot' of LTS members on these merger terms resulted in 4,906 votes in their favour and 6,138 against. The LTS informed the NUPB&PW that the proposed amalgamation should be dropped as the LTS members were against continuing merger talks. The NUPB&PW were suspicious as to the sincerity of the LTS leadership, since almost immediately after informing the NUPB&PW, amalgamation talks with the TA were started. The NUPB&PW suspected it had been used by the LTS to strengthen that union's hand in merger talks with the TA to whom it had now demonstrated there were alternative ways of gaining a foothold in the provinces and opening up employment opportunities for its members.

The LTS/Paperworkers amalgamation would have preserved LTS autonomy, given it a stake in the provinces and helped resolve the two unions' difficulties with the staffing of small cylinder machines. However, these industrial advantages were insufficient to overcome the LTS members' reservations, if not prejudices, that the NUPB&PW was an inappropriate partner. The NUPB&PW had 'lost' the possibility of resolving the small cylinder machine issue in London, of extending its influence into the composing room, of an easier advancement of its members into traditional craft printing areas and of consolidating its position to challenge the letterpress and litho craft unions as technological developments brought a decline in letterpress printing and a growth in lithographic printing.

The Monotype Casters and Typefounders' Society (MCTS)

This Society transferred its engagements into the NUPB&PW in 1962. It was founded in 1889 as the Amalgamated Typefounders' Trade

Society. Monotype Casters was added to its title in the late 1930s. It organised monotype caster attendants in London, Wales and the English provinces and regarded itself as a national union. However, outside London its membership was small. Of its 939 members 75 per cent were employed in London.

The union had come into existence because the LSC, and initially, the TA, refused to organise monotype caster attendants. As general print and newspaper employers introduced monotype composing machines at the turn of the century, the LSC and the TA viewed attendants as mechanics rather than printers. The linotype operator, organised by the LTS and TA, manipulated a keyboard, heated metal and distributed matrices. Unlike the linotype machine, the monotype required two operators – a keyboard operator and a type caster. When monotype machines were first introduced, the employers accepted TA jurisdiction over the keyboard but not over the type caster, arguing that the latter was semi-skilled work and required no knowledge of composition. In 1905, the TA temporarily gave up its claim to organise type casters, but in 1918 decided again to organise them. However, by this time provincial typecasters were organised in four unions – the TA, NATSOPA, NUPB&PW and the MCTS. The TA approached the other three unions to secure the transfer of their caster members to the TA. By 1948 NATSOPA and the NUPB&PW had transferred their monotype caster members to the TA but the MCTS retained pockets of membership in the provinces, rejecting TA suggestion it confine itself to London and conclude a reciprocity agreement with the TA.[7] The LSC, on the other hand, established control over keyboard operators on monotype composing machines but was disinclined to organise monotypecasters, who they regarded as non-craft employees. The MCTFS arose to represent the interests of these workers in London. It regarded itself as a mainline letterpress craft union and became recognised as such by its fellow craft unions. Over the period 1956–61 it was a party in the negotiations for a proposed six-craft-union merger.

In the continued pursuit of its policy of seeking merger with any interested union, the NUPB&PW's General Secretary and President in early 1962 attended the MCTS Executive Committee which agreed to call a National Delegate Meeting to gain 'the green light' to merge as a national branch into the NUPB&PW. The Delegate Meeting, held in London, voted by 168 votes to 3 that the MCTS transfer its engagements to the NUPB&PW and become a national branch of that Union. A ballot of all MCTS members voted by 480 votes to 75, a majority of 405, to transfer their membership to the NUPB&PW. Under the financial arrangements of the transfer, the MCTS paid £4,420 (the equivalent of £5.20 per member) into the NUPB&PW General Funds. A further £1,100 was paid by the MCTS into the NUPB&PW Officers' and Staff Pension Fund in respect of the pension liabilities of its General Secretary, Mr Cline and his Secretary.

The constitutional arrangements under the transfer of engagements were fourfold. First the Society became a nation-wide branch of the NUPB&PW at which it continued to operate as it had done as the MCTS and retained a high degree of identity and autonomy. Second, MCTS the General Secretary, Mr Cline, became Secretary of the National Branch and the MCTS President its Chairman. Third, the National Executive Committee of the MCTS became the National Branch Committee. Fourth the MCTS General Secretary was to attend the NUPB&PW National Executive Committee as a visitor for one year beginning in November 1962, but would not participate in its decisions; he was present in a strictly advisory capacity. The transfer of engagements to the NUPB&PW became effective on 20 July 1962. The MCTS brought nearly 1,000 craftsmen into the NUPB&PW and gave that union for the first time a presence in letterpress composing rooms. Within the NUPB&PW, the MCTS had retained sectional autonomy, had joined a more financially secure union, had secured the provision of NUPB&PW central services and benefits, and had joined, not only the largest union in the printing industry but one which had 40,000 craftsmen in membership. The merger also offered MCTS greater protection from encroachments on its job territory by other craft print unions and NATSOPA.

THE LITHO CRAFT UNIONS

The Amalgamated Society of Lithographic Printers and Auxiliaries (ASLP)

In May 1963 the ASLP and the NUPB&PW announced their intention to work together for the speedy transfer of engagements of the ASLP to the NUPB&PW as this was the quickest means of bringing the two unions together. Unlike an amalgamation it would not require a complete revision of the NUPB&PW General Rules and the ASLP existing rules could be adopted by the ASLP as either a national branch or a Lithographic Division within the NUPB&PW. It would also quicken the merger process. The NUPB&PW would not have to ballot its membership. For industrial reasons both unions wanted any merger completed in the shortest possible time. Formal amalgamation could have taken anything from six months to a year whilst a transfer of engagements would take as little as three months. The ASLP sought to preserve for itself a high degree of autonomy within an enhanced NUPB&PW. Under the terms of the transfer agreed in July 1963, the ASLP would join the NUPB&PW as its Lithographic Division in which it would continue to operate as the former ASLP subject to the general rules and policy of the NUPB&PW. The ASLP General Secretary, Mr Ron Emerick, would become a national officer of the NUPB&PW with the title of National Lithographic Divisional Secretary. The salaries of its General Secretary and Assistant General Secretary were to be paid from the NUPB&PW General Funds. The National Lithographic Divisional Secretary would be part of any NUPB&PW delegations to the P&KTF, the International Graphical Federation (IGF) and the TUC. The ASLP National Council and Executive Committee would become the Divisional Council and the Executive Committee of the Lithographic Division. The National Lithographic Divisional Secretary would conduct negotiations with employers and other unions affecting members of the National Lithographic Division which would have three seats on the NUPB&PW's National Executive Council. The National Secretary would automatically sit on the NEC. The title NUPB&PW was to be revised and a new one to be decided at a later stage by a joint working party after the transfer of engagements had settled down. The title of the NUPB&PW journal, *The Paperworker*, would be amended to include the word 'lithographer', or another appropriate word, and would have four to eight pages devoted to the affairs of the National Lithographic Division.

The capitation fee payable by the ASLP into the NUPB&PW General Fund was to be £5.20 for all adult male members of the Printers' Section, the Plate Preparers and the Small Offset Sections. For apprentices and women members of the Small Offset Section the capitation was to be £1 per head. In addition to these capitation fees, which totalled £43,215.20, the ASLP was to pay £13,500 into the NUPB&PW Officers' and Staff Pension Fund. Both these payments were to be made to the NUPB&PW by the ASLP liquidating investments from its General Fund. All former ASLP members would be entitled to receive the full range of NUPB&PW benefits (including dispute pay and unemployment benefit) as if their previous ASLP membership had been unbroken in the NUPB&PW. The NUPB&PW rules would contain provisions whereby the Lithographic Division could, if so desired, secede. The weekly contribution for Lithographic Division members to the NUPB&PW General Fund would be 6p for adult men, 4p for male apprentices and juniors, 7p for adult women and 3½p for junior women. These terms, like those offered to the LTS, were generous and reflected the NUPB&PW desire to merge with a craft union so as not to be isolated by the eventual formation of one craft union. A merger with the ASLP had the potential to open new job opportunities for its members in a growing section of the industry and thereby put the letterpress craft unions on the defensive.

On 6 January 1964 the result of the ballot of ASLP members on the proposed transfer of their engagements to the NUPB&PW was announced. It was as shown in Table 3.1. For the transfer of engagements to be approved, a two-thirds majority in favour from all members eligible to vote was required. Those who had voted, voted in favour of transfer by 2,758 votes – 75 per cent of those voting were in favour of merging with the NUPB&PW. However, the non-voters, the unsigned papers and spoilt papers all counted against the yes vote. When this was taken into account 4,817 had voted for and 3,193 against. To achieve the two-thirds of those eligible to vote as required under the Trade Union (Amalgamation) Act 1918, 5,340 yes votes were needed. The yes vote was 533 short of this target. Had 266 additional votes been cast in favour, the transfer of engagements could have been effected.

The Trade Union (Amalgamation) Act 1964 amended the legal requirement for the majority in favour in union merger ballots to a straight majority of those voting. If the ASLP ballot had been taken in the late autumn of 1964, rather than in 1963, the votes obtained in

Table 3.1
ASLP ballot vote on the merger with NUPB&PW

Section	Yes	No	Non votes	Unsigned papers	Spoilt papers	Total
Printers	3,598	1,733	602	87	1	6,021
Plate Preparers	667	211	71	12	2	963
Small Offset	552	115	1,026	15	1	1,026
TOTALS	4,817	2,059	1,697	114	4	8,691

favour would have been more than ample for the ASLP transfer of engagements into the NUPB&PW to have taken place. Had the transfer taken place, the NUPB&PW would have gained a foot-hold in lithographic printing and the NGA would probably have been isolated in the letterpress process, excluded from the litho revolution. The history of the NUPB&PW and subsequently SOGAT and the NGA would have been very different but for those 266 votes.

What was the basis of a merger between the ASLP and the NUPB&PW? The ASLP would have brought the NUPB&PW 11,000 craftsmen members thereby rising its craft membership to over 50,000. More importantly, the NUPB&PW would have gained a foot-hold in lithographic plate-making and printing at a time when that process was expanding and letterpress declining. A merger with the ASLP would have enhanced the employment opportunities and the possibilities of upgrading to craft status of NUPB&PW members. If the litho craft unions could not supply sufficient labour to litho printers and to letterpress printers converting their plant to litho, then the litho machine manager skills shortage could be overcome by upgrading to craft status lesser-skilled NUPB&PW members.

The ASLP, which had 11,000 members, was prepared to make a defensive merger with a larger union to guard against the LTS and the TA, which in total had 80,000 letterpress craft members claiming lithographic printing jobs. With the introduction of web-offset litho machines into provincial newspaper production, where the litho craft unions had no presence, the typographical unions challenged the ASLP's claim to be the sole provider of litho managers. They were prepared to accept that, in general printing, litho machines were the prerogative of the ASLP, but in the case of newspapers the TA and the LTS were not prepared to make the slightest concession to the ASLP's with regard to rights to this work. However, the NUPB&PW accepted that work done on web-offset machines was that of the ASLP.

The introduction of web-offset into provincial newspaper production led the typographical unions to seek an agreed formula to govern relationships between themselves and the lithographic unions. The need for this became acute with the announcement in 1963 by the *Daily Mirror* of its intention to invest £2m in web-offset machinery – the newspaper envisaged replacing all remaining letterpress and gravure machines in their Lavington House plant with web-offset equipment. The *Daily Mirror* intended that Lavington House become the largest web-offset factory in England. The ASLP feared that if it could not supply labour to employers introducing litho equipment or re-equipping with litho then the TA and the LTS would collude with the employers for the shortage to be overcome by retraining their letterpress members.

ASLP members' fears that joining the NUPB&PW would compromise their craft interests were to be overcome by the divisional status which would permit them to continue with their traditional industrial and democratic practices, policies and financial benefits subject only to the general rules and policies of the NUPB&PW. The NUPB&PW were offering the ASLP craft autonomy within the protection of a larger union in which there were already significant groups of craft print employees. The attraction of the NUPB&PW to the ASLP was put succinctly by the ASLP General Secretary when asked, at a conference held at Harrogate on 24 August 1963, what difference a merger would make to ASLP rank and file members:

> If the TA agreed they were going to work these machines (web-offset) what could we do on our own? By allying with the Paperworkers we would have more support, because, wherever there was a letterpress shop, there were Paperworkers, we would have a direct link with all letterpress shops in the country. We have only 50 branches; both the TA and the Paperworkers have about 200. It would make a great deal of difference as to how we could get control of web-offset.[8]

The ASLP General Secretary stressed that unless the ASLP had the support of a stronger union the typographical unions would take control of litho printing.

A further factor which attracted the ASLP to the NUPB&PW was finance. If the claims of the TA and the LTS to operate litho machines were to be resisted, interunion disputes were inevitable and would require resources if membership was to be protected. The ASLP had financial difficulties stemming from the 1959 six weeks' dispute in the general printing and provincial newspaper industry. Merging with the NUPB&PW offered the ASLP a stronger financial basis from which to resist typographical unions' claims to take over and then to control lithographic printing presses. Despite the industrial basis for the merger, the transfer of engagement could not take place because the legal conditions governing such a merger had not been satisfied. For the second time in two years the NUPB&PW had failed to attract a significant craft union to join its ranks despite being prepared to grant it a considerable high degree of autonomy within it. However, the Paperworkers remained committed to amalgamation with any union, craft or otherwise, as this would reduce the number of printing trade unions.

OTHER PRINTING AND PAPERMAKING TRADE UNIONS

The Book Edge Gilders' Trade Society

In 1961 The Book Edge Gilders' Trade Society disbanded itself and joined the London Bookbinders' Branch of the NUPB&PW. The Society, formed in 1889, organised those who gilded and polished with an agate the edges of books. The Society set its face against training apprentices. The NUPB&PW had rejected the view that book edge gilding was a separate trade but had always hoped edge gilders would eventually join with them

The assets of the Book Edge Gilders' Trade Society were just over £300 and were divided equally between the General Fund of the NUPB&PW and the funds of the London Bookbinders' branch. The members of the Society were accepted into the NUPB&PW as full members whilst its General Secretary was to sit on the London Bookbinders' Branch Committee for one year, after which he would have to stand for election to the Branch Committee in the ordinary way. The Book Edge Gilders' Trade Society members, in voting themselves out of existence, unanimously accepted the terms for joining the London Bookbinders' Branch.

The Papermould and Dandy Roll Makers' Society[9]

In 1962 the Papermould and Dandy Roll Makers' Society transferred the engagements of its 68 members into the NUPB&PW. This was a further step in the NUPB&PW policy of discussing merger as a means of resolving amicably with any printing union the ever-increasing overlapping of printing union interests in the light of technological developments. The Society's members performed a highly skilled task in making the wire 'dandy rolls' which had a raised wire design that was incorporated into the papermaking machine and run lightly upon wet pulp to produce a watermark. The dandy rolls made the watermark in banknotes, passports, driving licences, government documents, notepaper and cup final tickets. The transfer of engagements of the Papermould and Dandy Roll Makers' Society to the NUPB&PW became effective from 21 May 1962. The Society became a branch within the national union, with Mr Reid, its General Secretary becoming the Branch Secretary. The total capitation fees paid by the Society into the General Funds of the NUPB&PW was £317.

The Pattern Card Makers' Society [10]

This Society, founded in Manchester in 1865, had, until it was approached by the NUPB&PW in March 1963, never entertained merger with another union. The Society's membership was dependent upon the cotton industry, and when approached by the NUPB&PW its membership had been declining for a number of years. The Society also faced other problems, the most acute of which were the need to reduce current expenditure and the increasing number of members joining the superannuation list. The Society had a total membership of 176 and the jobs of its members were highly skilled and included assembling 'swatches' of clothes into pattern cards, the operation of serrating machines, and mounting patterns of ranges of dyed cloths. The Society was affiliated to the P&KTF but not to the TUC.

The Society held a Special Members' General Meeting on 27 May 1963 at the Oddfellows Hall, Manchester. The members agreed whole-heartedly to transfer their engagements to the NUPB&PW with effect from 1 July 1963. The Society became a special section of the Manchester Branch of the NUPB&PW. Its General Secretary, Albert Hodkinson became a full-time official of the Manchester Branch on which the former Pattern Card Makers' Society was to have two seats. The Society paid £400 as an agreed capitation fee was paid into the NUPB&PW General Fund.

RELATIONSHIPS WITH NATSOPA

Spheres of Influence

For many years 'spheres of influence' arrangements had existed between NUPB&PW and NATSOPA (see Chapter 1). In 1961 at a meeting of the two unions, the NUPB&PW listed a number of towns where they found the arrangements unsatisfactory while NATSOPA provided a list of complaints three times as long. On 30 June 1961 the NUPB&PW General Secretary issued a circular to branches clarifying the 'spheres of influence' arrangements. Difficulties continued however, and following discussions at General Secretary level it became clear that the information NATSOPA passed on to their branches varied from that given by the NUPB&PW to its branches. The two unions agreed that in future, even if it took some time, they would produce a statement to go out in identical terms to the members of both unions. The main features of this statement issued in 1963 were:[11]

(i) A NATSOPA town meant that employees in the warehouse, bindery, despatch, white paper department and assistants in the machine room were NATSOPA members.

(ii) An NUPB&PW town meant that employees in the warehouse, despatch, bindery and white paper departments as well as assistants in the machine room were NUPB&PW members.

(iii) The London set-up was a situation where all employees in the bindery and warehouse were NUPB&PW members but assistants in the Machine Room were NATSOPA members.

(iv) Where organisational rights had been conceded to NATSOPA, the Paperworkers would not accept further applications for membership. Similarly, where organisational rights had been conceded to the Paperworkers, the NATSOPA would not accept further applications for membership.

(v) Where towns were listed as the 'London set-up' the NUPB&PW would not accept into membership any more printing machine assistants, even in the houses where the Paperworkers had prior control before the establishment of agreed lines of demarcation. Similarly the NATSOPA would not accept into membership any more bindery and warehouse workers in houses where NATSOPA had control prior to the establishment of these agreed lines of demarcation.

(vi) It was jointly agreed that neither union would insist on the transfer of members at present doing the work of the other union in the towns named, but when the member left, retired or died, the branch listed as in control was to have the right of filling the vacancy.

(vii) Where it had been agreed that the *status quo* would prevail it meant new firms would follow the London set-up unless otherwise stated, and each union would remain in control of those houses they held at the time of these revised 'spheres of influence' arrangements.

(viii) Where the *status quo* prevailed, the Paperworkers or NATSOPA were entitled to replace the staff in houses which at the time of these revised arrangements were recognised locally as houses belonging to the one or the other union. Where the names of towns were given, the area of control was to extend to the area of the town administration only. Any change in town boundaries after these revised arrangements became operative was to be a matter for discussion between both unions.

(ix) New towns not listed were to follow the London set-up. If new organisation was undertaken and employees were accepted into membership of either union in new towns not listed, in contravention of the London set-up, the nomination forms were to be passed to the appropriate union so the London set-up could prevail.

(x) It was re-affirmed that, irrespective of whether a town was a Paperworker or NATSOPA one, the wholesale news section, motor drivers in general printing and periodical houses and individuals employed under the NUPB&PW Binders and Stationery Agreement, the Box Industry Agreement and the Paper and Board Agreement were to be members of the NUPB&PW. On the other hand, in a Paperworker town all employed in the printing machine room or publishing departments of newspapers were to be members of NATSOPA which also organised employees working under the Ink and Roller Agreement.

The General Secretaries of the NUPB&PW and NATSOPA urged their respective Branch Secretaries to make every effort to ensure that the list of towns and the spirit of the agreement were not infringed by either party. The 1963 revised arrangements resulted in 12 towns being classified as NATSOPA towns, 88 as Paperworker towns, 49 as the London set-up and three in which the *status quo* was to prevail. Merger between NATSOPA and the Paperworkers would have resolved many of these problems, but the Paperworkers' membership had turned down merger with NATSOPA in 1958. However, it was problems over these 'spheres of influence' arrangements that were the catalyst in 1965 for NUPB&PW and NATSOPA to begin amalgamation talks from which emerged the Society of Graphical and Allied Trades. Why had the proposed NUPB&PW/NATSOPA merger of 1956/8 failed?

The Proposed National Union of Printing and Allied Trades Workers

In the early 1950s, both the NUPB&PW and NATSOPA national conferences recorded decisions to seek closer working or amalgamation between their two organisations. The 1952 Delegate Council Meeting of the NUPB&PW approved a motion that the Union accept an invitation from NATSOPA to discuss amalgamation. The 1951 Governing Council of NATSOPA agreed amalgamation with the NUPB&PW be explored. Although from time to time talks over amalgamation had taken place between representatives of the two, so far nothing firm had transpired.

During 1955 the National Executives of NATSOPA and the NUPB&PW authorised their respective General Secretaries to explore the possibility of amalgamation. Talks were scheduled for November 1955 but were to be postponed because of the 1955/6 wage negotiations to revise the general printing and provincial newspaper industry wage basis agreements. In early 1956 the General Secretaries produced draft principles for an amalgamation of the NUPB&PW and NATSOPA and any other print unions willing to be associated with either these initial moves, or subsequent ones, designed to rationalise the printing union structure. The two unions, having accepted the guiding principles for merger, established a Joint Standing Committee to prepare a draft Rule Book for the new union and to agree procedures for the necessary ballot of the memberships in accordance with the Trade Union (Amalgamation) Act 1918. On 25 April 1956 the Joint Standing Committee invited other unions to join their amalgamation initiative. At this time the craft unions were exploring the possibility of creating a single craft printing union and none responded to this NUPB&PW/NATSOPA initiative.

On 9 May 1956 the NUPB&PW and NATSOPA publicly announced their intention to form a new, all-embracing national printing union to be called *The National Union of Printing and Allied Trades Workers* (NUPATW)[12] The new Union was to be based on a structure of trade divisions, geographical districts or areas and branches. It would cater for craftsmen, semi-skilled operatives, operators and unskilled auxiliaries employed in the printing, bookbinding, paper-making, graphical arts and allied trades. The customary demarcation lines between the existing printing unions would continue to be recognised by the new union so long as that was the desire of all unions in the industry.

The merging of the NUPB&PW and NATSOPA into a single organisation of 200,000 members was always going to be a formidable and difficult task. Considerable flexibility in approach to constructing the new organisation was essential, especially if the envisaged trade divisions were to retain autonomy. The principle of a Joint General Secretaryship was accepted, together with, for a transitional period, a duplication of officers and offices. Both unions agreed the membership ballot on any proposals for the creation of the NUPATW would be held no later than January 1957 and the NUPATW, if the outcome of the ballots was favourable, be established as soon as possible thereafter.

To demonstrate how a considerable measure of autonomy for interest groups might be achieved within the NUPATW, the Joint Standing Committee instanced the London positions in the two unions. It proposed the Printing Machine Branch, the London Bookbinders' Branch, the Machine Rulers' Branch, the London Central Branch, the London Women's Branch and the Circulation Representatives' Branch of the NUPB&PW continue in their present form within the new union. The NATSOPA London Machine, Revisers, Ink Rollers, Manufacturers and Auxiliaries' (RIMA) and the London Clerical Branches would continue as separate branches in the NUPATW. The magnitude of the task of achieving a successful amalgamation package was demonstrated in that the London branches alone of the two unions contained approximately 75,000 members.

However, the progress envisaged for the amalgamation talks was not achieved. The task of compiling a set of rules which needed to pay due regard to the traditions and customs of both unions proved extremely difficult. The talks proceeded more slowly than expected for two reasons. First, both the NUPB&PW and NATSOPA were heavily involved in the protracted general printing and provincial newspaper industry 1955/6 wage negotiations. Second, the NUPB&PW, after considering a set of proposals from NATSOPA, said they could no longer adhere to the original merger principles agreed by the Executive Councils of the two unions.

To avoid a breakdown in the talks, NATSOPA put forward revised proposals, but the Paperworkers responded by stating that the point had been reached where they must consult their members, via a ballot, on the situation. On 13 February 1958 the NUPB&PW declared the result of the ballot. Its membership had voted by 39,587 votes to 26,134 against continuing negotiations for an amalgamation with NATSOPA.[13] The ballot paper had asked a number of other questions. Eleven thousand three hundred and sixty-two members voted in favour of the automatic succession of the remaining Joint General Secretary when the other retired. However 38,696 voted in favour of a formula whereby if either Joint General Secretary retired a ballot vote should be taken, the successful candidate becoming sole General Secretary. If the remaining Joint General Secretary was not elected he would become the Assistant General Secretary. On the issue of an appropriate financial structure for the new union, 47,658 members voted for a system of branches having their own local funds, whilst only 8,343 voted for a system of central funding with the gradual elimination of local funds. Members of the NUPB&PW voted by 49,869 to 14,008 votes in favour of full-time branch officials being eligible for election to the National Executive Committee of the NUPATW.

The NUPB&PW members had effectively voted to retain in the new union their own system of branches with financial autonomy and an Executive Council upon which full-time Branch Secretaries could sit. Quite the reverse arrangements – central funding and an all-lay executive – operated in NATSOPA. These items now had to be included in amalgamation package if it were to be acceptable to NUPB&PW. NATSOPA members were unlikely to accept willy nilly Paperworkers' practices in the new union. Having been asked to indicate their wishes on the issues of the Joint General Secretary issue, the financial system, and the composition of the Executive Council, the NUPB&PW members were finally asked if they favoured giving their Executive Council discretionary powers to reach a compromise formula on these three issues. The NUPB&PW members voted by 33,119 votes to 30,733 (a majority of 2,386) in favour of their Executive Council having such powers.

On the basis of these ballot results, the NUPB&PW informed NATSOPA that amalgamation negotiations were at an end. NATSOPA made a similar statement. However, both unions were agreed on the continuance of the Joint Standing Committee which had tried to fashion an amalgamation package; they also re-affirmed their intention of continuing to work closely together. NATSOPA restated that it remained a supporter of amalgamation between the various unions in the printing industry.

Some aspects of the rationale behind the attempts to create the National Union of Printing and Allied Trades Workers was discussed in Chapter 2.[14] The amalgamation would have tidied up the organisational anomalies between the two unions and brought financial advantages in that the fixed costs of operating a union could be spread across a larger number of individual members. The merger would have enabled economies in expenditure through the elimination of the duplication of administrative support and in the longer run through a reduction in the number of full-time national and branch officials. The amalgamation would have reduced the fears of non-craft employees that the craft unions would combine to isolate them with a view to widening the craft/non-craft differentials, to preventing non-skilled employees gaining access to skilled work, to invading the job territories of NATSOPA and the NUPB&PW and to continuing with apprenticeships and other artificial barriers to adult entry to craft jobs.

Despite these pressures pointing to the desirability of amalgamation, the NUPB&PW and NATSOPA could not devise a mutually accept-able merger package. The negotiations floundered on fundamental differences in the governance of the two unions. NATSOPA was a centrally funded union and its branches had no financial autonomy. The NUPB&PW was not a centralised union. Its branches retained a proportion of the national subscription as well as levying their own branch contributions. Although the NUPB&PW branches had a degree of financial autonomy, they could not act contrary to the General Rules, collective agreements and policies of the NUPB&PW. Neither union was prepared to compromise on these issues. The hands of the NUPB&PW negotiations had been tied by a ballot of its members.

A second governance issue on which the negotiations collapsed involved the eligibility of full-time Branch Secretaries to serve on the National Executive Committee of the merged union. The NATSOPA Executive was a lay one and full-time Branch Secretaries were debarred from sitting on it. The reverse was the case in the NUPB&PW, where full-time Branch Secretaries were eligible to, and did, serve on the National Executive. NUPB&PW members had shown in their ballot that they wished to continue this system in the NUPATW. NATSOPA had been equally determined to retain the lay executive position.

Other governance issues upon which the amalgamation talks foundered included rule changes and the powers of delegation at the National Delegate Conference. On both these issues the two unions were diametrically opposed. In NATSOPA rule changes could only be sanctioned by a ballot of the whole membership, whilst in the Paper-workers rules could be changed by delegates to the Biennial Delegate Council. In NATSOPA, delegates to its Governing Council could not be mandated, whilst those to the NUPB&PW Biennial Delegate Council could.

The amalgamation negotiators could not resolve these fundamentally different positions. With the failure of the six craft union amalgamation talks, the pressures for a NUPB&PW/NATSOPA merger were reduced. However, the 1960 NUPB&PW Biennial Delegate Council had committed the Union to accept a merger approach from any union if it would reduce the number of print unions. In carrying out this policy, the Paperworkers had gained the MCTS (1962), the Book Edge Guilders' Trade Society (1961), the Papermould and Dandy Roll Makers (1962) and the Pattern Card Makers' Society (1963). However, merger negotiations with the LTS (1962) and the ASLP (1964) had failed. By 1964 the formation of the NGA indicated that the craft unions were now likely to come together. However, the craft unions favoured first the formation of one letterpress craft union, followed by the creation of one craft union and ultimately the creation of one union for the industry. This was not the approach of NUPB&PW and NATSOPA. They did not see the creation of one non-craft union as a prerequisite for the eventual emergence of an industrial union. They both favoured one union for the industry and were prepared to merge with any union in order to achieve this. They saw amalgamation as a desirable end in itself. If the NUPB&PW and NATSOPA were not to become separate isolated unions as a result of the amalgamation policies of the craft unions, they needed to come together quickly. When the NUPB&PW and NATSOPA began amalgamation talks in 1965 they could not afford to fail. They did not fail, but the organisational arrangements devised to achieve the amalgamation contained the seeds of their own destruction (see Chapter 5). It is now appropriate to examine the formation of the Society of Graphical and Allied Trades itself in February 1966.

NOTES

1. For a history of Typographical Association from its foundation to 1949 see A.E. Musson *The Typographical Association*, Oxford University Press, 1959. For a history of its evolution and development over the period 1950–63 see J. Gennard *A History of the National Graphical Association*, Unwin Hyman, 1990.
2. See National Union of Printing, Bookbinding and Paperworkers *Annual Report of the National Executive Council, 1959*, pp. 8–9.
3. See National Union of Printing, Bookbinding and Paperworkers *Annual Report of the National Executive Council, 1960*, p. 7.
4. For a full account of the PMB and the LTS dispute see National Union of Printing, Bookbinding and Paperworkers *Annual Report of the National Executive Council, 1962*, p. 15; National Union of Printing, Bookbinding and Paperworkers *Annual Report of the National Executive Council, 1963*, pp. 13–14; Printing and Kindred Trades' Federation *Annual Report 1962–63*, and *Report of 1963 Administrative Council*, pp. 42–45 and p. 85.
5. For a full account of these abortive negotiations see National Union of Printing, Bookbinding and Paperworkers *Annual Report of the National Executive Council, 1960*, pp. 7 and 8; National Union of Printing, Bookbinding and Paperworkers

Annual Report of the National Executive Council, 1961, p. 11; National Union of Printing, Bookbinding and Paperworkers *Annual Report of the National Executive Council, 1962*, pp. 2 and 3; and John Gennard *A History of the National Graphical Association*, Unwin Hyman, 1990, pp. 85–90.

6. This motion was moved by the Ruling, Manufacturing, Stationery and Box-making Branch. See National Union of Printing, Bookbinding and Paperworkers *Report of the Biennial Delegate Council Meeting, 1960*, pp. 292–6.

7. MCTS' relations were amicable with the TA despite its claim to be a national union. It rejected the TA's claims to be the sole representative body for monotype caster operators employed in the provinces. In 1959 the two unions agreed no dual members of both unions could resign or drop their membership of the MCTS when employed as caster operators in London or the provinces.

8. See The Amalgamated Society of Lithographic Printers and Auxiliaries of Great Britain and Ireland *Report of Special General Council Meeting to discuss the Alliance*, August 1963, p. 10.

9. For more information on the Papermould and Dandy Roll Makers see 'Dandy Roll Makers make their mark', *SOGAT Journal*, September 1975, pp. 12 and 13. The dandy roll put the watermarks into paper. It was sometimes called the riding roller or the watermark roller.

10. For more information on the Pattern Card Makers' Society see 'One Hundred Years Old: Pattern Makers' Proud Record' *The Paperworker*, June 1965, pp. 12–13.

11. For a fuller account see National Union of Printing, Bookbinding and Paperworkers *Annual Report of the National Executive Council, 1963*, pp. 17–22.

12. See *The Paperworker*, May 1956, pp. 9–11.

13. See *The Paperworker*, April 1958, pp. 3–6.

14. For a fuller discussion see 'Is One Union for Print a Practical Proposition?' NATSOPA Journal, November 1956, pp. 10–11.

CHAPTER 4

THE ACTUAL FORMATION OF SOGAT AND ITS RELATIONSHIPS WITH OTHER PRINT UNIONS

THE TERMS OF THE AMALGAMATION

The NUPB&PW being itself the product of a number of amalgamations feared little from trade union mergers. Its members had recognised the need for further mergers by the early 1950s. The 1956 Biennial Delegate Council Meeting expressed concern at the introduction of automation and electronic processes into the printing industry in that although in the long run it would benefit NUPB&PW members, the short-term impact would be felt in the form of redundancies. The members considered this problem was best tackled by closer co-operation with other print unions for the purpose of controlling the staffing of new machines prior to any agreement being made.[1]

The 1960 Biennial Delegate Council Meeting instructed the National Executive Committee to move immediately to make or accept any request that would bring about amalgamations of print unions and eventually lead to one industrial union. One motive for this was the emergence of large company groups in the industry. Such groups were motivated by the desire for greater and greater profit and the employment of the smallest possible workforce. To counter this development NUPB&PW members saw the creation of one union for the printing industry as essential, but in the meantime closer unity between the print unions was needed.[2] The 1964 Delegate Council reaffirmed its view that to counter the adverse effects of the implementation of automation and the growth of large-scale companies from mergers and take-overs greater unity amongst print unions should be pursued.[3] Unity was to be achieved by amalgamation and the strengthening of the Printing and Kindred Trades Federation.

It was against these conference decisions that in autumn of 1964 some 30 to 40 unresolved jurisdictional difficulties surfaced between the NUPB&PW and NATSOPA. Many of the complaints were minor but some had been outstanding for many years. When the two unions met to consider the complaints the NUPB&PW General Secretary said the only way to resolve permanently these complaints was to amalgamate and he proposed this task start immediately. NATSOPA considered this a positive recommendation and set of proposals which it would take back to the Executive Council. Given the open and straightforward way in which the amalgamation proposal had been put NATSOPA recommended it for consideration to their Executive Council.

NATSOPA's Executive Council decided to meet officially with the NUPB&PW to explore the possibility of amalgamation. The jurisdictional problems between the two unions were put aside for the time being. However, NATSOPA had a problem in that it had agreed to meet NGA to discuss closer working between the two unions and from which it was hoped a merger of the two unions would occur. NATSOPA proposed tripartite meetings between the NGA, NATSOPA and the NUPB&PW. However, the NGA did not respond and NATSOPA believed the opportunity for a wider amalgamation had been lost. It therefore decided to pursue amalgamation with the NUPB&PW.

In May 1965 the NUPB&PW and NATSOPA announced agreement on the central principles to guide the amalgamation. A new print union – the Society of Graphical and Allied Trades (SOGAT) – was to be brought into being with a total membership of 225,000 and representing at least two-thirds of employees in the printing industry. The merger was to be based on two principles. First, autonomy, under which the two unions would come together yet stay apart, with the aim of fully integrating over a period of years. Second, equality, so that the 47,000 members of NATSOPA would not feel that their interests would be swamped by those of the 172,000 NUPB&PW members in the new union.

A unique approach to amalgamation was adopted based on a two-pillar structure holding up the 'umbrella' organisation. The union was to be divided into two highly autonomous Divisions upon which a parent society – SOGAT – would rest. Every member of SOGAT would belong to one of the Divisions which were to be known as Division A and Division 1. Division A was to compromise the members of all branches, sections and chapels of the NUPB&PW immediately before the formation of SOGAT. Division 1 was to consist of the members of all branches, sectors and chapels of NATSOPA immediately before the formation of SOGAT. SOGAT was to rest on the two pillars of the Divisions until a National Conference to be held no later than 1969 gave further direction to the SOGAT National Executive as to how to proceed with the consolidation of the union. NUPB&PW and NATSOPA were to continue in two autonomous Divisions, retaining their present decision-making structures, subscription levels, benefits and trade practices but all in one parent union, SOGAT. Over time the Divisions would be gradually eliminated and a consolidated union would emerge. The rules of the new union were to be ten basic General Rules of SOGAT, the Rules of NUPB&PW (applicable to members of Division A) and the Rules of NATSOPA (applicable to members of Division 1). However, where there was a conflict between the rules of the Divisions and the General Rules the latter would take preference. The SOGAT rules were to be altered by a Rules Revision Conference to be held not later than 1969 and thereafter as determined by the Executive Council.

Under the proposed amalgamation arrangements, the NUPB&PW would retain all its funds, buildings, fixed assets and investment funds, just as it did as an independent union. The same would be the case with NATSOPA. The choice of two parallel structures was seen as a novel way of overcoming the difficulties of trying to marry two unions with fundamentally different structures. The NUPB&PW allowed full-time officers to serve on its National Executive Council whilst NATSOPA had an all-lay Executive. NATSOPA operated a centralised financial system whilst NUPB&PW branches were permitted autonomy to raise their own revenue which could be dispersed in any way so long as it was not contrary to national union's rules and policies. In the NUPB&PW rule changes could be approved by delegates to the Biennial Delegate Council meeting whilst in NATSOPA such changes required approval in a ballot of the whole membership. In the Paperworkers, delegates could be mandated at the Delegate Council whilst in NATSOPA this was not the case. In the Paperworkers, national officials were elected by a ballot of the membership but were not subject to re-election periodically. In NATSOPA national officials were elected by the members and were subject to re-election periodically.

It was on these constitutional issues that the 1956/8 amalgamation talks between the two unions had collapsed. The amalgamation panels realised if they tried to establish a unified constitutional and financial structure for SOGAT from day one of the new union the amalgamation talks would fail. It was essential a single non-craft union came into being as quickly as possible if the craft unions were not to exclude NUPB&PW and NATSOPA from a 'stake in the litho revolution'. A mechanism had to be devised, therefore, that would allow amalgamation to take place, recognise the important constitutional differences between two unions, and envisage these issues being resolved later as the two unions had developed a greater trust of each other from working together. Industrial considerations made a merger between the NUPB&PW and NATSOPA logical. The amalgamation talks could not afford to fail this time. To avoid constitutional and financial issues causing the merger talks to fail for a second time, the two unions adopted the unique approach to amalgamation described above. Normally the amalgamation panels would marry the Rule Books of the unions concerned and both sets of members in voting for or against the amalgamation, would express their views on the new proposed Rule Book. In the case of SOGAT, the amalgamation panels decided to amalgamate first and then devise a common Rule Book. It was not practical to adopt the conventional approach, since mutually acceptable compromises on the constitutional differences between the two unions would have been impossible in the early stages. The amalgamation talks would have collapsed. The industrial interests of the two unions could not permit this to happen.

The NUPB&PW and NATSOPA regarded the two-pillar structure as advantageous in that it ensured autonomy for the two divisions and did not permit interference from SOGAT. Both unions' benefits, procedures and prerogatives would remain and be subject only to the eventual role of SOGAT Rules. The NATSOPA General Secretary in addressing its 1965 Governing Council extolled the virtues of the proposed structure for SOGAT as follows:

> This is good, because it gets us over the hurdle of how we come together yet stay apart, how we begin in fact to take the first steps by an action which in the next part is a further process to the final action that might well take 8 or 9 years to complete. But from the beginning the important factor will be psychological. We will quickly understand ourselves so that soon, quite soon, after the amalgamation we should be talking

about the union itself, the Graphical Union rather than either just NATSOPA or the Paperworkers.[4]

To avoid NATSOPA members from opposing merger from a fear of being swamped by the interests of the larger number of NUPB&PW members, the principle of equity was applied in three areas – the National Executive Council, finances and officerships. The control, government and administration of SOGAT was invested in an Executive Council subject to the direction of the National Council which would formulate policy and receive and approve reports from the Executive. The Executive Council of SOGAT would be the Executive Councils of the two Divisions. It was to consist of 43 members, 24 of whom would be elected from and by members of Division A (viz the NUPB&PW Executive) whilst 19 were to be elected by and form the membership of Division 1 (namely the NATSOPA Executive). With 19 members from Division 1 and 24 members from Division A, NATSOPA members effectively had equal representation on the SOGAT National Executive Council. This level of representation, given the differences in the size of membership of the two unions, was generous.

Both NATSOPA and the NUPB&PW contributed equal sums of money to create SOGAT's original funds. Both unions contributed £150,000 to create a SOGAT headquarters' account of £300,000 made up of cash and investments.[5] The weekly contributions of the members were paid to the Division to which they belonged. Deductions from such contributions were allocated weekly to SOGAT funds – the sum of 1p (2d) per male member and ½p per female and junior member. The result was some £70,000 per annum for SOGAT-wide expenditure.

The equality principle also applied to the SOGAT officer corp. There was to be a Joint General Secretaryship of Tom Smith (NUPB&PW) and Dick Briginshaw (NATSOPA). In the event of resignation by ill health or otherwise, death or removal from office of one or other Joint General Secretaries, the remaining Joint General Secretary would become the sole SOGAT General Secretary. The President of SOGAT was to be the NUPB&PW's President since NATSOPA did not have such an office, but when the current holder left office there would be a ballot of the whole SOGAT membership to elect a successor. The Organising and Papermaking Secretaries of SOGAT were to be the existing NUPB&PW's Organising Secretary (Mr Vincent Flynn) and Papermaking Secretary (Mr E.B. White). To balance these three

NUPB&PW officers there were to be three Assistant Secretaries – Mr J.A. Harley, Mr O. O'Brien and Mr A.F. Davies – all from NATSOPA and who, like the Paperworker officials, were to retain responsibility within their own Division. The eight SOGAT-wide officers were thus drawn four from each union. Their salaries of the Joint General Secretaries would be paid in the proportion of 75 per cent from the Divisions and the remaining 25 per cent from SOGAT funds.

The NUPB&PW argued that the SOGAT Head Office be their own headquarters, namely 74 Nightingale Lane. NATSOPA opposed this, arguing that its members would see it as symptomatic of the NUPB&PW imposing its will and giving rise to fears that the amalgamation was not one of equal partners. NATSOPA saw the issue of the location of SOGAT's Head Office being decided by the SOGAT National Executive. NUPB&PW, on the other hand, argued that locating SOGAT's Head Office at that of the NUPB&PW would convince their members the amalgamation was not a NATSOPA 'take-over'. Eventually a compromise was agreed under which the final decision on the location of SOGAT's Head Office would be decided by the SOGAT National Council.

The amalgamation package was approved at a Joint Meeting of the Executives of NUPB&PW and NATSOPA held in August 1965. On 21 October 1965 the NUPB&PW called an interim, one-day conference at the Conway Hall, Red Square, Holborn, London, where a full report on the terms of the merger was endorsed. Further explanatory meetings were held in various parts of the country, culminating in a large meeting held in the Central Hall in London. The amalgamation terms were then put in to the NUPB&PW members in a national ballot which produced the following result:[6]

Votes for	66,900
Votes against	18,201
Majority in favour	48,699

In 1965 the NATSOPA Governing Council approved the terms for the merger. On 23 July 1965 an *ad hoc* NATSOPA conference, attended by some 2,500 delegates, endorsed the amalgamation package. During September 1965 further explanatory meetings were held in various parts of the country at which the amalgamation terms were endorsed. NATSOPA conducted at the same time as the NUPB&PW a membership ballot which produced the following result:

Votes in favour	18,271
Votes against	8,379
Majority in favour	9,892

This ballot produced a turnout of 65 per cent of those entitled to vote and was at the time the highest poll ever recorded in NATSOPA's history.

Following this proof of a substantial majority in both unions in favour of the formation of SOGAT, a joint meeting of the two Executive Councils, held on 16 December 1965, completed the amalgamation formalities. At the end of January 1966, the Registrar of Friendly Societies gave approval to the SOGAT Rules, the Instrument of Amalgamation and the General Rules of both Divisions. On 1 February 1966 the Society of Graphical and Allied Trades came into being. With 225,000 members it embraced three-quarters of the employees in the printing and allied trades and was the tenth largest union affiliated to the TUC. After half a century of endeavour an amalgamation between NUPB&PW and NATSOPA had been achieved.[7]

By its nature and constitution, SOGAT was an all-graphical union seeking to enhance and improve the general standards of its members. Although its members covered a multitude of crafts and a vast range of printing and papermaking machines, SOGAT was prepared to respect traditional demarcation and jurisdictional positions unless these could be changed by common consent. As a graphical union, SOGAT had legitimate interests to organise workers dealing with any aspects of pre-servicing, producing, post-servicing and distribution of the graphic image. The 225,000 SOGAT members in their two Divisions ranged from preparation of raw materials for printing, of paper and paper conversion and of ink-making to the distribution of finished products.

The founders of SOGAT felt they were creating an organisation that would provide the basis for establishing one union for the printing industry. Given the formation of the NGA and its desire to create one craft union for the industry, the formation of one union for the non-craft workers in the industry was a significant step forward in the direction of one union for the industry. For many, the formation of SOGAT meant it was only a question of time before one union for the industry as a whole became a reality.[8] SOGAT expected to become a significant force in the industry, to become, in fact, the most important union in the industry. This expectation was spelt out to the 1966 Division A Biennial Delegate Council Meeting by Dick Briginshaw the SOGAT Joint General Secretary:

> In doing so (that is coming together) we have already created an organisation which will become increasingly a great force in the production, servicing and distribution of the graphic image. We are important. We are if I may say so – and I don't think we want to boast about our industry – quite definitely the important union. We must have the confidence of our position, fully understand it and be prepared to use it. We are the important union in print, in ink, and in paper. If you ally that with the other descriptions which I gave just now of the pre-servicing, the actual servicing, the production and distribution of the graphic image then we are not overstating our position when we say we are the important union.[9]

RELATIONSHIPS WITH OTHER PRINT UNIONS, 1966–70

Society of Lithographic Artists, Designers, Engravers and Process Workers (SLADE)

SLADE and the PMB jointly negotiated with the Federation of Master Process Engravers for terms and conditions in process houses. In March 1967 SOGAT invited SLADE to consider the amalgamation of the two unions. SLADE debated the request at its April 1967 National Council Meeting and in October 1967 met with SOGAT to explore amalgamation. It was agreed that basis for a merger existed and amalgamation talks began. However, by October 1968 they had collapsed. A major difficulty had arisen in that SLADE insisted it have 12 seats on the SOGAT Executive Committee for all time. These seats would represent the interests of the SLADE Division. SOGAT would not accept that any group within it should keep into perpetuity all their old autonomies. Permanent representation was too high a price for SOGAT to pay for merger with SLADE. Over a 50-year period a number of independent unions had joined SOGAT and each would have liked to retain its autonomy rather than integrating fully into the wider union. If SLADE were permitted to retain permanently its

99

identity within the wider union then SOGAT would find itself faced with demands from other groups within the union that they be granted permanent representation on the Executive Council.

There was disappointment within SOGAT at the break-down of the SLADE merger talks because SOGAT believed the two unions could work together to the mutual benefit of their members. Within SOGAT's structure SLADE would have had a degree of autonomy relative to what could be offered by the NGA, into which SLADE would be expected to integrate with only limited representation rights. Delegates to the SOGAT National Council and Rules Revision Conference of 1968 were told that 'SLADE talks failed because SLADE wanted to unify without unification. It cannot be done. We understand the problems of the SLADE membership and their leaders. Time will change their attitudes.'[10] The SLADE General Secretary expressed disappointment at the break-down of the amalgamation talks to the SOGAT (Division A) 1970 Biennial Delegate Council Meeting of 1970. He stressed the impediment had not been the principle of amalgamation but the mechanics by which it would be achieved. The delegates were told:

> One cannot lose one's identity without at least getting to know people and fighting and soldiering with them. It is out of experience that you will gain, amongst the membership at rank and file level. We acknowledge that any formal division has to be eliminated, but the forfeiture of division must be a voluntary act on the part of the people concerned and must not be imposed from on high. There must in the next five years, emerge one industrial union for the printing industry.[11]

The National Graphical Association

The late 1950s and the early 1960s saw the rise of lithography relative to letterpress as the technical difficulties which had prevented lithographic printing from becoming more generally acceptable were overcome. The period saw a considerable number of web-offset machines introduced into the general printing and provincial newspaper industries and it was predicted that demand for such machines would expand at a quicker rate in the late 1960s and early 1970s. However, in the mid-1960s only one web-offset press was employed in the national newspaper industry. Although web-offset machines were being used for new types of work they were, by the mid- to late 1960s, increasingly being used to produce substantial amounts of work previously printed on letterpress, photogravure and sheet-fed lithographic machines. In the late 1950s and early 1960s the initial costs of installing web-offset presses and the cost of production per unit were high, exceeding those of machines based on other printing processes. There was an increasing demand for high-quality colour printing and it was this market demand that litho printing could satisfy. Web-offset presses could produce printed matter of high quality in one or more colours, were versatile and had a unique ability to produce acceptable multicoloured print at very high speeds.

In the mid-1960s staffing arrangements for letterpress and sheet-fed lithographic machines in the general printing and newspaper industries were well established. In letterpress machine rooms, the tasks of the machine manager were undertaken by members of the NGA. The tasks of machine assistants were done in some towns by members of SOGAT (Division 1) but in other towns by SOGAT (Division A) members. In the general printing industry, in machine rooms using sheet-fed lithographic machines, the duties of the machine manager were carried out by ASLP members and those of assistants by SOGAT (Division 1) members in some towns and SOGAT (Division A) in others. In the early 1960s the machine rooms of the majority of provincial and national newspapers consisted solely of letterpress machines. These staffing arrangements were covered in national agreements between the appropriate employers associations (BFMP or NS) and the trade unions.

The staffing of web-offset machines was not covered by collective agreements, and as they were introduced into lithographic or letterpress houses, staffing and union arrangements were the subject of separate house agreements. However, the introduction of web-offset machines in provincial newspaper houses and former letterpress general print houses caused interunion disputes between the ASLP on the one hand and the TA, STA and LTS on the other over whose members should undertake machine managing duties. The letterpress craft unions were prepared to accept the right of ASLP members to mind sheet-fed lithographic machines in the general printing industry. Indeed, in 1959 the unions involved had signed an agreement which stated that where the employment of either union contracted because of machinery operated by the other, those individuals affected could be retrained and transferred to the other union. However, the letter-press craft unions were not prepared to recognise the ASLP as responsible for providing the craftsmen on web-offset presses installed in provincial newspapers (where the ASLP had never had members) or in certain periodical houses. The difficulty arose because, although the presses were litho machines and so fell within the control of the ASLP, the work previously carried out in the provincial press had been undertaken on letterpress machines operated by members of the NGA or the STA. To resolve these difficulties, the ASLP and the NGA established in November 1965 a 'Joint Web-offset Committee' to consider union arrangement when web-offset presses were installed in provincial newspaper and certain periodical houses.

In addition to inter-craft union problems, the introduction of web-offset machines caused demarcation difficulties between the NGA and the ASLP on the one hand and SOGAT (Division 1 and Division A) on the other. SOGAT argued that neither its members nor those of ASLP or NGA had sufficient knowledge to manage web-offset presses. ALSP members required training in the techniques of handling web, whilst NGA machine minders, although familiar with web-fed presses, required training in the principles of lithography. Some 60 per cent of SOGAT machine assistants working on letterpress machines had had at least six years' experience on sheet-fed lithographic presses. Given the technical and operating requirements of web-offset machines, SOGAT saw no reason why its members should not have the neces-sary retraining to manage these presses. The ASLP and the NGA firmly rejected this claim.

Demarcation disputes between the NGA and the ASLP on the one hand and SOGAT on the other over the manning of web-offset presses were illustrated in three disputes in the mid-1960s – the opening of a new plant by the *Daily Mirror* in Belfast in 1965, the opening of a new plant by International Printers Limited at Southwark (Southwark Offset Limited) in 1964 and at the Co-operative Press, Manchester in 1965.

The Daily Mirror, Belfast

The first web-offset machine introduced into a national newspaper was at the *Daily Mirror* plant in Belfast. This happened just before the creation of SOGAT, but the former NUPB&PW had negotiated with the NGA and the company a settlement that gave non-craft machine room employees the same rights on the press as NGA machine managers. There was to be a 50/50 staffing based on one SOGAT operative and one NGA operative. All employees (both SOGAT and NGA) who were to run the press had, by and large, had no previous experience of litho presses. However, they could do the job efficiently. SOGAT had not achieved this situation without paying a price. They had made a concession from their traditional policy by allowing NGA's manning standards to increase to permit on print units a 50/50 ratio, whereas traditionally the ratio was 25/75 in favour of SOGAT. Although SOGAT had negotiated an 8 per cent increase on NGA rates in return for these concessions, they had difficulty in persuading the NGA that SOGAT members should have 87.5 per cent of the NGA rate. The SOGAT National Assistant Secretary told the 1968 National Council and Rules Revision Conference.

I have no time to deal with all the intricacies of the wages structure so far as web-offset is concerned, but the situation in Belfast is that our people on these printing units are doing the same job as the NGA, and in many ways are doing it more efficiently. I could go to the management tomorrow and get the same rate as the NGA. If the NGA were to co-operate, we could increase the rate, and yet they insist on the 87½ per cent differential, despite the fact that our people are doing the same job. This is the pitiful tale right throughout the web-offset field.[12]

However, when the *Mirror* introduced a double width web-offset press, serious difficulties arose and the machine stood idle for over nine months. The NGA and SOGAT could not agree on the staffing standards. The issue had not been resolved when the *Daily Mirror* building was blown up by the Irish Republican Army. SOGAT viewed the failure to an understanding with the NGA as a tragedy in that:

If we could have made a breakthrough in Belfast, then as regards the double width process that are going into the provincial daily newspapers where organisationally not only us but the NGA are weak and have not got the same bargaining power, we could have set manning and wages standards as a pattern for the whole of the web-offset introduction into the provincial press.[13]

Southwark Offset Ltd[14]

Southwark Offset Ltd, part of International Printers Ltd (IPL), produced periodicals and general printing products of the International Printing Corporation. Following a review in 1963 of its operation in London it was decided to build a new factory using web-offset presses and the most modern methods of plate-making to print a number of periodicals published by the Corporation and to undertake general printing work for other customers.

In January 1964, IPL presented a paper entitled 'Conditions Essential to the Establishment of the Web-Offset Factory in London' in which they proposed to bring to the new factory (Southwark Offset Ltd) a fresh approach to periodical printing in London. Any work produced in London was to be competitive with that produced in the provinces and if its proposals were unacceptable to the unions the new plant would be sited outside London and the future for the printing of periodicals and general print products in London would be in doubt. The company suggested the web-offset machines be manned at levels comparable with the provinces and operated on a double day shift system. In return it proposed to improve employment conditions, including a sick-pay scheme, a phased plan to bring in a fourth week's holiday at average earnings and a pension scheme. IPL proposed to employ at Southwark Offset redundant staff from the Odham's Long Acre site where printing was done on letterpress machines and the machine managers and assistants were members of the NGA and SOGAT (Division 1) respectively. The ASLP agreed that web-offset machines at Southwark Offset be manned by members of the NGA and SOGAT, and that a lithographic technician (an ASLP member) should retrain the NGA members in the necessary skills.

In May 1964 IPL began negotiations with the London Region of NGA and the SOGAT (London Machine Branch) about arrangements for staffing the web-offset presses. These resulted in separate agreements. The NGA agreed 1½ minders for each two-unit press and that an additional machine minder would only be required when the next two-unit press was installed. The SOGAT agreement covered the number of men to be employed on each shift to feed the paper on to the reel stands and to take the paper off the folder. In further discussions with both unions it was agreed that the machine minders should make the fullest use of assistants and a system of 'pool-manning' would operate.

IPL understood pool-manning to mean that all staff on each shift could be interchanged as the need arose. The NGA did not accept this view, arguing that when its members were not available SOGAT members would undertake duties which the NGA regarded as the prerogative of its own members. Pool-manning would have challenged the principle that craft work should only be carried out by craftsmen. The NGA had understood pool manning to mean that machine minders employed on all presses on each shift should be interchangeable and that a similar arrangement should operate amongst assistants. SOGAT saw pool-manning in the same way as IPL. This led the NGA to accuse SOGAT of being associated with the company's policies, of laying claim to joint control of web-offset presses and claiming craft status for their members on these presses.[15] SOGAT felt the NGA response to be *provocative*, pointing out that if staffing agreements were not kept, the new plant would close and arguing that no trade union could live in isolation since the behaviour of one affected others who, in turn, were therefore entitled to have a say about what went on.[16]

In July 1964, the NGA announced they were not prepared to accept even on an interim basis the agreed manning arrangements for Southwark Offset. In April 1965 they made a claim for 3½ minders on a four-unit press, i.e. 1½ more than had originally been agreed. The company rejected this demand whilst at the same time SOGAT threatened industrial action unless its members employed on the presses were paid at a rate close to the top rate paid to NGA members and were afforded full interchangeability of duties. In November 1965 the NGA informed IPL that the minimum number of staff required to run the four-unit presses at Southwark Offset was three machine minders and two minders in the case of each two-unit press. Between April and November 1965 a clash between the NGA and IPL had been avoided largely because the number of NGA members available for each shift at least equalled the number of machine minders the union felt necessary to operate the presses. However, when on 29 November 1965 the company brought into operation a two-unit press, the NGA chapel, following a National Executive Committee instruction, refused to operate the four-unit press with two machine minders. The company responded by saying Southwark Offset would close on 15 December 1965 unless the NGA ran the web-offset presses on the staffing originally agreed or on the basis of that staffing level while the matter was referred to conciliation or arbitration. The NGA would give no such undertaking but the P&KTF persuaded the company to delay the issuing of redundancy notices until 20 December. On that date a formula was agreed between the NGA and the IPL to resolve their dispute over the manning of web-offset presses. The Agreement included an inquiry into the dispute under the auspices of the TUC, but its form was to be agreed between all the parties. The TUC was to hear the parties on 16 February 1966 but the hearing never took place. Prior to the meeting the TUC had agreed to a SOGAT request that it be represented whereupon the NGA withdrew from the TUC inquiry claiming the TUC had departed from its terms of reference.

Further abortive attempts were made to resolve the IPL/NGA dispute including the company offering to ensure that if at any time while pool-manning was operating both machine minders were absent from a four-unit press it would not be operated solely by SOGAT members. On 4 April 1966 the NGA said it would no longer allow its members to work double shift and it gave notice that its members would not operate presses with less than 11 machine minders per shift and that absences for sickness and holidays would need to be covered by extra staff. In view of this the company decided it had no alternative but to close the works from 29 April 1966. Unsuccessful attempts were made to settle the dispute by the Ministry of Labour, the TUC and the P&KTF. Southwark Offset closed on 29 April 1966. On 1 May 1966 negotiations began between IPL, NGA and SOGAT (Division 1) to see if a basis could be found for a return to work. A formula was agreed on 5 May 1966 and work resumed at Southwark Offset that day. The significant points of the return to work were:

(i) Management accepted the joint approach made by NGA and SOGAT (Division 1) to operate a three-month experiment of a fully integrated staff so that the position could be reviewed by all parties in the light of experienced gained.

(ii) The unions agreed the total machine crews would be 34 plus one NGA overseer and would operate the presses as required, allowing for the normal incidence of holidays and sickness.

(iii) In the event of a person leaving the employ of the company during the three-month period they would be replaced by a member of the same union.

(iv) Integrated staffing meant all duties and responsibilities on the press could be delegated by the press room overseer, and the NGA and SOGAT gave an undertaking that their members would not prevent those of either union from performing any function on the press allocated to them by the press room overseer.

Meanwhile, on 2 May 1966 the Minister of Labour appointed a Court of Inquiry to inquire into the causes of the Southwark Offset dispute and a similar dispute at the Co-operative Press in Manchester (see below) and to undertake a wider inquiry into the problem arising from the introduction of modern printing techniques in the printing industry.[17]

The Dispute at the Co-operative Press, Manchester[18]

The Co-operative Press employed 150 production employees in its Manchester printing works which produced periodicals and general print products. Before the web-offset presses came into production in 1966 most of its work was on letterpress machines operated by machine minders and assistants who were members of the NGA and SOGAT (Division 1) respectively. There was a small lithographic section at the plant operated by ASLP members. In 1964 the company announced its intention to install a web-offset press to print a number of periodicals and, at a later date, a tabloid newspaper. Arrangements were made for representatives of ASLP, NGA and SOGAT to inspect the press at the manufacturer's works. As some of the work to be produced on the press had been printed previously on a rotary letterpress machine, the Co-op decided the crew for the new press should comprise craftsmen from both the ASLP and the NGA and assistants from SOGAT (Division 1). Initially these arrangements were accepted by the three unions and in January 1965 staffing levels were agreed whereby the number of assistants would be four, but this would increase to seven if two folders came into use.

When the machine was installed in the summer of 1965 difficulties arose between SOGAT and the craft unions over the duties which the various crew members would perform. The NGA insisted the machine should operate under the arrangements agreed nationally for sheet-fed lithographic machines, on which their members performed the more skilled and the assistants, drawn from SOGAT, the less skilled duties. SOGAT (Division 1) on the other hand, took the view that web-fed lithographic printing was a completely new process and that arrangements governing sheet-fed litho machines were irrelevant. It proposed the staffing of the new presses should enable their members to perform duties they undertook on rotary letterpress machines. This was unacceptable to the ASLP and the NGA because certain of these duties, e.g. control over stopping and starting the press, were performed by ASLP members on sheet-fed litho presses. Another SOGAT suggestion was that the press be staffed by an integrated crew drawn from the three unions and the machine should be staffed on an alternative basis by a member of SOGAT and a member of either the ASLP or NGA, each of whom would be responsible for all operations. This proposal would have permitted SOGAT members to perform duties normally carried out by ASLP members on sheet-fed lithographic presses and was, therefore, unacceptable to the ASLP and the NGA.

The Co-operative Press was unable to arrange joint meetings with all the unions present and when deadlock was reached at the branch level the dispute was referred to the national level. The ASLP continued to reject the proposal that SOGAT members should perform on the web-offset presses the duties they normally carried out on the rotary letterpress machine at the Co-operative Press. However, on 24 February 1966 the management informed the ASLP and the NGA that the press would come into operation on the basis of conditions previously agreed locally without prejudice to any national agreement that might be made. The machine did not go into operation as SOGAT refused to accept this arrangement. The company reported the dispute to the BFMP who suggested the matter to be referred to a Joint Conciliation Committee of the Joint Industrial Council. The ASLP and the NGA informed the P&KTF they would not attend any such meeting if SOGAT were present as to do so would give *de facto* recognition to SOGAT's claims. Although negotiations were resumed, a solution had not been found when the Cameron Committee began its hearings. In July 1966 all the parties finally accepted the formula below and the machine came into operation.

> Our web-offset press in Manchester shall run for a three month trial period with the staffing already agreed with the ASLP, NGA and SOGAT (Division 1). The management will appoint a man in charge who will delegate duties and responsibilities to the staff, the crew to be employed realistically over the whole range of duties on the press. We require an undertaking from the three unions that their members will not prevent members of any union from performing any function on the press allocated to them.
>
> The management will give an undertaking that a review of the unions can take place at the end of the trial period without prejudice to any subsequent agreement which may be reached

by the unions at executive level, or affect the outcome of the Court of Inquiry.[19]

The three disputes described above all involved a claim by SOGAT that its members should be allowed to perform a wider range of duties on web-offset presses than they carried out as assistants on sheet-fed lithographic machines. The claims took various forms. In one, SOGAT members were to perform on web-offset presses the duties they carried out as assistants on rotary letterpress machines. In its more radical form, SOGAT claimed web-offset machines should be staffed on an alternate basis by a member of SOGAT (Division 1) and a member of one of the craft unions, and that each man should be fully responsible for all operations on the presses. Both forms were attempts by SOGAT to get the craft unions to surrender their exclusive right to be machine minders in the printing industry. Why did SOGAT take this line?

SOGAT believed web-offset presses should be operated on a basis of integrated staffing as the traditional division of responsibility on presses between its members and those of the craft unions was artificial and undesirable in view of the technical and operating requirements of such presses. It was critical of the BFMP's approach to the staffing of these machines, particularly their decision to attempt to negotiate a national agreement covering the staffing of web-offset machines with the ASLP before entering into discussions about the numbers of machine assistants required. SOGAT believed the BFMP should have initiated joint discussions with all interested unions and adopted the policy that, in cases where employers did not want the benefits to be gained by operating web-offset presses with an integrated staff and were unwilling to face the interunion difficulties involved, then the presses should be staffed with the number of assistants required to operate comparable letterpress machines.

SOGAT denied it was challenging the control which the ASLP and the NGA had established for their members over web-offset presses. SOGAT believed no union had a prescriptive right of this kind with regard to web-offset machines and it was a matter to be resolved between the unions claiming an interest in the operation of these machines. SOGAT argued that neither its own members nor those of the ASLP nor NGA had sufficient knowledge to manage web-offset presses without some retraining. ASLP members required retraining in the web-handling techniques. NGA members, although familiar with web-fed presses, required retraining in the principles of lithography.

SOGAT saw no reason why its members should not be provided with the retraining necessary to enable them to operate web-offset presses. Machine assistants were well qualified in that some 60 per cent of those working on rotary letterpress machines had at least six years' previous experience on sheet-fed lithographic presses.

A further reason for SOGAT's attitude was a feeling it could no longer tolerate the traditional situation in which its members were unable to advance to the most responsible positions on presses, no matter how great their experience might be, because these were held by members of the craft union. It did not believe it right that the demarcation of duties between unions should prevent a person filling the highest positions on a printing press commensurate with their ability. SOGAT considered inadequate the facilities available for the upgrading of machine assistants by adult apprenticeship to the status of craftsmen. It was particularly concerned that in London its members were prevented by the NGA from benefiting from the existence of adult apprenticeships.

For SOGAT the creation of one union for the industry was essential if the problems arising from the introduction of web-offset presses were to be settled adequately. It recognised that the creation of one union would not in itself solve the problems facing the industry, but believed it would make their solution easier. SOGAT believed two all-graphical unions pursuing the necessity to protect their members' interests in a period of change must eventually come together. They were disappointed. The NGA always seemed to reject positive compromise designed to bring about an accommodation and continued to propagate outmoded views about exclusive craft rights.[20]

What were the objections of the craft unions to SOGAT's claim? The ASLP asserted that although SOGAT members had experience of both lithographic and letterpress machines, their experience did not include the operations involved in minding web-offset machines. The ASLP considered there were few members of SOGAT with sufficient knowledge of lithography to operate a lithographic press in a satisfactory manner without a year or two of intensive training under a lithographic printer. The ASLP would not accept that when a letterpress house transferred to web-offset the assistants should be allowed to perform on the new presses all the duties they had performed on letterpress machines.

The NGA accepted that SOGAT (Division 1) members had experience on both sheet-fed lithographic and web-fed letterpress machines but had no experience of the work carried out by the craftsmen concerned with the transfer of the printed image to the paper. The NGA acknowledged that a machine manager could be training to operate a web-offset press in six months, but doubted whether it was possible to train a person taken off the streets in the same period. It denied there was a lack of opportunities for SOGAT members to advance to the position and status of craftsmen. Opportunities for upgrading of non-craftsmen to the status of craftsmen existed in almost all departments of the trade, the NGA maintained, adding that it was significant that these opportunities had not been sought after enthusiastically. However, many of these opportunities for an adult apprenticeship, especially in London, were available only to people outside the industry. The NGA also considered it significant that although SOGAT (Division A) had at least as many machine assistants in membership as SOGAT (Division 1), it had made no claim for integrated staffing of machine crews.

THE CAMERON REPORT

The Court of Inquiry, under the Chairmanship of Lord Cameron, issued its report in January 1967. It reached two initial conclusions. First, the Southwark Offset and Co-operative Press disputes could only be settled within the existing framework of union organisation. Second, a settlement achieved in these two disputes should not be regarded as setting for the future a pattern or standard for the determination of staffing and operation of other printing machines similar to web-offset.

The Court recommended the settlement of the Southwark Offset and Co-operative Press disputes on the basis that the post of machine minder be filled by a member of one or other, or both, of the craft unions as agreed between them, and the post of assistant be filled by a member of SOGAT. In the case of Southwark Offset, the Court recommended the operation of a system of pool-manning whereby the machine minders employed on all presses on each shift be inter-changeable, and that similar arrangements operate amongst assistants. The Cameron Report also recommended the formal abandonment by SOGAT of its claim at the Co-operative Press to alternate manning. The Court took the view that at Southwark Offset and at the Co-operative Press the operation of integrated staffing should be that on those occasions when the number of NGA machine minders fell below a minimum level the leading machine minder would utilise the services of the assistants in a way which was practicable and proper in the light of the work being produced. This arrangement did not involve machine minders in training SOGAT members in operations which were normally carried out by the NGA. The Court's recommendations were interim ones in that there existed no effective means within the industry for settling disputes about staffing or jurisdictional disputes between unions on a satisfactory basis. Nevertheless, it said, 'we would gravely reprehend any further attempts by SOGAT to force acceptance in individual cases of the same or similar claims to those which precipitated the deadlock at Manchester'.[21]

The Cameron Report also examined the problems arising from the introduction of modern printing techniques other than web-offset presses. In this regard it made 17 recommendations of which the more important were:

(i) As a matter of urgency the two sides of the printing industry establish joint machinery for consultation and negotiations to replace the Joint Industrial Council for England and Wales.

(ii) New national machinery be established for dealing with disputes.

(iii) Both sides of the industry consider urgently alterations and modifications to the apprenticeship system to enable the emergence of a labour force capable of adapting to the skills required to meet the demands of a changing industry.

(iv) The amalgamation of existing printing trade unions into one representing the whole industry be pursued by all concerned with all dispatch.

SOGAT was highly critical of the Cameron Report.[22] It accused the drafters of the report of being inexpert, of knowing nothing at all about the printing and newspaper industry, and of showing, particularly in their reference to SOGAT, that they never really understood SOGAT's case. They claimed the report lacked any paragraph of original thinking and that it had bowed to expediency. Nevertheless, SOGAT welcomed the Court's call for one union for the industry. In February 1967 SOGAT advised the Minister of Labour that the union found the Cameron Report unacceptable but agreed to continue to participate in committees and councils of the printing industry established to discuss issues related to the implementation of new techniques.

SOGAT continued to pursue its policy of trying to achieve integrated staffing on web-offset presses. Towards the end of 1967 the NGA proposed a Joint Web-offset Committee consisting of representatives of the NGA, ASLP and SOGAT to discuss staffing on future web-offset installations. An essential part of the proposal was an agreement by the NGA and the ASLP to discuss opportunities for the progression of SOGAT members within the industry in return for SOGAT withdrawing its claim for integrated staffing. Although the three unions approved the arrangements, problems quickly arose. ASLP had reservations about the inclusion of general printing web-offset installations in the Committee's terms of reference whilst SOGAT announced its continued co-operation was subject to national newspapers being outside the Committee's remit. SOGAT intimated that, if it withdrew its claim for integrated staffing in the national newspaper field, it would simply negotiate independently on rates and staffing. The final break came when SOGAT refused to attend a meeting of the three unions at which the terms of reference for the Committee were to be finalised. However, a significant aspect of the abortive discussions was that SOGAT had pinpointed the two main considerations motivating its policy towards the staffing of web-offset presses. The first was concern that the traditional positions of its members on newspaper rotary presses were in danger of being virtually eliminated by the introduction of web-offset machines. The second was concern that their members would be denied opportunities for advancement to craft status.

In early 1968 the NGA suggested to SOGAT that there should be one union for all machine and composing rooms and that that union should be the NGA. It proposed a formula be worked out jointly by the two unions whereby there was progression from non-craft to craft in these departments. The proposals were totally unacceptable to SOGAT unless they were being implemented within the context of amalgamation. Although the door remained open for further discussions between the NGA and SOGAT to establish closer working and, ultimately, an amalgamation it was, in the summer of 1969, unrealistic to think that any real progress could be made whilst the NGA continued its policy of opposition to shared jurisdiction with SOGAT over web-offset machines. Relationships were also not helped by SOGAT's resistance to requests to transfer its members employed on small offset machines to the NGA under the terms of an agreement between the former ASLP (which transferred its engagements into the NGA in 1969) and SOGAT.

Developments in the litho field also led to disputes between SOGAT (Division A) and the NGA. A typical problem occurred towards the end of 1969 in connection with the operation of multi-lith machines engaged in the personalisation of cheques. This arose when a firm – where the work had previously been performed by the PMB of SOGAT (Division A) on vertical Miehles – closed down and the work was transferred to another office. At the time of the transfer new multi-lith machines were introduced, and because of the threat of redundancies SOGAT, claimed the right of its members to follow the job. The PMB also challenged the right of the NGA litho members to operate small offset machines. After a series of meetings a formula was reached that no redundancies would occur and that the machines would be operated on a 50/50 basis. Any new machines were to be operated by NGA members or by PMB SOGAT (Division A) members issued with NGA cards. The formula, unfortunately from SOGAT's perspective, firmly established recognition of the NGA's jurisdictional rights in this particular field.

However, in 1969 following the SOGAT National Council and Rules Revision Conference of November 1968, severe internal difficulties arose in SOGAT. These became so intense that the NUPB&PW/NATSOPA marriage ended in divorce in 1972. It is to the events surrounding this break that we now turn.

NOTES

1. See National Union of Printing, Bookbinding and Paperworkers *Report of the Biennial Delegate Council Meeting, 1956*, pp. 260–3.
2. See National Union of Printing, Bookbinding and Paperworkers *Report of the Biennial Delegate Meeting, 1960*, pp. 292–6.
3. See National Union of Printing, Bookbinding and Paperworkers *Report of the Biennial Delegate Council, 1964*, pp. 241–54.
4. See 'NUPB&PW and NATSOPA Amalgamation' *Supplementary Report to the NATSOPA Governing Council, 1965*, p. 22.
5. The NUPB&PW's £150,000 was £3,630 cash and £146,370 of investments. The NATSOPA's contribution consisted of £32,273 in cash and £117,727 in investments.
6. For a report on the ballot see National Union of Printing, Bookbinding and Paperworkers *Annual Report of the National Executive Committee, 1965*, p. 1.
7. See *NATSOPA Journal*, December 1965, Special Supplement Sheet.
8. See *SOGAT Journal*, February 1966, p. 10.
9. See Society of Graphical and Allied Trades (Division A) *Report of the Biennial Delegate Council Meeting, 1966*, pp. 64–7.
10. See Society of Graphical and Allied Trades *Report of the Executive Council to the National Council and Rules Revision Conference*, November 1968, p. 45.
11. See Society of Graphical and Allied Trades (Division A) *Report of Biennial Delegate Council Meeting, 1970*, pp. 60–3.

12. See Society of Graphical and Allied Trades *Report of Proceedings at National Council and Rules Revision Conference*, November 1968, pp. 65–6.
13. op. cit., p. 66.
14. See *Report of the Court of Inquiry into the problems caused by the introduction of Web-offset machines in the printing industry and the problems arising from the introduction of other modern printing techniques and the arrangements which should be adopted within the industry for dealing with them*, Cmnd 3184, HMSO, London, January 1967, pp. 23–8. This report is commonly known as the *Cameron Report* after its Chairman, Lord Cameron.
15. See 'Trouble Looms with NATSOPA' *NATSOPA Journal*, December 1965.
16. See 'Irresponsible Provocation' *NATSOPA Journal*, December 1965.
17. The members of this Court of Inquiry were the Honourable Lord Cameron (Chairman), D. Basnett, D.J. Flunder and G. Wood.
18. For an account of this dispute see the *Cameron Report*, pp. 28–31.
19. op. cit., para. 94, pp. 30–1.
20. See 'NGA/SOGAT relations: NEC Policy Statement' *SOGAT Journal*, September 1969, p. 5.
21. See the *Cameron Report*, para. 211, p. 66.
22. See *SOGAT Journal*, February 1967, p. 4.

CHAPTER 5

THE BREAK-UP OF SOGAT

ATTEMPTS AT INTEGRATION, 1966–8

Following the creation of SOGAT the task began of fashioning an integrated union. On 9 March 1966 the first meeting of the SOGAT Executive Council took place at which were established a number of sub-committees of which the most important were the Structure, Finance and Organisation Committees. These sub-committees began work on integrating SOGAT's two Divisions by encouraging branch and membership liaison between the two Divisions and by planning possible developments up to the SOGAT Rules Revision Conference. This was to be held no later than 1969 and would give further advice to the Executive Council concerning the integration of the two Divisions.

However, in reality, over the period February 1966 to November 1968, when the National Council and Rules Revision Conference met at Brighton, little progress was made towards the integration of Division 1 and Division A into one union. A common journal was introduced from February 1967,[1] the qualifications for holding SOGAT officerships were agreed,[2] the responsibility for wage negotiations was transferred from the Divisions to SOGAT so that a single union voice was heard in negotiations, and some rationalisation of administration was achieved.[3] The spheres of work of the officers were agreed, the contribution rate of the two Divisions for SOGAT funds was doubled to 2p per week for male members, and 1p per week for women members, and members of either Division could now attend, for a nominal sum, each other's convalescent homes.[4] Progress towards the integration of SOGAT in its first three years of existence had been slow.

Concern with the rate of progress towards the integration surfaced at the 1968 Biennial Delegate Council meeting of SOGAT Division A when its Midland Group successfully moved the following resolution:

> That this Conference is concerned with the lack of progress during the last two years towards the complete amalgamation of Division 1 and Division A into one union and instructs the Executive Council to take the necessary steps to bring this objective to a successful conclusion.[5]

A number of concerns were expressed. After two years of amalgamation the two Divisions still existed and even after the National Council and Rules Revision Conference there was still no prospect of a complete union. There was criticism of the multiplicity of full-time officials, some of whom, it was said, were performing duties which could be done by others who were by no means fully employed. Concern was expressed that little had been done to promote greater cohesion between local branches of the two Divisions. The Executive Council was urged to do more to promote local unity even to the extent of seconding a National Officer, whose main duty would be the promotion of local unity. Delegates were especially critical of the *SOGAT Journal*, claiming that it carried little news about Division A and nothing of interest to members employed in the papermaking and paper-conversion industries. Indeed, it was felt that the papermaking membership should be served by other full-time officers than just the Papermaking Secretary. Disquiet was expressed over the proposed balance of business at the National Council and Rule Revision Conference to be held in November 1968. Three days were to be devoted to policy-making and two days to rules revision. Two days was felt to be sufficient for policy-making as this period had been laid down at Divisional Conferences over a number of years.

Although the Division A Executive conditionally supported the Midland Group motion they sought to allay anxieties in two ways. First, they reminded the Delegate Council what had been achieved in bringing the two Divisions together, for example, basic negotiations had been transferred to SOGAT, national officers, under the leadership of the Joint General Secretaries, had defined spheres of work, and the union was operating at SOGAT House on the basis of SOGAT. Second, whilst admitting slow progress was being made in ending the divisional structure, delegates were warned that over-speedy progress could destroy the amalgamation since to quicken the pace could result in one Division seeing itself as being taken over by the other. Delegates were warned:

It was all very well saying let us quickly, destroy the Divisional structures but we do have a constitutional position prevailing. We have our Division 1 colleagues with their strong centralised system and we ours with the very strong branch system. I will say to Ray that it would be a very interesting exercise if, for example, Liverpool Division 1 branch suggested to Division A that they should amalgamate on the Division 1 basis. We are doing this type of thing by transferring to SOGAT certain major responsibilities and we are waiting to see, after the November National Council Meeting what the new form of SOGAT is going to be.

Nobody here should be under an illusion that after November there will have to be major surgery carried out in the areas up and down the country in reforming new branches, so if anybody thinks that we can, if you like, have a Division A take-over of Division 1, it will not be on. It has got to be on the basis of a new SOGAT structure.[6]

THE 1968 NATIONAL COUNCIL AND RULES REVISION CONFERENCE

The first National Council Meeting of SOGAT was held at the Metropole Hotel, Brighton in November 1968. It dealt with industrial policy, amendments to the ten basic SOGAT Rules and additions to the basic SOGAT Rules. Its decisions were further directions to the SOGAT Executive as to how to proceed with the consolidation of the union. On industrial policy, SOGAT became committed to the creation of one union for the printing and allied trades, to oppose any form of wage restraint legislation, government to resist any government legislation designed to restrict the freedom and rights of trade unions, to giving prior consultation and notice to unions effected by company mergers and take-overs and to re-align Labour Party policies to be more sympathetic to trade union principles. In addition, the National Council agreed some important collective bargaining objectives including the achievement of 92.5 per cent of the craft rate for all members employed as machine assistants, the upgrading to skill status for semi-skilled workers with at least five years' service and over 20 years of age, average earnings for holiday pay, the negotiation of sick pay schemes and a shorter working week.

However, it was the constitutional changes made by the National Council that were eventually to lead to the break-up of SOGAT. The first constitutional motion moved by Joint General Secretary Tom Smith instructed the Executive Council to abolish the divisional structure of SOGAT:

> That this Conference instructs NEC to make all necessary preparations for the abolition of the two Divisions and for one Rule Book for SOGAT and to report progress to this Governing Council as soon as possible but not later than October 1970.
>
> To assist towards this aim, motions for this Conference Agenda that cannot be implemented immediately, should be deemed in order and if passed by Conference be implemented at the first opportunity.[7]

The Executive Council was being given approximately two years in which to formulate the new structure for an integrated union. The second paragraph of the motion assured delegates that if, by the time of the next Conference there were propositions which had been carried at this Conference but not implemented, that would not prevent the 1970 Conference from taking whatever decision it wished on that particular issue. The motion, whilst recognising that some rule changes carried at the National Council might not be implemented immediately, nevertheless allowed that lobby to express their views. The motion was carried unanimously.

The Printing Machine Branch of Division A sought to make the SOGAT Object Rule that of Division A.[8] Although the SOGAT Executive Council opposed the PMB motion it was overwhelmingly approved by the delegates who accepted two main arguments. First, the current rule maintained the position of the two Divisions. Second, there should be a single set of objectives for SOGAT. It was not logical to assume that since a union had two divisions it must also have two sets of objectives. It was time SOGAT ceased being one union with two Divisions and two sets of objectives. The Divisions should come together with one set of objectives.

The SOGAT Executive Council proposed a SOGAT Executive Committee of 36 members elected 50/50 on a geographical (10 electoral areas) and trade (six groupings) basis. However, this proposal was rejected on a show of hands by 265 votes to 153. The EC argued that a Committee elected on this basis would be the first step ending the divisional structure as it would remove the two executive bases of the present SOGAT Executive Council. The proposed new Executive was designed to give the maximum amount of representation based on the principle of geography and trade and to ensure 50 per cent of the new Executive would be lay members. The Liverpool Branch of Division 1 sought to secure for the Ink and Roller Section direct representation on the new Executive Committee but this was defeated as was another Division 1 initiative which sought to give SOGAT an all-lay Executive which was the position pertaining in Division 1

The delegates from Division A opposed an Executive based on trade and geographical interests on a number of grounds. The proposal would retain the rule making reference to the two Divisions and two Divisional Executive Councils and would give SOGAT an overall elected Executive Committee whilst at the same time perpetuating two Divisions and two Executive Councils who could be different people from those elected to the main SOGAT Executive. Division A delegates felt a SOGAT Executive based on trade and geographical representation might hinder future possible amalgamation with other print unions.

Following the defeat of the Executive Council's proposals, the PMB of Division 1 proposed a SOGAT Executive of 36 people elected solely on a geographical basis. This proposal was the Division A Rule 3 which provided for an Executive on a regional basis and upon which could sit full-time Branch Secretaries. The proposed Executive would have authority to approve rule changes rather than the final authority in such matters resting with a ballot of the membership. Again this was the system operating in Division A (the former NUPB&PW). Despite opposition from the SOGAT Executive Council, the PMB motion was overwhelmingly carried.

The SOGAT Executive Council proposed a National Council attended by delegates on the basis of one for every 750 full members, delegates elected on a geographical basis, the Council meeting biennially during May or June, the duration of the Council decided by the Executive in the light of the volume of business and the Council receive a report of the stewardship of the Executive Council between National Councils. Delegates opposed these Executive Council proposals claiming they disenfranchised from representation at National Council small branches and all part-time branches in the two Divisions. It was pointed out, for example, that of the 21 branches in the North-west Region of Division A, only six would be entitled to representation at the National Council.

The Executive Council proposal was heavily defeated whereupon the London Central Branch of Division A successfully moved a motion to introduce a SOGAT National Council that would meet biennially, would be not less than five days in duration, would have delegates elected from branches (with each branch with a membership of not less than 200 being entitled to one delegate), would have a ratio of one additional delegate branch to every 500 members, would have power to confirm new rules, would decide the place of the National Council meeting and would allow observer status for branches with less than 200 members. This London Central Branch proposal was a virtual straight lift of Rule 5 of Division A. Despite opposition from the SOGAT Executive Council, the London Central Branch motion was overwhelmingly carried.

The PMB proposed new rules for SOGAT covering the role and function of its national officers and organisers. Once again, the proposed rules were straight from the corresponding rules in the Rule Book of Division A. The proposed rule on officers was carried but an amendment from the Manchester Branch of Division 1 suggesting candidates for national office be subject to an examination to ascertain their fitness and suitability for the duties involved was defeated. The Executive Council sought remission of the proposed rule on Organisers but this was rejected by delegates who then proceeded to accept the PMB motion. In opposing the PMB proposals on the functions of national officers, a delegate from the Glasgow Branch of Division 1 remarked that what was happening was a take-over of one Division by the other:

> This is taken solely from what has been happening in Division A. The whole idea of the Conference was to get together. Our Executive and our leaders had told us already that it would be a bringing together of the two rule books in an acceptable form to all of us, not a steam rolling, with one set of rules to be imposed upon the other group. This is what is taking place. We are talking about democracy but we have large groups and large branches in Division A steam-rolling through this Conference everything they want. We cannot do very much about it, and this is exactly what is happening and it should not be happening. This should be a marriage of two bodies, not a take-over bid. We have been talking about take-over bids and this is what is taking place. We have been taken over in one big fell swoop

as a Division and we are being incorporated into another Division with all their ideas and rules.[9]

The Bristol Branch of Division 1 unsuccessfully sought to secure, as soon as practicable, contribution rates and benefit scales which were common to both Division A and Division 1. It also unsuccessfully sought to establish that until the principle of equal pay for women had been established within the industry, women members should not pay equal contributions to men. The Executive Council had opposed the view that men's and women's contributions should not be equalised until equal pay had been achieved. Branches from Division A then sought to impose former NUPB&PW Rules in place of the existing SOGAT General Rule 8 – Administration – Benefits and Penalties, etc. The London Central Branch (Division A) successfully moved that the Executive Council be given powers to suspend incompetent and insubordinate Branch Officers subject to such Officers having the right of appeal to the National Council. The Ruling, Manufacturing, Stationery and Box-making branch (Division A) persuaded National Council delegates to give the Executive Council the authority to decide matters upon which the rules were silent. A third motion from the Leeds Branch (Division A) replaced the existing SOGAT position whereby the union could be dissolved by a simple majority of those voting to the Division A situation where dissolution required the consent of five-sixths of the members.

The PMB (Division A) succeeded in changing the SOGAT procedures for altering its general rules and replacing it with what was in fact Rule 6 (National Conference delegations) of the former NUPB&PW. In future, National Conference delegates were to be elected by ballot with representation on a divisional or area basis and were to be elected for two years. The PMB argued that what they were proposing was a tried and tested procedure which had worked equitably in Division A. Their motion was passed in the face of opposition from the Executive Council.

At the start of the fourth day of the Conference on 14 November 1968, Mr Edward (Teddie) O'Brien, an appointed delegate from Division 1, came to the rostrum to seek a meeting with the Executive Council and the General Secretary on the grounds that the SOGAT Executive resolutions had been defeated by mandated delegation and that the Executive Council 'have sat there like a load of dummies and have not said a word.'[10] When the President ruled the Conference would carry on, the Division 1 delegates left the hall. The Conference session was thereupon adjourned but the delegates were asked to stay around and be available to be called back if a resolution could be found to the difficulty. The Conference re-assembled at 2.15 p.m. and the President read a statement which he requested be heard in silence without interruptions. The President asked that when he had finished reading the statement, he would sit down in silence. The prepared statement was as follows:

The Division 1 delegates regret the situation that has arisen today. They have been activated in their protest by a strongly held feeling by the whole of their delegates that Conference regulations and Standing Orders covering the Conference had been breached in a way, out of control of the President of the Conference. Whilst it may be possible that no mandating meeting have taken place they hold the view that mandating nevertheless had been operating during the past days of the Conference. The delegates of Division 1 say honestly and sincerely that they came here with open minds, willing to listen to a logical presentation and vote accordingly. They found unacceptable the spirit of unreason and rejection of Executive Council proposals and the appearance of whole delegates seeking merely to defeat and humiliate their officers and Executive Council. They have witnessed the spectacle of delegates not having heard the debate, return to the hall immediately they knew the vote was to be taken and then voting in accordance with what can only be seen as a previously mandated position. They think that their dignity and standing and that of all delegates is impinged by this conduct and has led to the dissatisfaction that has found expression.

The delegates of Division 1 restate their desire for the widest fraternity in Conference in spite of all that has occurred because they firmly believe that the objective of a new union in SOGAT must be pursued. They regret that the Executive Council did not come forward with sufficient precise proposals that had been carefully worked out to enable Conference to deal with fundamental issues. They feel that many decisions of Conference so far taken will provide a rehash of Division A rules whereas the Deed of Amalgamation and the vote of the membership in the two former unions was, for quite definitely, the establishment of a new union. They believed that the SOGAT Executive Council should be supported by the whole Conference in turning its attention immediately after the Conference to establishing the single union and to this end to produce a cohesive policy at a re-call conference at the earliest time not more than a year from now. They, therefore, request that the statement be presented to Conference by the President.[11]

Following resumption of the Conference the London Machine Branch (Division 1) successfully persuaded the National Council delegates to establish a SOGAT Final Court of Appeal. Although the motion was, in fact, Rule 51 of the former NUPB&PW, the proposer remarked 'this is one Division A rule that is quite acceptable to us'.[12] The Executive Council had again been defeated in opposing the London Machine Branch resolution. After this, Division A Branches moved motions designed to add former NUPB&PW rules as addition rules to SOGAT rules on 25 issues. In 18 of these issues, including legal assistance, suspension and penalties, misconduct of members and formation of branches, they were successful. Four issues were remitted to the Executive Council and three (unemployment benefit, Christmas grants and the convalescent homes committee) were defeated.

SOGAT's first National Council and Rules Revision Conference had ended. The SOGAT Executive now faced considerable difficulties in preparing a SOGAT Rule Book based upon the Conference decisions. There had been 70 resolutions submitted to the Conference. Five had been from the Executive Council, three from Branches of Division 1 and 62 from Branches of Division A. The total number of resolutions submitted by the PMB (Division A) was 12, as was the number from the London Central Branch (Division A). Of the Executive Council motions, those on the composition of the Executive Council and the National Council had been defeated as was its opposition to proposed new rules on objects and National Officers. However, its motion advocating the end of the two Divisions had been accepted. With respect to additional rules to the SOGAT General Rules as opposed to changing the ten existing General Rules, there were 58 general resolutions of which 44 had come from Division A.

The 1968 Conference had been a Policy and Rules Revision Conference. All Branches had submitted policy and rules change propositions. However, the majority of proposed rules changes had been submitted by Division A Branches. This infuriated Division 1 delegates for

124

whom the Conference was to be the occasion when the SOGAT member-ship, via their elected representatives, decided how SOGAT developed in the future. However, SOGAT now had a Rule Book largely based upon Division A Rules. Delegates from Division A argue that this had arisen because the National Council and Rules Revision Conference had embraced principles voted for overwhelmingly and on many occasions unanimously. The only opposition to their propositions came from the Executive Council. The agenda had been dealt with in a proper manner. Division A propositions had been in order, had been moved, seconded, debated and a vote taken.

At the end of the Conference, Division A delegates had returned home feeling they had done a good job in that major steps had been taken towards abolishing the two Divisions and guiding principles for a united SOGAT had been laid down. Many felt that after nearly three years of amalgama-tion, their attempt to fashion a unified union had been sensible. Division 1 delegates had left the Conference with different feelings. They were not ready for a unified union based on the Division A Rule Book and consid-ered more time should be spent continuing as separate Divisions, working in association with each other and sharing a common title – SOGAT.[13]

DEVELOPMENTS: DECEMBER 1968 TO FEBRUARY 1972

Division 1 Rule Changes

When the SOGAT Executive Council published the proceedings of the November 1968 National Council and Rules Revision Conference it contained a preface which drew attention to the difficulties created by some of the decisions taken. A call to avoid recrimination and disunity was made. Although legal advice had been taken by Division 1, the SOGAT Executive Council began preparing a new Rule Book based upon the spirit and intentions of the Brighton Conference, intending to overcome the problems as they arose. The preface concluded:

The outcome of what will be a considerable and lengthy task will be presented, together with all advices obtained, to a further meeting of the National Council. The intention is to prepare a Rule Book on the basis of these declared intentions that will legally and sensibly comprise a whole acceptable for registration by the Registrar of Friendly Societies, and most important of all, acceptable to the membership.[14]

Following the Brighton Conference, Division 1 took legal advice which stated the results of the Conference were inoperable on three grounds. First, the Conference had placed both the Permanent Officers and the Divisional Executives in impossible positions because it was difficult to construct a Rule Book by means of a collection of separate and unguided committee decisions. Second, some individual rule alterations made nonsense and/or left uncertainties or gaps. The legal advice pointed to seven such examples:

(i)   Some Division 1 objectives had been eliminated in the new SOGAT objectives.

(ii) The Divisions had ceased to exist but the revised Rule Book nevertheless contained reference to Divisional Rules and Divisional contributions.

(iii) The original SOGAT rule governing the Executive Council had been revoked. It could be argued therefore the SOGAT Executive had been dissolved. However, the revised rule accepted at Brighton provided no machinery for electing a new SOGAT Executive.

(iv) No provision existed in the revised Rule Book for paying branch officials.

(v)   No provision existed in the revised Rule Book for contributions to SOGAT. The original rule allowed the SOGAT General Fund only 1p per week to meet all SOGAT benefits (unemployment, dispute, funeral, benevolent, fares, convalescent, etc). Division 1's legal advisers considered SOGAT would become insolvent.

(vi) The provision for rule alteration was obscure.

(vii) It was not clear whether there was more than one body controlling the Executive.

Third, the Executive had a situation in which they could be challenged at law. If they ignored or delayed acting on the Brighton decisions a member might seek an injunction. On the other hand, if they enforced the Brighton decisions there was the possibility of the union going bankrupt or a member going to the courts to establish that the new rules could not be implemented and must be ignored in whole or part. If the Executive selected which parts of the Brighton decisions they would implement they again faced the possibility of legal challenge. Division 1 was advised that once litigation started no one could predict the direction it would take or what the outcome would be, but the union would probably have at last three years litigation on its hands. The costs of legation would be prohibitive and carried the threat of tearing the union apart.

This legal advice caused Division 1 to ballot their members as to whether SOGAT General Rules should continue to have preference over divisional rules. In January 1969 Division 1 announced the ballot vote was 17,557 for and 1,605 against SOGAT General Rules remaining supreme. When Division 1 implemented this result, Division A contended the supremacy of SOGAT rules be restored otherwise how could SOGAT operate if decisions passed at its Executive could be ignored by one of its constituent bodies.

Against the background of these difficulties the SOGAT Executive Council appealed for calm so it could convene in the right environment sometime in 1970 another National Council to which it would put a new Rule Book that would be practical and workable. In reality the Executive Council was resisting implementing the decisions of the Brighton Conference and Division A members of the Executive argued for the 1968 National Council to be recalled so the difficulties in implementing it could be explained. They also urged SOGAT's solicitors be invited to produce draft rules for consideration by the SOGAT Executive Council and for submission to the National Council. Division A representatives on the Executive preferred not to push their view too far as they wished to maintain unity. However, this in no way allayed their fears that in resisting the implementation of the Brighton Conference decisions the SOGAT Executive Council was acting against the wishes of the SOGAT membership.

The Keys/Hooker Writ

The difficulties were brought to a head when two SOGAT members, Bill Keys and Rod Hooker (both members of Division A and the SOGAT Executive Council), wrote in December 1969 to the SOGAT Joint General Secretaries and then in January 1970 through a solicitor, to the Executive of Division 1. This was followed by Keys and Hooker then issuing a private writ against two members of the Division 1 Executive Council. The writ sought to establish that the amendments to the Division 1 Rules were invalid and void. The Keys and Hooker writ was a private action and not taken on behalf of the Division A Executive. In their letter to the Joint General Secretaries, Keys and Hooker argued they had considerable doubts that the SOGAT

Executive Council was acting lawfully in failing to implement the Brighton Conference decisions. They felt it imperative to seek legal advice but did not want to litigate because of the inevitable adverse publicity such action would have. Keys and Hooker stressed they had written their letter in the hope that 'it will not be necessary for us to seek any other way of putting things in order'.[15]

D.H.P. Levy & Co. Solicitors wrote to the Division 1 Executive saying they were acting on behalf of Keys and Hooker who had consulted them upon the situation resulting from amendments to the Rules of SOGAT made in accordance to changes in the rules of Division 1 made in January 1969. The letter informed the Division 1 Executive that they had advised Keys and Hooker these amendments were invalid and of no legal effect. The amended rules considered invalid fell into five areas:

(i)   That NATSOPA should constitute Division 1 of SOGAT only 'during the pleasure of the Executive Council of NATSOPA'.

(ii) The assumption of power by the NATSOPA Executive Council 'from time to time to revoke, modify or replace' any of the amendments to the NATSOPA rules.

(iii) The provision that in the event of conflict the General Rules of SOGAT should prevail over the Division 1 Rules 'unless the Executive Council (i.e. of Division 1) from time to time otherwise determines in respect of the whole or part of such rules'.

(iv) The provision, that in the event of any conflict between the decision reached by any Officer or Council or other authority of SOGAT on the one hand and the decision of any Officer, Council or other authority of NATSOPA on the other, the former shall prevail 'unless the Executive Council (i.e. of Division 1) otherwise determines'.

(v)   The declaration that the Trustees of NATSOPA shall be Branch Trustees only so long as NATSOPA constitutes Division 1 of SOGAT.

These amendments went far beyond a reinstatement of the objectives of NATSOPA. The 1968 National Council had adopted a new set of SOGAT objectives which were those of the former NUPB&PW with the result that NATSOPA objectives were no longer incorporated into those of SOGAT. The revised SOGAT objects would prevail over the Division's objects in the event of any conflict between them. Division

1 members were told, however, that the old NATSOPA Object Rule may have got accidentally revoked in the 1968 Rule Revision Conference with the result that 'the old rule must be reinstated as a matter of extreme urgency if Division 1 (NATSOPA) is to carry on its work'.[16]

The 1968 Rules Revision Conference had taken a number of important constitutional decisions. It had agreed any further alterations to the Rules of SOGAT had to be confirmed by its National Council. It had removed the power of both Divisions to alter their rules by the procedures laid down in their divisional rules. The rules of both Divisions, being part of the rules of SOGAT, could now only be altered by the National Council of SOGAT. The Rules Revision Conference had taken this decision on the grounds that the amalgamation would become unworkable if either Division could repeal their rules which were then at variance with the General Rules. The changes to the Division 1 Rules following the 1968 Rules Revision Conference, were in breach of SOGAT rules as changed by that Conference.

Keys and Hooker were deeply concerned that Division 1's unilateral action had put the whole amalgamation at risk and threatened to destroy the years of patient work leading to the merger. They felt the authority in the Divisions of one union to make rules of their own, at variance with the rules of SOGAT, was incompatible with the whole concept of amalgamation. Keys and Hooker hoped Division 1 would retreat from the action it had taken before they were forced to obtain a High Court adjudication upon the validity of the amendments to the Division 1 Rules. If Division 1 persisted with its rule changes, Keys and Hooker warned they would issue a writ to let the Courts determine the matters in dispute. In the High Court they would seek to have the Court (a) make a declaration that the amendments to Division 1 Rules were invalid and void, and (b) grant an injunction restraining each member of the Executive Council of Division 1 from exercising any of the powers purportedly conferred on the Executive Council by the amendments and by any of the rules of SOGAT other than in accordance with the provisions of the revised General Rules of SOGAT.

Dick Briginshaw, the General Secretary of Division 1 regarded the Keys/Hooker actions as a definite step in the disintegration, by one process or another, of SOGAT. He considered their action detrimental to the interests of SOGAT and to rules of that body. Unless the SOGAT Executive took some action against them, he warned, 'we shall not be able to get on to a positive discussion on policy in continuity of the work of the SOGAT Executive'.[17]

Events Post-Keys/Hooker Writ

At a Divisional 1 Executive Council meeting held on 26 January 1970 three things were agreed to be achieved at a special meeting of the SOGAT Executive to be held on 29 January. First, that SOGAT direct Keys and Hooker to withdraw their legal threat. Second, that SOGAT Executive Council then prepare a special supplementary report on the situation, explaining the legal advice obtained, and the considerations guiding the Executive in framing a set of rules for presentation to a SOGAT National Council to be held later that year. Third, that a supplementary report be presented to the Biennial Delegate Council meeting of Division A to be held in May 1970 and to the Governing Council of Division 1 to be held in June 1970.

Keys and Hooker, however, continued to hold the view that Division 1 had altered their rules to veto SOGAT, and unless this was rescinded they had no alternative but to pursue their action. Division A felt that only disunity could result from disciplining Keys and Hooker under SOGAT rules. The special SOGAT Executive Council held on 29 January 1970 considered a document which suggested Keys and Hooker withdraw the writ and that Division A discipline them under rule. The SOGAT Executive Council took the view that as they had not seen the document previously they needed time to consider it whilst Division A Executive Council members asked leave to retire to consider the document privately. When the meeting re-assembled it was quickly adjourned again. Division A members again met separately but felt they could not support the documents. When the Executive Council reconvened a number of its Division A members did not return, and those who did, walked out of the meeting early in its deliberation. The President ruled that as there were less than seven members of the Division A Executive present, the meeting was abandoned.[18] A further meeting held on 3 February 1970 was declared by the President to be inquorate and was subsequently abandoned. On this occasion insufficient members of Division 1 had turned up to provide the necessary quorum for their group. Subsequently, the Division A members of the SOGAT Executive conscientiously attended at the times and venues arranged to proceed with SOGAT business. But on every occasion the Division 1 Executive members did not turn up. However, the SOGAT officers from whichever

Division, were always present. As a consequence, no SOGAT business could proceed, except for that which could be dealt with by the Divisions separately.

Following the special meeting of the SOGAT Executive held on 29 January 1970, Division A Executive Council met on 2 February 1970 and unanimously agreed that the following proposition be sent to the Joint General Secretaries for the attention of the SOGAT Executive Council:

> Division A Executive Council are of the opinion that Division 1 acted unlawfully in carrying out a ballot and altering the Divisional Rules after the Brighton Conference. It, therefore, asks the SOGAT Executive Council to instruct Division 1 to return their Rules to the position as it existed prior to the Rules alteration registered in January 1969.
>
> Division A Executive Council request the SOGAT Executive Council to implement the decisions taken at the Brighton Rules Conference, bearing in mind Motion 27[19] carried at the Conference and have some printed and issued with the minimum of delay.
>
> If both of these requests are carried out, Division A Executive Council are prepared to request Messrs Keys and Hooker to withdraw their legal action against Division 1 Executive Council.[20]

On 3 February 1970 Division 1 Executive Council informed its membership of the situation that had arisen by circulating a pamphlet ('SOGAT (Division 1) Executive Council Statement on the Present Situation Affecting Division 1 in SOGAT'), by calling a special meeting of the Division 1 officers and by arranging a Special Conference of its Governing Council for 26 February 1970. In addition they agreed Division 1 would in future pay only the contribution laid down in the SOGAT Rules and the supplementary payments which had been agreed at a previous SOGAT Executive Council Meeting, would be discontinued. On 26 February 1970, the Special Governing Council of Division 1 was held but the only information available to Division A about its decisions were reports which appeared in the 'quality press'. In the light of this, Division A Executive Council informed its membership that:

(i) A difference of opinion existed between both Divisions, but Division A hoped some means would be found to settle the difference within a trade union framework.

(ii) Division A considered Division 1 had acted unlawfully in balloting their members and altering their Divisional Rules and they had asked the SOGAT Executive Council to instruct Division 1 to return to its rule position as existed prior to its rules alteration of January 1969.

(iii) Division A had requested the SOGAT Executive Council to implement the decisions taken at the Brighton Conference.

(iv) Two members of Division A had taken legal action against two members of the Division 1 Executive Council but it would be unwise for members to jump to any conclusions in regard to any of these matters.

(v) Ways and means be found for SOGAT to continue.

(vi) Division A Executive ask the SOGAT Executive Council, through the Joint General Secretaries, that the matter be referred to the Trades Union Congress.

On 6 April 1970 a Division A deputation saw Vic Feather, General Secretary of the TUC, to seek his help in settling the difference between Division A and Division 1 within the trade union movement rather than in the courts. Mr Feather subsequently met with representatives of Division 1 who made clear their refusal to discuss matters in view of the writ against Division 1. In these circumstances Mr Feather told both Divisions there was nothing he could now do, given the autonomy over their internal arrangements that unions affiliated to the TUC had.

On 20 April 1970 the Division A Executive were informed SOGAT had become involved in the writ issued against Division 1 because Mr Briginshaw claimed he had knowledge of a writ being issued against SOGAT. On hearing this news the Division A Executive sent the following resolution to the Joint General Secretaries of SOGAT.

Division A Executive Council, which consists of 24 SOGAT Executive Council members, refuse to endorse what they consider to be improper action or conduct taken by Joint General Secretary, R.W. Briginshaw, in instructing Division 1 solicitors to act on behalf of the SOGAT Executive Council in the action now proceeding in the High Courts of Justice entitled Keys and Hooker v Boulter and Butcher (first defendants) and the Society of Graphical and Allied Trades (second defendants) and in future no SOGAT policy decisions will be taken without consultation and approval of the SOGAT Executive Council.[21]

However, in an effort to find a solution to the problems, the Executive proposed a panel consisting of equal numbers from both Divisions to explore the matter. Division 1 was not prepared to go along with this request unless the Division A Executive took steps to have the Keys/Hooker writ withdrawn. The 1970 Division A Biennial Delegate Council meeting re-affirmed its faith in amalgamation but expressed concern that the 1968 National Council and Rules Revision Conference decision had not been implemented. The SOGAT Executive Council had a responsibility to implement the wishes of the Brighton Conference or to explain why they were unable to do so. The Executive Council had done nothing in 18 months. Delegates expressed their feeling that the failure to make progress towards the integration of SOGAT was leading to an anti-amalgamation feeling beginning to creep into Division A. These feelings were expressed by one delegate in the following way:

A certain section of our leadership (i.e. SOGAT-wide), against the wishes of the members, wishes to take over Executive control and to take over the control of this union and impose its will and its manners on us. This is foreign to us. We are a democratic society. We wish to remain a democratic society. The decisions come from this Conference. The Executive should acknowledge this. This Conference is sovereign when it comes to policy making decisions. It is the Executive Council's responsibility to carry out those wishes. If they find they are unable to do so they should call us back and tell us, or else get out, one or the other.[22]

The delegates reminded the Executive Council of the sovereignty of a delegate meeting, whether it be at divisional or SOGAT level. They also emphasised that although Division A believed in amalgamation it was not at any price, particularly if it meant replacing union democracy with dictatorship.

On 29 June 1970 the National Officers of Division A and Division 1 met, but the latter indicated, that they could not depart from the decisions of their Executive and Governing Councils, there was no possibility of the Brighton Conference decisions being implemented and, as far as they were concerned the Brighton Conference had been non-existent. Although there was still a desire on both sides to keep SOGAT in existence, there was still the question of on what terms and at what price. The suggestion there should be established a panel consisting of some seven to nine members of each Divisional Executive Council to consider how the two Divisions could work side by side was not without its problems. Division A had the commitment of its 1970 Delegate Meeting whilst Division 1 was unwilling to become involved whilst the legal action persisted. Indeed, Division 1 was adamant no SOGAT Executive Council meeting could resume so long as the legal action remained.

In July 1970 the General Officers of Division A met with Mr Ogden, QC, who, having read the Brighton Conference report expressed the opinion there were a number of decisions which could have been implemented but there were a great number which were ambiguous. Division A members at the Conference had been ill-advised and Division 1 could plead they were an oppressed minority. In discussing how the situation might be progressed, Mr Ogden advised against legal action but suggested alternatives. First, Division 1 might be persuaded to agree to a SOGAT Executive Council Meeting. Second, a National Council could be held. He volunteered that, if he were approached by both parties, he would be prepared to met counsel acting on behalf of Division 1, for an off-the-record exchange, with a view to finding accommodation between the parties. Following some discussion the Division A Executive proposed:

that this Division A Executive Council re-affirms their belief that the formation of SOGAT was correct in the interests of the membership. It states:

(i) that it will use the good offices of Mr M. Ogden, QC in an attempt to resolve the outstanding problems;

(ii) that it will notify Messrs Hooker and Keys to withdraw their writ provided Division 1 restore their rules as they stood prior to the Brighton Conference and regard to the veto;

(iii) that a re-call Conference be arranged as soon as possible so that the difficulties in implementing the rules decisions could be explained;

(iv) that the SOGAT Executive Council should present rules to the membership for their amendment and endorsement at a Conference;

(v)   that it is accepted that in the ultimate, the SOGAT Conference is the supreme authority.[23]

An amendment inviting Mr Ogden to try to find a solution to the problems confronting the union was also carried.

On 24 August 1970, the Division A National Executive authorised its General Secretary, Vincent Flynn, to advise Mr Briginshaw that Division A would not longer pay contribution income into the SOGAT account. Instead, it would open a special account into which it would pay monies normally paid into the SOGAT account until such time as the problems within SOGAT were resolved. In this event, authority would be given to the General Secretary to withdraw from this special account such sums as would be required to pay essential SOGAT administrative expenses, such as salaries of SOGAT officials and staff.

In September 1970, the regular monthly meeting of the Division A National Executive was attended, in an advisory capacity, by Mr Ogden. He outlined four possibilities as to how the problem of SOGAT ceasing to function might be overcome. The most desirable was that the SOGAT Executive Council should meet and function properly. Failing this, the SOGAT National Council should meet. The third possibility was litigation, which everyone wished to avoid, whilst the final option was to dissolve SOGAT. A fundamental difficulty was that it was virtually impossible for anyone to advise confidently as to which SOGAT Rules were in force and which were not. None of the new rules passed at Brighton had been registered, but that did not necessarily mean the old rules were still operating.

He advised there was much to be said for trying to force a meeting of a National Council by a request from 25 Branches with a total membership of 25,000. The request could seek the removal of the Executive Council or an understanding from the Executive Council to call a National Council or another Rules Revision Conference. The sole objective would be to obtain a meeting of the National Council and try to break the deadlock. Mr Ogden also advised Division A to consider writing to Mr Briginshaw expressing their deep concern about the position and urging a meeting of the SOGAT Executive Council, or alternatively the National Council, to resolve the situation; otherwise catastrophe lay ahead.

If it was impossible to get a meeting of the SOGAT Executive Council or a recall of the National Council then were two other alternatives:

litigation or dissolution. If it was decided to litigate then the Division A Executive Council could go to court to ask it to make an order that the National Council meet. There was every possibility the court would do this as they would not allow the present situation to continue indefinitely. Alternatively, Division A could intervene in the Keys/Hooker litigation, although the difficulty would be to speak as SOGAT. It would be an undesirable situation for Division A if Mr Briginshaw, as SOGAT General Secretary, acted for the SOGAT Executive Council in this emergency. Dissolution was seen as the unhappiest situation of all.

After Mr Ogden had finished his address the Executive Council considered a memorandum received from Mr Briginshaw in which he said it was becoming impossible to carry on the business of SOGAT and that this state of affairs could not continue. The time had arrived for either the Divisional Executive Councils to seek a path of agreement within the union or to seek an alternative of agreeing to disagree. Mr Briginshaw suggested, in an attempt to break the deadlock, that the Divisional Executive Councils appoint six of their members to join him in a round table conference without a chairman or an agenda. Those appointed would report back to their respective Executive Councils. None of the named persons in the High Court action affecting SOGAT or its Divisions would be amongst the six representatives from each Division.

Division A Executive had not taken out the writ and had no power to command its withdrawal. Division A was genuinely concerned to find a way out of the impasse and to make SOGAT fully operative with Mr Briginshaw as its General Secretary and the Divisions playing a subordinate and diminishing role. The fear of Division 1 members that they were being absorbed by Division A was seen as unfounded, as such a policy would weaken the organised strength of the members of both Divisions and undermine the concept of SOGAT as an organisation whose members enjoyed equal rights and shared equal responsibilities under a constitution fashioned by due democratic process. Division A remained deeply concerned at what it considered to be action which challenged the sovereignty of SOGAT and was preventing the consolidation of administration and control without which SOGAT could have no meaningful existence. Division A members considered that the alteration of Division 1 Rules constituted a right of veto which was prohibiting SOGAT's development. Division A proposed the deadlock be broken by the Divisions being removed and unity restored on the following basis:

   (i)   Keys and Hooker withdraw their writ;

   (ii)   Division 1 restore the position existing prior to the rule changes made at the Special Governing Council held in January 1969;

   (iii)   that either the SOGAT Executive Council, the two Divisional Executive Councils meeting jointly or a smaller group composed of equal members from each Divisional Executive meet to agree the method of achieving the ends stated above and, if the two Divisional Executives agreed, continue the tasks necessary to further the work to make SOGAT a living reality again;

   (iv)   the proposed meeting of a Committee of six representatives from each Division be held on 6 October 1970.

However, Mr Briginshaw insisted that the withdrawal of the action in the courts by Keys and Hooker was not negotiable and the issue be re-examined by Division A before the 6 October meeting. However, the Division A Executive Council continued to point out it had not given its tacit approval of the writ, the question of legalities was a matter of opinion and it would continue to seek solutions to the problems preventing the implementation of the Brighton Conference decisions.

The 6 October meeting considered a document entitled *An Agreement to Disagree*, prepared by the Division 1 Executive Council. The Division A delegation pointed out that the document contained a number of matters about which the two Divisions might differ, in particular the reference to actions of officers of Division A, that the writ had been issued by two individuals, acting in their individual capacity and the fact that they were members of the Division A Executive was coincidental. The Division A Executive was disappointed the document had not been made available prior to the meeting, especially as an answer to the proposals it contained was requested by Division 1 from Division A within 24 hours of its receipt. Division A requested a seven-day period to give a considered reply. Division 1 considered a further 48 hours sufficient time for Division A to take an effective decision. The General Secretary of Division A expressed disappointment that the two Divisions were now engaged in exchanging differences rather than exploring possible solutions to those differences, and added:

We must insist on having reasonable time to consider what you have said to us in the manner that its seriousness deserves. I assume that we, in Division A, are asked to discuss proposals, and not unconditionally to accept terms of surrender.[24]

The Dissolution of SOGAT

On 13 October 1970, Mr Briginshaw, the General Secretary of Division 1, issued the following statement to branches:

Your Executive Council has been advised by Mr Leo Price, QC that (subject to anything the Courts may say) the Division A Executive Council (NUPB&PW) had repudiated the Contract of Amalgamation and membership of SOGAT, as a result of their decision to discontinue their due payments into SOGAT funds. Your Executive Council are advised (subject to anything the Courts may say) that the Society of Graphical and Allied Trades, SOGAT, is no longer in existence.[25]

The decision to discontinue contributions into SOGAT funds had arisen from Mr Briginshaw's attempt to have the mandate regarding SOGAT finances transferred to him instead of the signatures of the two Joint Secretaries and a member of the Trustees. Relations between Division A and Division 1 continued to deteriorate, especially when Mr Briginshaw tried to have Division A leave the Borough Road premises. Division A considered they were being ordered out, despite Briginshaw's view that it was only an opinion that SOGAT was finished, and that the action was not just spite but vicious. By the end of October affairs had reached a critical stage and the October meeting of the Division A National Executive Council was advised by Thompson's solicitors:[26]

(i)   To accept a Receiver to be appointed for SOGAT funds on the grounds that throughout the whole episode Division A had expressed its concern for SOGAT. To oppose the appointment of a Receiver might be seen as taking a negative view.

(ii) The large SOGAT sign which had covered the former NATSOPA sign carved in the stone facia of 13/16 Borough Road had been removed. The SOGAT sign had not been reinstated and a small sign had been put up over the lintel of the entrance door. In addition, whilst formerly when people telephoned to Head Office, the telephonist answered 'SOGAT', the response now was the telephone number, but on being pressed the telephonist would say NATSOPA. Following the injunction the response had altered to NATSOPA/SOGAT. The understanding was that both the SOGAT sign and the telephone response fulfilled the requirements of the injunction.

(iii) There could be no certainty about the outcome of any trial as any decision was in the keeping of the Judge. There were however, certain possibilities. The Judge could decide SOGAT was effectively at an end. However, Division A did not want to end SOGAT, but continue it. One the other hand, the Judge could direct that a Conference be held but Division 1 would refuse to attend such a Conference. Division A could win its case through the legal process, but the law could not stop Division 1 from leaving the organisation.

(iv) There was no reason why Division A should not continue to use the title SOGAT as Division 1 had already reverted to the 'acronym' of NATSOPA.

(v) Division A should decide whether to continue with the fight through the courts and, possibly, win a victory, the effect of which would leave Division A in a position where all they had was the title. Division A could seek legally to retain the title 'SOGAT' but were advised they would have to pay of the order of £150,000 for this when they could have it for nothing. The original intention of SOGAT was now dead. Division A concluded that the title 'SOGAT' could be retained, but that given the exorbitant cost of litigation an out-of-court settlement be sought.

The October 1970 Executive Council meeting of Division A agreed to the appointment of a Receiver, to the recall of a Biennial Delegate Conference and to await a further report to be made to the Executive Council's November Meeting.

By the autumn of 1971 Division A's Counsel had come to the conclusion the Division 1 writ to end SOGAT be settled by mutual agreement outside the courts to avoid unnecessary expense. The Executive Council took the view that if there were to be a settlement outside the court procedure it would have to be (a) on the condition of title and (b) subject to the approval to the entire membership of SOGAT expressed through a ballot vote. On the issue of the title, Division 1 suggested Division A adopt the title 'National Society of Graphical and Allied Trades', but were reluctant to ballot their members on this. Discussions with lawyers continued and in November 1971 the following terms for an out-of-court settlement were agreed:

(i) SOGAT would be dissolved but the NUPB&PW would be immediately reconstituted as SOGAT.

(ii) The staff of SOGAT were to be absorbed into Division 1 and Division A.

(iii) The spheres of demarcation as existed prior to 1966 would continue. New areas and new recruitment would be subject to joint consultation.

(iv) After all outstanding SOGAT liabilities had been met the balance of funds would be divided as to first £300,000 equally, and any remaining balance in proportion as the per capita contributions of members of Division 1 and members of Division A.

(v) Each side would pay their own costs. The costs of the Receiver and Trustees would be borne from SOGAT funds.

(vi) Subject to a ballot vote of Division A members, Division 1 would assume authority to speak on behalf of its members.

The Division A National Executive Council accepted these terms at its November 1971 meeting. In addition it invited Mr H.W. Miles, the only elected SOGAT officer, to join Division A as a National Officer. The 1972 Biennial Delegate Council expressed regret at the break up of SOGAT but instructed the NEC to work for unity with all print unions to bring about one union for the industry.[27]

On 4 February 1972 in the High Court before Mr Justice Megarry, a Court Order was made giving effect to the NATSOPA and NUPB&PW agreement that SOGAT be dissolved. The Court Order re-established NATSOPA and NUPB&PW in the same position as prior to 1966. At the same time as the Court Order, a ballot of NATSOPA membership agreed that whilst retaining the acronym 'NATSOPA' the official title of the Society in future be the 'National Society of Operative Printers, Graphical and Media Personnel.'

The division of the assets of SOGAT between the two unions was not completed until 1974. On the formation of SOGAT, both unions had put in £150,000 of capital and subsequently made payments on a membership contribution basis. The Receiver's preliminary account to May 1973 reflected a balance of £268,710, although the final account was predicted to be in excess of £300,000. The two unions agreed that any figure below £300,000 be divided equally between them and that any sum in advance of £300,000 be divided in proportion to the contributions paid by each Division subject to two provisos. First, all elements making up the accounts were proven, and second the monies Division A paid into the accounts after 24 August 1970 be refunded to SOGAT (former Paperworkers) before the final division of the funds. By 1974 the Receiver had released £97,000 to each Society.

WHY THE BREAK-UP?

The break-up of SOGAT had happened for many reasons. Basically, it had proved impossible to accommodate a highly centralised union with a strong autocratic General Secretary and a decentralised union based on a democratic decision-making structure and a high degree of branch autonomy. However, there were other factors at work. There were those who perceived the formation of SOGAT, not as a new union but the reframing of their own union. Second, there were those who argued the Paperworkers never explained to its members the NATSOPA members' fears that the NUPB&PW would merely try to make SOGAT a bigger Paperworkers. Third, there were those who genuinely believed SOGAT was formed by equal partners and would continue as such as the divisional structure was dismantled. However, these expectations had been destroyed by the 'blatant' attempt by the Paperworkers at the 1968 Brighton Conference to make their Rule Book and industrial practices those of SOGAT. Fourth, there were those who blamed the break-up of SOGAT on the procrastination and vacillation of the SOGAT leadership. Fifth, there were those who blamed the break-up of SOGAT on the Keys/Hooker writ, which was regarded as an unwarranted attack on NATSOPA and SOGAT. There is no doubt that all these factors played a part in the disintegration of SOGAT.

New Union vs. Reframing the Old

NATSOPA believed the original idea and conception of SOGAT was right. The ten SOGAT General Rules were seen as a sound basis from which a new union could emerge. What did they see as having gone wrong? First, they considered there were fundamental differences of approach between themselves and the NUPB&PW in that NATSOPA viewed the amalgamation as forming a new union whilst the Paperworkers saw it as 'reframing' their own union. For NATSOPA a new union involved a progressive dismantling of the traditional rules and practices of both unions. Outmoded rules and procedures were to be replaced by a more democratic and efficient structure. If it were to function properly, SOGAT required a new structure, hence the NATSOPA support for a SOGAT Executive Council based on trade and geographical interests. This was a different basis than existed in both NUPB&PW and NATSOPA. It was disappointed the Brighton Conference had rejected such a proposal. It considered the SOGAT Executive had gone into the Brighton Conference divided under the improper pressures of various vested interests within Division A.

Take-over Fears vs. Bigger Paperworkers

NATSOPA was convinced that its members' fears of a take over by the NUPB&PW were never fully explained to that union's membership and that there were influential elements in the NUPB&PW for whom the creation of SOGAT was a larger Paperworkers' Union under another title. NATSOPA supporters of the amalgamation had had to work hard to overcome the genuine fear of their members of a take-over by the larger NUPB&PW. In the amalgamation campaign NATSOPA had dealt with this question openly and frankly. The divisional structure was conceived as temporary since the longer-term objective was the construction of a new union. The amalgamationists in NATSOPA had countered fears by stating that in the new union the voting superiority of the NUPB&PW would not operate. The proof they argued was that until the Brighton Conference this superior voting power was never exercised.

The problem of presentation and propaganda in the amalgamation campaign was much easier for Paperworkers than NATSOPA. The fear of numerical domination was not present and the NUPB&PW leadership conducted an amalgamation campaign in a different key to that of NATSOPA. It was possible, NATSOPA therefore argued, that a large number of NUPB&PW members might have considered that all they were being asked to do was to vote for a bigger Paperworkers' Union under a different title. The concept of a new union being created was underplayed by the NUPB&PW. NATSOPA firmly believed that from these campaign differences flowed the problems that ultimately caused the break-up of SOGAT.

The Paperworkers' 'Take-over' at 1968 Brighton Conference

The 1968 Rules Revision Conference was to have endorsed the actions during the first three years of SOGAT taken by the two Divisions in dismantling the Divisions and building SOGAT on the basis of its general rules. NATSOPA believed that in these three years, SOGAT had witnessed a diminution in the powers of the Divisions such that at Brighton what should have happened was an increase in SOGAT powers by consent, covering procedures, industrial practices, benefits, etc. NATSOPA had no doubt that a deliberate attempt had been made at the Conference by Paperworker delegates to impose the old NUPB&PW Rule Book as the revised and expanded SOGAT General Rules.

The Procrastination and Vacillation of the SOGAT Leadership

In the period immediately following the creation of SOGAT, NATSOPA was impressed by the immense efforts made by SOGAT officers and Executive Council members to establish the new union. However, NAT-SOPA argued that subsequently a sufficient majority was never established in SOGAT to overcome the procrastination of those who saw SOGAT as just another step towards a larger Paperworkers. For NAT-SOPA those with this attitude did not understand the original conception of SOGAT as a genuinely new union. As a result, those with this attitude were surprised when the new union concept was pressed during the years leading up to the Brighton Conference.

NATSOPA was convinced the procrastination, the lack of understanding of the real motives behind the creation of SOGAT and the foot-dragging of sectional interests had caused the momentum of the initial amalgamation to be lost. It had been hoped this momentum would coincide with a like movement in the NGA and so facilitate the establishment of a single printing union. NATSOPA blamed the break-up of SOGAT on the vacillating policy positions the SOGAT's Executive Council adopted at the Conference in the face of pressures from Division A, with the result the Brighton Conference passed rules and resolutions that were harsh, nonsensical and unworkable.

The Keys/Hooker Writ

NATSOPA viewed the Keys/Hooker writ as an attempt to force the SOGAT Executive Council to operate the unworkable Brighton Conference decisions, as a dictate and as an unwarranted legal attack upon itself and SOGAT. The SOGAT Executive Council was accused of failing to face up to the Keys/Hooker writ. The NATSOPA leadership believed the internal difficulties of working-class organisations should be kept out of the Courts. The writ was seen as motivated to bring about the disintegration of SOGAT. NATSOPA became increasingly frustrated when Division A would not take disciplinary action against Keys and Hooker or exert any pressure to persuade them to withdraw their writ. As a consequence, relations between the two Divisions went from bad to worse.

For the Paperworkers the break-up of SOGAT rested on two main factors – the personality of Mr Briginshaw and a belief that the amalgamation be based on democratic government determined by the membership through their elected representatives to the Delegate Council Meeting. In answering questions at the 1972 SOGAT Biennial Delegate Council Meeting of the original SOGAT, the General Secretary, Vincent Flynn explained the break-up in the following terms:

> There was fusion at shop-floor level and there was a good deal of evidence that amalgamation was working but there was one major difficulty. That was that one person wanted to run the show and he wanted to run it his way. He was never an innovator. He did not have the imagination to innovate anything. He was very unwilling, like a good many other unimaginative people, to take up the ideas of other people and he was terribly frightened that any ideas would challenge his position. The result was that he took the step of smashing anything that looked the least bit like any kind of challenge.[28]

The Paperworkers desire to maintain SOGAT as a democratic organisation as opposed to a union dominated by its Executive Council and senior officers was a non-negotiable issue. This was emphasised by the General Secretary of SOGAT when he told the 1972 Biennial Delegate Council:

There is talk abroad about one union for print and I want to make my position clear. I want one union for print but not just any union. We made great endeavours in Division A to bring about one union and I am sure that we will make great endeavours in the future, but I want to make this quite clear. I think I am speaking for my fellow officers and your Executive when I say that the one big union that we want to see is not a big union of big guys at a top table. It is a democratic union where the voice of the people is unimpeded and where the voice of the people and the views of the people become the policy of that one big union.[29]

The SOGAT merger had been dissolved. Divorce had been painful. The different personalities of the Joint General Secretaries and the fundamentally different constitutional principles of the NUPB&PW and NATSOPA could not be reconciled. The NUPB&PW, but now under the title SOGAT, had to pick up the pieces and continue to defend the industrial interests of its members. Despite the divorce with NATSOPA, it continued to see print union amalgamations and the creation of a single printing union as the only viable long-term option for advancing its members' interests in an industry undergoing rapid change. In 1982 it was to amalgamate again with NATSOPA. What were the general causes of this? It is to this we now turn.

NOTES

1. On the formation of SOGAT each of the divisions had its own monthly journal, namely, *The Paperworker* in the case of the NUPB&PW and the *Journal* in the case of NATSOPA. In June 1966 the SOGAT Executive Council agreed the publication, as from February 1967, of the *SOGAT Journal* in a magazine format to replace the former NUPB&PW and former NATSOPA monthly journals.

2. The two divisions had different procedures for the election and appointment of national officers. The qualifications for holding SOGAT office were: to be 55 years of age or less, to pass an elementary examination set by the Executive Council and to have at least six years' union membership. In April 1967, Mr Bill Miles, from the London Central Branch of Division A was elected National Assistant Secretary in the first and only SOGAT officer election.

3. The establishment of a single headquarters was a first priority. Accommodation, sought at Salisbury Square, London E4, was inadequate for the union's needs. Alternative properties for rent or purchase were only available at prohibitive rates. SOGAT, therefore, re-arranged its administration in the main properties it then owned.

4. At the time of its formation SOGAT had convalescent homes at Ayr, Filey, Bexhill and Rottingdean.
5. See Society of Graphical and Allied Trades (Division A) *Report of the Biennial Delegate Council Meeting, 1968*, pp. 221–4.
6. op. cit., p. 223.
7. See Society of Graphical and Allied Trades *Report of the National Council and Rules Revision Conference of the Society of Graphical and Allied Trades, 1968*, pp. 110–12.
8. There were at the time three sets of objectives – one for SOGAT and one for each of the divisions.
9. See Society of Graphical and Allied Trades *Report of the National Council and Rules Revision Conference of the Society of Graphical and Allied Trades, 1968*, pp. 159–60.
10. op. cit., p. 191.
11. op. cit., p. 192.
12. Society of Graphical and Allied Trades *Report of the National Council and Rules Revision Conference, 1968*, pp. 200–1.
13. For an account of how Division 1 viewed the National Council and Rules Revision Conference and subsequent events see Society of Graphical and Allied Trades (Division 1) *Executive Council Statement on the Present Situation Affecting Division 1 in SOGAT*, February 1970.
14. Society of Graphical and Allied Trades *Report of the National Council and Rules Revision Conference*, 1968, p. 5.
15. See letter dated 8 December 1969 from Mr W.H. Keys and Mr R.J. Hooker to Mr T.J. Smith and Mr R.W. Briginshaw, joint General Secretaries of SOGAT.
16. See letter dated 14 January 1970 from D.H.P. Levy & Co. to the Executive Committee of SOGAT (Division 1).
17. See inter-departmental memo dated 16 January 1970 from Mr R.W. Briginshaw to Mr T.J. Smith on the subject of SOGAT structure and rules.
18. No decisions had been arrived at. The standing orders set down a minimum of six members of Division 1 and a minimum of seven members of Division A.
19. Motion 27 was the National Council's instruction to abolish the SOGAT divisional structure and that motions that could not be implemented immediately be declared in order and implemented at the first opportunity.
20. See minutes of special meeting of SOGAT (Division A), held at 74 Nightingale Lane, London SW12 on 29 January 1970.
21. See minutes of special meeting of SOGAT (Division A), held at Kingsway Hall, London WC2 on 20 April 1970.
22. See Society of Graphical and Allied Trades (Division A) *Report of Biennial Delegate Council Meeting*, 1970, p. 172.
23. See minutes of the National Executive Council, SOGAT (Division A) meeting held at 74 Nightingale Lane, London SW12 on Thursday 16 July 1970.
24. See minutes of the National Executive Council, SOGAT (Division A) meeting held at 34/44 Britannia Street, London WC1 on Tuesday 6 October and Wednesday 7 October.
25. See minutes of the National Executive Council, SOGAT (Division A) meeting held at 34/44 Britannia Street, London WC1 on Tuesday 13 October 1970.

26. See minutes of a special meeting of the National Executive of SOGAT (Division A) held at 34/44 Britannia Street, London WC1 on Thursday 29 October 1970.
27. See Society of Graphical and Allied Trades *Report of the Biennial Delegate Council Meeting*, 1972, p. 229.
28. op. cit., p. 24.
29. op. cit., p. 24.

CHAPTER 6

THE FORMATION OF SOGAT (82): GENERAL CAUSES

The new SOGAT remained a firm believer in the rationalisation of the print trade union structure. As Division A of the former SOGAT its 1970 Biennial Delegate Council Meeting approved a Basingstoke branch motion 'that every endeavour be made by this society to accelerate the achievement of a single industrial union'.[1] In a short debate in which only the proposer spoke, the main arguments were that the print unions could not afford the luxury of internecine warfare and that to engage in such luxury would be suicidal. The 1972 Biennial Delegate Council approved a London Central Branch motion instructing the National Executive Council to work for unity with all print unions.[2] The real intention of the motion was to announce that the past was dead and SOGAT must look to the future firm in the belief that if print workers were to play their part in the advancement of the working class then further amalgamations were necessary.

In 1973, in response to the 1972 Biennial Delegate Council Meeting decision, SOGAT wrote to all print unions expressing their desire for greater unity which would ultimately lead to one industrial union. In the interim, SOGAT envisaged greater unity by *ad hoc* arrangements under which the print unions could protect and advance their members' interests. The letter went to SLADE, the NGA, the Scottish Graphical Association (SGA), NATSOPA and the National Union of Wallcoverings, Decorative and Allied Trades (NUWDAT). SLADE and the SGA responded positively. Amalgamation talks with SLADE, which started in December 1973, collapsed in 1974. Talks with the SGA were successful and a merger of the two unions took place in 1975 to form SOGAT(75). The NGA did not respond and during the first half of the 1970s SOGAT's relations with the NGA were particularly strained.

It was too early after the dissolution of the 1966 NATSOPA/ Paperworker amalgamation for re-merger talks. However, late in 1973 SOGAT and NATSOPA concluded a closer working agreement which redefined their sphere of influence arrangements in the light of technical change in the industry. Throughout the 1970s relation between the two unions remained amicable. In 1976 NATSOPA entered merger talks with the NGA, SLADE and NUWDAT. In 1977 NATSOPA was advised by these three unions that unless it could provide certain financial information the merger talks would continue on a three-union basis. In April 1978 NATSOPA sought to rejoin the three-union merger talks but it was told this was no longer possible. NATSOPA then approached the new SOGAT (SOGAT (75)) and in November 1978 merger talks began between the two. In April 1982 the membership of SOGAT and NATSOPA voted in favour of a merger and in July 1982 the Society of Graphical and Allied Trades (82) was born.

There were many pressures leading SOGAT to seek mergers. As well as Biennial Delegate Council decisions there were the continuing technological developments, most notably the decline of hot metal composing systems and letterpress printing. There were also the growth of multinational companies which was shifting the balance of bargaining power towards the employer and away from the print unions, the continued growth of an alternative printing industry based on import penetration of the UK print market, the expansion of in-plant printing and the growth of information systems based on electronic devices. In the mid-1970s and early 1980s the acceleration of the UK inflation rate and higher unemployment levels in the printing and papermaking industries were further pressures leading to the formation of SOGAT (82). The increasing unemployment amongst SOGAT and NATSOPA members arising from closures, mergers and redundancy led them to believe that declining employment opportunities should be reversed by means of union mergers.

A further pressure towards the creation of SOGAT (82) was the significant changes in the early 1980s in the legal environment surrounding the UK industrial relations system. The Employment Acts of 1980 and 1982 outlawed important SOGAT and NATSOPA industrial practices, but especially the 'blacking' of work not produced by unionised labour. This legislation made it more difficult for print unions in isolation to resist the implementation of changing techniques in the industry. The creation of one union for the industry seemed an obvious step. Yet another general pressure towards amalgamation was problems in the paper and paper conversion industries resulting from mill closures and the implementation of technological change, for example the standardisation of carton sizes and the use of plastics at the expense of paper for packaging materials. These factors pushing SOGAT towards amalgamation were encapsulated in a successful Merseyside Branch motion to the 1978 Biennial Delegate Council Meeting:

> This conference considers that in view of the growing numbers of problems that are facing all print workers i.e. the introduction of new techniques, computerisation, high speed papermaking machines which has resulted in redundancies, closures, etc and because of the chaotic situation arising out of the 1975 wage negotiations and the present lack of co-ordination between the unions in the initial Government wage policy, also many other issues with employers, the question of amalgamation of all print unions can no longer be postponed. This Conference, therefore, calls upon the NEC to make a determined approach to the other print unions to bring about one union in the industry that can only be in the interests of all print workers.[3]

TECHNOLOGICAL CHANGE AND DEVELOPMENTS: 1970s AND EARLY 1980s

The introduction of new techniques into the printing industry in the 1970s and early 1980s challenged the traditional lines of demarcation, the spheres of influence of the different printing unions, and threatened the jobs of their members. The implementation of new production techniques enabled the employers to undertake an offensive against the unions and use the threat of unemployment to set worker against worker when the unions' efforts needed to be focused on countering the actions of employers.

Technological developments led to inter-union problems between SOGAT and the NGA, particularly in London and Scotland. SOGAT was concerned the NGA was using these changes to encroach on traditional areas of SOGAT organisation catered for by the Printing Machine Branch, the Monotype Casters and Typefounders branch and its Scottish Graphical Division. An example of the SOGAT/NGA inter-union difficulties occurred at the HMSO establishment at Harrow when the management introduced a Linotron machine to do the work traditionally performed by members of SOGAT's Monotype Casters' Branch. The NGA claimed the sole right of handling the machine but SOGAT refused to concede this right and resisted by taking industrial action.

In a further incident in another town, the NGA refused to accept as assistants on a Linotron SOGAT members who were being redeployed from another area where redundancies were required. SOGAT was outraged about this situation because the NGA was prepared to accept as assistants individuals taken off the streets. There was a further incident in Liverpool involving the introduction of a double console machine which transferred work previously done by SOGAT members to an NGA area. It was only by taking a tough line that SOGAT retained a right to operate the press. There was a fourth incident involving a company introducing a photo machine traditionally operated by SOGAT Monotype Caster members into an NGA area. The NGA refused to work the new machine but would only allow SOGAT members to operate it if they took out NGA membership. The SOGAT members refused to do this.

These inter-union disputes stemmed from companies replacing hot metal systems by cold composition systems and the NGA claiming sole right to work photocomposition systems. The Monotype Casters and Filmsetters' Branch and the Scottish Graphical Division claimed that this work should be done by their members since Monotype Casters and Process Prover members had traditionally pulled proofs for reproduction. The Monotype Casters and Filmsetters' Branch was in a different position because it was a party to an agreement with the NGA that its members could work in these areas, which elsewhere were traditionally under the control of the NGA, on the condition that if SOGAT Monotype Casters and Filmsetters' Branch members left their jobs they were to be replaced by an individual holding an NGA card. This SOGAT Branch faced eventual extinction with the demise of the skills of its members who saw the NGA establishing the sole right to work in the printing industry.

In the machine rooms in London the SOGAT PMB faced similar problems to the Monotype Casters and Filmsetters' Branch in that other print unions claimed the right to do work the branch considered rightfully theirs. Where firms were replacing letterpress machines with litho machinery the PMB was faced with the NGA claiming the sole right to work litho machines, with the consequent loss of employment opportunities for PMB members. In national newspapers the NGA claimed the right to operate dia-presses which did the facsimile work of PMB members. At the same time all national newspaper employers were openly discussing the possibility of dispensing with hot metal production systems, and there was a real threat that the PMB would be removed from the industry. The PMB faced other problems. In the early 1970s there were in London some 180 small print firms that did not employ any SOGAT labour. This had arisen from NGA card holders setting up typesetting houses without engaging PMB members to do their press work or SOGAT Central London Branch members to do their traditional tasks in the press rooms.

The PMB and the Monotype Casters' Branches did not relish the position of being told by the NGA 'you can work in print if you hold an NGA card'. The PMB had experienced situations where its members had gone to work on small offset machines, which SOGAT in the past had done much to organise because the craft unions considered it below them to do so, only to be told by the NGA that if SOGAT members wanted to continue to work on small offset machines they must join the NGA. SOGAT realised that if it did not resist these pressures its members would face choosing between loyalty to their families or to SOGAT. The threats and the innuendoes from the NGA 'that if you did not join you could not continue to work in print'[4] was putting loyalty to SOGAT to the test.

The problems between SOGAT's and the NGA in Scotland centred around each union's claims to jurisdiction over lithographic presses introduced into traditional letterpress houses. These problems pre-dated the SGA amalgamation with SOGAT. The SGA controlled letterpress houses in Scotland whilst litho houses were controlled by the ASLP and subsequently the NGA when the ASLP transferred its engagements to that union in 1969. The NGA claimed to be the litho craft union in Scotland, and as litho machines entered letterpress houses controlled by SOGAT (Scottish Graphical Division) it claimed the right to staff these. The Scottish Graphical Division argued that the custom of the house should prevail and letterpress houses re-equipping with litho machinery should remain under its control. The NGA continued to reserve the right to recruit in Scotland all those categories of workers for whom it catered elsewhere in Britain unless SOGAT recognised the NGA's traditional rights in the litho field. However, in the spring of 1976 the two unions signed the 'Perth Agreement' which defined jurisdictional right between SOGAT (Scottish Graphical Division) and the NGA in the litho field in Scotland.

In the 1970s and early 1980s the employment security of SOGAT members, especially in London, was significantly undermined by technology. In the absence of an amicable compromise with other print unions SOGAT had no option but to defend the interests of its members in the best way it could. It did not seek differences with the NGA, but SOGAT felt it could not meekly accept the uncontrolled hostility the NGA had shown against its members. SOGAT found itself, with varying degrees of success, committing thousands of its members to industrial action against NGA encroachment into its traditional spheres of organisation and work. The alternative was to concede everything 'that moves in print' to the NGA, and SOGAT was not prepared to do this. The right to work in the printing industry could not depend upon which union card an employee held. SOGAT's position was summed up by its General Secretary in addressing the union's 1974 Biennial Delegate Council:

> But one thing I will say, to submit to the policies of the NGA in this moment of time we really ought not to be holding any further Biennial Conferences of SOGAT, we ought to hand them over to Bedford and let Bedford run SOGAT from the NGA headquarters.[5]

SOGAT took no pleasure in slanging matches with the NGA, since to win such matches could only be at the cost of another print worker losing their job. SOGAT sought one union, speaking with one voice, in and on behalf of the industry. However, this could only be a longer-term objective. In the short term, SOGAT need to seek accommodation with the NGA to end that union's invasion of its traditional areas of organisation. In March 1974 the SOGAT General Secretary wrote personally to the NGA General Secretary, John Bonfield, asking the two unions resolve their existing problems or SOGAT would have to fight back despite the fact that SOGAT had not attacked the livelihood of one NGA member. When John Bonfield saw fit to ignore the SOGAT letter the SOGAT Executive instructed SOGAT branches to use all possible means to defend the interests of its members against encroachments from the NGA.

In defending itself from NGA 'poaching', SOGAT was determined not to harm fellow trade unionists, to inform other print unions of its attitude since other print unions were concerned about the actions of the NGA, to make representatives to the TUC[6] and to maintain existing job opportunities for its members even if the NGA continued a policy of 'grabbing' every job resulting from a change in production technique. The policy of contesting the NGA's claim to legitimate SOGAT work was also based on a simple formula that where the product was the same but the process changed, the job should remain with the original union. SOGAT now decided to adopt a policy of refusing to accept work produced by NGA members in areas considered to be traditionally that of SOGAT. The policy was controlled through Head Office who were to be informed immediately of the introduction of any new techniques which might cause disputes over the spheres of influence between the two unions.

In 1976 relations between SOGAT and the NGA changed dramatically, helped by the desire of the new General Secretaries (Bill Keys and Joe Wade) and new General Presidents (Albert Powell and Les Dixon) of the two unions to start informal discussions with the objective of improving co-operation amongst the print unions. These informal discussions resulted in a SOGAT/NGA Joint Committee being established and quickly produced improvements in the relationships between the two unions in Scotland and London. In Scotland under the 1976 'Perth Agreement', SOGAT (75) recognised the traditional NGA areas. Where existing letterpress houses were changing to litho printing members of SOGAT so affected would remain members of SOGAT but that union would pay a licence fee of 15p in respect of each such member. SOGAT members covered by this licence fee wishing to work in a traditional litho printing shop under the control of the NGA would transfer their union membership to the NGA. The NGA/SOGAT (SGD) Joint Committee was to police the agreement. SOGAT committed itself not to intrude into the litho agreements held by the NGA and the Society of Master Printers of Scotland. However, problems between the NGA and SOGAT (SGD) over the control of litho printing machines arose again in the 1980s.

In the summer of 1976, the PMB, and the Monotype Casters, Filmsetters' and Typefounders' Branches of SOGAT and the NGA London Region were brought closer together. As a result it proved possible to introduce photocomposition equipment to the mutual advantage of both unions' members. The ending of the SOGAT/NGA jurisdictional and demarcation problems in London, like those in

Scotland, was seen as an important step forward in a possible amalgamation of the two societies. However, as in Scotland, difficulties were again to emerge in the early 1980s between the PMB and Monotype Casters, Filmsetters' and the Typefounders' Branches on the one hand and the NGA on the other.

Given that amalgamation between SOGAT and NGA could only be a longer-term objective, SOGAT tried, in the shorter term, to enforce the principle of its members 'right to follow their work'. This policy won the approval of the SOGAT Biennial Delegate Council of 1982, when a successful PMB motion applauded the actions of SOGAT in pursuit of one union in print but warned that, whilst following that policy the union should not lose sight of the members right 'to follow their work' as new technology was implemented. However, the reality was that employers were allowing the NGA to say that individuals could only work in the print industry with the permission of that union. For SOGAT, the enforcement of the right of their members to 'follow their jobs', was a message to the employers that as far SOGAT was concerned the NGA were not the be-all and end-all in the industry. In the longer term, amalgamation of all the print unions was the only policy that would close the option presently available to the employers of playing off one union against the other.

A further short-term option to counter the NGA's encroachment into SOGAT's traditional areas was to seek an amalgamation with NATSOPA. This would provide additional resources to withstand the NGA's offensive and offer the possibility of the NATSOPA Machine Branch providing industrial support in the case of NGA industrial action to undermine 'the follow the job' policy. A merger with NATSOPA also offered the possibility of new employment opportunities for SOGAT members in the clerical areas of national and provincial newspapers. In newspapers, computerised composition systems, which it was anticipated could replace photocomposition machines in the early to mid-1980s, would eliminate the need for composing rooms which were 100 per cent NGA organised. The tasks of typesetting, correction and page make-up of advertisements would be done by the computer whose keyboard would be controlled by employees in the advertising department where the recognised union was the NATSOPA clerical branch. Single key-stroking in newspapers would transfer work from an NGA to a NATSOPA area. The expansion of employment expected in the advertising and editorial departments of newspapers was a potential source of alternative employment for the members of SOGAT's Scottish

Graphical Division and the members of SOGAT's Monotype Casters and Filmsetters' Branch. The NGA had little or no presence in the advertising areas of newspapers and a merged SOGAT/NATSOPA union would make it easier to sustain this position, including co-operation, if necessary with the employer to undermine any NGA resistance to the introduction of computerised composing systems. Such a merger also offered the additional advantage that if the NGA called on its machine room members to take industrial action to protect its newspaper typesetter members then NATSOPA machine assistants could take, and then retain, control of the printing process in both provincial and national newspapers.

For SOGAT, the trade union movement derived its strength from the need to adapt to the changing industrial and political environment without compromising its basic principles. Trade unions did not have the option to remain static if they wished to survive. It was these principles that guided SOGAT's belief that it was not in the interests of workers to pursue sectarian interests but rather to promote policies that were in the common interest. It believed this was only possible by a single union, but in creating such a union care would be needed not to create some amorphous body which would diminish the right of debate at all levels in the union. SOGAT considered one union for the industry to be the only permanent solution to inter-union warfare stemming from the implementation of technological change. The NGA was not yet ready to take this step. It wished to create single craft union via a merger with SLADE before considering a link with SOGAT. In the meantime, SOGAT had to look after its own interests and seek mergers with other print unions. NATSOPA was the obvious candidate.

THE GROWTH OF MULTINATIONAL COMPANIES/ EUROPEAN COMMUNITY MEMBERSHIP

One of the most challenging problems SOGAT faced in the 1970s was an expansion in the number of multinational corporations in publishing and papermaking and the creation of a situation in which they would flourish via British membership of the European Economic Community in 1973 and the 1975 Referendum result that the UK remain in membership of the Community. In the decade 1964–74 the capital investment of multinationals in the Community grew by 300 per cent. The group of multinational companies shifted the balance of power away from labour and towards the employer. SOGAT was particularly concerned that multinational companies, especially those in the paper-making industry sometimes adopted anti-union attitudes. Given the readiness with which multinational companies threatened closure to gain concessions from the British Government, who were thereby less able to control the economy in the interests of working people, SOGAT believed that the sooner the printing trade unions abandoned their sectorial interests at both national and international levels the better. The print unions could not avoid the issue of how they might construct countervailing power to multinational companies both inside and outside the European Community. For SOGAT the answer lay in trade unions acting on an international scale, but SOGAT also recognised that this process could not even begin until the British printing unions spoke with a single voice in national and international trade union organisations. One union for the printing industry was clearly a necessary first step if the print unions were to construct a serious countervailing power to organised international capital.

THE CHANGED LEGAL ENVIRONMENT

A further pressure pushing SOGAT towards mergers with other print unions was the Employment Acts of 1980 and 1982 which were designed to reform alleged abuses of union power and to adjust an alleged imbalance in bargaining power against the employer. Some provisions in these Acts were direct challenges to the industrial practices of SOGAT. The 1980 Act restricted the circumstances in which a trade union could gain immunity from legal action when it was involved in secondary industrial action. SOGAT had used such action with effect in the 1980 wages and hours disputes with the BPIF (see Chapter 15). The Act also removed immunity for those who organised or took part in picketing at a place other than their own place of work. Controlled mass picketing had also been used in industrial disputes in the 1970s by SOGAT. The operation of the closed shop had been central to the industrial activities of the union for many years. The 1980 Act regulated the circumstances in which new closed shops could be established and challenged existing closed shops in that it made the dismissal of an employee in a closed shop situation on the grounds of non-union membership automatically unfair if the individual had conscientious grounds or other deeply held personal convictions against being a member of any trade union whatsoever or of a particular union.

The 1982 Employment Act built on the process started by the 1980 Act. It narrowed the definition of a lawful trade dispute to disputes between workers and their own employer and to matters wholly or mainly employment-related, for example pay and work allocation. One effect was to remove legal immunity for trade unions involved in an inter-union dispute. The consequences of this for printing unions in influencing the implementation of technological change in the industry unless one union could be achieved were obvious. The Act made provision for those damaged by unlawful industrial action to gain compensation from the union or unions involved, although the amount of such compensation was limited depending on the membership size of the union. The 1982 Act also outlawed the refusal of employees to handle goods from another firm because the goods were produced by non-union employees. This made the long-standing industrial practice of SOGAT and NATSOPA of refusing to handle work produced by non-unionists unlawful.

The 1982 Act also extended the 1980 Employment Act's closed shop provisions. Dismissal on grounds of non-union membership in a closed shop became now automatically unfair unless the closed shop had been approved in the last five years in a ballot of those working under the arrangements. Those dismissed in these circumstances could receive large compensation payments which the trade union enforcing the closed shop could be made to pay. SOGAT and NATSOPA adopted a policy of non-participation in ballots for the approval of existing closed shops. The 1982 Employment Act thus permitted circumstances in which non-unionists could continue to work in a closed shop situation and as such clashed fundamentally with the industrial practices of the two unions, particularly in national newspapers.

This changed legal environment, designed to undermine effective trade union action, together with the changing technological and economic environment of the printing industry made the ability of SOGAT and NATSOPA to protect and advance the interests of their respective members in isolation from the other printing unions more difficult. A common printing union policy towards the Employment Acts would be helpful but could only be a temporary solution, since in the absence of one union for the industry there was always the possibility that one or more union might break ranks over policy differences. Only a merger offered the possibility of real stability.

INCREASING INFLATION AND UNEMPLOYMENT

The early 1970s saw a sharp rise in the UK inflation rate which peaked at 25 per cent per annum in June 1975. From that date to mid-1979, the government's incomes and prices policy saw the inflation rate fall steadily to 10 per cent. However, in the early 1980s inflation surged again, reaching 21 per cent per year in the summer of 1980, after which it fell steadily. Throughout the 1970s and early 1980s, the wage increases of SOGAT and NATSOPA members, like those of other print unions, kept pace with inflation. Much of the accelerating inflation rate was accounted for by the oil price rises of 1973/4 and 1981/2, both of which plunged the British economy into recession from which the printing industry was not isolated.

During the period 1974–6 the industry witnessed an unprecedented number of closures of firms which led to large-scale redundancies and steep rises in unemployment amongst the SOGAT membership. In 1975, the union paid out £62,340 to its members in unemployment benefit payments. This was the highest payment of unemployment benefit in the history of SOGAT and its constituent societies. However, in 1976 the payment of benefit for unemployment rose to £76,821. In the second half of the 1970s unemployment amongst SOGAT members fell, whilst the average UK unemployment figure continued to rise. In 1979 the amount of unemployment benefit paid to SOGAT members fell to £39,818. Two years later the British economy found itself in severe recession with 3m people (12.1 per cent of the working population) out of work. Unemployment in the printing and paper industry in 1982 stood at 6 per cent. Rising unemployment stemmed from the rationalisation of company structures following corporate take-overs and mergers, closures, companies declaring redundancies to survive in the market place and increased foreign competition. The highest number of redundancies took place in papermaking and book production. In 1980 unemployment in the latter section stood at 8 per cent compared to 2 per cent for the industry as a whole. In the three and a half years to June 1982, 185 closures of printing firms, involving 27,500 redundancies were reported to the Department of Employment. At the formation of SOGAT there were 315,000 employees in the industry but by mid-1982 the figure was 249,000. Increasing unemployment amongst SOGAT members stemmed not only from economic recession but also from technological change. Rising unemployment put financial strains on SOGAT. In 1981 £475,774 was paid in unemployment benefit to its members, whilst in 1982 the figure was £274,368. These liabilities were only met because of an increase in subscription rates in 1980.

Rising unemployment and inflation were additional factors pushing SOGAT towards mergers with other print unions. An accommodation with NATSOPA would make adjustment to the changed circumstances and environment surrounding the industry easier, although it would remain a difficult adjustment to make. In a larger union it would be easier to deal with change, for example via redeployment and greater financial resources than if SOGAT continued as an independent union seeking to protect its members' interests regardless of those of other print unions.

THE GROWTH OF AN ALTERNATIVE PRINTING INDUSTRY

Import Penetration

The 1970s saw a sharp increase in the amount of imported print work into the UK (see Table 6.1). Although throughout the 1970s and early 1980s the value of exported printing goods exceeded that of imported goods, the industry's trade balance declined. The share of imports into the UK printing market rose over the period 1972–1982, from 9.4 per cent to 16.4 per cent. In 1982 British printers were competing against prices quoted by overseas printers which were as much as 45 per cent below the British 'costs only' prices and in some cases were below the British printers' costs of materials.

The book manufacturing industry was particularly affected by the loss of work abroad. By the mid-1970s a number of books, particularly children's books, were being typeset and printed in Hong Kong, Spain, the Canary Islands and Czechoslovakia. Throughout the 1970s an increasing amount of mail order catalogues, cardboard cartons and travel brochures were printed abroad. There were many reasons for the increased import penetration of print matter in the UK. Among the more significant were technological change, the higher UK 1970s inflation rate relative to other countries, the 'strong' value of sterling on foreign exchanges in the early 1980s, the high interest rate policy adopted by the incoming 1979 Conservative government and the high cost of energy in the UK relative to the other countries. Printing employers also blamed print union work practices, particularly the

Table 6.1
Imports: share of the home market, 1972–82

	Printed and Published matter (%)	Manufactured stationery (%)	Packaging (%)
1972	9.4	2.0	3.4
1973	10.0	2.4	4.2
1974	10.4	3.6	7.9
1975	10.8	3.9	5.0
1976	11.8	3.5	5.8
1977	11.8	3.6	6.2
1978	13.2	4.4	6.8
1979	13.2	5.2	8.0
1980	13.5	5.2	8.1
1981 (4th quarter)	16.4	6.5	10.5
1982 (1st half)	n/a	6.9	10.4

Source: *The Future of the Printing Industries*, Printing Industries Sector Working Party, NEDO, 1983.

ban on handling work from unrecognised sources. They contended that publishers, needing to re-establish their competitiveness, were turning to lower-cost non-traditional printing methods.

Technical developments enabled a book to be typeset in one country and printed and bound in another. A growing number of companies imported origination and printing from places like South East Asia and India, having established their own production capacity in those parts of the world. If the challenge of the growth of an alternative printing industry based on increasing imports of printed matter was to be overcome, the print unions needed a common strategy to deal with the problem. Although this could be achieved by loose associations (for example, the TUC Printing Industries Committee), a merger of unions was a more permanent solution. Amalgamation offered the advantage that job losses from increased imports could be managed via redeployment and retraining, etc., and markets recaptured as printers lowered costs of production as the unions accepted craft and non-craft labour flexibility. Individual unions would no longer be defending self-interest at the cost of jobs of other unions' members.

In-plant Printing

The 1970s saw a rapid growth of in-plant printing and binding whereby private and public sector organisations established their own printing and binding capacities rather than having this work done by commercial printers who employed SOGAT labour and adhered to the general printing industry wages and terms and conditions of employment as established by the BPIF and SOGAT Agreement. Companies introducing in-plant printing paid terms and conditions below those of the general printing industry. The 1976 SOGAT Biennial Delegate Council was told that local councils were running printing presses and paying 8–10 per cent below the rate of the general printing industry.[7] The individuals employed on in-plant printing and binding were either non-union or organised in a non-print union. SOGAT members were losing work to groups who were difficult to organise and who, if unionised at all, were members of trade unions with no intention of transferring members to SOGAT or any other print union. In-plant printing and binding developments caused bankruptcies amongst 'jobbing' printers and redundancy amongst SOGAT members. The growth of in-plant printing had considerable adverse impact on small print firms who lost, *inter alia*, work in advertising, circulars and educational materials.

Nationalised industries which established their own in-plant printing facilities did not employing print workers. In local authorities those employed on in-plant printing were often members of trade unions but not print trade unions. Delegates to the 1982 SOGAT Biennial Delegate Council were informed that Hampshire County Council had trebled their printing capacity and were printing five- and six-colour magazines, not only for themselves but for other county councils. They were producing textbooks and exercise books for schools and were encouraging other education authorities to purchase books from them. The employees doing this print work were members of NALGO. Other public sector organisations to which SOGAT was losing employment opportunities included the Portsmouth dockyards and Parliamentary printing. In the basement of the House of Commons were small litho/rotaprint machines operated by employees in membership of civil service unions. The 1982 SOGAT Biennial Delegate Meeting was informed that, if in-plant printing and binding in government establishments could be organised, then the union could gain 5,000 additional members.[8]

In the 1970s, in the private sector, in-plant printing expanded significantly in banking and insurance companies, where the employees involved were largely non-union. In the engineering industry, many household name companies, for example Balfour Beattie, Kenwood (where employees concerned were in membership of the T&GWU) and Marconi, developed in-plant printing capacity. By the early 1980s the QE2 had established on board a four-colour printing press with all its ancillary equipment. Previously two small printing companies in Southampton had the contract for all the QE2's printing requirements. These companies had now closed with a loss of employment not just for SOGAT members but also for members of other printing unions.

Given the job loss implications of the growth of in-plant printing and binding it was not surprising that calls for the organisation of workers operating these machines were made at Biennial Delegate Council Meetings. The 1974 Meeting carried a PMB motion calling on the NEC to organise people working in such shops. At the 1976 Meeting a Medway and Thanet motion asked the NEC to take up the organisation of in-plant printing workers with the TUC Printing Industries Committee. The 1980 Biennial Delegate Meeting saw two motions on in-plant printing. One, from the Scottish Graphical Division, argued that non-printing trade unions organising in the print industry were weakening print trade unionism and urged the NEC to continue its policy of attempting to organise in-plant printworkers into print unions. The second, from the Solent Branch, instructed the union to exercise more influence to protect SOGAT jobs in SOGAT-recognised areas and to bring pressure to bear through the TUC on in-plant printing as practised by such companies as Tesco under cover of the Union of Shop, Distributive and Allied Workers (USDAW) and the Meat and Livestock Commission under the cover of the National and Local Government Officers' Association (NALGO).[9] The 1982 Biennial Delegate Council also called on the TUC General Council to persuade non-print trade unions not to organise in-plant printing worker.

SOGAT's success in organising in-plant printing and binding workers was limited. By mid-1982 the Solent Branch had succeeded in gaining full recognition and organisation rights in only one private sector company undertaking in-plant printing, *viz.*, Zurich Insurance Company. Attempts to use the TUC Printing Industries Committee to gain some influence over in-plant printing and binding were equally unsuccessful. The loss of work from the printing industry from the growth of an alternative industry continued and remained a threat to all printing unions, not just to SOGAT. If the problem were to be resolved and increasing pressure applied to the TUC, then a common approach from the print unions was essential. Merger offered the best hope of this and in this sense the growth of in-plant printing and binding was an important factor in bringing about the formation of SOGAT (82).

Information Systems Based on Electronic Devices

The 1970s and early 1980s also saw the world of communications based on paper and ink processes come under challenge from a new communication 'world' based on electric devices such as Prestel, Oracle, Ceefax and videos. Teletext signals were broadcast to a house television receiver where the viewer with a decoder and key pad called up pages of text giving information on a wide range of subjects. Viewdata was a different system in so much as it came down a telephone line and cable. The system affected people's shopping habits by enabling individuals to order goods directly. Many companies involved in the investment of Teletext and Viewdata were either owned or controlled by employers with whom SOGAT had relationships. The new world of communications offered a challenge to newspapers, magazines, catalogues, etc. It was a world in which SOGAT had no stake, but in which unions like the NUJ did. However, SOGAT recognised that before calling for one union for the media, the union position must first be consolidated in the world of communications based on paper and ink processes. A merger with NATSOPA would be an important step along this road. Nevertheless, the increasing awareness of SOGAT members of the need to look beyond one union for the printing industry was recognised at the 1982 Biennial Delegate Council which accepted a Monotype Casters and Filmsetters' Branch motion calling upon the NEC to examine the possibility of amalgamation with trade unions inside the electronic and film communications industries.[10]

All these pressures simply confirmed SOGAT's long-held view that 'splendid isolation' from other print unions could no longer be possible. Inter-union competition between print unions needed to be replaced as soon as possible by total unity. SOGAT had had enough of being exploited by employers' bodies because of disunity shown between respective print unions. A particular example of this had been the 1980 wage negotiations with the BPIF, when SOGAT was prepared to settle with the employers but the NGA was not and, as a result, SOGAT was dragged reluctantly into a six-week dispute in the general printing and provincial newspaper industry (see Chapter 15). In March 1982 a single craft union in the industry came into being and in July a single predominantly non-craft union – SOGAT (82) – came into being. The next step would be the coming together of these two unions. However, this was to take nine years to achieve.

PROBLEMS IN PAPERMAKING AND PAPER CONVERSION

Foreign Competition

In the period 1967–1975 31 mills closed, 73 machines shut down and 17,100 paperworkers were declared redundant. In addition, there were part closures of 16 mills and 39 machines, causing a further 3,500 redundancies. It was the small mills that survived. Multinational companies, such as Wiggins Teape, Reed International and Bowaters were closing mills and machines. The second half of the 1970s saw no respite, with a further 25 mills closing, another 60 machines going out of production and 31,000 jobs lost.[11] By 1981 the UK had no major newsprint mill in operation at a time when it was the third largest newspaper consumer in the world. There were machines producing just over 100,000 tonnes of newsprint against an annual requirement of 1.2 million tonnes for national and provincial newspapers. Ten years previously the UK had been producing 840,000 tonnes per annum of newsprint. A similar situation existed in board-making. In 1981 there were only two board-makers left in the UK – Thames Board and Reeds of Thatcham. If Thames Board had ceased production that would effectively have killed the UK board-making industry. As with newsprint, the decline was the result of cheap imports, high interest rates and high energy costs, plus the fact that whisky was increasingly being exported by container rather than in flat cartons. The situation in the UK was that newsprint had virtually ceased production, board-making was in rapid decline and paper for book publishing was under severe attack from imported Scandinavian paper. What then had caused this decline?

A major factor was the natural advantage enjoyed by Scandinavia, Finland, Canada and many EEC member nations relative to the UK in terms of raw materials, water, fuel, power and taxation. These countries possessed enormous reserves of forests, particularly soft trees such as spruce, pine and fir, which are ideal for papermaking. With such forests on the doorstep, paper could be produced in integrated mills. The UK had nothing like enough trees to support its mills. Most wood had to be imported from the Nordic countries and from Canada. The

UK mills, with a few exceptions, were not integrated and the breaking down of imported wood pulp into fibres was an extra process adding to the cost of paper manufacture.

The Nordic countries and Canada had abundant supplies of water, and effluent problems were not serious. In the UK water was becoming more scarce and expensive as the population grew and the demands of industry increased. In the 1970s pollution was a serious matter in the UK and the standards of cleanliness demanded of mills for the purification of effluent was heavy. Though SOGAT regarded these social objectives as highly desirable they remained concerned that the extra financial cost involved would prove too much for some mills to bear. Unfortunately this proved to be so.

Fuel and power were also much cheaper in Scandinavia, Finland and Canada. Hydroelectric power was plentiful and oil was cheaper, since it did not bear a heavy tax as in the UK. The cost of fuel oil was higher in the UK than in Norway and electricity from the national grid was 100 per cent dearer in the UK than in Sweden. The UK papermaking industry was the fourth largest user of oil in the UK and the sixth largest user of energy and water. However, unlike its competitors overseas, it received no subsidy for these items from the UK government which was indirectly responsible for the price and supply of gas, electricity, coal and water.

However, the UK paper and board industry retained some competitive advantages. The most important were nearness to the market and quality service to the customer. The Scandinavians and Canadians had the advantage in terms of long-run, mass-produced goods, such as newsprint, whilst the UK had advantages in the special grades of paper. Over the period 1967–82 the UK paper- and board-making industry sought to close its competitive deficit. The industry improved the use of indigenous home materials, such as timber and waste paper. Integrated mills were established at Fort William, Sudbrook, Workington and Ellesmere Port. The industry sought to achieve a market niche in the production of the more valuable grades of paper. Attempts were made to enhance productivity levels by a series of measures, but these proved unsuccessful.

However, there was one disadvantage – 'price squeezing' – which the UK paper and board industry could not overcome by itself, since the Nordic countries could exert a 'double squeeze' on the UK mills. The Nordic Countries determined the price UK mills had to pay for Nordic wood pulp. They could raise the price of wood pulp but maintain the price of paper they exported to the UK market. To retain customers, UK mills maintained their price for finished paper whilst having to pay more for the raw materials from which it was made.

The paper- and board-making industry problems also stemmed from EEC tariffs and quotas. On joining the EEC on 1 January 1973, the UK had to adopt the Community's Common Customs Tariff (CCT) which meant, with certain exceptions, that after July 1977 the UK had to apply the same duties as the rest of the EEC on imports from countries outside the Community. Imports from Canada, whose paper had entered the UK duty-free under Commonwealth Preference, would now be subject until July 1977 to an annually rising scale of duties until UK/EEC harmonisation was complete. However, the UK did not gain the same treatment as the original six members of the EEC. Only the UK and Denmark, of the original seven EFTA countries, became full members of the EEC. The remaining EFTA countries including Norway, Sweden and Finland negotiated Trade Agreements with the EEC which, for most manufactured products, resulted in the mutual abolition of customs duties by July 1977. However, in the case of the UK, the duty-free position that had existed when the UK was a member of EFTA continued even though the UK was now a Community member.

However, paper and board other than newsprint was treated differently. The EEC insisted the industry in EFTA countries not joining the Community be included on a list of products to be accorded a complex package of protective arrangements. The result was that CCT, far from being abolished by July 1977, was subject to an abolition timetable which extended to 1984. Moreover, its first four stages (1973–6) were minimal reductions of 0.5 per cent. In addition, an important ceilings system operated whereby if the annual ceiling tonnage for imports into the EEC of a particular grade of paper was exceeded, any EEC member state could demand re-establishment of the original full CCT for the remainder of the year. For most grades of paper and board, this full rate was 12 per cent.

The UK paper and board duty position relative to her free trade partners in EFTA was awkward, since the Treaty of Rome aimed to establish steady expansion, balanced trade and fair competition. However, it would have been an unjust situation whereby the paper and board industry of the original 'six' was accorded special treatment whilst the UK continued with its duty-free position on imports from the EFTA non-candidates who had elected not to avail themselves of full EEC membership. Accordingly, it was agreed the UK re-introduce customs duties on imports of paper and board from the EFTA countries, starting at 3 per cent in 1974 and reaching a maximum of

8 per cent in July 1977. By this same date, the duty for the 'six' was also to be reduced to 8 per cent. This tariff harmonisation was then gradually abolished, reaching zero in 1984.

Sweden, Norway and Finland objected to the re-introduction of the duties given their previous free trade status for their imports into the UK. These countries insisted on UK duty-free quota provisions as a pre-condition of signing a Trade Agreement with the EEC, and on receiving from the British government letters of intent which set quotas for 1974 at four-fifths of the average tonnage levels for the period 1968–71, accepted that no annual quota could be less than any preceding one and that there be annual consultation and the arrangements subject to a review in 1975. To the disappointment of the paper- and board-making industry, the UK government set the 1974 quotas well above the minimum levels of 80 per cent of average imports over the period 1968–71 whilst those for 1975 were extremely generous to the EFTA countries. These high quota levels gave minimal protection to the industry when it most needed it if a permanent loss of jobs and produc-tion capacity was to be avoided. By contrast, the EEC paper and board industry, which was also going through recession, was protected by a 10.5 per cent tariff which applied to every tonne imported.

SOGAT was concerned about the rapid contraction of the paper- and board-making industry and the subsequent redundancies. Whilst this situation was unfolding, SOGAT made representations either singly and/or in conjunction with the employers on many occasions to the government. They told the Government a modern civilised society could not exist without a papermaking industry and pressed for a public inquiry on the grounds that it was a matter of public concern that hundreds of millions of pounds were being spent on imported products that could be manufactured in the UK.

In 1975, SOGAT launched its *Save Our Industry* campaign[12] setting out recommendations as to how, with the co-operation of the Govern-ment, the UK paper- and board-making industry could restore its com-petitiveness, be protected and thereby make a significant contribution to reducing the UK's balance of payments deficit. In the *Save Our Industry* document, SOGAT argued Government and public assistance was required to:

(i)   lessen the imports of paper and board from the Nordic coun-tries, whose percentage share of newsprint imports had increased since 1963 from 49 per cent to 78 per cent and in the case of

        printing and writing paper from 5 per cent to 33 per cent;
- (ii)   help with tariffs and quotas within the EEC;
- (iii) encourage the re-use of waste paper by assistance in the setting up de-inking plants;
- (iv) encourage the Forestry Commission in the planting and harvesting of a maximum number of trees, and the allocation of maximum supplies to the papermaking industry;
- (v)   lighten the cost of water usage and purification,
- (vi) ease the taxation burden on oil and fuel,
- (vii) assist the industry increase its capital investment, since without new investment the industry would continue to contract until it could no longer survive.

The document also listed measures to limit the share of the UK paper- and board-making market accounted for by imports and to reduce the dependence of the industry upon imported wood pulp. The document proposed strict enforcement of the limited quota of duty-free imports from Scandinavia with the application of a tariff on the remainder, relating import controls to the previous level of imports or the previous proportion of imports to total home consumption, and the introduction of import deposits.

Save Our Industry also advocated a greater role for UK forestry in supplying the wood pulp needs of the paper industry by stepping up future-tree planting programmes, identifying obstacles to higher rates of felling and home supply and linking contract supply terms with planning agreements for papermaking companies. SOGAT argued that, as a key user of both electricity and water, the paper industry should have a lower level of tariffs charged. It also suggested that a more stable and lower-cost supply of wood pulp was required.

The SOGAT *Save Our Industry* campaign resulted in the Government adding paper- and board-making to its list of industries to be included in its industrial strategy to regenerate the British manufacturing sectors. Paper and board had been originally excluded from that Strategy when it was first announced in 1975. In 1976 the Paper and Board Sector Working Party was established to examine strategies to revitalise the industry. One objective was to increase employment security for the industry's labour force by reversing the trend of increased import penetration. The Working Party called for a major effort by management, unions and Government to increase productivity, to concentrate production on profitable paper grades, to increase the use of waste paper and investment. It urged the industry to devise by the end of 1978 an agreed strategy on production and capital investment. It recommended a study be made of the printing and writing papers' sector to identify the quantity of investment required to improve competitiveness. The Working Party made a number of recommendations relating to training and employment, including special attention be paid to creating an environment in which the disadvantages of seven-day working were minimised. The industry was urged to promote improved communication and consultation between management and unions, especially on strategic issues at company level, to give manpower planning the highest priority both at company and industry level and to produce a well-trained work-force.

In early 1979 a paper- and board-making Industrial Strategy Conference identified world-wide competition and new technology as threats to the industry in the 1980s. The Conference noted demand for paper and board in the UK had fallen, the share of the home market taken by imports had risen steeply and UK production levels had changed little over the period 1963–77. The Conference saw the industry's basic problem as its dependence on imported wood pulp, particularly as the counties from which the UK purchased it were also competing with UK finished products. SOGAT consistently argued that this dependency could be reduced by concentrating on the more valuable and specialist grades of paper, by increasing the amount of home-produced pulp, by the use of recycled waste paper, by providing sufficient investment and by competing on fair terms with overseas competitors. However, with the fall of the Labour Government in May 1979 the Industrial Strategy programme ended as the incoming Conservative Government disagreed with public assistance for industry.

The UK paper- and board-making industry's economic fortunes could not be reversed without political action. A merger between SOGAT and NATSOPA would mean that calls for Government assistance to the industry were coming from an organisation of 250,000 whose members, directly or indirectly, were dependent on paper and paper conversion for their livelihood. An amalgamation with NATSOPA would strengthen SOGAT's voice in the decision-making forums of those organisations, such as the TUC and the Labour Party, which could influence or initiate political action to improve the fortunes of the paper- and board-making industry. In this respect the need for a larger, single political voice was an important factor in SOGAT's papermaking members supporting the proposal for the formation of SOGAT (82).

Technological Developments

In the 1970s the industry had to come to terms with implementation of technological change designed to lower costs by reducing labour requirements and increasing output. In the late 1970s the standardisation of carton sizes was clear to see in all supermarkets, where even the most casual observation revealed how few different cartons there were. In the 1970s the packaging sector witnessed an increase in the pace of technological change based on the increasing use of plastic and laser beam die casting. Paper bags were being superseded by plastic bags and plastic wrappings. Given the proportion of SOGAT's members working in paper bags and paper packaging, the union was rightly concerned about this trend. The growth in the use of plastics rather than paper in the manufacture of packaging materials lead to a growth of new skills in the industry – development in which non-print unions had an interest. The increased use of plastic saw an integration of the printing and packaging processes. The printing on plastics was ancillary to the needs of the products but an integral part of the manufacturing process. Tobacco manufacturers, for example were making greater use of plastic-based materials in their packaging and it was anticipated that in the near future the production of a cigarette and its container would be done in a single operation.

The 1970s' trend away from using paper as the basis of packaging materials was there for all to see. The decade witnessed a shift from paper bags to plastic carrier bags, well printed in colours to appeal to the younger generation. Another development was the growth in the use of the rigid plastic inner in a tough fibre outer in packing transistor radios and other electrical goods. Yet another innovation with implications for the papermaking industry was frozen foods, which required packaging materials which could withstand very low temperatures but which must protect the food from contamination. Plastic materials could do this, but paper could not. The spread of plastic-based packing materials and the integration of the production and printing processes led to unions unconnected with the printing industry claiming the right to organise the process. When the Amalgamated Engineering Union claimed the fitting of dies to come within its remit, SOGAT took the issue to a TUC Disputes Committee which awarded jurisdictional rights in SOGAT's favour.

Technological changes had produced a revolution in the lives of the consuming public and great changes in the employment security of

SOGAT members. The jump from buying sweets over the counter in a paper bag filled from a scoop to buying a tube of chocolate drops all ready packed in a plastic container was an everyday illustration of the move away from paper-based materials for packaging. With these changes came the need for new skills and the ending of clear demarcations between the production of packaging materials and the printing upon them. They also blurred the demarcation lines between the boundaries of SOGAT interests and those of other unions. SOGAT, therefore, viewed an amalgamation with NATSOPA as strengthening its resources to accommodate these changes.

NOTES

1. Society of Graphical and Allied Trades (Division A) *Report of the Biennial Delegate Council Meeting 1970*, p. 185.
2. Society of Graphical and Allied Trades *Report of the Biennial Delegate Council Meeting*, 1972, p. 229.
3. Society of Graphical and Allied Trades *Report of the Biennial Delegate Council Meeting, 1978*, pp. 252–5.
4. See Society of Graphical and Allied Trades *Report of the Biennial Delegate Council Meeting, 1972*, p. 230.
5. Society of Graphical and Allied Trades *Report of the Biennial Delegate Council Meeting, 1974*, p. 43.
6. Although at the time the NGA was not a TUC affiliate, the Industrial Relations Act (1971) was being repealed. The NGA sought to rejoin the TUC. SOGAT claimed the NGA had poached members without any regard to fellow trade unionists. Being outside the TUC meant SOGAT could not take the NGA to a TUC Disputes Committee.
7. Society of Graphical and Allied Trades *Report of the Biennial Delegate Council Meeting, 1976*, p. 370.
8. Society of Graphical and Allied Trades *Report of the Biennial Delegate Council Meeting, 1982*, p. 85.
9. Society of Graphical and Allied Trades *Report of the Biennial Delegate Council Meeting, 1980*, pp. 287–8.
10. Society of Graphical and Allied Trades *Report of the Biennial Delegate Council Meeting, 1982*, pp. 97–8.
11. Closures included Thames Board Ltd at Purfleet, Vale Board Mill at Denny, Kent Craft Mill at Northfleet, Wiggins Teape at Inverness and Domatar Papermill at Croxley.
12. See Society of Graphical and Allied Trades *Save Our Industry: The State of Trade*, 1975.

CHAPTER 7

THE ACTUAL FORMATION OF SOGAT (82)

RELATIONS WITH SLADE

Prior to 1966 the NUPB&PW had enjoyed very friendly relationships with SLADE. This had remained the case as the Union became SOGAT (Division A) and continued to be so with the reconstituted SOGAT. This friendly relationship resulted in SOGAT and SLADE concluding in the summer of 1973 a five-point agreement for closer working between the two unions. A Standing Joint Committee was established to promote closer co-operation and unity of purpose between the two unions in spheres of mutual interest. Items could be referred to the Standing Committee which consisted of six representatives of each union including their respective General Secretaries and Presidents. If the two General Secretaries considered the business of the Joint Committee required the co-option of additional members they had authority to make such co-option. The Standing Joint Committee met as required but not less than once every six months,. It had authority to delegate responsibility for the implementation of any policy recommendation endorsed by the respective National Executive Councils to any joint sub-committee if considered appropriate.

Just before Christmas 1973 SOGAT approached SLADE to explore the possibility of amalgamation. SLADE responded in positive terms, saying it envisaged a merged union that would allow individual interest groups sufficient autonomy to protect and advance their special interests whilst the combined union strength would be available for dealing with issues and problems which were common to all within the enlarged union. SLADE envisaged the claims and needs of the semi-skilled and unskilled employees and those of the craftsmen being accepted as equally valid and dependent one upon the other. SLADE foresaw a union where women would be regarded as equal partners and entitled to full equality of opportunities, wages and conditions. However, above all, SLADE desired a merged organisation which allowed men, women, skilled and unskilled to play a full role in developing the kind of life they would want, to have their full and proper share of the wealth they produced and to have greater control over the forces shaping their future. SOGAT was at pains to stress that as the largest union of the two it had no intention of being 'big brother' within any merged union. It envisaged the creation of an enhanced union based on the principle of democratic control by the membership.

The amalgamation talks were friendly. SOGAT's organisational structure as adopted at its 1972 Biennial Delegate Council (see Chapter 10) allowed for flexibility within the union's General Rules and would enable SLADE to join SOGAT and still retain a high degree of autonomy. SOGAT proposed SLADE have autonomous status as SOGAT's National Graphical Division, the secretary of which would be the SLADE General Secretary. Existing SLADE Branches would become branches of the National Graphical Division within which SLADE would continue its long-established industrial practices, including SLADE's White Card procedure for filling vacancies[1] and the negotiation of terms and conditions for its members on the basis of house, and not national, agreements. SOGAT envisaged the National Graphical Division would embrace existing craft groups in SOGAT, such as the PMB and the Monotype Casters and Typefounders' Branch as well as other craft groups joining SOGAT in the future via amalgamation. The National Graphical Division would represent the collective voice of craft members within SOGAT.

However, the amalgamation failed. SLADE sought to retain its autonomy in the enhanced union via a federal structure rather than the preferred SOGAT option of a divisional structure. SOGAT considered, on the basis of experience, that federal structures were an unwise practice within trade unions. A federal structure which had existed in SOGAT between 1966 and 1972 had ended in divorce. There was thus a fundamental and irreconcilable difference between the two unions. Despite the failure of the amalgamation talks, relations between SOGAT and SLADE remained cordial throughout the rest of the 1970s and early 1980s.

RELATIONS WITH THE NGA

Between 1972 and 1976 relations between SOGAT and the NGA were strained. Difficulties centred around the following issues: the NGA's attitude towards pay differentials in the 1974 wage negotiations with the BFMP, demarcation difficulties and the NGA's resignation from the TUC in 1972 over its inability to conform with the TUC policy of deregistration in opposition to the Conservative Government's Industrial Relations Act (1971). However, despite the strained relations the 1972 SOGAT Biennial Delegate Council Meeting approved a PMB motion which 'instructs the NEC to do all in their power to bring about one union for print and with this objective in mind, approach the NGA for discussions on amalgamation immediately'.[2]

The PMB considered discussions with the NGA to be the logical place to start because a merger between the two largest print unions would soon be followed by the creation of one union for the industry. The PMB, however, was seen by some SOGAT members as having parochial interest in a merger with the NGA in that it would ease finding alternative employment for its members as letterpress machinery was replaced by litho machinery. PMB members were already permitted by the NGA to operate litho machines provided they transferred membership from SOGAT to the NGA. Merger with the NGA would enable PMB members 'to follow the job' and to receive retraining to enter other jobs. Without a merger these opportunities would be denied to PMB members whose fate was expressed by Alex Brandon, the mover of the motion, in the following terms:

> Some unions have been able to follow the job and have their members retrained, but for those members of unions that this is denied, they face a printing industry that holds no future for them. One union for print would not solve all problems overnight but it would surely lend itself more readily in avoiding an industrial scrap-heap of trained workers who in most cases have given the best of their working years to print. It is a problem, quite frankly, that can effect many branches within our national union, and particularly with my own it is a matter of survival.[3]

SLADE, SOGAT and the NGA acted individually in presenting their 1974 wage demands to the BPIF. The three unions could not act collectively because the NGA objected to SOGAT's claim that any new monies gained should be paid to all three unions' members in equal amounts irrespective of gender, or craft/non-craft status. The NGA objected to the fact that such an increase would erode traditional percentage differentials between craft and non-craft workers. SLADE, however, was happy to accept SOGAT's position that any wage increases should be flat-rate and not percentage-wise.

SOGAT was particularly annoyed the NGA had raised the differential question in an editorial in its monthly journal *Print*[4]. Relations became even more strained when the SOGAT General Secretary asked the NGA how it would react if the three unions were offered by the BFMP the then existing Government pay norm of a £2.25 per week increase. The NGA responded by stating that traditional percentage differentials must be maintained. SOGAT's reason for preferring an equal money increase for all workers was simple: the rapid inflation of 1973/74 stemming from a sharp increase in oil prices hit the non-craft employees just as hard as craft employees. The hyper-inflation of the winter of 1973/4 was a unique situation which required original thinking if the adverse effects of rapid inflation on the wages and conditions of print workers were to be minimised. For SOGAT this was a unique situation and was not, therefore, the occasion to argue about traditional differentials as would have been the case in a normal situation. SOGAT considered the NGA had now become the 'Trojan Horse' of the printing industry in that, at a time of inflation rapidly eroding the purchasing power of wages, it seemed hell bent on holding back from protecting the lowest-paid in the industry from these ravages.

The first half of the 1970s witnessed many demarcation problems between SOGAT and the NGA as a result of the implementation of new techniques and new processes into the industry. In 1973 the two unions met to consider these problems. They agreed to establish a working party to examine the feasibility of uniting the two unions and to finding solutions to the immediate demarcation problems. The Working Party made two important decisions. First, there should be an end to the warfare between the two unions, and second, there should be a stand-off period of two years to allow talks on amalgamation to take place. The bloodletting would cease. The SOGAT accepted these two decisions. However, the NGA replied that although they were prepared to continue talks on amalgamation, their National Council had not discussed an agreed formula on demarcation issues.

The NGA continued its policy of encroaching on traditional areas of SOGAT organisation, but particularly those of the PMB and the Monotype Casters and Typefounders' Branch. On 7 March 1974 in an attempt to end this behaviour the SOGAT General Secretary wrote personally to the NGA General Secretary asking him to intervene, as he did not believe it to be in the interests of the working class or the industry to have open warfare between the two unions. The NGA General Secretary saw fit to ignore the SOGAT General Secretary's letter, whereupon SOGAT's response was to instruct its branches to defend their members' interests in any way possible.

The NGA found that for technical reasons it could not comply with the TUC policy of deregistration under the 1971 Industrial Relations Act.[5] It resigned from the TUC. Despite remaining on the Register of Trade Unions and Employers' Associations, the NGA committed itself not to use the Industrial Relations Act (1971) to promote its own interests. However, SOGAT's experience did not bear this out. The NGA had used the Act to promote its own interests without the slightest regard for the interests of other print workers. SOGAT informed the TUC that, when the Industrial Relations Act was repealed and the NGA applied to re-affiliate, SOGAT would not be prepared to see a red carpet laid out to fetch back the NGA into the TUC. When the Act was repealed in 1974 the NGA duly applied to re-affiliate to the TUC. SOGAT objected to this proposed re-affiliation. It was bitter about the NGA's behaviour because when SOGAT had received a letter from the TUC advising affiliates that it was 'open season' to poach members of those trade unions who remained on the Register they had told the TUC they would not behave in this way towards another print union, even if it registered under the 1971 Act. The NGA had a lot of explaining to do before SOGAT was prepared to withdraw objections to its re-affiliation. As far as SOGAT was concerned, the NGA's behaviour whilst outside the TUC had been anti-trade union, anti-working class and involved a total disregard for workers' common interests. SOGAT's position was supported by other print unions including SLADE, the SGA and NATSOPA. It was only when, in 1976, the senior officers of SOGAT and NGA were replaced by new officers determined to end the 'war' between the two unions that SOGAT withdrew its objection to NGA's re-affiliation to the TUC.

Related to the NGA's resignation from the TUC was that its General Secretary, John Bonfield, was the President of the International Graphical Federation (IGF) to which SOGAT was affiliated. SOGAT found it intolerable that John Bonfield could represent the British trade union movement on the European Trade Union Confederation (ETUC) of which Mr Vic Feather, the General Secretary of the TUC was the President. SOGAT refused to recognise that the General Secretary of a registered trade union could speak for all other British printing trade unions. It considered that, by remaining a registered union, the NGA had forfeited any standing within the TUC and any right to speak for British printing trade unions. SOGAT informed the IGF that if Mr Bonfield remained its President and continued to have contact with the ETUC they would have no alternative but to boycott IGF meetings. To SOGAT the choice facing the IGF was clear. Either they wished to continue with a President from a discredited print trade union or they wished the continued participation of a credible British print union. However, SOGAT did not take its opposition to the point of leaving the IGF.

In 1976, the relationships between SOGAT and the NGA changed dramatically, helped by the NGA's return to the TUC and the desire of the new General Secretaries (Bill Keys and Joe Wade) and the General Presidents (Albert Powell and Les Dixon) of the two unions to set in train informal discussions to improve co-operation between the print unions. Both SOGAT and the NGA saw such co-operation as vital if the unions were to defend their members' interests in the face of technological and economic change. The informal discussions resulted in the two unions establishing a dialogue and a sense of friendliness. In May 1976 SOGAT and the NGA agreed a 'basis of understanding', the core of which was an acceptance by both unions that they faced the most fundamental of changes in working practices and that the mutual recognition of the right of all workers to have a stake in the industry irrespective of the union card they held was the best way to advance. The 'new understanding' was seen as the first step along a difficult road which, it was hoped, would lead to the amalgamation of the two unions. As we saw in Chapter 6, the 'new understanding' resulted in the establishment of a SOGAT/NGA Joint Committee which produced significant improvements in SOGAT/NGA relations.

In September 1979 SOGAT began exploratory talks with the NGA about a possible merger to form a single union. The following joint statement was issued by the two unions:

The Executive Councils of the two largest unions in the printing and allied trades – SOGAT (205,000) and the NGA (115,000)

– have agreed to enter into immediate talks as to the feasibility of amalgamation between the two unions.

The ECs recognise that, whilst there has been a considerable
reduction in the number of unions within the industry in recent
years, it has become imperative that further endeavours be
made to improve the final objective of one union for the
industry.

New technology and competition from overseas have placed
many stresses upon the industry and its work-force and it is
seen by the ECs that an amalgamation would be a massive
step forward in securing the future.

Both ECs wish to re-emphasise that an amalgamation, if
successful, must be seen as yet a further step forward to a
single union and express the hope that at some future date
other printing unions will join them[6]

However, during these exploratory amalgamation talks, the NGA
entered formal merger talks with SLADE whilst SOGAT began formal
talks with NATSOPA. Both unions decided that in the light of these
developments it would be inappropriate to continue exploratory discussions on a possible SOGAT/NGA link-up.

THE FORMATION OF SOGAT (75)

In 1975, the Scottish Graphical Association (SGA), formed in 1853,
had five branches – Dumfries, Edinburgh, Glasgow, Kilmarnock and
Paisley. The union was not unaware of the conditions facing non-craft
workers in the industry as it had demonstrated in 1918 by setting up
an auxiliary section with membership open to all workers in printing
offices in Scotland. The period 1950 to the mid-1970s witnessed radical
changes in the technology of printing, including the use of film as
opposed to the use of metal type, the rise of computerised typesetting and the growth of lithography at the expense of letterpress. All
these developments threatened the craft members' employment security as they were mostly metal type compositors and letterpress
machine managers. The 1973 STA Delegate Meeting recognised the
need to adjust to this changing situation and agreed its title was an
anachronism which carried connotations that the union was not in tune
with the modern world of print. The union was retitled the Scottish
Graphical Association (SGA).

When SOGAT and the SGA began amalgamation talks the latter had 6,500 members employed in Scottish daily, weekly and local newspapers, magazines, book production, commercial printing houses and in the carton and packaging industry. Its membership fell into three categories: compositors (linotype operators, monotype operators, monotype caster attendants and proof readers), printing (letterpress, lithographic and flexographic) and printers' assistants (male and female). Outside of Aberdeen, Dundee, Edinburgh and Glasgow, the SGA organised ancillary workers in its Auxiliary Section which had its own rules, working agreements and arrangements. It had 32 branches covering every district in Scotland and organised more than 90 per cent of craftsmen on the letterpress side of the printing industry. It was affiliated to the TUC, the STUC of which it was a founder member, and the P&KTF. Although its prime concern was with affairs in Scotland, it was not so preoccupied with these affairs as to be indifferent to the struggle of print and other workers outside Scotland. For many years it had played a considerable part in improving wages and conditions in the Scottish printing industry.

What was the basis of the merger between these two unions? Over many years relations between SOGAT and the STA/SGA had been good. The SGA was motivated for merger by a number of factors. First, it did not see the prospect of a successful merger with any other print union. It believed that, as a small union, if it joined another small print union, such as NATSOPA, it would not be able seriously to influence future developments in the printing industry. It felt that to merge with the NGA would merely sustain the divisions between the craft unions and the other unions who had members working on jobs requiring lesser skills and responsibility. There was also a severe clash of personalities between Fred Smith, General Secretary of the SGA and John Bonfield, General Secretary of the NGA. The SGA was also concerned that joining with the NGA would result in the loss of its identity as the NGA constitution did not allow for special representation on its decision-making bodies. SOGAT, on the other hand, had a structure that would allow the SGA to retain a high degree of autonomy as a division within the enlarged union. Such autonomy was very attractive to the SGA.

Second, the SGA realised that as part of a larger union it would have greater protection in any inter-union disputes with the NGA that might arise in Scotland over the control of lithographic printing presses. The SGA was a highly nationalistic organisation, very proud of being

Scottish. Although most of its members worked in craft occupations it had always been a radical union and was the only print craft union with significant numbers of semi-skilled workers in its ranks.

For SOGAT, the SGA would bring 6,500 craft workers and fulfil its long-held desire to gain an amalgamation with a significant craft print union. Second, a link with the SGA would give them a 'bridgehead' into craft jobs in lithographic press rooms in Scotland, from which it could then attempt to make advances into such press rooms in England and Wales. This in turn would make it easier for SOGAT machine room assistants to graduate to the more skilled jobs. Third, the merger would be a further important step in SOGAT's objective of achieving one union for the industry as a countervailing power to the increased bargaining power of employers resulting from the implementation of new technology and the growth of multinational companies.

Informal discussions between SOGAT and the SGA concerning amalgamation resulted in the latter, in February 1974, holding a special meeting of its members to receive a report on these informal talks and to discuss the principle of amalgamation with SOGAT. The delegates to the meeting responded positively to the principle of amalgamation with SOGAT. In the ensuing amalgamation negotiations SOGAT was guided by the principle of not being 'big brother' and ensuring that the SGA should not lose its identity in the new union. The SGA was to become the Scottish Graphical Division of SOGAT, with its own rules, funds and retention of its traditional industrial practices. The Division would ultimately become a National Graphical Division into which SOGAT would admit other print craft unions and craft groups already within it. By the autumn of 1974 an amalgamation package had been negotiated and the SOGAT and SGA executives strongly recommended their respective members to accept the package. A procedure for completion of the amalgamation was also agreed. A meeting of SGA members would be held in October 1974 to consider the package and its consequences for the future operation of the SGA. If that meeting accepted the amalgamation package the SGA would proceed to ballot its membership. If the ballot decision was in favour of amalgamation then SOGAT would recall its 1974 Biennial Delegate Council and if that approved the amalgamation package SOGAT would ballot its membership.

The amalgamation package included an industrial union structure which retained the benefits of a federated system within a common constitution. The structure had been designed to allow differences of opinion on staffing and demarcation to be resolved within SOGAT's existing decision-making structures. Under the terms of the package the SGA would become the Scottish Graphical Division (SGD) of SOGAT and retain its own Executive Committee which would continue to determine those industrial matters which were directly, and solely, the concern of the former SGA. The SGA would be represented on the SOGAT National Executive Council and at its annual Trade Group Conferences, where policies on industrial matters were formulated. For a three-year period following the amalgamation, the SGA would have two seats on the SOGAT National Executive, after which former SGA representation would be in accordance with the SOGAT General Rules. A new trade section was to be created within SOGAT for the former SGA at which the basis of representation would be one delegate for every 250 working members. In addition, SGA trade representation would be assured in SOGAT's other trade sections. In Trade Section A (General Print) its representation would be one delegate for the first 200 members, one additional delegate for the next 500 members and one delegate per 1,000 members thereafter. In the Trade Sections C (Fibreboard), D (Newspaper Production and Distribution) and E (Carton, Multi-wall Sack, Rigid Box and Bag) the SGA would be represented by one delegate for not less than 50 members and one additional delegate for every 250 members thereafter.

The SGA was to have representation at the SOGAT Biennial Council Meeting on the basis of one delegate for the first 100 working members. A second delegate would be allowed up to 700 working members and thereafter there would be one additional delegate for each 500 working members. The Rule Book of the SGD would be the present SGA Rule Book amended to dovetail with the SOGAT General Rules. The General Secretary of the SGA would become the Secretary of the Scottish Graphical Division and a Divisional Officer of SOGAT as well as an *ex officio* member of the SOGAT National Executive Council with power to speak but not to vote. All existing officers and staff of the SGA would continue to hold office as officers and staff of the SGD. No officer or member of staff of the SGA would have their conditions of employment worsened as a result of the amalgamation.

In return for a capitation fee of £95,000, members qualified immediately for SOGAT benefits, *viz.*, dispute benefit, disablement benefit, benevolent grant, legal assistance, unemployment benefit, accident benefit, funeral benefit and convalescent home benefit. The £95,000 figure was arrived at by taking the value per head of members of

SOGAT and multiplying it by the number of SGA members. The holding of Special Funds by branches to provide additional benefits to those provided at national level was permissible under the SOGAT General Rules, hence, former SGA benefits would continue as the Scottish Graphical Division was to be treated as a branch of SOGAT. The weekly membership subscription to SOGAT for SGD members was to be 21p. Officers and staff of the SGA would become members of the SOGAT Officers' and Staff Pension Fund.

The SGA members voted by 2,602 votes to 2,195 votes, a majority of 407, to amalgamate with SOGAT. The Craft Section voted in favour by only 56 votes, whilst the Auxiliary Section majority was 341 votes. Following the result of SGA ballot SOGAT recalled, on 21 May 1975, its 1974 Biennial Delegate Council, which carried the following motion:

> That this recall Biennial Delegate Council endorses the actions taken by the National Executive Council in bringing about amalgamation with the Scottish Graphical Association in line with the decision of the 1972 Isle of Man Biennial Delegate Council Motion 163.[7]

Following this decision, SOGAT balloted its members on amalgamation. In August 1975 it was announced that a majority of 34,099 (53,326 votes to 19,227) was in favour of amalgamation with the SGA. On 30 September 1975 SOGAT (75) came into being and represented 90 per cent of workers in the Scottish print and allied industries.

In any union amalgamation talks there are conflicts over structure, contributions, benefits, the ambitions of the elected leadership and philosophy. All these had been reconciled in the SOGAT/SGA merger. However, two problems arose after the respective membership had voted for amalgamation. The first concerned the title of the merged union and the second the Political Fund and Political Objectives Rule of the new union. The difficulties over the title arose from the Trade Union and Labour Relations Act (1974) and the Trade Union Amalgamation Act (1964). The former laid down as a condition of the registration of a trade union that the Registrar 'should not enter the name of an organisation if that organisation has a name so nearly resembling any such name as to be likely to deceive the public'. The 1964 Act did not allow two unions amalgamating to retain their previous names or a name which could be construed by the public to be similar. SOGAT and the SGA had decided to call the new union SOGAT. However, the law forbade this, even though no other trade union at the time had a title resembling it. The problem was overcome by adding '1975' behind SOGAT and hence the legal title of the merged union became SOGAT (75), although the union was always referred to as SOGAT.

An extreme difficulty occurred concerning the Political Fund and Political Objectives Rule of SOGAT. SOGAT had a political fund but the SGA did not. Under the Trade Union Act (1913) when trade unions merge, separate approval has to be obtained for Political Fund Objectives for the merged union if both unions do not already have Political Fund Objectives. There were two options open to SOGAT. It could hold a separate ballot of all members after amalgamation to restore the Political Objectives Rule which had been removed from the date of amalgamation. Alternatively, it could stick to having a Political Fund and if the Registrar raised objection, take a ballot on political objectives. SOGAT had long recognised that industrial activity without political lobbying was incomplete. It decided to ballot members after the amalgamation to establish a Political Fund and Political Objectives rule. The ballot resulted in a narrow majority favouring the establishment of a Political Fund and Political Objectives Rule (see Chapter 15).

The creation of SOGAT (75) was as an important step towards the creation of one union for the graphical and allied trades. However, much work needed to be done if this objective were to be realised. Many had predicted the SOGAT/SGA talks would fail because the interests of craft and semi-skilled employees were incompatible. However, this did not take into account the fact that SOGAT's decision-making and financial structure had been shaped by the coming together of many craft and non-craft unions. Like other craft unions in print, the SGA retained the existence of its original societies as branches, as a result of which the SGD comprised 32 branches ranging from Glasgow, which contained one-third of the total membership, to branches such as Rothesay with less than 12 members. Only Glasgow and Edinburgh had full-time branch officials. By the mid-1970s complaints were being received at the lack of service the membership were receiving from the Divisional Office. The SGD retained its structured and operated precisely as it had done as the SGA. The situation could not continue and in October 1978 the SGD adopted a new structure. The Division was divided into three branches – the East Branch, the West Branch and the North Branch – each serviced by full-time officials. In 1984 the SGD became the Scottish Graphical Branch (SGB) and as such came fully into SOGAT. By the early 1980s, the SGD felt it had fully integrated into SOGAT and there was no longer any need for it to have a 'special' position with the union. This position had been necessary in 1975 because the SGA, as a small union, had feared losing its identity within the large SOGAT organisation and without this stipulation it the membership would never have voted for merger.

THE FORMATION OF SOGAT (82)

In 1978 when NATSOPA began amalgamation talks with SOGAT it organised administrative and clerical grades, copy holders, revisers, machine managers, machine assistants, photoprinters, linotype assistants, general assistants, ancillary staff, for example cleaners and doormen, ink makers, ink roller makers, type foundry assistants and sign and display employees. Although the word 'National' was in its title, 90 per cent of its members were employed in London and 50 per cent in newspapers. In the general printing trade, NATSOPA organised about 50 per cent of its potential membership. In 1969 it had formed a Technical, Administrative and Executive Section to cater for middle and senior management, for example company secretaries, labour relations managers and directors, but success in recruiting these grades had been limited.

Despite the break-up of the NUPB&PW/NATSOPA 1966 amalgamation, relation between the two unions in the 1970s were cordial. In 1973 SOGAT wrote to NATSOPA to seek greater unity by means of *ad hoc* arrangements under which the print unions could protect and advance the interests of their members. In sending the letter to NATSOPA, the General Secretary Elect of SOGAT, Vincent Flynn, sought to assure his members that 'there is no question at all of us doing any double shuffle over what happened on the dissolution of the original SOGAT'.[8] It was too soon after the divorce for amalgamation to be reconsidered. Nevertheless, in 1973 NATSOPA and SOGAT concluded an agreement redefining their spheres of influence to enable closer working.

In 1976 NATSOPA began merger talks with the NGA. Subsequently SLADE and NUWDAT joined these talks. In 1977 NATSOPA was unable to provide financial information to the four-union amalgamation panel and was advised that until it could provide the information it must withdraw from the talks. In April 1978 NATSOPA sought to rejoin the merger talks but was told the three-union movement could continue without NATSOPA until either a new union was formed or one or all three unions' members rejected amalgamation. Following this rejection, NATSOPA was attracted to SOGAT which, following its 1978 Biennial Delegate Council's re-affirmation of the need to work towards one union for the printing industry, sought further amalgamation initiatives. In November 1978 the following joint press release was issued by the two unions:

> Following decisions of the ECs of NATSOPA and SOGAT to commence talks as to the feasibility of amalgamation between the two unions, a meeting has taken place this weekend between representatives of the above mentioned unions.
>
> Considerable progress has been made in the talks, details of which will be subject to report to the full Executive Councils within the next fortnight.
>
> Both unions have undertaken, meanwhile, to use their best endeavours to present a united policy on all matters of common interest.[9]

On 24 April 1981 the General Secretaries of the two unions – Bill Keys (SOGAT) and Owen O'Brien (NATSOPA) – reported agreement on the principles to govern the amalgamation. During 1980 differences of opinion between the two unions centred over whether the merged union should have a lay executive, whether its rules should be changed by membership ballot and whether its officers should be re-elected periodically. However, the NATSOPA 1980 Governing Council voted to accept the SOGAT practices on these issues because at heart, NATSOPA desperately wanted the merger to take place. In September 1980 the SOGAT NEC agreed amalgamation talks should continue. The 24 April statement announced that differences of opinion previously existing between the two unions had now been resolved. Agreement had been reached on the structure and government of the new union, including the composition and powers of the NEC, the delegate conference, the officer structure, the principles governing the new Rule Book and the benefits to be paid to members of the merged union.

On 13 November 1981 a joint meeting of the National Executive

Councils of SOGAT and NATSOPA endorsed the amalgamation proposals and urged both sets of members to vote in favour of merger. The ballot of individual members of both unions was to commence in March 1982 with the result announced in April 1982. What was the package upon which the two sets of members would vote? Amalgamation between SOGAT and NATSOPA brought together as one society two unions with long and proud traditions. The merger was in many respects a natural development. There were areas and industries where both unions had common membership. For example, both unions catered for clerical workers and technical and supervisory workers as well as machine assistants and ancillary workers in general print and newspapers. The amalgamation panels ensured the best traditions and practices of each union were combined to create the best possible structure. The Society of Graphical and Allied Trades (1982) with a membership of 225,000 was the largest printing trade union in Western Europe and the UK. It organised 61 per cent of trade unionists in the UK printing industry.

Much consideration was given by the amalgamation negotiators to the officer structure for the new SOGAT (SOGAT (82)). In a number of areas the two unions had members doing the same job under the same employment conditions. There were other areas where each union had separate membership. The guiding principle for the amalgamation panels in determining the officer structure was to combine the expertise of both unions. SOGAT would have a Joint General Secretaryship of Bill Keys and Owen O'Brien. They would hold office until death, resignation, retirement or other removal of office of one of them when the position would revert to one General Secretary. The surviving Joint General Secretary would become the General Secretary of SOGAT which would have a General President, an Organising Secretary, a Papermaking Secretary and a Financial Secretary. These were all SOGAT (75) offices. NATSOPA had three National Assistant Secretaries whilst SOGAT (75) also had three General Officers. On merger, SOGAT (82)'s general officers would be the three NATSOPA National Assistant Secretaries plus the three SOGAT (75) general officers. Mr Jim Pointing, Mr Fred Smith and Mr Danny Sergeant were SOGAT (75) divisional officers. Fred Smith also held the title of Divisional Secretary. On the creation of SOGAT (82) these three divisional officers were given the status of general officers.

There were differences between the two societies concerning eligibility for election to the National Executive Council. In NATSOPA, full-time officers were debarred from election to the NEC. In SOGAT (75), any member could stand for election to the NEC. The amalgamation negotiators agreed that full-time Branch Secretaries should be allowed to stand for election to the NEC. In deciding the size of the National Executive Council, two considerations were paramount. First, the need to make the NEC as representative as possible, and second, not to establish an Executive that was too large and unwieldy. SOGAT would have an Executive Council of 36 members elected on a geographical basis, but would secure the widest possible representation by stipulating that no more than two members could be elected from any one branch. No more than one member from any particular chapel could serve on the NEC whilst another chapel was unrepresented.

The government of SOGAT (82) was vested in a Biennial Delegate Council at which representation would be on the basis of each branch with a working membership of not less than 100 members having one delegate, and a second delegate for branches with 700 working members. Thereafter, there would be an additional delegate for each complete 500 working members. This formula gave SOGAT a Biennial Delegate Council of 475. The first Biennial Delegate Council was to be held in 1984 but a special Policy Delegate Council would be held in May 1983.

In considering the branch structure for SOGAT (82) the amalgamation panels were aware that between them SOGAT (75) and NATSOPA had almost 250 branches. It was not feasible for SOGAT (82) to operate with this number of branches nor to operate with more than one branch in any particular town/area except in particular circumstances. The two unions were not only to amalgamate nationally from vesting day but were also to merge at branch/area level from day one. After careful consideration of all the differences involved, it was agreed to adopt the SOGAT (75) branch structure and branch boundaries for SOGAT (82). If such branch mergers were not in the interests of the members concerned, discussions would take place at the appropriate level to find an agreement that was in their best interests. SOGAT (82) would have as many full-time administered branches as possible with the ultimate objective of all members being serviced by full-time Branch Administrators.

The NATSOPA branches in London and Manchester were to remain as they were except that they would no longer be centrally funded. In the provinces, NATSOPA's role in the newspaper field was protected by the co-option to any merged Branch Committees of the former NATSOPA Branch Secretaries who would bring their specialised newspaper knowledge. The same principle applied for other specialised NATSOPA areas, for example ink and roller. The SOGAT (75) practice of branch allowances, whereby local branches could expend up to 40 per cent of the national contribution rate on branch administration was to continue in SOGAT (82).

A time limit was set by which branch amalgamations had to be achieved and during which branches would consider their officer structure and reform their branch committees to achieve the widest possible representation. In reconstituting branch committees, adequate representation was to be given for both NATSOPA and SOGAT specialist occupations/trades and industries in that particular branch. Branches were to complete amalgamation by no later than April 1983. However, the NATSOPA Clerical Branch (CAEP) would remain unchanged but the NATSOPA Technical, Administrative, Executive and Advertising (TAE&A) and the SOGAT Art, Technical, Administrative, Executive and Sales (ATAES) Branches would merge on vesting day. The SOGAT (ATAES) Manchester Office would be the central point for contributions and administration of this merged white-collar Branch. Whilst the NATSOPA's London Office (Caxton House) would service the southern areas of the Branch.

In considering the benefits to be provided by SOGAT (82) the amalgamation panels adopted the principle that whichever Society had the better benefit then that would apply in the new union. The financial structures of NATSOPA and SOGAT (75) were different. NATSOPA had a variable national contribution rate, the whole of which was remitted to Head Office. SOGAT (75) had a fixed national contribution rate, 40 per cent of which could be expended at local level by branches. SOGAT (82) adopt a single national weekly contribution rate of 73p, including the political fund, payable from July 1982. Branches would be permitted to establish their own local branch fund contribution.[10] NATSOPA and SOGAT (75) both had Stoy Hayward & Co. as their accountants who were asked to conduct a financial appraisal of each union. The exercise, based on each Society's 1980 audited accounts, showed NATSOPA's 'worth' per member to be double that of SOGAT (75) and NATSOPA would have a surplus on amalgamation. Following merger, this surplus was to be distributed in two ways. First, a lump sum would be paid into the SOGAT Officers' and Staff Pension Fund since NATSOPA had agreed to adopt this scheme immediately upon amalgamation. The sum of money to be paid would be determined by actuaries. Second, since NATSOPA branches did not have their own funds, there would be lump sum payments into SOGAT (82) local branch funds. These lump sum payments were to be regarded as 'per capita' payment by NATSOPA branches to SOGAT (82) branches.

Both NATSOPA and the SOGAT (75) Executive Councils saw the amalgamation package giving SOGAT (82) a solid basis as a strong and healthy union able to service its members. On 15 January 1982 SOGAT (75) and NATSOPA signed the Instrument of Amalgamation with Mr Len Murray, the TUC General Secretary, acting as witness. On 29 January 1982 the SOGAT (75) recalled Delegate Council voted overwhelmingly in favour of the merger package. Of the 366 delegates present only three voted against the proposed package. The final stage of the process was completed when the memberships of SOGAT (75) and NATSOPA voted in favour of the merger. SOGAT (75) members voted by 57,405 to 26,169 in favour and NATSOPA members voted by 17,100 to 13,539 in favour. SOGAT (82) came into existence on 3 July 1982. The General Secretaries of the two unions remarked that 'This major step of joining two old and proud trade unions must be seen as yet a further step towards the final objective of creating one union in the graphical and allied trade.'[11]

DIFFERENCES FROM THE 1966 AMALGAMATION

When NATSOPA and the NUPB&PW created SOGAT in 1966, they never really amalgamated. The two Divisions were created, two Executive Councils existed and only met occasionally as a SOGAT Executive Council to administer matters where they could agree. SOGAT had three different Rule Books, different subscription levels, a non-elected National Executive Committee and suffered from a clash of personalities at General Secretary level. In reality, two sovereign National Executive Councils, forming themselves into separate Divisions, came together by appointment as a new National Executive Council for SOGAT. The members of NATSOPA and the NUPB&PW had been asked to wait for some future date before a full amalgamation would be achieved. The merger never took place on the basis of negotiating a new Rule Book which set out decision-making, financial and officer structures and in which the different philosophies of the two unions were reconciled.

The 1982, amalgamation had a firm basis. The SOGAT (82) Rule Book had been agreed by a joint meeting of the SOGAT (75) and NATSOPA Executive Councils in November 1981, by the Governing Council of NATSOPA, by the Re-call SOGAT (75) Biennial Delegate Council in January 1982, and finally by a ballot of the respective membership in March/April 1982. The members of the two unions knew the new structure, the new Constitution and had indicated their view thereon. The members had received the fullest amount of information on the amalgamation.

The 1982 amalgamation package was the result of three years' negotiations. One union with one national contribution rate and a new National Executive Committee of 36 members elected directly by the membership would come into office within three months of vesting day. In SOGAT (82) all members would pay the same national contribution. This was unlike 1966, when one Division paid one contribution nationally but the other Division had a different structure of contributions. SOGAT (82) branches had the option to establish local funds where they did not already have them.

Another important difference relative to 1966 was that NATSOPA was prepared to concede to SOGAT (75) the principle that full-time Branch Secretaries could serve on the National Executive Council, that National Officers would not be subject to periodic re-election, that rule changes could be confirmed by the Biennial Delegate Council and not have to wait until a ballot of the membership and that SOGAT (82) would not be a centrally funded union. The major reason for NATSOPA's acceptance of these constitutional principles was that technological changes in the industry were weakening its industrial strength. SOGAT was the only union with which a merger was a serious possibility. NATSOPA's attempt to merge with NGA, SLADE and NUDWAT had failed. NATSOPA had had to leave these talks in 1977 because it was unable to provide answers to questions about its finances. When these matters had been settled, the NGA and SLADE dismissed in an off-hand manner NATSOPA's request to rejoin the talks. Given that the craft union route was cut off, NATSOPA had little choice if it wished protection from technological changes and other problems, such as the NGA's challenge to its rights to organise in the non-manual areas of newspapers, but to seek an accommodation with SOGAT. The alternative was isolation with the prospect of joining an NGA/SLADE/SOGAT (75) merged union at some point in the future from a position of weakness. If an accommodation was to be reached with SOGAT, then it would have to concede the principle of a centrally funded union, an Executive Council on which full-time branch officials could sit, the non-periodical re-election of national officers and the approval of union rule changes by the Delegate Council Meeting.

In addition, the relationship between Bill Keys, General Secretary of SOGAT (75) and Owen O'Brien, General Secretary of NATSOPA was much more friendly and constructive than that which had existed over the period 1966–72 between Mr Briginshaw, the General Secretary of NATSOPA and first Tom Smith and then Vincent Flynn, the General Secretaries of SOGAT. There was no clash of personalities at the highest level to prevent the successful creation and consolidation of SOGAT (82). Matters were assisted in that Owen O'Brien was close to retiring age and the problems associated with a relatively long period of a Joint General Secretaryship were unlikely to persist or even arise.

The founders of SOGAT (82) regarded the new union as providing a springboard for recruitment of new members on an unprecedented scale. Prior to the amalgamation, NATSOPA and SOGAT were often organising in the same areas, which meant competing against each other rather than working in unity. SOGAT (82), on the other hand, being broadly based, would provide impetus and the opportunity for a significant recruitment drive in areas currently largely unorganised. In the clerical areas of paper and printing production an enormous recruitment potential existed, and there were also organisational areas that remained untapped, for example sales forces in printing, ink and office supplies and papermaking.

The creation of SOGAT (82) was seen, especially by the former NATSOPA, as a means of protecting existing organisation rights amongst clerical groups in general printing and provincial newspapers. This area was being encroached on by the NGA. The creation of SOGAT (82) would make it possible to defend these organisational rights more strongly than would be the case as two separate unions. There was also a strong feeling that SOGAT (82) would facilitate solutions to the problems arising from the introduction of new technology into the office. The problems arising from the implementation of word processors and microfiche systems would have to be faced by office workers in the same way as production workers had had to face the implementation of new technology.

NOTES

1. Under this procedure any vacancy was to be offered to the longest-unemployed member of the union. If no unemployed members wished to fill the vacancy the second priority was unemployed members in the branch where the vacancy occurred. If no unemployed members in the branch wished to fill the vacancy then it could be offered to existing employed members in the branch where the vacancy occurred.
2. Society of Graphical and Allied Trades *Report of the Biennial Delegate Council Meeting, 1972*, pp. 229–30.
3. op. cit., p. 230.
4. See *Print*, February 1974, p. 5.
5. For an explanation of this see J. Gennard *A History of the National Graphical Association*, Hyman Unwin, 1990, pp. 294–300.
6. See *SOGAT Journal*, December 1979, p. 3.
7. See *Society of Graphical and Allied Trades (SOGAT) and Scottish Graphical Association: Proposed Amalgamation*, Re-call 1974 Biennial Delegate Council Meeting, May 1975, p. 2.
8. See Society of Graphical and Allied Trades *Report of the Biennial Delegate Council Meeting*, 1974, p. 44.
9. See *SOGAT Journal*, December 1979 p. 3
10. At the time of the formation of SOGAT (82) the existing level of branch contributions in SOGAT (75) varied from nothing to 30p per week.
11. See *SOGAT Journal*, May 1982, p. 3.

CHAPTER 8

THE MERGER OF SOGAT (82) AND THE NGA (82): THE CREATION OF THE GRAPHICAL, PAPER AND MEDIA UNION (GPMU): GENERAL CAUSES

By mid-1982 there were three main trade unions in the printing and paper industry. The two production unions were SOGAT and the NGA which was now a single-craft union. In publishing and newspaper production the major non-manual employees' union was the National Union of Journalists. In the spring of 1983 SOGAT and NGA re-affirmed their commitment to one union for the media, communications and allied industries and in particular to their own amalgamation. A joint statement said:

> SOGAT and the NGA agreed that in order to achieve this objective there is a compelling necessity to promote a better understanding between the two unions of our mutual problems; to develop closer working relationships, to strive for better inter-union climates and take urgent steps to resolve some of the outstanding issues between the two unions.
>
> The economic recession and the disregard of the interests of working people by this Government, the dreadful misery and degradation of unemployment, compounded by the threats of challenges of new technology required a strong and united trade union response, and thus could be more effectively developed by the creation of one union for the media, communications and allied industries.

> SOGAT (82) and NGA (82) representatives will recommend to their respective National Executive Councils to look favourably towards re-opening discussions at the earliest opportunity, bearing in mind the current discussion between the NGA and the NUJ.[1]

The SOGAT 1984 Delegate Council Meeting accepted that with the current warfare between the two unions there was an urgent need for them to amalgamate speedily into one union and that such action should take place as a matter of urgency.[2] The delegates re-emphasised the need for the print unions to unite into one body and have collective strength in what was bound to be a difficult future. The longer SOGAT and the NGA were apart, the greater the opportunity for inter-union conflict as the implementation of new technology increased the overlapping interests of the two unions.

Amalgamation talks between SOGAT and NGA continued throughout the 1980s. The two panels met regularly in 1983 and 1984 and made progress. However, from autumn 1984 to February 1986 there were no meetings. During this period relationships between the two unions reached an all-time low because of inter-union disputes stemming from the implementation of new technology in the provincial newspaper sector. The amalgamation talks were not broken off and in March 1986, in the light of common problems being suffered by members of the two unions in the Wapping dispute (see Chapter 19), talks recommenced with both SOGAT and the NGA pledging themselves to reach an agreed amalgamation 'package' within 12 months. However, this proved optimistic and a package was not agreed until March 1990. This 'package' was accepted by the National Executives of the two unions, their Delegate Meetings and, in December 1990, by their respective memberships in a ballot. Vesting day for the merged union, to be known as the Graphical, Paper and Media Union (GPMU), was to be 1 July 1991. However, this was eventually postponed until 30 September 1991 (see Chapter 9). What were the reasons for the creation of the Graphical, Paper and Media Union?

There were five underlying factors behind its formation. First, there was the need for the print unions to speak with a single united voice to the TUC and the Labour Party if they were to influence the content of legislation repealing that of the Conservative governments of the 1980s and 1990s. This legislation, together with the Conservative Government's economic policies shifted significantly the balance of bargaining power towards the printing and papermaking employers. Second, both unions realised that whatever their views on the European Community, the completion of the Single European Market in 1992 and the political and economic disintegration of Central and Eastern Europe in the late 1980s and early 1990s would have profound economic implications. Both events offered multinational companies in the printing and papermaking industry the attractive option of establishing plants and/or transferring production to areas where wages were low and unions weak. Given that the prospect of European-wide collective bargaining was slim, SOGAT and the NGA recognised the need for legislation originating from the European Commission for the creation of a social dimension to the European Community. The ability to speak with one voice to the European Commission and the Social and Economic Committee and to international graphical trade union bodies such as the International Graphical Federation and the European Graphical Federation as well as the European Trade Union Confederation (ETUC), was a first necessary step if they were to increase their influence on the development of a social dimension to the European Community.

A third pressure leading to the formation of the GPMU was the changing balance of bargaining power in favour of printing and papermaking employers in the 1980s. This stemmed from the implementation of new technology, anti-union legislation and the changed economic circumstances resulting from increased international competition and deflationary economic policies. If SOGAT and the NGA remained separate, the employers would use their enhanced bargaining power to undermine the employment conditions of print workers. A fourth pressure was the need to improve the resource base of the printing and papermaking unions. Both SOGAT and the NGA recognised that merger would provide a more secure financial base from which to resist employer 'offensives'. A fifth factor leading to the formation of the GPMU was the implementation of technological change in papermaking and the printing industry which led to inter-union disputes between SOGAT and the NGA with, on occasions each union 'colluding' with the employer to undermine the interests of the other. Both realised that to continue in this vein would simply enhance the employer interests.

A SINGLE VOICE IN THE LABOUR PARTY AND THE TUC

The balance of bargaining power in the 1980s shifted significantly in favour of the printing and paper employers. One factor in this was successive pieces of employment legislation – the Employment Acts of 1980, 1982, 1988 and 1990 and the Trade Union Act (1984). If SOGAT and the NGA were to have a significant influence on the content of the employment and trade union legislation which eventually led to the repeal of that introduced in the 1980s, then they needed to speak with one voice and take a high profile in organisations that would have the power to change the 1980s employment legislation. The ability of SOGAT and the NGA to influence the policy-making bodies of the TUC and the Labour Party in deciding priority areas for the repeal of the Conservative Government employment legislation would be enhanced as a single union of 300,000 members rather than two separate unions – one with 130,000 members (the NGA) and the other with 170,000 (SOGAT). The NGA General Secretary underlined this point in addressing the 1990 SOGAT Biennial Delegate Council when he told delegates:

> We are often faced with the same problems, but we express different opinions: two voices divided saying different things. We frankly cannot afford that any longer.
>
> There has to be one voice for print workers, that of the GPMU. We have to be able with one voice to tell the Labour Party what legislation we want as print workers when they are returned to Government, what workers rights were believe are necessary for print workers, what opportunities legislation there should be, that there should be justice for all and a social system that puts right before might. A single voice of 300,000 print workers with credibility that will be listened to.[3]

THE SINGLE EUROPEAN MARKET AND THE EVENTS IN CENTRAL AND EASTERN EUROPE

Both SOGAT and the NGA recognised the implications for their members of the completion of the Single European Market and the economic and political disintegration of Central and Eastern Europe. Both unions dealt with printing, paper and graphical reproduction employers who were already established companies on mainland Europe. Events in Eastern Europe offered employers the attraction of establishing plants in areas where wages were low and unions were weak or non-existent. Given that the prospect of European-wide collective bargaining to counter this was as yet remote, SOGAT and the NGA appreciated the need to establish minimum employment standards in the European Community. This involved being able to influence the Community's decision-making bodies by speaking with a single and united voice. As the largest printing and paper union in Europe, the GPMU would be able to increase its influence in the European Graphical Federation (EGF), International Graphical Federation (IGF) and the European Trade Union Confederation. All these organisations lobbied government institutions, such as the European Commission and the International Labour Organisation (ILO), to introduce common international standards to regulate labour markets.

The Single European Market permits the free movement of labour and capital. Whilst transnational companies were ready to take advantage of the Single Market, SOGAT and the NGA were still striving to achieve a single print union. Further delays in achieving this objective were becoming a luxury. The implications for SOGAT and NGA members of the events in Central and Eastern Europe were spelt out by the NGA General Secretary when he told the 1990 SOGAT Biennial Delegate Council:

> The change which will take place from a command to a market economy is going to bring to Eastern Europe massive unemployment. They are already crying out for investment at any price. They are connected by road and rail to Western Europe. We are going to be faced with the kind of competitive problems that we were faced with some 15 years ago when we look at Hong Kong and Taiwan.[4]

Central and Eastern Europe had an abundance of cheap labour but no trade unions. It was an 'employers' dreamland', with massive implications for maintaining UK print wages and conditions of employment. By the early 1990s West German and French print multinational employers were already investing in Eastern Europe whilst Robert Maxwell was moving into Hungary, and the four major German multinationals – Burda, Springer, Butelsmann and Bauer – had divided up East Germany between themselves in terms of distribution and production zones.

THE BALANCE OF BARGAINING POWER

New technology, by blurring demarcation lines and altering skill content tipped the balance of bargaining power in favour of employers. SOGAT and the NGA acknowledged that if they remained separate the employers would use their enhanced bargaining power to the detriment of their members. To engage in mutually destructive inter-union conflict would increase further the bargaining power in favour of the employers. The two unions predicted that if amalgamation did not happen derecognition and individual employment contracts which, by the late 1980s, were common for non-manual employees in the newspaper industry, would become a day-to-day event in the mainstream printing industry.

In the 1980s, emboldened by anti-union legislation and changed economic circumstances, some employers in printing and papermaking industries embarked on an attack on trade union organisation, challenged the continuation of National Agreements and made no secret of their objective to de-unionise their companies. SOGAT and the NGA membership declined and their ability to deliver improvements in their members' pay and conditions was weakened. By 1990 both unions faced a common problem of anti-union employers and a realisation neither could be victor in destructive inter-union fights over a diminishing pool of jobs and potential members. If SOGAT and the NGA did not join forces they would find themselves squabbling over the demise of effective trade unionism in the printing industry. They could not afford the luxury of going back over past disagreements. If they did not achieve a single union the future would be bleak given the non-union objective to which some employers in the industry aspired.

IMPROVED RESOURCE BASE

Both SOGAT and the NGA desired to create a merged organisation which would give their members a more secure financial base than could be provided separately by each union. It was accepted that one union, by removing inter-union conflict, would enhance its ability to retain and attract members. A merged union would mean that in future negotiations the production work-force would speak with one voice and would not be pitted one against the other. More resources could be devoted to producing one claim instead of two to the BPIF, the Newspaper Society and company groups not in the employers' associations. A merger also held the attraction of combining the services of the two unions to give a more efficient service to its members.

TECHNOLOGICAL DEVELOPMENTS IN THE 1980s

Papermaking

The 1970s and 1980s were a tumultuous period for the papermaking industry. Production capacity was reduced by nearly 1m tons and most companies made significant losses. During the 1980s, the number of papermills fell from 171 to 123, whilst 30,000 jobs were lost. One hundred and forty two papermaking machines closed. The industry suffered from high interest rates, high exchange rates, high inflation and high energy costs coupled with low paper prices and falling demand. In the early 1980s, there were many who predicted the industry was in terminal decline.

However, during the mid- and late 1980s the industry made a remarkable recovery and experienced a period of continual growth. By 1990 UK paper consumption at 10m tons was well in excess of 1979 levels despite there being 30 per cent fewer mills. By 1990 productivity levels were 80 per cent higher than 1979. Economic growth created a new confidence which in turn brought major new investments, a significant amount of which was by foreign-owned firms, the opening of two new pulp and papermills and a spate of mergers and take-overs as companies sought to establish a market leadership position before the advent of the Single European Market in 1992.

However, this upturn brought problems which increased the pressures towards the SOGAT/NGA merger. Corporate merger significantly changed the ownership of the British papermaking industry. The concentration of ownership, with its threats to the bargaining power of SOGAT, was described in 1990 as 'probably the most challenging and potentially most difficulty issues the union will face'.[5] In 1990, 49 of 111 papermills in the UK were foreign-owned. Nineteen were US-owned, seven Finnish-owned, three New Zealand-controlled, three Swedish-owned and two Australian-owned. These 111 mills belonging to 71 companies employed 33,000 people of which 20,200 were manual employees and 7,800 staff employees. Financial restructuring through corporate mergers and take-overs was predicted to accelerate in the 1990s with many older paper companies disappearing to be replaced by pan-European or multinational companies which were expected to dominate the industry by the turn of the century.

By the late 1980s the implications of the increasing concentration of ownership in the industry were apparent. First three foreign-owned companies (British Tissue, Scott Ltd and Kimberly Clark) withdrew from the national agreement between the British Paper and Board Industry Federation and SOGAT. Second, three new papermills opened in the late 1980s – Bridgewater, Shotton and Caledonian – decided not to be parties to the Federation\SOGAT National Agreement. Third, the management methods of some multinational papermaking companies, together with the opportunism of some traditional producers, posed a further threat. Fourth, a further decline in the number of companies working under the British Paper and Board Industry Federation Agreement was expected, leading to a growth in decentralised company/plant bargaining with an inevitable additional call on SOGAT's finances and resources. Fifth, SOGAT's future in the industry was under threat. Two new mills – Shotton and Caledonian Irvine (both Finnish-owned) – had secured single-union agreement with the Electrical, Electronic, Telecommunications/Plumbing Union (EETPU) despite the fact of that union having only 4 per cent of total manual union membership in the industry.[6] SOGAT organisation was also threatened in the late 1980s by some employers derecognising it, removing its check-off arrangements, introducing single bargaining arrangements and radical changes to existing payment systems by the implementation of single-status, individual employment contracts, merit pay and profit sharing schemes. Sixth, SOGAT had become concerned that multinational and pan-European companies would take advantage of their enhanced bargaining position by undermining SOGAT members' existing terms and conditions of employment. Indeed, by 1990 some US-owned papermaking companies had succeeded in eliminating Sunday premia and holiday premia payments.

If SOGAT was to maintain a presence and some influence in the UK papermaking industry then a response to these threats was essential. If the enhanced bargaining power of the employers was to be counter-balanced, SOGAT could not remain isolated as an independent union. Link-ups with other unions in the papermaking industry were unlikely since SOGAT was for all intents and purposes the industry's union. It needed to improve its resource base.

The General Printing Industry

Origination

The early 1980s saw the introduction into a number of London printing firms of photocomposition and which led to inter-union disputes between the NGA and the Monotype Casters and Filmsetter's Branch of SOGAT. Under hot metal systems the NGA organised case hand compositors, linotype operators and proofreaders. SOGAT organised copy readers, monotype operators, revisers and linotype assistants. Photocomposition blurred these demarcation lines and the NGA adopted the policy that all jobs arising from the implementation of new technology in origination areas belonged exclusively to them. It was prepared to pursue this policy at the expense of SOGAT including, if necessary, collaboration with employers and crossing SOGAT picket lines.

SOGAT, however, considered that photocomposition systems required computer back-up, which it saw as providing an opportunity to create additional employment opportunities for their composing room members. It argued that on the implementation of new technology the staffing of composing rooms be shared equally between SOGAT and the NGA members currently employed in this area, with the necessary retraining requirements being met. The composing room functioned because of the dual efforts of the two unions' members, SOGAT felt that since a 'new world' of working was emerging it must state clearly the right of its members to gain employment benefits, not redundancy, from the implementation of photocomposition systems. These sentiments were well expressed in a motion from the Revisers and Ink Roller Manufacture Auxiliaries' (RIRMA) Branch to the 1983 SOGAT Biennial Delegate Council:

> That this SOGAT '82 Policy Conference resolves that where and when photocomposition is introduced in composing areas, SOGAT '82 members must be guaranteed equal staffing in all aspects of the computer operations.[7]

Photocomposition involved keyboard inputting. The machines had a keyboard operation at one end whilst the copy came out as a pulley-made plate at the other. This was then sent down to the machine room. Photocomposition eliminated the clear demarcations between previous SOGAT assistant jobs and 'core' NGA jobs. The members of the NGA claimed that in the past they had set the type. Since inputting on photocomposition systems performed the same function, the NGA claimed inputting should be their preserve. SOGAT argued that computer-based composition systems destroyed or fudged demarcation lines and in such situations their members had a right to operate equally with NGA members photocomposition systems.

Photocomposition developments also affected national newspaper production. In Fleet Street, SOGAT formed federated chapels to protect SOGAT jobs and to achieve a partnership and an eventual amalgamation with the NGA on a 50/50 basis. The NGA's behaviour in the early 1980s with regard to the implementation of photocomposition systems led some SOGAT activists to suspect the NGA's motives for amalgamation on grounds that the NGA agreed with the rallying cry of one union in print but gave the impression when it talked about one union that they literally meant a bigger NGA, regardless of the interests of other print trade unions.

The Press Rooms

In the 1980s new technology implementation blurred the previously clear demarcation lines between SOGAT and the NGA job territories in the machine room. The inter-union difficulties were most acute in London, where the NGA claimed sole right to jobs that had previously been accepted as belonging to the members of the PMB of SOGAT. The bitterness of their members towards the NGA's behaviour was well expressed in a motion they successfully presented to the 1983 SOGAT Biennial Delegate Council:

> That the SOGAT '82 Special Delegate Conference expresses grave concern at the continued encroachment by the NGA on SOGAT areas of work.
>
> In particular, their actions in the London area whereby they appear to be in collaboration with employers to eliminate SOGAT machine room operatives from traditional presses, to the extent that in many recorded instances where dubious liquidations of companies occur one week, with consequent re-opening of the same factories under new names a week or so later but only employing NGA members to the exclusion of SOGAT operatives.
>
> In these circumstances, whilst recognising that one union for

the industry can be the best long term solution to advance and protect the interests of all workers in the industry, this Conference directs the NEC to adopt a policy of resolute and determined opposition to each and every encroachment. To this end, all resources at SOGAT's disposal should be used to protect our members' interests and in particular the withdrawal of all supplies and services within the control of SOGAT, such as ink and paper or board should be imposed, irrespective of any legislation, past, present or future.

In conclusion, the NGA must be made to realise that we shall not allow one union for the industry to come about via the elimination of SOGAT and will, therefore meet their incursions head on.[8]

SOGAT saw one union for the industry as the best way to protect its members against attacks they were experiencing from a number of quarters. However, it passionately believed that one union for the printing industry could only be achieved when SOGAT and the NGA had mutual respect for each other, when they respected each other's traditional spheres of influence and thereby protected one another. SOGAT was outraged that the NGA seemed to believe the only way in which it could serve its members was by encroaching upon SOGAT's spheres of influence and attacking SOGAT's position in a most un-trade-union-like fashion. SOGAT's activists remained firmly committed to the view that until one union for the printing industry could be achieved SOGAT needed to protect its members by whatever means necessary. The union could not stand idly by and watch NGA walk over its members. Although it was determined to strive for one union for the industry, if only on the grounds that unity is strength, under no circumstances was SOGAT prepared to see this achieved by the NGA stealing their members' jobs.

The aggressive attitude of the NGA towards SOGAT in London was debated at the 1984 Biennial Delegates Council which carried unanimously a PMB motion:

This conference completely rejects the policy of the NGA concerning new technology and to that end supports any SOGAT branch or branches that are forced into a situation of opposing the NGA in reiterating SOGAT '82 previous policy of the right to follow the job.[9]

The NGA was criticised for claiming a 'God-given right to all jobs stemming from the implementation of new technology'.[10] The PMB argued that although in the future its membership might still continue to decline, it would not allow anyone to lead it to the slaughter house. Its Branch Secretary told delegates, 'My branch will fight to its last member before we allow anyone to cut us up and spread us out to all parts of the globe'.[11]

SOGAT believed it could work with the NGA in a united fashion but that the NGA must accept that all benefits from new technology implementation were not to go to the NGA. All SOGAT members had a right to follow their job, and if there were to be misery in the form of redundancies from the implementation of new technology, then that misery must be shared by all the parties concerned, including NGA members. SOGAT members considered they had a right to undertake the new jobs arising from the implementation of new technology in the press areas as they had always worked in that area. They had a legitimate expectation that they would continue to work there.

In 1989 relationships between SOGAT and the NGA in the general printing trade deteriorated even further as the NGA concluded single-union agreements for press rooms with employers opening 'greenfield sites' or, as in the majority of cases, relocating existing machinery to new premises. In some cases, employers and the NGA had adopted a single-union agreement because, *inter alia*, technological change in the press rooms was eliminating the need for semi-skilled labour. Robots could now be used to fit the reels of paper to the machines. However, in the vast majority of cases the NGA was concluding single-union agreements because the machine manager's job was being deskilled by the introduction of computer-aided control mechanisms (e.g. automatic colour register). The NGA compensated for this by its members undertaking tasks which previously they had regarded as lesser skilled, for example stacker driving and handling paper, and which traditionally had been SOGAT jobs. This behaviour of the NGA was regarded by SOGAT as nothing more than the stealing of their machine assistants' jobs.

In companies introducing the latest high-tech printing machines, a significant way in which SOGAT lost jobs was that NGA members would not retrain SOGAT members unless they joined the NGA. This, happened for example, at Royale's Colour Inserts, and CB Dorey's Westerham Press. SOGAT also lost members where firms closed down and moved to new sites. For example, when Colliersearle relocated outside London to Basingstoke, 16 SOGAT jobs were lost. They were offered redeployment to Basingstoke, but only if they joined the NGA. SOGAT regarded this as yet another example of the NGA stealing their members' jobs, reducing their future job opportunities and forcing SOGAT members into the NGA as the only means whereby they could retain employment. By mid-1990 there were 23 companies with which the NGA had concluded single-union membership agreements thereby excluding SOGAT from their press rooms.[12]

The justified anger of SOGAT members at the NGA behaviour spilled over at the SOGAT 1990 Biennial Delegate Council whilst discussing the following motion from its London Machine Branch:

> NGA Encroachment – Single Union Recognition. That this BDC is deeply concerned at the policy of encroachment being pursued by the NGA to achieve single union representation on printing machines, this being achieved by re-classification of machine assistants duties up to a junior NGA minder status, or by agreeing to carry out the recognised duties of SOGAT assistants to enable managements to sack SOGAT assistants. This action to include complaints through the TUC procedures where necessary.
>
> That this BDC supports fully the NEC policy of defending the rights of SOGAT members to work on printing machines and further instructs the NEC to take whatever action is necessary to defend SOGAT's rights to machine room areas.
>
> That this BDC supports the issuance of a policy statement from the NEC drawing direct comparison between the action of the NGA in seeking single union recognition on the press with those of the EETPU in Wapping.[13]

An amendment to the motion from the Greater Anglia Branch proposed the deletion of the last paragraph on the grounds that further slanging matches with the NGA should be avoided if the two unions were to go forward positively. Although the motion, as amended, was carried, emotions were high. The NGA was accused of being muggers, poachers, and anti-trade union in that despite having worked with and alongside SOGAT members for years, they were now actually going into work and doing SOGAT jobs. A delegate from the Multi-trades Branch urged:

206

I want to make it absolutely clear a message must go to the NGA to let them know that we do not appreciate their actions, we do not appreciate keeping on hearing about management getting involved with these single deals or enforcing them. We do not appreciate the NGA making the preference of a single union agreement. We have to be honest with each other. The reason we are putting forward motions of this nature is because we are losing a membership battle against people who are being forced into the NGA because that is the only means of employment. That is not trade unionism, that is not looking after the best interests of the industry.[14]

SOGAT was further outraged in that the NGA was concluding single-union deals more often than not behind the backs of SOGAT branch officials and openly continued his policy unabated after the terms for the amalgamation of the two unions had been reached in March 1990.

SOGAT complained to the TUC about the NGA behaviour as it considered that the alternative options of disengaging from the amalgamation talks or just accepting what the NGA was doing would lose the union credibility in the eyes of its members. SOGAT's request in March 1990 to the NGA that now an amalgamation package had been agreed it should not sign any more single deals fell on deaf ears. At a joint meeting of the two unions held on 15 March 1990 the NGA General Secretary responded to SOGAT's request that the NGA cease signing single-union agreements:

in relation to the machine room situation, the NGA cannot take on board the proposal put in totality because we do not think it practical and to a large extent is outside our control in terms of being able to deliver. At the same time we are suggesting that once the proposals are through both conferences, for the entire period of the campaign and ballot we will do our utmost to ensure there is the most positive and stable position in the industry we can possibly achieve.[15]

In April 1990, a TUC Disputes Committee met to consider the SOGAT and NGA inter-union problems in the machine rooms. SOGAT had laid 23 specific complaints against the NGA, arguing that it was not the machine assistant whose job was disappearing under new technology but that of the no. 3 machine manager. At the hearing, the

NGA argued that the problem was not just related to the three companies in the three cases being heard by the Disputes Committee – Artisan Press, Jarrolds and Redwood & Burn – but to the whole industry. The Disputes Committee accepted the pointlessness of considering the three cases in isolation and requested an inspection visit to receive further information from both unions. SOGAT was concerned at this decision and requested the TUC Disputes Committee to issue a directive to the NGA to the effect that, in the meantime, they must not sign any more single-union agreements. The Disputes Committee replied that it was not within their authority to give such an instruction but they would request, through the TUC General Secretary, that the NGA did not sign any further deals. The NGA General Secretary told the 1990 SOGAT Biennial Delegates Council that when his union formally received this TUC request it would cease signing any further single-union agreements covering commercial web-offset press without the consent of SOGAT and the TUC. However, he stressed that this commitment would end unless there was a successful merger ballot.

SOGAT accused the NGA of breaking procedures, of concluding single-union deals, of colluding with employers in companies withdrawing recognition from SOGAT, of causing SOGAT to lose members, of failing to negotiate jointly with SOGAT over the introduction of new technology into commercial printing press rooms, of creating redundancies amongst SOGAT members and of being 'muggers'. The NGA, for its part, criticised SOGAT as 'poachers turned gamekeepers' and reminded SOGAT of its behaviour towards the NGA in provincial newspapers, of the non-implementation of the Kessler Award (see below), of disputes in newspapers where SOGAT members had crossed NGA picket lines and of SOGAT's refusal to negotiate jointly with the NGA and the NUJ over the implementation of new technology in the provincial press.

SOGAT recognised technological developments were moving against its members in the machine rooms and that the TUC, at best, could only give them a temporary respite from the NGA's encroachment on their traditional job territories. Without amalgamation with the NGA it foresaw its problems in printing machine departments could only increase. Any truce would only be temporary because technological developments would not stand still. Whilst SOGAT and the NGA remained separate unions, the employers would set them against each other forcing them to compete for jobs and influence at the expense of each others' jobs and employment conditions. Both unions recognised that they would cease to influence effectively developments in the industry as separate unions. Amalgamation offered the only long-term solution if SOGAT were to have any influence and control in the printing and paper industry of the 1990s.

Newspapers

Provincial Newspapers

Over the period 1984–7 the implementation in provincial newspapers of direct entry systems from advertising departments caused serious inter-union disputes between SOGAT and the NGA despite them being involved in merger talks. The introduction of direct entry/front-end systems for the typesetting, editorial and advertising functions of producing a newspaper offered the prospect of increased bargaining power and job opportunities for SOGAT at the expense of the NGA, which had controlled the newspaper production process based on hot metal and photocomposition. Under hot metal processes the functions involved in producing a newspaper fell into separate and easily definable categories. In the advertising department, staff who were either in membership of SOGAT or in most cases of no union at all, produced advertising copy, whether received by telephone or as space sold by advertising staff and then generated by typewriter. This copy was subsequently processed and sent to the composing room, which was 100 per cent NGA organised, for typesetting, reading and page make-up. In the editorial department, journalists who were either in membership of the NUJ or in most cases no union, created copy by the use of a typewriter. This copy was subsequently processed and prepared by sub-editors. Hard copy was then sent to the sub-editor prior to being passed to the NGA compositor for typesetting. All contents of a newspaper, whether news or adverts, were typeset by NGA compositors, who also corrected their work and then assembled it in page form. The compositors' work went to the foundry where the NGA stereotyper members produced a plate for the printing process which was controlled by NGA machine managers.

The processes involved in photocomposition were not radically different from those which characterised hot metal. Compositors, by the use of VDUs on line to the photocomposition system, manipulated, recalled and corrected copy. The output from photocomposing units was a bromide paper which was subsequently assembled and made up into pages by NGA compositors. The made up pages were reproduced as a lithographic plate which was used for printing.

Direct entry, however, brought a radical change by introducing into the advertising department VDUs which were linked directly with a typesetting computer. The functions of the advertising staff replaced those of the typesetting and correction functions. It transferred key-stroking from an NGA area to one which was the province of SOGAT. Exactly the same displacement occurred between the composing and the editorial areas. Direct entry meant the advertising and editorial functions replaced stages of the production process traditionally controlled by the NGA. The implication of direct entry for SOGAT was the potential expansion of jobs in the advertising area at the cost of the composing room.

Three unions – the NGA, the NUJ and SOGAT – had an interest in the outcome of the implementation of direct entry systems in the production of provincial newspapers. Two of these unions – SOGAT and the NUJ – perceived such implementation would enhance their bargaining power and employment opportunities at the expense of the third – the NGA. SOGAT was convinced the NGA's influence in the industry would decline. By taking up a neutral position between the provincial newspaper employers and the NGA, SOGAT felt it could quicken the pace of the NGA's decline and the advent of its own enhanced bargaining power and employment opportunities. It believed its interests were best served by assisting neither the NGA nor the employers in disputes over the introduction of direct entry systems from the advertising area. SOGAT was not prepared to assist the NGA because of that union's past behaviour towards SOGAT members.

The NGA feared that if the three unions involved could not agree a common policy for the acceptance of the implementation of new technology in provincial newspapers the result would be inter-union disputes, mutual self-destruction and de-unionisation of the industry. In March 1984 the NGA issued a document entitled *The Way Forward – New Technology in the Provincial Newspaper Industry: An NGA (82) Initiative*, which sought to provide all parties – employees, union and employers – with a stake in the industry's future and a share of the benefits arising from the implementation of new technology. It hinged on four principles. The first was the need for the three unions to be united. The second was that 'unity of action' could be achieved only if all parties saw gains from co-operating with the introduction of new technology. The third envisaged a new concept of the 'origination area' combining advertising, editorial and composing functions. It proposed that origination comprise advertising, marketing, administration, editorial and composing as a single entity in which union membership would be distributed equally between SOGAT, the NUJ and the NGA. The fourth principle was that typesetting remain a unionised operation with only union members operating the new technology systems.

The NGA was unable to persuade SOGAT and the NUJ that *The Way Forward* should be the agreed approach for the acceptance of direct entry systems in provincial newspapers. In November 1984 negotiations between SOGAT and the NGA produced an agreed division of union membership of advertising departments on a 50/50 basis except where either union already had 100 per cent membership. In May 1985 SOGAT wrote to the NGA saying it was now unable to accept a joint 50/50 national membership agreement for recruitment of clerical and tele-ad staff in provincial newspapers. This followed a Consultative Conference held on 16 April 1985 of SOGAT branches with Newspaper Society members. The dominant view expressed at this conference was that clerical recruitment was an area belonging to SOGAT in that they had a national agreement with the Newspaper Society giving them recognition and negotiating rights for white-collar staff, including clerical and advertising staff. In addition, SOGAT was party to local agreements in many Newspaper Society companies.

To accept the 50/50 formula was seen by delegates as selling out areas where SOGAT had organisation for those where it had not. Other delegates expressed the view that although they understood the trauma of the compositors' jobs becoming defunct, SOGAT members should not delude themselves that if the situation was the other way around the NGA would bother itself about the plight of SOGAT members. Another argument put forward was that the national agreement covering the recruitment of non-manual employees in the provincial newspaper industry had not stopped the NGA from encroaching into these areas. In fact, SOGAT members had witnessed blatant NGA encroachment. The NGA plan for a 50/50 recruitment drive in clerical and advertising areas of newspapers was regarded as nothing more than a crude solution to its problems stemming from new technology eliminating traditional composing methods. The NGA's real motive was seen as taking over SOGAT members' jobs in the advertising departments of newspapers despite a national agreement under which the Newspaper Society recognised SOGAT as the appropriate union in this area. The NGA's argument that its members should 'follow the work' into the advertising department was seen as merely a cover for claiming the right to organise clerical staff in newspapers and to achieve its own institutional survival.

After SOGAT rejected the proposed 50/50 agreement, relationships with the NGA severely deteriorated especially when SOGAT refused to assist the NGA in the *Wolverhampton Express and Star* and the *Kent Messenger* disputes. Matters were not improved when, during the dispute the NGA was involved in with Boxfoldia in Birmingham, SOGAT allowed its machine assistants to be retrained to operate the company's lithographic presses. Matters got even worse as a result of SOGAT's behaviour at the *Liverpool Post and Echo*. In October 1985 the paper announced the introduction of direct entry systems from the editorial and advertising departments. SOGAT refused to participate in a tripartite response with the NGA and the NUJ and became involved in discussions with management to reach an agreement allowing its members to perform functions traditionally carried out by NGA members. Over the period January 1986 to December 1987, SOGAT continued to conclude direct entry agreements with a number of employers in the provincial newspaper industry in order to protect its job territory in the advertising area. In seeking to gain benefit from its policy for clerical and production members, SOGAT demanded that where new technology was implemented its members involved should receive no less than the basic rate a compositor would have received.

SOGAT/NGA inter-union problems in the provincial press centred around SOGAT's willingness to undermine the NGA by refusing to negotiate jointly with it, by crossing NGA picket lines, by doing NGA work in the machine room and by adopting a neutral stance when employers found themselves in difficulty when introducing direct entry systems from the advertising department and/or the editorial areas. The direct entry agreements concluded by SOGAT over the period 1986 to end 1987 enabled the NGA to retain control over contributed advertising copy. However, in 1988 armed with assurances from SOGAT that they would help companies that experienced difficulties in implementing technological change with the NGA and the NUJ, provincial newspaper employers challenged the NGA's retention of contributed copy. Once again SOGAT foresaw that if employers succeeded it would bring more work for its members at the expense of the NGA. The NGA's response to employers' attempts to end their hold on contributed copy was to engage in a number of unsuccessful disputes. These disputes, exemplified by that at the *South Wales Argus* led the NGA to conclude that, if employers could establish a low wage inputting section with SOGAT's support, it would be better to accede to demands for the establishment of NGA inputting sections, which would at least retain an NGA influence and involvement. SOGAT resented this and continued its neutral stance towards disputes between the employer and the NGA with the objective of enhancing work opportunities for its members and recruitment opportunities for itself.

SOGAT's behaviour in provincial newspapers led the NGA to lodge formal complaints under the TUC's Disputes Principles and Procedures. A TUC Committee, chaired by Professor Kessler, recommended a formula which identified the divisions of work between the two unions and provided for joint negotiations and closer working relationships at chapel level. The formula was rejected by SOGAT but accepted by the NGA. Following SOGAT's rejection, the NGA requested a formal TUC Disputes Committee hearing on its complaints. In 1988 the Committee issued an award supportive of the NGA's position on direct entry from the advertising area.[16] The NGA complained that SOGAT had acted, and was continuing to act against NGA interests by signing new technology agreements in the advertising areas and cited as examples the action by SOGAT at the *Evening Post*, Reading, the *Lancashire Evening Post*, Preston and the *Evening News*, Worcester. The NGA argued that the issue was an industry-wide problem and the Disputes Committee should deal with it on this basis. SOGAT, on the other hand, considered the Committee should deal with the differences between the unions case by case and make awards on an individual basis.

Since the NGA and SOGAT could not resolve their differences privately, the TUC Disputes Committee had no option but to make an award. It therefore recommended that neither union should sign or reach an understanding with any provincial newspaper about the introduction of new technology within the advertising area unless it was with the agreement of the other union and in accordance with the 'Kessler Formula' which stated:

(i)   All classified advertisement copy, sold and received over the telephone by either tele-ad sales staff and/or tele-ad canvassers be input directly. This copy was not to be re-set by the NGA origination department.

(ii) Copy for updating or alteration of previous advertisements already processed by SOGAT members would, when received

213

over the telephone or post, be input directly by the advertising staff who originally processed the advert.

(iii) When classified copy was handed over the counter and there was no facility for direct input in the front counter reception area, it should be input into the system by the NGA. The introduction of direct input into the front counter reception area was not be impeded, and where this occurred, classified copy over the counter would be directly input by SOGAT.

(iv) All other classified advertisement copy not covered by (i), (ii) or (iii) above would continue to be input into the system by the NGA.

At each provincial newspaper the two unions were recommended jointly to negotiate arrangements which enabled their members to gain improved terms and conditions of employment and that there should be no compulsory redundancy. The NGA and SOGAT were advised to ensure full trade union organisation was established in the areas covered by new technology. However, the TUC Disputes Committee award was never implemented. The clock could not be turned back and SOGAT was not prepared to return what it had gained to work jointly with the NGA.

Unfortunately, SOGAT's advancement in provincial newspapers proved only temporary. By the late 1980s all three print unions had retreated significantly in the newspaper battle. The NGA had experienced reductions of staff in the composing room by a half to two-thirds of their previous size. Employers had substituted cheaper, non-unionised labour receiving up to, in some cases, £100 per week below the negotiated rate. SOGAT had suffered derecognition and its members had experienced enforced redundancy, reduced pay and conditions, extended normal working hours and more bank holiday working. By 1990, moves towards individual contracts were being experienced by SOGAT members in white-collar areas whilst the Newspaper Society announced its intention to reduce the coverage of the National Wage Basis Agreement to minimum rates of pay, hours and holiday. However, by late 1990 many Newspaper Society affiliated companies were no longer operating the agreements whilst others were withdrawing or failing to grant recognition to SOGAT, particularly in clerical areas. Over the period 1985 to 1989, the number of SOGAT members employed in provincial newspapers fell from a peak of 8,000 to just over 4,000.

Trade unionism in newspapers suffered terribly in the second half of the 1980s. SOGAT found it difficult to resist the combination of new technology, aggressive management and anti-union laws. SOGAT and the NGA realised they could make temporary gains at the expense of each other whilst they remained separate unions. Employers' behaviour would force them, whilst they remained separate, to look after their own corners. Any truce would not last since employers would set the two unions against each other. Both unions acknowledged they would never be able as separate unions to re-organise the provincial newspaper industry, to reverse the trend towards individual contracts and to restore collective bargaining. Only amalgamation offered the possibility of a lasting solution to these problems.

Wholesale Newspaper Distribution

In the late 1980s, SOGAT not only suffered set-backs in newspaper production, but also in newspaper wholesale distribution. Many regional publishers established their own networks for the distribution of freesheet newspapers and leaflets. More sophisticated sorting and addressing equipment was expected to become available in the early 1990s threatening SOGAT members' employment security as these developments would provide door-to-door delivery of paid forms. There was also the threat that, should national newspaper titles be lost to traditional newspaper wholesaling, existing wholesale houses would be left with only short-run periodicals, local newspapers and magazines and could cease to be cost effective thus resulting in the loss of further traditional areas of SOGAT members' employment. The union decided to work together with established wholesalers to ensure an efficient and fast-turn around business for newspapers, magazines and periodicals.

The 1980s saw freesheet newspapers grow in number and circulation. In 1984 the value of advertising in weekly freesheets overtook that of weekly paid newspapers. After 1986 the value of advertising in all newspapers saw increases in real terms, but freesheet newspapers took a larger proportion of the total market, largely at the expense of the national press. However, by 1990 the same 20 companies controlling over 50 per cent of weekly freesheet newspaper circulation controlled 50 per cent of the weekly paid-for circulation.

Freesheet newspapers threatened job opportunities for SOGAT members employed in newspaper distribution. Freesheets were delivered at major railway and underground stations by self-service (bundles piled high) or by young women and to people's homes by various methods, for example pram, milk-float or pedal cycle, for payments ranging from 25p to £2. All this was happening whilst SOGAT wholesale distribution members sought to maintain their employment and uphold decent wages. Freesheet newspapers were printed 50 per cent in unionised shops and 50 per cent in non-unionised shops. SOGAT faced the challenge of how to eliminate the printing of free newssheets in non-union houses and ensure they were printed in union houses and distributed by legitimate wholesalers. Freesheet newspaper growth caused the closure of paid-for newspapers and redundancies amongst SOGAT members. In the early 1980s, the *Islington Gazette*, published for 120 years, closed, as did the *Tottenham and Hornsey Journal* which had been published for 125 years. The *Croydon Advertiser* and the *Kentish Times*, both of which were long-established papers employing many SOGAT members, closed. Members' concerns over these threats from the growth of freesheet newspapers were raised at the 1983 Biennial Delegate Council Meeting in a successful motion moved by the London Central Branch:

> This Conference of SOGAT '82 deplores the attitude of the printing unions in their failure to apply a positive opposition thus creating an erosion of job opportunity in distribution and instructs the NEC to organise in this area without delay.[17]

SOGAT remained opposed to freesheets because they competed with paid-for newspapers, opened up an area of exploitation of young children and destroyed legitimate employment within newspaper distribution. In the early 1980s SOGAT was the only print union persistently objecting to the printing of freesheets. The NUJ and the NGA initially supported the production of freesheets. However, in Scotland, SOGAT exercised tight control over freesheets due to the fact the union organised employees from the compositor and machine manager downwards on the printing of freesheet newspapers.

By 1984 SOGAT employment in the distribution of national newspapers was threatened from the distribution of these papers by road haulage in which the recognised union was the T&GWU. National newspaper owners alleged that the traditional transport sources of distribution were inefficient and an alternative distribution system should be supported. Wholesale distribution was one of the life bloods of SOGAT and created many jobs for its members with good staffing and realistic wage levels. In both Manchester and London the national newspaper delivery vehicles driven by SOGAT members were serviced by employees in the same union. SOGAT opposed attempts by national newspaper employers to switch distribution from traditional transport sources. The 1984 Delegate Council Meeting agreed that a message be sent to the national newspaper owners stating that any attempts on their part to repudiate current methods of working or staffing levels would be met with the strongest possible force.

By 1990, the Murdoch and Maxwell companies had developed interests in newspaper distribution. For Maxwell this was through Newsflow and for Murdoch through his Circle K newsagent and convenience chains as well as a minority stake in TNT. The dominant feature of the 1980s in the distribution of national newspapers was undoubtedly the withdrawal of News International from traditional distribution methods. This action was subsequently followed by nearly every national newspaper publisher. The use of TNT to by-pass the British Rail system and to provide a direct delivery to London newsagents was introduced during the Wapping dispute. Soon afterwards, Maxwell set up the Newsflow operation. In TNT, the T&GWU was the recognised union, whilst sole recognition rights for Newsflow employees were granted to the NUR. These moves excluded SOGAT from traditional areas of organisation. At the 1988 Biennial Delegate Council Meeting an emergency motion on distribution was accepted because of the concern with national newspaper titles transferring from rail to road and the concentration of this road transport in the hands of TNT and Newsflow. Associated with these changes in newspaper distribution were considerable redundancies amongst SOGAT drivers, train packers, station men, etc.

SOGAT's concern about the increasing concentration of newspaper wholesale distribution was raised at a motion to the 1989 TUC and Labour Party Conference. This was followed by SOGAT launching a campaign on the issue of monopoly control in wholesale distribution of newspapers and magazines. In early 1990 News International reduced the number of regional wholesalers with which it dealt from 1,000 to 182 regional franchises. With TNT carrying all News International titles plus the *Daily Telegraph* and *Sunday Telegraph* and Newsflow handling most other national newspapers, changes were forced upon retail newsagents. Although the established large wholesalers such as John Menzies, W.H. Smith and Surridge Dawson saw their profit margins squeezed by an enforced tendering process, the small wholesalers were decimated. The tendering process caused the total demise of the independent Sunday wholesaler and with it the SOGAT agreement with the Sunday wholesalers employers' association. Members of the Federation of London Wholesale Newspaper Distributors (FLWND) also suffered badly. So many member firms failed to survive, that in October 1989 SOGAT was informed that the FLWND would merge with the Association of Newspaper and Magazine Wholesalers. Many smaller wholesalers had gone out of business or been taken over by larger companies. This, in turn, gave big wholesalers an unexpected boost in some areas of their business, for example, Sunday newspapers and the distribution of magazines, periodicals and weeklies.

The national newspaper industry had originally dismissed the possibility of News International going direct to retail. However, by 1990 it looked as though London would be the Achilles' heel for home delivery which was being championed by the Mirror Group. Publishers sought faster turn-around times and a better service from the wholesaler. TNT was running an efficient wholesaling practice in London, offering an alternative to the existing trade and in this way they remained a serious threat to the established method of wholesale distribution. Although TNT lost a number of wholesale franchises in 1989, unfortunately for SOGAT only two of the lost franchises was gained by W.H. Smith and John Menzies, both of whom employed many SOGAT members. The others went to independents that did not employ any SOGAT members. With the advent of the 1992 Single European Market and the associated opening of the Channel Tunnel, SOGAT foresaw a further threat to its members employed in the wholesale distribution of magazines and newspapers.

The loss of SOGAT jobs in wholesale distribution was serious. Prior to the mid-1980s the industry had been very labour-intensive with little mechanisation. A stable, permanent labour force was supplemented by casual employment, with 'casuals' being supplied by the SOGAT London Central Branch. The union needed alternative employment opportunities for its London and provincial wholesale newspaper and periodical distribution members. This was more likely to happen via an amalgamation with the NGA than by merging with a large general union. One impact of technological change, increased product market competition and employment law changes in the 1980s was that in that decade SOGAT's membership fell by over one-third, which had implications for its finances and ability to service its membership effectively.

Amalgamation with the NGA offered a means of alleviating this problem. Although the case for one union for the printing industry had long been championed by SOGAT and the NGA, it had taken a long time, for various reasons, for the two unions to enter serious negotiations to achieve this end. These negotiations were to be protracted, difficult and at times acrimonious. It is to the negotiations to create the Graphical and Media Union that we now turn.

NOTES

1. See *SOGAT Journal*, April 1983, p. 2.
2. See Society of Graphical and Allied Trades (82) *Report of the Biennial Delegate Council Meeting, 1984*, p. 285. The motion, which was 'with current disputes going on, the urgent need for unions within print is to amalgamate speedily to one union', was moved by the London Women's Branch. The Glasgow and West of Scotland Branch amended the motion, accepted by the Women's Branch, to include 'such action to take place on the conclusion of the BDC as a matter of urgency'.
3. Society of Graphical and Allied Trades (82) *Report of the Biennial Delegate Council Meeting, 1990*, p. 21.
4. Op. cit., p. 22.
5. See Report on Papermaking Industry presented by George Beattie to the Society of Graphical and Allied Trades (82) *Report of the Biennial Delegate Council Meeting, 1990*, p. 18.
6. Amongst craft employees the EETPU had 21 per cent of union membership compared with 49 per cent for the AEU and 3 per cent for UCATT. Amongst unionised process workers 85 per cent were in SOGAT, 5 per cent in the T&GWU and 2 per cent in the GMBU. Taking all manual workers, the percentages were SOGAT 70 per cent, AEU 9 per cent T&GWU 5 per cent, EETPU 4 per cent, GMB, 2 per cent and UCATT 1 per cent. Despite the traumas of the 1980s, trade union membership held up remarkably well. Throughout the 1980s trade union density remained almost constant.
7. Society of Graphical and Allied Trades (82) *Report of the Biennial Delegate Council Meeting, 1983*, pp. 57–8.
8. Op. cit., pp. 119–20.
9. Society of Graphical and Allied Trades (82) *Report of the Biennial Delegate Council Meeting, 1984*, p. 283.
10. Op. cit.
11. Op. cit.
12. These companies included Royale's Colour Inserts, C.B. Doreys, Colliersearle, Artison Press in Leicester, Jarrolds in East Anglia and Redwood & Bun in Bristol. In fact, the companies ranged from Southampton to Carlisle and Wales to the Wash.
13. Society of Graphical and Allied Trades (82) *Report of the Biennial Delegate Council Meeting, 1990*, p. 59.
14. Op. cit., p. 60.

15. Op. cit., p. 25.
16. See TUC *Congress Report, 1988*, pp. 12–14.
17. See Society of Graphical and Allied Trades (82) *Report of the Delegate Council Policy Conference, 1983*, p. 95.

CHAPTER 9

THE ACTUAL MERGER OF SOGAT (82) AND THE NGA (82)

The NGA (82) came into being on 29 March 1982 with the amalgamation of SLADE and the National Graphical Association.[1] The latter had been created by an amalgamation in January 1964 of the London Typographical Society (LTS) and the Typographical Association (TA).[2] Between 1964 and March 1982, five other print unions transferred their engagements into the NGA.[3] Over the period 1964 to 1991 the NGA's membership diversified from a craft to an industrial base. On its formation in 1964 it was a union of compositors, readers and letterpress machine managers. At the time of the merger with SOGAT, in addition to these groups it organised telegraphist operators and technicians, stereotypers and electrotypers, litho plate-makers, litho machine managers, litho artists, designers and engravers, camera operators, tele-ad operators, wage clerks, sales staff, supervisors, tin printers, silk screen printers, pre-press, press and finishing trades in the wallcoverings' industry. In March 1991, NGA membership stood at 130,000. Another feature of its membership was a growing number of female members. In 1972 it had only 203 female members, but by 1991 this figure had increased to 8,000.

A misconception about the NGA was that it was a predominantly newspaper-based union. At the peak of its membership, only 10 per cent were employed in provincial newspapers and 5 per cent in national newspapers. Eighty-five per cent of its membership were employed in the general printing, packaging and tin printing industries. It had no members in the papermaking or ink-making industries. The NGA had members working in England, Wales, Northern Ireland, Scotland, the Republic of Ireland, the Isle of Man and the Channel Islands.

THE AMALGAMATION NEGOTIATIONS, 1983–90

In the NGA merger negotiations, SOGAT was guided by a number of basic principles. First, its members should not be required to pay contribution increases over and above that agreed in the SOGAT Rules of 10p per week per year. SOGAT members did not want to pay in a merged union the higher rates that existed in the NGA but only those rates already agreed for SOGAT members. Second, there be no reduction or freezing of the SOGAT Branch Allowance for a period of time to equalise the levels in the two unions. SOGAT branches retained 40 per cent of the national contribution whilst NGA branches retained 21 per cent. Third, there would be no compulsory merging of chapels. Chapels should be encouraged to merge but not be compelled to do so. Chapels would elect their own representatives on the basis of existing procedures. SOGAT was not prepared to accept dictation from the national level as to what the chapel structure and representation in the merged union should be. SOGAT wanted one chapel within each of the companies where the merged union would be represented. However, the reality was that in SOGAT 80 per cent of the companies in which it had representations, had more than one chapel.

Fourth, any amalgamation at national level must be reflected at branch level and at the date of amalgamation SOGAT branches should know their future. SOGAT was seeking a 'branch blueprint' mapping out how the branches of the two unions would be merged. The principle to underlie the 'blueprint' was that wherever possible there would be no break-up of existing SOGAT and NGA branches. In adopting this principle, SOGAT realised it meant larger branches in the merged union but believed the only alternative would be to start the exercise as though the two unions were starting with a blank sheet and let the merged union decide the new boundaries. This, however, would mean the breaking up of the majority of existing SOGAT branches, and to gain acceptance for this from branches would be 'well nigh impossible'.

Fifth, in the merged union no SOGAT members should suffer reduced financial benefits relative to those already being received. National benefits should remain at no lower level than existed in SOGAT at the time of any amalgamation. Sixth, the special interests of SOGAT's 30,000 members employed in papermaking and paper conversion be adequately provided for and the word 'Paper' be included in the title. Some senior

SOGAT officials had been disappointed when SOGAT (82) was formed that the word 'Paper' was not in its title.[4]

Although the amalgamation panels met regularly in 1983 and 1984, they did not meet at all from autumn 1984 to February 1986 as the prospects of negotiating a package were low given the inter-union warfare between the two unions in the provincial press. The amalgamation talks were revived in March 1986 with both unions pledging themselves to reach agreement within 12 months. The 1986 SOGAT Biennial Delegate Council recognised the difficulties of merging two unions with different cultures and long-established traditions but nevertheless felt negotiations should proceed at a more urgent pace. The delegates requested a full report on the progress of amalgamation talks be made in 1988 and, if at all possible, before. As requested, the 1988 Biennial Delegate Council received a document entitled *Interim and Progress Report on the Amalgamation Talks Between SOGAT (82) and NGA (82)*, which reported that agreement had been reached on a decision-making structure for the merged union, on its senior officerships, on the election of the National Executive and on the Delegate Conference.

The merged union would have a National Council/National Executive Council comprising 40 members elected on a geographical basis by and from the members. There would be no provision for separate or sectional representation. The first NC/NEC would hold office for a three-year term, but after that its term of office would be two years. On the initial NC/NEC there would be guaranteed equality of representation for former SOGAT and former NGA members. After the initial NC/NEC had completed its term of office, future NC/NEC would be on the principle of 'best person government' with no guaranteed representation for former SOGAT and former NGA members. To ensure there was no perpetuation of the 'guaranteed representation' principle, the amalgamation ballot paper and the new union's Rule Book would state that after the three-year interim period, guaranteed representation would cease. It had also been agreed that the new union would not place any restrictions on eligibility for election to the NC/NEC. SOGAT permitted lay members and full-time Branch Secretaries to be elected to its NEC. The NGA permitted only a 'lay' executive. In the interest of gaining a successful amalgamation package, the NGA was prepared to accept that the SOGAT system should operate in the new union.

The only organisation that would be recognised at the shop-floor level in the new union would be chapels. SOGAT and NGA chapels would be encouraged wherever possible and practical to amalgamate. This would be on a voluntary basis but where this proved difficult the approach would be to encourage, at house level, the formation of an imperial chapel. However, whether this happened would be left for discussion and agreement between the chapels concerned. Although there would be no enforced chapel amalgamations, it was envisaged that chapel mergers would progress in a positive manner as branches amalgamated.

The merged union would hold a Delegate Council Meeting biennially thus continuing the existing practice of the two unions. The Delegate Council Meeting would consist of approximately 500 delegates and branch representation would be one delegate per 600 members with an additional delegate for each complete additional 600 members. The merged union's first Delegate Meeting would determine industrial and other policy issues whilst the second Delegate Meeting would be a rules revision and industrial and policy issues conference.

Previous amalgamations in which both SOGAT and the NGA had been involved had usually resolved the issue of the General Secretaryship of the new union by the mechanism of a Joint General Secretaryship. However, the General Secretaries of SOGAT and the NGA both had considerable periods of office in front of them. A similar position existed with the Presidents. The amalgamation panels agreed that a Joint General Secretaryship which would last for many years was not practicable and agreed a procedure to decide who would be General Secretary within the new union. In the event of an amalgamation package proving acceptable to the two memberships, before vesting day a second ballot vote of the membership of two unions would take place to decide which of the two existing General Secretaries would become the General Secretary of the new union. Whoever was unsuccessful would become the Deputy General Secretary which would be designated in the Rule Book as the merged union's second most senior officer. The same procedure would operate to decide which of the existing two General Presidents would take the posts of General President and Vice President within the merged union.

The amalgamation panels had agreed that in the new union the SOGAT subscription level would become the basic level of contribution and the 10p per week annual increase currently provided for in the SOGAT Rule Book would also operate. The merged union would provide a minimum level of benefits for all members equal to SOGAT's current level of benefits. In addition, it was accepted there would be a supplementary Provident Fund and a supplementary Dispute Fund into which all NGA members, prior to vesting day, would continue to contribute and in return receive supplementary unemployment and dispute benefit payments. It would be optional for former SOGAT members to pay into these funds and in return receive the supplementary benefits.

The *Interim and Progress Report* stressed there were a number of areas where agreement was still to be reached. These included the location of the Head Office of the new union, the timetable for completing the amalgamation talks, branch boundaries, branch allowances, the Officers' and Staff Pension Fund, and the rules of the merged union. The report contained some draft proposals concerning branch amalgamations, the central feature of which was the period of three years after the formation of the new union for local branch mergers to be worked out. This suggestion was purely for discussion and consultation and not imposition. Its guiding principle was the 'minimum disturbance' to existing branch boundaries of the two unions. The 1988 SOGAT Biennial Delegate Council overwhelmingly carried the *Interim and Progress Report* on the amalgamation talks.

The negotiations over financial and branch boundary issues were difficult and at times acrimonious. At an amalgamation meeting held on 27 January 1989, the NGA argued that the branch merger talks were making little progress and if both unions waited until all the branches had reached agreement the amalgamation would not materialise. The NGA suggested three options. First, the unions could abandon the talks and inform the branches they must merge and make progress. Second, they could take the branch boundaries 'blueprint' document off the agenda, put it to one side and concentrate on securing an amalgamation. Third, following withdrawal of the branch boundaries 'blueprint' the National Executive of the new union be given the right to determine all branch boundaries. In taking this action the new Executive should consult with the existing SOGAT and NGA branches, but if branch mergers could not be achieved within a period of three to five years, then the National Executive should impose branch mergers. In implementing this third option, the guiding principle would be one geographically based branch for each area. This third option was the NGA's preferred way of resolving the branch boundaries issues.

The NGA also indicated that it was against the continuation of the

SOGAT Clerical, Managerial and Sales Branch as a national branch. However, SOGAT argued that if the NGA-preferred option for dealing with branch boundaries was accepted then the final decision on the status of the CMS Branch should be decided at a later date by the National Executive. The NGA expressed its strong opposition to SOGAT's Electrical and Technical Services Branch continuing as a national branch. This branch had been set up to recruit all electricians in the printing industry and SOGAT branches already having electricians in membership had been expected to transfer these into the branch, although few had done so. The branch had a membership of 419 and a seat on the SOGAT Executive. The NGA feared national branches within the new union might lead to some of its own small groups of membership, for example the press telegraphists, to demand similar status in the new union.

In April 1989, SOGAT withdrew the branch boundaries 'blueprint' document recognising the only way to move the merger talks forward was to have the question of branch amalgamations decided within the new union. SOGAT, in the interests of gaining a successful amalgamation package, accepted the NGA's view with one exception, namely, that the Executive of the new union, after discussion and consultation with the branches should bring branch structure proposals for consideration by the first National Delegate Meeting of the new union to be held in 1993. In considering these Executive Council's proposals the delegates would have authority to accept, amend, refer back or reject all or part of the proposals. Following the 1993 Conference there would be a three-year period in which the branch proposals would be implemented. The 1996 Delegate Meeting would receive a progress report on branch structure and branches which had not complied with the 1993 agreed branch structure proposals would have the opportunity to appeal to the Delegate Meeting who would be the final arbiters on branch merger disputes. No branches would be forced to amalgamate before 1996. Branches which had not merged by then and subsequently lost their appeal to the 1996 delegate meeting, would be forced to merge as per the 1993 agreed branch structure proposals. SOGAT had persuaded the NGA to agree that the final arbiter on branch boundaries would be the Delegate Meeting and not the National Executive Council, as preferred by the NGA.

In April 1989 the NGA accepted that although they were opposed, in principle, to national branches within the new union, SOGAT's CMS Branch would continue in the merged union. In return SOGAT agreed that the branch would not recruit or take into membership former NGA members in areas where the NGA had recognition or organisation. Only a Delegate Meeting would have power to change the status of the CMS Branch. Another problem branch was the Electrical and Technical Services Branch which had been formed when the 'Fleet Street' electricians left the EETPU and joined SOGAT. The NGA's opposition to the continuation of this Branch was different from that towards the CMS Branch. Although the Branch had been recruiting electricians in the papermaking sector outside London, the NGA was adamant the Branch remain in the new union as a purely London-based branch. After much debate SOGAT accepted this view as they believed the issue could not be allowed to stand in the way of achieving an acceptable amalgamation package. The Electrical and Technical Services Branch would have no organisational remit on a national basis, and would be limited to the London area.[5]

There was considerable discussions as to the location of the Head Office of the merged union since neither the SOGAT Head Office at Hadleigh in Essex or the NGA Head Office in Bedford was suitable. In January 1989 an investigation of the issue was undertaken by the Financial Secretaries of the unions assisted by professional advice and given certain guidelines, such as any new Head Office should be easily accessible and within easy reach of main motorway, rail and air links, and be able to accommodate meetings of the Executive and the increased number of officers and staff. The ideal would have been to move to a new Head Office, but the investigation of the Financial Secretaries revealed that whatever location was chosen a new Head Office would be expensive. The amalgamation panels agreed, after much debate, that the new union's Head Office would have to be one of the two existing Head Offices. Neither union, however, would agree to the other's Head Office being that for the new union. It was agreed that a trade unionist be approached to look at the two Head Offices from an accommodation, travel, location and other related matters, point of view. Moss Evans, former General Secretary of the T&GWU, was given the task of deciding which union's Head Office become that of the new union. His recommendation, accepted by the SOGAT, was that the NGA's Head Office was the more suitable for the merged union.[6]

SOGAT had an Officer and Staff Pension Fund to which all the officers and staff at whatever level were members. However, the NGA had three different pension schemes – the SLADE Superannuation and Pension Fund, the Litho Printers' Superannuation Fund and the Pension Fund for Officers and Staff – all of them for Head Office personnel. The NGA did not provide a national pension facility for branch officials and staff. It was up to each NGA branch to make its own pension arrangements for staff and officers. However, after lengthy discussions between SOGAT Officers' and Staff Pension Trustees, SOGAT's professional advisers and the NGA it was agreed the SOGAT Officers' and Staff Pension Fund become the pension fund of the merged union. Those already in NGA national officers' and Staff Pension Schemes or branch pension schemes would not be required to transfer into the new union's pension scheme.

In January 1989 SOGAT announced its aim was to complete the merger talks by April 1989, put the proposal before the Executive Councils of the two unions, followed by a special Recall Delegates Conferences during May, June and July, membership ballots at the end of July 1989 and vesting day for the new union to be mid-1990. The NGA thought this timetable optimistic and proposed the talks be completed by July 1989, the National Executives receive reports in August and September, special Delegate Meetings be called and the ballot of the memberships take place in January or February 1990. However, because of difficult negotiations over the financial structure of the new union the timetable for completing the amalgamation was not agreed until early 1990. The amalgamation package would be put to the respective Executives in April 1990 and considered by the Delegate Meetings of the two unions in May 1990 in the case of SOGAT and June 1990 in the case of NGA. A ballot of the two memberships would take place in November 1990 with the result announced on 20 December 1990. If the membership ballots produced a vote in favour of amalgamation this would be followed by the General Secretary election, then the General President election, then the NEC elections and vesting day for the new union would be July 1991.

Initially it had been agreed the national contributions to the General Fund of the new union by the members of the two unions would be equalised over a five-year period. Given that SOGAT branches retained 40 per cent of this contribution, but NGA branches only 21 per cent, NGA members would pay more into the General Fund than SOGAT members. Over the five-year period, SOGAT members would pay their normal 10p per week increase each April as provided for in the SOGAT Rules, whereas NGA(82) members would have only a 3p or 4p increase in the final year to achieve, within the five-year period, full equalisation of contributions to the new union.

However, in late 1989, the NGA became concerned about the financial projections for the merged union even though these predicted a surplus in the first few years of operation of the new union. The predicted surplus was below the £2m considered necessary by the NGA if the new union was to be viable. Two alternative proposals, both of which would mean SOGAT members paying an increase in subscriptions over and above that currently agreed in the SOGAT Rules were put forward. SOGAT rejected both these proposals and tabled its own. One suggested subscriptions for members of the new union should increase annually by the 10p per week already agreed for the first two years of the new union's operation. During that two-year period the Executive Council of the new union would assess the new union's income and expenditure and then put to a Rules Revision Conference of the merged union firm proposals on contribution rates. A second proposal was there be a 10p contribution rate rise in each of the first two years of operation of the new union whilst the Executive Council explored the possibility of a two-tier contribution system being introduced in the merged union subject to the agreement of a delegate meeting. SOGAT considered these proposals ensured the new union began on a firm financial footing whilst careful consideration was given to the establishment of a fairer financial structure for the longer term.[7]

Although the NGA remained convinced that an increase in contributions was necessary, it agreed, in the interests of securing an amalgamation package, that the present SOGAT increase introduced in 1983 of 10p per week implemented each April, should apply for the first two years of the new union. However, this acceptance was conditional on the first Delegate Meeting of the merged union considering proposals on the future structure of contribution rates and such proposals, once approved, being accepted by a ballot of the membership. SOGAT accepted that the final decision on future contribution rates should lie with the membership, although this was contrary to its existing practice whereby the final authority on contribution increases lay with the delegates to the Biennial Delegate Council.

SOGAT branches would continue to retain up to 40 per cent of the General Fund contributions at the time of merger and the NGA branches 21 per cent. However, from the first 10p a week increase, branches could retain 3p with the remaining 7p going the national union. The same would apply to the 10p increase in the second year. However, the first Delegate Council Meeting of the merged union, to be held in 1993, would receive proposals to equalise the branch allowance. Branches would be able to table a motion on the branch allowance. The 1993 Delegate Council Meeting of the new union would finalise the equalisation of branch allowances and the membership would decide on contribution rates.

THE AMALGAMATION PACKAGE

The Name of the Union

The merged union was to be called the Graphical, Paper and Media Union (GPMU) with its Head Office located at Bedford. The inclusion of the word 'Paper' in the title was in recognition of the interests of SOGAT's papermaking members. The GPMU, with 300,000 members, was the largest printing and paper trade union in the world and the sixth largest union affiliated to the TUC.

Contributions

At vesting day, the national contributions for full members would be £1.66 per week. The rate would apply until April 1992 when it would increase by 10p per week. A further 10p increase in the rate would apply from April 1993. At the 1993 Delegate Council Meeting the Executive Council would table proposals to equalise contribution rates and the branch allowance. Any increase in contribution rates approved at the Meeting would require confirmation in a membership ballot before implementation. In accepting these proposals, SOGAT fulfilled its commitment to its members that they would not have to pay higher contribution rates or the branches receive lower branch allowances as a result of any amalgamation package.

Benefits

All benefits provided for in the SOGAT Rule Book would be maintained in the GPMU. An unemployment benefit of £10 per week for ten weeks would be payable from the General Fund. Contributors to the Supplementary Provident Fund would receive a 'top-up' payment of £23 for ten weeks and then a payment of £33 for a further 16 weeks. A Dispute Benefit of £12 per week for 20 weeks would be payable from the General Fund. Those contributing to the Supplementary Dispute Fund would receive a 'top-up' of £48 for 20 weeks. Retired NGA members would receive from the Supplementary Provident Fund an annual superannuation grant of between £12 and £20 based on their length of full membership.

Any former SOGAT members or new members who opt to contribute to the Supplementary Funds would accrue entitlement from the date they first paid subscriptions to the funds. All former NGA members were required to contribute to the Supplementary, Provident and Dispute Funds. All former SOGAT members were to have the option of contributing to the Supplementary Provident/Dispute Funds. After vesting day, all new members working in traditional NGA areas would be required to contribute to the Supplementary Funds. New members employed in traditional SOGAT areas would have the option of contributing to the funds.

In the case of the NGA Provident Fund all income from investments was paid into that fund. It was inappropriate in the new union for the General Fund investment income to be transferred to the supplementary funds of which all former NGA members but not all former SOGAT members would be beneficiaries. However, to ensure viability of the Supplementary Provident Fund, the new union proposed to transfer properties investments from its General Fund to its Provident Fund. SOGAT was angered by this action, viewing it as transferring money to the almost exclusive use of former NGA members rather than for the good of the wider membership of the new union.

SOGAT had achieved its objective that national benefits in the new union should be at a level at least equal to those existing in SOGAT and that none of its benefits should be reduced as a result of amalgamation. It was optional for former SOGAT members to pay increased weekly contributions to gain supplementary unemployment and dispute benefit. The SOGAT convalescent home benefit would be available to all GPMU members who would have access to rest and recreation centres at Ayr in Scotland and Rottingdean in Sussex.

Chapels

All chapels would continue to elect FOC/MOCs to conduct the affairs of the chapel. No compulsory amalgamation of chapels would take place and they would continue to operate as they were currently

231

structured until they decided to merge. These arrangements meant that SOGAT had achieved its objective of its members not having to accept dictation from the national level on the chapel structure and representation.

Branches

Both SOGAT and the NGA in the main operated geographically based branches which for the most part were serviced by 'full-time' branch officers. The GPMU would continue and expand the concept of 'full-time' administered branches, providing it improved the service to the membership.

Branch Structure

The SOGAT CMS Branch would continue as a national branch. However, it would not recruit or take into membership former NGA members 'from areas where that union had recognition or organisation. The SOGAT Electrical Technical Services and Plumbing Branch would not have a national organisational remit, but would be limited to London. The GPMU Executive Council would consider the future branch structure and submit, branch structure proposals to the first GPMU Delegate Meeting to be held in 1993. In considering branch structure proposals the delegates would have authority to accept, amend, refer back or reject all or parts of the proposals. The 1996 Delegate Meeting would receive a progress report on branch structure and branches which had not complied with the agreed structure proposals would have the opportunity to appeal to the Delegate Meeting which would be the final arbiters on the proposals. If a branch lost its appeal then it would have to comply with the Executive Council's branch structure proposals.

Branch Rules

Both NGA and SOGAT branches were semi-autonomous and their constitutions and methods of operation varied from branch to branch. However, all branch rules, before they become operative, would require the endorsement of the Executive Council of the GPMU. A set of guidelines would provide the minimum standards to be contained within the rules of a GPMU branch.

Branch Allowances

SOGAT branches received a branch allowance of up to 40 per cent. NGA branches received an allowance of 21 per cent. In the GPMU, of a 10p increase in basic contributions 3p would be allocated to the branches and 7p to Head Office. However, this would apply for only the first two years of the GPMU. The first delegate meeting would receive from the Executive Council proposals designed to equalise the branch allowance.

Regions

Nine regions[8] would exist as electoral constituencies for representation to the National Executive Council, for consultation with Executive Council and for the exchange of information. Each region would hold an annual Consultative Conference but would have no authority to determine GPMU policy. The CMS Branch would be a region for the purpose of Executive Council elections but in all other elections its members would stand for election as representatives of the region in which they worked. Existing NGA regional officials and SOGAT organisers would become GPMU officers accountable to the Executive Council and charged to assist branches in the particular geographical area for which they were responsible. The allocation of work to regional officers/organisers would be done by GPMU Head Office.

The National Executive Council

The initial GPMU Executive Council would be 40 members made up of 20 former NGA representatives and 20 former SOGAT representatives. It would hold office for three years and three months but subsequent Councils would sit for two years. After the initial GPMU Executive Council subsequent ones would consist of 37 people elected on the basis of 'best-person' government. There would be no restrictions on eligibility of members for election to the Executive Council. Lay members and members employed as 'full-time' branch officials could seek nomination and election. Any rule changes agreed at the 1993 GPMU Delegate Meeting in regard to eligibility for nomination and election to the Executive Council would not apply until the 1996 Executive Council Elections. The longer time period of office for the first Executive Council was to provide the continuity considered necessary to deal with the consequences and problems arising from the amalgamation. It was to bring proposals to the first Delegate Meeting to resolve, on a permanent basis, issues the amalgamation panels had resolved temporarily. An initial Executive Council with guaranteed representation was necessary if the members of the two merging unions were to be satisfied their interests would be properly considered by a Council charged with forwarding proposals on important issues to the initial Delegate Meeting.

The Biennial Delegate Council

The number of branch delegates at the Biennial Delegate Council was to be determined on the basis of one delegate for all branches with a membership of up to 600 and an additional delegate for each complete 600 members. The first Delegate Conference, due to be held in June 1993, would consider proposals from the Executive Council on financial issues, general policy and branch amalgamations. In 1994, the second GPMU Delegate Council would be a full policy and rule change meeting.

The Women's Committee

The GPMU National Executive Council would be advised by a Women's Committee whose constitution would be set down in the Rule Book.

Journal

A union journal published ten times per year would be distributed free to all members. There would also be a quarterly publication.[9]

Officer Structure

The GPMU would have the following officers – General Secretary, Deputy General Secretary, General President, Vice President, Assistant General Secretary, Financial Secretary, Organising Secretary, a national officer with particular responsibility for papermaking, boardmaking and conversion and as many additional officers considered to be necessary for the conduct the affairs of the union and service effectively the membership. The General Secretaryship would be determined by a ballot of the membership. The unsuccessful candidate would become

234

the Deputy General Secretary. The posts of President and Vice President would also be determined by the same mechanism.

The Vice President position would exist only so long as it was occupied by either the current General President of SOGAT or the current General President of the NGA. The Assistant General Secretary post would continue only so long as occupied by the current Assistant General Secretary of the NGA. At vesting day there would be two joint Financial Secretaries but should either of them leave or retire then the remaining 'Joint' Financial Secretary would become the Financial Secretary. The retention of a Papermaking Secretary fulfilled SOGAT's commitment to its papermaking members to protect their special interests within the GPMU. SOGAT constantly argued that the merged union would be employing too many officers. It preferred a reduction in the number of national officers but when this could not be obtained it was content to accept that the Executive Council determine the GPMU officer establishment.

An amalgamation package had been agreed, but there were those in SOGAT who considered it had been achieved at the price of too many concessions. There were those, however, who considered that even if this were the case, given it was inconceivable that SOGAT's candidate would not gain the GPMU General Secretaryship, concessions could be gradually taken back. The amalgamation talks had lasted over six years during which time the balance of bargaining power between the two unions had changed. In the early stages of the talks the NGA had the greater need for the amalgamation as it sought a common union approach to the implementation of new technology in provincial newspapers so as to protect its compositor members. It was prepared to make concessions to SOGAT and to resist attempts to provoke it into breaking off amalgamation talks. SOGAT too wanted an amalgamation but considered that by 'spinning out' the talks it could render the NGA less powerful with SOGAT gaining an even better amalgamation deal. However, by the late 1980s SOGAT's enhanced bargaining power in newspapers had not materialised and the NGA was forcing it out of the press rooms in the general trade. It was SOGAT which now saw the greater need for the amalgamation and was now prepared to make concessions it would not have considered earlier. The NGA recognised it could now gain even more concessions. Tony Dubbins, the NGA General Secretary was prepared to squeeze the last possible concession from SOGAT but not to the extent SOGAT left the amalgamation talks.

SELLING THE PACKAGE TO THE MEMBERSHIP

In April 1990 the SOGAT National Executive Council recommended the amalgamation package go to a ballot of the membership, and the May 1990 Biennial Delegate Council should start a day earlier to allow full discussion of the amalgamation package. Tony Dubbins, NGA General Secretary, addressed the May 1990 SOGAT Biennial Delegate Council whilst Brenda Dean, SOGAT General Secretary, addressed the NGA June 1990 Delegate Meeting. At the SOGAT 1990 Biennial Delegate Council, Brenda Dean, General Secretary, moved on behalf of the National Executive Council the following motion which was carried by 262 votes to 44.

> This Biennial Delegate Meeting of SOGAT(82) endorses the terms concluded for the amalgamation of SOGAT(82) and the NGA(82) to form the Graphical, Paper and Media Union and agrees that the terms be put to a ballot vote of the membership with a recommendation to vote for amalgamation.[10]

SOGAT now began a campaign amongst its membership to secure a 'yes' vote for the merger. The October 1990 issue of the *SOGAT Journal* was an amalgamation special issue explaining to the members why lay activitists, Branch secretaries and national officers were committed to amalgamation and why, in their own words, they supported the amalgamation package.[11] SOGAT also distributed to its membership a list of materials, including a 'question and answer' booklet giving the reasons why the National Executive Council strongly recommended amalgamation and so the members would know exactly what they were voting for. These materials presented sound industrial reasons for the amalgamation, for example, a single union for workers in the industry, more muscle power in negotiating better pay and conditions, enhanced services and the elimination of wasteful duplication of effort. Some materials produced were also on the lighter side, a bit of fun, albeit with the same serious underlying message. The SOGAT amalgamation materials aimed to make members talk about the issues themselves since it was probably the most important issue upon which they had being asked to vote. The General Secretary, Brenda Dean remarked, 'I am absolutely certain that it is the most vital decision SOGAT (82) members will have taken for decades and the one which will effect the future of their union, beyond all others'[12]

After a long campaign the ballot result on amalgamation was announced on 20 December 1990. For SOGAT, 74,883 members voted in favour of merger and 13,078 against. For the NGA, 51,859 members voted in favour of merger with SOGAT (82) and 19,212 against. The long-held dream of a single production union for the printing, publishing, packaging and papermaking industries had been achieved. The GPMU inherited a rich and proud legacy from both SOGAT, whose roots went back to 1786 as the Journeymen Bookbinders of London, and the NGA, which had evolved from various typographical societies originating in the 1790s. Although SOGAT and NGA were the results of many previous amalgamations none had ever been so momentous as the creation of the GPMU.

Four main arguments had been used to persuade SOGAT members that amalgamation with the NGA was in their best interests. First, that merger was not being pushed. Second, there were benefits to be gained from a merger, and third, amalgamation was not new to SOGAT. The fourth argument was that there were no other real alternatives. Neither union could be accused of rushing in to the amalgamation. The merger talks had been conducted over a period of nearly a decade. The negotiations had been tough, necessitating give and take on both sides. An agreement had been fashioned which had cost the members nothing but which gave them a lot.

There were numerous benefits for SOGAT members from merger with NGA in that a carefully constructed new union provided a stronger and more efficient organisation at all levels – chapel, branch and national. The GPMU would be better able to represent former SOGAT members and to offer them enhanced services. A single print union would make better use of resources, end duplication of effort and secure a stronger financial base from which to operate. It was stressed in selling the package that neither SOGAT nor the NGA could hope for a second opportunity to merge if the present attempts failed and that although both unions could probably survive with or without each other, they would both be weakened along the way. Both SOGAT and the NGA accepted they had moved as far as they were able to meet each other's need and the future of their unions now lay in the hands of their members. If amalgamation was voted down then it was likely the two unions would go their separate ways. SOGAT had given the maximum concessions. There were no more to be given. The NGA would not have contemplated any further concessions to SOGAT. It would have been pointless for the two unions to meet again to negotiate a revised package.

Amalgamation was not new to SOGAT, as it was itself the product of numerous amalgamations with smaller unions. Amalgamation with the NGA was a logical step in what had been a continuous process for the best part of 200 years. By voting to create the GPMU, SOGAT members would be taking the last step in the amalgamation of trade unions in the paper and printing industries, but the first step towards the eventual creation of one union for the media. However, amalgamation with the NGA was not sold as a cure-all for SOGAT's industrial problems but as giving its members a broader base from which to resist the current industrial and political threats they faced. The failure to amalgamate, it was pointed out, would not resolve the inter-union disputes between SOGAT and the NGA. It was only by coming together in one union that such problems could be permanently resolved.

The NGA/SOGAT marriage was not born out of love for each other. It was a merger born of the necessity of both unions to represent and protect their members in the industries in which they worked. The SOGAT members were presented with a package, not a perfect one by any means, but one which would form the basis of a new union. A major argument in selling the NGA merger to the SOGAT membership was that any other option would be second best. Other possible options were not as attractive in terms of offering the possibility of maintaining some influence and control in the paper, printing and media industries of the 1990s. The SOGAT General Secretary told the 1990 SOGAT Biennial Delegate Council that 'None of the other options will be as good as the one you have before you now, warts and all!'[13]

What were the alternative options considered by SOGAT?[14] There were three. One option was to remain an independent trade union. A second was to merge with a general trade union such as the T&GWU or the GMBATU. The third was a merger with Manufacturing, Science and Finance (MSF). The option of remaining an independent trade union bore no serious examination. It would prevent SOGAT from making industrial progress since there was no way in which it could just carry on as before. SOGAT had no option but to address immediately restructuring to provide a solution to the inter-union problems between itself and the NGA. The 1988 SOGAT Delegate Council Meeting was told by Brenda Dean:

> Yes, I suppose we could stand alone as a union and survive, or even progress, but is it really an option to stand alone when

we look around and see the difficulties experienced by other unions and read in the press this morning about the big mega-union that is going to be formed between the AEU and the electricians? Do we really want to stand alone? It might be conceivable at the moment to stand alone, and the easiest option, but it is not the best option, and it is not meeting our responsibilities to our members.

As General Secretary I believe – and I believe you hold this view too – that we are not just talking about survival for our members. It is my job and your job to ensure survival and progress, for our members. If we really are sincere in our commitments to the future for our members and sincere about our place in the future, we will not take an apathetic and complacent attitude. We will face this challenge and go forward. We will meet that challenge, each giving and taking and each expressing tolerance. The time has come to stop talking and support the work on amalgamation.[15]

The option of joining a general union was seen by SOGAT members as something that might be forced upon the union if a merger with the NGA were rejected. SOGAT could find itself as an autonomous section in a larger union. This was not what SOGAT members wanted. Their preference was a link with a union which represented the needs of workers employed in papermaking, ink-making, printing, paper conversation and distribution. Supporters of an amalgamation with NGA stressed that joining a general union would do nothing to solve the inter-union problems between SOGAT and the NGA.

The MSF option was a second-best or third option. For SOGAT the preferred option was merger with the NGA followed by subsequent marriages with the NUJ, and the media and telecommunication unions. The formation of the GPMU was a strong position from which to launch the creation of such a union. Only a union covering paper, print, media and communications could protect SOGAT members given that the world was getting smaller and the Single European Market was going ahead. SOGAT recognised a first step to a media union could not be achieved unless SOGAT and the NGA merged.

The SOGAT campaign to persuade its members to vote for the amalgamation package had involved all levels and areas of the union. It was the biggest team effort and campaign ever conducted by the union.[16] The national officers and Head Office staff played key roles in the development of the materials for the campaign. At organiser, branch and chapel level, officers and individual members played effective roles in explaining the amalgamation terms, the reasons why amalgamation was important and why the members should use their vote.

PRE-VESTING DAY ELECTIONS

The Braidwood Affair

The original vesting date for the GPMU was 1 July 1991. However, this was postponed until 30 September 1991 because the NGA taken aback by the high turnout of SOGAT members in the amalgamation ballot, needed to organise a campaign to increase the chances of their General Secretary winning the GPMU General Secretary election. The NGA realised that if SOGAT turned out a similar number to vote in the ballot for the General Secretary election, then Tony Dubbins would lose out to the SOGAT General Secretary, Brenda Dean, The NGA had estimated that a relatively low vote of SOGAT members compared to NGA members would ensure their General Secretary become the GMPU General Secretary.[17] Legal complications internal to SOGAT became an excuse for delaying the original vesting day by three months so that an election campaign amongst SOGAT members could be planned by the NGA. The internal problems for SOGAT began in March 1990 when a retired member, Mr K. Braidwood, complained to the Certification Officer for Trade Unions that neither SOGAT General President, Danny Sergeant nor Ted O'Brien and Fred Smith, both SOGAT General Officers, had stood for re-election during the previous five years as required under the 1984 Trade Union Act. The Certification Office declared in favour of Braidwood's complaint and SOGAT was obliged to seek nominations for the position of General President. There was only one nomination, the current General President, Danny Sergeant, who was thus re-elected unopposed.

Following the Certification Officer's decision to uphold Braidwood's complaint, on 19 December 1990, the day before the amalgamation ballot result was known, although the result must by then have been known, the NGA informed SOGAT they could not agree to initiate the General Secretary election until General President position in SOGAT was known. They said it would be no longer possible to keep to the 1 July vesting day. Following Danny Sergeant's re-election, the

NGA decided their General Secretary and General President should seek nomination for re-election since they had both been elected to their current offices over five years ago. Both Tony Dubbins and Bryn Griffiths were re-elected unopposed as General Secretary and General President respectively of the NGA. Ted O'Brien and Fred Smith, the SOGAT General Officers against whom Mr Braidwood had also laid a complaint decided to retire early. Ted O'Brien retired in June 1991 followed by Fred Smith in July 1991.

SOGAT opposed Braidwood's complaint on three grounds. First, they argued, as a retired member he was not entitled to make a complaint under the 1984 Act. Second, Messrs Sergeant, O'Brien and Smith did not have a vote on the SOGAT National Executive Council and were not members of that body. Third, the General President election under the GPMU procedures, if endorsed by the members in the amalgamation ballot, would remedy any breach of the law in so far as Danny Sergeant's position was concerned.

The Certification Officer declared Mr Braidwood to be a SOGAT member, O'Brien and Smith were members of the NEC as explicitly stated in the SOGAT Rule Book, and Danny Sergeant was a member of the National Executive Council and in any case was also covered by the provisions of the 1988 Employment Act which provided for the periodic re-election of General Secretaries and General Presidents. The Certification Officer also ruled that whilst accepting that an election to the General Presidency of SOGAT was inconvenient in the run-up to the GPMU vesting day, this was a 'self-inflicted' problem since the General President election should have been held in March 1990.

In the light of the Certification Officer's ruling, SOGAT considered four options. One was to ignore the declaration, in which case Mr Braidwood would apply to the courts to enforce the decision. Ignoring the courts would lead to sequestration of SOGAT's assets. Second, the decision could be challenged, in which case the problem would be the grounds for such a challenge. Third, the union could comply with the decision. Four, attempts might be made to persuade Mr Braidwood not to pursue the matter. However, Braidwood was unwilling to drop his complaint and his legal advisers wrote to the General Secretary of SOGAT on 28 November 1990 in the following terms:

> Our client has passed to us his correspondence with you concerning the complaint that he has in respect of your union's failure to hold ballots for the election of three members of its

principal executive committee who have not been elected to their posts within the last five years.

We have seen the declaration of the Certification Officer and noted the fact that you stood for re-election in November 1988 on the basis that the union would otherwise be vulnerable to legal action.

We have advised our client who has the assistance of the Commissioner for Rights of Trade Union Members that it would be appropriate for him now to apply to the Court for an enforcement order.[18]

Further correspondence with Mr Braidwood came to nothing and the Executive Council endorsed Danny Sergeant's decision that he offer himself for re-election as General President. SOGAT in the meantime was advised by the NGA that the elections for General Secretary and General President in the GPMU should not go ahead until the SOGAT candidate for President was known, and the position of the other SOGAT officers clarified.

SOGAT arranged a consultation with its QC Mr Eldred Tabachnik on 20 December 1990. The NGA attended and was represented by its General Secretary, General President and its legal adviser, Ian Kershaw. The SOGAT QC confirmed his advice that Danny Sergeant seek immediate re-election. Prior to this meeting the NGA's view had been that this was essentially a SOGAT problem and they should not become involved. However, on subsequent legal advice the NGA concluded that to continue this stance would be unwise. Ian Kershaw advised that at the 20 December meeting, Mr Tabachnik had made a comment which, if applied, to the NGA might mean that in:

the absence of a 1984 Act ballot that technically the position of General Secretary or General President (of the NGA (82)) is vacant.

If that were right, you would not be eligible to stand as General Secretary or General President of the GPMU, as under clauses 8 and 9 of the Instrument of Amalgamation that ballot is limited to the persons holding the offices of General Secretary and General President.

It would be possible for a member of SOGAT (82) or the NGA (82) to obtain an injunction stopping you (Mr Dubbins) or Mr Griffiths from standing in the GPMU elections. I do not think you should run the risk.

In conclusion, therefore, I recommend that you (Mr Dubbins) and Mr Griffiths do submit yourselves for re-election under the 1984 Act.[19]

On 10 January 1991, the NGA National Council endorsed this legal advice believing that it could not in all conscience contemplate any action that might debar Tony Dubbins or Bryn Griffiths from office in the GPMU on a legal technicality. Despite the NGA policy of non-compliance with the government's trade union laws, its National Council felt the situation had to be faced and to do otherwise than support re-election would be an abdication of its responsibility to the membership. Tony Dubbins and Bryn Griffiths were subsequently re-elected unopposed as General Secretary and General President respectively of the NGA.

Following the elections for the GPMU General Secretary and General President, Mr Braidwood made a further complaint to the Certification Officer that the SOGAT Papermaking Officer (George Beattie) and Organiser (John Mitchell) had not stood for re-election under the 1984 Trade Union Act and had been elected to office more than five years previously. The Certification Officer again upheld Mr Braidwood's complaint, but in view of the pending amalgamation date, decided to take no further action than to instruct both George Beattie and John Mitchell not to attend the last statutory Executive Council Meeting of SOGAT. They complied with this.

The GPMU General Secretary and General President Elections

The two candidates were Brenda Dean, General Secretary of SOGAT and Tony Dubbins, General Secretary of the NGA. The ballot result was declared on Wednesday 29 May 1991 and was:

Tony Dubbins	78,654 votes
Brenda Dean	72,657 votes
Majority	5,997

The turnout of NGA members was 70 per cent, and that of SOGAT members was 65 per cent. The election had been hard fought and at times the fight had been bitter. Some 25 per cent of SOGAT members voted for Dubbins and some 15 per cent of NGA members for Dean. Tony Dubbins became General Secretary of the GPMU on 30 September 1991 whilst Brenda Dean became its Deputy General Secretary.

The two candidates in the election for General President of the GPMU were Danny Sergeant, the SOGAT General President, and Bryn Griffiths, General President of the NGA. The result was declared on Tuesday 23 July 1991 and was:

Bryn Griffiths	66,588 votes
Danny Sergeant	51,649
Majority	14,939

The turn-out in the election was 43 per cent for SOGAT members and 66 per cent for NGA members. Of SOGAT members 25 per cent voted for Bryn Griffiths and 15 per cent of NGA members voted for Danny Sergeant.

Why had 25 per cent of SOGAT members voted against the SOGAT candidate in these elections? The London members had been disappointed by the outcome of the Wapping dispute. The Greater Merseyside Branch had been in dispute for some time with the national union whilst the Scottish Graphical Branch had never forgiven Brenda Dean whilst she was the SOGAT Manchester Branch Secretary, for persuading the 1984 Delegate Meeting to vote against the facsimile transmission of origination work for newspapers into Scotland. Other craft groups were aggrieved that the union, in recent years, had concentrated heavily in wage negotiations on increasing the pay of lower-paid members to the detriment of craft differentials. Machine assistants were unhappy at SOGAT having made no industrial response to the NGA blatant attempts to remove them from press rooms. Other activists were unhappy that the union journal had become too dominated by a 'Women in SOGAT' section. The Braidwood affair had enabled Tony Dubbins to mount an election campaign amongst SOGAT members, which would have been impossible with the original time scale for the General Secretary election.

Nevertheless, there were many SOGAT members who were proud that their union's profile had been raised in the eyes of the general public, that the administration of the union had become streamlined and that important industrial advances for the lower-paid members, particularly its women, had been gained. However, these feelings, together with a natural loyalty to SOGAT were insufficient to outweigh the industrial discontent of other sections of the membership.

On 30 September 1991 the GPMU came into being. SOGAT and the NGA ceased to be independent trade unions. The achievement of one production union had at long last been accomplished. However, it was not seen as the end of the amalgamation road but as the beginning of a new one, towards the eventual establishment of one union for the media.

NOTES

1. For an account of the evolution and development of The National Graphical Association and its constituent unions over the period, 1950–90, see J. Gennard *A History of the National Graphical Association*, Unwin Hyman, 1990.
2. For an account of the first 100 years of one of the constituent unions of the London Typographical Society see E. Howe and H.E. Waite *The London Society of Compositors*, Cassells, 1949 and for the Typographical Association see A.E. Musson *The Typographical Association*, Oxford University Press, 1954.
3. These were the Association of the Correctors of the Press (1965); the National Union of Press Telegraphists (1965); the National Society of Electrotypers and Stereotypers (1967); the Amalgamated Society of Lithographic Printers and Auxiliaries (1969) and the National Union of Wallcoverings, Decorative and Allied Trades (1979).
4. See Society of Graphical and Allied Trades (82) *Report of the Biennial Delegate Council Meeting, 1990*, p. 58.
5. This decision was to apply only if a merger was achieved. If there were no merger the Electrical and Technical Services' Branch would continue as a national branch within SOGAT.
6. On the formation of the GPMU, Graphic House, the Head Office of the former NGA was renamed Keys House, after Bill Keys, a former SOGAT General Secretary, 1975–84.
7. See 'Last Ditch Effort to Save SOGAT–NGA Amalgamation' *SOGAT Journal*, December/January 1989/90, p. 4.
8. These nine regions were London, the Home Counties, South East, North East, North West, Midlands, Wales and the West, Scotland and Ireland.
9. The first issue of this publication, entitled *Spectrum*, appeared in May 1992.
10. Society of Graphical and Allied Trades (82) *Report of the Biennial Delegate Council Meeting, 1990*, p. 35.
11. See 'GPMU – Putting the Members First' *SOGAT Journal*, October 1990, p. 21.
12. Op. cit., p. 12.
13. Society of Graphical and Allied Trades (82) *Report of the Biennial Delegate Council Meeting, 1990*, p. 39.
14. Op. cit.,
15. Society of Graphical and Allied Trades (82) *Report of the Biennial Delegate Council*

Meeting, 1988, p. 22.

16. In the NGA campaign in support of the amalgamation with SOGAT two points of opposition were raised. First, there was concern that merger would result in skill dilution. Second, there was concern the greater numbers in SOGAT would prevent their General Secretary becoming the leader of the new union. NGA members were reassured on their first concern in that SOGAT members would only proceed to craft status through the recognised routes. On the second issue SOGAT members did not turn out in large numbers to vote whereas NGA members did. On the 'differential turn-out factor' there was every chance the NGA General Secretary would become the GPMU General Secretary.

17. The two candidates at one stage publicly exchanged insults and allegations against each other. The membership of the two unions were appalled. Having accepted that merger was in the best industrial interests they were now witnessing the two potential leaders criticising each other.

18. *Print*, Jan./Feb. 1991, p. 3.

19. Op. cit.

PART II

CONSTITUTIONAL AND FINANCIAL STRUCTURE

CHAPTER 10

DECISION-MAKING STRUCTURE DEVELOPMENTS

MEMBERSHIP TRENDS

Table 10.1 shows the membership of the NUPB&PW/SOGAT (Division A) over the period 1955 to 1972. Its membership showed an overall slow but steady increase but at points in time a fall in membership was recorded for example in 1957 and 1959. The largest absolute fall in year-on-year membership changes (minus 9,644) occurred in 1971. The 1957 fall was due to loss of women members in part-time employment whilst the decline in the following year resulted from closure of a number of papermills and a fall in employment in the printing and binding trades. Membership peaked in 1970 at 192,920.

The Rule Book of the NUPB&PW/SOGAT (Division A) listed occupations that qualified for membership of the union. In 1955, 55 occupations were listed but in 1964 the Biennial Delegate Council tidied up the 'Qualification for membership' rule. The NUPB&PW had organised in some fields for many years but the rule did not reflect this. Some membership increases had been in new occupations and it was important, especially if the NUPB&PW were taken by another union to a TUC Disputes Committee, that its constitution recognised that the union organised such workers. This would also be a useful point in disputes with other unions over organisational rights.

Individuals were admitted into NUPB&PW/SOGAT (Division A) as full members or junior members. However, no applicant over 50 years of age could be admitted as a full member without the permission of the National Executive Council. The junior member category was open to men up to the age of 20 or the commencement of the final year of their apprenticeship and to women up to the age of 18. Although

Table 10.1

Membership of the NUPB&PW and SOGAT (Division A), 1955–72

Date	Membership
1955	158,813
1956	163,061
1957	160,710
1958	158,065
1959	157,396
1960	166,374
1961	171,064
1962	172,592
1963	177,621
1964	180,665
1965	186,474
1966	not available
1967	not available
1968	180,262
1969	not available
1970	192,920
1971	183,276
1972	183,990

Source: *Annual Report*, National Executive Council for NUPB&PW and SOGAT (Division A) 1955–72.

applications for membership were submitted to a branch which had authority to accept or refuse an application, the final authority on admission lay with the National Executive Council.

Table 10.2 shows the membership of SOGAT over the period 1973 to 1981. In 1978, the membership for the first time exceeded 200,000. Membership peaked in the following year at 205,784 having grown every year since 1971. Owing to adverse economic conditions, SOGAT's membership declined in 1980 and 1981. Although the recruitment of new members had not stopped it could not keep pace with redundancies from factory and mill closures.

The SOGAT Rule Book listed occupations that qualified for membership. In 1976, in a further tidying up exercise, SOGAT members engaged in the production of playing cards and games were included amongst the list of occupations qualifying for membership.

Table 10.2
Membership of SOGAT/SOGAT(75), 1973–81

Date	Membership
1973	187,580
1974	192,723
1975	195,522
1976	194,312
1977	199,583
1978	203,352
1979	205,784
1980	197,048
1981	not available

Source: TUC *Congress Report*, 1973–81.

In 1988 'printers' were removed from the list and replaced by the category 'all letterpress printers, photogravure printers, lithographic printers, flexographic printers and all engaged in any other form of printing'. The 'qualification for membership' rule was all-embracing and detailed every job function carried out by SOGAT members with the sole exception of the different printing processes. Many members of the Scottish Graphical Division had retrained from letterpress to other printing processes and other print unions were not adverse to telling such members that SOGAT was no longer the appropriate union to organise them. If all printing processes were included in the 'qualification for membership' rule there could be no confusion amongst members that after retraining SOGAT was still their appropriate union.

Individuals were admitted to SOGAT as full or junior members. Although membership applications were submitted to the branch, which had authority to accept or refuse an application, the final authority on admission lay with the National Executive Council. The junior member category was open to men and women up to the age of 20 years. The decision that full membership start at 20 years of age was taken by the 1974 Biennial Delegate Council on the grounds that the age of the majority had been lowered from 21 to 18 and the union's collective bargaining policy was to lower the age at which the adult rate of pay would operate. The 50 years age limit on the admission of applicants except with the sanction of the National Executive Council had been removed in 1972.

Table 10.3 shows that over the period 1982 to 1991 the membership of SOGAT fell in every year. The union had worked hard at recruitment, including the introduction of new services available to its present members and to potential recruits. A further fall in membership particularly, in the London Branches, occurred in 1989. Membership decline reflected the economic recession, the employers' offensives against the union (especially in newspaper production and wholesale distribution) in the form of derecognition, technological change eliminating many SOGAT and NGA roles and the EETPU taking over jobs which had traditionally been done by SOGAT. This steady decline throughout the 1980s in membership was in contrast to the steady growth of the 1970s, and had adverse effects on SOGAT's finances.

Over a 35-year period the membership of NUPB&PW/SOGAT diversified. In 1955 the NUPB&PW was mainly a union of machine managers, machine assistants, bookbinders, warehouse personnel, bindery workers, wholesale distribution workers and transport drivers. At the time of its amalgamation with the NGA in addition to these groups, SOGAT organised revisers, readers' assistants, linotype assistants, monotype casters, typefounders, filmsetters, pattern card makers, dandy roll makers, ink makers, silk screen printers, electricians, compositors, wage clerks,

Table 10.3
Membership of SOGAT(82), 1982–91

Date	Membership
1982	225,155
1983	213,605
1984	210,462
1985	205,916
1986	199,594
1987	196,231
1988	183,213
1989	176,144
1990	not available
1991	not available

Source: TUC *Statistical Statement*, 1982–90.

clerical staff, advertising staff, sales staff, technical, supervisory and administrative staff and executives. A feature of its diversifying membership was a growing number of female members. However, in the 1980s SOGAT's female membership fell in relative terms more than its male membership. Between 1982 and 1991 SOGAT's male membership fell from 161,267 to 113,057, a drop of 48,210 or 30 per cent. Its female membership, over the same period, fell from 75,393 to 44,161, a drop of 31,232 or 41 per cent.

A common misconception about SOGAT was that it was predominantly a newspaper union. At the peak of its membership, SOGAT had only 8 per cent of members employed in national newspapers, 12 per cent in provincial newspapers and 15 per cent in paper and paper conversion manufacture. The largest trade sector of SOGAT members was by far the general printing industry, followed by papermaking and paper conversion. Newspapers were third. In the 1980s, technological changes and the shift of newspaper distribution from rail to road significantly reduced the number of SOGAT members employed in newspapers. At the time of SOGAT's merger with the NGA its newspaper membership was below 5 per cent of its total membership.

ORGANISATIONAL PROBLEMS AND WIDENING THE MEMBERSHIP

The increasing diversification of SOGAT membership was not due solely to mergers but also reflected expansion into new areas such as supervisors, sales, administration and technical employees. In the late 1980s when SOGAT attempted to recruit in 'high-tech' areas, where it found competition with the EETPU, which believed it had an unalienable right to recruit where, when and how it chose.[1] The impact of technological change and increased employer bargaining power were powerful incentives for SOGAT to extend its membership base into new areas.

There was controversy within the NUPB&PW as to whether overseers, supervisors and other persons in charge of NUPB&PW members must or may be members of the union. The 1960 Biennial Delegate Council rejected a Reading Branch motion that those in charge of NUPB&PW members must be members of the national union.[2] Four main arguments were presented in favour of supervisors being compelled to join the union. First, it would strengthen the case for 100 per cent trade union organisation. Second, the majority of supervisors had been promoted from the shop floor where they had been NUPB&PW members. When promotion took place the individual had the choice of whether they wished to remain a union member or not. This option should be removed. Third, improvements in the wages and conditions of supervisory staff were based on production workers and employment conditions improvements were passed automatically to overseers and supervisors. Given that overseers and supervisors bene-fited from NUPB&PW actions it was reasonable they should be members of the union. Fourth, overseers and supervisors in the union would create greater harmony on the shop floor as the possibility of discrimination against employees on the grounds of union membership by supervisors would be minimised.

However, those who opposed overseers and supervisors joining the NUPB&PW feared they would insist on attending chapel meetings which might cause problems with employers. The first loyalty of over-seers and supervisors was to the company and not the union. If supervisors refused to be members then the NUPB&PW chapel might have to take industrial action giving rise to difficulties with the employers. The issue of supervisors, overseers and clerical workers, with the exception of clerical staff in the general printing and news-paper industries, having to be members of SOGAT (Division A) was raised by the National Executive Council at the 1966 Biennial Delegate Council.[3] The proposal that supervisors, overseers and clerical workers may be members of the SOGAT (Division A) was accepted by dele-gates but an amendment from the Aylesbury Branch that they 'must join' the union was defeated. The Executive considered circumstances had changed since 1960. First, technical developments taking place in the industries in which SOGAT (Division A) operated meant it was necessary to organise supervisory grades. Second, supervisors who formerly saw themselves as 'the servants' of higher management were now looking to trade unions to provide them with industrial protec-tion. Third, the union was receiving approaches from supervisory staff for membership. They had grievances against their employers and were looking for an organisation to process and resolve those grievances. Four, if SOGAT (Division A) did not organise overseers and super-visory staff then other unions would do so.

In 1972 SOGAT established Art, Technical, Administrative, Executive and Sales (ATAES) to cater for the needs of supervisors, administrators, clerks, technicians, computer programmers, systems analysts and managers. In 1974, the ATAES Section was established as an autonomous unit within SOGAT. It was felt the union's existing organisational structure did not provide a suitable means for non-manual workers to obtain proper representation. SOGAT decided non-manual members must be organised separately from its manual member chapels and branches. The ATAES was established as a nation-wide branch with its own full-time officials assisted by two organisers. Initially the branch grew rapidly and then progressed more steadily but was described in 1985 as the 'only growth area on the industrial front'.[4]

The creation of SOGAT (82) was regarded as providing a spring-board for recruitment of new members on an unprecedented scale. Prior to the formation of SOGAT (82), NATSOPA and SOGAT were often organising in the same area which meant they were competing against each other rather than working together. SOGAT (82), being broadly based, was to provide the impetus and opportunity for a significant recruitment drive into areas currently unorganised. In the clerical areas of paper and printing production an enormous recruitment potential existed but other areas remained untapped, for example sales forces, ink and office supplies and papermaking. Unfortunately these recruitment expectations were never fulfilled.

Efforts were made in the 1980s to retain and attract into SOGAT young people by increasing their opportunities to participate in the Society's affairs. In 1980 District Councils were permitted to elect a young delegate (under 20 years of age) to represent the Group in regional youth activities, to attend the Biennial Delegate Council as an observer and to attend all meetings of the Group with the right to participate in its business but without the power to vote. The National Executive Council reviewed the contribution and benefit levels of young members as well as their representation and partici-pation in SOGAT's decision-making machinery.[5] The 1983 Delegate Meeting sought the establishment of a Youth Committee to bring to the attention of the leadership of the union the industrial prob-lems young members faced. In 1990 branches were encouraged to elect or appoint a Youth Delegate to their Branch Committee. These measures were to prevent young people becoming an isolated section of the union feeling they had no input to make. The expec-tation was that the union would develop a pool of young people who would generate an interest in and raise the profile of young people's interests in the union by having a real say at all levels. These decisions were implemented and were well received by the young members in the union. However, redundancies and lack of recruitment by employers during the economic recession of the 1980s took their toll on these initiatives and their impact on the retention and recruitment of young people into SOGAT was not as great as expected.

Over the period 1982 to 1991 SOGAT lost 79,500 members which represented a fall of some 34 per cent, whilst in the years 1984–90 employment in the printing, paper and publishing industries increased by 20 per cent. The main membership losses were in sectors where SOGAT had high membership concentrations, for example newspapers, paper and board, magazines and books. Four factors were exerting pressure on SOGAT's membership. First, the economic recession of the first half of the 1980s resulted in closures of factories and mills whilst those that survived reduced the numbers they employed. Second, the implementation of technological change resulted in the loss of many semi-skilled and unskilled jobs, for example in the bindery and warehouse, which had traditionally been undertaken by SOGAT members. Third, traditionally SOGAT had recruited members through its direct involvement in the supply of labour to employers in national newspaper production and wholesale distribution through its operation of the closed shop. In the 1980s both these recruitment methods came under attack. The Government removed legal protection from the closed shop and national newspaper employers, because of technical developments, gained access to alternative supplies of labour. Fourth, SOGAT's traditional areas of organisation were undermined by national and provincial newspaper employers, who derecognised SOGAT particularly in the clerical, sales and managerial areas, and by the NGA and the EETPU, both of whom were prepared to conclude single-union deals with employers to exclude SOGAT completely.

SOGAT gave much thought as to how it might reverse this decline in membership given that in the past it had achieved a high level of organisation without having to give recruitment work a high priority amongst its activities.[6] In an attempt to reverse the falling membership, organisers gave a higher priority to recruitment, additional organisers were appointed, a more professional approach to recruitment was adopted and a more professional image for the union was cultivated. By 1990 SOGAT had 11 organisers working in geographical areas under the direction and control of the Organising Secretary and who performed many duties including representing the members in negotiations, servicing the local branch, especially part-time ones, and recruiting new members. The union raised the awareness of the importance of recruitment and organisers to spent more time on recruitment activities relative to industrial duties. A Ruling Stationery and Packaging Branch motion that 'organisers shall have, as their priority, the duty to organise into membership employees in companies in the printing and allied trades where there is no existing SOGAT organisation'[7] resulted in a tied vote at the 1984 Biennial Delegate Council[8] where upon the President declared the motion not carried. When the branch re-presented the motion to the 1986 Delegate Meeting, it was easily carried. However, by the late 1980s organisers on average, were spending 25 per cent of their time, or just one day per week, on recruitment work compared to 5–10 per cent in the early 1980s when the union had more organisers in the field.[9]

In 1989 the NEC appointed two new organisers on the condition their duties were restricted solely to recruitment and they worked with other organisers to encourage branches to develop recruitment strategies that dovetailed with their own work. The increase in time spent by organisers on recruitment together with the appointment of two new organisers demonstrated the union's commitment to improving its membership level. However, what was really required for branches was to change their attitude towards recruitment and provide more time for organisers to carry out recruitment work systematically. The response of the branches, however, was mixed.

SOGAT did, however, adopt a far more professional approach to recruitment. The union launched a new recruitment drive centred around three elements. First, new recruitment materials stressed to prospective members the services SOGAT could offer them, including an industrial and domestic legal service, good quality health and safety information and a high degree of industrial servicing from national officers, organisers, branch and chapel officials. Second, a branch information profile was produced which, when analysed against the background of local conditions and resources, identified where recruitment effort could constructively be directed. Specific groups were targeted as part of this systematic approach. In the 1980s the number of female manual workers in the jobs traditionally organised by SOGAT had risen only slightly. For women employed in clerical jobs there had been an increase of 9.5 per cent. Although SOGAT stressed the industrial needs of women, such as cervical and breast cancer screening and child-care facilities, it realised that it had to be seen to be addressing those problems effectively. To this end, in 1990 SOGAT held a one-day conference for SOGAT women, the aim of which was to promote and encourage activity and participation by women within SOGAT. The conference was to be held annually. However, attempts to recruit women met with little success.[10] The third element of this more professional approach to recruitment was the introduction of a branch team concept involving the organisers, the branch committee, and the branch and chapel officers. The lynchpin of the concept was a branch officer assuming responsibility for co-ordinating branch recruitment activities with those of the organisers. The development of the branch team concept did not take off.

The fourth element in SOGAT's attempts to reverse the decline in its membership was to change the image of the union from one of a 'cloth cap' manual workers' organisation to a highly professional union relevant to the needs of the microprocessor revolution. The union improved its communications with the members through the branches by direct mailing and computers. The Head Office computer was linked to branch offices to give them regular, fast 'telex'-type print-outs. A press relations policy was introduced to ensure better presentation of the union's points of view to the national media and to the membership and to co-ordinate the union's publicity work through publications, leaflets and advertising. In January 1989 SOGAT appointed a Press and Media Officer, a move which was welcomed by the 1990 Delegate Council Meeting as essential to the union's well-being and to the promotion of the benefits of belonging to SOGAT.

In attempting to recruit new members SOGAT was disadvantaged by its relatively high contribution rate compared to those of non-print unions recruiting in the same areas. It reformed its contributions structure to attract members and retain existing members. The 1984 Delegate Council Meeting agreed that part-time workers whose contractual hours of work did not exceed 16 per week and whose gross wage was less than 50 per cent of the lowest adult minimum earnings level in the SOGAT/BPIF agreement be allowed reduced contributions. It accepted that the NEC should establish a reduced scale of contributions for organisational purposes, and that women members taking maternity leave and who had indicated they would return to work after confinement pay reduced contributions for up to 26 weeks from the time maternity pay expired. However, membership continued to decline and further financial incentives for individuals to take out or retain membership were approved. In 1986, part-time working members were classified as full members and received the full range of SOGAT financial benefits. Reduced subscriptions were available for up to one year after maternity pay had expired. The 1988 Delegate Council approved a reduced contribution rate of not less than 25 per cent for organisational purposes, although it would be reviewed every six months and the maximum period of its operation would be three years or until such time as recognition for the members concerned had been achieved.

However, despite all these constructive efforts, SOGAT was unable to stem the decline in membership. If it had not devoted such time and resources to reverse this fall in membership it would probably have been even greater. The impact of the decline on SOGAT's financial resources and industrial bargaining power was substantial.

THE NUPB&PW/SOGAT (DIVISION A) DECISION-MAKING MACHINERY, 1955–72

The basis of the NUPB&PW/SOGAT (Division A) organisational structure was that members were grouped into branches which were geographical and/or trade-based. The branches were organised into ten groups whose purpose was to secure uniformity of employment conditions, greater harmony between branches and to promote the work of the union. These branch groupings had no policy-making role in the union.[11] For purposes of election to the National Executive Council these groups compressed into five Divisions. The policy-making body of the union was the Biennial Delegate Council to which branches sent delegates and at which policy was decided on the basis of motions submitted by branches and the National Executive Council. Between Delegate Council Meetings, the governing body was the National Executive Council which was accountable to the delegates for its activities via the provision of annual reports which required the approval of the Delegate Council. The implementation of union policies, rules and agreements was the responsibility of the National Executive Council on whose behalf a team of national officers, the chief of which was the General Secretary, elected by the whole membership (see Figure 10.1) acted. The channel of communications in the NUPB&PW/SOGAT (Division A) was chapel to branch to National Executive Council and vice versa. Branches had direct access to the National Executive Council.

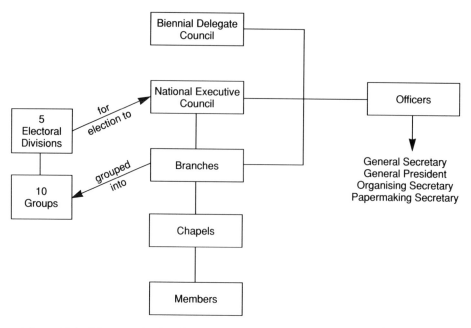

Figure 10.1   The organisational structure of the NUPB&PW/SOGAT (Division A)

Table 10.4 shows the number of branches in the NUPB&PW/SOGAT (Division A) for each year over the period 1955 to 1972. The largest branches had full-time secretaries but the number of such branches never exceeded 36. The table also shows the number of branches confined to papermill workers, bookbinders and to print trade members. The number of branches declined from a peak of 231 in 1962 and the decline accelerated after the 1968 Division A Conference accepted that wherever possible branches should join together to provide full services in the district. Although the great majority of members were attached to the branch nearest their place of work there were exceptions to this. In London there were five branches: the London Central Branch, the Printing Machine Branch,[12] the London Women's Branch,[13] the Circulation Representatives' Branch whose offices were in London but which had members throughout the UK,[14] and the Ruling, Manufacturing, Stationary and Boxmaking Branch. In addition to the London-based branches, there were trade-based nation-wide branches of which the most important were the Papermould and Dandy Roll Branch and the Monotype Casters and Typefounders' Branch which was predominantly a London-based branch.

Table 10.4
Number of NUPB&PW/SOGAT (Division A) branches, 1955–72

	Total	Mill only	Binding only	Print only
1955	229	60	16	19
1956	230	65	15	21
1957	227	61	16	20
1958	231	63	14	18
1959	227	62	14	21
1960	226	64	12	24
1961	227	61	12	25
1962	231	63	11	23
1963	227	61	11	23
1964	225	61	11	23
1965	221	60	8	21
1966	221	61	7	23
1967	217	56	7	21
1968	211	52	7	19
1969	198	50	7	17
1970	185	50	5	16
1971	179	45	6	17
1972	174	42	6	16

Source: *Annual Report*, National Executive Council.

The 1960s saw NUPB&PW/SOGAT (Division A) attempt to organise non-manual employees in the printing and paper industry. The main attention focused on technical, administrative and executive grades of employees. However, there were problems in that some branches were doubtful about having such workers, particularly managers, in membership. In 1970 the National Executive Committee set up a sub-committee to examine the question of organising amongst non-manual employees and particularly how they might be accommodated within the existing decision-making structure. As a result of this examination, SOGAT (Division A) in 1972, established a new branch called the Art, Technical, Administrative, Executive and Sales (ATAES) Branch to cater for the interests of non-manual workers. It was a nation-wide branch with its own officers. Members of the Branch could not call on the services of the local SOGAT (Division A) branch in which they lived; they were serviced by their own officers.

In 1963 the NUPB&PW adopted a policy of creating full-time branches whilst the London branches were asked to explore the possibilities of mergers. In 1965 the London Bookbinders' Branch and the London Central Branch following a series of inter-union disputes decided to merge.[15] Branch mergers gained a further impetus when the 1968 Delegate Council accepted there should be moves towards the membership being serviced by a full-time Branch Secretary. In August 1968 the principles to govern branch mergers were agreed. First, no merging of branches or discussions about merger should take place without the prior consent of Head Office and without the presence at such discussions of a national officer. Second, where the NEC decided, after consultations with the members, certain branches should amalgamate there should be no question of any particular branch contracting out. Third, where branch mergers took place, the question of the purchase of an appropriate property would be decided by the NEC and not by local branches. Proper training facilities were to be given for the new Branch Secretary before taking the job. Following the acceptance of these principles, branch mergers accelerated. Between 1969 and 1972 the number of branches fell by 24 via mergers.

In 1955 the NUPB&PW National Executive Committee comprised 24 representatives elected by the membership from five electoral divisions together with the General President, General Secretary, Organising Secretary and the Papermaking Secretary. Not more than two representatives from any branch could be elected to the Executive, except for electoral Division 1 (London) where the maximum was three. Over the period 1955 to 1972 attempts at Biennial Delegate Council Meetings to increase the size of the National Executive Committee were defeated as were attempts to gain automatic representation for the larger branches. A major change to the NEC composition occurred at the 1968 Delegate Council Meeting when the Ipswich Branch successfully moved a motion which meant some groups losing a seat at the cost of smaller groups. It was envisaged that this would encourage people of ability and not merely those from the large groups to seek election, would mean no matter what branch a member belonged to their voice would be heard and would rectify the situation whereby the union allowed its members with ability to be lost through the misfortune of belonging to the smaller branches.

The merger of the London Bookbinders' and the London Central Branch in July 1965 resulted in the Ruling, Manufacturing, Stationery and Boxmaking Branch (RMSB) writing to the NEC questioning

London representation on that body. They had expected the rule confining a London Central Branch representation on the NEC to three would apply. Prior to the merger, the London Central Branch had three representatives on the NEC and the Bookbinders' Branch two. The merger meant the London Central Branch now had five representatives on the National Executive. The Ruling, Manufacturing, Stationary and Boxmaking Branch was told that as the two bookbinders' members had been elected prior to the merger they were elected for the full period of the NEC office. The RMSB rejected this, arguing that the London Central Branch representation on the NEC conflicted with the general rules of the union and asked the NEC to re-examine the position. When the NEC confirmed its decision, RMSB Branch gave notice to raise the matter at the 1966 Delegate Council Meeting.

At the Delegate Council the RMSB Branch succeeded by 182 votes to 118 in having the section of the NEC 1966 Annual Report dealing with London Central Branch representation on the NEC following its merger with the London Bookbinders' Branch referred back. The Delegate Council then proceeded to defeat an NEC motion that the maximum number of representatives from any branch in electoral Division 1 (London) be increased from three to four. The NEC did not propose to increase the number of seats for Division 1. The London Central Branch, with 28,000 members, was the union's largest branch and held a number of agreements with employers' associations in its own right. The total membership of the other branches in London was 25,500. The NEC argued it was inequitable given the size of the London Central Branch to deprive it of adequate representation on the NEC. LCB membership equalled the total of all other London branches. The LCB was only seeking further representation which would give them half of London's NEC seats. Opponents argued that if the motion were passed it could give rise to a situation whereby one-third of the NEC came from only two branches, thereby, reducing seats for other London branches and giving larger branches the opportunity to elect NEC members at the expense of smaller branches. Others opposed the NEC on the grounds that the real issue was the best method of electing the NEC so that it represented, within the framework of 24 members, as many interests as SOGAT represented in the printing and paper industry.

Although one-third of the SOGAT (Division A) membership was female, only two women sat on the NEC. To ensure that the industrial interests of women members were understood and discussed, the

1968 Delegate Council established a Women's Advisory Committee. The Committee was to reduce the work of the general officers and the NEC by undertaking all preparatory work on women's issues and giving their advice to the NEC who would then decide whether to act on that advice. However, there was strong opposition to the establishment of a Women's Advisory Committee on the grounds that it was only advisory, represented a special sectional interest and that it was a self-inflicted problem that women were underrepresented on the NEC because they did not seek nomination to it. The NEC also opposed the Committee arguing that if women members were seeking equality they should work together to win seats on the NEC where they could influence policy-making rather than establishing a committee which was seen as an attempt to create a union within a union.

An important NEC sub-committee was the Appeals Committee which dealt with disputes between members and their branch. Over the period 1955 to 1972 the Appeals Committee usually upheld the branch decision. A high percentage of cases before the Appeals Committee involved members of the London Central Branch.[16] A Final Appeal Court, consisted of 24 lay members elected from, and by, the delegates to the Delegate Council. It was the body to which members could appeal from the NEC Appeals Committee. The Final Appeal Court met in April and October each year. As a rule, the Final Appeal Court upheld NEC Appeals Committee decisions.

The Delegate Council was the NUPB&PW/SOGAT (Division A)'s 'parliament'. It met every two years with authority to approve the National Executive Committee's annual report, determine policy, determine (until 1966) financial questions and to change the union's rules. Representation at the Delegate Council was related to the size of the branch. In 1955 the basis of representation was that each branch or group with a membership of not less than 250 was entitled to one delegate. The formula for additional branch delegates was one for each complete 500 members. The 1960 Delegate Council reduced the minimum branch or group size for a delegate to a membership of not less than 200, justified on the grounds small branches had the democratic right to share in the formulation of the rules and policy of the union. The NEC unsuccessfully opposed the move, arguing that the union had 110 branches with less than 200 members and 25 branches with 50 members or less and that when this was realised chapels with membership of 50 or more would demand automatic representation on the Delegate Council.

Prior to 1966, the supreme authority on financial matters (changes in subscriptions and benefits) was the membership. The NEC persuaded the 1966 Delegate Council that the supreme authority on financial questions should become the Delegate Council. The pressure for the change was the rejection by the members, in a ballot, of the 1964 Delegate Council decision to increase subscription rates. The change established the principle that once a Delegate Meeting had decided a change in subscription or benefits that decision was binding upon the membership and not subject to confirmation by a membership ballot. The delegates to the 1964 Delegate Council had, after considerable discussion, decided it was in the best interests of the whole membership to increase subscriptions. This action had been taken in full knowledge of all the facts but had been rejected by the membership. When members found themselves in trouble with employers they expected adequate resources to be available from the union to protect them. Because of this need, the NEC stressed the union could no longer afford to let the 'could not care less member' determine the future of the union by membership ballots on financial issues. The NEC was not removing democratic rights from the members since every branch could mandate its delegates on any motion to be debated at the Delegate Council. The Delegate Council as the supreme authority on all matters continued in the reconstituted SOGAT, SOGAT (75) and SOGAT (82).

In 1955 the rules of the NUPB&PW could only be changed every four years. However, the RMSB Branch persuaded the 1964 Delegate Council that the Rules should be able to be changed at each Council Meeting. Four years was seen as too long to wait for rule changes and as encouraging many rule amendments from branches motivated by the attitude 'we shall not have a chance to do so again for four years'. The RMSB Branch believed that if the opportunity existed to amend the rules every two years then gradually over time the number of proposed rule changes would fall and when changes were proposed their necessity would be easier to demonstrate. The changing of rules at each Delegate Council continued as the practice in SOGAT post-1972, in SOGAT (75) and in SOGAT (82) until the 1988 Delegate Council returned to the pre-1964 situation of rules revision at every other Delegate Council.

THE 1972 CONSTITUTIONAL CHANGES

In October 1971 the NEC undertook an examination of SOGAT's decision-making structure. It was designed to create a structure to cope with the increasing pressures imposed on the membership by rapid technological change, the creation of larger production units, company mergers, the emergence of multinational companies and government interference in industrial relations through the Conservative government's Industrial Relations Act (1971) which sought to provide for the first time in the UK a comprehensive legal framework surrounding the industrial relations system and to impose legal obligations and responsibilities on trade unions and employers and their organisations. To combat these developments, it was necessary to provide an up-to-date industrial service whilst at the same time promoting greater member participation within SOGAT. The structure had changed little since its formation in 1921 although its membership was now larger and more diversified. SOGAT wanted to create new benefits for new groups of people but was keen at the same time not to push the old values aside. The NEC justified its proposed fundamental changes on the grounds that for too long the union had operated on the tolerance by the majority of the members of an outdated system.[17]

The SOGAT National Executive submitted proposals to the 1972 Delegate Council for a new structure covering six areas: the Biennial Delegate Council, Annual Trade Conferences, the Executive Council, the group system, the Papermaking Advisory Committee and the Women's Advisory Committee. The proposals had three main objectives: greater membership participation, greater membership involvement in considering workplace issues and an NEC embracing both trade and area interests. In introducing the proposals the General Secretary outlined two reasons for the change. First, the present structure had not, as some claimed, lasted for over 50 years. The structure had changed and evolved over the years and the union intermittently had held *ad hoc* trade conferences for papermaking, fibreboard, wholesale newspaper distribution and other specialised interests. These *ad hoc* conferences had not met the expectations of either the NEC or the delegates involved. Second, a new structure was needed because the rate of change was very rapid and outside pressures from government and other agencies were so great that SOGAT could not afford a long slow gestation period. The General Secretary emphasised that if the delegates accepted The *Structure of the Society* document they would not be keeping ahead of events but merely reacting to them.

The document proposed that every branch with a working membership of 100 or more be represented at the Biennial Delegate Council by at least one delegate. To have a second delegate a branch required

700 members with an additional delegate for each further full 500 members. This proposal aimed to ensure wide representation at future Delegate Council meetings but at the same time to avoid a situation where a branch of 12 or 30 members would be represented. The proposal gave an additional 28 delegates to the Delegate Council Meeting and married two things. It maintained some kind of relationship with the present structure but did not pack the Delegate Council Meeting with small unrepresentative groups. The NEC would pursue with vigour the merging of small branches and the practice of observers from branches attending the Delegate Council would discontinue.

The Structure of the Society Document proposed six Annual Trade Conferences covering general print, binding and stationery; paper and board mill; fibreboard packing case; newspaper production and distribution; carton, multi-wall sack, rigid box and paper bag; and technical, administrative, executive and clerical. The number of representatives to attend each Trade Conference would be determined on a proportional representation basis. No individual member other than an elected full-time branch officer could be a representative to more than one Trade Conference. Branches within a particular trade sector and the National Executive Council would submit motions to the Annual Trade Conference which would then submit motions to the Delegate Council. The decisions of the Annual Trade Conferences were to be recommendations to the next Delegate Council or, in the interim period, to the Executive Council. Although the Trade Conferences would be advisory, it was anticipated that the effects of their work would be positive. The Annual Trade Conferences would deal with trade matters so Delegate Council Meetings would not be lumbered with motions on industrial matters. By the same token, the Trade Conferences would not be saddled with debates on funeral benefits, etc. Although the Delegate Council would continue to deal with matters of high policy, Annual Trade Conferences would prevent situations at the Delegate Council Meeting where members from one trade section voted on matters affecting exclusively another section.

The *Structure of the Society Document* proposed an Executive Council of 32 members of which 20 would be Trade Section representatives and 12 area representatives. The Executive Council, in addition to representatives from geographical areas, would now also reflect the trade sectors in which SOGAT had membership. In proposing an NEC of trade and geography interests the document sought to achieve a situation whereby all groups had representation on the NEC but at the same time the numerical position of the larger branches and trades was acknowledged. In the past, the union's Executive Council had never had representation from the multi-wall sack, wholesale newspaper distribution or the fibreboard trades.

On the question of the branch groups system it was proposed that if the Trade Conferences were successful then the 1974 Biennial Delegate Council would be invited to phase out the group system. The Annual Trade Conferences would involve more people in decision-making on a more democratic basis. Each Annual Trade Conference would address issues of direct relevance to the groups concerned. This was not the situation with branch group meetings. It was impracticable to operate both systems since there would be no single chain of responsibility and authority and the financial cost would be beyond the Society's means. Although the Trade Conference system would be more expensive than the branch group system, the *Structure of the Society Document* argued that this would be more than offset by increased membership involvement in the affairs of the Society via the Trade Conference system.

The *Structure* document proposed the abolition of the Papermaking Advisory and the Women's Advisory Committees. The Papermaking Advisory Committee had been established in 1966, against the background of no members with papermaking experience serving on the National Executive Council. Members of the Committee were unhappy, claiming that no clear thought had been given to its functions beyond saying that it was advisory. Within the Trade Conference structure papermaking members would be able to make recommendations to the NEC and the Biennial Conference. The Women's Advisory Committee had not served its purpose and had found it difficult to segregate men's and women's interests when reviewing industrial problems. The Women's Advisory Committee had not proved effective as a way of dealing with the problems confronting the women members of the union. The General Secretary told delegates: 'I do not think there are many exclusively women's problems any more than there are exclusively men's problems.'[18]

The proposed reform of SOGAT's structure recognised the union consisted of various trade sections which had connections between each other but which nevertheless had their own special and peculiar industrial practices. The *Structure* document asserted that it was prudent to produce new arrangements that acknowledged this situation. The opposition to the *Structure* document came mainly from London and Merseyside and centred around four arguments: cost, a change in the distribution of power within the union, sectarianism and the opinion that the existing structure worked well. It was argued that the new structure would be more costly than the existing one and thereby a waste of members' money. The second argument was that the proposals surrendered control of the union to the National Executive Council. Motions passed at Annual Trade Conferences would only be recommendations to the next Delegate Council or in the interim to the NEC. Unless there was an immediately following Delegate Council the document effectively meant the NEC would control the fate of the union between Delegate Council meetings. A third argument against the *Structure* document was that Trade Conferences put the union into separate boxes which it might difficult to climb out of. Branches might want to use a Trade Conference as a tactical measure to get something defeated so that it could not appear at a future Delegate Meeting. Likewise, a branch could have a motion carried at a Trade Conference only to be told the topic of the motion was not a matter for the Trade Conference but for the Delegate Council. The opponents predicted the new structure could lead to 'dillying and dallying' between the two bodies.

A fourth argument was that nothing under the existing structure prevented SOGAT from tackling the technical problems affecting the industry or the government's legislative interference into industrial relations. If the present structure had evolved as claimed by the General Secretary, then there was little case for a completely new structure. The present one was adequate to deal with the union's current industrial problems and any difficulties arising from a more legally regulated industrial relations system. If the NEC genuinely desired to devise a completely new and updated structure, their opponents said this could easily be done within the union's present decision-making mechanisms which had stood the test of time.

The Biennial Delegate Council

The 1972 Delegate Council accepted the NEC's *Structure* document by 194 votes to 135 to give the decision-making structure shown in Figure 10.2. The Scottish Graphical Division was added in October 1975 on the merger with SGA. The Delegate Council then went on to consider amendments to the Document. It accepted there be a Trade

Conference to cover art, technical, administrative, sales and clerical members and that the basis of representation at the Paper and Board Mills Trade Conference be one delegate per 750 members instead of the one per 1,000 members originally proposed. Paper and board membership had fallen from 40,000 to 30,000 and by granting a ratio of one delegate to 750 members, representation at their Trade Conference would remain at 40 as originally planned in the *Structure* document. However, delegates rejected a motion from the Solent Branch to lower the number of members required by a branch to gain representation at the Annual Trade Conference. The Solent Branch argued that if it was necessary to extend democracy and membership participation at Trade Conferences, then the best way to achieve this was to reduce the number of members required for a branch to have the right to a delegate, to give members from the shop floor an opportunity to attend Trade Conferences and to prevent Trade Conferences being dominated by Branch Secretaries, many of whom would not be working at the trades. The delegates also rejected an NEC's motion to end the system of observers at the Delegate Council. The system had been introduced in 1966 but only three observers had attended the 1968 Delegate Council Meeting, five at the 1970 Meeting and four at the 1972 Meeting. The NEC argument had been that the reduction to 100 members in the minimum size of branch for representation made observers from unrepresented branches unnecessary.

A perennial issue at Delegate Council was an age limit for delegates. In 1980 it was agreed that delegates from the branches had to be 65 or less in the case of men and 60 or less in the case of women at the date of the Council Meeting. The Delegate Councils of 1956, 1960 and 1964 had, on the advice of the NEC, defeated attempts by the London Central Branch (1956), the London Bookbinders (1960) and the PMB (1964) to impose an upper age limit on delegates. NEC argued that if members over the age over 60/65 were playing an active part in chapels and paying full subscriptions they should have the right to attend the Delegate Council, where their knowledge and practical experience would be of value and that the best people to judge who were the right representatives from the branch were the branch members themselves. By 1980 the NEC had changed its mind arguing an upper age limit on branch delegates would encourage younger members to attend the Council Delegate Council.

By the late 1970s, concern was being expressed that Delegate Councils spent too much time on changing rules and not enough on debating

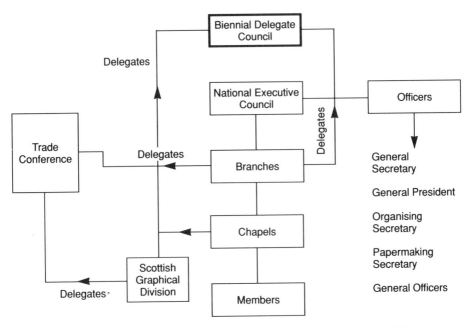

Figure 10.2   The organisational structure of SOGAT/SOGAT (75)

policy issues. This led the Edinburgh Branch at the 1978 Delegate Council to suggest that changes to the union's rules be dealt only with at every other conference, but the suggestion was rejected. The Edinburgh Branch argued that more time should be spend debating policy questions as the Rules had stood the test of time and need only be debated at alternate conferences. The branch was supported by the NEC which argued that having rule changes as the first part of the Delegate Council business and the policy motions as the second part often meant the latter went through without debate. At the 1980 Delegate Council, the Yorkshire Ridings Branch re-ran the Edinburgh motion pointing out the Council spent 3½ days considering rules, and important though this was, insufficient time was left for discussion of policy issues. The 1978 Delegate Council had considered 66 propositions on rule changes whilst the 1980 Council was considering 197 motions covering 54 rules. The Yorkshire Ridings Branch had the support of the NEC which accepted the Delegate Council needed sufficient time to deal with industrial and political issues important to SOGAT as a trade union and not get 'bogged down' with rule changes. However, the motion was again defeated. The Merseyside Branch at the 1984 Delegate

Council was also unsuccessful in persuading delegates to accept that 'revision or amendment of rules should be dealt with at alternative Delegate Councils'. Nevertheless, the ATAES Branch was successful without debate in persuading the 1986 Delegate Council to accept the following motion:

> Conference is concerned that too much time is taken up with the revision of the General Rule Book which means that important policy matters do not receive the attention they deserve. We, therefore, instruct the NEC to give detailed consideration to the matter with a view to placing before the 1988 Biennial Delegate Council a motion designed to alleviate the problem.[19]

In giving effect to this motion, the NEC proposed to the 1988 Delegate Council that the revision of rules be dealt with at alternative Delegate Councils. The NEC argued this would give more time to discuss policy issues and would allow one Delegate Council to consider both rule changes and policy issues and the next to consider policy only. In the past, policy motions had been hurried through and many decided in the final session of conference. At the 1984 Delegate Council, 28 motions had been carried without debate and the equivalent figure for the 1986 Council was 42. The NEC proposal that rules be changed every four years was carried by 178 votes to 162.

Trade Conferences

A seventh Annual Trade Conference to protect and advance the interests of clerical workers was introduced in 1974. It was felt that these members should have the same rights as any other members with respect to sectional and trade meetings. It was considered that the interest of clerical members and ATAES members would be best served if they had their own Trade Conferences. The ATAES Branch was comprised of managers and supervisors whilst clerical staff were working people with different problems. The establishment of a seventh Trade Conference was opposed on the grounds that six were ample and to add to them would be a waste of money. Others argued there were clerical workers in membership of ATAES and that this Branch adequately represented their needs since clerical employees had a kinship with managers and supervisors.

There was a wide difference of opinion about the effectiveness of the Trade Conferences. The London Central Branch proposed to the 1976 Delegate Council, for three reasons, that Trade Conferences be abolished. First, they were seen as a waste of time and money which could be better spent in some other direction. Second, their achievements were nil in that a proposition carried at a Trade Conference was opposed by the NEC when it came to the Delegate Council. If a proposition was lost at a Trade Conference then it was lost forever when a Delegate Council might have carried the proposition. Third, they dealt with little real business and apathy abounded. What had started as a health exercise had soon lost its effectiveness. Members had become frustrated about what could be achieved at Trade Conferences. Matters that were passed at local branches were often found by the Trade Conferences to be 'superfluous' because they could not be discussed as a result of government pay policy or had to be submitted to Head Office. Supporters of the Trade Conference system considered that they allowed chapel officials to gain experience to do their jobs and were an excellent training ground and a introduction to trade union conferences. Supporters also argued that the Trade Conference provided a means for members to meet others working in the same industry from other areas, that Trade Conferences were still in their infancy, and although they were not perfect they should be reformed and not abolished. When the motion to abolish Trade Conferences was put to the vote it was overwhelmingly defeated.

The General Secretary, Bill Keys, then moved a motion that Trade Conferences be held biennially and in the opposite year to the Delegate Council Meeting. He admitted that Trade Conferences had not come up to expectations in that they had not brought greater involvement from the workshop, but he added that they were in their infancy and should be allowed to develop. He assured delegates that the decisions of Trade Conferences would be endorsed by the NEC unless they conflicted with another section of the industry. He argued that biennial Trade Conferences would reduce costs, and that by having Trade Conferences on alternate years to the Delegate Councils there would be more time to get more grassroot members involved in the business of the Conference. The vote to make Trade Conferences biennial was carried by 190 votes to 169. The Delegate Council then abolished the Clerical Trade Conference on the grounds there would still be branch autonomy for clerical workers and ATAES members but they could come together in one Trade Conference to discuss common problems.

Biennial Trade Conferences were abolished by the 1978 Delegate Council but the NEC was given authority to call special trade meetings if and when the need arose. Trade Conferences had been set up to meet the challenge of the changing patterns of the industry, increasing government intervention in pay determination and the need for greater involvement from the shop-floor. These objectives were still valid but it had to be recognised that the Trade Conferences had not fulfilled expectations. They were no longer serving the interests of the wider membership and the money to finance the Trade Conferences could be used more effectively. Their timetables had been dramatically shortened and some were completing their business in less than one day, with additional speakers being drafted in to 'pad out' the Conference. For some, Trade Conferences were a duplication of effort, costly and slow in their reaction to technological change. However, some delegates strongly defended the Trade Conference system. It was argued they had not had a fair test and had achieved much in the short period of their existence, for example the opportunity to meet fellow members and to share the experiences gained on the shop-floor. The system had provided a 'stepping stone for new boys' in that they gained experience of public speaking and arguing the members' point of view. The Conferences had given the various trade interests in SOGAT a forum where they could debate improvements in their specific working conditions. During the government's restraint on wages (1975–8) the Trades Conferences had been inhibited, but with the movement back towards free collective bargaining they would come into their own. In closing the debate on the abolition of Trades Conferences, the General Secretary summarised the case for abolition as follows:

> The Trades Conferences were designed to see lay membership involvement, to see feedback from the shop floor but it has to be acknowledged that at these Conferences invariably were getting the same motions coming up and indeed we are having great difficulty in keeping them going half a day let alone a day. There is a constant padding of them and when people say 'hang on until we get into a freer position so far as legislation is concerned' it is like waiting for God to turn up – he is never going to turn up.[20]

Trade Conferences were abolished by 177 votes to 171, a majority of six.

The National Executive Council

The 1978 Delegate Council also reformed the composition of the National Executive Council which in future would be elected on a solely geographical basis and its size reduced from 32 seats to 31. This return to the system which had prevailed prior to 1972 was on the grounds that the trade section representation was grossly unfair. The General Print, Binding and Stationary Section elected 12 representatives which meant one NEC representative for every 7,800 members. The Paper and Board Mill Section had four members on the NEC giving a ratio of one for every 8,500 members. The ratio for the Fibreboard Packing Case Section was one to 11,250 members, for the Carton, Multi-wall Sack, Rigid Box and Paper Bag Section one to 14,000 members and ATAES Section one to every 2,700 members. The NEC proposals provided a more reasonable proportional representation on the NEC in that no one group/branch would be in a more advantageous position than any other. They also removed the anomaly of the present system whereby a full-time Branch Secretary had two opportunities to gain a seat on the NEC whilst lay members had only one. If Branch Secretaries were unsuccessful in the election to a trade section seat then they could then stand for a geographical constituency. This right was denied the lay member.

THE LOCATION OF HEAD OFFICE

The 1976 Delegate Council accepted that authority for deciding the location of SOGAT's Head Office should be changed from the National Executive Council to the Biennial Delegate Council. The background was the decision in 1975 of the NEC to transfer SOGAT's Head Office from Nightingale Lane in London to a new Head Office at Hadleigh in Essex.[21] In 1934, when the NUPB&PW purchased Nightingale Lane it had 50,000 members. By the early 1970s it had 200,000 members. Head Office, throughout these years, had constantly grappled with the problems of matching service to the membership with the office space available. To service its growing membership, in the early 1970 the union had to close the canteen and the rest room and convert the Board Room at Nightingale Lane into offices. However, the problem of inadequate office space remained. Larger offices were needed not only to provide effective administration but to develop additional facilities required by the membership, for example the establishment of a research/projects department and the need to cope with government legislation in the fields of health and safety, equal pay, sex discrimination and pensions. The National Executive Council and the Final Court of Appeal needed housing and facilities were required by those members who came to Head Office under the appeals disciplinary procedure. Nightingale Lane could not house any of these essential developments.

The NEC required a new property that would be freehold, would contain 18,000 square feet of office space and would require only a limited amount of money additional to the selling price of Nightingale Lane. Over a three-year period, 87 properties were examined, the majority of which were in central London. In most cases where the amount of office space met the requirements of the union the lease had to be purchased. The high building costs in the centre of London meant the purchase price of such leasehold properties was in excess of £1½ million, which was beyond the union's resources. The NEC looked beyond Greater London but in most cases the accommodation available required major structural alterations or the price was too high. The South East Essex Branch drew the NEC's attention to land available at Hadleigh which had planning permission from the local authority for the erection of a building and which offered SOGAT a development site at minimum additional costs. The contract was signed with a view to occupying the premises in September 1976. Hadleigh would house all the union's present services, provide accommodation for meetings of the NEC and the Final Appeal Court and additional office space for education services, any enlargement of the NEC and officers corps that might arise from future amalgamations. Hadleigh was 30 miles from central London on the main London–Southend Road and was well served by rail. The building at Hadleigh cost about half that of a comparable building in London. The sale of Nightingale Lane provided over half the costs of building Hadleigh and the further costs were offset by the sale of the SOGAT Edinburgh Branch Office which had remained empty since the removal of the Branch to other premises.

In challenging the transfer of Head Office from Nightingale Lane to Hadleigh, the London Central Branch complained that Head Office was going to the 'mudflats near where the prison hulks used to load'. Members of the LCB felt there should have been more consultation with the membership about the move, pointing out that no report on the move had been given to the 1976 Delegate Council. Defending the NEC decision the General Secretary stressed that the move was long overdue, as services to members were in danger of breaking down entirely if larger premises were not found. Hadleigh, although not palatial, would facilitate provision of the services the members required. Nevertheless, the NEC decided not to oppose the view that in future any decisions on the location of Head Office rest with the Delegate Council and not the NEC.

BRANCH DEVELOPMENTS

New Branches

In the early 1970s SOGAT began recruiting technical, administrative and executive staff in the printing, paper and allied trades. The Art, Technical, Administrative, Executive and Sales (ATAES) Branch had been established but was not primarily concerned with organising non-manual workers in general print or newspapers but rather such workers in papermaking, paper conversion and multi-wall sack manufacture. In these industries non-manual employees were unorganised and unions outside of print and paper, notably the former ASTMS, were threatening to start recruiting them. To compete with ASTMS, SOGAT had to be as professional as that union and felt compelled to organise supervisors, administrators, technicians, managers, etc. in the papermaking industry into a separate section from its manual worker members. SOGAT had experienced instances of managers in papermills saying they would not join SOGAT if they had to deal with the part-time Branch Secretary for whom they were responsible in the work situation as far as discipline and supervision were concerned. Recruitment of non-manual workers was also threatened by SOGAT's image. Non-manual workers prized their status as managers and were reluctant to be associated with shop-floor workers. The SOGAT leadership was prepared to pander to this sense of status if it meant SOGAT could recruit such employees, could remain the only union in papermaking and paper conversion organising technical, sales, administrative and executive staff and could thus keep out competing unions.[22]

The 1976 Delegate Council accepted the ATAES Branch be allowed to conduct its own business as a national-based branch in the normal manner, as any other branch. It was no longer administered from Head Office, having removed to offices in Manchester. Its officers were assisted by two organisers. However, problems arose between the ATAES Branch and other SOGAT branches over the recruitment of clerical workers. In March 1976 the NEC agreed principles to be followed in deciding whether clerical members should belong to their local SOGAT branch or to the ATAES Branch. The principles laid down:

(i) Where clerical members belonged to branches with full-time Branch Secretaries they should remain with that branch unless, after consultation with Head Office, agreement was given to their moving.

(ii) Where there were Group or Combine Agreements covering clerical and ATAES members, clerical should remain with the ATAES Branch.

(iii) Where clerical members belonged to branches with part-time Branch Secretaries, the evaluation should be on the service the branch could provide. If the branch could not give the appropriate service then members should belong to the ATAES Branch.

(iv) Because of policies that had been adopted within the union, situations had arisen in certain areas where there were organised clerical workers in the local branch and ATAES members in the ATAES Branch. In such circumstances, one branch was to be made responsible for the members concerned.

These principles not only recognised the historical development in SOGAT of the organisation of white-collar workers but also provided the proper basis for organisation, namely what is best for the member. They helped to end the alienation of the ATAES Branch from local branches and to stem potential recruitment losses because the question of which branch should organise clerical workers remained unresolved. The ATAES gained membership steadily until the late 1980s. In 1988 the Circulation Representatives' Branch merged with ATAES, but the enlarged branch retained the latter's name. In the following year the London CAEP and ATAES amalgamated on 31 March 1989 to form the Clerical, Management and Sales (CMS) Branch giving a nation-wide working membership of 12,500. It also completed the process of unifying the separate SOGAT branches representing white-collar members. CMS had a female membership of over 40 per cent, which was higher than in any other SOGAT branch. There were five women on its branch committee.

The Scottish Graphical Association joined SOGAT in 1975 and became its Scottish Graphical Division (SGD) containing 32 branches of which only two – Glasgow and Edinburgh – were full-time administrations. The remaining branches had to rely on part-time Branch Secretaries and, when available, the assistance of the Divisional Office. By the mid-1970s, member complaints were being received at a growing rate about the lack of service from the Divisional Office. The 1977 SGD Delegate Meeting remitted to the Divisional Executive Committee a number of solutions to these problems. In 1978 a Recalled Delegate Meeting agreed a new structure. The Division was divided into three branches – the East Branch, the West Branch and the North Branch – each serviced by a full-time Branch Secretary. The new structure, approved by the Recalled Delegate Meeting, came into operation on 2 October 1978. The new structure had not been devised in isolation. The SOGAT General Secretary and General President had been involved, as had a working party of the NEC and the NEC itself. In December 1982 the SGD decided to end its divisional status and to become the Scottish Graphical Branch (SGB) of SOGAT. Its special status in the union was seen as no longer necessary and there was a need to cut the cord that linked the SGD with the old SGA. Although the NEC endorsed the SGD being granted branch status, the end of divisional status could only be granted by a Delegate Council. The 1984 Delegate Council accepted that the SGD become a branch on the condition that it did not use this new status to extend its membership outside its traditional areas, for example to organise in papermaking. In 1988 the Glasgow and West of Scotland and Dundee Branches joined the SGB.

In 1989 a new national branch of SOGAT – the Electrical and Technical Services Branch – was formed when the 1,000-strong London Press Branch of the EETPU voted by a majority of two to one to leave that Union. This was the biggest defection from the EETPU since its 1988 expulsion from the TUC for poaching other unions' members. The London Press Branch recruited in electrical, plumbing, electronic, communications and technical services in industries where SOGAT had traditionally organised. The former EETPU Press Branch Secretary, Sean Geraghty, became full-time Secretary of the new London Press Branch. In 1991, however, the Branch merged with SOGAT's Multi-trades Branch.

Branch Mergers

The encouragement of branch merger to create full-time administrations and better servicing to the membership continued in SOGAT

(75) and SOGAT (82), whose organisational structure is shown in Figure 10.3. However, the 1974 Delegate Council rejected an NEC *Fusion of Branches* document[23] which outlined the principles to govern the merger of branches for the creation of full-time branch administration. The NEC document stressed it was not condemning the fruitful service part-time Branch Secretaries had given over the years to the union. Technological developments and changing company structures meant the Branch Secretary's job was getting harder and the common goals of the membership could no longer be maintained on the basis of part-time branches. Small branches could not exploit organisational potential but full-time ones, by employing organising staff, would be in a better position to do so. A multiplicity of small part-time branches caused financial problems and duplication of services within the union as a whole. The document acknowledged that, on a voluntary basis, SOGAT had seen a rapid movement towards branch mergers, but the pace had not been fast enough and needed to be quickened.

The *Fusion of Branches Document* was a statement of intent. Its proposals were not to be arbitrarily imposed, and its guidelines were indications of what the NEC would ideally like to see. If the princi-

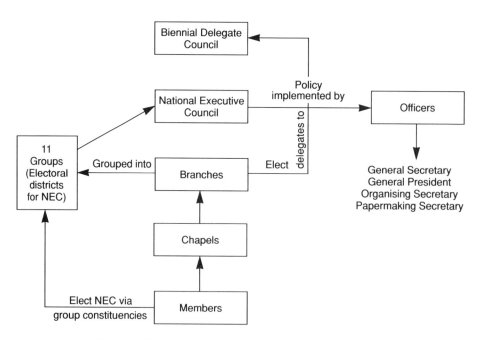

Figure 10.3   The organisational structure of SOGAT (82)

ples embodied in the document were acceptable, the NEC would consult with and listen to the views of the branches and their members. The proposals were designed to create a new image and to provide a more efficient and effective organisation than currently existed. The NEC was not forcing the issue and committed itself to vary its proposal if branches could demonstrate that, by so doing, the members would be better serviced.

However, there was opposition to the *Fusion of Branches* document. Some delegates argued its acceptance would permit the NEC to trespass on branch autonomy. The opposition was well expressed by a delegate from the Hartlepool Branch:

> We believe in an organisation like ours, the only way to obtain fusion is by persuasion not compulsion. To force branches which are used every day to fighting for their very existence with employers etc. to fuse will only provoke resistance and defections within our union, and to say the least will cause lasting bitterness. This union, as it has been rightly said, is the product of amalgamation but amalgamation by consent. We in Hartlepool want no part of a shotgun marriage. Like most virgins we want to be persuaded. What we say is don't be impatient, we will fuse, but by consent.[24]

The Delegate Council refused to endorse the NEC's *Fusion of Branches* document. However, branch mergers continued on a voluntary basis, gathering pace in the late 1980s as SOGAT's membership fell. In 1973 SOGAT had 165 branches. By 1976, this had fallen to 142, of which 99 were part time. As shown by Table 10.5, the number of branches fell from 87 in 1986 to 60 at the time of the merger with NGA. By the end of 1988, 95 per cent of SOGAT members were in full-time branches. In 1973 the Papermould and Dandy Roll Branch went out of existence and its members joined their appropriate local branch. In 1986 the Monotype Casters and Filmsetters' Branch merged with the PMB whilst in January 1988 the Ruling, Stationery and Packaging Branch and the Revisers, Ink and Roller Makers and Auxiliary (RIRM) Branch amalgamated to form a new branch called the Multi-trades Branch. Both branches recognised, in the face of an employers' offensive, future anti-trade union legislation and industrial changes within their various sections, the need to maintain and improve their services to the members. The creation of the Multi-trades Branch was the first merger in London between

Table 10.5
Number of SOGAT (82) branches, 1986–91

Date	Number of branches	Full-time branches	Part-time branches	Working members in full-time branches	Working of members in part-time branches
1986	87	45	42	—	—
1987	76	44	32	150,616	10,703
1988	67	41	26	143,405	8,085
1989	64	38	26	168,466	8,730
1990	60	37	25	160,686	8,310
1991	62	36	24	150,000	8,000

Source: Annuals Reports, 1986–91, National Executive Council.

a former NATSOPA branch and former SOGAT branch since the amalgamation of the two unions in 1982.

In February 1987, in what was described by the SOGAT General President as a 'historic landmark', the London Central Branch and the Greater London Branch, formerly the London Women's Branch, amalgamated.[25] This brought to an end the tradition of a separate women's organisation dating back to the formation, in 1874, of Women Employed in Bookbinding which led the way for the first of a new wave of women's unions to be set up in the 1880s around the time of the famous 1889 match girls' strike at Bryant and May. Although the two Branches were under pressure from the NEC to amalgamate, the Equal Opportunities Commission under the Sex Discrimination Act (1975) carried out an investigation into the Branches and their areas of work. The Commission concluded there was discrimination between men and women because of the existence of the separate branches and the patterns of work and job opportunities. As a result, a non-discrimination notice was served on SOGAT in September 1986 and in the following November the London Central Branch voted by 2,317 votes to 1,708 and the Greater London Branch by 737 votes to 356, in favour of merger. New membership cards were issued and male and female members were to have equal access to vacancies notified through the call system for jobs in the general print, in warehouses and distribution and in Fleet Street newspapers. Job vacancies were to be allocated by seniority with length of membership of either branch counting equally. The merger terms guaranteed places for the former Greater London Branch on the new London Central Branch Committee, on branch delegations to the SOGAT Delegate Council and on the London District Committee.

THE FORMAT INTERNATIONAL DISPUTE

This dispute began in 1976 as a quarrel between the London Central Branch on the one hand and Format International and the London Women's Branch on the other. It not only embittered the relationship between the two Branches but developed to involve the company, SOGAT Head Office, ACAS, the NEC, the Final Court of Appeal and other print unions. Format International was a small firm in South London employing 10 men and 20 women. In March 1976 the company sent the London Central Branch a letter stating that the men were claiming work which had previously been done in the firm by women, and they found it difficult to understand what the men were claiming for since they were already working four or five and a half nights a week overtime (20–5 hours a week overtime). When SOGAT Head Office first heard from the employer about the dispute in June 1976 they did not regard it as being difficult to resolve. The London Women's Branch was prepared to return to the *status quo* but the London Central Branch continued 'blacking' work produced by the women. Meetings of the parties to solve the issue took place but no progress was made. On 8 October 1976 the London Central Branch chapel at Format International walked off the job. They had not been called out on strike.

On 26 October 1976 the General Secretary, Bill Keys, wrote to the two Branches seeking a meeting and pointing out that the union was being brought into disrepute and he could not sit back and watch one SOGAT Branch on strike against another. A demarcation dispute over equal pay and sex discrimination was not acceptable to the NEC and the London Central Branch was acting contrary to union policy as well as illegally. Shortly after this action by the General Secretary, the two Branches agreed a formula for resolving the dispute. There would be an immediate return to work on the conditions existing before the men walked out over their claim to do women's jobs. As to the 'jobs' that were the immediate cause of the dispute, both Branches arranged for their officials to meet with the MOC/FOC's to resolve the difficulties. The NEC decided to establish an NEC Committee of Inquiry.

However, when the men walked off the job, the women undertook the work the men were previously doing. When instructed by the NEC to stop this they refused, arguing that to do so would result in Format International closing down, and in them becoming unemployed, when they were not the ones who had caused the problem. In November 1976 the NEC asked the women to explain why they had refused to carry out NEC instructions and asked the General Secretary to intervene again in the dispute. In the following month ACAS became involved, but still no solution could be found. The NEC Inquiry Report, published in December 1976, recommended that both Branches and their officers observe SOGAT rules, no hostile action and no stoppage of work should take place by either Branch arising from the inter-branch dispute without the authority of the NEC, and any members failing to abide by the recommendations be disciplined. The NEC Report considered that the London Central Branch members, by leaving their place of employment, were in default of SOGAT General Rule 20 and recommended the Branch discipline the members concerned. It re-affirmed its instruction to the London Women's Branch that they cease performing work previously done by men and urged both Branches to abide by union policy. Five months after the NEC Report, the London Central Branch summonsed its members to appear before the Branch Committee which had ruled these members involved in the Format International dispute had no case to answer. In January 1977 the London Women's Branch chapel members at Format International appeared before the NEC who ruled they had acted improperly by refusing to obey its instruction. However, in view of the pressures being exerted on the chapel, the NEC decided to impose no penalty but repeated that the women should only carry out the work they performed before the dispute began. The London Central Branch was disappointed at the NEC's action and accused it of bias in favour of the women. At the end of 1977 another formula to end the dispute was proposed. Nine of the 10 men involved in the dispute would be reinstated for a period of two weeks but only four would commence work. The other five would receive a minimum payment of £1,000 plus two weeks' pay in lieu of notice. This formula was rejected by the London Central Branch whereupon the suggestion was made that an independent person be appointed to find a solution. This too was rejected by the London Central Branch which in April 1978 held a Delegate Meeting which considered four options. First, there be·a 10p levy placed on all members of the Branch to support the members employed at Format International. Second, the Branch withdraw contributions to Head Office until a satisfactory settlement was reached. Third, those in breach of the union's rules be disciplined. Fourth, the Branch Committee call a one-day stoppage through the industry in support of the Format International chapel. The General Secretary advised the Branch that what they were proposing was contrary to SOGAT Rules. The advice was disregarded and the Delegate Meeting voted for the 10p levy, that contributions to Head Office be withdrawn and that disciplinary action be taken against those acting contrary to rule.

The next stage in the dispute was the Final Appeal Court's award to vary the NEC decision to expel the women for not carrying out its instructions to one of censure, since they considered the pressures exerted upon the women were unjust. On 4 May 1978 the NEC endorsed its view that the London Central Branch was acting contrary to the union's rule and instructed its national officers to negotiate a return to work formula. A basis for a return to work was reached which provided for an independent chairman, for the 10 men to return to the payroll for a period of two weeks, for the optimum staffing level to be four, for those not re-engaged to receive £1,000 compensation, and for additional labour, when Format International's business picked up again, to be recruited from the two Branches. The NEC instructed the London Central Branch of this formula. However, the Branch put forward alternative proposals that the FOC be re-instated, the 10 members involved return to work at Format International and the women cease the work they were currently doing and give it the London Central Branch chapel. The NEC rejected these proposals, arguing that replacing women by men would be illegal, that the workload of Format International had, as a result of a two-year stoppage declined to such an extent that the re-instatement of four people was the most that could be achieved and that, the company preferred to close rather than reinstate the FOC.

The NEC reacted to the non-payment of subscriptions decision by issuing a summons against the London Central Branch and its officers for not complying with SOGAT General Rules, by directing the Branch to forward the Minutes of the Delegate Meeting and to forward a cheque for £50,000 outstanding in contributions to the national union. The London Central Branch refused to attend the NEC to discuss these instructions. The NEC stood on the principle that SOGAT Rules were to be observed by all branches, that Delegate Councils determine the rules and that no branch can flaunt them. The NEC therefore placed before the 1978 Delegate Council an emergency motion which instructed the London Central Branch to withdraw its decision not to pay contributions to the national union. The motion was to restore the authority of the union and confirm the principle no branch could contract out of the National Rules. When the emergency motion was called, the London Central delegation left the Delegate Council despite having accepted the President's ruling that delegates leaving the meeting would be excluded from the remainder of the Delegate Council. When the London Central delegates left the hall, the NEC emergency motion was carried unanimously and the President ruled that all London Central Branch motions on the Delegate Council Agenda fell.

When the London Central Branch issued court proceedings against SOGAT the NEC told the General Secretary to defend the action. The matter came to court on 1 November 1978 but an out-of-court settlement was reached under which the President acknowledged that following the withdrawal of the London Central delegates from the 1978 Biennial Delegate Meeting the exclusion of the London Central Branch delegation from the remainder of that conference was unnecessary. In return, the London Central Branch regretted that it had felt compelled to pass a resolution to withdraw contributions to the national union but wished it made known that it had never implemented the resolution. The NEC also agreed to use its best endeavours to change the rules so that no emergency motions criticising any branch or its officers would be considered until the session during which such a resolution was tabled. Messrs Chard, Gardner and Huggett, all London Central Branch members, would be reinstated as members of the National Executive Council. In return, the London Central Branch would call off the pickets at Format International immediately upon the General Secretary using his best endeavours to have Format International honour the terms agreed with him in a letter dated 12 May 1978. There would be an inquiry by a member of the Bar into the reasons why SOGAT had not secured a return to work of all male members who worked for Format International and into relations between the London Women's Branch and the London Central Branch. The inquiry committee would then make recommendations. All disciplinary charges outstanding against officers of the London Central Branch would be withdrawn. Thus ended one of the more distressing inter-branch disputes in SOGAT's history.

RANK AND FILE ATTEMPTS AT CONSTITUTIONAL CHANGE

There were frequent, but unsuccessful, attempts by branches at the Delegate Council Meetings to reduce the minimum size of branch membership for representation there. The objective was to achieve representation for every branch regardless of its size. There were three main reasons for this. First, whatever the size of a branch it should have the right to be at the Delegate Meeting, to participate in its discussions and report to members on what had happened. Second, there were some branches, particularly papermill ones, that were too small and too isolated for merger with other branches, and if they were forced to amalgamate the members concerned might leave the union or become apathetic, leaving room for non-unionism. Third, it was argued that so long as there were branches that did not have the right of representation at the Delegate Council there were disenfranchised members. However, the counter-arguments always carried the day. The NEC was satisfied that the Delegate Council represented fairly the broad interests of the membership in terms of groups and branches, that to increase its size would substantially increase its costs and that the amalgamation of branches would ultimately end small branches.

The 1976 and 1978 Delegate Council Meeting rejected motions from the North West Group (1976) and the Glasgow and West of Scotland Branch (1978) that SOGAT hold annual conferences instead of biennial ones. The same arguments were used at both meetings. The supporters of annual conferences considered that an increasing number of motions at biennial conferences were being put to the vote after being only formally moved and seconded, that restrictions of finance and workload were not valid reasons for refusing annual conferences, that there was increasing political interference by the government in wage bargaining and in industrial relations law, and that wages and conditions were changed annually. Given all these developments, it was felt that to wait two years to determine a common policy was too long. The need for annual conferences had become imperative. The opponents of annual conferences, including the NEC, argued successfully against them on grounds of both cost and administration. Having annual conferences would not reduce the number of motions submitted, the NEC argued, the additional administrative burden at branch and Head Office level would become unbearable, the cost would be prohibitive and the quality of service to the membership would be jeopardised unless extra staff could be recruited, and that would mean increased contributions.

Over the period 1955 to 1991 there were a number of attempts by rank and file delegates to change the size of the National Executive Council. The 1974 and 1980 Councils sought to increase its size. At the former, an attempt was made to gain two extra seats on the NEC whilst the latter witnessed efforts to increase its size by one seat. In both cases the group of branches concerned – the North West in 1974 and East Anglia Group in 1980 – argued that their proposals would improve the representative nature of the NEC. For example, the 1974 motion sought representation on the NEC for clerical members. The NEC successfully opposed both attempts to increase its size, arguing that if this were to happen it would not give greater proportional representation but rather give overrepresentation to certain groups and areas.

NATSOPA had an all-lay Executive Council and at the SOGAT 1984 and 1988 Delegate Council Meetings former NATSOPA Branches – Manchester (1984) and London Clerical (1988) unsuccessfully attempted to introduce an all-lay Executive Council for SOGAT. It was argued that such an NEC would broaden the democratic basis of the union by making its structure shop-floor based, would develop the continuity of rank and file involvement in decision-making between Delegate Councils and the NEC and would provide a union in which lay members gave instructions to the paid officials about how the union should be run; thus the situation of a union dominated and controlled by full-time officers would end. The supporters of an all-lay Executive Council also considered SOGAT was based on two common but contradictory principles. First, the union claimed to be democratic, and second, it advocated 'best-person' government. However, the overwhelming majority of NEC members were full-time branch officers, and this situation led to decisions being taken in the light of the interests of paid officials rather than those of the membership, and also to too much power being concentrated in too few hands. It was also argued that branch officers were elected to assist members with their industrial problems and not to sit on the NEC – this could in fact lead to full-time officers getting out of touch with their memberships, seeing membership of the NEC as their highest priority and devoting their energies to canvassing for votes to further their careers.

In successfully opposing proposals for all-lay Executive Councils, the

NEC marshalled a number of arguments. First, it was wrong to disenfranchise any SOGAT member from offering themselves to serve on the NEC. Second, full-time secretaries brought expertise to the NEC and it would destroy the fundamental principle of the right of a person to present themselves to the membership if full-time officials were debarred from the NEC. Third, in the final analysis it was the membership who decided who they wanted to represent them, whether on the NEC, as General Secretary, as General President, and so on. The membership, it was stressed, must have the right to express their views as to who should represent them. The case against an all-lay Executive was well summarised by the Greater Manchester Branch Secretary at the 1988 Delegate Conference in the following words:

> I refute categorically the denial of my right as a trade union officer to stand for the NEC or anyone else in this union. I will not bear with anyone who seeks to take that right away from me. I have spent my time on the shop floor, my best friends are on the shop floor and I will never move away from them. If anyone on the platform, any NEC member or anyone else, moves away from the people on the shop floor the remedy is to remove him. Do not make second class citizens.[26]

Organisers were appointed by the NEC but at five Delegate Council Meetings – 1974, 1976, 1978, 1980 and 1986 – there were unsuccessful attempts to change this situation and submit organisers to election by the whole membership. The main arguments used in support of the election of organisers were the democratic right of the members to decide who represented them at every level, that organisers had industrial duties – including negotiating on behalf of the members – and members should decide who represented them in such situations and that being selected rather than elected meant no accountability to the membership in general. If it was important to retain the democracy in SOGAT then there should be no exception to official positions being subject to ballot. Those who wished to retain the appointment system argued that no system was perfect but the present one was as fair as you could get; under a ballot system a small branch would have little chance of one of its members being elected even though their candidate might be the best for the job and under an electoral system candidates could be elected yet their abilities be unknown to the electorate. The selection system was also justified on the grounds that organisers had special responsibilities and it was only through the appointment system that the union could sustain the good work undertaken by organisers. The principle of election of organisers was inappropriate. The NEC believed the selection of organisers was not only efficient but produced an effective organising staff. All applications from candidates for organisers' positions were examined closely. A shortlist was drawn up and candidates sat a written and oral examination. The NEC thought it inappropriate to make organisers accountable through the balloting system when they were policy implementators and not policy-makers.

The issue of periodic re-election of national officers was another perennial at Delegate Council Meetings. The issue was debated at the 1956, 1968, 1984, 1986 and 1988 Councils on motions from the London Central Branch (1956, 1968 and 1984) and the London Machine Branch (1986 and 1988) but on each occasion the Delegate Council voted to retain the system that once officers had been elected they should not stand for re-election. The London Machine Branch was attempting to have introduced the former NATSOPA practice of periodic re-election of national officers. Those supporting periodic re-election presented four main arguments. First, they argued that chapel officials, chapel committee and branch committee members faced periodic re-election and this should apply to national officers. All officers in the union would be accountable to the members, have to stand on their record and be democratically elected and re-elected. Re-election would ensure accountability of all officers in that their record would be put on the line to enable the members to decide if they should remain in office. If re-election was good for lay members then it was good for national officers. There was no substitute for the support of the membership expressed in a ballot. A second argument used by the 're-election school' was that if periodic re-election would discourage good candidates from standing for national office, then they could not be good candidates in the first place. Third, no reason could be seen why there should be any fear by the existing national officers or any future aspirants, as a really foul deed or massive feat of mismanagement would be needed for an officer to be defeated in a re-election ballot. Fourth, it was argued that, if the membership felt their interests were not being reflected by the people who represented them, then they should regularly call their representatives to account.

The NEC always opposed moves to make national officers stand for re-election. They used six main arguments. First, national officers were accountable to NEC which had authority to dispense with the services of an officer. The procedure provided a fair hearing for the officers to defend themselves. Second, national officers were policy implementors and not policy-makers and it was therefore illogical to make them accountable for policies to which they had not been party in deciding. National officers would demand a vote at the NEC thus upsetting the principle of proportional representation which determined the size of the NEC. Third, the current system had operated in the interests of the membership. Officers were not periodically looking over their shoulders and did not base their actions on what was popular rather than what was in the greater interests of the whole membership. Fourth, re-election would influence the type of candidates coming forward. Individuals would not give up a stable job as a branch officer or organiser to be judged periodically. Fifth, the union would be involved in continual ballots. Finally, it was argued that ballots did not really determine the competency of officers and there was a danger re-election would result in national officers providing excellent service to the large chapels and branches at the expense of the quality of service to the small chapels and small branches.

NATIONAL OFFICERS

The NUPB&PW and SOGAT (Division A) the general officers were the General Secretary, the General President, the Organising Secretary and the Papermaking Secretary. When SOGAT was reconstituted in 1972 its general officers were these four officers plus one general officer. This was to accommodate into the officer structure Bill Miles, who had been elected an officer of the original SOGAT. The 1974 Delegate Council Meeting agreed not only that Bill Miles should become a general officer but also that two divisional officers be elected by ballot of the membership. When its membership was 50,000 the NUPB&PW had four general officers and in 1974 with a membership of 170,000 it had only five officers. Industrial matters were now more complex, officers were stretched to their limits and the NEC was concerned that the quality of service to the membership would decline. The divisional officers would be below the status of a general officer but higher than that of an organiser. The divisional officers were retitled general officers by the 1980 Delegate Council Meeting. The title of divisional officer had been adopted as future amalgamations were seen as developing on the basis of trade divisions. However, apart from the creation of the SGD, there were no divisions in the union.

The two divisional officers carried out functions across the whole union and they were referred to as national officers both in correspondence to Head Office and when they met with employers. Since the divisional officers had *de facto* national coverage, to change their title was logical even though there would be no change in their functions.

The NUPB&PW/SOGAT (Division A)/SOGAT Rule Book made no provision for a Financial Secretary who historically had been a member of Head Office staff and was responsible under the General Secretary for the administration of Head Office, of the union's funds and for the day-to-day income and expenditure of the union. In addition, the financial secretary drafted documentation on behalf of the union but could not sign documents. The NEC considered that the Financial Secretary should have the same standing as all other officers but that the system of appointing the Financial Secretary should continue. Permission was sought from the 1978 Delegate Council Meeting to spell out in the Rule Book the functions of the financial secretary. The officer was still to be appointed and to be accountable to the General Secretary. By listing their responsibilities in the Rule Book, financial secretaries would be more conscientious of their responsibilities. This NEC position was accepted by the 1978 Delegate Council Meeting.

The general officers of SOGAT (82) were the General President, the General Secretary, the Organising Secretary, the Papermaking Secretary and six general officers. The 1986 Delegate Council Meeting reduced the number of general officers to five while the 1988 Delegate Council reduced it to four. The NEC argued that on its formation, the total membership of SOGAT (82) was 204,000 and with four named officers plus six other general officers giving a ratio of one officer per 25,000 members. By 1988 the total membership was 161,000, with an officer complement of eight giving one officer per 26,000 members. On the basis of these figures, the NEC successfully argued that eight officers were sufficient to cover the trade interests in SOGAT (82) and there was no need to restore the officer complement back to nine.

The General President, the General Secretary, the Organising Secretary, the Papermaking Secretary and all other general officers were elected by a ballot of the whole membership, but the rules did not allow for their periodic re-election. No general officer could continue in office after they reached state retirement age. The general officers were also members of the NEC and as a result subject to re-election periodically under the Trade Union Act (1984). However, SOGAT's attitude to this legislation was 'business as usual' unless ordered to hold re-elections by a court order following a complaint by an individual member. This policy held until 1990 when Mr Braidwood threatened to trigger the 1984 Act (see Chapter 9). The Employment Act (1988) made General Secretaries and General Presidents, whether or not they were members of the NEC, face re-election every five years by a postal ballot of the membership from July 1989. In October 1988 the SOGAT General Secretary, Brenda Dean, informed the NEC she intended to stand for re-election immediately to avoid any likelihood of SOGAT being subjected to legal action through the courts for being in breach of the Employment Act (1988). As the senior officer she was the most exposed to a challenge under the law. It also meant the re-election ballot would be a normal SOGAT workplace ballot rather than the postal ballot which would have had to be used after July 1989. In addition to Brenda Dean, a nomination was received from Mr Bob Hills of the Maidstone Branch. In February 1989, Brenda Dean was declared re-elected with a overwhelming majority. The voting figures, on a 39.8 per cent turnout, were as follows:

B. Dean	43,517
R.E. Hills	13,657
Majority	29,860

The SOGAT General President, Mr Danny Sergeant, decided not to submit himself for re-election preferring not to co-operate with the Conservative government's anti-trade union legislation. However, eventually he did so under the threat of court action from Mr Braidwood.

The General President chaired the Delegate Council Meeting and all meetings of the National Executive Council with the right to speak on all questions. The President assisted the General Secretary in industrial issues and supervised the work of Head Office in the absence of the General Secretary. In this sense, the General President was also the Deputy General Secretary. However, the most important role of the President was to act as chief custodian of the union's constitution and the will of the membership as decided at the Bienniel Delegate Conference. Respect and dignity surrounded the office of President, who was without favour, binding every member in the union to its decisions, rules and proceedings decided by the members. The President ensured that no member or group of members contravened the union's constitution or principles because of their position. Over the period 1955 to 1991, SOGAT and its constituent unions had six Presidents – John McKenzie (1954–67), Vincent Flynn (1968–9), Bill Keys (1970–4), Albert Powell (1975–82), Brenda Dean (1983–4) and Danny Sergeant (1985–91). All set, and achieved, high standards. They wielded their authority at the NEC and Delegate Council Meetings with dignity and impartiality that was impressive. Whether it was a speaker from ·'the front bench' or from 'the floor' the same impartial treatment was given.

The General Secretary was the senior officer with the right to speak on any business at the Delegate Council Meeting and at the NEC and its sub-committees, but with no right to vote. The Secretary was automatically a delegate at all national conferences and those of any organisation (TUC, Labour Party, IGF, etc.) to which SOGAT was affiliated. The General Secretary was the Editor-in-Chief and responsible to the NEC for the conduct and control of the monthly journal. Over the period 1955 to 1991 SOGAT and its constituent unions had five General Secretaries – Bill Morrison (1947–61), Tom Smith (1961–70), Vincent Flynn (1970–4), Bill Keys (1974–84) and Brenda Dean (1985–91). Bill Morrison became General Secretary in 1947 having previously been Secretary of the London Central Branch since 1938. His period of General Secretaryship was best remembered for the achievement of the 40-hour working week (see Chapter 15). He unified, in his position as President of the P&KTF, the hours reduction claim. The success of this claim was in no small way due to Bill Morrison's leadership and personal endeavours.

On 11 January 1961, Tom Smith (26,454 votes) defeated John McKenzie (24,784 votes) and Vincent Flynn (14,521 votes) to become General Secretary. In February 1966 he became Joint General Secretary of SOGAT. Before election as General Secretary he had been, since 1951, the Secretary of the London Central Branch. Tom Smith dedicated himself to the members and took the initiative in suggesting the formation of the original SOGAT. He worked hard and did not spare himself, often at to the expense of his health. In December 1968 he suffered a heart attack from which he fortunately recovered. He received strong advice from his colleagues to take a period of convalescence and to take things easy until his retirement in November 1970. However, this advice was not heeded and he continued to work even harder. The result was that he undoubtedly worked himself to death. He died in his office on 3 August 1970 after having attended a meeting of the SOGAT (Division A) Executive Council.

In 1970, Vincent Flynn (22,469 votes) defeated Bill Keys (22,182 votes), Albert Powell (13,915 votes) and Cliff Phillips (11,285 votes) to become the General Secretary of SOGAT (Division A) and then subsequently of the reconstituted SOGAT. Since 1961 he had been the Organising Secretary. He was passionate about the need to involve young people in the affairs of SOGAT and the wider trade union and labour movement. He was a powerful speaker in terms of both style and presentation, and people would often listen to him in awe. His election came relatively late in his working life and meant there was insufficient time to develop the union as he would have liked. Among his proudest moments were the 1971 one-day strike by SOGAT against the Industrial Relations Act and the part he played in the release of the five dockers from Pentonville Prison in July 1972. SOGAT's support for the one-day strike over the 1971 Act was disapproved of by the TUC. This led Vincent Flynn to go to the rostrum at the 1971 Congress and accuse the TUC of being a crab because it always moved sideways. This did not endear him to the TUC leadership. However, Vincent Flynn never lost his commitment to the working-class movement.

In 1973, Bill Keys (27,577 votes) defeated Albert Powell (12,438 votes), John O'Leary (9,780 votes), John Selivry (8,992 votes), Alec Brandon (7,404 votes) and George Harrop (5,842 votes) to become the General Secretary. Between 1961 and 1970 Bill Keys had been Secretary of the London Central Branch and between 1970 and 1974 he had been SOGAT General President. On becoming General Secretary he changed SOGAT from being an inward-looking organisation to one heavily involved in wider trade union issues. He believed SOGAT had a responsibility to be active within the TUC, the Labour Party and society at large. He was an internationalist and forged links with unions throughout the world in a wide range of industries.

Of his many achievements two stand out. One was his co-ordination of the trade union political fund ballots campaign in 1985. The Trade Union Act (1984) required members to re-affirm their support for unions continuing with their political funds. He spearheaded the campaign and volunteered SOGAT as the first union to go to ballot, which ended in a resounding victory (see Chapter 14). Other unions followed and all unions with political funds persuaded their members that political funds should continue. He also achieved a number of important steps towards the development of one union for the industry by means of the 1975 merger of the SGA and SOGAT and then the 1982 merger of NATSOPA and SOGAT (75). His biggest disappointment was the failure to persuade the London Central Branch in 'Fleet Street' members to accept *Programme for Action* as the basis of the implementation of new technology in national newspapers.

At the wider trade union level Bill Keys made a significant contribution to shaping TUC policy in his role of Chairman of the Employment Policy and Organisation Committee, the Printing Industries Committee, the Media Committee and the Equal Opportunities Committee. He also served on the TUC's Finance and General Purposes Committee, and as one of its 'elder statesmen' was the trade union nominee for the Committee of Inquiry which resolved the national steel strike (1980) and the national water strike (1983). He was one of the seven senior TUC leaders who tried to resolve the miners' strike of 1984/5 (see Chapter 13). He was a TUC nominee on the Commission of Racial Equality, the Manpower Services Commission and the Central Arbitration Committee.

On 21 September 1983 the NEC were informed by Bill Keys he had given consideration to the instability that would prevail in the union over the next few years arising from five senior officers retiring within a short time of one another over the period April 1986 to November 1988. Bill Keys was due to retire on 1 January 1988 but felt it to be in the best interests of SOGAT that his position should be dealt with first. The NEC accepted his suggestion the union proceed to a ballot for his replacement, since whilst it was not Keys' intention to retire earlier than necessary a General Secretary Elect would facilitate an orderly changeover. Bill Keys retired early in March 1985 to co-ordinate the trade union political fund ballot campaign.

On 21 March 1984 the result of the General Secretary Elect ballot was announced: Brenda Dean (25,454 votes) defeated Danny Sergeant (13,935 votes), Dennis Hills (13,872 votes), Ted O'Brien (13,706 votes), John O'Leary (9,980 votes), Maurice Suckling (9,317 votes) and Alan Shaw (3,142 votes). A woman from Manchester was to lead a printing union for the first time in the 500 years of the printing industry's history. Dean had previously worked for the Manchester Branch – the largest outside London – for which she started working as a secretary at the age of 16 for the then Manchester Branch Secretary, Joe Sheridan. As Manchester Branch Secretary she increased membership involvement and created a strong sense of family unity by holding successful social events. Membership was doubled and good relationships formed with national newspaper employers in Manchester.

She was elected President of the union when Albert Powell stood down on the grounds of ill health. This established her on the national scene for the first time, although she had already received public notice through her radio and television appearances. As General Secretary she raised SOGAT's profile on a wide range of issues, including supporting Save the Children, Childline and One World, as well as bringing child victims of the Chernobyl nuclear disaster and the Azerbaijan earthquake to the union's convalescent home at Rottingdean for a holiday and health treatment. A wide spectrum of SOGAT membership took part in these events.

Brenda Dean introduced major changes to increase the participation and involvement of female SOGAT members. She built up morale and the involvement of the general membership to back her in persuading the NEC to approve the major financial reforms that were desperately needed to build funds after the Wapping dispute (see Chapter 19). She pioneered an advanced computer system so that every SOGAT branch was linked to Head Office for financial and information services. She enabled the introduction of education and training courses and broadened SOGAT's image away from that of a closed 'Luddite' organisation. Other initiatives for which she was responsible included the appointment of a full-time Press and Publicity Officer, *inter alia*, to revamp the union's journal.

Brenda Dean played a leading role on the General Council and was the first female officer to join the National Economic Development Council. She was also Deputy Chairperson of the National Women's Commission and took on many voluntary roles to enhance the union in an era in which the government strove to reduce the impact of trade unionism on society.

In the Wapping dispute her communication skills enabled her to capture the moral high ground, frequently putting News International at a disadvantage. However, by using every legal weapon handed to them by the Thatcher government, News International won the day – but only after Dean had extracted compensation for her members for the virtual destruction of their jobs. During the dispute it was sometimes hard to hold the union together as provincial members tired of the perceived intransigence of their London colleagues. The split was prevented and Dean took much of the blame from the London members for ultimately calling off the dispute after a year's struggle. The London members' feelings were never finally soothed and this was a factor in her narrow defeat by Tony Dubbins in the election for General Secretaryship of the GPMU.

Dean had seen a merger with the NGA as in the best interests of her members. Several of her predecessors had tried, and failed, to achieve one union for the industry. It was one of her greatest achievements that she finally drove this through even though she knew she was putting her own job on the line.

MONTHLY JOURNAL

The monthly journal was the link between the NEC and the members in the workshops and the papermills. It was the official organ of the union and the recognised medium for conveying information to the membership. The monthly journal of the NUPB&PW was entitled *The Paperworker* and the Editor-in-Chief was the General Secretary. Its last issue was in January 1967, having commenced publication in May 1940. The *Paperworker* had a high reputation and had carried the kind of material the majority of the membership wanted. The *NATSOPA Journal* also ceased publication at the same time and SOGAT (Division A) and SOGAT (Division 1) produced the *SOGAT Journal* covering the whole union.

In May 1972, the first issue of the monthly journal of the reconstituted SOGAT appeared under the title of the *SOGAT Journal*. In May 1974 its format changed to magazine style. However, sales remained disappointing and the NEC frequently complained much more could be done by branches to promote sales and urged chapels and branches to assist to achieve this objective. Nevertheless, the 1972 Delegate Council Meeting rejected a proposal that the *Journal* be distributed to the membership free of charge.

By 1984 the *Journal's* circulation was 35,000 per month, which was a low figure in comparison to the membership size of the union. However, in 1986 the *Journal* was launched in a new format, made free to the membership, the print run increased from 33,000 to 60,000 per month and for reasons of economy was published only 10 times a year by combining monthly journals July/August and December/January. In 1987 judges in the TUC trade union journal competition considered the *SOGAT Journal* was a very close contender for first prize in the magazine section in that it was well designed and full of articles for the members that were relevant without being heavy or over long. In 1988, for the second year running, the *SOGAT Journal* was picked the second-best union magazine by judges in the TUC annual trade union journal competition.

NOTES

1. See Society of Graphical and Allied Trades (82) *Annual Report of the National Executive Council, 1987*, p. 1.
2. See National Union of Printing, Bookbinding and Paperworkers *Report of the Biennial Delegate Council Meeting, 1960*, pp. 142–8.
3. See Society of Graphical and Allied Trades (Division A) *Report of the Biennial Delegate Council Meeting, 1966*, pp. 67–70.
4. See 'ATAES Branch Celebrates Ten Years of Achievement' *SOGAT Journal*, March 1985, pp. 6–7.
5. Society of Graphical and Allied Trades *Report of the Biennial Delegate Council Meeting, 1982*, pp. 252–3.
6. For a fuller discussion of SOGAT's attempts to reverse its decline in membership in the 1980s, see Society of Graphical and Allied Trades *Report on Recruitment*, to the Biennial Delegate Council Meeting, 1990.
7. Society of Graphical and Allied Trades (82) *Report of the Biennial Delegate Council Meeting, 1984*, p. 155.
8. Society of Graphical and Allied Trades (82) *Report of the Biennial Delegate Council Meeting, 1984*, pp. 155–61.
9. Op. cit., p. 5.
10. It reported 'It is clear that the area where we are not having full success is the recruitment of women'. See Society of Graphical and Allied Trades (1982) *Annual Report of the National Executive Council, 1989*, p. 1. The report considered that the union's contribution rate might be a factor in this.
11. There were, nevertheless, bound to hold two meetings with full representation from the branches and two meetings of the Group Executive Committee each year.
12. See 'PMB Celebrates 75 years' *The Paperworker*, February 1966, pp. 20–6.
13. See 'The Only One of its Kind: Run by Women for Women' *The Paperworker*, January 1967 pp. 14–26. By the late 1960s the London Women's Branch had 10,000 members. The Branch was the only one in the UK which was run entirely by women for women.
14. See 'The Paper Must Get Through' *The Paperworker*, July 1963 pp. 7–10. The Circulation Representatives Branch was a national branch. The chief responsibility of its members was to see that their particular publication reached every sales point in their area on time. The 'reps' were not newspaper salespeople but their efforts usually resulted in increased sales in their area. They were their paper's ambassadors, the link between Fleet Street and the remotest village. By no means all members of the Circulation Representatives Branch were representatives of newspapers. About 30 per cent were employed by the national magazine groups. For these members the emphasis was on selling rather than distribution.
15. For an account the terms upon which this branch merger took place see 'Binders and Central Branch to Join' *The Paperworker*, April 1965 pp. 10–11. The Binders Branch voted 1,411 to 715 in favour of merger and the Central Branch by 6,729 and 6,469. For a 'brief' history of the London Binders see 'Passing of the London Binders: Two Hundred Years of History' *The Paperworker*, May 1965, pp. 18–28.
16. In 1956, 1957, 1961, 1962, 1963, 1965 and 1967 over 90 per cent of the cases dealt

with by the NEC Appeals Committee involved members of the London Central Branch.

17. See Minutes of meeting of National Executive Council, SOGAT (Division A) held at Royal Victoria Hotel, St Leonards on Sea on Thursday and Friday 30 September and 1 October 1971.

18. See Society of Graphical and Allied Trades *Report of the Biennial Delegate Meeting, 1972*, p. 32.

19. See Society of Graphical and Allied Trades (82) *Report of the Biennial Delegate Meeting, 1986*, p. 173.

20. See Society of Graphical and Allied Trades *Report of the Biennial Delegate Council Meeting, 1978*, pp. 58–65.

21. For a fuller discussion of the reasons for this see 'Why SOGAT is On the Move. In More Ways Than One' *SOGAT Journal*, October 1975, p. 15.

22. For more information on the ATAES Branch see 'The ATAES: What's in it for Me?', *SOGAT Journal*, December 1975, p. 13; 'New ATAES Drive on White Collar Recruitment', *SOGAT Journal*, January 1976, p. 9; 'ATAES Branch Celebrates Ten Years of Achievement', *SOGAT Journal*, March 1985, pp. 6–7.

23. The 1934 Council had carried a motion on the merger of small provincial branches. The 1968 Council had accepted a motion calling for the merger of branches and the creation of full-time branch secretaries.

24. See Society of Graphical and Allied Trades *Report of the Delegate Council Meeting, 1974*, pp. 104–9.

25. See 'End of an Era for London Women' *SOGAT Journal*, May 1987 and 'The Golden Age of the 1950s', *SOGAT Journal*, June 1987, pp. 12–15.

26. See Society of Graphical and Allied Trades *Report of the Delegate Council Meeting, 1988*, p. 39.

CHAPTER 11

THE FINANCIAL STRUCTURE DEVELOPMENTS

The main fund of SOGAT and its constituent unions was the General Fund into which were paid members' contributions, entrance fees, fines levies and interest from investments. From the Fund were paid benefits and grants, legal costs, affiliation fees, deputation and delegate expenses, the union's contributions as an employer into the Officers' and Staff Pension Fund, national administration costs (employees' salaries, wages, postage, telephones, etc.) and group and branch expenditure. Branches retained a proportion of the national contribution rate (the branch allowance) to cover local management expenses but they could raise their own funds provided their methods conformed with the objects of the union. The General Fund contained the resources from which the union protected and advanced the living standards of its members. It was the 'fighting fund' so maintaining it at healthy levels was crucial to SOGAT's ability to protect its members.

THE GENERAL FUND

Table 11.1 shows the balance of the General Fund and the excess of income over expenditure for the period 1955–91 inclusive. By 1965 inflation was eroding surpluses and the amount of working capital per employed member was precariously small at £1.30. However, despite efforts to control costs and despite increased member contributions from October 1966, working capital per member continued to fall. By 1973 increasing rates of inflation had considerably increased administrative costs in addition to which SOGAT now faced the costs of holding Trade Conferences. In the following year, the balance of the General Fund improved due to several factors: a revaluation of properties, £97,000

301

Table 11.1
NUPB&PW/SOGAT (Division A)/SOGAT/SOGAT (75) and SOGAT (82): the General Fund, 1955–91

Date	Balance of fund (£)	Excess of income (£)
1955	1,318,635	+74,069
1956	1,386,208	+70,997
1957	1,419,029	+178,418
1958	1,555,746	+155,304
1959	1,665,082	-518,321
1960	1,091,244	+106,051
1961	1,140,348	+224,839
1962	1,233,352	+101,856
1963	1,358,143	+123,296
1964	1,450,392	+90,666
1965	1,548,956	+98,773
1966	1,332,692	+50,881
1967	1,486,412	+212,505
1968	1,487,016	+180,881
1969	1,489,974	+184,163
1970	1,497,274	+69,230
1971	1,544,933	+103,150
1972	1,565,109	+32,376
1973	1,632,543	+79,551
1974	2,693,157	+96,697
1975	2,719,705	-26,200
1976	2,504,030	-310,096
1977	2,781,311	+169,418
1978	2,889,752	+143,100
1979	4,094,532	+586,908
1980	4,390,548	+348,948
1981	4,497,531	+150,436
1982	4,073,832	-370,753
1983	5,128,421	-919,381
1984	5,417,544	+289,123
1985	5,639,268	+221,724
1986	5,313,858	-325,410
1987	5,719,909	+106,051
1988	6,415,201	+345,292
1989	7,255,837	+478,592
1990	8,084,856	+479,019
1991	8,219,698*	+134,842

Source: *Financial Statements*, 1955–91
* to 31/3/91

received as an interim payment from the Administrator overseeing the dissolution of the original SOGAT, £25,555 standing in the original SOGAT contribution account, and £80,426 received from the dissolution of the P&KTF. All this meant that 50p per member per year was added to reserves. However, given the increasing rate of inflation and growing unemployment amongst members, this increase proved to be inadequate and the General Fund went into deficit in mid-1975. The amounts of unemployment benefit paid out in 1975 and 1976 were the highest in the history of the union. Contribution rates had not kept up with increases in wages and inflation. Nineteen seventy-seven saw SOGAT drawing on its overdraft facilities. To meet its commitments the union was forced to redeem investments. However, as inflationary pressures eased in the late 1970s the state of the General Fund improved. In the early 1980s, increasing unemployment amongst the membership again caused the Fund's balance to decline, although in 1984 the Fund showed a surplus of £289,123 (due mainly to the sale of the Bexhill Convalescent Home).

During the year to 30 September 1986, SOGAT experienced in the Wapping dispute the most financially crippling era in its entire 200 years history. Following the end of the dispute many stringent financial measures were introduced to contain the deficit, but the union's financial position remained perilous. In the early 1990s economic recession returned to the UK economy with adverse effects for SOGAT finances. The half year to 31 March 1991 saw the union suffer a significant drop in working members but the continued operation of financial control measures enabled SOGAT to record an operating surplus of £134,842 after allocations to cover future liabilities whilst the assets of the General Fund rose to £8.5 million.

Income

Contributions

The major source of income into the General Fund was the member's weekly contributions. In 1955 the contribution rates of the NUPB&PW varied by trade sector (printing and binding and papermills) by gender and by scales. There were five scales of contributions for male and female members in printing and binding and in papermills, six scales for men and four scales for women. The top rate of contribution for men in printing and binding was 12p per week whilst for women the rate was 6p. In papermills the highest scale of weekly contributions was 7p for men and 4p for females. Papermill rates were lower than printing and binding because papermill members did not have to contribute to the National Superannuation Fund.

The 1956 Delegate Council approved weekly contribution increases of 2½p for male and 2p for female members in printing and binding and of 2p for male and 1p for female members employed in papermills. This was the first increase in subscriptions since 1935. The NEC justified the increases on the grounds of increased living costs since 1939, increases in union expenses since 1939, the facts that it had been 21 years since the last increased subscriptions, that inflation had risen by 150 per cent since 1939, that existing contributions did not cover administration costs, that the branches received a higher branch allowance than in 1939 and the proposed increases were much less in proportion to wage rates in 1956 relative to 1939. Before the Second World War, the wage rate of a craftsman in a Grade 1 town was £3.87½. In 1956 the wage rate had risen to £9.75, an increase of approximately 152 per cent. The proposed average increase in weekly subscriptions was 35 per cent and unemployment and dispute benefits were also being increased. The debate on the increase in weekly contributions brought a clash of interests between delegates working in printing, who supported the increases, and those working in papermills, who opposed the size of the increase on the grounds that, there was no closed shop in papermills and since union membership was therefore voluntary, there was competition for membership with the T&GWU and GMWU.

In 1960 membership contributions increased by 1p per week across the board to clear the NUPB&PW overdraft with the Midland Bank which had been used to support dispute benefit payments to members involved in the 1959 six-week dispute in the general printing and provincial newspaper over a wage increase and the introduction of a 40-hour working week. This increase was accompanied by the abolition of Scale C contributions for members employed in printing and binding, although it continued for members employed in papermills. The 1964 Delegate Council approved increases in all contribution scales of 1½p for men, 1p for women and ½p for juniors on the grounds that prices were continuing to rise, staff wages were increasing, administration costs were escalating and members' wages over the period 1939 to 1964 had increased in proportionally much greater terms than the proposed weekly subscription increases. No compensating increases in benefits were proposed as the NEC felt it wiser to accumulate the union's reserves so that it could meet any challenges from employers or other unions with the adequate resources. However, when these proposed increases were put to a membership ballot, they were rejected by 43,352 votes to 35,185 – a majority of 8,167. As a result of this ballot decision, the 1966 Delegate Council changed the ultimate authority on financial questions from the membership to the Delegate Council. The 1964 Delegate Council, on the advice of the NEC, rejected an Edinburgh Branch attempt to simplify the contributions structure by introducing a uniform two-scale contribution structure (Scales A & B) for all members regardless of whether they worked in print or papermaking. The NEC felt this proposal was too radical for its time, would lead to steep increases for lower-paid members and would not assist in competing for membership with other unions.

The 1966 Delegate Council not only increased the weekly subscriptions of SOGAT (Division A) but accepted a further reform of the contributions system by introducing an automatic ½p per week increase per member every January with effect from 7 January 1967 on the condition that the position was reviewed at each Rules Conference.[1] This established the principle of annual increases in contributions and eliminated the problem of debating the need for increased subscriptions which came up every four years at the Conference. However, the delegates rejected a move by the London Women's Branch to introduce equal contributions for male and female members on the grounds that the lower-paid members in papermaking would have to pay double the current contributions and the time was not right for such change. Following representations from the Midland Group, the NEC, after careful consideration, decided in the light of the government's pay freeze, introduced in July 1966, to forgo the automatic ½p a week increase due in January 1967.

Nineteen sixty-eight saw a further rationalisation of the SOGAT (Division A) contributions structure when the Trade Scale E for papermill members was abolished and the scales for papermill members were brought into closer unanimity with those in the binding and printing sections. In 1972 SOGAT took the final step in the rationalisation of its contribution structures by accepting one scale of contributions for men, women and juniors by eliminating sectional (print and binding and papermills) contributions. This had a threefold effect. First, it gave a considerably increased sum of money to the national union. Second, it simplified the bookkeeping activities at both national and branch level. Third, it enabled officials to concentrate on improving the service offered to the membership rather than on balancing the books. The 1972 Delegate Council introduced a contribution scale for Art, Technical, Administrative and Executive members of £12 per annum payable annually, quarterly or monthly in advance.

The 1974 Delegate Council dealt with a batch of rule changes designed to create a 'unisex Rule Book' in which women would pay equal contributions for equal benefits. However, the Council turned it into something far more. Delegates accepted the annual increase in weekly contributions should be 2p from October of each year – instead of 1p – and 10p per month for ATAES members instead of 5p. However, they were not prepared to wait until 1975 – the year when equal pay legislation became fully effective – before women members shouldered the burden of full contributions. The Manchester Branch successfully argued for equality of contributions and benefits between male and female members from October 1974. The effect of these decision was that the adult weekly contribution rate became 21p from October 1974 and the junior rate 12p per week with a further 2p from October 1975.

In 1976 adult contributions to SOGAT increased to 30p per week and those of juniors to 21p whilst the automatic annual increase in weekly contributions raised from 2p to 4p from October 1977. A move by the Solent Branch to link contributions to basic wages in National Agreements was defeated. The 1978 Delegate Council again rejected moves by the Solent Branch to relate contributions to wages. The Branch argued that linking contributions to wages would remind members of what they received in return for their subscriptions, but opponents said it would be too complicated and members would need pocket calculators to work out their contributions. The Delegate Council, however, approved an NEC motion that the annual automatic weekly increase in contributions should be 6p given that SOGAT had the lowest sum per head of membership of all the printing unions and, in real terms, the union's contributions were less than one-third their value of 40 years ago. The 1983 Special Delegate Meeting called to consider SOGAT's finances, agreed that the annual automatic increase in the weekly subscriptions should be 10p from April 1984 and the adult rate should be 79p per week. There were no further increase in SOGAT's weekly contribution rates other than the automatic annual 10p increases while it remained an independent union.

In the second half of the 1980s, changes in contribution rates were motivated by the need to attract new members and retain existing members, particularly female members taking a break from work, usually to have children. From 1984 at the request of an organiser and a branch committee, a reduced national contribution rate could be charged for organisational purposes, for example to attract part-time workers, but the cash benefits available to such members would be reduced and any reduced rate set would be reviewed every six months by the NEC. However, in 1988 this reduced rate for organisational purposes was fixed at not less than 25 per cent of the adult contribution rate, to be reviewed every six months by the NEC, and to continue for a maximum period of three years or until such time as recognition for the members involved had been achieved. SOGAT attempted to recruit part-time employees by permitting those working 16 hours or less per week and whose gross wage was less than 50 per cent of the lowest adult minimum earnings level set down in the SOGAT–BPIF Basic Wage Agreement to pay reduced weekly subscriptions. The 1986 Delegate Council accepted that part-time workers in membership of SOGAT be treated as full members and entitled to full benefits. It sought from 1984 to retain members leaving their employment to take maternity leave by permitting them to pay reduced contributions for up to 26 weeks from the time maternity pay expired (from 1986 this period became 52 weeks). A further financial incentive to retain members was introduced in 1986. In certain circumstances members in arrears with their subscriptions were to have a longer period of time to meet their arrears before they were expelled. In 1986 in an effort to attract and retain members employed by Remploy, it was agreed that Remploy members pay only 50 per cent of adult rate and be exempt from the automatic annual weekly increase.

The NEC had discretion any powers if they considered it essential during any dispute lock out or serious depletion of funds to impose a levy.[2] If the NEC wished to continue the levy for a longer period or in excess of the maximum level of such a levy, then approval of the membership in a ballot was essential. In 1956 the maximum levy was raised from 1½p to 2½p, the first increase in this figure since 1925. In 1982 the raising of a maximum flat-rate figure levy was replaced by a figure determined by a percentage of the adult contribution rate.

Branch Allowances

However, a certain percentage of the national contribution (known as the Branch Allowance) was retained by the branch to meet its local management expenses. If branches did not spend all the Branch Allowance they were required to return the balance to the Head Office. Should they exceed the allowance, branches funded the difference from their own resources. In 1955 the NUPB&PW's Branch Allowance was 33.33 per cent, having been increased to this level from 25 per cent by the 1948 Delegate Council at the suggestion of the NEC. The Branch Allowance was debated at eight Delegate Council Meetings over the period 1955 to 1991. The 1956 meeting rejected a London Central Branch motion that the allowance be increased from 33.33 per cent to 40 per cent. The same motion, this time from the Leeds Branch, was rejected by the 1964 meeting. However, in 1968 the Branch Allowance was increased to 37.33 per cent on a motion from the Leeds Branch to the Delegate Council meeting. Six years later the allowance was increased to 40 per cent which was its level when SOGAT merged with the NGA. In 1976 the Dover Branch unsuccessfully sought to reduce the allowance to 38 per cent whilst the 1983 Special Delegate Council rejected a Darlington Branch motion that the allowance be reduced from 40 per cent to 35 per cent. The 1988 Delegate Council rejected a Multi-trades Branch attempt to raise the allowance to 42 per cent. Attempts by the NEC at the 1986 Delegate Council to restrict the allowance to branch administration expenses was defeated.

The Branch Allowance issue was important in the balance of power between the national union and its local branches which had autonomy within the constraints of National union's Rules, policies and industrial agreements. Branches could raise their own local funds but were expected to meet their management costs – staff, postage, meetings, etc. – from the Branch Allowance. If branches felt unable to or would not increase local subscriptions there was a temptation to request a larger Branch Allowance. If this was conceded then the national union's income fell, giving rise to consideration of cuts in services to the membership, reduction in benefits and a lowering of industrial protection. The General Fund was the only fund available to protect every member equally. If the membership were willing to pay higher national contribution rates then it was easier to accommodate the local and national need to fund existing or new expenditure. In the absence of increased national subscriptions, an increase in the Branch Allowance could only be at the expense of the national union finances, and vice versa. There was a constant tension between the branches and the national union as to whether the distribution of the members' national contributions between local and national needs was right. If the Branch Allowance was too high then the national union's ability 'to do things for the membership' would be reduced. On the other hand, if the branch allowance was too low then the national union enhanced its power and influence over the branches whose full-time officials would find it more difficult to provide membership services. If the branches were constantly short of money and local funds could not be increased, then branch autonomy would be threatened as the national union could make the receipt of additional income conditional on, for example, reductions in certain items of branch expenditure.

However, changes in the size of the branch allowance only occurred when both branches and the national union gained mutual advantage from doing so. If a proposed change was seen as significantly altering the balance of power between branches and the national union then it was always rejected. In 1968 the branch allowance was increased from 33.33 per cent to 37.5 per cent. It had remained unchanged for 20 years. The branches argued that it was necessary to adjust the allowance to balance more fairly the impact of rising inflation on the escalating costs of branch administration. In 1960, in the aggregate, branch expenditure on management expenses exceeded the amount available from branch allowances by some £170,000. By 1967 the figure had risen to £332,000. The branch allowance meant that branches could spend 33p in every £1 of national contributions on local administration, but in reality they were spending 43p. The present branch allowance was inadequate to meet the rising costs of branch expenditure. An increase to 37½p in the £1 would only lighten the burden, and branches believed it was imperative that increased expenditure be met by an increase in the amount of money available to the branches from the national contribution.

The NEC of SOGAT (Division A) opposed the increase in the branch allowance on the grounds that the branches, instead of facing their membership, telling them the position bluntly and asking for an increase in local contributions, were taking the easy course of trying to convince delegates to take another slice out of what was necessary for the national union. It would be foolish to support an increase in the branch allowance as the national union needed funds to face the problems of the future and to carry out the wishes of the membership. If the national union was strapped for cash it was pointless passing resolutions to take action against employers, as resources would not be there to back up such action. In 1974 however, the NEC supported a motion to increase the allowance to 40 per cent on the grounds that since the 1968 Delegate Council the administrative costs of running branches had increased sharply and branches were spending 48.5p in the £1 from local funds to meet their management expenses instead of 37.5p as assumed by the branch allowances. The branches needed extra cash if they were to continue to service their membership effectively. They need the national union to assist with extra resources. At a time of increasing inflation, more money was needed at both branch and national levels, a situation which called for an increase in national contribution rates and an increased Branch Allowance.

The 1956 and 1964 Delegate Council Meetings rejected attempts to increase the Branch Allowance from 33.33 per cent to 40 per cent on the grounds the national union's funds should be strengthened otherwise the union would wither away as the General Fund could not be built up. Both Delegate Councils accepted the first priority must be to build up the General Fund. Many branches did not need 40 per cent of the national contributions to meet their branch management expenditure, but if they were to be allowed to retain 40 per cent they would spend up to that level regardless. Delegates in 1964 were told:

> what is the use of us asking for a 3d [1p] a week increase and then sending it back to the branches when in fact it is to build up the General Fund that we are asking for the increase.[3]

In 1988 the Multi-trades Branch unsuccessfully attempted to increase the branch allowance to 42 per cent. It sought to redistribute national resources towards the branches against a background of declining membership and a desire to maintain the present level of service to the membership. The argument was that if servicing was not maintained in the present industrial climate members would leave the union. Most branches in the union, it was stated could not contain their management expenses within the 40 per cent and excess of expenditure over branch allowance income was over £2.75m. A further contention of the Multi-trades Branch was that the national union had reduced the number of organisers and the costs of union recruitment had been passed onto the branches without any corresponding increase in income from the union's National Fund.

The motion was opposed by the NEC which argued the national union could not afford the increase in the Branch Allowance to 42 per cent as it would reduce the income to the General Fund by £200,000, the equivalent of a 5p increase in contributions. It was unlikely the members would be willing to pay increased national contributions to offset this. The NEC argued that branches should increase local fund contributions and not remove from the national union resources desperately needed to provide benefits and services to the membership. The delegates were told that, if the motion were carried, effectively they would be telling the national union to cut benefits, cut services or increase national contributions. In support of its position, the NEC made much of the fact that over the period 1983 to 1987 the total assets of the branches had increased from £12m to £19m, whilst the assets of the national union had stagnated at £5m. The national union could not be accused of accruing to itself a nest egg of money at the expense of the branches.

Investment income

The second major source of income to the General Fund was interest from investments and income from the rent of properties. With continuing inflation in the early 1960s, the NUPB&PW considered investing in properties which held their value and, if anything, showed an increase in price. By contrast, depositing money in the bank or in securities, because of low interest rates, meant a rapid loss in terms of its real value. In the 1960s the NUPB&PW steadily increased the number of properties it owned. The union gained rental income and an appreciation in the value of its properties. In 1960 the value of the NUPB&PW's freehold properties was £300,711, and by 1970 they had a market value of £325,840. By 1980 the value of freehold properties held by SOGAT amounted to £2.2m and ten years later to £2.6m.

The investment policy of the NUPB&PW in the late 1950s and early 1960s was to invest in government gilt edge stocks and local authority stock and bonds. These investments had the advantage over industrial stocks and shares in that the money could not be lost since the initial sum invested was paid back at a later date with interest. The central government and local authorities could never, in effect go bankrupt. Since taxes and rates could, as a last resort, be levied to pay back investment owed to individuals or organisations. The NUPB&PW always felt comfortable with such investments as they did not represent investments in capitalist enterprises and nor they could be presented as gambling irresponsibly with the members' money. However, unlike industrial equities, government gilt edge stock and local authority bonds did not give rise to capital growth. For example, in 1960, £100 invested in a government bond in 1947 was only worth £58.50 because over the period 1947–60 retail prices had risen by 71 per cent. However, over the same period industrial equities had increased in capital value. In 1947 the Trade Union Unit Trust had been formed so that trade unions could take advantage of the share market to not only maintain but increase the real value of their assets. Trade Union Unit Trusts enabled a capital appreciation because the companies in which the investments were made established sums of money which guaranteed the capital value of the company shares for all time. By spreading investments across many different companies in many different industries unit trusts helped trade union investors to overcome the main risks of investing in industrial equities, namely, that the company in which the purchase of shares had been made went bankrupt, resulting in a complete loss monies invested. Loss in some company investments would be more than offset by gains from investments in others. The Trade Union Unit Trust, unlike other trust companies, was managed by a committee of trade union officials advised by professionals and financiers.

In 1961 the NUPB&PW invested £100,000 in Trade Union Unit Trusts. This was censured by 1962 Delegate Council which approved a PMB motion opposing the principle of national union funds being invested in unit trusts. Four years later the Delegate Council agreed by 172 votes to 144 to rescind this decision and to give the NEC authority to invest further monies in Trade Union Unit Trusts. The NEC had no intention of overinvesting into Unit Trusts but wanted flexibility to invest further amounts if warranted by the circumstances. The arguments put forward for and against investing in Trade Union Unit Trusts were the same at both Delegate Councils.[4] The opponents argued that unit trusts were run for profit, did not in fact always make a profit, could fall in value as well as increase and had high management charges. If the union invested in local government bonds this would not only be a good thing for the labour movement but would keep down local government rates as it reduced the need for local authorities to borrow money on the money markets where interest rates were relatively high. It was pointed out local government bonds and central government gilt edge securities were safe, unlike the stock market where money tended to be invested in some 'great financial venture' which could go down. In addition to these financial arguments, the opponents of Trade Union Unit Trusts contended that, if the union acquired an interest in private enterprises and there was subsequently a dispute between working people and the owners of the company in which the union had shares, the union might be reluctant to take industrial action against the company for fear of affecting adversely the return on its investments. Trade union funds, they pointed out, were for the use and benefit of members – for the working class – and not to bolster the capitalist system by reducing the propensity of trade union members to undertake industrial action.

A third set of arguments against unit trusts were ideological in nature. The stock market was viewed as a vicious system because it gambled with the lives and well-being of the British people. To dabble on the Stock Exchange was regarded as poisoning the spirit of the trade union movement since it would mean entering the capitalist world of 'dog eat dog'. The NEC was accused of selling the soul of socialism and crossing the line that took the union into the capitalist camp. It was regarded as immoral for socialists or people with socialist ideals to invest in the capitalist system.

The supporters of investing in unit trusts pointed out that some 43 trade unions were participating in the scheme, that capital losses were being experienced on gilt edge stock and government bonds, but that the value of unit trusts had increased greatly relative to the original investment. Although the value of unit trusts could decline, this was unlikely to happen in an inflationary market, and the union's £100,000 investment in unit trusts was now worth £1,063 per unit, which amounted to another £6,300 in capital value. Supporters pointed out that banks held the funds of the union and invested them in capitalist industry and that the union had little control over where the banks invested their funds. The same was true of local government investments. Trade Union Unit Trusts, on the other hand, offered a situation where by the trade union could control where their money was invested. This argument was well expressed by a delegate at the 1966 Delegate Council:

> The point is this. You are investing this money anyway either through the banks or through local government. The interest

that is earned by that investment, even if it is your Co-op movement is earned by the exploitation of the workers they employ. The Trade Union Unit Trust can control what enterprise your money is invested in. We feel that here you have a situation where the trade union can control the money that is invested and take away from bank mangers what will happen to your money and the conditions under which the employees in those industries are employed.[5]

Expenditure

The amounts of money expended from the General Fund on benefits to members over the period 1955 to 1991 inclusive is shown in Table 11.2. Marriage dowries benefit for women members was abolished in 1956. Nineteen sixty-eight saw an unsuccessful attempt to increase the level of unemployment benefit and to pay equal benefit to male and female members. In 1980 an attempt to abolish unemployment benefit was rejected as was an attempt to increase its level to £10 per week for adult members and £7.75 for junior members. These levels, however, were eventually accepted by the 1986 Delegate Council. Two years previously the Delegate Council had rejected the proposal that unemployment benefit be denied members for a 12-week period if they received redundancy compensation payments over a certain size. In 1972 there was an unsuccessful attempt to improve the level of funeral benefit and to give members the option of choosing either a lump sum on retirement or as funeral benefit. The level of funeral benefit for junior members was raised in 1984 from 50 per cent to 75 per cent of the adult member rate.

THE 1983 FINANCIAL MEASURES

Prior to their amalgamation in July 1982 to form SOGAT (82) both NATSOPA and SOGAT (75) showed surpluses on their balance sheets. Over the period 1979–81 both unions recorded surpluses, albeit that they were small and reducing in size each year. However, in the first half of 1982 the two unions went into deficit and SOGAT found itself unexpectedly in the red. A financial projection drawn up in June 1981, based on the accounts of NATSOPA and SOGAT (75) showed an estimated surplus of £875,000 on a year's operation. However, a revised projection made in October 1982 and utilising the 1981 accounts

Table 11.2

NUPB&PW, SOGAT (Division A), SOGAT, SOGAT (75) and SOGAT (82): payment of benefits, 1955–91

Date	Unemployment benefit (£)	Funeral benefit (£)	Benevolent grants (£)	Accident benefit (£)	Dispute benefit (£)	Total expenditure (£)
1955	2,062	13,835	1,731	3,239	10,913	275,453
1956	31,640	13,858	2,327	3,314	2,481	311,474
1957	8,155	14,722	3,364	5,404	445	309,219
1958	13,662	15,464	3,434	5,281	610	344,247
1959	10,730	15,744	3,089	5,267	690,056	1,090,311
1960	3,349	15,476	3,245	5,972	550	404,744
1961	9,194	22,695	3,888	9,423	606	399,606
1962	13,896	24,174	3,608	10,273	499	535,818
1963	13,982	25,625	3,756	10,797	616	529,774
1964	8,776	22,717	3,956	11,469	1,905	596,955
1965	7,294	23,233	4,733	11,519	11,167	626,070
1966	10,285	24,701	5,297	11,429	25,927	739,912
1967	15,682	24,447	5,385	14,101	2,076	683,336
1968	11,110	25,092	4,801	14,518	0	763,292
1969	9,911	27,058	4,863	15,142	2,846	816,787
1970	14,627	28,354	4,523	14,329	19,198	1,084,594
1971	51,924	30,381	4,819	12,486	380	1,107,465
1972	24,230	24,108	3,520	8,916	17,247	952,516
1973	13,692	28,343	4,935	14,535	59,613	1,359,680
1974	7,212	30,015	4,852	17,890	75,205	1,642,330
1975	62,340	31,778	6,003	20,799	34,220	2,108,755
1976	76,821	34,825	6,901	24,611	7,763	2,728,040
1977	55,657	32,485	8,284	50,284	4,099	2,861,642
1978	66,396	33,568	7.199	54,826	39,660	3,366,245
1979	39,818	33,914	6,717	53,769	1,233	3,509,576
1980	99,177	33,926	6,045	45,272	29,655	4,591,798
1981	475,774	30,910	6,375	37,050	31,751	5,566,114
1982	274,368	24,138	4,850	28,060	113,034	5,020,357
1983	478,746	59,088	8,373	43,212	53,585	11,468,583
1984	254,809	48,541	9,045	35,069	117,805	9,561,989
1985	222,628	49,622	7,332	34,195	14,529	10,268,747
1986	218,786	45,794	6,209	30,779	467,839	11,890,701
1987	250,516	44,788	7,917	29,860	170,836	11,396,134
1988	178,504	46,327	7,232	17,641	8,212	11,071,102
1989	197,251	53,695	8,107	11,309	1,770	11,080,574
1990	226,102	52,652	9,414	9,652	1,318	10,831,225
1991	180,822	31,830	4,957	4,580	0	5,728,261

Source: *Financial Statements* 1955–91.

suitably updated, showed a shortfall of £649,000. This movement of £1.5 m from a projected surplus of £875,000 to an estimated deficit of £649,000 had to be addressed.

SOGAT called a Special Delegate Meeting on 25 May 1983 to consider the grave financial position and to consider whether it could continue as a coherent independent organisation, democratically structured, defending the industrial interests of its present and future membership. The General Secretary told the meeting the union was fighting for its survival and they could not avoid making fundamental changes in order to improve the union's finances. What had gone wrong? SOGAT's financial plight stemmed from the Government's economic and social policies which had led to factory and mill closures and redundancies with a consequent loss of membership. This problem had been reinforced by the separate but related problem of increased administration costs and benefit payments, particularly unemployment benefit.

In 1979 the combined membership of NATSOPA and SOGAT was 260,248. At the time of the Special Delegate Council, SOGAT's membership was 227,485, giving a membership loss of 32,763 between the two points in time. All the signs suggested that membership would continue to decline in the near future. January 1982 had seen further redundancies in the paper and printing industries being registered with the Secretary of State for Employment whilst the National Economic Development Council's Printing Industries Sector Working Party had published in 1981 an assessment of future prospects for the industry which predicted a further fall in employment in the 1980s from a low of 45,000 unemployed to a high of 84,000. In the economic recession of the early 1980s, SOGAT membership loss had been adversely affected to a greater degree than other print unions and most other TUC-affiliated unions.

The loss of 32,763 members represented a drop of £1.3m in income. In the face of this loss the union had sold investments to the value of nearly £800,000 which, in turn, meant that the revenue SOGAT received in interest from its investments fell. The excess of expenditure over income had yet another adverse effect on the union's cash flow – the union had to draw down heavily on its overdraft facilities thereby increasing its banking charges. The increasing unemployment amongst members not only reduced income but generated increased expenditure on unemployment benefit. In September 1980 the total unemployment benefit paid out by SOGAT (75) and NATSOPA was £100,157. At the end of 1981 this had risen to £482,401 and was likely to increase as the Government continued its deflationary economic policies. This adverse financial situation also impacted at branch level, with branches having to engage in cost-cutting exercises and being forced to increase their subscription rates. The union had examined its administrative costs at the national level, but the General Rules meant benefits had to be paid. The loss of income to the General Fund, which was the life-blood of the union in struggles with employers, was serious. The General Secretary, Bill Keys, told delegates:

> A trade union, in many ways, is similar to a commercial concern. A commercial concern can have the finest product in the world but unless it has the finance to promote and sustain that product, then the product will die. A trade union can have the finest policies in the world but to sustain those policies and to promote the common good it must have adequate finance.[6]

The financial position was becoming desperate and something had to be done. The NEC brought forward proposals to deal with the situation. Longer-term solutions were limited since it was impossible to predict the long-term future with any certainty. The NEC ruled out an approach based on improving the service to the membership but eliminating benefits. It concluded that benefits and the same quality of service to the membership would be maintained and the means of achieving this policy must be met. Given that sources of funding to achieve these objectives had to be found – and the imposition of a levy on the membership was firmly rejected – the NEC presented a package of measures designed to increase revenue, reduce expenditure and give SOGAT an annual surplus of £199,731.

For every 1,000 members SOGAT lost, given a contribution rate of 76p per week in April 1983, the income forgone was £39,520 per annum divided 60/40 between national funds and local funds. The NEC sought an increase of 10p per week in contribution rates to operate from the first week of October 1983 and proposed that the present 6p per week automatic annual increase in contributions be raised to 10p per week as from April 1984. To help delegates evaluate the contribution rate increases being proposed, the NEC made comparisons with 1939. At that time, the NUPB&PW contribution rate represented 1.72 per cent of a member's wages or, nearly an hour's wages. If the same percentage were to be paid in 1983 the contribution rate would be £1.53 per week and this ignored the fact that since 1939 the branch allowance had increased from 25 per cent to 40 per cent. Taking this into account, in order to maintain the value of the national union contribution relative to 1939 the rate should be £1.91 per week. The NEC proposal would give a weekly contribution rate of 86p from October 1983 and 96p from April 1984. The delegates accepted these proposed increases. However, they rejected an NEC proposal that in order to meet organisational or special circumstances a reduced contribution rate could be charged. The proposal was to help recruit part-time employees and low-paid workers who had been identified as a substantial source of new recruits. The NEC believed these groups would not otherwise be attracted to SOGAT given its relative high weekly contributions compared with the T&GWU and the GMBU, both of which were organising such employees. The delegates were concerned the NEC was introducing an open-ended rule, and felt that the provision for 'special circumstances' was open to abuse. They also felt it was wrong to charge part-time workers already in the union full contribution rates but to allow newly joined part-time workers a lower rate. It was not the contribution rate which deterred potential members but the level of service they received, the delegates protested.

To reduce expenditure the NEC successfully proposed that the Bexhill convalescent home be closed and sold, the viability of the Ayr convalescent home be kept under review, paying guests should be charged a realistic rate and that the maximum period of time members (retired or otherwise) could spend at the convalescent homes be reduced from three weeks to two weeks. The NEC, however was unsuccessful in an attempt to reduce national union expenditure by transferring the payment of affiliation fees and delegate's expenses to Trade Councils from the General Fund to branch funds. The delegates argued that some branches were experiencing financial difficulties and would simply disaffiliate from Trade Councils, which would be seen by other trade unions as SOGAT divorcing itself from the wider trade union movement. The delegates asserted that financial problems were not solved by shifting the burden from one pocket to another.

The NEC also agreed to tighten up day-to-day administration at Head Office and to examine ways of reducing costs. It announced that four organisers who were due to retire in the near future would not be replaced and that Caxton House, the headquarters of the former NATSOPA, would be sold. The price of the *Journal* was increased to 10p per copy and further staff savings would accrue from the forthcoming early retirement of Joint General Secretary, Owen O'Brien. The NEC was pleased with the outcome of the Special Delegate Meeting. The delegates had not drawn back from taking hard decisions. They had not taken too little action too late. The finances of the union began to improve over the period 1984–91, and only in 1986 did the union's expenditure exceed its income. This was the year of the Wapping dispute following which major financial reforms were introduced. Budgets were set for particular activities, a contingency fund was established and special allocations were made, for example for the Biennial Delegate Council, so that income requirement for these items had been fully budgeted for by the time they fell due.

CONVALESCENT HOMES BENEFIT

SOGAT and its constituent unions had convalescent homes designed to restore to health and vigour the members shocked by an accident, which occurred either at work or outside of work, that had befallen them. In 1955 the NUPB&PW had three convalescent homes – at Hastings (opened in 1925), Filey (opened in 1925) and at Ayr (opened in 1948) – placed so as to meet the convenience of the members. Southern England and Wales were served by Hastings, Yorkshire and the Midlands by Filey and Scotland and Northern England by Ayr.

In 1955, it was decided to replace the Hastings home because of rising maintenance costs, administrative difficulties and problems with the recruitment and retention of staff. The union purchased a site on the sea front at Bexhill and built a home to its own specifications. The Bexhill convalescent home opened on 3 October 1958. In 1961 the Hastings home was sold for £9,750 having been originally purchased freehold at £6,000 in 1925. In 1983 SOGAT sold the Bexhill home for £1.3m. The merger of NATSOPA and SOGAT (75) meant that SOGAT (82) acquired the NATSOPA Rest and Recreation Centre at Rotting-dean which had opened in September 1965. The 1976 Delegate Council agreed to the closure of the Filey home on the grounds the union could not afford to support three homes and more than adequate convalescent facilities could be provided by two homes. The 1988 Delegate Council rejected a proposal that the Ayr convalescent home be closed. Although when SOGAT merged with the NGA it had two convalescent homes – Ayr and Rottingdean – pressure was mounting to close the former which required work on its structure and facilities.

In 1955, the welfare of each convalescent home was put under the supervision of a panel of four members plus the General Secretary and the General President. The four members, who served for two years, were elected by and from the delegates attending the Delegate Council. In 1964 the condition was introduced that members of the Convalescent Homes Committee must be under retirement age, whilst 1972 saw the ending of London and the Home Countries having two representatives on the Committee. On the creation of SOGAT (82) responsibility for the everyday running and welfare of the convalescent homes was given to the National Executive Council and the Convalescent Homes Committee ended. The Greater Manchester Branch unsuccessfully sought at the 1986 Delegate Council to bring back the old Convalescent Homes Panel but with an important addition. The Panel would meet every six months and report to both the NEC and to the Delegate Council. This position was justified on the grounds that the NEC's record on convalescent homes had not been good. Since 1974 the NEC had proposed the closure of all three convalescent homes. The Greater Manchester Branch claimed that letting the NEC have charge of the day-to-day running of convalescent homes was 'like putting a fox in charge of chickens'. The NEC defended its record, pointing out that the convalescent homes were supervised by the Finance Committee of the NEC which was the only body that could recommend expenditure on the homes. To have the Panel as well as the Finance Committee reporting to the NEC on convalescent homes was viewed as a duplication and a waste of time and money.

Convalescent benefit was available to any member recovering from illness or who was in danger of a breakdown in health. In 1966 the benefit was restricted for retired members to the winter period (October to April) and in 1984 this winter entitlement was extended to their spouses and to their widows. However, the benefit was always unavailable to members suffering certain illnesses, such as tuberculosis, serious heart problems, fits, or infectious or contagious diseases. Until 1976 the benefit was withheld from members who had contracted illnesses through immorality or drunkenness, but in that year it was made available to such members on the grounds that if a period of convalescence would help them 'dry-out' then the benefit should be available. In 1983 the availability of benefit was reduced to two months, it having been three months for many years previously. Members admitted to a convalescent home received a grant. In 1955 this was £2 but it was increased to £3 in 1964. Ten years later, it was increased to £5 and in 1980 to £10, which was the level prevailing when SOGAT merged with the NGA. In 1974 a travelling allowance of £1.25 was introduced for homeward journeys from convalescent homes where the journey exceeded 100 miles. This was increased in 1976 to £1.75 and in 1980 to £2.

By the early 1970s the convalescent homes were causing the union financial problems. They were little used by the working membership, their cost of upkeep was increasing astronomically, their losses were increasing (see Table 11.3), paying guests were highly subsidised and expensive structural repairs were necessary. In 1973 in the light of these problems the NEC initiated a review into convalescent homes. Its terms of reference were to establish the extent to which the homes were occupied, to ascertain the financial commitment of SOGAT per category of patient at the three convalescent homes and to examine whether greater use could be made of the homes, particularly bearing in mind the desire of the 1972 Delegate Council to provide educational facilities for union members. The report noted that over a four-year period the occupancy of the three convalescent homes by working members was about 22 per cent whilst their use by retired members and friends had increased. It concluded that the convalescent homes were not fulfilling the purpose for which they had been established, namely, convalescence for members working at the trade who were recovering from illness. The report showed that all members working at the trade who were recovering from illness could be accommodated in one home. A further finding of the report was that the loss on the three homes was running at over £100,000 a year and was likely to increase in future. The cost per patient per home varied but averaged out at about £51 per week, yet people who were not working at the trade were allowed to stay at the Homes for £15 per week. A further feature referred to in the NEC report was that in the near future major structural alterations in all three homes estimated to cost £500,000 would be necessary. Of every £1 of a member's contribution 8p went to the maintenance of the three homes. The report recommended that the Society could not afford to keep its convalescent homes.

The NEC review was presented to the Delegate Council in 1974 – the first time it had ever received a comprehensive report on the convalescent homes. In the light of its review, the NEC proposed the three convalescent homes be closed as soon as practicable. The case was summarised to delegates by the General Secretary Elect in the following words:

Table 11.3
NUPB&PW SOGAT (Division A)/SOGAT/SOGAT (75) and SOGAT (82): loss of convalescent homes, 1956–91

Date	Loss	Loss as % of income
1956	32,015	8.3
1957	34,038	7.0
1958	37,299	7.5
1959	40,390	7.1
1960	47,226	9.2
1961	46,053	7.9
1962	49,611	7.8
1963	50,493	7.3
1964	55,469	8.1
1965	58,996	8.1
1966	65,621	8.3
1967	62,962	7.0
1968	68,483	7.3
1969	72,253	7.2
1970	76,919	7.1
1971	83,210	6.9
1972	64,034	6.7
1973	101,089	7.0
1974	100,788	5.8
1975	248,276	7.1
1976	168,725	7.0
1977	170,657	5.6
1978	146,443	4.2
1979	160,580	3.9
1980	182,627	3.7
1981	242,197	4.2
1982	181,622	3.9
1983	411,060	3.9
1984	339,766	3.4
1985	292,376	2.8
1986	301,755	2.6
1987	333,745	2.8
1988	393,614	3.3
1989	380,065	3.2
1990	414,585	3.6
1991	237,839	4.1

Source: *Financial Statements*, 1955–91

We do not believe that this Society can continue to support a situation where less than 21 per cent of the bed space in the Homes is being utilised by the working membership. We do not believe we can continue to support a situation where the working membership who are recovering from illness can be accommodated in one Home with all the necessary services that are required. We do not believe that we can continue to have this astronomical drain on the funds with the further monies that we are going to have to expand plus the cost of probable structural alterations unless you are prepared to accept – and don't someone tell me that I am threatening, I do not do things like that – there has got to be a violent increase in contributions if you want to maintain these Homes open in their present form.[7]

In response to opposition, the NEC accepted an amendment from the Watford Branch that two, and not three, convalescent homes be closed. However, this was rejected as the delegates approved a Manchester Branch amendment that only one convalescent home be closed. The NEC was given authority to decide which home would close. The Manchester amendment carried the day on the argument that money should not be the sole motivator in deciding the future of the convalescent homes, but rather the main consideration should be the health of the members. However, delegates then went on to say that none of the three homes should close.

The 1974 Delegate Council decision reflected a hesitancy to remove or interfere with a well-established holiday and convalescent home facility for the member whether they be working or retired. However, this seemed to be in contrast to the indifferent attitude of the membership to the homes in that less than 1 per cent made use of them. The NEC told the 1976 Delegate Council that if convalescent home benefit were maintained, then adequate facilities could be provided by two homes, and that by closing one home considerable savings could be made. The delegates accepted that the Filey home should close but any further closures or sales of homes must be approved by the Biennial Delegate Council.

The closure of convalescent homes also surfaced at the 1978 Delegate Council when an unsuccessful attempt was made to prevent further closures until the membership had been made aware of the circumstances for doing so. In 1980 the Edinburgh and Forth District unsuccessfully sought to abolish the convalescent homes benefit. They argued that the closure of Filey had been insufficient and the drain on the union's funds from convalescent homes benefit was getting worse. They pointed out the long-standing problems of decline in the use of the Homes by the working membership, continuing excess of expenditure over income and continuing subsidies to non-working members and their guests. It was stressed that SOGAT existed to provide industrial protection for its members, something that the 'millstone of the convalescent homes' inhibited. The resources devoted to convalescent homes would be better used to improve the quality of industrial services offered to the membership. Convalescent homes had been first provided in specific economic and environmental conditions. They had been fashioned when members' incomes were low and before the National Health Service existed. With the modern welfare state it was unnecessary to continue to provide from the union's own funds a benefit which was superfluous to the needs of the members in the 1980s. However, the supporters of the retention of the two existing convalescent homes won the day, arguing that the National Health Service was under attack, that two homes, one in the North and one in the South, met the needs of the membership and that there had been a definite lack of effort by the NEC to publicise the convalescent homes.

At the 1983 Special Delegate Council delegates were told that over the nine-month period to May 1983 the Bexhill and Ayr homes had lost £181,622, the creation of SOGAT (82) meant acquiring the Rest and Recreation Centre at Rottingdean which was in close proximity to Bexhill, and all members recovering from illness or injury could be accommodated in one of the two homes in the South. The NEC proposed the Bexhill home be closed down and sold, the viability of the Ayr Home be kept under review and paying guests at the remaining homes be charged economical tariffs. The delegates voted to close and sell the Bexhill home. The Humberside Branch moved the closure and sale of the Ayr convalescent home on the grounds that all the convalescent homes should close because they were draining from the union the life-blood whereby it gave industrial protection to the membership. However, this motion was defeated on the NEC argument that the union wanted to try and maintain convalescent benefit for all members who wanted to go to the homes and this meant at the present time retaining those at Rottingdean and Ayr.

Plans to sell the Ayr convalescent home and use the funds to develop the Rest and Recreation Centre at Rottingdean were rejected by delegates to the 1988 Delegate Council. The decision was reached after a series of debates which reflected both the financial and the emotional arguments on what had been a contentious issue at Delegate Councils since 1974. Balanced against heartfelt pleas to maintain convalescent facilities for members, the General Secretary warned that refusal to act might mean being forced into selling both homes in the near future. The sale of the Ayr house was estimated to raise £700,000. This would then to be used to carry out essential maintenance, modernisation and extension of the Rottingdean Rest and Recreation Centre. In addition, money was to be used from the General Fund to upgrade the standards of facilities at Rottingdean. To ensure members from Scotland who used the Ayr home did not lose out they were to be flown, free of charge, to Gatwick and met at the airport to be driven to Rottingdean. The union was in a difficult financial state and would need to spend £250,000 just to maintain the two homes at an acceptable standard. To do this would put SOGAT into deficit unless there was an increase in contributions. The NEC felt the union should find a way of keeping the convalescent home provision without its financial burden. Ayr was an old building with a conservation order which made extensions difficult. It was not as popular with the members as Rottingdean and guests had to share dormitory accommodation instead of having a single room. It cost SOGAT £158 more per person per week to house members at Ayr rather than Rottingdean. The NEC warned that if its plans were not approved the union would be faced with selling both homes in the near future.

However, the two homes continued to require expenditure to maintain a reasonable and acceptable level of repair. Rottingdean, which had had no major structural repairs for over 20 years, now required such expenditure. Ayr required expenditure on both its structure and its facilities. At the time of the SOGAT/NGA merger the Rest and Recreation Centre at Rottingdean and the convalescent home at Ayr were still in being. Since its opening in 1948 over 15,500 members and spouses had stayed at the Ayr home.

THE NATIONAL SUPERANNUATION FUND

When the NUPB&PW amalgamated with the National Union of Bookbinders and Machine Rulers in 1921 each union had its own superannuation fund and this situation continued after the merger. Both funds experienced difficulties and in 1937 a Special Interim Delegate Conference considered the unsatisfactory state of the two Superannuation Funds. To solve the problem, the NEC proposed to abolish the two schemes and replace them with a unified fund into which male members would pay 2½p per week and female members 1p per week. This sum would be additional to the normal weekly subscriptions. The superannuation benefit was fixed at 50p per week, to qualify for which a member required at least 25 years' membership and must have reached retirement age. The 1937 Special Interim Delegate Conference overwhelmingly accepted the NEC proposals and following a ballot of membership they become operational for members employed in the binding and print sectors. However, the Papermill Section members voted to terminate superannuation benefit and from 1939 the benefit was only available to the printing and binding membership.

However, the unified superannuation scheme did not work as well as had been expected, mainly through the effect of the war on the fund's income. An NEC sub-committee examined the situation and suggested proposals whereby the Fund could be put on a sound footing. Its recommendations were endorsed by the Executive Council which decided to seek approval for them at the 1944 Delegate Council. However, this meeting was postponed in response to a request from the government that travelling should be avoided wherever possible. The 1944 Delegate Council Meeting was eventually held in January 1945 at which the Executive Council sought authority to submit to a ballot vote alternative proposals. The proposals were first, that contributions to the Superannuation Fund be increased to 4½p per week for men and 1½p per week for women with a sliding scale of benefit from 50p per week to 62½p per week depending on the length of union membership. Second, failing agreement to increase the contributions, a reduced scale of benefit (30p to 50p per week) related to length of membership be adopted. The Executive emphasised the impossibility of producing any other financially sound scheme except in return for a contribution rate that would be prohibitive. They were confident that their proposals would make the scheme financially viable for some years. However, the debate went against the NEC with the delegates rejecting a sliding scale of benefit and instructing the NEC to submit a more businesslike solution to the Fund's problems to the 1946 Delegate Council. The settlement of the vexatious problem of superannuation benefit had been postponed and the NEC was sent back 'to the not very agreeable task of making bricks without straw'.[8]

The NEC claimed its proposals to the 1946 Delegate Council were not based upon sentiment and expediency but on financial realities.

They sought a contribution rate for both male and female members of 7p per week in return for a pension of 50p per week. However, the delegates rejected these proposals preferring to accept a motion from the Midland Group which proposed to keep the present contribution rates to the Fund unchanged but to introduce a sliding scale of benefit varying from 30p per week to 50p per week depending on the length of membership. In 1948 the NEC sought to secure superannuation benefit for the future by proposing female members be given the option of subscribing to the Fund on the same basis as men and qualifying for benefit at the age of 65 as for men. However, this suggestion was rejected.

In 1952 it was decided that an annual superannuation bonus payment of £5 be made to men and women. This continued until December 1956. The 1956 Delegate Council accepted, in the light of the rising number of claims on the Fund, that men and women contributing to it should pay another ½p per week whilst the benefit scales be increased by 10p and the annual bonus to £5 per year. However, the continued rise in the number of pensioners continued to cause concern. By 1962 the fund was heading for insolvency. Attempts had been made at the 1958 Delegate Council to make contributions to the Fund voluntary, as members should decide whether or not they wished to contribute to the Superannuation Fund, particularly as central government protected its senior citizens by way of the state pension scheme. The 1962 Delegate Council also considered the issue of superannuation. The Midland Group sought to increase subscriptions to the fund to 5p per week for men and 2p for women in the belief this would establish a healthy Superannuation Fund. There was no reason why superannuation contributions could not be increased year by year as with general contributions. The NEC opposed these proposed increases pointing out the Fund had a rising deficit and contribution increases were merely tinkering with the problem as they would, at best, only cover the Fund's liabilities for another two years. The NEC asked the Midland Group to withdraw its motion pending a full inquiry and the convening of a special Delegate Conference to consider how the Fund could be put on a sound basis. The Midland Group refused to withdraw its motion which was heavily defeated.

The General Secretary then moved that an inquiry be made into the state of the national union's Superannuation Fund, a full report be issued to the membership and a special conference be called to decide the future of the fund at a convenient date after the issue of the report.[9] The Midland Group wanted the enquiry to ensure the continuity of the Fund but lost its attempt to decide the future of the Superannuation Fund before the report was complete. An Interim Delegate Council Meeting was held in London on 29 October 1963 to consider the Report into the Superannuation Fund and two main proposals. Proposal 1 in the name of the NEC stated:

That the National Superannuation Fund in its present form should be discontinued, the cash balance being used to provide existing pensions and those liable to occur within the next five years and that existing pension commitments be met together with the pensions of those who would normally qualify within the next five years. That those eligible and awaiting pensions shall continue to pay National Superannuation Fund contributions at the new scale of 2/6d [12½p] per week both for men and women with the option of withdrawing from the Fund and sacrificing any benefit if desired. And that, if necessary, the General Fund shall be utilised to assist in discharging these obligations.[10]

Proposal 2 also in the name of the NEC urged:

That the National Superannuation Fund be continued, but the contributions shall be increased to 1/6d [7½p] per week for men and 1/– [5p] per week for women and that the words '40 years of membership and over 12/– [60p] per week be deleted from General Rule 28, clause 2' this change being in respect of any present or future recipients.[11]

The sole object was to find a solution to the problem either by ending the fund or by making it financially sound for the future. The first proposal gave an opportunity to end the Fund. The second proposal set down conditions under which the Fund could continue if the majority opinion was against ending it. The NEC was in no doubt that securing a fully financed Fund was impossible. Nevertheless, it realised that if the fund were to continue it was necessary to collect the maximum amount of money possible, otherwise, given the continual rise in the number of pensioners, the fund would keep getting into difficulties. The NEC accepted the actuarial advice that the highest contribution rate that might be extracted from the members was 7½p

Bill Morrison, General Secretary (1947–60)

John McKenzie, General President (–1967)

Tom Smith, General Secretary (1960–70)

Albert Powell, General President (1974–83)

Vincent Flynn, General President (1967–1970), General Secretary (1970–74)

per week. Amendments that the contribution rate to the Super-annuation Fund be 6p for both men and women, that it be 5p and women members have the option of withdrawing from the Fund and sacrificing benefit and that the subscription rate be 5p for men and 2½p for women were all defeated. The NEC gained the impression from the debate on Proposal Two that the majority of delegates wished the Superannuation Fund to continue one way or another. However, when Proposal Two was put to the vote it was defeated.

The Interim Delegate Meeting proceeded to debate Proposal 1 which sought to end the Fund without undue hardship. The NEC spelt out the scenario it envisaged if the proposal to end the Fund were rejected:

> We thought we should give you the opportunity to end the Fund under reasonable conditions without undue hardship. If you choose otherwise that is your affair but a choice to continue will assuredly lead to a progressively growing community of pensioners, living longer and longer, with the aid of surgery and medical science who are drawing longer and longer from the Superannuation Fund if it continues, or from the General Fund if it does not, for which those at work pay more and more and which, due to inflation, is worth less and less.[12]

By 1963 the superannuation benefit was worth only half of what it had been in 1946. When Proposal 1 was put to the vote it was defeated. The Interim Delegate Council had left the NEC in a difficult position. On the one hand, it had voted against the continuation of the Fund, but on the other hand, it had also voted against the ending of the Fund. Half the delegates were pulling one way and half were pulling the other. One half was trying to continue the Fund and the other half trying to wind it up. The result was that the Conference made no decision.

In an attempt to resolve this dilemma the Leeds Branch proposed to the 1964 Delegate Conference that before a final decision was taken on the superannuation fund there be a national ballot of all contributing members in which they would state whether they wished the superannuation fund to continue, but the ballot papers would inform the members that if they favoured continuation there would be a need for an increase in superannuation fund contributions. The Leeds Branch was saying that a Delegate Meeting could not decide, so let the members decide. The Delegate Council had forfeited the right to decide. However, the motion was defeated by 189 votes to 177. Motions to wind up the Fund and distribute the balance to contributing members in accordance with the sums paid by them were defeated as was a Glasgow Branch suggestion that the Fund be ended by limiting the period for which benefit would be paid to three years. Like the Leeds Branch, the London Bookbinders' Branch felt the members should decide the future of the superannuation fund by a ballot in which they would have a choice. One option would be to increase contributions to the Fund to 1/3d (6p) per week for men and women, with the present level of benefits continuing. The second option would be to commute the fund to a retirement fund with the present pensioner members continuing to draw their pensions. The Bookbinders' motion was defeated by 130 votes to 114 on the basis of two perennial arguments. First, the union had been built up by the older members who, after a period of service, to the trade and the industry had to retire. These 'class warriors' should be looked after in their old age. Second, women were a burden on the fund in that they paid in less than men but, because they retired five years earlier, they took more out of the Fund. This could only be overcome, it was argued, by equality of contributions, but the London Bookbinders' motion did not provide for this. The 1964 Delegate Council had debated all the arguments for the ending of the fund but they had all been rejected. The NEC assumed the Council favoured the continuation of the fund and proposed conditions on which the fund should continue. However, opponents of the fund argued that the cost of a 'pay-as-you-go' pension system had now reached the stage where it was too prohibitive, that too many of those in support of continuing the scheme were motivated by sentimentality about looking after people who had spent their time and energy promoting members' interests in the days when it was difficult to be a trade unionist, and that what was being proposed was unfair to women in that the number of superannuated women was small and they paid into the fund to help the male members of the union. Although at present female members tolerated this situation, whether this would continue to be the case if they had to pay an increase in contributions of 200 per cent was debatable. The NEC motion to continue the superannuation fund on the basis of increased contributions was defeated by 190 votes to 102. Like the 1963 Interim Delegate Council, the 1964 Delegate Council had bucked the issue and voted against either continuing or ending the fund.

This farcical situation could not continue, and in 1965 a Special

Interim Conference of representatives of contributors into the super-annuation fund was held. The meeting approved the following resolution:

> That the Superannuation Fund (General Rule 28) be wound up on 31 December 1965 after which date no further superannuation contributions shall be taken, no further applications be accepted for this benefit and pensions of existing superannu-atants shall cease. Any remaining assets in the Superannuation Fund, after the 1965 accounts have been finalised, shall be shared among the superannuatants in proportion to the benefit scales.[13]

When put to a ballot of subscribing members, the resolution was carried by 32,460 votes to 8,501 votes, a majority of 23,959. The decision to terminate the superannuation fund was regretted, but the hard facts were that members were not prepared to increase their contributions and expenditure from the fund exceeded income by over £29,000.

Table 11.4
NUPB&PW/SOGAT (Division A): the National Superannuation Fund, 1955–66

Date	Income (£)	Expenditure (£)	Surplus (£)
1955	114,107	104,111	9,996
1956	122,355	106,088	16,267
1957	138,054	115,115	22,940
1958	138,896	121,855	17,041
1959	133,124	129,413	3,711
1960	144,686	135,486	9,382
1961	142,169	146,057	−3,888
1962	130,935	154,605	−9,670
1963	144,235	156,706	−12,471
1964	145,069	169,195	−24,116
1965	145,538	174,623	−29,085
1966	10,972	79	10,893

Source: Financial Statements, 1955–66.

Calculations to divide the Superannuation Fund's assets began in April 1966 by which time all its investment had been liquidated at a loss of £60,000 and the monies placed in a deposit account. The money from the sale of investments plus interest from the deposit account amounted to £159,041.63 and the NUPB&PW decided to make a share in the fund equal to £1.23. The rates of pension in 1965 were 35p, 40p, 45p, 47½p and 60p per week. The common denominator was 2½p, which would count as one share. This meant a 35p per week pension would have 14 shares, a 40p pension would have 16 shares, and so on. The number of pensioners in the superannuation fund as at 31 December 1965 was 6,746 designated as follows:

1 member at 35p	=	14 shares
1,269 members at 40p	=	20,304 shares
959 members at 45p	=	17,262 shares
8 members at 47½p	=	152 shares
1,252 members at 50p	=	25,040 shares
3,257 members at 60p	=	78,168 shares
		140,940 shares

£159,144.75 was divided by 140,940 to give a sum of £1.13 per 2½p share. The application of this formula resulted in the union's pensioners receiving the following amounts which were paid out via the branches in May 1966:

35p members received	£15.81
40p members received	£18.07
45p members received	£20.32½
47½ members received	£21.45
50p members received	£22.57
60p members received	£27.10

This distribution was in accordance with the instructions given by the Special Interim Conference of representatives of contributing members. After distribution, £4,750 was left over and this plus interest was transferred to the General Fund.

THE OFFICERS' AND STAFF PENSION FUND

This Fund began in December 1938 and provided for officers (national and branch) and staff a pension based on final pay and a death benefit. In 1955 the percentage of retirement salary payable as a pension varied from 30 per cent to 50 per cent of final salary for officers and organisers depending on the years of service. For staff, the final pension varied from 20 per cent to 50 per cent of final salary, depending on the length of service. In 1962 the percentage of final salary payable as a pension for officers and organisers was increased from 35 per cent to 55 per cent and for staff from 35 per cent to 55 per cent. In 1964 the pension arrangements were changed. After 10 years' service officers and organisers were to receive 35 per cent of final salary as a pension increasing by 1 per cent for each completed year thereafter with a maximum of 55 per cent. For staff, after ten years of service the pension would be 25 per cent of final salary increasing by 1 per cent each completed year thereafter up to a maximum of 55 per cent. In 1988 the death-in-service benefit was increased for both staff and officers from twice to four times annual pensionable balances whilst for the first time a children's benefit was introduced whereby on death in service there would be a pension payable to children equal to 25 per cent of the member's prospective pension for one child and 50 per cent for two or more children. If there was no surviving spouse then the benefit with regard to the children would be doubled. On a member's death in retirement, children's pensions would be based on the member's pension at death. These benefits were available only to full-time employees of the union and, from 1982, to part-time employees who were at least 20 years old and worked 16 hours or more per week.[14]

The pension and death benefit responsibilities of the Fund were met from its assets which were managed by an independent trust advised by professional actuaries and administrators. As shown by Table 11.5, the assets of the Fund increased from £123,060 in 1955 to £21,741,318 by 1991. The liabilities of the Fund were met by interest from its investments. The income from the subscribers (i.e. the union's employees) was a percentage of their salary or weekly wage. In 1956 the employee contribution was 2.5 per cent which increased to 5 per cent in 1968 and 7 per cent in 1988. Up to 1966 the union (employer) contribution into the Fund was a fixed amount 2p per week for each member but from 1966 it was a percentage of the total annual gross salaries of the subscribers to the Fund. This figure was originally 19 per cent but in 1986 the sum to be paid by SOGAT as the employer became determined by the Trustees on the advice of the Actuary. The amount contributed was not to be less than 10 per cent and not more than 19 per cent. In 1988 the amount of employer contributions, into the Fund became not less than twice the employee contribution. The Officers' and Staff Pension Fund was originally valued by the Actuary every four years but in 1978 biennial valuations were adopted.

By the early 1960s the rising cost of pensions was reducing the Fund's surplus. The NUPB&PW attempted to rectify the situation by increasing the Fund's investments so that the increased interest could fund the pension liabilities. This policy of 'scraping the barrel' to invest brought some temporary respite but the position remained precarious since more and more pensions would have to be paid in future years. The 1962 actuarial valuation of the Fund revealed a deficit of £105,133, but when the 1966 valuation revealed a deficit of £427,705 the NEC decided to act. Unless the subscribers to the Fund and the union were prepared to face up to the situation the Fund would have to be wound up. Proposals were placed before the 1966 Delegate Council to remove once and for all the Fund's deficit and establish it on a firm footing. The first proposal, which was accepted, increased the employees contribution from 2.5 per cent of pay to 5 per cent. The second, which was also accepted, changed the basis of the employers' contributions from a fixed sum to a percentage of gross salaries. Although wages had risen and staff had increased, the income into the Fund had not increased pro rata to meet increased costs. By making a payment based on a fixed amount, the Fund was in a position whereby the employers' contributions could not increase as wages or staff levels changed. The NEC saw this as the 'basic and root cause' of the Fund's trouble. To ensure that the Fund was maintained on behalf of the employees and to be secure in the knowledge that the money was there to meet the union's obligations to its employees when they retired, the NEC proposed successfully that contributions be 19 per cent of the total annual gross salaries of all contributing members.

The impact of these measures was to reduce the actuarial deficit of the Fund in 1970 to £121,884. The NEC ordered a professional investigation into the Fund, the purpose of which was to suggest not only how to bring the Fund back to the point where it was no longer in deficit but to make available new and improved benefits to the members. The report identified new fields of investment for the Fund

334

Table 11.5
NUPB&PW SOGAT (Division A)/SOGAT/SOGAT (75) and SOGAT (82): the Officers and Staff Pension Fund, 1955–91

Date	Income (£)	Expenditure (£)	Surplus (£)	Balance of funds (£)
1955	21,732	6,391	15,341	123,060
1956	23,721	6,353	17,368	140,454
1957	24,955	7,136	17,819	158,272
1958	25,954	6,712	19,242	177,514
1959	26,895	6,663	20,232	197,746
1960	28,468	8,291	20,177	217,923
1961	29,550	10,176	19,374	234,297
1962	33,894	13,409	20,485	257,782
1963	32,149	15,981	16,168	273,950
1964	36,663	19,083	17,580	291,530
1965	38,676	18,905	19,771	311,301
1966	42,076	20,575	21,501	332,802
1967	43,567	23,893	19,674	352,476
1968	59,614	28,431	31,183	383,659
1969	88,118	29,166	58,952	442,611
1970	102,499	29,675	72,824	515,435
1971	125,245	32,145	93,100	608,535
1972	95,456	25,865	69,591	678,126
1973	149,041	43,224	105,818	783,944
1974	190,343	61,600	128,743	916,393
1975	235,291	78,577	156,714	1,073,107
1976	314,825	86,744	228,081	1,240,290
1977	325,209	136,975	188,234	1,950,102
1978	334,889	161,229	173,658	2,115,401
1979	473,508	144,797	328,711	2,590,430
1980	633,375	206,815	426,560	3,180,312
1981	750,028	282,425	467,603	3,472,819
1982	711,015	213,190	497,825	4,348,149
1983	2,015,312	716,551	1,298,761	9,158,346
1984	1,404,978	649,562	755,416	10,822,086
1985	1,459,329	887,559	571,770	12,330,550
1986	2,474,036	854,624	1,619,412	14,959,040
1987	1,840,312	1,189,280	651,032	20,801,168
1988	1,883,522	1,229,549	653,973	16,587,608
1989	2,115,402	1,540,773	574,629	20,345,092
1990	2,121,285	1,365,503	755,782	17,105,910
1991	1,084,627	657,891	426,736	21,741,318

Source: *Financial Statements*, 1955–91

and suggested additional income could be obtained if decisions agreed by the employers and employees as to the financing of the Fund could be implemented without waiting for approval at the next Delegate Council. The 1972 Delegate Council accepted these suggestions. As a result the Fund's underlying deficit was removed, with the actuarial valuations of 1978, 1980, 1982, 1984 and 1986 all showing surpluses. The 1988 valuation revealed an actuarial deficit of £215,000 which was rectified by the contributions into the Fund being increased in line with the Actuary's recommendations. At the point that SOGAT ceased to be an independent union, its Officers' and Staff Pension Fund was in a satisfactory position, paid a good pension and the employer contribution was at least twice that of the employee.

SERVICES TO MEMBERS

SOGAT and its constituent unions over the period 1955–91 provided legal assistance at the discretion of the NEC to members who met with accidents resulting in personal injury or who contracted suspected industrial diseases during their employment or in search of employment and to members in connection with wrongful dismissal, arrears of wages and claims for holiday pay. In 1974 legal assistance was extended to two other circumstances. First, members injured going to or from any union meeting authorised by any national, branch or chapel officer, and second, to members requiring help as a result of lawful picketing during an industrial dispute or any action authorised by the NEC. In 1976 the legal assistance scheme was extended further to cover members employed as drivers in relation to charges brought against them for alleged offences against the Road Traffic Acts during the course of their employment. This did not cover situations where charges were brought against a member for alleged driving under the influence of drink. Legal assistance was also available to relatives of deceased members whose death was due to accidents or diseases or where the deceased member had claims pending at the time of death. In 1984 the NEC was given authority to grant, at its discretion, legal assistance to a member's immediate dependants or dependent children.

In 1991 SOGAT's legal services, which were among the best in the trade union movement, expanded to cover conveyancing, financial advice, wills and protection on the roads. The lawyers for the SOGAT were Robin Thompson & Partners and Brian Thompson & Partners.

This relationship with Thompson's dated back to 1947 when the NUPB&PW employed W.H. Thompson solicitors. This was the same year that Robin and Brian Thompson joined the firm. Through nearly 45 years of change the relationship grew and strengthened. It survived various amalgamations. The 1991 changes meant Thompson's were not just there to help members when they suffered an injury at work but also to protect members and families in other ways.

The NUPB&PW did not provide an educational and training service for its members and chapel officials preferring to rely on the TUC and the P&KTF. However, new branch secretary courses were run from Head Office. By 1974 the SOGAT NEC was concerned about the poor response of the membership to the educational opportunities available and expressed disappointment that courses arranged by the TUC, Industrial Training Board and other educational bodies had to be cancelled through lack of support. However, by the late 1970s and early 1980s there had been an improvement in the interest shown by members in educational courses and an increasing number were attending TUC courses.

A major criticism made of TUC courses by SOGAT members was that they were too general in nature and did not meet their needs. In July 1985, SOGAT met with TUC Education Officers to discuss how SOGAT might better utilise the resources and expertise of the TUC National Education Centre in developing and running SOGAT-based courses. It agreed that the structure of existing TUC courses could easily be used as a framework for specifically SOGAT-based courses. SOGAT materials were used for the preparation and running of pilot joint TUC/SOGAT courses covering pensions, equality issues, FOC/MOC skill needs, health and safety and youth issues. The 1986/7 training programme included four-day chapel officials' courses held in regional centres throughout the country and which examined the role of SOGAT representatives at the workplace and in the wider trade union movement. Health and safety courses started in line with the 1986 Delegate Council decision that the union's health and safety representatives receive a minimum level of training. The 1986 Delegate Council called on the NEC to institute a co-ordinated system of training with regard to newly elected chapel officers and to develop training courses that met the particular needs of women members. In 1987, SOGAT began, through its Research and Education Department, a comprehensive annual training programme of 50 courses held in centres around the country. The programme provided in each district area two chapel officials' courses, one on pensions, one for women members and one for young members. In addition, separate provision was made for the training of health and safety representatives. SOGAT's own courses were complementary to, and not a replacement for, TUC Education courses. They were run in collaboration with the TUC Regional Education Officers who supplied the tutors and venues with SOGAT supplying the course materials and, where appropriate, input from a branch officer.

In 1981, SOGAT appointed a Health and Safety Adviser to help develop activities in the field. In June 1985 the NEC decided that health and safety should become a separate department within the union. In 1986, in the case of hearing defects – deafness or tinnitus – SOGAT negotiated a 'no-fault compensation scheme' which enabled members who could demonstrate deafness caused through exposure to noise at work to receive automatically a fixed sum of compensation rather than having to rely on protracted and expensive litigation. This led to an increase in accident and ill health claims and the average settlement paid out in compensation was £1,300. Although few SOGAT members were profoundly deaf, far too many had had their hearing impaired and their quality of life worsened by noise in the workplace. Health and safety advice was seen by SOGAT members as one of the major services provided by the union, and in the late 1980s SOGAT increased its activities in this area to help reduce the level of work-related ill health, injury and death suffered by its members.

NOTES

1. See Society of Graphical and Allied Trades (Division A) *Report of Biennial Delegate Council Meeting, 1966*, p. 75.
2. In 1955 the maximum period for which such a levy could operate was three months but by 1991 it was six months. In 1955 the maximum levy that could be imposed was 5p per week for male adults and 2½p per week for women. By 1991 the maximum level was 50 per cent of the adult weekly contribution.
3. See National Union of Printing, Bookbinding and Paperworkers *Report of the Biennial Delegate Council, 1964*, p. 139.
4. See National Union of Printing, Bookbinding and Paperworkers *Report of Biennial Delegate Council, 1962*, pp. 215–20 and Society of Graphical and Allied Trades (Division A) *Report of Biennial Delegate Council, 1966*, pp. 195–203.
5. See Society of Graphical and Allied Trades (Division A) *Report of the Biennial Delegate Council, 1966*, pp. 200–1.
6. See Society of Graphical and Allied Trades *Report of the Special Delegate Council to Consider the Financial Position of the Society, 1983*, May, p. 226.

7. See Society of Graphical and Allied Trades *Report of Delegate Council Meeting, 1974*, p. 49.

8. See C.J. Bundock *The Story of the National Union of Printing, Bookbinding and Paperworkers*, Oxford University Press, Book 5, Chapter 54, p. 478.

9. See National Union of Printing, Bookbinding and Paperworkers *Report of Biennial Delegate Council, 1962*, pp. 198–9.

10. See National Union of Printing, Bookbinding and Paperworkers *Report of the Proceedings of the Interim Delegate Council Meeting, 1963*, p. 37.

11. Op. cit., p. 8.

12. See National Union of Printing, Bookbinding and Paperworkers *Report of the Proceedings of the Interim Delegate Council Meeting Concerning the National Superannuation Fund* (General Rule 28), 1963, pp. 43–4.

13. See Society of Graphical and Allied Trades (Division A) *Balance Sheet, 1966*, pp. 2–3.

14. The 1968 Biennial Delegate Council accepted that the minimum age at which employees could enter the Officers' and Staff Pension Fund be reduced from 20 years to 18 years.

PART III

THE WIDER TRADE UNION AND LABOUR MOVEMENT

CHAPTER 12

RELATIONS WITH WIDER PRINT UNION BODIES

SOGAT and its founding unions were members of four wider print union organisations. These were the Printing and Kindred Trades' Federation (P&KTF) which was founded in 1901 and disbanded in 1973 the International Federation of Commercial, Clerical, Professional and Technical Employees (FIET), the International Federation of Chemical, Energy and General Workers (ICEF) and the International Graphical Federation (IGF) from which SOGAT withdrew in 1976.

THE PRINTING AND KINDRED TRADES' FEDERATION

Structure

The P&KTF's aim was unity of action amongst its affiliated unions, to obtain uniform working conditions in different sectors of the industry, to prevent the occurrence of strikes and in the event of disputes arising to encourage their settlement by peaceful means, to establish a central fund for mutual assistance and to conduct research and inquiry work. It was the collective voice of the print unions. In 1955, 16 unions with a total membership of 320,525 affiliated to the P&KTF. The NUPB&PW accounted for some 50 per cent of this affiliated membership. By the time of its dissolution in 1973 seven unions with a total membership of 218,354 were affiliated. The peak of its membership was 1971, when its nine affiliates had a total membership of 405,793. Unions paid contributions to the P&KTF in proportion to their membership levels. The NUPB&PW/SOGAT (Division A)/SOGAT were major providers of funds to the Federation.

The affiliated unions retained and guarded jealously their autonomy, and Rule 6(a) of the Federation stated that 'the Federation shall not interfere in the internal management of any union, nor its rules and customs'. However, the P&KTF had authority in certain areas. Where a dispute between two or more affiliated unions over demarcation of work or organisation could not be settled by the unions concerned, the matter could be referred to the P&KTF Arbitration Board whose decision was binding on the parties. The Federation, on behalf of its affiliates, negotiated agreements with employers' organisations on hours of work, holidays and the pay of apprentices. Throughout the period 1955 to its dissolution, it frequently sought to negotiate with the major printing employers' organisations industry-wide minimum standards of sick pay, pensions and compensation for redundancy. Wages, however, were solely the concern of the individual unions. When the print unions made a collective approach on wages it was the unions acting together with the Federation playing a co-ordinating role by providing common facilities, preparing the claim and issuing reports. The Federation *spoke* collectively for its affiliates to the TUC and to government departments. It only *acted* collectively for its affiliates when they gave it authority to do so.

The policy-making machinery of the Federation consisted of membership ballots, its Administrative Council and its Executive Committee.[1] The Administrative Council was appointed annually. Each affiliated union had at least one representative on the Council but each was entitled to additional representatives in proportion to their size. The NUPB&PW had 21 representatives whilst the original SOGAT had 33 representatives. At the time of the Federation's dissolution in 1973 the reconstituted SOGAT had ceased to be active in the Federation following a disagreement regarding organisational rights and the P&KTF's role in the legal action by NATSOPA against SOGAT. The Council met as and when it had business to transact but had to hold an Annual Conference in May of each year.

The Council appointed a President, a Vice President and 15 members from its own ranks to act as an Executive Committee to run the affairs of the Federation between Annual Conferences. At least one member of the Executive had to be a woman. Until 1958 Miss M.G. Wallis of the NUPB&PW occupied this seat. She was replaced by Miss M. Hogarth, also of the NUPB&PW, and who remained on the Executive Committee until 1965. Miss O. Day of SOGAT then held the seat for one year before being replaced by Mrs Chubb of SOGAT, who occupied the seat up to the point SOGAT ceased to participate in the

Federation's affairs. The General Secretary of the NUPB&PW, Mr Bill Morrison, was the Vice President of the Federation in 1955 and became President in the following year. He held this post until 1960. In 1956 John McKenzie of the NUPB&PW became a Trustee of the Federation, a post he held until he became in 1965 a member of the Executive Committee; he left this office in 1968. In 1960 the NUPB&PW General Secretary, Tom Smith, became a member of the Executive Committee and served in this capacity until his death in August 1970. Vincent Flynn became an Executive Committee member in 1967 and Bill Keys a member in 1970. Both served the Federation in this capacity until SOGAT withdrew from participation in its affairs.

The major officers of the Federation were the General Secretary, who was also the Treasurer, the Assistant General Secretary and the Assistant Secretary. The General Secretary of the Federation in 1955 was Mr J. Fletcher who was a Typographical Association member. In 1958 he was replaced by Mr Granville Eastwood, the Federation's Assistant General Secretary. He reached retirement age during 1971 but accepted the Federation's Executive's invitation to continue in office for a further period not exceeding two years. He finally retired in 1973 after 30 years' service divided equally between the offices of General Secretary and Assistant General Secretary. Granville Eastwood was succeeded as Assistant General Secretary by Mr Stan Carter, a member of the Manchester Branch of the NUPB&PW who held this position until his appointment in 1967 to the post of Research Officer for SOGAT. On Mr Carter's departure the office of Assistant General Secretary was abolished leaving a General Secretary. The post of Assistant Secretary ended in 1962 but was revived with Mr Carter's departure when Miss Gloria Hart was appointed Assistant Secretary. Following the retirement of Mr Eastwood, she assumed the office of Acting General Secretary until the establishment in 1974 of the Printing Trade Unions' Co-ordinating Bureau of which she became Secretary.

NUPB&PW and SOGAT at the Administrative Council

The NUPB&PW, SOGAT (Division A) and SOGAT played an active part in the affairs of the Federation although SOGAT, in line with its 1972 Delegate Council decision that the P&KTF be wound up, withdrew from participating at all levels in the activities of the Federation. SOGAT allowed their affiliation fees to lapse and in January 1973, because of arrears of contributions, SOGAT ended its connection with the Federation. Prior to 1972, as well as participating in debates at the Annual Administrative Council, NUPB&PW proposed a motion designed to restore unity amongst the Federation's unions following disputes between affiliates during the 1955/6 wage negotiations with the Newspaper Society and the BFMP. The motion proposed a meeting of two or three representatives of each union in the Federation to devise a basic wage structure for the industry. At the 1960 Council the NUPB&PW successfully moved a motion to restrict the amount of permitted overtime to be worked by affiliated unions' members as the length of the working week was reduced in BFMP and Newspaper Society offices. They sought to prevent the amount of permitted overtime in the collective agreements being increased by the same amount as the length of the working week was reduced.

The NUPB&PW successfully submitted a motion to the 1962 Administrative Council, requesting the Executive Committee consider an extension of representation on the Executive in the event of affiliated unions merging. Three years later the NUPB&PW successfully committed the P&KTF not to approve any further incentive schemes unless they contained a clause providing for bonus payments to be included in the calculation of holiday pay. At the 1971 Council, SOGAT (Division A) persuaded delegates that since young people attained the age of majority at 18 with the power to vote, the period of service for an indentured apprenticeship be reduced and the adult rate be payable at 18 years of age rather than 21.

By the late 1960s SOGAT had become disillusioned with the Federation to such an extent that it proposed to the 1969 Council that the Federation be wound up, although this proposal was rejected. Dissatisfaction continued and at the 1972 Council SOGAT proposed the P&KTF be wound up at the earliest suitable date. This was also rejected.

Co-ordinated Wage Claims, 1955–71

In anticipation of the termination of the 1951 five-year stabilisation agreements the Federation held a meeting of the unions concerned to see if a common approach could be agreed for the renegotiation of these agreements. Eleven unions, including the NUPB&PW attended the meeting but the LTS and the ACP said they would make their own approaches. Eleven unions went forward collectively with a wage

346

claim of a new basic provincial craft rate of £10.50 with a London upward differential of 57½p, 87 per cent of the proposed craft rate for semi-skilled workers, 85 per cent for general assistants and 75 per cent of the male Class 3 rate for women, incorporation of the cost of living bonus into basic wages and one grade for all employees in the provinces. After many hard bargaining sessions with the employers, the unions' members accepted a new basic craft rate of £10.31½ in London, £9.75 in the provinces, a cost of living bonus scheme of 5p a point above the Index of Retail Prices figure of 150, stabilisation for three years and a series of measures designed to increase the supply of skilled labour to the employers. The revised agreement for NUPB&PW members became operative from January 1956.

The separate negotiations between the BFMP and the Newspaper Society on the one hand and the LTS and the ACP on the other broke down, as did those between the two employers' organisations the TA. The two disputes were referred to Court of Inquiry, but during the early stages of the TA Inquiry the employers and the union announced they would resume negotiations immediately following the Report of the Court of Inquiry into the London dispute. The Report urged, *inter alia*, that further efforts be made to establish comprehensive national machinery on a two-tier basis (one for craft unions and one for non-craft) for the negotiation of wages and conditions in the industry. Four craft unions (the LTS, ACP, TA and ASLP) made agreements in May 1956 with the BFMP and the Newspaper Society and which disturbed relativities with the unions that had settled in January 1956. Meetings took place between the employers and the 'January' unions to adjust their settlement in the light of the May agreements. The employers quickly agreed to parity of craft rates between the 'January' and 'May' unions but refused, initially, to concede proportionate increases for non-craft employees. However, the employers subsequently agreed to do this, much to the approval of NUPB&PW members.

The lack of unity amongst the print unions during the 1955/6 wage negotiations led the NUPB&PW to submit the following motion to the 1956 P&KTF Administrative Council:

> That, in the opinion of this Conference, recent events have demonstrated a serious lack of unity between the unions affil-iated to our Federation. As a means of restoring this unity Conference instructs the General Secretary to call a meeting of two or three representatives from each union in the

Federation, such meeting to endeavour to devise a basic wage structure for the industry.[2]

The Paperworkers argued that there was 'an atmosphere' between craft and non-craft employees in the industry and that bitterness and bad feelings should be forgotten and the two groups sit down together to solve the problem. The LTS moved and the TA seconded an amendment to the NUPB&PW's motion. The amendment proposed:

> Conference accepts the recommendations of the Court of Inquiry for a two tier wage structure for the industry. In order that this can be achieved the Conference requests the Federation officers to act as convenors for calling together the affiliated unions at two meetings; one for craft workers and the other for non-craft.[3]

Both the Paperworkers' resolution and the LTS amendment sought to secure unity by devising wage negotiation machinery which would prevent the problems of the past from recurring. The LTS wanted a two-tier structure. It envisaged that if there was one tier for craftsmen and one for non-craft then those 'non-craft' unions with craft members would put the case for those members at the Craft Group Conference. Unions with both craft and non-craft members would put the case of their members to both sections. For the LTS and the TA a two-tier structure was the only practicable way of solving the craft/non-craft wage differential problem. The LTS amendment was defeated by 46 votes to 25 whilst the NUPB&PW motion was carried by 47 votes to 25.

At a meeting called by the Federation in February 1957, two sets of proposals for the future wage negotiation machinery emerged. The first included the clause that there be a basis of agreement between all the unions, craft and non-craft, for a period of five or ten years and that that basis should include agreement at a preliminary union conference on what amount the unions would claim and what the percentage craft/non-craft differential should be. All the unions, craft and non-craft would negotiate as one body. These first proposals acknowledged that, as the unions could not have individual autonomy, as in the past, and at the same time have unity in a wages structure, there should be acceptance that a union could withdraw from a united movement and a small sub-committee deal with the question of percentage differentials and present a report. The second set of proposals, largely the work of the

LTS, contained four elements. First, there should be an initial conference of all craft unions to discuss the craft demands. At the same time there should be a conference of non-craft unions for the same purpose. The second element involved a conference of all unions to agree on the percentage of the craft rate to be claimed by the non-craft unions. Third, the negotiations with the employers and the craft and non-craft unions would proceed, not jointly, but side by side. The fourth element envisaged consultation and reports on the progress being made by both sections through information given to the Federation and at subsequent joint union conferences.

Both sets of proposals were discussed at a further conference and the second set were approved as they would unite the Federation and the unions within it and avoid the problems of previous wage negotiations. It was envisaged that disunity between the unions would end. They were now to divide into craft and non-craft interests and those unions with both craft and non-craft members would participate in negotiations and consultations when both groups interests were considered.

In April 1958 the Federation initiated discussions to devise a basic wage structure in readiness for the negotiations to revise the agreements with the BFMP and the Newspaper Society due to end in April 1959. A meeting of the craft sub-committee took place on 17 June 1958 and the one for the non-craft unions the following day. NATSOPA sent a delegation to the craft union meeting. The craft unions objected and it was apparent that if NATSOPA remained some of the craft unions would withdraw from the attempts to devise an agreed wage structure. The LTS General Secretary suggested that NATSOPA belonged to the second tier of negotiations and that they should therefore leave the meeting. This they did, claiming their exclusion was unconstitutional and an insult. Getting no satisfaction from the P&KTF to their complaint, NATSOPA disaffiliated from the Federation in January 1959, stating that re-affiliation would not happen until there was a change of attitude by the P&KTF.[4]

Following the acceptance of a two-tier wages structure, discussions on the details of claims proceeded at separate meetings of craft unions and those unions with non craft and women members. There was full consultation between the two groups and agreement was reached as to the claims to be presented to the BFMP and NS to replace the wage agreements due to terminate on 20 April 1959. Although the 1959 wages claim (for a 10 per cent increase) and hours claim (for a 40-hour working week) were both collective claims, they were not made under the auspices of the Federation. They were the result of a collective approach by two groups of unions in which the Federation fulfilled a liaison role whilst its General Secretary was closely associated with the negotiations. As the hours and holiday agreement was between the Federation and the BFMP and the Newspaper Society, the 40-hour week claim was presented by the Federation's General Secretary. The Wages and Hours Agreement made following the 1959 dispute was to operate to 6 August 1962, but in 1961 consideration would be given as to whether there was justification for a reduction in hours and/or an increase in basic wages to commence from the first full pay week in September 1961. These 1961 negotiations resulted in an agreement for wage increases, a 41-hour week in 1961 and a 40-hour week by September 1962.

In January 1962 the Federation arranged a meeting of unions to ascertain whether there was a general desire to renegotiate on a collective basis the wages agreements due to terminate on 6 August 1962. Eight unions (including the NUPB&PW and NATSOPA) favoured a collective approach to the BFMP and the Newspaper Society. As in 1959, the collective claim was not a Federation movement but a group of unions acting collectively. However, the 1962 claim included a demand for three weeks' paid holiday and a change to the Apprentices' wage agreements. These were Federation agreements and could claim a Federation movement. On wages, the Federation acted as a liaison and its General Secretary was closely associated with the negotiations. The 1965 wages agreements were stabilised until 31 March 1965.

In December 1964 nine unions, including the NUPB&PW, formulated a collective claim for new wages agreements with the BFMP and the Newspaper Society. The claim was confined to wages so, as in 1959 and 1962, the collective wages movement was the unions acting together and not a Federation movement. However, as in the past, the P&KTF acted as liaison and its General Secretary was closely associated with the negotiations. The 1965 agreements became operative in May and terminated on 31 December 1966.

In July 1966, six unions, including SOGAT, readily agreed to take a collective approach to the employers, but negotiations with the employers were not opened until December 1966 because of delays in reaching agreement amongst the six unions about the nature and scope of their claim and the difficulty of obtaining agreement to drop 'domestic' claims so as to concentrating on an increase in the basic rate. A settlement was not reached with the BFMP and the NS until October 1967 and only then after the imposition of an overtime ban in provincial daily newspaper offices. The agreements were stabilised to 30 October 1969. The NGA refused to be involved in a collective wages movement to replace these agreements, arguing that delays in reaching a wage settlement in 1966/7 had not been due to employers but to the unions, first by disagreeing over what the claims should be, and second by their lack of unity during the negotiations. In the light of this SOGAT decided to pursue its own wage claim.

Hours of Work

The 1937 hours and holiday agreement between the P&KTF and the BFMP and the NS established a 45-hour working week, continued the one week's paid annual holiday (granted in 1919) and provided three years' stabilisation. In 1940, as the country was at war, the Federation postponed re-opening negotiations on hours of work. However, in March 1946 the P&KTF submitted a claim to the BFMP and the NS, for a 40-hour working week and a fortnight's paid annual holiday. The employers rejected the claim but following a Court of Inquiry, a settle-ment was reached which provided for a 43½-hour working week and two weeks' paid annual holiday. Both parties, however, accepted the principle of the 42½-hour week and agreed to work towards it when the industry's labour shortage had been overcome.[5]

The NUPB&PW supported the NATSOPA motion to the 1958 Administrative Council that 'this Society urges the P&KTF to press on with collective representation for the establishment of a 40 hour week in the general printing trade.'[6] NATSOPA argued that print employees wanted a 40-hour week, that greater leisure time was part of the advancement of society, that productivity per head in the British printing industry had increased by 25 per cent and that the industry's labour shortages had been overcome. The three-year wage agreements with the BFMP and the NS signed in 1956 were to terminate in April 1959 and the unions now wanted the 40-hour working week included in the 'shop-ping list'. On 1 December 1958 the nine unions submitted their claims that the hours and holiday Agreement (1946) be amended to provide a working week of 40 hours. The employers rejected the claim and in June 1959 the nine unions' members ceased work and did not resume it until 6 August 1959. The return to work formula included reducing the standard working week for day workers to 42 hours. The 1959 Hours and Holiday Agreement was to operate for three years but in 1961 consideration could be given to whether a further reduction of hours and/or an increase in basic wages should operate from September 1961, and if a settlement could not be made by 30 June 1961, the matter would be decided by a judicial inquiry.

In December 1960 the nine unions presented to the employers the balance of their 1959 claims to be granted in 1961. The employers said that, provided the industry could get the labour it needed, they would concede, by stages, a 40-hour working week. The unions told the employers that if they granted the claims on hours without delay then they would talk about the labour supply situation. On 30 June 1961 an Hours, Wages and Labour Supply Agreement was signed between the BFMP and the Newspaper Society on the one hand and the ten printing unions on the other under which the standard working week was reduced as from September 1961 to 41 hours and from September 1962 to 40 hours. The printing unions thus became the first group of manual workers in Britain to achieve the 40-hour working week on an industry-wide basis. The P&KTF President told the 1962 Administrative Council Annual Conference:

> But it is, manifestly, the 40-hour week that makes the greatest impact on the imagination. For this has been the aim not only of the printing unions but the whole British trade union movement for more than one cares to remember. As in so many other fields of industrial endeavour, the honour of effecting the final breakthrough to this desirable objective has fallen to the printing unions. But, as we now recall this achievement, we shall remember that it – and the wage increase to which I referred – flowed directly from a six week stoppage of the industry and the longest set of continuous negotiations in the history of industrial relations in this country.[7]

Holidays

The Hours and Holiday Agreement (1946) provided for two weeks' annual holiday with pay. In 1957 the Federation adopted an Executive Committee report that when circumstances were opportune an approach be made to the BFMP and the Newspaper Society with the first priority being a shorter working week and the second a third week's annual holiday. Following the achievement of the 40-hour working week, the 1962 Administrative Council Annual Conference carried a Monotype Casters and Typefounders' Society motion:

this conference considers that in view of the fact that a large number of printing offices engaged in the production of newspapers, periodicals and general printing are now operating a third weeks' holiday pay for the benefit of their employees, application should be made for the third weeks' holiday with pay for all printing trade workers before the termination of the present agreements with the British Federation of Master Printers and the Newspaper Society in August next.[8]

Three weeks' annual holiday, included in the unions' claim for the 1962 wages negotiations had been rejected by the BFMP and the Newspaper Society. However, it was part of the 1962 Wages Stabilisation Agreement that if at some time during the life of the Agreement the unions considered the circumstances warranted it, the employers would make an objective assessment of the position and consider whether there was justification for an additional week, or some lesser period, of holiday. In October 1963 the Federation considered the time was opportune for an application for the third week's paid holiday. In March 1964 the employers replied there was no justification for a further week's holiday but that they would consider some improvement in holidays if ways could be found of maintaining production and avoiding increased costs. The Federation rejected the view that improvements in holiday pay must be self-funding. Months of bargaining took place in which the employers maintained that if longer holidays were granted 'extra labour' would be required at once. The Federation contended that manpower issues should be dealt with separately by a joint committee representing both sides of the industry. Eventually, the Federation negotiators obtained an agreement, ratified in January 1965, for the introduction of a third week's annual holiday in return for the unions accepting the setting up of a Joint Committee on Manpower. Both sides accepted that the issue of an adequate labour force in a changing industry was too serious a matter to be the subject of 'horse trading' across the table during negotiations for improved wages and conditions. The Joint Manpower Committee would make a careful study of the present and future manpower needs of the industry.

However, by 1966 the Committee was not functioning as intended. It had concentrated on short-term manpower problems raised by the employers and had given no consideration to long-term requirements. However, the Ministry of Labour agreed to undertake an analysis of the industry's long-term manpower needs in the light of economic and technological changes. Not all unions accepted their obligations under the Committee's terms of reference, whilst the employers attempted to widen its terms of reference to include matters the unions thought more appropriate for collective bargaining. When Mr O'Brien, the Independent Chairman, and the employers insisted the Cameron Court of Inquiry (see Chapter 4) be considered by the Committee, the NGA objected and withdrew from the Committee to be followed quickly by SOGAT, SLADE and ASLP. In 1967, the Joint Manpower Committee ceased to function.

In 1971 the Federation opened negotiations with the BFMP and the Newspaper Society to amend the Hours and Holiday Agreement to provide for a fourth week's annual holiday to be taken during the summer period. The P&KTF argued that if the claim were granted it would bring the British printing industry into line with the industry in other countries, would bring provincial newspapers into line with national newspapers and provide more leisure time which was felt necessary given the pace of modern industry. Although initially the BFMP and the Newspaper Society rejected the claim, agreement was reached in 1972 for the staged introduction of a fourth week of annual holiday from 1974. Print manual workers were again the leaders in obtaining four weeks' paid holiday on an industry-wide basis.

The Federation campaigned not only for an increase in paid holidays, but also for holiday pay to be based on average earnings rather than basic rates. The Federation had adopted this policy in 1951 but the employers had rejected demands in 1952 and 1953 for holiday pay based on average earnings. The Federation in 1958 reconfirmed its policy but delayed a renewed approach to the employers pending the 1959 wage negotiations in which the top priority was the 40-hour week and a 10 per cent wage increase. Following the 1971 Federation Administrative Council Annual Conference the employers were again approached with a claim for average earnings holiday pay. The unions argued that it denied the principle of 'holidays with pay' to give workers who went on holiday less money than they would receive during the same period had they been at work. Workers needed more, not less, money when they went on holiday. The Federation argued that the employers had already conceded the principle of average earnings by making provision for payment during holidays of average work measurement bonuses. In rejecting the claim, the BFMP and the Newspaper Society stated that to concede to it would increase the annual wage bill by 2 per cent. By the time of its dissolution the

Federation had still not achieved holiday pay on the basis of average earnings.

Sick Pay, Pension Scheme and Redundancy

The NUPB&PW supported an unsuccessful TA resolution to the 1954 Federation Administrative Council proposing an investigation into the practicability of an industry-wide sick pay scheme. Four years later, a similar STA motion, backed by the NUPB&PW, was submitted to the Federation Executive which conducted an inquiry into the extent and nature of sick pay schemes then operating in the industry. On the basis of the results the Federation decided that a sick pay scheme be deferred until a more appropriate time. Although the issue of an industry-wide sick pay scheme was raised on subsequent occasions when the Federation was considering its negotiating priorities, it was never included in claims to the BFMP and the Newspaper Society.

Efforts by the P&KTF to persuade the BFMP to adopt an industrial pension scheme failed completely. The first post-Second World War approach to the employers for such a scheme had been in 1953. The 1964 NUPB&PW Delegate Council voted for a transferable pension scheme to be set up within the industry with all existing pension schemes that where not transferable to be altered in order to comply. The differences between the unions and the employers were clear. The Federation wanted a scheme in which there would be a uniform subscription and benefit and which accepted the principle of transfer of pension rights for workers changing their jobs. The BFMP, however, consistently argued that a pension should be a reward for service to the firm. The BFMP was prepared, however, to co-operate with the unions to persuade member firms to introduce house schemes.

This remained the situation until August 1965 when the National Board for Prices and Incomes in their report on the industry's wages settlement recommended for consideration as a means of overcoming the fear of redundancy the introduction of an industrial pension scheme. This was welcomed by the Federation and the employers agreed to discuss the subject. However, before approaching the employers, the Federation conducted a survey of pension schemes already in operation. The survey showed 73 per cent of men and 42 per cent of women in the industry were covered by 'house' pension schemes. This compared with a figure of 60 per cent provided by the

BFMP in February 1967.[9] The Federation concluded that the unions must make up their minds just where an industrial pension scheme stood in their list of negotiating priorities. To bring the matter to a head the Federation recommended that when the current wage negotiations with the BFMP and the Newspaper Society were concluded, the unions should agree that in the next round of negotiations the main priority should be an industrial pension scheme rather than a further increase in wages. This recommendation did not find favour with affiliated unions. Inconclusive talks took place with the Newspaper Society as to the possibility of extending the limited operation of the Newspaper and Printing Industries' Pension Fund Scheme (NPIPFS) which allowed a worker to transfer from one employer to another within the scheme, taking their pension rights with them.

Given that many workers in the general printing and provincial newspaper trade were already covered by 'house' pension schemes, it was unlikely that even a national campaign would secure the overwhelming support of union members for an industrial pension scheme. Members already in 'house' pension schemes would not support by industrial action efforts to obtain pensions for workers not already covered. The Federation concluded that affiliated unions should be asked directly whether they were prepared to agree to a collective approach to the BFMP and the Newspaper Society on behalf of members not covered by pension schemes, and if so, whether they supported seeking to persuade employers to introduce 'the NPIPFS Scheme' into offices where there were presently no pension schemes. SOGAT was not attracted by the idea but NGA and SLADE were. However, in 1970 the Federation decided that an approach to the BFMP and the Newspaper Society for an industry-wide pension scheme should be deferred indefinitely.

The 1958 P&KTF Conference considered a report on problems in the newspaper industry. It identified the need for a common approach between affiliated unions on a policy for compensation for redundancy when newspapers closed. Approaches were made to the NPA, the Newspaper Proprietors' Association, the Newspaper Society and the Scottish Daily Newspaper Society for agreements to provide for compensation for redundancy on the basis of one month's salary for each year of service. As a first step, the Federation decided, claims should be made to newspaper employers and the BFMP should only be approached when precedents had been established elsewhere. A claim was made to the NPA in 1958 for compensation on the basis of one month's wages for each year of service. This was rejected. The NPA argued that as a 'non-trading' organisation it could not provide a redundancy fund, but said a clause might be added to the existing National Agreement to cover redundancy compensation payments. Eventually the employers offered to provide for minimum compensation of one week's wages for each year of service to be increased in accordance with the individual circumstances of closures. However, negotiations were suspended when the NPA issued, in 1963, their Memorandum *Efficiency and Production*, which dealt with, *inter alia*, compensation for redundancy.

In 1959 the Scottish Daily Newspaper Society announced that it considered a collective agreement covering redundancy compensation on behalf of its member firms to be impracticable. The Newspaper Society told the Federation that although the time was inappropriate for a redundancy compensation agreement, they were prepared to discuss the issue. However, in 1960 it notified the Federation of its rejection of the claim for a redundancy compensation agreement. In 1963 the Federation adopted the compensation levels for redundancy shown in Table 12.1.

This scale had been devised in the light of experience in attempting to base compensation on one month's pay for each year of service. One problem had been the widely varying circumstances in which firms had had to close down. The Federation and the unions, in pressing compensation claims, had been forced to consider the financial resources available in each particular case. Varying amounts of compensation had been secured but the Federation policy remained one not of accepting compensation of less than one week's wages for each year of service. If this could not be achieved, individual chapels decided whether or not to accept lesser amounts.

Table 12.1
Proposed level of redundancy compensation

Years of service	Compensation
Less than 5 years	1½ weeks' wages for each year of service
5 years to less than 15 years	2 weeks' wages for each year of service
15 years and over	3 weeks' wages for each year of service

Source: *Annual Report*, 1962/3, Printing and Kindred Trades' Federation.

The Redundancy Payments Act (1965) notwithstanding, Federation policy remained as agreed in 1963. Each affiliated union, when faced with redundancy, tried to secure compensation terms not less favourable than Federation policy. In 1967 the BFMP and the Newspaper Society were again approached for a compensation for redundancy agreement but the employers maintained that the Federation's proposals did not form a suitable basis for an agreement or understanding covering the whole industry and it was impractical to make a national agreement on redundancy compensation. Although the Federation was unable to achieve such an agreement, it continued its policy of reaching agreements on compensation for redundancy with individual companies and groups of companies. In 1968 it produced a model compensation for redundancy scheme which was accepted by all its affiliated unions. Its main objective was to provide redundancy pay based on two weeks' wages for each year of service between the ages of 18 and 65. It sought to protect employment as far as possible but, if redundancy became unavoidable, to supplement the minimum provisions of the Redundancy Payments Act (1965). In practice, in the majority of instances where NUPB&PW members were unfortunate enough to find themselves redundant either through closure or part closure, the employers paid the Federation scale of redundancy compensation even though in some cases the union had no agreement with them.

Dissolution of the Federation

By the late 1960s, in the light of union mergers and with the prospect of future marriages, the future of the P&KTF was being questioned. At the 1969 Administrative Council Annual Meeting, SOGAT proposed the P&KTF be wound up, its assets be distributed amongst affiliated unions, affiliates each appoint a national officer for liaison purposes and meetings be arranged from time to time when matters of mutual concern occasioned them. Local Federations were to be replaced by unions encouraging their local officials to meet under the auspices of liaising officers. SOGAT's case was simple. The industry was down to two major unions – itself and NGA – and the time was ripe to wind up the Federation as its days were numbered. Bob Willis of the NGA, speaking on behalf of the Federation Executive, opposed the motion arguing that SOGAT's case was based on the desirability of one union and the need for amalgamation, but that no case had been made for dissolution. He advised that the P&KTF be left as it was for as long as there were affiliated unions. When put to the vote the SOGAT motion was defeated by 37 votes to 26. The NUJ, STA, NGA, SLADE, NUWDAT, and the Sign and Display Union voted against.

Following discussion at the 1970 Annual Conference, the Federation Executive consulted affiliates as to its future. They were asked if the services provided by the Federation should continue with an unaltered constitution or if, in the light of developments in printing trade union structure, the constitution should be amended. Affiliates were also asked, should neither of these courses be acceptable, if they wished consideration to be given to the dissolution of the Federation and to the setting up of a TUC Industry Committee. SOGAT and NATSOPA favoured dissolution. The other affiliated unions expressed a desire for the Federation to continue.

However, SOGAT proposed to the 1972 Annual Conference 'that steps be taken to wind up the Printing and Kindred Trades' Federation at the earliest suitable date and under suitable conditions, having regard to the rights and claims of employees of the Federation.' The motion was seconded by NATSOPA but after a lengthy debate was defeated by 40 votes to 34. The President (John Bonfield) said the Federation Executive would take on board the point emphasised in the debate that the constitution needed streamlining in the light of modern conditions. He hoped the unions whose views about winding up the Federation had not been sustained would nevertheless support the Federation both in the work of streamlining its constitution and the industrial problems they faced. However, later in 1972 SOGAT, in the light of its 1972 Delegate Council decision that the P&KTF had outlived its usefulness and should be wound up, ceased to attend meetings of the P&KTF Executive Committee. This decision also followed a disagreement regarding organisation rights, the alleged role of the Federation in NATSOPA's legal action against SOGAT (see Chapter 5) and the fact that two of the affiliates, the NGA in particular, were registered under the Industrial Relations Act (1971) (see Chapter 13). Remaining on the Register was contrary to TUC policy and, as a loyal affiliate of the TUC, SOGAT found it intolerable that P&KTF unions remained registered. However, in carrying out its policy of non-attendance, SOGAT did not cut itself off from contacts with other unions in the industry. It continued to hold direct discussions with individual unions on problems of mutual concern.

Following its 1972 Annual Conference the Federation set up a sub-committee to examine how its constitution might be modified. The sub-committee recommended the Federation become a purely co-ordinating body, a function that even the fiercest critics of the Federation had admitted was still necessary. It proposed a Printing Trade Union Co-ordinating Bureau which would co-ordinate union activities whenever the unions felt this was desirable. The Bureau would cater for all foreseeable contingencies. If one union for the industry were established then the Bureau could be disbanded at any time. On the other hand, if it were felt in the future that something on the lines of the Federation was required, the nucleus of machinery, staff and premises would be available. The Bureau would operate from 1 October 1973.

The constitution for the Bureau was unanimously approved at the 1973 Annual Conference. It was then put for endorsement by each of the affiliated unions. Six of the seven unions signified their acceptance but NATSOPA declined unless arrangements were agreed, prior to the establishment of the Bureau, as to how the Federation funds would be distributed among the affiliated unions. The Executive Committee told NATSOPA that the Bureau was not a device for winding up the Federation but a genuine attempt to provide machinery for co-ordination of union activities, and only in the event of the Bureau failing to fulfil this function would the question of its dissolution and the distribution of funds arise. On 4 July 1973 NATSOPA gave six months' notice to disaffiliate from the Federation or the Bureau 'as the case may be'.

In the circumstances the Federation saw no alternative but to defer the setting up of the Bureau until 1 February 1974 by which date NATSOPA would have left the Federation. By then, the Bureau which was accepted by the remaining affiliated unions could become operative. During 1973 efforts were made by the Federation to persuade SOGAT to accept membership of the Bureau. In September 1973 the P&KTF President wrote formally to the President of SOGAT inviting his union to re-affiliate. However, the SOGAT NEC rejected this invitation concluding that no useful purpose would be served by becoming a member.[10] The Bureau would do little to achieve unity amongst print unions. Under its banner they would still defend their sectional interests instead of building a common front. Inter-union disputes would continue with the only winner being the employer. SOGAT wrote to all unions suggesting a meeting to explore ways of providing a vehicle that could express a unity of action and lead to a single print union.

Danny Sergeant, General President (1985–91)

Bill Keys, General President (1970–4), General Secretary (1974–85)

Owen O'Brien, Joint General Secretary (1982–3)

Brenda Dean, General President (1983–5), General Secretary (1985–91)

In October 1973 the P&KTF Executive recognised that in the absence of SOGAT and NATSOPA the proposed Printing Trade Unions Co-ordinating Bureau could not be effective. At their November meeting the Executive decided to call a Special Conference of the Administrative Council to which a resolution dissolving the Federation and abandoning the Bureau would be submitted. The Special Conference, held on 17 December 1973, agreed to dissolve the Federation, to refund all affiliation fees paid since 26 April 1972, to distribute the remaining assets of the Federation among the affiliated unions and to abandon the Bureau.[11] SOGAT received 40 per cent of the Federation's assets.

THE INTERNATIONAL GRAPHICAL FEDERATION (IGF)

In 1889 the first international graphical trade union was formed when typographers meeting in Paris decided to join together internationally. Seven years later the Lithographers' International was born and in 1907 the bookbinders followed by setting up their own international union in Nuremberg. In 1939, these three separate international organisations came together with the intention of creating an all-embracing International. It was not until 1946, however, that, at the invitation of the P&KTF a co-ordinating committee to draft a constitution for the new body was established. The inaugural conference for the International Graphical Federation (IGF) met in Stockholm in May 1949. The IGF was to protect and further the occupational, economic and industrial interests of printing workers. It was a non-political body intended to co-ordinate activities on technical matters, for example union responses to technological change in the various sectors of the industry. It provided information on terms and conditions of employment in the printing industry in the countries of member unions and on health, safety and welfare matters. It would also inform affiliated unions of disputes member unions had with employers.

The IGF did good work in bringing together print workers of many nationalities to exchange their views. In many practical ways the IGF, for example by offering financial assistance in disputes, assisted unions in various parts of the world. The IGF's policy was decided by Congress which met every three years and to which the Paperworkers and subsequently SOGAT until it disaffiliated in 1976 always sent a delegation. The IGF Executive Committee was made up of 15 people, the President, Vice President, General Secretary, three representatives from each of the three Trades Boards plus three further members appointed by the Trade Groups of the country in which the IGF had its headquarters. There were three Trade Group Boards covering typography, lithography and bookbinding which discussed matters specific to those trades. The decisions of the Boards were presented for approval to the Congress. Between meetings of the Executive Committee matters were run by the Bureau which comprised of four representatives of the country in which the IGF headquarters was located plus the General Secretary and President.

Over the period 1955 to 1968, considerable discussion and strong feeling was engendered amongst IGF affiliates over the affiliation of unions who

> it was suggested would give their loyalty to the Communist dominated World Federation of Trade Unions rather than the IGF.[12]

The attitude of the NUPB&PW, and subsequently SOGAT, was that if at all possible the introduction of political and ideological discussions into the IGF should be avoided and the International concentrate on the industrial interests. To do otherwise would open the door to the IGF spending most of its time and energy arguing about issues better dealt with in the political sphere. However, the NUPB&PW, and SOGAT, took the view that whilst it might be contrary to the IGF constitution to allow Soviet trade unions to affiliate, this would not prevent them continuing to make contact with the trade unions of any country in the world if it was in the interests of their members to do so. The 1964 Congress of the IGF confirmed the policy decision made at its inaugural Congress to uphold the free trade union movement and the principles of freedom and democracy. It pledged itself to strengthen the International Confederation of Free Trade Unions whilst retaining the autonomy of the IGF. It instructed affiliates to continue to co-operate with other international trade union secretariats. On the basis of these principles, the IGF was content for its affiliates to work in continuous contact with unions not as yet affiliated to the IGF in order to propagate of the ideas of free and democratic trade unions with the objective of persuading them to join the IGF.

The attitude of affiliated unions to Communist-based unions was polarised by the request in 1964 for re-affiliation from the French bookbinding union, FFTL. The union was affiliated to the World Federation of Trade Unions via its affiliation to the French Communist-based trade union centre, the CGF. Its membership was 80,000. However, the union denied strongly that its members had communistic leanings. The attitude of the NUPB&PW, and subsequently SOGAT, was that FFTL should be admitted to the IGF. However, on the advice of the IGF Executive Committee the 1964 Congress deferred a decision on admitting the FFTL whilst the union's political position was clarified. In February 1965 the Executive approved the affiliation of the FFTL by a small majority. Under the IGF constitution decisions were only valid if at least three members of each Trade Board Group voted in favour. This had not happened with this decision but the Executive decided the condition of Trade Group approval need not be observed in this case of the FFTL affiliation. However, the majority of affiliated unions took a different view, arguing that the constitution must be observed. As a result, in November 1965 the Executive put into abeyance its decision to admit the FFTL until the 1967 Congress when the February 1965 decision could be put to vote. The 1967 Congress voted to admit the FFTL, a decision fully supported by SOGAT.

The IGF provided support ranging from statements to financial assistance for affiliates involved in major disputes with employers. In April 1959 the P&KTF asked the IGF to send circulars to its affiliated unions asking them not to handle work which was placed in their countries as a result of a dispute situation in the UK general printing industry. The IGF passed to continental unions information to stop the transfer of British printing orders and in most cases this happened. In some countries print unions had to make real sacrifices in doing this. In Germany and Denmark print unions were sued and ordered to pay compensation to print employers in their countries for refusing to print work that had been diverted from Britain. The support of the IGF unions to UK print unions in the six-week dispute with the BFMP and the Newspaper Society in the summer of 1959 was seen by the NUPB&PW as a practical demonstration of the real value of international trade unionism.

NUPB&PW and SOGAT officials occupied important positions in the IGF. In 1955 Mr Killingback, a member of the NUPB&PW National Executive Committee was elected Chairman of the Bookbinding Trade Group whilst in 1961 John McKenzie was elected to the Bookbinding Trade Group Board. Bill Morrison, General Secretary of NUPB&PW was a member of the Executive Committee. His successor as General Secretary, Tom Smith, also served the IGF in this capacity. Arising from the 1963 IGF Congress the NUPB&PW

nominated Mr Torode, General Secretary of the Sign and Display Union, for the vacant post of IGF General Secretary but the nomination was later withdrawn.

By the early 1970s SOGAT was concerned the IGF was not serving the interests of the international working class and was not a particularly dynamic organisation.[13] It considered the activities of the Trade Group Boards to be non-existent, arguing that full boards meet at Congress and without exception all the business was disposed of within two or three hours. In the Congress itself, at its main session, for which was allowed 1½ days, very little was done outside of receiving the Trade Board's reports and electing the officers. There was rarely discussion of matters affecting print workers throughout the world, such as for example the behaviour of multinational companies. In between Congresses little happened. In fact, it had become a joke at SOGAT Head Office that the union only received two letters a year from the IGF, one asking for its contributions which were £25,000 per annum and one thanking the union for the receipt of its contributions. Following the 1973 IGF Congress SOGAT attempted to change the IGF constitution. Its views were shared by other British affiliates – the NGA, SLADE and NUWDAT.

The four British unions submitted to the 1976 IGF Congress proposals for a fundamental change to its rules. The IGF Executive also submitted proposals with which the British unions parted company in a number of important ways. Whereas the Executive wished to retain the Trade Board principle the British unions wished to abolish them, but allowing for them to meet if matters of importance to a specific section of the IGF needed to be considered. The British unions also proposed the IGF move its headquarters from Berne to Brussels because of the increasing importance of the work of the European Trade Union Confederation which had been established in 1973 to lobby the European Community decision-making bodies. When put to the vote, after a heated debate the British proposals were declared lost, although the voting was 57 for, 57 against. The Chairman cast his vote against the UK changes.

The British unions, which contributed 34 per cent of the IGF revenue, thereupon decided to withdraw from the Congress but before leaving they made it clear that they subscribed to the need to strengthen and support the activities of the IGF through a reform of its rules. The British unions had been prepared to accept an American proposal that a Commission be established to review the IGF constitution. This had not been acceptable to Congress. The inability of the four British print unions to convince the IGF Congress to reform itself so that urgent problems facing print unions such as new technology, multinational companies, unemployment and social and economic developments could be dealt with effectively, led each of them to recommend to their National Executive Committee withdrawal from the IGF. The Scandinavian unions proposed discussions between the IGF and the British unions to effect a reconciliation. The NGA, SLADE and NUWDAT entered these discussions and agreed that efforts be made through the constitution of the IGF to achieve compromise proposals which would meet with approval at the 1979 Congress. In the meantime, German and French unions indicated that if a compromise solution proved impossible then they would support at the 1979 Congress the British proposals submitted to the 1976 Congress. In the light of this the NGA, SLADE and NUWDAT decided to remain IGF affiliates.

Although SOGAT attended the initial meetings with the Scandinavian unions, they decided in 1977 to withdraw from the IGF believing they could no longer justify paying £25,000 per annum to an organisation whilst seeing nothing in return for it. The decision was not taken lightly as SOGAT had worked hard over many decades to establish international brotherhood. However, it remained convinced that the IGF as presently constituted did not serve the interests of working people. The General Secretary, Bill Keys, described the IGF in the *SOGAT Journal* as 'at best an expensive club, which permits a jaunt overseas every three years'.[14] The saving on the IGF affiliation fees was used to expand the union's international contacts at much less cost and to greater effect. In 1990 as the British trade unions embraced the European Community, SOGAT applied to re-affiliate to the IGF but no decision had been made on its application by the time SOGAT merged with the NGA.

THE INTERNATIONAL CHEMICAL, ENERGY AND GENERAL WORKERS' UNION (ICEF)

The NUPB&PW and subsequently SOGAT affiliated to the International Industrial Organisations and General Workers' Union which had a pulp and paper section. The International subsequently changed its title to the International Federation of Chemical and General Workers (ICF) and in 1976 to the International Federation of Chemical, Energy and General Workers (ICEF), which represented 6 million

365

employees in 58 different countries. 1988 saw the International moving its headquarters to Brussels.

The NUPB&PW found affiliation to the International particularly valuable in the late 1950s and early 1960s because of the problems the UK papermaking and paper board industry faced and would face consequent upon the creation of the European Common Market in 1957 and the European Free Trade Area in 1958. The basic problem for the British papermaking and board-making industry was that its raw materials were imported from abroad whilst countries from which the industry imported its raw materials had firms that manufactured their own pulp and also had their own papermills. The NUPB&PW feared competitor firms from overseas might be tempted to supply their own country's manufacturers at a lower price than they would UK papermills. International trade union co-operation was necessary to deal with the problem. As a result, the International spent many hours attempting with national governments, Common Market and EFTA institutions to find a solution to this problem, but without much success

However, in 1970, following a disagreement between SOGAT (Division A) and the International the former ceased to play a full part in its affairs. In 1974 SOGAT decided to become active again, believing that in a world increasingly dominated by multinational companies it was only by co-operation between trade unions on an international basis that the power of such companies could be redressed. SOGAT participated in November 1975 in a three-day conference held in London to consider the common problems besetting workers in all countries employed in paper- and board-making. These included multinational companies, industrial democracy, trade union representation, health and safety and collective bargaining objectives.[15] This meeting of the Pulp and Paper Division of the ICF formed a permanent World Council for the Bowater company to implement agreed programmes, exchange information and statistics, make appeals for solidarity of action and to organise bargaining campaigns and organisation campaigns within Bowaters. The meeting also agreed a common objective of all affiliates achieving official recognition by the company as both discussion partner and bargaining agent on international problems, especially investment and employment programmes. The Bowater Council gave top priority to practical international programmes to help organise the unorganised of the company and to secure recognition for local unions as bargaining agents. The major collective bargaining objective for the Bowater World Council was the harmonisation of the best conditions of employment prevailing in the company.

However, despite SOGAT's high profile in the ICF, the 1978 Delegate Council Meeting was faced with a South East Essex Branch motion that the union withdraw from the ICF. The International was seen as being too conservative and discouraging of affiliates with radical positions, as having an attitude of 'I'm all right Jack' with no concern outside their own boundaries. It was accused of not being a genuine international body and of having senior officers that were reactionary. Opposing the motion, the General Secretary, Bill Keys, argued that the threats to the paper- and board-making industry were international and the union needed to work through an international body like the ICF. He stressed that SOGAT would remain an affiliate only as long as it was of value to its members to do so. The South East Essex Branch remitted its motion to the National Executive Committee. SOGAT continued to play an active part in its activities but at the 1980 Delegate Council, the South East Essex Branch asked why more information on the ICEF had not been provided, since a condition of its motion being remitted was that 'an in-depth report had been promised'. Membership of ICEF was maintained because it was the only body through which SOGAT could work in the international field, it was taking a lead internationally, had established three committees on technology, investment and multinational companies that were important to SOGAT and it made representations to the EEC on tariffs and quotas which were relevant to the industrial interests of SOGAT members. Delegates were told, 'It has worked for us and as long as it continues to work for us we shall use it. The day it ceases to, we will pull out.'[16]

During the November 1979 meeting of the ICEF Pulp and Paper Division Steering Committee, SOGAT successfully proposed that if the ICEF were to be effective then a planned approach to future strategy for its activities in paper and board was needed. All participating unions were agreed that the structural and economic changes sweeping the industry required as an urgent priority international liaison. To this end, three sub-groups were set up in automation and technological unemployment, trade and international investment restructuring and multinational company bargaining. These groups, consisting of technical experts from affiliated unions, had a mandate to press ahead with defining present trends, future developments and particular strategies in their areas. The groups were to report to a Steering Committee which would take strategic decisions on an international basis to safeguard the future employment of the members of affiliated unions. The sub-groups identified high interest rates, high inflation, environmental protection legislation and scarcity of raw materials as major factors contributing to the increased cost of future investment programmes in new papermills. Successive advances in technology had been directed at increasing the size and speed of mills along with productivity improvements from the introduction of automation around the machines. The implications of these changes for workers in the paper and pulp industry was heavy job losses as older plants closed in favour of new automated plants. The future trend would be towards automation and away from the traditional skills of the machine operators who would be replaced by workers with the skills required to feed in and interpret computer data.

In the 1970s SOGAT campaigned to reverse the decline in the UK paper and board industry. Its campaigns highlighted the industry's problems but the growth and importation of paper and paper products from overseas countries could not be ignored. As a result SOGAT adopted a higher profile within the ICEF European Co-ordinating Committee for Paper and Board to increase its knowledge and understanding of what was happening within the EEC and Scandinavian countries. It was particularly concerned to influence policy and initiate multinational discussions with the objective of ensuring the survival of the UK papermaking industry and the livelihoods of its members working in that industry.

In 1988 the European Co-ordinating Committee was restructured by the setting up of a new committee called the European Federation of Chemical and General Workers (EFCGU) with four sectional subcommittees – chemical, oil and pharmaceutical, rubber and plastics, glass, ceramics and cement and paper and pulp. These sub-committees were made responsible for examining specific problems existing in their sectors at Community level and for the presentation of proposals to the Executive Committee. Membership of the EFCGU was open to national unions affiliated to a national trade union confederation affiliated in turn to the ETUC. The objectives of the Federation, an affiliate member of the ETUC, included promoting the interests of all employees, overcoming social, economic and environmental problems within the EEC and promoting co-operation between member unions. In addition, it sought consultation and negotiation with the EU and

employers and promoted education, health and safety and equal opportunities. In addition to EU country unions, the Federation also included
the Scandinavian papermaking unions. The EFCGU held its first
meeting in May 1988 at which it was agreed to exchange information,
to promote co-operation between affiliated unions, to enhance the
protection of employees and to promote the consultation and education in the framework of the EU institutions and the promotion of
equal opportunities.

SOGAT officials held prominent positions in the ICEF. In 1987 for
example, Brenda Dean, General Secretary of SOGAT was elected to
the Executive Committee to represent the women members of the
ICEF and was appointed Chair of the International Women's
Committee. In 1989 George Beattie, the Papermaking Secretary of
SOGAT became President of the European Paper Sector Committee
of the European Federation of Chemical and General Workers
which included 43 affiliates from 17 countries. Although the position
was part-time, it gave SOGAT a strong voice amongst the European
unions and an influence on international developments in the paper-
board industry. George Beattie also served on the Management
Committee and Executive of the EFCGU. This had also been the case
with Mr White and Mr O'Leary, previous Papermaking Secretaries of
the union.

THE INTERNATIONAL FEDERATION OF COMMERCIAL, CLERICAL, PROFESSIONAL AND TECHNICAL EMPLOYEES (FIET)

FIET, the world organisation for white-collar trade unions groups
together 8m employees in banks, insurance, commerce and industry
and is one of the largest international trade union secretariats. SOGAT
joined FIET in 1988 on behalf of its membership employed in technical, administrative and executive jobs. It played an active part in this
International and was represented at many conferences and working
groups organised by FIET covering such issues as the impact of technical change upon clerical workers, performance-related pay and its
challenge to trade unions, the recruitment of senior staff into recognised trade unions rather than separate management groups, equal pay
for work of equal value, equal social security for men and women and
'model' arrangements for employees asked to work abroad.

OTHER INTERNATIONAL ACTIVITIES

By the time SOGAT ceased to be an independent trade union it had long recognised that with the advent of the Single European Market and the rapidly changing situation in Central and Eastern Europe international trade union solidarity and co-operation was more important than ever as an integral part of trade union activity. Awareness alone was not enough, and SOGAT realised the need to develop its international dialogue if it were to represent effectively its members. SOGAT saw its commitment to international trade union solidarity involving more than just active participation in international trade union secretariats. As a result, it had a tradition of visiting countries as the guests of sister unions. It maintained fraternal links with unions around the world, always sent messages of support to other unions in their time of need and often advertised in publications in the UK to highlight the plight of union brothers and sisters in Southern Africa. It made frequent donations to international organisations such as the El Salvador Solidarity Campaign and affiliated to many international bodies such as War on Want, Amnesty International, Chile Solidarity, the Anti–Apartheid Movement and One World. Its affiliation to the UK-based Trade Union Friends of Palestine went back to a Delegate Council decision of many years perviously.

NOTES

1. In places where two or more branches of affiliated unions existed such unions were obliged to instruct their branches to form a local federation. All unions affiliated to the P&KTF were responsible for their branches becoming members of local federations.
2. See Printing and Kindred Trades' Federation *Annual Report 1955,* and *Report of the Administrative Council,* May 1956, pp. 36–41.
3. Printing and Kindred Trades' Federation *Report of the Administrative Council, May 1956,* p. 37.
4. NATSOPA re-affiliated in 1960. See also J. Moran *NATSOPA: 75 Years,* Heinemann, London, 1964, p. 118.
5. For a discussion of this dispute see J. Child *Industrial Relations in the British Printing Industry,* Allen & Unwin, Part V, Chapter 18, pp. 299–303.
6. Printing and Kindred Trades Federation *Annual Report, 1957/8,* pp. 32–6.
7. Op. cit., p. 14.
8. Op. cit. pp. 71–4.
9. Printing and Kindred Trades Federation *Annual Report, 1971/2,* p. 53.
10. See *SOGAT Journal,* December 1973, p. 1.
11. See Printing and Kindred Trades Federation *Final Report, 1973/4.*

12. See National Union of Printing, Bookbinding and Paperworkers *Annual Report of the National Executive Committee, 1955*, p. 7.
13. For a more detailed discussion of the reasons for this see 'Why the British Unions Pulled Out of the IGF' *SOGAT Journal*, December 1976, pp. 8–9.
14. Op. cit.
15. For a fuller discussion see 'International Solidarity Action Agreed by World Paper Unions' *SOGAT Journal*, January 1976, p. 18.
16. See *SOGAT Journal*, July/August 1980, p. 14.

CHAPTER 13

RELATIONS WITH THE TRADES UNION CONGRESS

PARTICIPATION IN CONGRESS AFFAIRS

In From the Cold, 1955–75

Although in 1955 the NUPB&PW was the 15th largest TUC affiliate and sent a 20-strong delegation including the General Secretary and the President to Congress, the union's role in TUC affairs throughout the 1950s was minor. No motions were submitted to the Annual Congress, delegates rarely contributed to debate and the NUPB&PW Executive Annual Report seldom mentioned the TUC.[1] However, at the 1958 NUPB&PW Delegate Council Meeting a composite motion from the Nottingham and Manchester Branches instructed the NEC 'to nominate, at the opportune time, one of the principal officers for the TUC General Council'[2] on the grounds that the union took insufficient interest in the wider trade union movement. The motion was opposed by the NEC on whose behalf the General Secretary told delegates he had declined from standing for the General Council against the sitting member for the printing unions, Bob Willis from the LTS so as to avoid dissension between craft, semi-craft and non-craft unions. His workload made it difficult to attend the General Council and its sub-committee meetings, and it was in the interests of the NUPB&PW that he retained his position as P&KTF President. In the light of this information the motion was withdrawn, but in 1960 the Nottingham Branch again raised the issue of one of the officers being nominated for the General Council. This was, however, defeated, with the NEC arguing that any such nominee should be a national official.

In marked contrast to the 1950s, between 1961 and the 1966 merger with NATSOPA, the NUPB&PW submitted six motions to Congress covering topics of industrial concern to its members. One called for protective measures to help the papermaking industry (1963) and another that workers have the right to representation during visits by the Factory Inspectorate. Another advocated a trade union stance on wider issues such as the power of multinationals and the need for public ownership (1964). Following his election as General Secretary in 1961, Tom Smith proposed the NUPB&PW motions and/or contributed to Congress debates – especially those on printing industry matters and on incomes policy – at every Congress during his first seven years in office.

A number of factors lay behind the NUPB&PW's change of attitude towards the TUC. First, the NUPB&PW viewed the British government's decision to join the European Free Trade Association (EFTA) as a threat to the jobs of its papermaking members and concluded that measures to protect the industry were more likely to be obtained from Government if a broad-based campaign of support were developed. This motivated the union's emergency motion on this issue to the 1963 Congress on the need for Government action to protect the papermaking industry from import competition (see Chapter 2). Second, the adoption of incomes policy by successive governments from the early 1960's 'politicised' the issue of pay determination. Incomes policy applied to all and it was difficult for individual unions or groups to act in isolation from the policy. The Paperworkers had a tradition of branch autonomy and strong workplace organisation, and many chapels resented governmental attempts to restrict plant bargaining. Unions could only be represented in any dealings with the government by a collective voice expressed by the TUC. If the NUPB&PW's voice was to be heard in this process, then it had to raise its profile within the TUC.

Third, the implementation of new technology in the printing industry was creating inter-union problems. A higher profile in the TUC might be helpful in that the union's position would be better understood when taken to a TUC Dispute Committee over jurisdiction or demarcation issues by another union. The question of who was to operate new technology was likely to continue as a source of inter-union friction and the NUPB&PW considered it would be no bad thing if it were to gain allies and friends in the TUC through being seen as an active participant in wider trade union bodies. The merger with NATSOPA gave further impetus to these developments as that union's General Secretary, Richard Briginshaw, was a member of the TUC

General Council having been elected to the printing and paper industry seat on the Council following Bob Willis' resignation in 1965 on accepting the TUC nomination to the National Board for Prices and Incomes.

From its formation in 1966, SOGAT, the 10th largest affiliate, played an increasingly active role in the TUC. In the late 1960s and early 1970s, motions were submitted to Congress on safety at work (1971), and for changes in social security provisions which disadvantaged women (1973). The union also raised at Congress wider issues, such as Britain's economic problems, the need to develop world trade (1967) and support for those struggling for democratic rights in fascist Spain (1969). On the industrial front, SOGAT proposed a TUC campaign to achieve the 35-hour working week throughout industry (1972) and became particularly associated with opposition to the Health government's 1971 Industrial Relations Act. The SOGAT Joint General Secretaries – Tom Smith, Vincent Flynn (from 1970) and Richard Briginshaw – were regular contributors to Congress debates, but increasingly other members of the union's delegation also participated. For example, five members of the SOGAT delegation spoke at the 1973 Congress. In 1970, the first ever TUC Youth Award was presented to Glasgow SOGAT member, Janette Harkness.

On a less happy note, SOGAT (Division 1) became embroiled with the NGA in disputes over the manning of web-offset presses in the newspaper and general print industries and which resulted in TUC intervention on several occasions (see Chapter 4). In 1970, as trade union membership grew rapidly and many unions expanded into new job territories, SOGAT made four unsuccessful appearances before a TUC Disputes Committee. These concerned recruitment and recognition rights for clerical workers at Bowater, Newport, drivers at the Manchester Evening News and F.J. Whelan and processing staff at Littlewood's Pools in Liverpool and Glasgow.

The growing importance SOGAT attached to participation in the TUC was further reflected in the submission of motions proposing changes in the method of electing the General Council.[3] SOGAT argued that only those unions in the Trade Groups which formed the basis of General Council representation should vote for their Trade Group representatives. Under the prevailing system, all affiliated unions voted for the entire General Council and this gave much power to a few large unions who assumed, in the words of Vincent Flynn, the role of 'adoptive parents'. In 1965 this situation resulted in 8.6 million votes being cast

374

for candidates in the Printing and Paper Trade Group, the unions in which had a total membership of 264,293. SOGAT considered that the choosing of representatives on the General Council should be returned to the 'natural parents', viz, only the unions who were in the Trade Group. The main counter-argument was that those elected to the General Council were not elected delegates from their union or Trade Group, but as representatives of the whole movement. The whole Congress therefore voted on who sat on the General Council. SOGAT's motion was not supported by the biggest unions and was defeated at the 1972 and 1973 Congresses. With the break-up of the original SOGAT, Bill Keys stood, unsuccessfully, in 1972 and 1973 against Briginshaw for the Printing and Paper Trade Group seat on the General Council. Brenda Dean, then a Manchester branch official, was unsuccessful in gaining election to one of the women's seats on the General Council.

Towards Centre Stage, 1975–91

The victory in 1975 of Bill Keys over Owen O'Brien of NATSOPA in the election to succeed Richard Briginshaw on the General Council reflected SOGAT's growing influence within the trade union movement and marked the beginning of a period in which that influence was consolidated and deepened. Whilst carrying out the wide range of tasks given to him by the TUC, Keys used the time he served on the General Council (1975–85) to advance and promote SOGAT policies. In respect of motions and amendments submitted by SOGAT to Congress there was a noticeable shift towards the major issues of the day confronting the wider trade union movement, for example pay restraint, return to free collective bargaining and public expenditure cuts and withdrawal from the National Economic Development Council, as it had become 'a dialogue with the deaf' under the Thatcher government.

Matters of particular concern to SOGAT members were brought to Congress in the early 1980s. In an attempt to balance the concentration of press ownership into a few hands, SOGAT persuaded Congress that a publicly-owned National Printing Corporation should be established to encourage a wider variety of publications and democratic debate. The crisis in the paper manufacturing industry in the early 1980s led SOGAT to submit an emergency motion to Congress, proposing a series of measures – a lower sterling exchange rate, reduced energy costs,

375

increased domestic supply of raw materials and import controls – which it believed necessary if closures were to be averted. However, at the same time, SOGAT also brought to the movement's attention the need to improve the conditions of and opportunities open to the poorest and most disadvantages members of society. Thus, in 1977, the union condemned the withdrawal of invalid tricycles for the disabled and advocated increased benefits for the long-term jobless. In 1982, in response to rising youth unemployment, the union called for proper training programmes, decent wage rates and the right to union membership, whilst the 1984 Congress approved a SOGAT motion seeking a substantial increase in the old age pension. In the late 1970s SOGAT took a strong stand against racists and fascist organisations which blamed black workers for rising unemployment and social deprivation by arguing that social conditions were a product of the economic system and asserting that racism posed a challenge to the principles of trade unionism. It urged the TUC to campaign to counter such divisive ideas.

On the floor of Congress, SOGAT participation continued to grow, with five speakers – apart from the General Secretary – reaching the rostrum in 1981 and 1984 and four in 1985. In 1982 Carollyn Baikie became the second SOGAT member to win the TUC Youth Award. In 1983 came the first major change to the method of electing the General Council since its creation in 1921 when Congress agreed affiliated unions with 100,000 or more members have 'automatic' representation on the Council. Unions with 250,000 or more members were entitled automatically to two seats on the General Council, thus giving SOGAT two seats.

During his ten years on the General Council, Bill Keys played a leading role not only in raising SOGAT's profile and standing within the labour movement but also in the development and work of TUC committees. As Chair of the Equal Rights Committee he worked to combat and eradicate discrimination against women and black workers. He persuaded the General Council that ethnic minority problems were industrial problems and not issues that should be the responsibility, as hitherto, of the Council's International Department. The period when he chaired the Printing Industries' Committee and the Media Working Group was one in which inter-union rivalries and bitterness were inflamed as provincial newspaper employers implemented new technology. The anti-union legislation introduced by the Thatcher governments in the early 1980s thrust the Employment Policy and Organisation Committee, which Keys chaired, into the trade union and media spotlight as the movement sought to adjust to operating in a more restricted legal environment. To mark his service on these TUC Committees, including its Finance and General Purposes Committee, Bill Keys was awarded the Gold Badge of Congress on his retirement from the General Council in 1985.

With the succession of Brenda Dean in 1985 to the SOGAT General Secretaryship the essential thrust of SOGAT's policies and level of participation in the TUC continued. However, relationships between SOGAT and the TUC became strained over the latter's attitude towards the behaviour of another affiliate union, the EETPU, in the News International dispute. In 1986, SOGAT was angered over the TUC's reluctance to take firm and immediate action against the EETPU and then in 1987 to its 'copping-out' of disciplining the EETPU despite mounting evidence of that Union's deep complicity in the Wapping dispute.

Over the period 1985–91 issues taken up by SOGAT in TUC motions included opposition to the imposition of VAT on print products (1987), greater protection for workers in the event of company take-overs (1990), more union involvement in occupational pension schemes (1986) and for unions to have a statutory right to recognition from employers (1990). At the 1988 Congress, the union called for a TUC campaign to alert workers to the growing menace of repetitive strain injuries (RSI), and seconded motions demanding greater provision and availability of cancer checks for women, and tighter restrictions on noise at work. It also brought to the fore the interests of its Remploy members by advocating the provision of more jobs at decent wages for the disabled. In the international sphere SOGAT sought the support of Congress for emergent workers' organisations in South Africa and Eastern Europe and also on Middle East issues. Members of SOGAT's TUC delegations contributed to Congress organisational as well as policy debates. For example, in 1987 in seconding a motion on union organisation and recruitment, Brenda Dean emphasised the importance of the trade union movement making itself more attractive to the growing numbers of women workers.

Brenda Dean served on the General Council and was a member of the Employment Policy and Organisation Committee, of the Equal Rights, Women's, International, Trade Union Education and Economic Committees, as well as being on the Media Working Group and chairing the Printing Industries Committee. She also served on the Special Review Body established by the 1987 Congress to examine

377

union organisation, membership and prospects for growth. In 1989 the number of places allocated to women on the General Council was increased and Pam Thomas, a SOGAT NEC member, employed at the Neath plant of David S. Smith, was elected to the Council. In the following year she topped the poll in the women's section, and served on the Equal Rights, Social Insurance and Industrial Welfare, Trade Union Education and Women's Committees.

Over the period 1975 to 1991 SOGAT was involved in TUC Disputes Committee hearings on 13 occasions. They were mainly with the NGA over jurisdictional rights in the advertising areas of provincial newspapers and in the machine rooms of the commercial printing industry. Two disputes were with the NUR over membership and recognition rights for newspaper distribution workers at Newsflow Ltd. In both these cases the Disputes Committee found against SOGAT. However, the most serious inter-union dispute involving SOGAT which reached a TUC Disputes Committee were with the EETPU. In 1983 SOGAT's decision to accept into membership the London Press Branch of the EETPU almost led to its expulsion from the TUC. In 1987 the TUC's *de facto* endorsement of the EETPU's single-union deal with United Paper Mills at their Shotton 'greenfield site' particularly angered SOGAT. Further conflict between the two union's occurred in 1988 when the EETPU signed a single-union agreement to represent paperworkers at the Caledonian Paper Mill, another 'greenfield site', in Scotland, but before the matter reached a TUC Disputes Committee the EETPU had been expelled from the TUC.

In the latter part of 1982 SOGAT was informed that the NGA had invited officers of the EETPU Press Branch to discuss transferring their engagements into the NGA. SOGAT considered that if this happened the balance of power between the unions in the national press would be disturbed. SOGAT took the initiative and approached the Press Branch who said they were interested in joining SOGAT because they were disgusted by their treatment by the leaders of the EETPU over a long period of time. The EETPU stated that its Press Branch was not available for transfer to any other union. However, Press Branch members resigned from the EETPU and applied to join SOGAT. The TUC sought assurances that SOGAT would not break 'Bridlington procedures' and risk exclusion from the TUC. To force the issue, SOGAT issued membership cards to the 'Fleet Street' electricians but did not to collect contributions. The EETPU referred the matter to the TUC and on 26 August 1983 a Disputes Committee made the following award:

After considering the oral and written evidence of both unions, the Committee find that SOGAT(82) by accepting into membership members of the EETPU despite objections by the EETPU and by seeking recognition from the NPA, have acted in breach of the TUC's Disputes Principles and Procedures.

The Committee award that SOGAT(82) shall exclude forthwith the members of the EETPU they have taken into membership and shall cease recruiting amongst electricians employed by national newspapers in London and claims for recognition in respect of these electricians.

The Committee's firm view is that it is in the best interests of the individuals concerned to re-join the EETPU.[4]

SOGAT refused to comply with the award, arguing that the TUC had broken its own Rules and Procedures and that the Press Branch antagonism towards the EETPU was such that if they were not admitted to SOGAT non-unionism in a vital part of Fleet Street was a real possibility. The TUC told SOGAT that it either complied with the award forthwith or its membership of the TUC was in jeopardy – a Disputes Award was binding and there was no right of appeal against a Disputes Committee decision. A plea by SOGAT to the whole General Council on 26 October 1983 failed to change the TUC decision and the union was told it must comply with the award by 2 November 1983 or be suspended from the TUC with a recommendation for expulsion at the next Congress. The SOGAT NEC decided to comply with the award. In doing this SOGAT had taken account of the 'costs' of being expelled from the TUC. These included the fact that it would no longer be represented on the General Council or its sub-committees, would be barred from attending meetings of the TUC Regional Councils and from affiliation to Trades Councils, would be excluded from the Printing Industries Committee. SOGAT would also lose access to the 'Bridlington procedures' to safeguard against the poaching of its members. These costs were judged to overweigh the benefits of retaining the Press Branch members. However, in December 1988, following the EETPU expulsion from the TUC, the 1,000-strong Press Branch voted by a majority of 2–1 to join SOGAT. These events severely strained relation between SOGAT and EETPU, and although the latter had had its members returned in 1983, it was determined to even the scores. Wapping was to give the EETPU this opportunity (see Chapter 19). On the other hand, SOGAT had 'mended its fences' with the TUC and could now continue to play a leading role in its affairs and continue to raise its own profile in the wider trade union movement.

ATTITUDE TOWARDS MAJOR POLICY ISSUES

Incomes Policy

1955–74

Although it was 1961 before a British government introduced a formal incomes policy, calls for wage restraint had regularly surfaced during the post-war period.[5] In 1956 the TUC, with NUPB&PW support, rejected the government's plea for wage restraint arguing that as long as prices continued to rise wages would follow. However, the 'Pay Pause' of 1961 with its 'Guiding Light' of 2–2.5 per cent signalled the intention of the Government to intervene directly in wage setting. The 1962 TUC Congress rejected the 'Guiding Light' and expressed support for the TUC boycott of the National Incomes Commission[6] which had been established to 'oversee' wage increase restraint. The NUPB&PW's attitude had been determined by its 1962 Delegate Council which opposed a national wage policy and a policy of wage increases being related solely to productivity. The Council had argued that factors such as the cost of living and the level of profits needed to be taken into account and that the trade union movement had to be able operate within a framework of free collective bargaining. It was against this background that the NUPB&PW backed a resolution, opposed by the TUC General Council, of the Boilermakers' Union expressing complete opposition to any form of wage restraint.

The 1964 TUC Congress took place just before the General Election in which the Labour Party was offering a voluntary productivity, prices and incomes policy as the central plank of the economic strategy of a Labour government. Of eight motions on the agenda dealing with wages, three opposed any incomes policy but in an effort to avoid discussion on the issue and thereby possibly damage Labour's electoral chances, all eight were contained in a resolution which accepted incomes policy provided it was based on social justice and applied to profits as well as wages. The NUPB&PW was the only union to vote against the composite resolution as its delegation felt bound by the Delegate Council's decision of opposition to all forms of wage restraint.

380

The Labour Party won the October 1964 election and in February 1965 agreed with the TUC and the employers' organisations a Statement of Intent for a Productivity, Prices and Incomes Policy. In April 1965 the Government established the National Board for Prices and Incomes, to police the voluntary policy, the central plank of which was an incomes norm increase of 3–3.5 per cent with exceptions in the case of greater productivity, of labour shortages and of the lowest paid. However, by the time of the 1965 TUC Congress, the voluntary policy was under strain and the Government threatened to tighten the policy. To avoid this, the General Council established an early warning system for vetting whether affiliated unions' wage claims were compatible with the voluntary productivity, prices and incomes policy. In July 1966 the government imposed a six-month statutory freeze on wages and price increases and made it a criminal offence for unions to organise industrial action to force an employer to implement a pay increase, the introduction of which had been recommended to be delayed by the National Board for Prices and Incomes. This was followed by a statutory productivity, prices and incomes policy providing for a 'nil norm' for income increases, except where increases were self-funded by changes in working practices or were to elevate low pay problems. It operated until the end of 1967. The 1966 TUC Congress narrowly voted to continue supporting the Labour Government's economic strategy but the 1967 Congress, against the advice of the General Council, voted for the repeal of the legislation giving effect to the Government's statutory productivity, prices and incomes policy.

The 1966 Delegate Council meeting of SOGAT (Division A) was urged by the General Secretary to support the TUC voluntary 'vetting machinery' but the delegates rejected this and passed a Glasgow/London Central composite motion which re-affirmed the union's policy of opposition to all forms of wage restraint and support for the implementation of Clause 4 of the Labour Party constitution.[7] Delegates accepted that there was no justification for an incomes policy whilst 1 per cent of the population owned 40 per cent of net capital and 5 per cent owned 70 per cent of all personal property. The Council rejected the Government's argument that the only alternative to an incomes policy was mass unemployment. Delegates also expressed concern that prices could be raised immediately but wage increases delayed for four months. These views of the Delegate Council were expressed by the SOGAT (Division A) General Secretary at the 1966

TUC Congress when he told delegates many trade unionists earn less the £11 per week, but if price increases had been restricted the trade unions could have helped the government.

Although by 1967 SOGAT (Division A) considered the Government's prices and incomes policy a hallow sham, its General Secretary tried unsuccessfully to persuade the 1968 Division A Delegate Council to remit a motion expressing opposition to the TUC's Wage Vetting Committee. Delegates were insistent that the TUC adhere to its role to assist affiliated unions in their efforts to improve wages and conditions. They opposed any form of wage restraint legislation, urged support for any branch taking action under the constitutional authority of the NEC and acknowledged the conflict of loyalties which many trade unionists were experiencing over whether they could support a Labour Government doing things the movement would never support under a Conservative Government. At the 1968 TUC Congress support for the wage vetting procedure was narrowly accepted but SOGAT (Division A) maintaining its opposition to all forms of interference in free collective bargaining, voted against the continuation of the wage vetting procedure. In 1969, however, SOGAT (Division A) had the gratifying experience of watching Congress reject incomes policy and thus come into line with SOGAT policy.

The 1970 SOGAT (Division A) Delegate Council re-affirmed the union's complete opposition to the prices and incomes policy, to all forms of wage restraint and to the TUC vetting machinery but expressed support for the restoration of free collective bargaining. The hardening of SOGAT (Division A)'s opposition to the Labour Government's incomes policy was symptomatic of an ever-growing disenchantment throughout the trade union movement with the government's economic strategy. Although the Wilson Labour Government continued its productivity, prices and incomes policy, its credibility diminished and was effectively ended by a wave of strikes in 1969/70, only to be formally terminated with the defeat of the Labour Government in the 1970 General Election.

Although the incoming Conservative government of Ted Heath abolished the Prices and Incomes Board, repealed government legal powers to restrict wage increases and publicly renounced a formal incomes policy, wage restraint was pursued by other means. The Government restrained wages in the public sector by its 'N-I' policy designed to reduce each successive pay settlement to 1 per cent lower than the previous one. This was reinforced in the private sector by the threat of unemployment, i.e. by refusing or withdrawing state aid to companies experiencing financial difficulties. The trade union movement rejected both strands of this approach and between 1970 and 1972 the TUC was united in opposition to wage restraint in the public sector and pledged to give no support to prices and incomes policy unless it became an integral part of an economic strategy which included control of rents, profits, dividends and prices as well as securing a redistribution of income and wealth.

However, in the summer of 1972, the Heath Government adopted an interventionist role and invited the trade unions and employers' organisations to discuss with it a voluntary prices and incomes policy. The TUC entered these talks but when they ended without agreement. In November 1972 the Government imposed a statutory pay standstill which was followed in April 1973 by a statutory 'norm' of £1 plus 4 per cent to be enforced by a Pay Board. The 1972 SOGAT Delegate Council re-affirmed the union's aim to pursue the interests of its members free from outside interference. When the Government imposed its pay freeze, SOGAT called for a conference of TUC unions to plan co-ordinated action against the policy. SOGAT insisted the Government's refusal to take meaningful action to control food prices, rents, dividends and profits was proof that the real aim of the policy was to freeze wages in the interests of profits. A Special TUC held in March 1973 voted by a large majority for a day of protest against the pay policy. The vast majority of SOGAT members stopped work on 1 May 1973 along with more than 1½m other workers.

The 1973 TUC Congress considered breaking off talks with the Government about the economy and ceasing to co-operate with the Pay Board. By a narrow majority the view prevailed that the General Council continue talks with the Government and co-operate with the Pay Board. The Government, in November 1973, introduced Stage 3 of its pay and prices policy which included a norm of 7 per cent or £2.25 per week increase whichever was the higher and threshold payments linked to the Index of Retail Prices. SOGAT, along with the TUC, rejected the policy and called for an immediate return to free collective bargaining. However, in January 1974 the Government faced a national miners' dispute and in February 1974 called a General Election on the basis of 'who runs the country'. The Government was defeated; although the Conservative Party returned the most seats it was insufficient to give an overall majority. A minority Labour Government, headed by Harold Wilson, took office in March 1974.

1975–79

After the problems involved in trying to operate, over the previous decade, a statutory incomes and prices policy, the Labour government made a 'social contract' with the TUC covering a voluntary approach to wages and economic policy. It represented an attempt to broaden the scope of trade union involvement in determining economic strategy and policy in return for limits to wage increases, improvements in the 'social wage' and the introduction of legislation favourable to unions. The 1975 TUC Congress accepted a £6 per week across the board increase for 12 months from July 1975 on the understanding that the government restrained price increases, taxed the wealthy and implemented measures to combat rising unemployment. SOGAT, however, supported the alternative strategy which opposed any interference in free collective bargaining, advocated more state regulation of the economy and committed unions to industrial action in pursuit of more holidays, a shorter working week, less overtime and a £40 per week minimum wage. SOGAT wanted to see the Labour government honour their pledge to bring about the fundamental and irreversible shift in the balance of wealth and power in favour of working people and their families. To do this, SOGAT believed the Labour government had to challenge the basis of the society in which people lived, as society was still based on class and privilege.

The acceptance of the £6 policy by the TUC left SOGAT having to decide whether to live with this situation given its long-standing opposition to any interference with free collective bargaining. In the end, the union decided it would be wrong to disregard the wishes of the majority of working-class people and it backed the TUC decision. SOGAT members would gain nothing from a path of confrontation with the employers and the government if in so doing they isolated themselves from the wider trade union movement.

When the SOGAT Delegate Council met in May 1976, delegates were faced with an emergency motion from the NEC pledging support for the TUC/government-agreed guidelines for wage increases for the next 12 months of 5 per cent with a minimum increase of £2.50 per week and a maximum of £4. There was also a motion from the Glasgow Branch calling for a return to free collective bargaining, a rejection of wage restraint, a freeze on prices, control of imports and capital exports, a cut in arms expenditure and increased tax on the wealthy. The debate at the Council centred around the extent to which delegates were prepared to carry their opposition to Government policy. The NEC argued that, unpalatable as some polices might be, the Government must remain in office if social justice were to be achieved, and to criticise constantly the Labour Government was unfair given the economic problems they had inherited. Delegates supporting the Glasgow motion emphasised the need for a radical change in Government policy and accused the Government of accepting 'the false premise that wages are the main cause of inflation'. Delegates were urged to be consistent and keep to the tradition of being one of the few enlightened unions who had always defended free collective bargaining. The Glasgow motion was passed by 203 votes to 164, but when the NEC emergency motion supporting the TUC Guidelines was put to the vote it was carried by 232 votes to 157. The membership was balloted on the TUC Guidelines which were accepted by 51,293 votes to 7,889. It was a decision made reluctantly in the hope that at the end of the year the sacrifice would have been worthwhile.[8]

At the 1977 TUC the prospects of a third year of wage restraint, falling standard of living, and increasing inflation resulted in delegates rejecting the government's proposed 10 per cent maximum wage increase for the following 12 months. The General Council supported a return to free collective bargaining, with the proviso there be a 12-month gap between settlements. Bill Keys seconded an amendment opposing the 12-month interval and, although this was defeated by 7.1 million votes to 4.3 million, the SOGAT NEC decided not to abide by Congress policy. The Executive justified its decision by referring to the mounting pressure for action on wages at shop-floor level and to commitments, given to members when accepting Stage 2 awards, that negotiations would be re-opened when that phase of the pay policy ended. If the 12-month gap were adhered to, then the union was breaking faith with its membership. The 1978 SOGAT Delegate Council, reflecting the growing disillusionment with the Social Contract throughout the trade union movement, carried the following motion from the PMB which stated 'This Conference is appalled at the way the Labour Government has applied its strict control over wages while allowing profits and prices to increase sky high, and urges the NEC to oppose any future wage restraint'.[9]

The 1978 TUC took place amid speculation that the Prime Minister Jim Callaghan was about to call a General Election. In the event he did not, and the delegates went on to reject the government's announcement of a 5 per cent 'norm' for the next 12 months. It passed a motion, supported by SOGAT, calling for a return to free collective bargaining, a 35-hour week, development of the public sector and a new agreement on economic strategy and social priorities. The SOGAT 1978 NEC's Annual Report expressed regret over the extension of wage restraint and warned that it would create difficulties and confrontation with the government. This prediction came true in the 1978/9 winter wage round in which a wave of strikes, mainly by low-paid workers in the public sector made the Labour government unpopular. In April 1979, the Government lost a vote of confidence in the House of Commons and was voted out of office at the ensuing General Election. The incoming Conservative government rejected incomes policy preferring to base its pay strategy on increasing unemployment and on legislation to weakening trade union organisation in the longer term. Despite the Tory government's declared approach, the basic stance of SOGAT towards wage restraint, which had only altered briefly during the early period of the Social Contract, was restated at the 1986 Delegate Council in a Scottish Graphical Branch motion:

> In view of recent statements made by prominent members of the Labour Party leadership, Conference re-affirms opposition to wage restraint through any form of incomes policy, instructs the NEC to place in front of the next TUC and Labour Party Conference a motion giving total support to free collective bargaining from which can be gained maximum benefits and conditions from employers.[10]

Industrial Relations Reform

In Place of Strife, 1969

In 1965 a Royal Commission under the chairmanship of Lord Donovan was established to examine the contribution of the UK industrial relations system to Britain's competitive deficit and the role the law might play in reforming the system. In 1968 the Donovan Commission Report was published, recommending that trade unions should be strengthened in terms of controlling their members and shopstewards and in increasing their membership, that collective agreements be comprehensive and that disputes procedures be reformed. It saw little role for the law in reforming the UK industrial relations system. In January

1969 the Government published a White Paper entitled *In Place of Strife*, in which it set out possible legislation based on the Donovan Report to reform the industrial relations system. Many proposals were straight from the Report, for example the right of a worker to join a trade union, to protection from unfair dismissal and the right of a union to recognition. However, the White Paper contained three proposals which angered the trade union movement. The Secretary of State for Employment was to have power to order a ballot before strike action and to impose a 28-day 'cooling off period' whilst the dispute went through the disputes procedure in the case of unconstitutional strikes. Failure to comply with such orders would result in workers being liable to financial penalties. In the case of inter-union disputes an Industrial Board would decide between one union and the other and non-compliance with the Board's award would render unions liable to financial penalties. Matters were inflamed when the Labour Government announced in the March 1969 Budget that it intended to introduce immediately a short bill on industrial relations containing these 'penal clauses' and leaving the enactment of the main Donovan proposals to later.

The SOGAT Executive Council responded quickly to *In Place of Strife*, arguing its proposals would be disadvantageous to SOGAT and its members. It supported the TUC opposition to the 'Penal Clauses' Bill and urged the re-call of Congress. Many SOGAT members participated in a 3,000-strong lobby of a TUC Conference of Executives held in February 1969 whilst 1,000 expressed their opposition in a demonstration outside SOGAT House before Joint General Secretary Richard Briginshaw, a member of the TUC General Council left to attend the April meeting of the General Council. On 1 May 1969 thousands of SOGAT members went on strike in protest at the Government's proposed legislation whilst the Executive Council accused the government of being swayed by media campaigns against the trade unions and called upon the TUC to organise a 24-hour national stoppage if the Government persisted with its plans to translate the proposed legislation into law.

In June 1969 a Special Trades Union Congress considered the General Council's document entitled *Programme for Action*, which contained alternative proposals to those of the Government. It proposed that affiliated unions inform the General Council of unauthorised and unconstitutional stoppages of work involving their members and that they follow TUC advice on how to deal with them. Affiliated unions were to inform the General Council if stoppages were contemplated over inter-union disputes, to desist from action until the TUC had considered the case and to strive to get members back to work if stoppages were 'unauthorised'. SOGAT supported *Programme of Action* which was carried by the Special Congress. The Government had committed itself to reconsider its legislative proposals if the trade union movement could provide alternatives which met the Government's objectives. After ten marathon meetings between the General Council and the Prime Minister, Harold Wilson, the Government withdrew its proposed legislation in return for a 'solemn and binding undertaking' by the unions to operate the proposals contained in *Programme for Action*. The Government then introduced in early 1970 an Employment Bill to enact the Donovan Commission recommendations, but it was overtaken by events when the June 1970 General Election produced a victory for a Conservative Party, which was committed to the introduction of a comprehensive legal framework for the UK system of industrial relations.

The Industrial Relations Act, 1971

The Industrial Relations Act sought to reduce the legal immunity of trade unions in industrial disputes, to increase the rights of individual employees, including the right to decide whether or not to be a member of a union, to regulate the internal affairs of trade unions so their rules conformed to certain standards, to impose limited financial compensation on registered unions committing unfair industrial practices and to make collective agreements legally binding unless the signatory parties inserted a clause to the contrary. The Act established the National Industrial Relations Court to deal with cases arising from the Act including ordering strike ballots and 'cooling off' periods in the case of serious industrial disputes.

At a Conference of Union Executives held in March 1971, the TUC General Council recommended a campaign of non-compliance with the Act involving non-registration by affiliated unions, inserting non-legally binding clauses in agreements, strict observance of TUC 'Bridlington Principles' over recognition from employers and non-co-operation with the institutions such as the NIRC and the Commission on Industrial Relations established to enforce the Act. The General Council was authorised to help towards the costs borne by any union as a result of contravening the Act whilst a future Labour government was committed to repeal the Act. At the 1971 Congress, union opposition hardened when delegates voted, against the wishes of the General Council, not to 'strongly advise' but to 'instruct' affiliated unions not to comply with the Act.

From the outset SOGAT took a defiant attitude towards the Act. In December 1970 the NPA secured an injunction restraining NEC members from encouraging members to take part in a protest stoppage against the Industrial Relations Bill. SOGAT was the only print union to call out its members and the injunction covered the whole of SOGAT (Division A)'s members, not just those employed in national newspapers. The TUC strategy of seeking amendments to the Bill as it went through Parliament would, the NEC believed, lead only to minor concessions and encourage the government to present the legislation as the will of the people. Furthermore, the Executive considered the General Council's 'recommendation' to affiliates not to register to be too weak and suggested that they had chosen the path of compromise. SOGAT therefore submitted a motion to the 1971 Congress seeking to make it a condition of affiliation to the TUC that unions were not registered and that existing affiliates who failed or refused not to register be expelled. SOGAT wanted to prevent the General Council's 'strong advice' not to register from being eroded by unions seeking registration to gain financial and recognition benefits available only to registered unions. If one union registered, this would encourage others to do the same. Although the Congress agenda contained a motion 'instructing' unions not to register, SOGAT argued the only way the unity of the movement could be safeguarded was by making it clear, before the event, that any union who registered would be expelled from the TUC.

In moving the SOGAT proposal, Vincent Flynn warned of 'the possibility of people slipping into registration quietly'[11] and condemned the General Council for 'turning its face against taking any industrial action to fight the Bill'[12]. The seconder, Bill Keys, argued that 'the moment of truth has come for this Congress. ... The key of this Industrial Relations Act is this question of registration.'[13]

In the event, the composite, moved by the AUEW and supported by the TGWU calling upon Congress to instruct unions not to register, was carried by a large majority. But the question of what to do about affiliates who did register could not be avoided. SOGAT itself was not immune from such pressures. At its 1972 Delegate Council meeting, a Midland Group/Northern Group composite motion deplored the Industrial Relations Act, but went on to propose:

> should the Society become exposed to incursions from other unions or should we be faced with a situation of TUC affiliated unions becoming registered in significant numbers ... the NEC shall have authority to withdraw any notice of de-registration.[14]

Those supporting the motion argued that union opposition to the legislation was fragmenting and the Act was being accepted, step by step, due to a lack of leadership from the TUC which had already advised unions to pay fines imposed by the NIRC and to defend themselves before it. However, the motion was strongly opposed by the General Secretary, Vincent Flynn, who argued this was not the time for 'fence-setting', and the proposal was duly defeated.

The delegates then carried two motions from the London Central Branch. The first congratulated the Executive for refusing to register and asked the TUC to take 'the severest measures' against any union which registered. The second condemned the TUC General Council for their 'retreat' from the policy of non-cooperation with the agencies established by the Act, and called for an emergency TUC in order to re-affirm the non co-operation policy. Earlier, the Conference had been addressed by TUC General Secretary, Vic Feather, who appeared to hand an olive branch of union co-operation to the government. Replying to Vic Feather, Vincent Flynn called for 'boldness' in the struggle against the legislation and emphasised the need to rally the strength of the ten million 'ordinary men and women in the trade union movement'. He concluded, 'I think that the TUC must give the leadership which it can give because I know that there are those who are willing to be led and they are not only in SOGAT'.[15]

By the 1972 Congress the credibility of the Industrial Relations Act had been damaged severely. Closed shops continued, collective agreements habitually contained legal enforceability disclaimers and the NIRC and CIR were still boycotted by the unions. The NIRC had ordered, in May 1972, a 'cooling off' period when the NUR and ASLEF banned overtime and imposed a work-to-rule in support of an improved wage offer. After the unions' members voted by 6–1 in a ballot to continue their action, the credibility of these procedures was damaged. The Industrial Relations Act's credibility fell further in July 1972 when five London dockers, members of the T&GWU, were jailed for defying an NIRC injunction to stop picketing a container depot which had doing work previously carried out in the docks. Their imprisonment triggered off an national dock strike, widespread stoppages in other industries and the threat by the TUC General Council to call a one-day national protest strike. The NIRC indicated it would consider an application by the jailed dockers to purge their contempt but, when the official solicitor visited them in prison, they refused to purge their contempt. The next day a similar case involving picketing by TGWU members was judged by the House of Lords, which held the national union responsible for the action. On this basis the dockers were released. An editorial in the August 1972 *SOGAT Journal* congratulated:

> The workers in Fleet Street (who) in common with other SOGAT members, showed wonderful solidarity with their fellow workers when they stopped work in protest ... but (this writer) finds it hard to believe that there was no collusion between the judiciary and the Government ... Laws are not ends in themselves ... they must be related to morality and they must be related to justice.

The delegates to the 1972 TUC met in an atmosphere of confidence that the Act had been neutered. However, by a 2–1 majority, Congress followed the General Council's advice to permit unions to appear before the NIRC to defend themselves. SOGAT was in the minority in supporting a strengthening of the non co-operation policy. Despite the previous 'instruction' to affiliated organisations concerning non-registration, 32 (with a total membership of half a million), remained registered. With little opposition, these unions were suspended from the TUC. By 1973 the Industrial Relations Act still remained a potential threat to trade unions although its effects, because of non-registration and non co-operation, were not as adverse as first feared. In January 1974 the Conservative Government called a General Election for 28 February 1974 at which it lost office. The incoming Labour Government immediately set about repealing the Industrial Relations Act, a task which was completed by summer 1974. Reviewing the Industrial Relations Act in *SOGAT Journal* just before the 1974 General Election, Vincent Flynn remarked that 'We in SOGAT have played an honourable part in the fight against the Industrial Relations Act. We stood firm when others in the movement wavered'.[16]

The Thatcher legislation, 1980–90

The Conservative Government led by Mrs Thatcher pledged to restrict what it considered to be excessive trade union power and to this end passed five Acts of Parliament – the Employment Act (1980), the Employment Act (1982), the Trade Union Act (1984), the Employment Act (1988) and the Employment Act (1990). The Thatcher Government pursued a step-by-step approach, rather than attempting to pass one all-embracing Act, as the Heath Government had done. The trade union movement's opposition to these Acts did not succeed in either removing the legislation or damaging its credibility.

The Employment Act, 1980

The 1980 Employment Act limited picketing to an employee's own place of work, restricted secondary action to direct customers or suppliers of the firm in dispute, required 80 per cent of all employees to vote in favour of new closed shops, curtailed unfair dismissal and maternity rights, abolished union recognition procedures and made state funds available for union postal ballots. The 1980 TUC Congress endorsed the view that the legislation could be neutralised by ignoring its provision and continuing existing arrangements and agreements with employers. SOGAT believed the Government's low-key presentation of its legislation disguised the fact that it was a major assault on workers' organisations and their individual rights and a reactionary backlash against the effectiveness of trade union organisation. As part of the TUC campaign of opposition to the 1980 proposals, a 140,000 strong national demonstration took place in March 1980 followed by a 'Day of Action' in May. Despite an injunction by *The Daily Express* against the print unions to prevent the 'Day of Action' and opposition from some members, around two-thirds of SOGAT's membership obeyed the NEC instruction to stop work for the day and to participate in rallies and demonstrations. An estimated 6,000 SOGAT members marched in Bristol and Birmingham, 8,000 in Edinburgh and Sheffield, 9,000 in Manchester, 15,000 in Glasgow, 20,000 in Liverpool and tens of thousands in London. SOGAT called for the repeal of the Employment Act (1980) and, under the auspices of the TUC Printing Industries Committee, refused together with other print unions to use the provisions of the Act and resisted any attempts to introduce non-union labour or undermine trade unionism in the printing and paper industries. SOGAT warned its members and the wider trade union movement that complacency towards the Act was not an option.

The Employment Act, 1982

The 1982 Employment Act narrowed the definition of a trade dispute to one between workers and their employer 'wholly and mainly' about terms and conditions of employment, thus making inter-union disputes, solidarity and 'political' disputes illegal. The Act also subjected existing closed shops to periodical review by a ballot of those working in them, outlawed contract clauses specifying the use of unionised labour, removed legal immunity from industrial action targeted against non-union companies, gave employers the right in certain circumstances to dismiss selectively strikers and permitted those claiming loss as a result of trade unions taking unlawful action to sue the union for limited damages and to seek injunctions. However, the real threat to SOGAT's industrial power and financial stability was not damages but injunctions which, if not obeyed, could lead to unlimited fines for contempt of court and to sequestration of its assets.

On 5 April 1982 the TUC convened a conference of union executives at Wembley to consider an eight point strategy of opposition to the 1980 and 1982 Employment Acts. Affiliated organisations were to boycott closed shop ballots and state funds for union ballots. Affiliates involved in disputes with employers were to consult other unions, the TUC Disputes Principles and Procedures were to be observed and employee representatives on Industrial Tribunals were to boycott cases concerning union membership. Where an affiliate was confronted with legal action by an employer, the General Council would co-ordinate action, including industrial action, and provide financial assistance from a defence fund. However, support would not be given automatically. Support would depend upon the General Council being satisfied that the union's action was justified, that support from other parts of the union being assured and that the views of the TUC on the affiliate's behaviour had been taken into account. Affiliated unions would conduct amongst their members campaigns of opposition to the 1980 and 1982 Employment Acts.

The 1982 SOGAT Delegate Council meeting re-affirmed its policy of non-co-operation with the Employment Acts and urged the TUC to declare 'that an injury to one is an injury to all', and in the event of one union being attacked others would support it financially and industrially. During the debate, the need was emphasised to make members aware that the legislation was not an attack on Head Office nor trade union officials but on their individual rights. The General Secretary, Bill Keys, warned the time was fast approaching when words against the legislation would have to be translated into action and this might involve defying the law. In his capacity as Chairman of the Employment Policy and Organisation Committee, he also warned delegates to the 1982 TUC Congress that when the union movement was tested under the legislation and it would be judged by the speed, decisiveness and unity with which it responded.

The first major test of the trade union movement's opposition to the Employment Acts came in autumn 1983 with NGA's dispute with the Messenger Newspaper Group.[17] In July 1983, six NGA members employed at Finewood Ltd, a subsidiary of the Messenger Newspaper Group, in Stockport, were dismissed after going on strike over wages and conditions. Finewood, owned by Eddie Shah, transferred production of its freesheet newspapers to its non-union Bury and Warrington plants. When the NGA responded by asking advertisers to cease using Messenger Group newspapers, by instructing its members to 'black' the company and by picketing the Bury and Warrington plants, the company sought a High Court injunction under the Employment Acts instructing the union to cease its 'unlawful' activities.

The NGA, regarding the company's behaviour as a threat to wages and conditions in the entire printing industry, refused to comply with the injunctions and stepped up picketing at Warrington. As a result they were fined £50,000 for contempt of court, after which picketing continued on an even greater scale resulting in the NGA being fined a further £100,000 and the High Court ordering sequestration of all its assets. In protest at this attack NGA members shut down all national newspapers for two days and, after talks with Messenger broke down, the union resumed its picketing at Warrington. When a further fine of £525,000 was imposed, the NGA called a one-day strike throughout the printing industry for 14 December 1983. To demonstrate to printing employers it was not taking this action in isolation from the rest of the trade union movement, the NGA requested a statement of support for its action from the TUC.

SOGAT was closely involved in supporting the NGA in a dispute which was seen as having serious implications for print unions and the trade union movement. A joint print union committee co-ordinated support for the NGA, whilst SOGAT members from London, Portsmouth, Glasgow, Lancashire and the North of England joined the picket line at Warrington. The SOGAT attitude was that the NGA's fight was a fight for all unions and SOGAT members were urged to join the NGA picket lines. For SOGAT the responsibilities of the rest of the trade union movement to the NGA were clear. It saw no point in passing motions of opposition to the Employment Acts and then, when the test of resolve came, in walking away from the situation. The trade union movement had to support the NGA in every way possible.

The NGA's request for a statement of support for their one-day stoppage was given by the TUC Employment Policy and Organisation Committee. However, TUC General Secretary, Len Murray, immediately pointed out that the General Council was not bound by a sub-committee decision, and he would recommend rejection of the recommendation when it was considered by the General Council. Len Murray's argument was that if the General Council issued a supportive statement, it would be encouraging the NGA to defy injunctions, which would then put the TUC in contempt of court. The General Council duly declined, by 29 votes to 21, to express support for the NGA one-day strike, but pledged financial aid to the union. In the light of this decision, the NGA called off the proposed stoppage, purged its contempt, agreed to abide by the court's injunctions and to pursue the dispute by other means.

SOGAT unanimously condemned the TUC General Secretary for publicly disowning a decision of a TUC sub-committee, for action contrary to the decisions of the Wembley Conference, and for failing to support a union defending its members' interests when the union movement was under the greatest legal attack in its history. It considered the General Secretary's behaviour had divided the trade union movement and weakened the resolve of the working class to resist the anti-working class Employment Act.[18] The 1984 Delegate Council carried unanimously a Greater Manchester Branch motion congratulating the NGA for its stand in defending the right to mount effective pickets and to take secondary action.

The General Council's argument that they were concerned about the legality of the TUC's position had they expressed support for the NGA proposed a one-day strike, was rejected by the 1984 TUC Congress. Whilst accepting that the General Council determined when unions in conflict with the law received TUC support, they backed the NGA's stance in the Messenger dispute and reaffirmed the decisions of the Wembley Conference. However, the damage had been done, and the credibility of the TUC's opposition to the Employment Acts had suffered a serious setback. If the TUC thought its actions in the Messenger dispute would improve its relationships with Government such hopes were quickly dashed. The Government banned trade union membership at the GCHQ intelligence-gathering centre at Cheltenham and insultingly dismissed the TUC's offer of a 'no strike' agreement. In March 1984 the

Government committed itself to give every assistance necessary to British Coal to defeat the NUM who began a strike over potential pit closures. This dispute was to last over 12 months and the miners were forced to return to work without an agreement (see below).

The Trade Union Act, 1984 and the Employment Acts, 1980 and 1990

In 1984, Parliament passed the Trade Union Act which provided for secret ballots for election to union Executive Committees whose voting members had to be directly elected at least once every five years. The Act also provided for a secret ballot before a union could call industrial action and retain legal immunity. Third, provision was made for a secret ballot on a periodic basis to ascertain the union's members wished the union to continue with a political fund.

The response of the SOGAT to the 1984 Act was to call upon the TUC to have no further dialogue with the Government. It considered the Tories had attacked workers and their unions by creating unemployment to breed fear of redundancy and reluctance to fight for improved wages and conditions. The introduction of anti-union laws was designed to undermine the movement's ability to fight back against unemployment. In September 1984, SOGAT, because of the far-reaching consequences of the legislation for all levels of the union, called a special conference of branch and area officials. The General Secretary told the delegates the law now meant chapels and branches must give careful consideration to their actions when involved in issues such as secondary industrial action, closed shop ballots or expulsion from the union. This new situation required that chapels and branches keep the national union informed as to what they were doing and contact Head Office for advice. Branches and chapels undertaking their own actions could expose the national union to fines and/or sequestration of its funds. Industrial action had to be controlled at Head Office and the union work as a united union. The 1984 Act was designed to pressure union leaders into exercising much tighter control over the activities of workplace representatives.

The attitude of SOGAT to the Employment Acts (1980 and 1982) was to ignore them and conduct business as usual unless challenged by an employer or member. However, this attitude could not be taken with respect to the re-affirmation of the political fund. To refuse to ballot would result in SOGAT having no right to spend money on political purposes and no right to have a Political Fund. To allow such a situation would weaken the ability of SOGAT to protect and advance the interests of its members. SOGAT therefore balloted its members successfully over the retention of its Political Fund.

Following their 1987 General Election victory, the Conservative Government continued its trade union reform programme. The 1988 Employment Act made illegal the disciplining of union members who refused to abide by majority ballot decisions to undertake industrial action, outlawed industrial actions to gain or enforce the closed shop, made dismissal for non-membership of a union automatically unfair and appointed a Commissioner for the Rights of Trade Union Members to assist financially members pursuing legal action against their union. In industry-wide disputes, unions were to hold separate industrial actions ballots for each workplace and to declare results separately. The Act made provisions for the re-election of union Presidents and General Secretaries and for all members of union executive bodies to face re-election by secret postal ballot at least every five years.

The TUC opposed the 1988 Act claiming it imposed technical regulations on unions and allowed maximum scope for malcontents to disrupt unions and their procedures. SOGAT strongly disapproved of the outlawing of industrial action to defend or establish a closed shop, and of making the dismissal of non-trade unionists illegal. To deny unions the right to discipline members who disobeyed a lawful strike instruction was seen as illogical in that if a majority voted in favour of industrial action the minority could ignore it and carry on as normal but if the majority voted against industrial action no such liberty applied to the minority in that case. Indeed, if that minority went on strike, they could be dismissed lawfully. SOGAT also objected to the law, and not its members, deciding when and how national officers should be elected. Delegate Council Meetings had repeatedly voted against the re-election of national officials and the 1988 Delegate Council voted not to change SOGAT's General Rules to comply with the 1988 Act. However, it accepted that where ballots were legally imposed on the union it should apply for the public funding.

The trade union movement sought from 1989 to mitigate the effects of the 1980s industrial relations legislation by working for the election of a Labour Government and for European Community directives rather than by active defiance. However, the anti-trade union legislation continued with the 1990 Employment Act, which had three main objectives: the abolition of the pre-entry closed shop,[19] the removal of immunity from all forms of secondary action and the regulation of unofficial industrial action. The 1988 Act had made post-entry closed shops unenforceable. The 1990 Act made the refusal to employ a person because they were or were not a member of a trade union or because they would not agree to become a member or because they ceased to be a member illegal. Although the TUC General Council could see no evidence to justify the legislation, for SOGAT the outlawing of secondary action and the pre-entry closed shop went to the heart of its traditional industrial practices whereby it had protected and advanced the living standards of its members. Brenda Dean, the SOGAT General Secretary, considered that from SOGAT's standpoint the 1990 Act was in some respects far more damaging than its predecessors as it was clear proof the 'steam has yet to run out of the Thatcher-inspired crusade against organised labour'[20]. For SOGAT the 1990 Act was nothing more than a monument to the extremism and irrationality of the Conservative government's campaign, against the unions which had no parallel elsewhere in Europe.

Repeal of the 1980s' Legislation

The 1990 TUC was the setting for a debate to define the attitude of the movement towards industrial relations legislation. By the second half of the 1980s the TUC and its affiliates had accepted some elements of the 1980s legislation should stay. There was considerable support for the view that restrictions on some forms of secondary action, secret ballots before industrial action and secret elections for National Executive Committees should be retained by a future Labour Government. The trade union movement, including SOGAT, accepted that the legal framework which had surrounded the industrial relations system in 1979 could not be restored. The unions would have to seek from a future Labour Government a new framework of legal rights for workers and unions.

A number of factors had caused this shift in SOGAT's position. First, the 1985 TUC called for a positive framework of law to be agreed with the Labour Party. The subsequent joint TUC–Labour Party document entitled *People At Work: New Rights, New Responsibilities*, promised to replace the trade union legislation enacted since 1979 by 'a positive framework of law' to establish the freedom to organise, to negotiate, to withdraw labour, to establish the right for union members to have a secret ballot on decisions relating to strikes and for the election of union executives to be based on secret ballots. The *People At*

Work document was approved at the 1986 Congress.

Second, in response to a fall in membership from 12.2m in 1979 to 9.1m in 1987, the TUC established a Special Review Body to consider how to increase membership and promote trade unionism. Its first report drew attention to the relationship between successful new membership recruitment and the need for unions to gain recognition from employers. As the law stood, there was no imperative on employers to grant recognition even where unions had a majority of the work-force in membership. In addition, there were no legal barriers to derecognition. Legislation in the field of union recognition was attractive to both the TUC and SOGAT. The shift towards support for a new legal framework was given further impetus by the advent of the Single European Market in 1992 and by the speech of Jacques Delors, President of the European Commission to the 1988 Congress where he stressed the importance of the 'Social Charter' in guaranteeing workers certain rights, including that of being covered by collective agreements.

The SOGAT Delegate Council meeting welcomed the Labour Party's pledge, given at the 1989 Conference, to restore many of the union rights removed by the Conservative Government but considered they did not go far enough in correcting the overwhelming swing in the balance of power towards employers stemming from the current industrial relations legal framework. In moving the NEC motion, Brenda Dean listed the principles that would influence SOGAT's attitude towards future legislation introduced by a Labour Government.[21] It would have to prevent the reoccurrence of disputes like that at Wapping, to prevent the sacking of SOGAT members after a democratic strike ballot, to prevent derecognition, to give workers who join unions the legal backing for recognition where an employer refuses, to prevent the setting up of separate companies in disputes which have the effect of making picketing illegal, to provide the right to picket and to undertake secondary action where the workers have a genuine interest and involvement in the dispute. On the closed shop she said the SOGAT Rule Book listed as an objective the achievement of 100 per cent trade union membership and the union would expect a future Labour Government to recognise this fact and not outlaw working towards that 100 per cent membership. An emergency motion from the London District deploring a statement made in December 1990 by Tony Blair, Labour Party spokesman on employment, that there would be no re-introduction of legal protection for the closed shop from a future Labour Government was carried. It was being argued such a Government should pass a law to protect the closed shop, which was so important to the printing unions, where a majority of the workforce balloted in favour of it.

At the 1990 TUC, SOGAT seconded a composite motion which supported replacing the Conservative legislation with new laws which still placed some restrictions on unions' ability to carry out certain activities. Those unions advocating this approach were referred to as the 'new approach' supporters. On the issue of secondary industrial action, they supported that such action be subjected to a ballot and restricted to 'where there is a direct interest of an occupational or professional nature' whilst on the closed shop they considered there was a need to pursue 100 per cent membership in ways that were not inconsistent with the right of employees to belong or not to belong to a trade union. The 'new approach' also supported the establishment of a specialist Industrial Court with a conciliation role, with powers of enforcement and to award damages but not prevent a union from carrying out its lawful business by imposing the total sequestration of a trade union's income and assets. When the vote was taken the General Council's statement, *Employment Law: A New Approach*, and the composite motion seconded by SOGAT were both carried. At the point at which SOGAT merged with the NGA its official policy was to support a new legal framework of employment law for unions and for individual workers and to reject a return to the situation of the 1970s characterised by flying pickets, unlimited secondary action and strikes without ballots. SOGAT believed the 1970s' situation would not be supported by most of its members or by any political party, least of all the Labour Party.

The European Community

In 1957 the British Government announced it would not be joining the Common Market. The TUC agreed with the Government but recognised serious disadvantages, both economic and political, which would follow if the UK remained aloof from developments in the rest of Europe. The NUPB&PW accepted the necessity of Britain participating in the creation of a European trading agreement but was concerned as to the impact of any extension of free trade on the British papermaking industry, especially the small mills. The union held talks with the papermaking employers and with the TUC and informed its members they were watching the position carefully. In 1959 the UK Government signed an agreement along with Sweden, Norway, Denmark, Austria, Switzerland and Portugal to establish the European Free Trade Association (EFTA). The first reduction in tariffs took place in July 1960 with the objective of the complete elimination of tariffs by 1970. The NUPB&PW feared that as tariff walls were built around the EEC the Scandinavian papermakers would increasingly divert production to the UK market.

In 1961 the British Government re-opened negotiations to join the EEC. This decision was supported by the TUC provided Britain's 'special needs' could be accommodated regarding relations with the Commonwealth, the position of the agricultural industry and governmental 'independence of action'. On a show of hands, the 1961 Congress backed the General Council's policy of awaiting the outcome of the Government's negotiations before taking a decision about joining. The NUPB&PW delegates supported this position following the decision of a special meeting of the NEC called to discuss the question. However, at the 1962 Congress, although a similar 'wait and see' stance was accepted, the NUPB&PW voted for a defeated motion opposing Britain's entry into the Common Market. This decision stemmed from the 1962 Delegate Council accepting a motion from the London Central Branch opposing entry as 'a threat to print workers and the working class generally'[22] and urging the TUC to press for an alternative policy of expanding trade with all countries. The purpose of the Common Market was seen as strengthening capitalism and preventing Britain from taking industries into public ownership whilst the Council of Ministers yielded enormous power over economic, commercial and social policy without seeking the consent of national Governments. Supporters of the EEC questioned the way opponents seemed to consider the French and Germans not to be trade unionists and pointed out that many employment conditions in the Common Market were superior to those existing in the UK. The General Secretary however, urged delegates to see what the entry terms were before rejecting entry and said the union's papermaking members wanted Britain in the EEC to divert from this country imports entering under reduced tariff arrangements with the EFTA. However, in January 1963 the negotiations on Britain's proposed entry into the EEC collapsed.

Attention was refocused on developments inside EFTA. As import duties between member states were progressively lowered, the NUPB&PW became increasingly alarmed about the impact on the British papermaking industry. The union submitted a motion to the 1963 TUC urging the Government to recognise the need for special treatment for the papermaking industry within EFTA, to retain tariffs in EFTA at existing levels or extend the period for reductions, to introduce quotas for Scandinavian imports, to review Commonwealth tariffs to ensure British industry traced under equal conditions and to negotiate cheaper charges for the industry's fuel and water requirements. The jobs of 100,000 employees in papermaking were at risk, including many employed in isolated mills with little prospect of alternative work. The TUC indicated their support for the NUPB&PW and gave assurances of an early approach to Government. However, when the NUPB&PW, other unions with interests in papermaking and the TUC met with the Board of Trade little transpired. The unions argued only an extension of the timetable for the elimination of tariffs would save the papermaking industry. The Board of Trade's response was that employment in the industry had risen since the formation of EFTA and that a more effective way of dealing with the industry's difficulties would be informal discussions with the Scandinavian governments.

In May 1967 the Labour Government applied for membership of EEC. The TUC Council welcomed this but felt it unwise to comment itself until the negotiations were more advanced. It also said that affiliated unions would be consulted before a final decision was made. Prior to the 1967 Congress, SOGAT took action in support of its opposition to the Common Market, by collecting information about setting up a printing industry consortium inside the EEC and by making a donation to the Labour Committee for the Five Safeguards on the Common Market. However, in November 1967 the French government again applied their veto to Britain's application but on taking office in June 1970 the Conservative Government re-opened negotiations to join the EEC.

By a large majority and on the condition that Congress would make the final decision, the 1970 Congress supported the General Council view the trade union movement reserve its position until the final entry terms were known. However, the 1970 SOGAT (Division A) Delegate Council carried a Basingstoke Branch motion urging every effort be made to prevent Britain's entry into the EEC and to resist attempts to hold a national referendum on the issue. SOGAT continued to publicise the case against entry, pointing out that even the UK Government admitted entry would cause labour costs to rise leading to the loss of markets and a widening trade deficit. The EEC, SOGAT considered, had its roots in the Cold War division of Europe and argued that this narrow outlook be reduced by a cut in arms expenditure and investment in industry and social welfare.

In June 1971, negotiations for Britain's entry into the EEC were successfully concluded with an entry date set for 10 January 1973. The 1971 Congress was told that, since the negotiations had failed to secure the TUC's objectives, the General Council opposed entry. They were particularly concerned over the likely impact on the balance of payments and of higher food prices on workers' standard of living. The TUC launched a campaign against Britain's entry into the Common Market and the 1972 Congress committed a future Labour Government to withdraw from the EEC unless new terms could be negotiated and these were approved by the British people. The 1972 SOGAT Delegate Council reaffirmed the union's opposition to entry and condemned the Government for refusing to consult the people. The 1973 TUC voted to take no part in 'all committees, institutions and organisations to which it was entitled to participate within the EEC'.[23]

The Labour Government, elected in October 1974, pledged to renegotiate the EEC entry terms and to hold a referendum on continued membership. When the Government announced the renegotiated terms and that it would hold a referendum on continued membership on 5 June 1975 both the TUC and SOGAT rejected the terms and campaigned against continued membership. The 1974 Delegate Council had not only reaffirmed its opposition to the Common Market but called upon the Labour Government 'to withdraw immediately without the sham of renegotiation'.[24] It considered the case for entry and continued membership had been disproved by the experiences of membership. The referendum result was a 2 to 1 majority in favour of continued membership and the TUC accepted the Government's invitation to nominate to EEC Committees 'now that the decision of the British people had been made'.[25] The 1975 Congress agreed to turn 'the rich man's club into a working man's club'[26] by seeking democratic control over the European Parliament, greater control by the Parliament over EEC institutions, reforming EEC policies in workers' interests, extending industrial democracy and by resisting any 'irrevocable steps' towards European union without the consent of the British people. SOGAT fully supported this approach.

For both the TUC and SOGAT, the dominant issue related to EEC membership in the late 1970s was rising unemployment. SOGAT's main concern was the continuing problems in papermaking. As imports increased rapidly and mill closures and redundancies showed little sign of abating, SOGAT demanded a reduction in duty-free quotas from EFTA countries permitted under arrangements made with the EEC. At the same time, with SOGAT's support, the TUC sought to reform

EEC policies and institutions despite the 1980 Delegate Council demanding withdrawal from the EEC. This decision had been heavily influenced by SOGAT's belief the UK papermaking industry had suffered more than any other industry as a result of Community membership and worse would follow when the Scandinavian producers gained duty-free access to the EEC in 1984.

SOGAT maintained an interest in EEC developments at a more general level. In 1980, Bill Keys was elected as one of two TUC representatives on the advisory committee to the European Social Fund. SOGAT delegate Mike Hicks successfully intervened at the 1981 TUC to argue support for the affiliation to the ETUC of the largest trade union centres in France, Portugal and Spain which had been refused ETUC membership on political grounds. This policy was confirmed by the 1982 Delegate Council on the argument that multinational companies did not recognise national boundaries and neither should trade unions.

In 1981, the TUC re-affirmed its policy of withdrawal from the Common Market and stated its desire for this to be included in the next Labour Party election manifesto. Community membership was seen as having caused the de-industrialisation of Britain and balance of payment problems whilst its 'free market' philosophy ran contrary to the unions' belief in a planned economy. Delegates to the 1982 SOGAT Delegate Council supported the TUC policy of withdrawal which included campaigning for this to happen. Although attempts to reverse the decision to campaign for withdrawal were defeated subsequently, TUC enhanced interest in Community developments was reflected in successful motions supporting Community directives on equal pay for work of equal value and on extended industrial democracy.

The changing attitude of British trade unions towards the EEC peaked at the 1988 TUC in the unanimous endorsement of the General Council's report entitled *1992: Maximising the Benefits – Minimising the Costs*, in the unanimous acceptance of an APEX motion setting out union preparations for the advent of the Single European Market in 1992, and in the standing ovation accorded to Jacques Delors, President of the Commission of the European Communities. He spoke of a 'social dimension' to the Single European Market which would include a platform for workers' rights including rights to union membership, to collective bargaining agreements, to information and consultation and to life-long education. He concluded by telling delegates that the movement had a major role to play – 'Europe needs you'. The TUC General Secretary told delegates to the 1988 Congress:

We know that the European Community will not go away and that 1992 cannot be deferred. There is a vital influential role for the TUC in the European Community. In this country we will get little help. The Government will resist the idea of consulting and working with trade unions towards 1992. Fortunately, there is another Europe with which we can work.[27]

Following the 1988 Congress, the TUC established a Committee on European Strategy to co-ordinate work on 1992. SOGAT's General Secretary, Brenda Dean, served on this Committee.

After the 'Euro-euphoria' of the 1988 Congress, delegates to the following Congress set about seeking improvements in the social regulation of the Single European Market. Motions were carried on the rights of migrant workers in the Single Market, equal rights for women and the attainment of EEC environmental standards in Britain. At the 1989 and 1990 Congresses, delegates continued to support the General Council's approach but some delegates sought to temper the unions' new found enthusiasm for Europe by warning by all means support the social dimension but to do so with an awareness of its potential difficulties as well as its promises. Such reservations found an echo in SOGAT, and Danny Sergeant, the union's President told delegates to the 1990 Delegate Council in his Presidential address:

Whilst there are many aspects we welcome about the European Social Charter on Workers' Rights, there are many of us who have doubts about putting too much expectation on it and do not regard it as a panacea to solve all our problems. British unions may be relying too heavily on the Social Charter, as employers will be obliged or forced to recognise the collective bargaining rights of workers. In many respects, it will need to be strengthened and developed before we can fee confident about it.[28]

At the 1990 TUC Congress, SOGAT seconded three EEC-related motions. The first called for greater co-ordination between TUC representatives on the European Commission's Health and Safety Advisory Committee and union safety specialists in Britain. The second advocated a concerted European trade union campaign to provide full protection for workers following privatisation or take-over, especially with regard to occupational pension schemes. The third drew attention to the need for unions to strengthen links with East European trade unionists to combat the activities of pan-European companies.

THE NEWS INTERNATIONAL DISPUTE, 1986

SOGAT's dispute with News International was the longest dispute in which it and its constituent unions had ever been involved. The dispute is dealt with in detail in Chapter 19. The dispute, which began on 24 January 1986, was sparked off by News International transferring the production of the *Sun, News of the World, The Times* and the *Sunday Times* from Fleet Street to a new plant at Wapping in East London. As a result of the dispute News International dismissed the 5,000 strikers who were members of SOGAT (4,500 strikers), the NGA, AUEW and EETPU. This last named union had concluded a deal with News International to undertake production jobs at Wapping that had traditionally been performed by SOGAT and NGA members. Both SOGAT and NGA had accepted the introduction of new technology at the Wapping plant but it was the conditions attached to this acceptance that were the root cause of the dispute. News International wanted the implementation of new technology with the unions accepting no closed shop, a non-strike clause, a different disciplinary procedure to apply to chapel officials than to employees and for the company to have the unfettered right to manage. News International was not interested in a negotiation agreement. The company had prepared its grounds for a dispute and made a declaration of war.

The NGA and SOGAT complained to the TUC claiming the EETPU was in breach of TUC Rule 13 in that its actions were detrimental to the interests of the trade union movement by collaborating with an employer and that the final result had been the dismissal of 5,000 members of other unions affiliated to Congress. The two unions detailed evidence of the involvement from the summer of 1985 of EETPU Southampton and Motherwell Branch officials in facilitating the employment of people at Wapping and Kinning Park to undertake tasks usually performed by print workers. Despite assurance from the EETPU leaders that recruitment had ceased, the print unions presented evidence of the union's continuing involvement in hiring new staff. The EETPU was summoned to appear before the 5 February 1986 meeting of the General Council to answer seven specific charges against them. These were that they had jeopardised the chances of an agreement with News International by refusing to participate in a joint approach despite formal advise from the TUC to do so, that by assisting production at Wapping they had 'imperilled' the jobs of union members employed at Bouverie Street and Grays Inn Road, that they had assisted in the recruitment of a new work-force for the News International plants and this was intended to gain the EETPU sole recognition rights, that their members had produced a *Sunday Times* supplement in breach of other unions' existing agreement with the company, that they had continued recruitment for the Wapping plant despite assurance from their national secretary this had ceased and that the EETPU had entered into an 'agreement or arrangement with News International' without the agreement of the other unions.

The EETPU presented a detailed defence of its position and for the first time in TUC history a union was permitted to bring a lawyer into an internal meeting. The General Council found five of the seven charges made against the EETPU had been established and the union's actions had been detrimental to the interests of the trade union movement and contrary to the declared principles of Congress. Without division, the General Council issued a number of directives to the EETPU. The union was not to conclude any agreement with News International or enter into unilateral talks with them, was to desist from recruiting News International employees, to do nothing to assist the company to recruit staff and to give an understanding to accept or act on the General Council's directive by 12 February or face the possibility of suspension from the TUC. When it was proposed the EETPU be instructed to order its members at Wapping to stop doing the sacked printers' work, the General Council was advised such a directive would constitute unlawful secondary action.[29] As there was no dispute between the EETPU and News International, it was argued that such an instruction from the TUC would result in the EETPU and/or News International applying for an injunction to prevent the directive being implemented. The TUC decided the EETPU should 'inform' their members at Wapping that they were engaged on work normally done by members of the print unions who had been dismissed by News International.

Brenda Dean strongly opposed this action, arguing that the General Council's directives to electricians must 'have teeth' or they would lack credibility. Five thousand trade union members had been dismissed and members of another affiliate were doing their work. Dean argued that since the General Council had already accepted that this was the situation they now had to take the responsibility of instructing the EETPU to tell its members to stop doing the printers' work. The only argument employed to prevent this happening was the claim that the TUC could not issue 'an illegal directive' and if the Courts made such a ruling then the TUC's six other directives to the EETPU would also be nullified.

Ray Buckton, the ASLEF General Secretary, rejected the TUC's view and asserted that the basic principles of the trade union movement would go 'to the dogs' if they accepted that 'anyone can do anyone else's job of work at any time the lawyers say so'.[30] Buckton moved the EETPU be instructed to tell its members not to do printers' work, but the proposal was lost by 15 votes to 14. After a meeting lasting 13 hours, the General Council decided the EETPU members employed at Wapping and Kinning Park should be 'informed' they were doing other trade unionists' work. The TUC General Council had sent out a clear signal that was unwilling to defy the anti-trade union legislation. If SOGAT and the NGA decided to challenge the law, they would have to do so without the backing of the TUC. The significance of the TUC decision was not lost on News International who, four days after the TUC decision, but 14 days after they had first obtained an injunction against SOGAT, complained to the Courts that the original injunction had not been obeyed. This resulted in SOGAT being fined £25,000 for contempt of court and in the appointment of sequestrators to take control of all the union's funds and assets. SOGAT compared the TUC's decision to that of the burglar being caught in the act and told he could keep what he had stolen so long as he promised not to burgle the house again.

At the 1986 TUC Congress, SOGAT and the NGA sponsored a successful motion, supported by the NUJ, which condemned 'the anti-union laws which have been instrumental in assisting Robert Murdoch to dismiss 5,500 British workers'.[31] The motion went on to reject the 5 February decision of the General Council not to direct the EETPU to tell its members to refrain from doing printers' work. Finally, attention was drawn to the public declaration of Wapping EETPU members that they would support action by their union to achieve an honourable settlement for all concerned. Despite pressure from the General Council, the print unions refused to withdraw the motion. The General Council's actions were defended by the AEU, who argued that too much time had passed and the EETPU had confirmed they would have embarked on legal action against the TUC in February 1986, and by the TUC General Secretary, Norman Willis, who stated that the General Council had done all it could, within the law, against the EETPU.

The General Council was accused by SOGAT of hiding behind the skirts of lawyers and the Tory legislation. Delegates were reminded that TUC policy on GCHQ was unlawful but had been supported by the

EETPU and that the TUC circular at the start of the News International dispute asking all unions to tell their members not to cross picket lines had been another unlawful request. In the Wapping dispute, however, people were asked to shy away from testing the law. Both SOGAT and the NGA felt their members were entitled to more, especially as the possibility of the TUC coming into the conflict with the law was not due to a threat from an employer but from another affiliated union. Brenda Dean considered the News International dispute would rank in history books alongside with Tolpuddle and Taff Vale and told delegates that, having found the activities of the EETPU detrimental to the interests of the trade union movement, it was not good enough for the General Council to have told the EETPU to inform its members they were performing the jobs of print workers. Without the EETPU, she told delegates, Wapping could not have happened and those working there should have been told 'not to cross the picket lines and not to do SOGAT(82) members' work'.[32] Although the dispute could only be resolved by negotiation, SOGAT considered the passing of their motion would deter other employers who were watching the Wapping dispute following News International's action. Despite the opposition of the General Council, the SOGAT/NGA motion was carried by 5.8 million votes to 3.1 million. SOGAT reminded the General Council that this decision meant if negotiations with News International failed then the General Council would be required to tell the EETPU they must instruct their members at Wapping to stop doing the work of printers.

In 1986, the issue of disciplining the EETPU arose again when the minutes of a meeting held in May 1985 between the EETPU General Secretary, Eric Hammond and News International came to light and proved conclusively that Eric Hammond had given the company the go-ahead to print the four titles at Wapping.[33] At the same time the visit of the EETPU's National Secretary, Tom Rice, to the USA in April 1985 with Pole-Carew[34] became known. These two new pieces of evidence directly contradicted elements of the EETPU statement, to the February 1986 Special General Council meeting, about its role at national level in the months before the News International dispute broke. However, on 24 November the TUC Finance and General Purposes Committee rejected the print unions' argument the TUC implement the 1986 Congress decision regarding the EETPU. The TUC General Secretary contended that since the case had been heard against the EETPU on 5 February 1986 it would be double jeopardy to re-open disciplinary proceedings. SOGAT and the NGA were informed they would have to file a new complaint against the electricians' union if they wished to pursue the matter. The two print unions argued that references to 'double jeopardy' were inappropriate as any decision of the General Council was subject to ratification by Congress which had already indicated what should happen to the EETPU. Moreover, they argued, new evidence had emerged showing the electricians had mislead the General Council. However, after a wideranging and lengthy debate, the decision not to take further action against the EETPU was supported by 23 votes to 21.[35] The General Council then went on to advise all the unions, including the EETPU, with an interest in News International to meet to discuss the basis of a common approach to the company.

The General Council's decision was described as 'dreadful' by the SOGAT General Secretary. It had shied away from carrying out Congress policy and applying its own rules because of threats of legal action by an affiliated union. On 5 February 1987, under threat of sequestration of its funds and assets for a second time, SOGAT's National Executive Committee voted by 23 votes to 9 to end the News International dispute. Its reverberations continued and were raised again at the 1987 Trades Union Congress. As additional evidence emerged of the extent of the EETPU leadership's secret involvement with News International, the TUC came under increasing pressure to discipline that union. At the 1987 Congress, the General Council received another rebuff when the delegates supported SOGAT's contention that the General Council had failed in November 1986 to carry out the policy agreed at the previous Congress.[36] Speaking on behalf of SOGAT, its President, Danny Sergeant, reminded delegates how the EETPU's General Secretary had made statements to the TUC which were totally at odds with subsequent revelations. Acceptance of the TUC's 'double jeopardy' argument, Sergeant claimed, was a 'cop out' and was an indication that some General Council members wanted the issue over and done with. Although the SOGAT motion to the 1987 Congress expressing rights of traditional print unions to organise and be recognised at Wapping had been ruled out of order, its President made it clear the struggle to achieve this would continue. In a supporting speech, the NGA's General Secretary concluded that as for the EETPU, the TUC report was 'an indictment of their treachery, collusion and unprecedented behaviour'.[37] The TUC's General Council had failed throughout the Wapping dispute to get its supreme policy-making body – the Congress – to endorse its actions towards the EETPU behaviour in the dispute. The 1986 Congress had not approved the General Council's recommendations the EETPU inform its members to cease undertaking the jobs of print workers. The 1987 Congress had refused to endorse the General Council's decision not to carry out the 1986 Congress decision when new commending evidence of the EETPU collaboration with News International came to light.

THE COAL MINING DISPUTE, 1984–5

On 6 March 1984, Mr Ian McGregor, Chairman of the National Coal Board informed the National Union of Mineworkers (NUM) of his plans for the future of the industry in which he stressed the need for a planned contraction to take account of the change in the market since the development of the original 'Plan for Coal' agreed by government, unions and the Coal Board in 1974. Over the financial year 1984/5 coal output was to be reduced by 4 million tonnes to 97.4 tonnes with a loss of some 20,000 jobs. On 9 March the NUM Executive voted to give official sanction to strikes due to start in Scotland and Yorkshire over pit closures. Strikes had already been called in Durham and Kent. At the beginning of the strike, several areas continued working. In South Wales an earlier decision against striking was effectively reversed as pickets from neighbouring pits persuaded miners to join the strike. However, the Nottingham miners voted against joining the strike. Although some later joined the strike, many continued to work throughout. On 3 March 1985 a Special Delegate Meeting of the NUM accepted there should be a return to work without a signed agreement. So ended a strike that had seen the Government give a blank cheque to subsidise the losses of British Coal and its customers, huge bills for policing, great damage to the fabric of society, the cost to the pits, limitless antipathy developing between working and striking miners and above all the bitter financial and personal suffering of miners and their families.

The 1984 Congress pledged total support for the miners' struggle to save pits, jobs and communities and appealed to other workers to make the dispute more effective by banning the total movement of coal or oil. The miners received tremendous help from other trade unions, but SOGAT was the most supportive. The SOGAT NEC quickly gave its support to the NUM. Branches adopted mining districts whilst chapels adopted individual collieries. There were regular levies on membership in the branches to provide financial support. In addition, there were voluntary levies at the chapel level and collections were taken at Delegate Meetings. The 1984 Delegate Meeting pledged total support to the NUM in the firm belief the miners' fight was a fight for the whole trade union and labour movement. They were seen as fighting against the Government's policy of the de-industrialisation of Britain, for the expansion of the mining industry and the growth of the economy. The Delegate Meeting instructed all branches to join with others in the trade union and labour movement in setting up support groups in their towns to organise financial and active support for the miners and their families. They also called upon the TUC to call for total and unstinting support for the NUM from all affiliated unions including a national weekly levy to sustain the miners and their families.

In June 1984 SOGAT's Scottish Group in support of the miners sent a convoy of lorries which contained over 30 tons of groceries collected by chapels and branches throughout Scotland and which went to the six main strike headquarters in Scotland where facilities had been set up to provide meals for miners' families. Another convoy was sent in September. In June 1984 visitors from the SOGAT *Daily Mirror* chapel took two lorry loads of foods for striking miners and their families when they visited the Yorkshire area of the NUM. In July the West Midlands Branch delivered £1,200 of food to their 'adopted' colliery of Lytleton at Cannock in Staffordshire. In September 1984 the biggest ever food convoy bringing supplies for miners' families was organised. SOGAT had organised £100,000 worth of food which was despatched from London in 26 lorries. Hired from BRS and driven by members of London Central Branch and other London branches, the lorries had taken two days to load with food and essential supplies at the Co-op warehouse in Edmonton, North London. £100,000 had been collected in a matter of weeks after an appeal to all SOGAT Branches from General Secretary Bill Keys. The National Executive added a donation from national funds. The lorries drove to Yorkshire where they split up and went to different areas of the Yorkshire coalfield where strike centres and food kitchens provided meals for miners and their families. Some went also to Lancashire, North Derbyshire, Nottinghamshire and Staffordshire.

The London Central and London Machine Branches provided over 2,000 turkeys and an unlimited number of children's toys and annuals for miners' families for the Christmas of 1984. In addition, London SOGAT Branches and chapels laid on Christmas parties for the children, discos for the older children, toys and turkey dinners for families in almost every mining community throughout Britain. During the mining strike, branches and chapels raised nearly £1m for the miners and their families. SOGAT reached every mining community in the country. The resources were raised from regular weekly levies, sweepstakes and auctions. The London Women's Branch sent delegations on virtually every trip to the mining communities. They collected stacks of food, clothing and money and stood on picket lines in every part of the country.

THE SCOTTISH TRADES UNION CONGRESS (STUC)

The NUPB&PW, SOGAT (Division A), SOGAT, SOGAT (75) and SOGAT (82) all played leading roles in the affairs of the Scottish Trades Union Congress. After the merger of SOGAT and the SGA, SOGAT (75) represented over 95 per cent of printing workers in Scotland. SOGAT and its constituent unions regularly placed on the STUC agenda motions on wider trade union and political issues. Members of the delegation, which was always led by the President, participated frequently in Congress debates. In 1968 the STUC widened representation on its General Council resulting in the print unions gaining a seat on the council. Bob Gillespie was SOGAT's largest-servicing member of the STUC General Council and was a member of its major sub-committees including its Economic Committee. The upfront role of SOGAT and its constituent unions in STUC affairs was much appreciated by the STUC officials. SOGAT was a consistent supporter at the STUC of the establishment of a Scottish Assembly.

NOTES

1. Bill Morrison, the NUPB&PW General Secretary was in 1955 elected Chairman of Scrutineers whilst the NEC Annual Report for 1959 stated 'history was made for our union when Len Bellinger from Oxford was awarded the Gold Badge of Congress in 1959'.
2. National Union of Printing, Bookbinding and Paperworkers *Report of the Biennial Delegate Meeting, 1958*, p. 211.
3. See 'SOGAT Launches New Bid to Reform TUC' *SOGAT Journal*, July/August 1973.
4. See Society of Graphical and Allied Trades (82) *Report of the National Executive Council, 1982/3*, pp. 20–1.
5. Between 1948 and 1950 the Labour Government operated a wage freeze. It was relatively successful but broke down in 1950 in the face of falling real wages as prices increased on the fear of the Korean War developing into a world war. In 1956 the Government established the Council on Prices, Productivity and Incomes (the Cohen Committee) to educate, *inter alia*, collective bargaining partners of the dangers of inflation on economic prosperity.
6. Wage settlements could be referred to the National Incomes Commission for an inves-

tigation as to whether they were compatible with a given level of inflation. However, wage settlements had been implemented before their reference to the Commission, which was chaired by a barrister flanked by independents rather than by direct representatives of employers and the unions.

7. See Society of Graphical and Allied Trades (Division A) *Report of the Biennial Delegate Council, 1966*, pp. 232–44.

8. See Society of Graphical and Allied Trades *Annual Report of the National Executive Council, 1975*, p. 1.

9. Society of Graphical and Allied Trades *Report of the Biennial Delegate Council Meeting, 1978*, pp. 287–8.

10. Society of Graphical and Allied Trades (82) *Report of the Biennial Delegate Council Meeting, 1986*, p. 190.

11. See *TUC Congress, 1971*, pp. 430–1.

12. Op. cit. p. 430.

13. Op. cit. p. 431.

14. See Society of Graphical and Allied Trades *Report of the Biennial Delegate Council Meeting, 1972*, pp. 230–2.

15. Op. cit., pp. 26–7.

16. See *SOGAT Journal*, June 1974, p. 10.

17. For a detailed account of the Messenger dispute see J. Gennard *A History of the National Graphical Association*, Unwin Hyman, 1990, p. 485–92.

18. Bill Keys was later to reveal he had wanted to resign from the General Council over their handling of the Messenger dispute, but was dissuaded from doing so.

19. The then Secretary of State for Employment, Mr Michael Howard, described this measure as consigning 'the closed shop to the dustbin of history where it belongs'.

20. See *SOGAT Journal*, June 1990, p. 11.

21. See *SOGAT Journal*, June 1990, p. 34.

22. See National Union of Printing, Bookbinding and Paperworkers *Report of the Biennial Delegate Meeting, 1962*, p. 247.

23. See *TUC Congress, 1973*, p. 575.

24. See Society of Graphical and Allied Trades *Report of the Biennial Delegate Council Meeting, 1974*, p. 244.

25. See *TUC Congress, 1975*, p. 222.

26. Op. cit., p. 223.

27. See *TUC Congress, 1988*, p. 567.

28. See Society of Graphical and Allied Trades (1982) *Report of the Biennial Delegate Meeting, 1990*, p. 6.

29. See L. Melvern *The End of the Street*, Methuen, p. 212.

30. See *TUC Congress, 1988*, p. 468.

31. Op. cit., p. 466.

32. Op. cit., p. 468.

33. See *SOGAT Journal*, December, 1986, p. 3.

34. Pole Carew was a well-known anti-print union employer. He had succeeded in defeating the print unions in a bitter battle at the *Nottingham Evening Post* over the introduction of new technology in the mid-1970s.

35. See *Trades Union Congress, 1987*, p. 42.

36. Op. cit., p. 455–7.

37. Op. cit., p. 456.

CHAPTER 14

RELATIONS WITH THE LABOUR PARTY

THE POLITICAL FUND

The NUPB&PW

The income and expenditure of the NUPB&PW Political Fund over the period 1955 to 1964 is shown in Table 14.1. The main items of expenditure were affiliation fees to the Labour Party, the Scottish Labour Party, the Northern Ireland Labour Party, delegation fees and expenses, by-election insurance fund premium and grants and donations. At the time of General Elections the union made donations to the Labour Party General Election Fund. The NUPB&PW donated £500 to the Party's 1955 General Election Fund and £1,000 to its 1959 General Election Fund. In General Election years (1955, 1959 and 1964) the Political Fund spent more than it received in income.

The main source of income was contributions from those members paying the Political Fund subscription. In 1955 the annual contribution to the Political Fund contribution was 5p per annum for adult men and women and 2½p for juniors. However, 50 per cent of the contribution was retained in the branches so the annual fee paid into the National Political Fund was only 2½p per adult union member. Under the Trade Union Act (1913) individual members had the right to opt out of paying the Political Fund contribution. In the NUPB&PW, 75 per cent of members exercised this right with only 30,000 paying into the Political Fund. In 19 branches, including the PMB, 75 per cent of the members paid into the Fund. In 15 branches, including the London Bookbinders and the Circulation Representatives, the Political Fund contribution was paid by between 50 and 75 per cent

Table 14.1
NUPB&PW: The Political Fund, 1955–64

	Income	Expenditure	Balance of Income Over Expenditure	Balance of the Fund
	(£)	(£)	(£)	(£)
1955	1,824	2,248	424	4,847
1956	1,716	1,644	72	6,563
1957	2,220	1,770	450	5,369
1958	1,919	1,781	138	5,569
1959	2,069	3,955	−1,886	5,273
1960	2,184	1,836	348	5,687
1961	2,824	2,355	535	6,222
1962	2,568	1,883	752	6,974
1963	2,605	2,408	265	7,239
1964	2,647	2,816	−102	7,137

Source: *Balance Sheet and Accounts*, 1955–64, NUPB&PW

of the members. In 35 branches, including the London Central Branch, between 25 per cent and 49 per cent of the members contributed to the Political Fund. In 158 branches less than 25 per cent of the members contributed to the Political Fund. These branches included the London Women's, the Ruling, Manufacturing, Stationery and Box Making and Manchester. Some members did not pay into the Political Fund because as individual members of the Labour Party they paid an individual membership fee. Nevertheless, given the membership size of the union, the number paying into the Political Fund was relatively small, a situation described by the General Secretary as deplorable.[1]

By the late 1950s the financial state of the Political Fund had deteriorated to such an extent that financial problems had arisen. In 1956 the Fund reached the stage where its income was insufficient to cover its annual liabilities even though the union affiliated to the Labour Party on a figure less than the number of members actually paying the Political Fund contribution. The Fund suffered three problems. First, the number of members opting out of paying the Political Fund subscription was increasing. Second, from 1 January 1957 the affiliation fees to the Labour Party increased by 50 per cent, from 2½p per member per annum to 4p. Third, whilst the balances of the Central

Political Fund had declined to dangerous levels, those in the branches totalled a £3,500 surplus but this money was unavailable to the Central Fund. In July 1957 the Executive Council concluded that without increased income to the Fund, it would be difficult to meet the union's affiliation fees liability to the Labour Party. The General Secretary was instructed to publish in the *Paperworker* an article explaining the financial problems of the Fund and impressing upon all members the necessity of paying the Political Fund contribution. In doing this, the General Secretary explained to members that the Labour Party, because of its composition, traditions and mission, was most likely to assist the trade unions. Branches were urged to work to achieve 75 per cent of members contributing to the national Political Fund.[2]

These difficulties with the Political Fund led the London Book-binders' Branch to submit to the 1958 Delegate Council a motion expressing concern at the reduction in political fund contributors, a trend which it considered did not truly reflect the attitude of the members towards the labour movement. The second part of the motion asked the NEC to consider changing the Political Fund rules to enable greater support for the Fund. The London Bookbinders' motion was carried and the NEC brought proposals to the 1960 Delegate Council designed to establish the Political Fund on a sound financial footing.[3] These were:

(i)   2½p of the full weekly adult contributions each quarter be the contribution to the Political Fund except for those members contracted out of paying the Political Fund subscription. This gave an annual contribution to the Political of Fund of 10p payable quarterly.
(ii) the contribution to the Political Fund be allocated two-thirds to the Central Political Fund and one-third to the Branch Political Fund.

The NEC proposals were carried unanimously. However, they were rejected in a ballot vote of Political Fund contributors. The union was disappointed by the result and appealed to branch secretaries, chapel officials, mill collectors and all active members to do more to persuade their colleagues of the necessity of paying into the Political Fund, as it was a small sum compared with the results they would gain by becoming contributors.

The 1962 Delegate Council was the third in succession at which a scheme to put the Political Fund on a sounder financial basis was debated. The Liverpool Branch successfully moved 'that this Conference urges the National Executive to examine every possibility of increasing the Political Fund'.[4] It was supported by the NEC who pointed out that 45 of the 228 branches in the union did not have a single subscriber to the Political Fund and there were 14 branches represented at the Delegate Council which had no Political Fund subscribers. In 1948 when NUPB&PW membership stood at 120,000 there were 47,534 paying the political contribution. In 1961, with a membership of 169,000, there were 56,478 contributors to the Political Fund. If the 1948 standard had been maintained, then in 1961 there would have been 66,000 subscribers. The NUPB&PW had lost ground every year. The 1964 Delegate Council received NEC proposals designed to put the Political Fund back on its feet. The contribution to the Political Fund was to be 1p per week for all members. This would do three things: change the contribution basis from annual to weekly, eliminate the lower contribution rate for junior members and increase the contribution levied to 21p per member per year. Quarterly collecting of the Political Fund had caused endless trouble. Although in 1964 the number of members paying the Political Fund had increased since 1962 this was seen merely as a good start on a long road.[5] This proposed increase in the Political Fund contribution was carried by the Delegate Council and subsequently by a ballot of Political Fund paying members. The Delegate Council then went on to allocate the contributions to the Political Fund two-thirds to the Central Fund and one-third to the Branch Political Fund. This too was subsequently approved in a ballot of Political Fund members. Although the branch percentage was reduced, the absolute sum received by the branches increased. This increased income to the national fund, met the increase in Labour Party affiliation fees which rose in 1965 to 5p per member and permitted the union to affiliate on the actual number of members who paid the political subscription. This increase in contributions (with effect from 1 April 1965) and the change in its distribution between the national union and its branches did much to put the Fund on a sound basis (see Table 14.2).

SOGAT (Division A)/SOGAT

The income and expenditure of the Central Political Fund of SOGAT (Division A) and SOGAT over the period 1966–75 inclusive is shown

Table 14.2
The NUPB&PW/SOGAT (Division A)/SOGAT/SOGAT (75) and SOGAT (82); the Political Fund: central, 1965–91

	Income	Expenditure	Balance of Income Over Expenditure	Balance of the Fund
	(£)	(£)	(£)	(£)
1965	6,232	1,681	4,551	5,536
1966	8,382	1,870	6,512	12,048
1967	8,097	1,732	6,365	18,413
1968	7,556	1,873	5,683	24,096
1969	7,789	2,038	5,751	29,877
1970	8,267	4,985	3,282	33,149
1971	14,973	3,099	11,874	45,023
1972	12,338	3,187	9,151	54,196
1973	15,629	4,689	10,940	65,324
1974	16,440	46,280	−29,840	35,254
1975	14,336	9,806	4,530	39,784
1976	13,965	10,628	3,337	43,121
1977	17,387	14,931	2,456	45,577
1978	18,339	20,253	−1,914	43,663
1979	18,918	34,241	−15,323	28,340
1980	19,758	17,465	2,293	30,633
1981	51,090	22,996	28,094	58,727
1982	35,709	22,806	12,903	71,630
1983	143,232	101,612	41,620	123,928
1984	112,799	67,213	45,586	169,514
1985	128,447	101,142	27,305	196,819
1986	140,853	103,574	37,279	234,098
1987	131,894	273,249	−141,355	92,743
1988	121,915	83,932	27,983	120,726
1989	117,288	121,282	−3,994	106,732
1990	115,430	132,637	−17,207	89,525
1991	59,720	72,906	−13,196	76,339

Source: *Financial Statements*, 1955–91.

in Table 14.2. The main items of expenditure from the Fund were the same as those for the NUPB&PW. At the time of General Elections, SOGAT (Division A) and SOGAT made donations to the Labour Party General Election Fund. SOGAT (Division A) donated £2,000 to the Party's 1970 General Election Fund whilst SOGAT donated £40,000 in total to the Labour Party for the two General Elections held in 1974. The effect of these 1974 donations was that in that year, Political Fund expenditure exceeded income by £29,840.

In 1964, the NUPB&PW's Political Fund had a deficit but, as Table 14.2 shows, the balance of the Fund increased in every year of the existence of SOGAT (Division A). Prior to the February 1974 General Election, the SOGAT Central Political Fund had a balance of £65,324 despite affiliation fees per member to the Labour Party having increased to 7½p in 1971, to 10p in 1972 and 12½p in 1973. Three factors enabled the Fund to reach this strong position. First, the number of members paying the political contribution had increased significantly relative to the late 1950s and early 1960s. Second, the Political Fund contribution had increased from one penny per week (1d) to one pence per year (2½d) from the introduction of decimalisation with effect from 20 February 1971. Third, the Fund was receiving interest income from investments. In 1968, for the first time, an investment of £10,000 was made from the income of the SOGAT (Division A) Political Fund with the London Borough of Haringey at 8 per cent for ten years. Interest payments from this investment added £4,700 per year to the Fund's income. A further investment was made in 1969 when £10,000 was invested in the Borough of Basingstoke for ten years at 9.75 per cent. SOGAT (Division A) had hoped to make further investments to make the Political Fund self-supporting from interest payments from investments but was unable to do so.

SOGAT(75)

SOGAT's amalgamation with the SGA led to difficulties concerning the Political Fund and the Political Objectives Rules of the merged union. The SGA did not have a Political Fund but SOGAT did. The law required that if two unions were amalgamating and one did not have a Political Fund then a ballot should take place before amalgamation of the union without a political objectives rule to embrace such a rule. Alternatively, a ballot could take place after the amalgamation had become effective to restore a Political Fund in the new union.

SOGAT and the SGA decided SOGAT(75) would hold a Political Fund ballot after vesting day.

The ballot to approve the Political Fund rules for SOGAT was conducted in January 1976. Of the 174,297 ballot papers sent 126,677 (73 per cent) were not returned. Of those who voted, 27,799 favoured the proposed procedure for the establishment of a Political Fund whilst 19,592 did not. A second ballot was held between 9 February 1976 and 5 March 1976 to approve the furtherance of political objectives. In this ballot, 25,665 voted for the resolution whilst 24,493 voted against, a majority of 1,172. The former SGA had previously always rejected the establishment of a Political Fund. Shortly after the ballot only 38,000 SOGAT members (22 per cent) were contributors to the Political Fund. Of the 143 branches in the union, 81 had subscribers to the Fund whilst 62 (43 per cent) branches had no members contributing to the Political Fund. This unsatisfactory position led the PMB to submit successfully a motion to the 1976 Delegate Council deploring the lack of support for the Political Fund and urging the NEC to campaign amongst the whole membership to strengthen substantially the financial position of the Fund. The motion also expressed concern that some branches did not apply the Political Fund rule and that only with a strong Fund could SOGAT gain industrial advancement for its members via the political lobbying process. The late 1970s saw a slight increase (up to 25 per cent) in the proportion of members contributing to the Political Fund.

The main item of expenditure from the SOGAT Political Fund was affiliation fees to the Labour Party, the level of which continued to increase. By 1980 they had reached 32p per year per member when the amount of annual income received by the Fund per contributing member was only 31p. However, the 1980 Delegate Council appreciated the potential problem of the Central Political Fund and increased the weekly contribution to the Fund to 2p per week with effect from October 1980. The Political Fund's resources had also been put under strain by SOGAT's contributions to the Labour Party's General Election Fund. In 1979 the Central Political Fund showed an excess of expenditure over income of £15,323 due entirely to the £15,351 donation made to the 1983 General Election Fund. To relieve the pressures on the Fund and to provide much-needed cash, the union's General Fund purchased the Political Fund investment in the Borough of Basingstoke for £10,000. The investment had been due to mature on 31 March 1979.

In arguing for the Political Fund contribution to increase to 2p per week, the General Secretary described the affiliation of SOGAT members to the Political Fund as 'nothing short of disgusting' and laid the blame for this at the feet of branch secretaries who were accused of working on the principal of contracting members out in advance rather than operating the practice that when individuals joined the union they paid the political levy and they had to make a deliberate effort to contract out of it.[6] The Labour Party affiliation fee increased to 40p per annum per member in 1981 and to 50p in 1982, and the General Secretary warned that if the proposed increased contribution was not agreed then SOGAT would reduce substantially the number of members it affiliated to the Labour Party and thereby lessen its influence in the decision-making bodies of the party. The delegates unanimously carried the proposed increase and its immediate effect was to produce a large surplus of £58,727 for the Fund in 1981.

The 1978 Biennial Delegate Council agreed a number of changes to the SOGAT Political Fund Rules. The NEC wished to update the rules to meet the current circumstances. The Certification Officer had directed SOGAT's attention to certain requirements needed in its Political Fund Rules. He had sent model rules which SOGAT was asked to include within its Political Rules. The major change as part of the updating of the Rules was the establishment of a Political Executive to administer the political activities of the union, subject to the policies of the Delegate Council, and to deal with political questions between BDCs. SOGAT and its constituent unions had long been involved in political activity but they had never had a steering committee to implement the political policies emanating from the Delegate Council or the NEC. The Political Executive would perform this function. It consisted of five members of the NEC plus the General Secretary and the General President. Its prime function was to give effect to the political decisions of the BDC and to ensure that Parliamentary candidates, who the union nominated, represented the views of the union and observed the broad policies established by the BDC. Although the Delegate Council was the only body that could determine the number of Parliamentary candidates the union would sponsor, the Political Executive would have the authority to approve support for the constituencies for which SOGAT-related candidates were nominated. The general principle for determining whether support was given was whether there was a reasonable chance of winning the seat. If it was 'a lost cause' the union would not waste money supporting the candidate and the constituency. Branches submitted nominations for Parliamentary candidates who had to have been members of the Labour Party for at least five years. Candidates, however, were to be examined by the Political Executive to ensure they accepted the political philosophies of SOGAT as determined by the Delegate Council.[7] The Political Executive presented a report to the Delegate Council on its activities, including whether support for Parliamentary candidates should be retained. This was the mechanism whereby the union would deal with situations where Parliamentary candidates had, for whatever reason, since their adoption moved away from supporting SOGAT policies.

SOGAT (82)

The income and expenditure from SOGAT's Political Fund is shown in Table 14.3. In 1987 the balance on the Fund was reduced from £234,098 to £92,743 due to financial support given to the Labour Party in the 1987 General Election. In 1989, contribution income to the Fund declined by £7,239 in a year when SOGAT's affiliation fees to the Party increased by £14,436. In the following year, the Fund sustained a deficit of £17,207 as contribution income declined by £9,507 and affiliation fees increased by £15,970. The deficit was partly offset by donations from branches totalling £5,142. Although in the first half of 1991 branches donated a sum of £8,850 to the Central Political Fund this was insufficient to reverse the decline in the balance of the fund.

The creation of SOGAT(82) saw the number of contributors to the Political Fund rise from 71,392 to 121,151, an increase of over 40 per cent. One impact of the formation of SOGAT(82) was to increase to 63 per cent the proportion of the membership paying the Political Fund subscription. Nevertheless, there were still 17 branches with no members paying the political levy. Only six branches had every member contributing to the Political Fund. There was a wide variation in contributors between branches. The Greater Manchester Branch had 98 per cent of its members paying into the Fund whilst the Monotype Casters and Filmsetters' Branch had only 37 per cent. In the London Women's Branch contributors accounted for 15 per cent of branch membership whilst in the PMB, the LCB and the Ruling, Stationery and Packaging Branch corresponding figures were 58 per cent, 53 per cent and 50 per cent respectively. The ATAES Branch had 31 per cent of its members paying the Political Fund. The number of contributors

Table 14.3
The NUPB&PW/SOGAT (Division A)/SOGAT/SOGAT (75) and SOGAT (82); the Political Fund: branches, 1965–91

	Income	Expenditure	Balance of Income Over Expenditure	Balance of the Fund
	(£)	(£)	(£)	(£)
1965	2,857	709	2,148	8,300
1966	3,864	1,542	2,322	10,622
1967	3,273	1,580	1,693	12,315
1968	3,387	803	2,584	14,899
1969	3,143	2,511	632	15,531
1970	3,191	3,089	102	15,633
1971	5,984	1,988	3,996	19,629
1972	4,486	2,235	2,251	21,932
1973	6,602	2,077	4,525	26,747
1974	7,548	24,064	−16,516	9,889
1975	7,749	4,653	3,114	13,009
1976	7,203	1,900	5,303	18,306
1977	9,500	1,921	7,579	26,249
1978	10,220	2,017	8,203	34,452
1979	11,141	24,111	−12,970	21,482
1980	12,687	9,958	2,729	24,311
1981	29,231	15,703	13,528	37,739
1982	22,358	12,563	9,795	47,534
1983	91,219	81,720	9,499	57,033
1984	68,726	24,822	43,904	100,937
1985	82,550	40,128	42,422	143.359
1986	85,948	40,517	45,431	188,790
1987	83,839	180,305	−96,446	92,324
1988	79,091	38,097	40,994	133,318
1989	73,174	55,566	17,608	148,926
1990	69,478	57,681	11,797	160,723
1991	34,754	28,867	5,887	166,610

Source: *Financial Statements, 1955–91.*

in former NATSOPA Branches was much higher relative to the former SOGAT (75) Branches. In the London Machine Branch, the RIRMA Branch and the London CA and EP more than 95 per cent of members contributed to the Political Fund.

Throughout the 1980s the number of SOGAT members paying the Political Fund contribution declined as follows:

1984	121,175	(63 per cent of working membership)
1986	112,404	(63 per cent of working membership)
1988	100,110	(65 per cent of working membership)
1990	87,267	(65 per cent of working membership)
1991	82,731	(67 per cent of working membership)

At the time of SOGAT's merger with the NGA, there were only five branches that did not have a single member paying the political levy whilst there were eight branches with 100 per cent contributors. However, a wide variation continued to exist between branches as the following examples illustrate:

London Machine Branch	100 per cent
Multi-Trades Branch	87 per cent
Yorkshire Ridings Branch	59 per cent
LCB/GLB	55 per cent
PMB	48 per cent
ATAES	36 per cent

SOGAT was a supporter of the Labour Party campaign for Political Fund contributors to become individual members of the Labour Party at a reduced membership fee. Appropriate application forms and accompanying literature were supplied to branches in January 1989 but the response to the initiative was disappointing. By October 1989, only 147 Political Fund payers had become Party members. In April 1990 the number had reached 460. The Political Executive was concerned about those branches which appeared to be making little effort to encourage members to pay into the Political Fund and stressed that a well-funded and effective Labour Party was an integral part of the labour movement and essential if SOGAT were to protect and advance the industrial interests of its members.

SOGAT supported the Labour Party proposal that rather than having an affiliation fee and then appealing separately to unions for

425

General Election Funds there should be a basic affiliation fee plus an additional element in respect of a General Election Fund. This meant contributions per member increased from 75p in 1988 to £1.45 in 1991. However, these proposals posed the union the difficulty of meeting this restructured affiliation fee to the Party. To overcome this the Political Executive successfully recommended to the 1990 Delegate Council that the weekly subscription to the Political Fund be increased from 4p to 5p with an annual increase of 1p thereafter.

The Trade Union Act (1984) required trade unions to ballot their members at least once every ten years to see whether they wished to retain a Political Fund. In 1985, SOGAT began this process by launching a campaign entitled 'Keep Your Voice in Parliament'. A number of arguments were used. First, the campaign stressed the different legal treatment between companies and trade unions with regard to spending money on political purposes. Employers could and did spend money freely on political purposes to safeguard their interests. They were not required to consult their shareholders or customers. Trade unions, in contrast, had to establish, by ballot, a separate Political Fund for the purpose and individual members could contract out of paying into the Political Fund. Second, the Political Fund had been set up because experience had taught trade unions it was in their interests to secure a voice, and representation, in Parliament. Workplace conditions were influenced by Parliament's decisions concerning the rate of inflation, unemployment, health and safety and sex discrimination laws, the provision of health care, education and pensions. SOGAT had played an important part in gaining improvements and greater rights for working people and had found it necessary to pressure governments through direct negotiations and/or by Parliamentary representation.

Third, by voting to retain the Political Fund, two conflicting sets of individual rights could be reconciled. If there was a vote to retain the Fund then those who wanted to contribute could do so. At the same time, individuals could, if they so wished, still retain the right to contract out of paying the political levy. On the other hand, if the vote was against retaining the Political Fund then only the rights of those who did not wish to contribute would be protected, since those who wished to contribute to the Fund would be denied the chance of doing so. No member would be compelled to pay the political level and the ballot was not about paying the political levy but about the union being able to express a view on behalf of its members. If the union had no Political Fund it would be unlawful in the future to run campaigns like 'Save

Our Industry', which had resulted in considerable financial assistance from the Government to the papermaking industry and thereby protected the jobs of many paperworker members. For the union to campaign against the imposition of VAT on books, magazines and newspapers, which could cause the loss of 20,000 jobs, would become illegal if the union lost its Political Fund. These 'political representations' were about industrial issues but could only be achieved by political activity either inside or outside Parliament.[8]

A fourth argument used in the campaign was it could not be good for democracy if trade unions, which represented over 11m people plus their families, were denied a voice in Parliament. Political issues were often industrial issues, particularly employment law. It would be the height of hypocrisy if employers could have representatives in Parliament but trade unions could not. SOGAT believed for trade unions to be the only organisations that could not promote their own interests in Parliament would be not only inequitable but would be the equivalent of trade unions taking a vow of silence whilst all other organisations were pushing sectional interests.

SOGAT was the first union to ballot on the retention of a Political Fund. This was a deliberate decision of its General Secretary, Bill Keys, who chaired the Trade Union Co-ordinating Committee established to oversee for all unions their Political Fund campaigns and to secure 'yes' votes for a retention of the Funds. Bill Keys felt it essential for his credibility and for that of the Co-ordinating Committee that if they were to have influence on other unions' campaigns then he must deliver a retention vote first of all in SOGAT. The ballot result announced on 7 May 1985 was a landslide 'yes' vote in favour of retention of the Political Fund. There were 91,760 votes to retain the Fund whilst 25,947 voted against – a majority of more than three to one in a turn-out of 57 per cent. The result reflected many SOGAT members' resentment at outside attempts to interfere with their right to maintain a Political Fund.

The SOGAT result was a tremendous impetus to other unions and not one Political Fund retention ballot was lost. All produced large majorities in favour of retention. SOGAT's campaign was seen by the Trade Union Co-ordinating Committee as a 'model for all' to follow. It had involved great personal effort and planning. SOGAT had carefully explained the issues to its members in its campaign literature. They understood the importance of the decision they were being asked to take and were keenly aware of the need to keep their political and Parliamentary voice.

REPRESENTATION IN PARLIAMENT

House of Commons

The NUPB&PW, SOGAT (Division A) and SOGAT did not sponsor Parliamentary candidates. Attempts at Delegate Council meetings to have sponsored candidates were always defeated, but the SOGAT 1976 Delegate Council voted to sponsor candidates for Parliament. Delegates accepted that the union should exert more pressure in the political arena in defending the industrial interests of its members by sponsoring up to three candidates for Parliament. Moving the proposition, the General Secretary, Bill Keys, said the union's rules already allowed for sponsored candidates but use had not been made of the provision. However in the 'Save Our Industry' campaign for the papermaking industry, it had become clear that there was little point having Political Objective Rules if the union did not have the means to pursue these objectives. If SOGAT candidates were selected, the union was prepared to pay a proportion of the individual's election expenses and make a contribution of £350–£450 towards the salary of the secretary/agent in the constituency depending whether it was a country or urban area.

The 1978 Delegate Council approved the conditions for the sponsoring of Parliamentary candidates. The BDC was given the ultimate authority on the number of candidates who could submit themselves for nomination as sponsored candidates. However, the Political Executive was given power to adopt in any constituency a candidate who was not a member of the union but who, in the view of the Political Executive, would follow the aims of SOGAT. This decision to sponsor non-members stemmed from the union's experiences of its political campaign to save the papermaking industry. SOGAT had convinced many MPs to accept its case and advocate it in Parliament, but the union believed it would have been even more effective if it had sponsored MPs in the House. There were Labour MPs with papermills in their constituencies who gave much assistance in the papermaking industry campaign. They were not SOGAT members but clearly had SOGAT's interests at heart. The Delegate Council also approved that sponsored candidates be subject to review periodically as to whether they were still committed to SOGAT's aims and policies. The Parliamentary candidates were known as the Parliamentary Panel. Although the Political Executive recommended to the BDC that whether or not the Parliamentary candidates, or any of them that were members of the Parliamentary Panel preceding a General Election, be retained upon the panel, the final decision in this regard rested with the BDC. The union wanted to protect itself from the situation of agreeing to a certain individual representing SOGAT as a sponsored candidate and then finding later that their attitude and general credentials had changed so much since their adoption that they could no longer represent effectively the industrial interests of SOGAT members in Parliament. The motivation for this procedure had come from the behaviour of Mr Reg Prentice, a former Labour Government Cabinet Minister and T&GWU sponsored who, in 1976 whilst an elected Labour member for the Newham North East constituency, crossed the floor of the House and became a member of the Conservative opposition.

Sponsored candidates agreed to stand only as Labour Party candidates. The Political Executive selected the candidate from the Parliamentary Panel and then the constituency for which they were to be nominated. It had the power to remove any person from the Panel and there was no appeal against such a decision. However, if a candidate were removed from the Panel then the Political Executive had to seek approval for their action from the BDC. Members of the Parliamentary Panel elected to the House of Commons attended the BDC where they presented a report on their Parliamentary activities. Any member or non-member elected to Parliament as a SOGAT representative and who had been adopted by the Political Executive and then lost their seat at a subsequent General Election and could not find employment, received a grant from the Political Fund until they gained employment again. However, this was not to be an open-ended commitment in terms of time. Sponsored SOGAT MPs received out-of-pocket expenses at the discretion of the Political Executive and the 1976 Delegate Council accepted that provision should exist for SOGAT to give a maintenance allowance to each MP in the House that it sponsored.

On 27 September 1979 Bob Litherland became SOGAT's first MP when he won the Manchester Central by-election with 5.9 per cent swing in his favour. He was a bookbinder by trade and had worked for the Manchester Print Group, previously known as Hird, Hoyle and Sight, for 26 years. He had been a Manchester City councillor for eight years. He worked consistently in the House of Commons to ensure SOGAT's views were heard and tabled numerous questions, forwarded to him by the union on various subjects such as health and safety, mill closures and redundancy. SOGAT (82) had two sponsored MPs since NATSOPA had sponsored Ron Leighton, Labour member for Newham North East since 1979 and who was a member of the London Machine Branch of NATSOPA. He had worked at the Amalgamated Press, the *Reveille* and the *Daily Mirror*. From 1951 to 1979 he worked in the machine room of the *News of the World*. He had been a chapel committee member at the *Sun*, *Reveille* and the *News of the World*, a Governing Council delegate for many years and chairman of Standing Orders of the NATSOPA Governing Council. In the House of Commons, Ron Leighton specialised in industrial relations and trade union affairs. His expertise was recognised by fellow MPs who, in 1983, made him Chairman of the All Party Select Committee on Employment which monitored the work of the Department of Employment. He worked continuously to ensure the interests of NATSOPA and then SOGAT (82) members were represented effectively in the House of Commons. In 1982, during a speech by a Tory Employment Secretary on the closed shop in the printing industry, Ron Leighton intervened 17 times, setting a record for the number of interventions by a Member of Parliament.

In 1990, the Political Committee agreed that should Gerry Sutcliffe, Assistant Secretary of SOGAT's Bradford Branch, be selected as a Parliamentary candidate then he would receive union sponsorship. However, he failed to make selection for a Parliamentary seat. SOGAT also gave support to members who were selected as Parliamentary candidates but were not seeking union sponsorship. However, none of these were successful in being elected. In 1988 Bob Gillespie, a national officer of SOGAT, was selected as the Labour Party candidate in a by-election in the safe Labour seat of Govan in Glasgow. However, despite being a hardworking candidate who struck a chord with local people, and despite fighting a vigorous campaign, he was defeated by Jim Sillars, the Scottish National Party candidate, whose victory was a massive protest against Mrs Thatcher's Conservative government and a backlash against Labour, who were seen as incapable of defeating her.[9]

The European Parliament

Following the passing of the Single European Market Act (1987), designed to introduce from 1 January 1993 freedom of movement between the 12 member states of the European Communities for both labour and capital, SOGAT saw the need for a voice in the European Parliament. To this end, the 1990 Delegate Council empowered the

NEC to sponsor a European MP in accordance with the Political Fund Rules. To give effect to this decision the NEC approached Barry Seal who had been nominated by its Bradford Branch and Gary Titley who had been nominated by CMS, Central Lancashire, Greater Manchester and Manchester Central Branches. Both candidates were accepted as SOGAT-sponsored European MPs. From 1990 to the creation of the GPMU both kept SOGAT informed of developments in the European Community that were of interest to the union and its members.

THE LABOUR PARTY

Annual Conference

The NUPB&PW, SOGAT (Division A) and SOGAT always sent their full delegation to the annual conference but never proposed a motion at any Labour Party Conference between 1955 and 1975. However, the delegation, via the General Secretary, contributed to Conference debates. For example, at the 1960 Conference the NUPB&PW's General Secretary spoke against a resolution calling for a policy of unilateral nuclear disarmament. He argued in favour of the implementation of the Labour Party–TUC statement on defence which backed continued membership of NATO.

SOGAT(75) sent 7 delegates to the Party Conference. They voted on the basis of National Executive Council and BDC policy. Only if the Conference debated an issue on which SOGAT had no policy was the union's policy decided by a majority vote of the members of the delegation. This was also the case with SOGAT (82). At the 1979 conference, SOGAT successfully moved a composite motion condemning the lack of diversity, access and balance in the private newspaper industry. In the following year, the union successfully moved a motion expressing opposition to any defence policy based on the use of or threat of use of nuclear weapons. However, the delegations did on occasions contribute to debates on incomes policy, employment law and the Common Market.

SOGAT (82) sent 14 delegates to the Party Conference. It was active in the business of the Conference in terms of moving and seconding motions, contributing to debates and asking questions on the NEC Report. In 1982 SOGAT spoke in favour of a motion which expressed total opposition to the Tory Government's anti-trade union legislation. In 1983 the union successfully moved a motion on public ownership as a means of bringing future prosperity to the British people. SOGAT's higher profile was not intended to associate the union more openly with wider issues facing the Labour Party as it had a good reputation in this regard, but to influence directly Labour Party policy-making bodies on issues such as the repeal of the Conservative Government's anti-trade union legislation. SOGAT's delegation played a role in the Labour Party Conference over the period 1982 to 1990 out of proportion to its size.

National Executive Committee

SOGAT sought, unsuccessfully, to have its President, Albert Powell, elected via the Trade Union Section to the Labour Party National Executive Committee. His vote varied from a low of 91,000 in 1978 to a high of 1,114,000 in 1974. SOGAT in 1985 succeeded in having one of its national officials elected to the Labour Party's NEC when Ted O'Brien received 3.6m votes in the Trade Union Section ballot. This was the first time in the history of SOGAT and its constituent unions that direct representation on the NEC had been achieved. It was a remarkable event in that SOGAT, although large in printing trade union terms, was relatively small in relation to the large general and white-collar unions.

In subsequent years, Ted O'Brien was re-elected to the Labour Party NEC and he played an active role on numerous NEC sub-committees and in the Policy Review Groups. Whilst SOGAT was responsible for his nomination to the NEC, he was not a representative of SOGAT on that body. His election required the support of other unions and the constituents to whom he was accountable as a member of the NEC were all unions affiliated to the Labour Party. Ted O'Brien had to remind delegates to the 1988 Delegate Council of this constitutional situation when the London CA and EP Branch moved a motion noting that the union's representative on the Labour Party NEC had voted for the closure of *Labour Weekly* and urging that SOGAT adopt a policy of re-opening *Labour Weekly*. In opposing the motion on behalf of the NEC, Teddie O'Brien, *inter alia*, told delegates:

> There is a side swipe in the motion about how I voted on the NEC. I do not approve of that at all. When you have the honour to be nominated by the SOGAT union to be a nominee to the Executive there is a reliance on the support of all other

union voting in the particular section, therefore, the responsibility of an NEC member is much wider than actually sitting on the Executive; just as we hope that the National Executive that we elect speaks for the national union rather than the parochial branch aspects.[10]

Constitutional Reforms

The late 1970s saw the development of pressures for greater democracy within the Labour Party centring around the reselection of Labour MPs, the election of the leader and deputy leader of the Party and the issue of the NEC, not the Parliamentary Labour Party, having control of the Party's General Election Manifesto. At the 1980 Labour Party Conference, SOGAT voted for the compulsory reselection of MPs, an extension of the franchise for the election of the Leader and Deputy Leader and for the re-establishment of a three-year rule with respect to changes to the Party's constitution. The SOGAT delegation voted against the National Executive having sole control of the General Election manifesto and for the adoption of an electoral college for electing the Leader and the Deputy Leader of the Party. In January 1981 a special Labour Party Conference met at Wembley to consider the mechanics of an electoral college for electing the Leader and the Deputy Leader. The delegation eventually supported the formula proposed by USDAW under which the trade unions would have 40 per cent of the votes and the constituencies and the Parliamentary Labour Party 30 per cent each.

In 1981 there was a Deputy Leader election contest between Mr Tony Benn and Mr Dennis Healey, the existing Deputy Leader, which was won narrowly by the latter. The SOGAT delegation voted for Tony Benn but the 1982 Delegate Council delivered a rap over the knuckles to the NEC for the way in which it had backed Tony Benn. Delegates refused in a close vote of 165 against to 157 in favour to 'endorse the decision of the NEC to nominate Tony Benn for the position of Deputy Leader of the Labour Party'.[11] However, the meeting did approve the report of the Political Executive which reported its support for Tony Benn. The Council was dissatisfied with the procedure adopted in deciding to support Tony Benn rather than the principle. In defending their action, the NEC said they had taken into account the policy decisions of the union. Second, they argued Tony Benn had consistently advocated greater democracy in the Labour

Party and this was fully in line with SOGAT policies. Third, Benn was seen as a person making the right statements and meaning what he said. Fourth, the NEC pointed out that Tony Benn had supported every one of SOGAT's policies, for example import controls, withdrawal from the Common Market, the abolition of the House of Lords and opposition to incomes policy. Dennis Healey, on the other hand, opposed nearly all of SOGAT's policies. Finally, the NEC argued that the union would have stood on its head if it had supported Healey who opposed SOGAT's declared policies. They had taken a principled stand and supported the individual best able to articulate the union's ideas. Those opposing the NEC action argued that the decision to support Benn had been made without any consultation with membership or the branches. The members expected to have a say in the election and were disappointed that they did not. The NEC was accused of having backed Benn before the runners had even been nominated for the race and the NEC was told it should have waited until all the candidates were known before making a declaration of support.

Michael Foot resigned as the Leader of the Labour Party following the 1983 General Election defeat. In the ensuing leadership ballot at the 1983 Annual Conference, SOGAT voted for Neil Kinnock as Labour Party Leader and for Roy Hattersley as Deputy Leader. This action was taken after consultation with branches which had used a number of different methods to solicit the membership's wishes, for example a ballot, a meeting of interested members, writing to chapels and writing to members. Thirty-six branches covering 72,716 members expressed their views. Of these, 97 per cent favoured Neil Kinnock for Leader and 54 per cent Hattersley for Deputy Leader.[12] Following Labour's defeat in the 1987 General Election the Kinnock–Hattersley leadership was challenged by Tony Benn (for leadership) and Eric Heffer (for Deputy Leader). Following consultation with the Political Fund paying members, SOGAT backed the successful re-election of Kinnock as Leader and Hattersley as his Deputy at the 1987 Annual Conference. In 1988 John Prescott challenged Roy Hattersley for the Deputy Leadership of the Party but SOGAT, again after consulting the membership, supported the successful re-election of Roy Hattersley.

Following its defeat at the 1987 General Election, the Labour Party undertook a major review of its policies. In 1990, the Party published the results of its Policy Review which had covered seven areas:

(i) *Competing For Prosperity*, report on a productive and competitive economy
(ii) *A Talent-based Economy*, report on people at work
(iii) *A Fairer Community*, report on economic equity
(iv) *A Commitment to Excellence*, report on consumers and the community
(v) *A Modern Democracy*, report on democracy for the individual and the community
(vi) *A Better Quality of Life*, report on the physical and social environment
(vii) *A Power For Good*, report on Britain and the World

The SOGAT Political Executive and subsequently its National Executive Council considered in depth the proposals contained in each Policy Review Paper. It concluded that the Policy Review gathered together, in a detailed manner, the range of policy views covering British society and reflected that a Labour government would be a caring, compassionate and responsive government to the needs of the ordinary people in British society. Apart from the report *A Power For Good*, the NEC agreed that all be supported by the SOGAT delegation to the 1990 Party Conference. The report *A Power For Good* proposed changing Labour Party's policy from a unilateral to multilateral stance. This was contrary to SOGAT's policy of unilateralism and therefore the NEC told the union's delegation to the 1990 Conference to oppose this section of the Policy Review. SOGAT supported the Policy Review as an all-embracing statement on what democratic socialism should mean in Britain and as providing a basis upon which the Labour Party could improve its credibility with the electorate.[13]

In 1987, the Labour Party Conference, as part of moving eventually to decision-making on the basis of one member one vote, agreed that the future selection of Parliamentary candidates be by an electoral college in which the trade union constituency would have 40 per cent of the votes. The trade unions would consult members directly as to the candidate(s) for which these 40 per cent of votes should be cast. SOGAT supported this principle of an electoral college for the purpose of selecting Parliamentary candidates and the principle of one member one vote. The Labour Party also advocated reform of the trade union 'block vote' at the Annual Conference. The trade unions had 90 per cent of the votes at this Conference and cast them on occasions as a 'block' one way or the other and not in proportion to the support for or against the issue amongst their members. Some argued the 'block voting system' was an electoral liability to the Party and should be replaced immediately by one member one vote. SOGAT supported the need for a balance of interests between those of affiliated trade unions and those of individual members. It accepted that the proportion of votes controlled by the trade unions at Conference be reduced to 70 per cent but any further reduction be in relation to increases in individual membership. To this end, SOGAT supported the Party's mass membership campaign and agreed to persuade Political Fund paying members to become individual members of the Party. However, SOGAT had little success in persuading Political Fund payers to become individual Labour Party members.

ATTITUDES TOWARDS MAJOR POLITICAL ISSUES

Disarmament

In 1958, the NUPB&PW Delegate Council approved an Edinburgh Branch motion denouncing the government's agreement to allow American rocket bases and the carrying of 'H' bombs by the American air force. The motion instructed the NEC to protest, via the TUC, to the Government and ask for summit talks to bring peace. The mover argued that while some delegates might feel that the motion would not help the situation, it was vital to keep the issue in the public eye and bring pressure to bear on the government, since to use the nuclear deterrent meant genocide. Some delegates argued that the nuclear issue was the most important issue debated at the Delegate Council as everything discussed 'will come to nothing if we do not do something about the bomb'. The 1960 Delegate Council accepted an emergency motion from the Bolton Branch urging the TUC to demand the withdrawal of all American bases and troops from Britain. In making this decision the BDC was influenced by the shooting down of an American 'U2' spy plane over Russia.

The PMB proposed successfully to the 1962 Delegate Council the trade union movement to support the unilateralist view at TUC and Labour Party Conferences. The mover argued that although the bomb was supposedly a weapon of defence, history showed whenever nations acquired weapons because others had them eventually the weapons were used. The NEC opposed the motion, drawing parallels with the 1930s when, it was claimed, pro-disarmament demonstrations had almost led the nation into slavery. The NEC argued that if a Labour Government were elected then it should hold a referendum on the nuclear deterrent. Comparisons with the 1930s were rejected since the logic was that every nation should have the bomb. War between the major powers, the supporters of the motion argued, would end humanity. It was claimed that somebody had to make a start and renounce nuclear weapons. A proposition, at the same Council, from the Ruling, Manufacturing and Boxmaking Branch, condemning nuclear tests and calling on the Government and the Labour Party to renounce the use of nuclear weapons and to take disarmament initiatives, was carried unanimously.

The NUPB&PWs unilateralist policy was reaffirmed by the 1964 BDC. It welcomed the Test BAN Treaty signed by the US, USSR and Britain the previous year as a first step towards disarmament. The British government was urged to renounce nuclear weapons and bases in Britain to strengthening its ability to oppose the spread of weapons to the other nations. It was also suggested the British Government submit a disarmament plan to reconcile East–West differences, work for a European treaty to replace NATO and the Warsaw Pact and to create a nuclear-free zone.

From the mid-1960s until the end of the 1970s, the nuclear disarmament debate virtually disappeared from the agenda of SOGAT Delegate Council Meetings.[14] The USA and the USSR signed a Strategic Arms Limitation Treaty (SALT) in 1972 and followed this with a second treaty in 1979. However, the coming to power of Mrs Thatcher in the UK and Ronald Reagan as the President of the USA was seen by some as creating a potentially dangerous period in international relations. Both had always displayed a bellicose manner towards the Soviet Union. Nevertheless, the 1980 BDC carried a Scottish Graphical Division motion welcoming SALT II as an important contribution to world peace and calling for the strengthening of links with Soviet trade unions so that SOGAT could play its part in promoting peace and *détente*. In addition, the 1980 Delegate Council called on a future Labour government to pursue an independent socialist foreign policy entailing the removal of all nuclear weapons from Britain and Europe, the phasing out of Polaris with no replacement by Trident, cutting arms expenditure by half, converting arms production to 'socially useful products' and scrapping NATO and the Warsaw Pact. In the early 1980s SOGAT maintained its opposition to the new missile systems (Cruise and Trident) which it was estimated would introduce 2,000 new nuclear weapons to Britain. SOGAT also opposed the massive and qualitative escalation of the 'arms race inherent in' Star Wars.

At the 1988 BDC, the ATAES Branch argued that the Labour Party should give a commitment in the election manifesto to hold a national referendum on the question of unilateral nuclear disarmament once they came to power. Labour had lost the last three General Elections and, it was argued, probably the Party's biggest single handicap was defence policy. The mover stated the branch's proposal was not a renunciation of unilateralism, but a recognition of its unpopularity with the electorate. The opposition to the motion claimed that problems experienced during the election campaign due to the bias of the mass media would be repeated in the event of a referendum. The NEC opposed a referendum, arguing that the Labour Party should put unilateralism in the manifesto and fight to win. The ATAES motion was lost and the Conference went on to re-affirm SOGAT's non-nuclear policy.

At the 1990 BDC an NEC motion, seconded by the Surrey and Sussex Branch, sought to jettison the union's policy unilateral nuclear disarmament. It 'welcomed Labour's Defence Policy Review as the best way of defending Britain, and the surest road to achieve the greatest possible international peace and disarmament'.[15] The motion welcomed the progress made by the superpowers, in particular the Intermediate Nuclear Force (INF) agreement and advocated that a Labour government put 'British nuclear weapons into the disarmament talks' and work for the creation of a nuclear-free Europe. The NEC position was counterpoised by a West of Scotland and Scottish Graphical Branch motion, seconded by Greater Anglia, which declared that Conference:

'reaffirms all existing SOGAT policies on nuclear disarmament ... (and) its total commitment to Unilateral Nuclear Disarmament ... recognises that the Labour Party Policy Review is fundamentally flawed and will be exposed as contradictory in the run-up to the next General Election.[16]

The motion called on conference to reaffirm the need for Britain to end its dependency upon nuclear weapons, to remove all US weapons, to use the money saved for socially useful and employment-creating policies and to congratulate those trade unions which had stood by their principles on the issue.

In moving the NEC motion, General Secretary Brenda Dean acknowledged the issue of nuclear weapons had been a major and sometimes emotive debate within the labour movement since the war. The background was that after three election defeats, the Labour Party had embarked upon a review of policy but, at SOGAT conferences, there had been no in-depth detailed discussion of nuclear weapons since 1982. She stressed that none of the policies the trade union movement desired could be enacted unless Labour was elected and that unilateralist defence was a major factor in why people had not voted for Labour in the last election. The Party was now proposing international negotiations to remove nuclear weapons, cancel the fourth Trident submarine and adopt a 'no first' policy.

The unilateralists reminded delegates it had been SOGATs General Secretary who had convinced the 1982 Labour Party Conference that unilateralism should be in the election manifesto. The 1983 election, they claimed, had been lost for many reasons other than defence policy, e.g. internal divisions, an interim Party Leader, post-Falklands patriotic fervour, whilst the Labour Party leadership had never put the unilateralist policy to the electorate during the 1987 campaign. Supporters of the NEC's position pointed out that polls and doorstep canvassing showed unilateralism was an election-loser amongst the public as well as the SOGAT membership. The number one priority had to be the election of a Labour Government for, until this happened, everything else SOGAT wanted to see was 'way down the line'. The world situation had changed, with the prospects for international disarmament transformed by the new situation in Eastern Europe. The only way Britain could influence events was by actively participating in the disarmament talks. The unilateralists were accused of remaining with policies which failed to come to terms with these new circumstances.

Those supporting the unilateralist position argued they could not be expected to accept something simply because it was contained in Labour's Policy Review, and neither should the union be asked to perform a policy somersault. Delegates were reminded that the 1979 election had been lost on a multilateralist policy, and the Party's credibility with the electorate would diminish if they were perceived to be completely changing their position. The British 'independent initiatives' promised in the Policy Review report would be constrained by the need to abide by NATO policy, whilst the retention of Trident represented an escalation of the arms race. The argument advanced in support of the NEC's stance was not that it would give better defence but that it would be attractive to the electorate, but opponents said if that was the sole criterion then the Party should support the anti-union laws or anything else that appealed to the floating voters. When the vote was taken, the NECs motion was carried by 173 votes to 122.

Public Ownership

The NUPB&PW was a strong supporter of public ownership and the 1960 Delegate Council re-affirmed its long standing belief in nationalisation. It regarded a public ownership ideology as essential for a trade union committed to the introduction of socialism. It became concerned in the early 1960s when sections of the Labour Party began to discuss openly the possibility of dropping from its constitution Clause 4 which committed the Party to the common ownership of the means of production. The 1962 Delegate Council re-affirmed the union's belief in socialist principles and deplored attempts to renegotiate with the TUC and the Labour Party the socialist concept of public ownership as contained in Clause 4 of the Party constitution. The following Delegate Council also re-affirmed the union's belief in the principle of public ownership to protect national and economic interests threatened by monopoly. Twelve years later the 1976 Delegate Council confirmed SOGAT's belief that Clause 4 was the bedrock of the union's faith in socialist aims and called for the expulsion from the Labour Party of all factions refusing to accept Clause 4 or anyone working or speaking against its principles.

Vietnam war

The 1966 SOGAT (Division A) Conference opposed USA foreign policy in Vietnam claiming the ever increasing build-up of its military forces in that country was a danger to world peace. Delegates considered that only on the basis of the 1954 Geneva Agreement, to which the British Government was a signatory, could peace be restored in Vietnam. Concern was expressed that the British Government's support of US intervention in Vietnam contravened its obligations under the Geneva Agreement. SOGAT (Division A) repeatedly called, without success, upon the British Government to disassociate itself from USA military policies in Vietnam. The 1968 Delegate Council unequivocally re-affirmed the SOGAT (Division A) policy towards the Vietnam war. SOGAT always remained unconvinced by the British government's argument that its objective, along with that of the USA Government, was to have the fighting stopped, have negotiations started, reach a settlement allowing the people of South Vietnam to live in peace and under a government of their own choice, but the North Vietnamese were unwilling to de-escalate the war.[17] SOGAT retained this policy until the end of the Vietnam war in 1975.

Racism

Immigration and Race Relations

The NUPB&PW had a long tradition of opposing racism and fascism. Many of its members had been active in the printers' anti-fascist movement in the 1930s both in combating Mosely's British Union of Fascists and as participants in the Spanish Civil War. The 1960 NUPB&PW Delegate Council viewed with alarm the resurgence of Nazism and racial hatred in Germany. General President, John McKenzie, condemned the oppression of the black majority in South Africa and the British government's mildly reproachful attitude to events in that country. The 1962 Delegate Council debated immigration into Britain. The NEC was instructed to move a resolution at the next Labour Party and TUC conferences calling for the compulsory medical examination of all immigrants into the UK to protect the National Health Service from having to deal with infectious diseases brought into the country. However, a second unsuccessful motion on immigration moved by the PMB provoked a heated debate.

The PMB wanted action on two fronts. First, all immigrants should serve a qualifying period of 12 months' residence in Britain before having access to social security benefits. Second, unless there was a reciprocal agreement all foreign visitors should be charged for any medical attention received. The mover stated that what small progress had been made in Britain towards socialism was the result of bitter struggle. Capitalists wanted to use immigrants to lower wages, but if those wishing to come to Britain knew they would have to stand on their own feet for 12 months, only those with a sense of responsibility would emigrate. As for visitors paying for medical treatment, the PMB said this would only apply to those who could afford it and not to ordinary working people. Opponents argued that the motion was not based on socialist principles and British capitalism had a record of subjugating colonial people.

The 1966 SOGAT (Division A) Delegate Council expressed alarm at increased racial propaganda and described the Labour government's *White Paper on Commonwealth Immigration* as discriminating against Commonwealth citizens. The government's proposals were a major concession to racist ideas and a spur to racism. Supporters of this view argued that immigration levels were determined primarily by job prospects and that without any controls the numbers coming into Britain halved between 1954 and 1958/59 as unemployment rose. People did not go to other countries to be unemployed. Current policy, it was argued, amounted to a colour bar, since only 8,500 vouchers had been issued to Commonwealth immigrants on the basis that there was a shortage of jobs, houses and social services yet five times that number of white 'aliens' had been allowed in. Immigrants were overwhelmingly young people looking for work and legislation was necessary to prevent discrimination in housing and employment. It was seen as the duty of trade unionists to be supportive of 'our coloured brothers' and to revive the international spirit of solidarity which had been lacking for some years in the trade union and labour movement.

In December 1972, SOGAT's National Organiser, Bill Miles, writing in the *SOGAT Journal*, drew attention to a Department of Employment report on race relations at work. Whilst the report found most employees had good relations with black fellow workers, it criticised the unions for responding only to pressing problems and for hoping these could be dealt with by the existing machinery. SOGAT considered these criticisms had to be seen within the context of the pressures union leaders were under to support many different causes and that discrimination suffered by the whole working class could not be split into separate fragments. London Community Relations Officers commented upon the situation in the national newspaper industry where no black printers or workers, save for a black assistant in the canteen, were to be seen. However, in 1975, Johnny Dar became SOGAT's first black full-time organiser. He was born in India, joined the NUPB&PW in 1957, served as a Father of the Chapel at a Bowater papermill before becoming Chair of the Sittingbourne and Kemsley Branch.

The Fascist Threat

The 1974 SOGAT Delegate Council expressed opposition to all forms of racial discrimination and committed itself to defend all workers against any form of discriminatory practice. The issue of racism had been raised more sharply by the growth of fascist organisations like the National Front, the National Party and the British Movement. SOGAT related the rise in racism to rising unemployment and cuts in housing and education services. It viewed discrimination and prejudice as undermining the unity upon which the trade union movement was founded. The only winners were the employers and those politicians and groups who used racism to divide, divert and weaken the trade union movement. The September 1976 *SOGAT Journal* contained an article written by the General Secretary, Bill Keys,[18] which described fascists as enemies of the working class and opposed to everything for which the labour movement stood. By attacking immigrants the fascists avoided offering concrete solutions to the real problems and by appealing to national interest they undermined the strength and unity of the labour movement.

SOGAT placed a motion on the agenda of the 1976 TUC to alert the movement to the nature of fascist activity and strategy and to initiate a campaign to counter these ideas. All workers were urged to oppose the twin evils of unemployment and bad social conditions which were the product of the capitalist system. The Government was called upon to ban provocative marches and demonstrations designed to inflame racial hatred and intolerance against ethnic minority groups. The TUC was asked to deliver the clear message that the development of fascism would not be tolerated in the UK and the unity of all workers was required to combat it.

At a more practical level, SOGAT actively supported the struggles of racial minorities. This was best seen in the case of the *Daily Jang* which was published in Urdu for Pakistanis in Britain. The newspaper was owned by a Karachi millionaire and, with the exception of the editor, the entire staff joined SOGAT. In the summer of 1976 the work-force occupied the plant in a dispute over working conditions. After 90 days in dispute the SOGAT members emerged with significant concessions from the employer. They were considerably aided by support from other SOGAT members both on the picket line and by means of financial assistance.

An emergency motion from the Solent Branch, supported by the NEC, was carried at the 1978 Delegate Council. It welcomed the setting up of the 'Printers and Media Workers Group Against the Nazis' aimed at uniting all those opposed to fascism irrespective of political differences. SOGAT was asked to support this organisation at every level. The mover pointed to the growing respectability of racist ideas and warned delegates not to underestimate the threat posed by the fascists to socialists, ethnic minorities, Jews, homosexuals or active trade unionists. Delegates were reminded that TUC and Labour Party policy on racism had emerged from a resolution submitted by SOGAT, which regarded racism as a challenge to the very nature of the labour movement. The union was concerned that despite an unprecedented number of attacks on people from ethnic minorities the law had proved inadequate to protect them. Provocative marches had been permitted through areas with large immigrant populations.

At the 1983 Delegate Council a London CA and EP motion called upon the NEC to mount an active campaign against all forms of racist and fascist activity, to affiliate to the Anti-Nazi League and to reiterate that membership of a fascist organisation was contrary to the interests of the union. Reference was made to the defeat of the National Front in the late 1970s and to the corresponding drop in the Anti-Nazi League's profile. However, in areas of deprivation and rising unemployment fascism was re-emerging. The Anti-Nazi League needed to be revived to help remove the dangers of the fascists attracting unemployed youths.

Within SOGAT, there was progress on the racial equality. In 1988 the IPC Magazine chapel appointed an Equality Officer. When new union offices were opened in Sittingbourne, Kent, the local branch decided to name them the John Dar Building and guidelines for the elimination of race discrimination in employment were circulated to all branches. The 1989 BPIF agreement committed the employers and SOGAT to promote actively equal opportunities irrespective of race, religion or gender. Work-place-level management and union chapels were called upon to promote and encourage applications from members of ethnic minorities who were underrepresented in gaining access to skilled jobs. The 1990 Delegate Council gave a strong lead on equal opportunities and positive action. Noting with concern the continuing levels of discrimination practised by employers in all sectors of the printing industry an NEC motion stated:

> Therefore, chapels and branches are directed to translate SOGAT equal opportunities policies and agreements into positive action by ensuring that jobs and training are offered to women as well as men, to black workers as well as white workers.[19]

The motion directed branches and chapels to examine their internal procedures to ensure that no indirect discrimination existed and to use the Equal Opportunities Commission and the Commission on Racial Equality codes of practice, as well as TUC guidelines, to eliminate race discrimination. Employers perpetuated discrimination, the NEC argued, because they profited from it.

NOTES

1. See '*A Serious Situation: Political Fund Running Down*' The Paper Worker, October 1957, pp. 8–10. Only one branch – Kilbagie in Scotland – had 100 per cent of its members contributing into the Political Fund.
2. Op. cit.
3. See the National Union of Printing, Bookbinding and Paperworkers *Report of the Biennial Delegate Council, 1960*, pp. 240–5.
4. See the National Union of Printing, Bookbinding and Paperworkers *Report of the Biennial Delegate Council, 1962*, pp. 199–202.
5. See the National Union of Printing, Bookbinding and Paperworkers *Report of the Biennial Delegate Council, 1964*, p. 167.
6. See Society of Graphical and Allied Trades *Report of the Biennial Delegate Council, 1980*, p. 195.
7. See Society of Graphical and Allied Trades *Report of the Biennial Delegate Council, 1978*, p. 187.
8. See '*The Fundamental Democratic Right to Express a View*' SOGAT Journal, April 1985, pp. 2–3.
9. See '*Inquest Begins into Labour's Shock Defeat at Govan*' SOGAT Journal, December 1988/January 1989, pp. 6–7.
10. See Society of Graphical and Allied Trades (82) *Report of the Biennial Delegate Council, 1988*, p. 158.
11. See Society of Graphical and Allied Trades *Report of the Biennial Delegate Council, 1982*, pp. 195–202.
12. See *Report of the Political Fund Executive Sub-Committee* to the 1984 BDC, p. 405. Eric Heffer and Peter Shore received no support for the leadership in the consultation exercise. Roy Hattersley received 3 per cent support. In the case of Deputy Leader there was almost 100 per cent support it should be Kinnock were he unsuccessful in the leadership contest. To work out the members' second choice as Deputy Leader, votes were excluded from Neil Kinnock and transferred to the other candidates. This gave the following result: Hattersley 54.4 per cent, Michael Meacher 21.3 per cent, Neil Kinnock 3.8 per cent, leave to the delegation 1.3 per cent and no return 19.3 per cent.
13. See *Report of the Political Committee* to the 1990 BDC, p. 2.
14. However, the pages of the *SOGAT Journal* regularly highlighted the burden of expenditure on weapons of war at a time when the British economy was suffering from a lack of investment and severe balance of payment problems.
15. See Society of Graphical and Allied Trades (82) *Report of the Biennial Delegate Council Meeting, 1990*, p. 120.

16. Op. cit., p. 121.
17. See Society of Graphical and Allied Trades (Division A) *Annual Report of the National Executive Council, 1968*, p. 23.
18. See 'Purveyors of Hatred – No Platform for Nazis' *SOGAT Journal*, September 1976, pp. 2–4.
19. See Society of Graphical and Allied Trades (82) *Report of the Biennial Delegate Council Meeting, 1990*, p. 84.

PART IV

RELATIONS WITH
EMPLOYERS

CHAPTER 15

THE GENERAL PRINTING TRADE AND PROVINCIAL NEWSPAPER EMPLOYERS: (1) WAGES AND HOURS MOVEMENTS, 1955–91

The main employers' organisation in the general printing trade in the UK was the British Printing Industries Federation (BPIF), known until 1974 as the British Federation of Master Printers (BFMP), which had been formed in 1901. Up to, and including, the 1980 wage negotiations, the Master Printers negotiated with the print unions jointly with the Newspaper Society (NS), formed in 1920 to represent the interests of firms engaged in the production of provincial daily and weekly (including London suburban) newspapers. The majority of NUPB&PW and subsequently SOGAT members were employed in the general printing industry and worked under the BPIF/BFMP agreements.

THE JOINT INDUSTRIAL COUNCIL

From 1919 to 1966, there was a Joint Industrial Council for the Printing Industry, consisting of BFMP and NS representatives and representatives from unions affiliated to the P&KTF. The Council had no authority to negotiate wage agreements but did operate conciliation machinery for dealing with industrial disputes and had an Apprenticeship Panel to regulate apprentice matters and a Health Committee.

Following the 1959 dispute the Council almost collapsed although good work continued to be done at local level. Both sides agreed there was justification for revising the constitution of the Council and the passage of time meant it was no longer necessary to retain certain objects because they had long been achieved by mutual co-operation or rendered obsolete by government legislation. In January 1960, the employers submitted detailed proposals for a revised constitution. The most important were that the JIC's objective of securing complete organisation of employers and employees throughout the trade be deleted, that the size of the Council be reduced from 80 to 68, that the Council meet annually instead of quarterly, that the JIC should not concern itself with disputes arising as to the meaning, operation, or construction of agreements and that if a dispute of a 'local character' were not settled by a JIC Committee it should be referred to an independent chairperson whose decision would be binding.

The NUPB&PW regarded these proposals as of little value[1] but in June 1960 the unions submitted counter-proposals. They proposed the complete organisation clause remain, the Council meet at least twice a year, disputes arising from claims for revision of national agreements be outside the scope of the JIC and local disputes procedures remain unaltered. The employers accepted the unions' proposals with one important exception. They were not prepared to retain the 'complete organisation' clause. It had been a source of bad feeling for many years because of the unions' support for NATSOPA's attempts to invoke the clause in their desire to organise clerical workers, a purpose the employers' claimed, for which the clause had never been intended.[2]

For the unions more was involved than the organisation of clerical workers, as the aspiration of complete organisation of employers and workers in the industry was a central pillar of the JIC constitution. Its deletion would be a significant departure from the principles on which the JIC had been founded. For the unions, the employers' desire to delete the 'complete organisation' clause reflected a wish to undermine union organisation and possibly introduce an 'open house' policy. The strength of feeling in the NUPB&PW over the issue was such that they preferred to terminate the JIC rather than delete the 'complete organisation' clause. The full JIC referred the deadlock back to the constitutional sub-committee for further consideration.

The deadlock was not broken until January 1962 when both sides accepted the insertion of a footnote to the 'complete organisation' clause to the effect the JIC had no powers to secure organisation of either side of the industry and that the responsibility lay with the parties. In October 1963 the first full meeting of the JIC for three years approved a revised constitution, the main features of which included reducing the number of full JIC meetings to two, the number of standing committees to four and that disputes arising from the revi-

450

sion of agreements be outside the scope of conciliation by the Council. The NUPB&PW's General Secretary, Bill Morrison, was appointed to the General Purposes Committee. In October 1964, after a gap of five years, the JIC Annual Convention was resumed.

However, in April 1966 the JIC dissolved itself because of continuing problems over the operation of the disputes procedures. The dissolution decision was deferred to allow time for arrangements to be made for the establishment of alternative joint machinery to deal with apprentice and health matters. Nevertheless, by mid-1968 SOGAT accepted health and safety measures be dealt with by joint action via the offices of the P&KTF, the BFMP and the Newspaper Society. The Printing and Publishing Industry Training Board absorbed the JIC training responsibilities.

THE 1955–6 NEGOTIATIONS

Towards the end of November 1955 the NUPB&PW acting collectively with NATSOPA, the STA, NSES and MCTF, agreed with the BFMP and the NS weekly increases of 92½p for craftsmen, of 77½p for semi-skilled adult male workers and 60p for women. These revised rates became operative from January 1956. Shortly after their implementation a serious situation developed consequent upon disputes between the LTS and ACP and the London Master Printers' Association and the TA with the BFMP.[3] Although the NUPB&PW was not in dispute with the employers, the London dispute led to unemployment amongst its members, to whom it made special payments. All adult men received £3.50, male juniors £1.75, adult women £2.50 and girls £1.25 per week. These payments were funded by the union obtaining a cash advance from its bankers against the security of its investments. Given these union 'casualties' were confined to the London area, the NUPB&PW issued a financial appeal to its London Branches. The response was good and raised £5,059.10p which proved more than sufficient to finance the 'casualties'.[4] It also meant the union did not have to draw on the facilities offered by its bankers. However, it decided, in order to cover any such future situations, to build up reserves of £200,000.

Following the settlement in May 1956 with the craft unions, the NUPB&PW entered negotiations with the BPMP and the NS. It proved an easy matter to obtain the revised May 1956 craft rates for its craft members in the English provinces, London and Scotland. There was, however, tremendous difficulty in obtaining further increases for its

451

non-craft and women members. The May craft unions had stated, during negotiations with the BFMP and the NS, that the increased craft rate they were asking for would settle wage differential between craft and non-craft workers and any subsequent increases granted to non-craft workers could result in an application for a further increase by the craft unions. With respect to female employees the employers were adamant that the rates agreed in the January 1956 settlement were adequate if not generous. The NUPB&PW, however, was equally determined that its non-craft and female members should have an increase in wages. Although on several occasions the negotiations almost broke down, the NUPB&PW succeed in its objectives and obtained the same increases for these two groups of its members in the general printing and provincial newspaper industry that had been achieved in the May 1956 settlement with the craft unions.

The NUPB&PW craft members, who wanted the benefit of the increased craft rate as soon as possible, loyally supported the union in its policy of refusing to settle for one section of its membership only. During negotiations the Paperworkers' union had been associated with the NSES, MCTS, NATSOPA and the STA. After the BFMP and the NS revised the craft rate the NUPB&PW told the NSES and the MCTS that as they were exclusively craft societies it had no objection to them settling. The STA were in the same position as the NUPB&PW and refused to settle for their craft members until a satisfactory settlement had been reached for their non-craft members. NATSOPA could have notified the employers earlier than the Paperworkers of their members decision to accept but refrained from doing so until the result of the NUPB&PW's ballot on the employers offer was known. NATSOPA had not been prepared to see the NUPB&PW completely isolated if its members had rejected the employers' terms.

THE 1959 DISPUTE

The 1958/9 negotiations saw, for the first time since the end of the Second World War, a united approach by nine print unions, under the auspices of the PKTF, to the BFMP and the NS. The claim was for a 40-hour standard working week, a 10 per cent increase in wages, a reduction in the London/provincial craft differential, the continuation of the cost of living bonus, a three-year stabilisation period, the abolition of the provincial wage Grade 2 and the semi-skilled workers to receive 82.5 per cent of the craft rate, general assistants 85 per cent and women

66.66 per cent. 'Domestic claims' would be the concern of the individual unions. Accordingly the NUPB&PW submitted to the BFMP a series of domestic claims including the jobs of folding machine minders and precision slitting machine operators be upgraded into Class 1, that the Class 4 occupational grade be abolished and all other operations be reclassified into three classes and that machine extras be more realistic to current prices and be increased by the same percentage as basic rates.

The question of the 40-hour working week was a P&KTF–BFMP/NS issue so the claim was put to the employers by the P&KTF General Secretary. After the 1956 dispute the unions had agreed a two-tier wage structure – one for craft and one for non-craft. The craft and non-craft union claims on wages proceeded side by side and not together. However, the Chairman of the craft group – Bill Morrison, General Secretary of the NUPB&PW – was also chairman of the non-craft group so there was one spokesman for the two separate groups of workers. When the negotiations began in December 1958 the employers described the unions' proposals as 'staggering' and suggested that the present agreement, due to terminate in April 1959, continue for a further 12 months or alternatively they were willing for the matter to be submitted to arbitration. The unions rejected both a continuation of the present agreements and the use of arbitration, arguing that an arbitrator would be influenced by the general economic policy of the government which was to prevent any improvements in working conditions, either by way of reduced hours or increased wages.

In view of the attitude of the employers, the unions' in April 1959 placed a ban on excessive overtime working but agreed that firms which from 20 April were prepared to operate a 40-hour week and observe the final settlement on hours and wages be excluded from the dispute. In May as the result of the ballot a series of industrial sanctions were to be introduced to break the deadlock. The measures were to be a ban on overtime, a ban on the extension of shift working, a policy of non-co-operation in the workshop, the withdrawal of participation in incentive schemes and the tendering of strike notices if subsequently considered necessary. Eighty per cent of the votes cast supported this policy of the progressive implementation of sanctions. The actual figures were 108,116 in favour and 25,926 against.[5] Armed with support for a progressive build-up of industrial sanctions, the unions again met the employers who submitted a document containing a tentative list of 22 points or suggestions dealing with labour supply, productivity improvements, new processes and method study. The unions said the document should be withdrawn as it was too revolutionary.

On 21 May the employers offered a reduction of hours from 43½ to 42½, a wage increase of 2.5 per cent, stabilisation and continuation of the cost of living bonus provided the unions accepted practically all the 22 points tabled by the employers at the last meeting. The unions rejected the offer as 'totally inadequate' but at a further meeting conceded that the hours claim might be met by a phased reduction spread over three years and the 10 per cent wage increase be met by granting 5 per cent immediately, a further 2.5 per cent in a year's time and a further 2.5 per cent after that. In return, the unions would discuss efficiency questions. The BFMP and NS, however, insisted any further offer be conditional upon the unions agreeing in advance to the implementation of methods of improved efficiency. Negotiations had reached deadlock and on 3 June 1959 the industrial sanctions authorised in the membership ballot became effective. By 20 June, 120,000 members of the nine unions involved ceased work.

However, in July 1959 informal talks between the unions and the employers under the auspices of the Ministry of Labour considered formulas to bring about a restart of negotiations. The unions pressed for the restart of talks under an independent chairman who might guide and assist the negotiations but who would not have the powers of an arbitrator. The BFMP and the NS desired an independent third party with authority to give decisions on issues on which the two sides could not agree and that both sides must accept any such decision. The talks made little progress, but following further intervention by the Ministry of Labour the two sides agreed to restart negotiations under an independent chairman to be appointed by the Ministry. The independent chair would preside at joint meetings of the parties and help them towards a settlement. The chair would advise, control and guide the discussions to this end. If the parties failed to reach agreement on any points they would submit the recommendations of the independent chairman on the points to their constituents as part of the final settlement for acceptance or refusal by those constituents.

With the support of both sides, Lord Birkett was appointed independent chairman and joint discussions began on 14 July 1959. A week later the BFMP/NS increased their offer on basic rates to 3.5 per cent, that the standard working week be reduced to 42 hours, and stabilisation be for three years and in return the unions accept conditions covering labour demarcation, work study and new processes. The NS made an additional offer of an enhanced payment of 25p per week to employees on provincial morning and evening newspapers who were already working 40 hours or less per week. The revised offer was rejected by the unions in that it had to be 'earned' by acceptance of conditions when they considered the contributions made by the workers in the industry since 1945 were of themselves worthy of reductions in hours and increases in wages. The unions suggested the 40-hour week be introduced gradually but by no later than January 1962. As the negotiations proceeded, well over 120,000 men and women remained on strike. 4,000 firms and almost 1,000 provincial newspaper offices were affected by the stoppage.

The real breakthrough in the dispute came when Lord Birkett put forward four suggestions. First, the two sides should settle between themselves the 'basic requirements' provision for greater productivity. Second, the unions' domestic claims be settled along with the 'basic requirements'. Third, a 42-hour week be fixed for at least two years with provision for a judicial inquiry, binding on both sides, if there was disagreement about any further reductions in hours. Fourth, the basic wage increase be 4.5 per cent stabilised for two years and if there were a claim for further increases at the end of the period, it be referred to the judicial inquiry if there was a failure to agree. On 29 July 1959 the BFMP and the NS accepted this proposed settlement despite considering a 4.5 per cent increase in basic rates as being too high. Despite some initial difficulties, a return to work formula was agreed by both sides on 31 July. Work resumed on 6 August 1959, seven weeks after it had stopped and after considerable financial sacrifice by the members of the unions involved. The return to work formula contained provision for no victimisation and both sides committed themselves to observe it scrupulously.

On 2 September 1959 it was announced that nine of the ten unions in the collective hours and wages movement had accepted the proposed agreement in ballots.[6] There were 108,582 votes cast in favour of acceptance of the agreement and 34,901 against. The NUPB&PW members voted by 50,975 votes to 14,248 (a majority of 36,727) to accept the agreement. The cost of the dispute to the NUPB&PW was some £750,000 which was almost half of the value of its General Fund as at 31 December 1959. One union – the NSES – voted by a majority of 507 against acceptance of the agreement.[7] Under the terms of the settlement the standard working week was reduced to 42-hours, the basic minimum grade rates were increased by 4.5 per cent with agreed 'extras' for readers and keyboard operators, stabilisation for three years, the cost of living bonus continued and all unions made manpower concessions. Although the agreement would run for three years, consideration would be given in 1961 as to whether there was justification for a further reduction of hours and/or an increase in basic wages to operate from the first week in September 1961. If it proved impossible to negotiate a settlement by 30 June 1961 then the application was to be referred to a general inquiry whose decision would be binding on both parties. The form of such an inquiry would be decided by Lord Birkett.

General manpower concessions were made by all unions covering the maximum use of craft skills, increased shift working, the introduction of work study, of new processes and of changes in methods of production, apprentice quotas and the apprenticeship training period. The London Central Branch and the PMB of the NUPB&PW accepted that an apprentices could be indentured up to the age of 16½ if they had remained at school until 16. The London Central Branch also agreed to the introduction of a block of 20 apprentices additional to the normal quota. The London Women's Branch accepted the introduction of extra girl learners to cover any cases of difficulty in supplying demands for labour. The employers agreed to meet with the NUPB&PW to discuss within the next 12 months the classification of certain larger folding machines and a limited list of machines for which the union considered an extra based on skill and responsibility might be paid to women. However, the employers were insistent that the NUPB&PW understand this did not imply they accepted the principle of the payment of extras to women.

The NUPB&PW was not fully satisfied with the outcome of the 1959 strike. It regarded the settlement as an interim one awaiting final settlement in 1961 through a judicial inquiry should the employers again prove difficult. However, the Union had made significant progress in improving the relative position of its women members. The Union's policy had been for many years to obtain 75 per cent of the non-craft male rate for them. During the negotiation other unions had suggested that there was psychological value in securing for women 66.66% of the craft rate. NUPB&PW agreed to this as it would give a higher basic rate to women compared with the male craft rate. Progress had been made in this direction since the beginning of the last war. In London in 1939 the craft rate was £4.45 per week and the women's rate £2.10, 46 per cent of the craft rate. After the 1959 settlement the craft rate in London was £11.50 and the women's rate £6.76, 59 per cent of the craft rate. In the provinces the weekly Grade 1 craft rate in 1939 was £3.87½ and the women's rate £1.60, 44 per cent of the craft rate. Following the 1959 dispute, the respective figures were £10.73 and £6.39, giving women 60 per cent of the craft rate.

SEPTEMBER 1962: THE 40-HOUR WEEK ACHIEVED

In September 1960 the unions and the BFMP and the NS met to reach agreement on the form a judicial inquiry should take if the 1961 negotiations over the balance of the 1959 claims broke down. Both sides preferred a settlement to be reached by direct negotiation but felt it wise to have the judicial inquiry procedure settled so if direct negotiations broke down provision would have been made. Both parties considered it better to decide the form in a rational atmosphere rather than wait until they were in the middle of negotiations when it might be more difficult to reach agreement. Any inquiry would be conducted by one individual and both sides agreed Lord Birkett be invited to undertake the task if necessary.

In December 1960 the ten unions submitted their claim that the balance of the 1959 claims to be granted. In March 1961 the BFMP and NS recommended to their members a further reduction in hours of work and a further increase in wages provided the unions meet them on the labour situation. When pressed for details the employers replied:

> Providing the industry can get the labour it needs we are prepared to negotiate an agreement which will give you, by stages, a 40-hour week and the balance of the 10 per cent wages claim. If you do not do anything on labour we can do nothing.[8]

The unions responded by rejecting staged increases and told the employers they should implement the 40-hour week and the balance of the 10 per cent wage increase in September 1961 subject to mutual agreement on labour requirements. The employers refused but it later emerged they had the following timetable in mind: a 2.75 per cent wage increase be given in September 1961, followed by a further 2.75 per cent increase in September 1962. They also envisaged one hour's reduction in the standard working week in September 1961 with the 40-hour week operative from September 1963. The alternative offer was a 5.5 per cent increase in pay in September 1961, one hour's reduction in September 1962 and the 40-hour week from September 1963. The implementation of either offer was subject to the employers receiving satisfaction from the unions on labour requirements. The unions' response was that a complete settlement be implemented no later than August 1962 and there be a staggering of the reduced working week and wage increases. There should be a 5.5 per cent increase in wages and one hour's reduction in the working week in September 1961. The reduction of a further hour would take place in March 1962. The unions accepted agreement be conditional on there being a mutually agreed settlement on labour which, given that circumstances varied so greatly from union to union, could only be done by individual union discussion with the employers.

The BFMP/NS response was that individual talks on the labour supply should begin immediately with individual unions since the employers' attitude to the staged introduction of both wages and hours adjustments would depend on how this issue was settled. The unions readily agreed to talks on labour supply problems on an individual union basis. By 11 May all the unions, with the exception of the ASLP, had concluded agreements with the employers covering increased labour supply. The NUPB&PW agreed on behalf of its bookbinders and machine rulers members a bonus block of 175 apprentices additional to normal recruitment. The London Central Branch accepted additional labour whilst the London Women's Branch agreed to 100 bonus girl learners. Negotiations on wage and hours adjustments were renewed. The employers offered a 2.75 per cent wage increase in September 1961, an hour's reduction in September 1961, a 2.75 per cent increase in September 1962 and the 40-hour week also from September 1962. The employers subsequently amended their offer on wage enhancements to increases of 5.5 per cent from September 1961. The unions recommended acceptance of these proposals to their executives and in turn to their members. In the ensuing ballots all the unions' members expressed majority support for the proposals: 61,700 NUPB&PW members voted for the proposed settlement and 3,740 against, giving a majority in favour of 57,960.

On 4 September 1962 the 40-hour working week was introduced into the general printing and provincial newspaper industries. The 40-hour working week had been the aim not only of printing unions but of the whole trade union movement. The honour of effecting the final breakthrough had fallen to the printing unions. The industry was first to achieve the 40-hour standard working week for manual workers across a whole industry. It had flowed directly from a six-week stop-page of the industry in 1959 and the longest set of continuous negotiations in the history of UK industrial relations. The NUPB&PW's General Secretary, Bill Morrison, who was also President of the P&KTF, had led the unions in the 1959 and 1961 negotiations and considerable credit was due to him for the results achieved by his skill in having kept the ten unions together until a successful finish.

1967: THE END OF THE COST OF LIVING BONUS

A cost of living bonus was first included in the basis wage agreements with the BFMP and the NS in 1951. These agreements ran for five years and the function of the cost of living bonus was to protect the real level of wages during the stabilisation period. The bonus was a flat-rate payment made every six months in relation to movements in the Index of Retail Prices. The cost of living bonus was continued in the 1956–9, the 1959–62, 1962–5 and the 1965–6 agreements. Without the cost of living bonus the NUPB&PW, like other print unions, would have been reluctant to accept stabilisation. The employers were prepared to accept the bonus on the assumption the prevailing rate of inflation remained low. When inflation began to increase in the late 1960s the employers questioned the relevance of the cost of living bonus.

In December 1964 nine unions, including the NUPB&PW, met to consider a collective approach to the BFMP and the NS when the current wage agreement terminated on 31 March 1965. At a further meeting held on 22 December agreement to go forward on a collec-tive basis was made with the P&KTF acting as liaison and its General Secretary being closely associated with the negotiations in the same way as in 1958–9, 1961 and 1962. The claim was for a 5 per cent increase for each of three years, a three-year stabilisation period, increases in the cost of living bonus, partial consolidation of the cost of living bonus and a reduction in the London/provincial differential. A difficult issue in the negotiations was the length of the period of stabilisation. The unions wanted three years but the employers preferred 21 months – March 1965 to December 1966. The unions eventually accepted 21 months.

The original wage offer by the employers was 20p immediately and 30p in 1966. After months of further negotiations the BFMP/NS increased their offer to 75p per week in two instalments – 45p imme-diately and 30p in 1966. The negotiations appeared to be breaking down but in informal talks the employers indicated they were prepared to pay 52½p at once and a further 60p in January 1966. In return, the unions agreed to forgo the first three-point rise above 108 in the cost of living bonus. Of the existing cost of living bonus the employers agreed 35p be consolidated immediately and a further 35p in January 1966. An attempt to persuade the employers to revert to the six-monthly instead of annual adjustment of the cost of living bonus failed.[9] These proposed terms were accepted by the unions' members and became operative from 17 May 1965.

However, on 14 May the Minister of Economic Affairs referred the settlement to the newly-formed National Board for Prices and Incomes (NBPI) because it appeared to be out of line with the recently announced Government policy on productivity, prices and incomes. The unions condemned the Minister's action particularly in bringing within the Board's terms of reference an increase of 15p negotiated three years earlier and a bonus of 37p provided under a previous agreement in respect of the 1964 cost of living bonus payable from the beginning of 1965. The Board issued its report on 17 August 1965[10] and criticised the settlement as inconsistent with the Government's productivity, prices and incomes policy. It also recommended the cost of living bonus be eliminated when the next national wage settlement was made.

In July 1966 five unions, including SOGAT, agreed on a collective approach to the employers. The BFMP and the NS, in acknowledging the unions' request to terminate the existing agreement in December 1966, had stated 'we shall not be prepared in any new agreements to include the provision for a cost of living sliding scale'.[11] However, the unions were agreed that the cost of living bonus should continue and a firm stand be taken by the unions' negotiators on this particular point. On 3 November 1966, six unions, including SOGAT, submitted a claim to the BFMP and the NS for increases in the basic weekly craft rate of £1.75 in two stages (87½p on 1 January 1967 and 87½p on 1 January 1968), maintenance of present male basic wage differentials, an increase in the women's rate to 75 per cent of the craft rate, continuation of the current cost of living bonus provision but with 10p per point for adult women as well as adult men adjusted at six monthly intervals from 1 January 1967, abolition of provincial Grade 2 and a two-year agreement to run from 1 January 1967 to 31 December 1968.

The TUC's Incomes Policy Committee informed the P&KTF the proposed claim was incompatible with the Government's policy of severe restraint on incomes increases and should not be pursued. Against this background, negotiations began on 6 December 1966. The BFMP and NS could see no grounds, given the industry's economic position, for an increase in basic wages and in any case an increase would be in breach of the Government's incomes movement criteria for the period of severe restraint. They proposed existing agreements continue for the time being. The employers were opposed to any continuation of the cost of living bonus. They considered members should earn more by effective productivity schemes which were capable of sharing measured results and felt the unions could encourage the introduction of such schemes in suitable cases. The unions sought an immediate payment of 50p per week to compensate for the fall in real wages and as a prerequisite to talks on the original claim. The employers argued that the Government would not allow the payment and even if they did the employers could not afford it. The only situation in which they would consider wage increases was if there was an increase in production and a revision of traditional work practices.

Throughout the negotiations, the unions continued to attach importance to retention of the cost of living bonus. Its retention was, however, just as vigorously resisted by the employers who repeatedly quoted the recommendation of the NBP&I that the cost of living bonus be eliminated when the next national wage agreement was made. During subsequent meetings, whilst feeling it should be retained, the unions decided, in order to make progress, not to press the principle of the continuation of the scheme until a later stage. The employers, on the other hand, made it clear that so far they were concerned the cost of living bonus scheme was ended. In an effort to make progress, the unions proposed an immediate increase of 50p to remedy the injustice their members had suffered by the reduction in their real wages since the last cost of living adjustment had been made. However, the BFMP and the NS insisted they were not prepared to agree any wage adjustments whatever that were not matched by greater productivity. In an effort to move matters forward, it was agreed without either side conceding on the principle of the 50p to leave the matter in abeyance and each union would examine separately the productivity proposals the employers had in mind.

The employers' productivity proposals were flexibility of labour, assessment of staffing and rating of equipment, measurement of individual output, use of women on typewriters producing work for reproduction and the use of the employees on more than one job in newspaper houses. Early in August 1967 the BFMP and the NS confirmed they were prepared to settle based on consolidation of the current cost of living bonus (45p for men and 38p for women) and wages increases of 62½p per week for craftsmen, from 55p to 59p for non-craft men and 40p for women providing their productivity proposals were met. The unions rejected these suggestions saying that unless the employers substantially improved their wages offer and withdrew the more onerous conditions attached to it, they would have no alternative but to embark upon industrial action. When the employers refused to consider any improvement to their wages offer, the unions concluded the negotiations had gone as far as they could peacefully.

An informal meeting between the two sides was held on 27 September 1967 at which BFMP and the NS made a revised offer of an 80p per week increase providing the unions made further concessions on productivity. The unions' considered 80p inadequate given the employers' proposals on productivity and the abolition of the cost of living bonus. On 16 October 1967 the unions imposed an overtime ban in all NS offices. Although the ban led to production difficulties in provincial daily newspapers, it failed to produce a resumption of negotiations. On 26 October the P&KTF General Secretary, at the request of SOGAT, arranged an informal meeting with the employers at which it was agreed to resume negotiations. They centred on the nature of the employers' productivity proposals. On a number of occasions, during a 12-hour negotiating session, talks almost broke down. Eventually a settlement was reached providing for immediate increases in wages of 80p for craftsmen with a further 70p 12 months later. There were pro rata increases for non-craft employees. Women received weekly increases of 50p. Provision was also made for the cost of living bonus to be consolidated into the basic rate. In return, the unions agreed a number of proposals to increase productivity via flexibility of labour and retraining and transfer of craftsmen. Agreement was reached on a procedure for the assessment of staffing and rating of machines and equipment. There was no provision, however, for continuance of the cost of living bonus scheme. The agreement was to continue until 30 October 1969. SOGAT members voted in December 1967 by 57,260 votes to 15,221 to accept these proposals which became operative from 30 October 1967. The Ministry of Labour had indicated that it considered the settlement, given the range of productivity concessions and the discontinuance of the cost of living bonus, consistent with the Government's productivity, prices and incomes policy.

THE 1974 DISPUTE: BIG ADVANCE FOR THE LOW PAID[12]

In January 1974 SOGAT set out six basic principles it hoped to secure from the BFMP and the NS. It wished to eliminate the lowest male classification (Grade 4). Unless this grade could be eliminated, women members would continue in second- and third-class status economically and industrially. Equally the union was determined to increase Grade 4 rates of pay on the grounds that low rates in an agreement pulled everybody down. Second, SOGAT sought a wage increase of £7.62 per week. Third, the union wanted a threshold arrangement as a safeguard against substantial increases in the cost of living. Fourth, an adjustment of machine extras, which had last taken place nearly 21 years ago, was sought. Fifth, SOGAT sought an increase in overtime rates from time and quarter to time and a half. Sixth, the union requested the introduction of average earnings for holidays, arguing it was indefensible that a member should go on holiday with less money than they normally enjoyed.

The application of these principles was open to negotiation. Other items in the claim included the reduction of the working week to 35-hours, bereavement leave and maternity leave. SOGAT hoped the three other major print unions would agree to present the claim jointly but NATSOPA refused to be part of a collective movement because it included the NGA, a registered union under the Industrial Relations Act (1971). The NGA refused to support a claim that did not maintain craft differentials. As this attitude cut across SOGAT policy, it in turn refused to enter negotiations jointly with the NGA. However, SLADE accepted that special circumstances existed and presented a joint claim with SOGAT.[13] The employers' first offer was weekly increases of £2.30 for Class 1 (Craftsmen), £2.13 for Class 2, £2.01 for Class 3 and £1.96 for Class 4. Women were to receive the Class 2 increase. In addition, they proposed a threshold clause which provided that if the Retail Price Index rose by seven points above its October 1973 figure, a 'flat extra' of 40p for men and 36p for women would be added. Thereafter, every one-point increase would yield another 40p for men and 36p for women. All other parts of the SOGAT claim were rejected. SOGAT, SLADE and NATSOPA told the employers the offer was derisory and unless they offered a more realistic sum there was no point in continuing the negotiations.

Within a fortnight the employers presented a second offer ranging from a £2.65 weekly increases for Class 1 to £2.25 for Class 4. SOGAT found this offer unacceptable. Throughout the negotiations the employers offered the minimum limits laid down under the Conservative Government's counter-inflationary policy. SOGAT argued that even under this policy provision existed for a further 1 per cent for flexibility and, this being the case, weekly increases possible were: for Craftsmen £3.00, for Class 1 £3.00, for Class 2 £2.80, for Class 3 £2.70, for Class 4 £3.31 and for women £2.70. It was envisaged that women would move into Class 3, thus eliminating Class 4. The employers rejected the suggested formula.

Why had the employers rejected SOGAT's initiative? The elimination of Class 4 would mean women – with the introduction of equal pay – would get no less than a Class 3 worker. The BPIF/NS attitude was to hold down the lowest-paid male rates because if the lower male rate was raised the floodgates would open to women. The employers were not interested in social justice arguments. Further meetings were held to overcome the impasse. The employers made their third offer of increases of £3.05 for Craftsmen – Class 1, of £2.82 for women and Class 2, of £2.67 for Class 3 and £2.67 for Class 4. They agreed women would receive a further increase with effect from 7 October 1974, calculated so the rate for women with three years' experience after training would be 95 per cent of the lowest male rate at that date. The effect of this offer was to make the lower-paid worse off. By offering women 12p extra they were attempting to buy them off from the 60p they would receive by eliminating Class 4.

SOGAT found the offer unacceptable but agreed to meet the BFMP and the NS on 5 April 1974 at which the employers put their 'final' offer. On wages, the only adjustment to the offer was a further 5p to Class 4 workers. The offer on threshold payments remained unchanged from the first offer. The claim for enhanced overtime rates and reduced hours of work were rejected on the grounds of costs as was the claim for holiday pay at average earnings. The employers considered bereavement leave was unsuitable for national arrangements whilst maternity leave was best covered by social legislation. The BFMP and the NS rejected the claim for the abolition of Class 4. They claimed they could not enter into any forward commitment on this issue bearing in mind the implications of the Equal Pay Act.

Having reviewed the progress of the negotiations, SOGAT balloted its members with advice to vote against the employers' offer. In doing this SOGAT was influenced by the accelerating rate of inflation in the economy and the fact that for far too many years the union had accepted wages and conditions that were small reward for the skill and responsibility of its members' jobs. The union was convinced that as long as it allowed women and men in lower grades to be treated as third-rate citizens in relation to wages, all the grades above them would be pulled down. It believed its members must once and for all stand up and defend the right to have decent wages and conditions. The result of the ballot was 28,984 in favour of the employers' offer and 33,034 against.

Following the ballot rejection, SOGAT issued instructions that branches and chapels submit the following claim to individual employers:

(i)   the immediate abolition of the Class 4 category where it still existed
(ii) an immediate increase for craftsmen – Class 1 of £3.05 per week, for Class 2 and Women of £2.82p and for Class 3 of £2.70 – and women ultimately to move into Class 3
(iii) a threshold clause to provide that where the Retail Price Index rose by seven points above the October 1973 figure of 185.4 (old index) a flat increase of 40p for men and women be added
(iv) payment of average earnings for holidays as from 1 July 1974
(v)   100 per cent increase for all listed machine extras
(vi) elimination of overtime payments at time and a quarter and replacement by time and a half

Firms that did not grant the claim by 31 May 1974 would be subject to a complete ban on overtime. In addition, it was agreed to withdraw all SOGAT members from NS offices where its six-point demand had not been met by 6 June 1974.

It was apparent early in the dispute that the employers were going to make a stand. SOGAT members closed down the Dickinson–Robinson Group, where its activities came under the BFMP agreement, and certain of their mills. A calculated risk had been taken in calling out these groups of members. Dickinson–Robinson had a reputation of being at the forefront of the BFMP attempts to retain a pool of low-paid employers. If the members had not come out the union would have been in difficulty. In the event, not only did SOGAT members come out but so did the non-unionists who then joined SOGAT. At the end of the first week 10,000 members were out on strike and another 100,000 committed to industrial action of some kind. SOGAT members in the papermills responded positively when asked to stop paper supplies as did members working in wholesale distribution. Although a number of firms conceded SOGAT's claim these were not the large company groups. However, the response of SOGAT members in provincial newspaper offices to a request to withdraw their labour was patchy.

The Government intervened into the dispute early in its second week, first as a fact finding exercise and second by arranging for SOGAT to meet the employers via the Conciliation Officer of the Department of Employment. This meeting, however, proved abortive. Later SOGAT met the Secretary for Employment, Mr Albert Booth, at the House of Commons and the union was told by a senior civil servant that the Pay Board had ruled the threshold clause at variance with the Government's counter-inflationary policy. This became a focal point for both sides to intensify the dispute. SOGAT formed the impression the BFMP and the NS wanted to destroy them as an effective force. For this reason, the union decided to close down the whole printing industry. As a first step it hit those parts of the national press in London and Manchester who had interests covered by the BFMP or the NS. Of these five large groups – News International, Associated News, Thomson Newspapers, Westminster Press and IPC – two (News International and Associated News) conceded before the stoppage took place. The SOGAT 'Fleet Street' membership responded magnificently. The *Financial Times*, *The Times* and the *Daily Mirror* closed and remained so until the dispute was resolved. The day following the closure of the national press, SOGAT leaders were invited to meet Michael Foot, the Employment Secretary, who asked the union to address three points – the wages, the threshold, and the elimination of Grade 4 – because he believed the union's demand to establish principles was a stumbling block. The union told the Minister that even if it had the authority it was not prepared to make concessions in those areas.

Within two hours of leaving the Employment Secretary, SOGAT was approached by the employers for a meeting. After nearly 24 hours of talks the basis for an agreement was reached. Grade 4 was eliminated from March 1975. Men in Grade 4 would move into Grade 3 and receive a consequential wage adjustment. From October 1974 women in the industry would receive 95 per cent of the Grade 3 rate and in March 1975, 97.5 per cent of the Grade 3 rate or the classification rate, whichever was the greater. Any increases caused by a triggering of the threshold arrangements would be on top of this. SOGAT had achieved its main objective. As a safeguard against substantial rises in the cost of living, arrangements for special supplementary payments over and above the minimum grade rate were agreed. These arrangements would operate for 12 months from October 1973 to 16 November 1974. If the Retail Price Index rose by seven points above 185.4 a flat increase of 40p per week would be paid to adult men and women. For every subsequent one point rise above the figure of 185.4 a further increase of 40p per week for adult males and women would be paid.

With effect from the first pay day in November 1974 the listed machine extras in the national agreements would increase by 80 per cent subject to absorption where any person was already receiving a specific higher extra related to a machine. An examination would be conducted of machines basic to binding, finishing and warehousing which were not listed in the agreements. The increase in the weekly minimum grade rate for craftsmen and Grade 1 was £3.05, Grade 2 and women received £2.82 and Grades 3 and 4 £2.67. As part of implementing equal pay adult women received a further increase of £1.28 with effect from 7 October 1974 and a further 65p in March 1975. The BPIF and the NS set up machinery within the industry with the intention of introducing average earnings for holidays to be phased in between 1 July 1975 and 30 June 1976. The machinery would also provide for the introduction of time and a half for overtime payments from 1 July 1975. The wage increases were paid from 6 May 1974 with the threshold to apply from the first pay day following 21 June 1974. These dates did not really satisfy SOGAT but they had to judge whether it was in the members' interests to continue the dispute over this issue. The union had achieved its six principles, of which four would be applied in the lifetime of the proposed agreement and the other two shortly after the 1975 agreement came into effect. To have continued the dispute would have meant the withdrawal of the employers' offer. On balance, the union decided to take the risk. When put to a ballot of the membership, the proposed settlement was accepted by 47,299 votes to 2,041, a majority of 45,258.

So ended one of the most bitter disputes in which SOGAT had entered. It had lasted three weeks. The General Secretary told the membership:

Firstly, let me say – we succeeded. I am not normally given to boasting – indeed it is a quirk of character I do not normally have – but why should we not say outright what we achieved, despite all the odds that were ranged against us.

We did not just win a three week battle. We captured a major objective in the war that has been waged since the creation of our industry – the war of the low paid and exploited women.[14]

The union had stood alone against the BFMP and the NS and won. The benefits gained for the low paid and women were objectives SOGAT had striven to gain for many a decade. SLADE had been particularly supportive of SOGAT. It had supported them in the original negotiations on behalf of the low paid and then by their actions in the dispute.

SOGAT learned some lessons from the dispute. Some of its own members had been found wanting in the dispute whilst other unions had had difficulty in supporting SOGAT in that their own members had accepted the employers 'final offer'. SOGAT could not morally compel these unions to support them. These pressures convinced SOGAT that the sooner there was one voice for the print worker in the industry the better. Nevertheless, SOGAT's members had stood up under extreme circumstances and acted as an industrial union for the first time in its long history. However, the union knew it was ill-equipped to have become involved in a dispute of this magnitude. It had endeavoured, through circulars to branches and meeting branch secretaries to keep the membership informed of events, but there was often a time-lag in communications particularly to the shop floor, for in the period of the dispute, all officers were fully extended. Head Office of the union needed a better telephone system. The dispute demonstrated that the union required more telephone lines into the building and this was done after the dispute. SOGAT at the time of the dispute had no research department. It had relied on memory and Labour Research. Following the end of the dispute the union established a Research Department. A constant cause of worry throughout the dispute was the financial state of the union. The imposition of a levy on the membership at the time of the dispute was not really satisfactory. The dispute demonstrated SOGAT's need for a special separate 'Fighting Fund' which could be built up by weekly contributions of all members and used only for the pursuit of industrial action. After the end of the dispute SOGAT renamed its 1973 Exigency

Fund a voluntary 'Fighting Fund' to which members/branches could send donations.

THE 1980 NEGOTIATIONS: 37½-HOUR WORKING WEEK ACHIEVED[15]

In January 1980 SOGAT submitted a claim to the BPIF and the NS for a 37½-hour standard working week and a £80 per week minimum earnings level for Grade 1 operatives in the provinces (£91.18 in London) with proportionate increases for Class 2 (£74.74) and Class 3 (£71.23). The claim for a 37½-hour standard working week for day, double day shift and night shift workers was seen as the first step towards a 35-hour week for the industry. On wages the minimum grade earnings claimed were inclusive of the consolidation of existing supplements in part or in whole. Negotiations with the BFMP and the NS opened on 12 February.

For over a decade, BDC meetings had called for a shorter working week. The 1970 Council instructed the NEC to seek a shorter working week in all national agreements. Two years later it considered the time had come to achieve a reduction in the working week to 35 hours. It instructed the NEC to place motions on the Conference Agendas of the TUC and the Labour Party calling for a united effort by workers to obtain the 35-hour week. The 1976 Delegate Council recommended the NEC pursue the policy of a shorter working week when negotiations took place on all national agreements, with the objective of securing a 35-hour week for all SOGAT members. It accepted the reduction of the working week to 35 hours be pursued with a further one week's extra holiday irrespective of any government-imposed wage limits.

However, SOGAT did not claim the 37½-hour standard week just because it was union policy. The reduction in the standard working week was a bargaining priority adopted by the 1979 TUC. In addition, SOGAT argued that at the European level the TUC supported the ETUC programme for action, adopted in May 1979, which called for a 10 per cent reduction in working time to be implemented as a move towards a reduction in the working week to 35 hours. SOGAT also argued that workers in the UK had a longer working year (actual hours of work per year), a longer working week (average weekly hours of work) and shorter holidays than workers in any EEC country.

In addition to the fact that a shorter working week was SOGAT, TUC and ETUC policy, the union justified its claim by asserting that if it did achieve a reduction in the working week it would not be the first union to breach the 40-hour barrier. By 1980 in the UK 15 per cent of full-time male manual workers had basic hours of 39 or less, and 21 per cent full-time non-manual workers had a basic week of 35 hours or less. Reducing working time in the general printing and provincial newspaper industries would not, therefore, set a precedent for other industries. They claimed this was true also in terms of industry-wide agreements, since in the lock, latch and key industry hours of work had been reduced to 37½ as far back as 1972. In electrical contracting normal hours had been 38 since 1975. In 1979 the National Agreement in the engineering industry, which covered 1½m workers, had provided for a reduction in working hours to 39 from November 1981 as well as a fifth week's holiday phased in from 1982. SOGAT pointed out that not only had workers in other industries secured a reduction in the working week but so had some print workers. For example, in Scotland a 39-hour week had already been achieved in the general printing industry and in September 1980 a 37½-hour standard working week would operate in provincial newspaper wholesale distribution.

SOGAT also justified its hour reduction demand on the grounds that if it conceded the industry would remain competitive. It claimed that the usual employer arguments against shorter working weeks – increased costs, lost competitiveness and higher unemployment – were disproved by the facts. Most studies of working time saw long hours of work as a reflection of inefficiency, in that long hours had adverse effects on morale, performance and absenteeism and encouraged the extensive use of outdated machinery thereby inhibiting investment in new processes. In France and Germany advances in productivity had resulted from increased output despite a greater reduction in working hours than had occurred in Britain. Shorter hours had not impacted adversely on Britain's European competitors. The evidence suggested a reduction in hours of work formed part of a positive cycle of productivity, growth and employment.

SOGAT argued that a reduction in the working week would reduce unemployment, particularly that resulting from the implementation of new production techniques. The union considered new techniques should not only contribute to future economic growth but to social progress in the form of shorter working time. The granting of its claim for a 37½-hour standard working week throughout the industry would, SOGAT claimed, create 360,000 jobs and a move to 35-hour would create 750,000 jobs. The union was convinced that unemployment would be reduced by reducing the working week and this could be achieved without adverse effects upon costs or output. The struggle to reduce the standard working week in the printing industry had been long. In the last 60 years the print unions had reduced the working week from 48 hours to 40. Since 1937, the standard working week had been reduced by just five hours. There had been no reduction in working hours on an industrial basis for nearly 20 years. SOGAT believed the time was now ripe for a further reduction.

The wage claim of £80 was a reaction to inflation experienced in 1979 and to the inflation rate expected in near future. All forecasts predicted that inflation was unlikely to increase rapidly in the year 1980/1 whilst taxation was unlikely to be reduced. SOGAT calculated its members needed at least 15 per cent more money to buy the same goods in 1980/1 as they bought in 1979. The union appreciated that its wage claim would be costly to the industry but recognised too that price increases were costly to its members. SOGAT had not created the present levels of inflation. The £80 claim was therefore based on current and future inflation trends. The claim reflected other pressures. The SOGAT membership employed in BFMP firms was spread across three classes of operatives and there were different patterns of earnings between and within these classes of operatives. Some members were simply on the basic BPIF minimum rates whilst others earned extras through shift working, overtime working or incentive schemes. The NEC also had to take into account that successive rounds of income increase restraints in the 1970s had left an untidy wage structure through supplements that were still not consolidated into basic rates. Consolidation that had taken place had different effects on patterns of work. Existing consolidation had not produced a single penny in new money to members earning minimum rates and those who were low paid. On the other hand, consolidation produced new money for shift workers and workers on either incentive schemes or overtime. The supplements meant actual pay for shift working and overtime did not reflect the agreed rates in the agreement and shift workers only received 20 per cent of the grade rate and not 20 per cent of the minimum earnings level. With such diversity within its membership employed in the general printing trade it was impossible for SOGAT to please everybody. However, the union firmly believed its claim ensured that all its members were treated fairly.

On 22 February 1980 the BFIF and the NS offered an increase of

12.5 per cent (£7.96 at Class 1 level) on the minimum earnings level for the Provincial Craft/Class 1 rate. No offer was made to reduce the working week but the employers stated that before entering into any commitment on hours the union must agree provisions for greater productivity, flexibility and use of labour. SOGAT replied that their attitude to the employers' proposals to improve the economic performance of the industry would depend on a realistic offer on wages and hours. At a further meeting, the employers improved their offer from £7.96 to £10.96 new money (Class 1) with proportionate increases to other grades and accepted the principle of the introduction of a 37½-hour week in two stages – 39 hours from 30 March 1981 and 37½-hours from 30 September 1982. They rejected consolidation of the flat-rate supplement payments. SOGAT rejected this revised offer.

At a meeting on 11 March 1980 lasting over 14 hours, the employers improved their offer, both on new money and on the reduction of the working week. However, they were not prepared to consolidate any of the flat-rate supplements. Equally SOGAT was not prepared to settle unless some consolidation was affected. A classic stand-off position had emerged. The employers finally presented what was described as their 'final offer' which increased new money to Craft/Class 1 to £12.79, to Class 2 £11.83 and to Class 3 £11.20. In addition, they consolidated into these rates £3.96 for Class 1, £3.86 for Class 2 and £3.80 for Class 3. As a result, the minimum increase in grade rate for Class 1 became £16.75. The corresponding figures for Classes 2 and 3 were £15.69 and £15.00 respectively. The flat-rate supplement was reduced to £5 for all grades. The percentage increase in the minimum grade rate was 20 per cent for Grade 3, 20.4 per cent for Class 2 and 20.6 per cent for Class 3. Consolidation did nothing for members on the flat rate but attracted fair sums of money for those working shifts and overtime. In 1979 problems had arisen in bonus houses and in the 1980 negotiations the employers' negotiators were under specific instructions not to consolidate any flat-rate supplements because of the adverse effect on unit costs in bonus houses and the creation of non-recoverable on-cost would both have affected the viability of many firms leading to closure in some cases. Following the 1980 negotiations the minimum earnings guarantee was £75.

On hours of work SOGAT accepted a phased reduction in the length of the working week. It was reduced to 39 hours from 5 January 1981 and to 37½-hours from 5 July 1982. The general printing industry became the first major industry to breakthrough the 40-hour week and establish a 37½-hour week. This was a significant step towards SOGAT's long-term goal of the 35-hour working week. The agreement was not to terminate earlier than 23 April 1981. SOGAT members voted by 51,987 to 8,898, a majority of 43,089, to accept the BFMP/NS offer.

Although SOGAT and the BPIF and the NS had made a peaceful settlement, this was not the case with the NGA which, in March 1980, launched a campaign of industrial action to gain 'interim agreements' with individual BPIF member firms to provide for an £80 per week minimum earnings level, a £75 per week basic rate and the phased introduction of a 37½-hour standard working week via a 1½-hour reduction in April 1980 and a further one-hour reduction in April 1981. This policy proved successful and by the end of May 1980 the majority of NGA members who worked under the BPIF agreement were covered by 'interim deals' which met the union's claim in full. The effect was that a National Agreement no longer existed between the NGA and the BPIF. Two structures were now operating in the industry. One was the SOGAT National Agreement with the BPIF/NS made in 1980 and the other the 'interim agreements' with the NGA. If this situation continued it was unlikely that the BPIF would retain its National Agreement with SOGAT. However, the BPIF and the NGA wanted to see a National Wage Agreement reinstated. In the 1981 wage negotiations the BPIF objective was the re-establishment of the National Agreement. SOGAT was told if this proved impossible then there would be no alternative but to negotiate on a firm-by-firm basis. Apart from the problems of servicing such arrangements, SOGAT recognised that it meant a wider disparity of rates would emerge.

All the unions (SOGAT, NATSOPA and NGA) and the BPIF saw advantages in re-establishing a National Agreement, if only for the stability it would give to the industry. Although the 1981 negotiations were difficult, the National Agreement was re-established. The BPIF refused to rationalise the date of the implementation of the 37½-hour working week between those set out in the 1980 National Agreement and those in 'house agreements' which had improved on the 5 July 1982 date of the National Agreement. The employers were also difficult over the bonus calculator, as they tried to break the link between basic wages rates and bonus. On the issue of wages the employers increased their offer from nil to £7.50 for Craft/Class 1, to £6.96 for Class 2 and to £6.60 for Class 3, giving a minimum earnings level of £74 in the provinces and £74.82 in London.

A further result of the NGA–BPIF/NS dispute was that the Newspaper Society announced that they would conduct future negotiations alone and not jointly with BPIF as in the past. Although SOGAT had, since 1980, a Recognition and Procedure Agreement with the Newspaper Society the vast majority of its members in provincial newspapers were either covered by a 'house agreement' or the BPIF/NS Wage Basis Agreement. SOGAT hoped to use this separation to strengthen its agreement with the Newspaper Society – which although had benefits in advance of the BPIF agreement – had some limitations.[16]

WAGES MOVEMENTS: 1981–1991

The BPIF

Over the period 1981 to its merger with the NGA, SOGAT gained improvements in pay and conditions for its members employed in BPIF firms. In 1981 the minimum earnings guarantee was £74 per week in the provinces and £74.82 in London. By 1991 the minimum earnings guarantee in the provinces had risen to £148.88 (an increase of 101 per cent) and in London to £149.84 (an increase of 100 per cent) for a full standard week. These minimum earnings levels were for adult employees and excluded overtime earnings. In 1984 SOGAT finally succeeded in having the £5 flat-rate supplement to basic rates, and which was a hangover from the TUC/Labour Government Pay Policies of the mid-1970s, consolidated into the minimum grade rate and thereby count for shift and overtime premium. The consolidation was on a phased basis. On 1 January 1985, £2 was consolidated, a further £1 on 1 October 1985 and the final £2 on 1 April 1986. It had been a source of annoyance to SOGAT's members that their premium payments had been based on rates below the agreed minimum rates. The BPIF argued that the industry could not afford consolidation because of a slowdown in orders which meant many machines stood idle.

In 1987 SOGAT requested in the annual wage negotiations that the employment conditions of part-time and temporary workers be made comparable to those of full-time employees. The BPIF said they were prepared to discuss any evidence SOGAT had of problems with these workers after the new National Agreement had taken effect on 24 April 1987. To provide its negotiators with full information, SOGAT undertook a survey amongst its branches to ascertain how many part-time and temporary workers were employed in BPIF member companies and whether they enjoyed pro rata conditions to full-time employees and if not what the differences were. The employment conditions of temporary and part-time workers was also an item in the unions' 1988, 1990 and 1991 wage claims to the BPIF. In 1990 the employers agreed to meet with SOGAT during the lifetime of the agreement to discuss the position of part-time and temporary workers in the industry. However, little had been achieved by the time SOGAT amalgamated with NGA.

SOGAT failed to convince the BPIF that Class 3 should be eliminated. This was a priority issue in SOGAT's collective bargaining agenda, having been the subject of successful motions at the Delegate Councils of 1980 and 1982. It was included in SOGAT's claim to the BPIF in 1989, 1990 and 1991. In the 1980s some BPIF companies had eliminated Class 3 at the local level but it still remained, mainly in small companies. By 1989 SOGAT considered the time had arrived for the elimination of Class 3 at the local level to be recognised in the National Agreement. However, the BPIF rejected this, arguing that Class 3 still had relevance in the industry and was best dealt with at the local level.

In the 1989 wage negotiations SOGAT finally, with effect from 24 April 1990, achieved its objective of the adult rate becoming payable at 18 instead of 20. The issue had been raised at the 1980, 1983 and 1984 Delegate Councils and had been included in the annual wage claims of 1986, 1987, 1988 and 1989. The unions' argument was simple. A person in the 1980s in all walks of life was an adult at 18, yet in the general printing industry they were treated as juveniles until the age of 20. Members under that age who had completed their formal training and were doing exactly the same job as a member who was 20 and over did not receive the adult rate.

However, improvements in wages over the period 1981 and 1991 were not given for nothing. SOGAT in return made concessions in the deployment of their members designed to improve efficiency and productivity. They accepted the need for management initiatives to increase efficiency and productivity and assist in maintaining employment. The union committed itself to co-operate fully at national, branch and local level in changes necessary to achieve increased output and lower unit costs through a more effective use of people, materials and machines. Improvements in efficiency and output could only be achieved at individual company level and discussions between management and SOGAT chapel representatives identified and implemented the necessary changes. However, these discussions were limited in scope, covering flexibility, staffing, arrangement of hours and changes in the methods of production.

In the 1985 wage negotiations SOGAT agreed to encourage the introduction of the working of double day shifts, night shifts or treble shifts to meet the production requirements of the industry and accepted that the arrangement of working hours be left for each house to determine in the light of the needs of production and distribution. They also accepted the ending of demarcation lines between warehouse, bookbinding, print finishing, stationery, carton converting and printing departments. There was to be early consultation and full co-operation with employers over the adoption and development of new processes and new types of machines. In 1989 SOGAT accepted further measures to promote flexibility of labour and in the following year agreed to the redeployment of employees to other departments on a short- or long-term basis when a company's production requirements demanded this. SOGAT also accepted treble shift working and national provisions on efficiency and productivity be applied locally through genuine efforts at company level to improve productivity.

However, over the period 1981 and 1991 there were items in SOGAT's collective bargaining agenda with the BPIF which it did not achieve, for example the reduction of the standard working week to 35-hours, the abolition of Class 3 and pro rata working conditions for part-time and temporary workers. A demand for a 35-hour standard working week was included in the annual wage claims of 1986, 1990 and 1991 but the employers refused to make any concessions.

The Newspaper Society

Production Workers

In April 1983 the minimum earnings guarantee level for SOGAT members in provincial newspaper houses was £88.16. By April 1990 the figure had increased to £128.38, an increase of 46 per cent. In 1991 the Newspaper Society ended its National Agreement with SOGAT terminating a 70-year tradition of national pay bargaining for regional newspapers. The Newspaper Society considered changes in technology and employment structures had made national bargaining less relevant for its employees than in the past. In 1985 the flat-rate supplement was consolidated into minimum grade rates over a four-year period whilst the age at which the adult rate was paid was reduced to 19 upon completion of three years in the industry. However, by the late 1980s the balance of bargaining power had moved sharply in favour of Newspaper Society member firms relative to their employees. As a result, post-1985 the Newspaper Society made offers to SOGAT only on wages and holidays and rejected all other items including a reduction in weekly working hours, additional payments for overtime undertaken without a specific finishing time, Boxing Day be paid at double time plus one day off in lieu, and a re-examination of differentials between weekly and daily houses.

When the Newspaper Society decided to terminate the National Agreements held with SOGAT they regarded it as the final act in a process they had been working towards for a number of years. The NS considered the print unions so weakened and the conditions of their members so eroded they had no fight left. In the event SOGAT and the NGA convened on 14 March 1991, a meeting which was attended by 250 chapel and branch officials from both organisations and which agreed a joint campaign and claim for the review of agreements. The claim was not merely that there should be no pay cuts but that all chapels press for a 9 per cent increase in house rates and other payments, no erosion of conditions and a model disputes procedure to give members the right to have trade union representation during the hearing of any grievance. SOGAT area organisers undertook the task, with branch officers, of drawing the campaign together. However, the outcome of the negotiations was mixed. In some houses pay increases of 5 per cent were simply imposed upon SOGAT members together with new disciplinary and grievance procedures in which the first stage involved participation by Newspaper Society representatives. On the other hand, in the South and South West some chapels secured a 9 per cent pay increase with no erosion of terms and conditions. However, in a number of instances derecognition took place and individual contracts were issued whilst in many branches, particularly in the Midlands and the North East, members were made redundant. SOGAT realised that regaining influence in the provincial newspaper industry would be a long haul. The 1990/1 National Executive Council Report sumed up the position:

We do of course have a very long way to go to win back from employers the full protection that union membership affords

477

their employees but given the will and unity we are resolved to do so no matter how long it may take.[17]

Clerical Workers

In 1984 the minimum earnings level for clerical workers in daily provincial newspaper offices reached £93.34 and in weekly offices £84.34. At the time the NS terminated the National Agreement the minimum earnings level in daily provincial newspaper offices had increased to £130.34 and to £118.44 in weekly houses. The 1985 revision of the National Agreement saw the introduction of the adult rate at 19 upon completion of three years experience in the industry or 20 years of age, whichever was the sooner. However, post-1986 the Newspaper Society, as with production workers, offered only increases in wages and holidays and rejected all other claims, for example the 35-hour working week, a re-examination of differentials between weekly and daily bonuses and that workplaces producing papers on three or more days per week be classified as daily houses.

NOTES

1. See National Union of Printing, Bookbinding and Paperworkers *Annual Report of the National Executive Council*, 1960, p. 5.
2. The unions told the employers that the clause had previously proved of little assistance to NATSOPA and was hardly likely to prove more so in the future. On the issue of the organisation of clerical workers the unions were prepared to 'let sleeping dogs lie'.
3. For more details on these two disputes see J. Gennard *A History of the National Graphical Association*, Unwin Hyman, London, 1990, pp. 374–9.
4. The unspent balance was returned to the branches.
5. Amongst NUPB&PW members, 51,318 voted in favour and 12,002 against.
6. The collective movement of nine unions became ten on 22 June 1959 when NATSOPA accepted an invitation from the other unions to join them. From that date, NATSOPA took full part in negotiating the final settlement.
7. The proposed settlement was rejected by the NSES mainly because of a proposed clause for the introduction of auxiliary workers into the foundry. A satisfactory resolution to the difference was agreed on 7 December 1959.
8. See Printing and Kindred Trades Federation *Annual Report 1960/1*, p. 21.
9. The annual adjustment had been accepted in 1962 and the P&KTF had calculated that men had lost £16 on bonus and women £12 over the period of the agreement (1962–5).
10. See National Board for Prices and Incomes '*Wages, costs and prices in the printing industry*' Cmnd 2750, HMSO, London, August, 1965. It was the first wages settle-

ment on which the Board had been asked to report. There was wide publicity in the press and on radio and television.

11. See Printing and Kindred Trades Federation *Annual Report, 1967/8*, p. 7.

12. For detailed accounts of this dispute see 'The Offer We Must Refuse' *SOGAT Journal*, May 1974, pp. 6–7 and 'Over Three Weeks Battle with the Master Printers: A Big Advance in the Long War for the Low Paid', SOGAT Journal, July-August 1974, pp. 2–3.

13. Although the NGA and NATSOPA presented their claims separately, the basic details on wages, revision of overtime and a 35-hour week were similar to SOGAT's claim.

14. See 'Our Three Week Battle with the Master Printers: A Big Advance in the Long War for the Low Paid' in *SOGAT Journal*, July-August 1974, p. 2.

15. For a more detailed account of these negotiations see '37½-Hour Week, £80 Class 1' *SOGAT Journal*, March 1980, pp. 4, 5 and 11 and '20 Per Cent Plus Breakthrough in Shorter Hours', *SOGAT Journal*, April 1980 pp. 2 and 3.

16. See Society of Graphical and Allied Trades, *Annual Report of the National Executive Council, 1981*, p. 3.

17. See Society of Graphical and Allied Trades (82) *Annual Report of the National Executive Council 1990/1*, p. 32.

CHAPTER 16

THE GENERAL PRINTING TRADE AND PROVINCIAL NEWSPAPER EMPLOYERS: (2) OTHER EMPLOYMENT CONDITIONS AND TRAINING

HOLIDAYS

Prior to its demise, the P&KTF negotiated agreements covering hours and holidays with the BPIF and the NS. At the time the unions agreed to dissolve the P&KTF, annual paid holidays in the general printing and provincial newspaper industry were four weeks. Over the period 1975 to 1991 SOGAT's policy on holidays centred around three issues. First, it wished to increase the paid annual holiday entitlement. Second, it sought pay for statutory bank holidays at average earnings or some alternative formula, whichever was the greatest. Third, it tried to obtain increases in the minimum paid holiday entitlement on the basis of years of service with the same employer.

The 1978 Delegate Council called for the inclusion in the 1979 annual negotiations with the main employers' organisations a claim for five weeks' paid holiday[1] to enable members to gain maximum benefits from the implementation of new technology. The 1980 Delegate Council committed negotiators to seek a further week's paid holiday in all national agreements, stating that this be the third priority after obtaining the maximum possible monetary increase for the membership.[2] The following Delegate Council instructed the NEC to claim a 35-working week and an additional week's paid holiday as this would help alleviate rising unemployment amongst the membership. Further, it ranked this the highest priority in the union's collective bargaining agenda to the extent of involving, if necessary, the membership in industrial action in its support. The first Delegate Council of SOGAT (82) ranked the achievement of an additional week's paid holiday as the next highest priority in negotiations at national level after the maximum possible increase of new money had been obtained. Its justification was a belief that this would create additional employment opportunities for SOGAT members to offset those jobs lost as a result of the implementation of new technology and the economic recession of the early 1980s. By the mid-1980s, Delegate Councils replaced the highest priority in negotiations from one of achieving the maximum possible increase in new money to one of the achievement of a shorter working week and a fifth week's paid annual holiday.

As a result of the 1986 annual negotiations with the BPIF and the NS, print workers maintained their tradition of being 'leaders' in achieving significant breakthroughs in changes in the amount of annual paid holiday for manual workers on an industry-wide basis. SOGAT had included a demand for five weeks' paid holidays in its 1983 wage claim to the BPIF and the NS but this had been rejected. However, in the 1986 negotiations the two employers' associations agreed to the phased introduction of five weeks' paid holidays. From 1 January 1986 paid annual holiday entitlement was increased from four weeks to four weeks and two days. From 1 January 1987 holiday entitlement became four weeks and three days, whilst from 1 January 1988 it was enhanced by a further day. From 1 January 1989 paid annual holiday leave in the general printing industry and provincial newspaper houses became five weeks.

The 1990 Delegate Council instructed the NEC to pursue with vigour the attainment of six weeks' annual holiday for all SOGAT members. The delegates were persuaded by a number of arguments. First, it would be in the spirit of the concept of reduced working hours, and second, it would give opportunities for more people to be employed in the industry. Third, six weeks' holiday would give people more time off from work and this would be beneficial given the greater pressure on workers in the late 1980s/early 1990s to perform to higher standards and quality. Fourth, increased holidays would improve the quality of life for those who helped to earn and create the nation's wealth and would allow parents to spend more time off with their children. The demand for six weeks' paid holiday was included in the 1991 claim to the BPIF but was rejected by the employers, who argued that, in a time of economic recession, the demand was unrealistic.

The issue of additional holidays for years of service with one employer was raised at the 1974 Delegate Council. It was proposed that ten years' service with the same employer should bring an extra three days holiday, 15 years' service, four days, 20 years' service five days, 25 years' service eight extra days and 30 years ten extra days. However, the issue was never pushed at national level although some extra holiday based on length of service was gained in 'house agreements'.

From the mid-1970s, the issue of the basis of payment for statutory holidays was a perennial item at SOGAT Delegate Council Meetings to the extent that a delegate to the 1988 Council remarked it was in danger of getting into the Guinness Book of Records.[3] Although average earnings for annual holiday entitlement had been achieved in 1972, statutory bank holidays were paid at the hourly rate. SOGAT members wished for consistency in the basis of payment for holidays. The loss of earnings on statutory holidays was in most cases the result of local agreements which gave additional payments in the form of productivity bonuses, oil-up and wash-up times and change-overs. All these additional payments to the hourly rate were discounted for statutory holiday pay. Delegates to the BDC complained that the different basis of pay for annual holidays than for statutory holidays caused confusion amongst SOGAT members and the wage offices of the printing firms. However, by 1988 many companies had brought payment of statutory holidays into line with annual holidays and SOGAT no longer accepted the BPIFs justification for refusing to rectify a long-overdue holiday payment anomaly.

The regular demand from delegates that statutory holidays be paid at average earnings or some alternative formula meant it was a regular item in the unions 'shopping list' to BPIF. The payment for statutory holidays at average earnings was rejected by the BPIF in 1987, 1988, 1989, 1990 and 1991. In 1987 the claim was for payment at average earnings or basic rates plus 25 per cent, whichever was the greater. The BPIF negotiators rejected the claim on the grounds that the issue was best dealt with at local level.

SICK PAY SCHEMES

Negotiations for an industry-wide sick pay scheme had been the responsibility of the P&KTF before its demise. However, it had registered little success in achieving an industry-wide minimum standards sick pay scheme. The 1978 Delegate Council urged the NEC to press for a comprehensive sickness scheme to operate in the general printing industry and provincial newspapers and that this scheme should be on a par with schemes operating in private sector manufacturing, local government, the civil service and clerical workers. Two years later the BDC again committed SOGAT to negotiations with all the employers' associations (not just the BPIF and the NS) with which it had National Agreements, to work towards a national sick pay scheme.

In 1986 Delegate Council instructed the NEC to pursue with the BPIF a national sick pay scheme at least equal to that obtained from the Society of British Printing Ink Manufacturers. Delegates accepted that sick pay was not a privilege of the few but a basic worker right. Employers should not be allowed to opt out of their duty to their employees because workers had the misfortune to fall ill or suffer injury through an accident whilst in their employ. Although some chapels had negotiated a sick pay scheme with their employers, there were many companies which either did not pay for sickness or used discretion or bias in deciding who received sick pay. Delegates were told that 30 per cent of SOGAT members (21,000) who worked under the BPIF agreement were employed in companies without sick pay schemes. A national sick pay agreement would bring cover to these members.

In its 1987 annual wage claim to the BPIF, SOGAT sought to establish a national sick pay scheme. The BPIF agreed to undertake a study to provide up-to-date information on the coverage and application of sick pay benefits in the industry. The study would be completed by 31 October 1987. At the earliest opportunity following the completion of the study, and prior to the expiry of the 1987 National Agreement, SOGAT and the BPIF would meet to exchange information and to consider jointly the possibility of establishing an industry-wide fallback sick pay scheme. Both parties accepted that participation in the study did not commit them to the establishment of an industry-wide sick pay scheme and that it was not the purpose of the study to affect company sick pay schemes already established.

In 1988, SOGAT again pushed for a national sick pay scheme but was only able to pursue the BPIF to encourage member firms to introduce sick pay arrangements at 'house level' subject to the individual company's ability to meet the costs of the administration and benefits provided and subject to such arrangements being supported by facilities for monitoring and controlling levels of sickness absence. This encouragement took place in conjunction with a SOGAT campaign at branch level for the introduction of a national sick pay scheme. A claim for an industry-wide sick pay scheme was included in the 1990 claim to the BPIF but it was again rejected. This led the 1990 Delegate Council to condemn the NEC on its achievements to date in its pursuance of a national sick pay scheme in the general printing industry. Delegates considered the situation unacceptable, particularly when set against a background of a Tory Government undermining the National Health Service and the National Insurance system. It was vital that SOGAT sought long-term coverage for its members when absent from work through illness. The demand for a national sick pay scheme was put to the BPIF in 1991 but once again was rejected on the basis that the majority of BPIF member firms already operated a sick pay scheme. SOGAT had not achieved its longstanding objective of an industry-wide sick pay scheme by the time it merged with the NGA.

INDUSTRIAL PENSION SCHEME

The P&KTF had long sought a transferable industrial pension scheme but had not achieved this by the time of its demise in 1974. However, the issue was taken up by SOGAT when its 1978 Delegate Council called upon the NEC to open talks with the BPIF and the NS to produce a Pension Fund for SOGAT members working in the general printing trade. Two years previously SOGAT had re-affirmed its policy that a pension scheme on a non-contributory basis was a worker benefit by right. In the 1983 annual negotiations the BPIF agreed to establish a Joint Working Party to examine, with SOGAT, the feasibility of establishing a pension scheme to which BPIF member firms and employees would subscribe on a voluntary basis.

SOGAT decided their members interests in the working party's deliberation would be best served by a common approach with the NGA. Discussions were complex but in April 1985 the principles to underpin an industry-wide pension scheme were agreed. However, all the work to reach this stage was undone when the Government published its Green Paper on the future of the social security system and which contained a proposal to end the Supplementary Earnings Related Pension Scheme (SERPS). The need to take this possibility into account meant it was December 1985 before a new draft scheme was agreed. This was a major step forward for thousands of SOGAT members employed in small firms who now, like their fellow members employed in medium and large size enterprises, could become members of a proper pension scheme. However, the time taken to fashion the scheme concerned the activists, and the 1986 Delegate Council, by 203 votes to 166, deplored the lack of information given to members regarding the progress of the working party towards shaping an industry-wide pension scheme.

After two years of difficult planning by the Joint Working Party, a voluntary industry-wide, transferable money purchase pension scheme for the printing industry was launched. It was known as the Printing Industries Pension Scheme (PIPS) and became operative on 1 June 1986.[4] The scheme topped up the existing state basic pension and state earnings-related payments. Normal retirement age in the scheme was 65 for men and 60 for women. The Prudential Assurance Company Ltd were the professional administrators, investors, insurers and promoters of the scheme. The scheme was open to all companies within the industry. The trusteeship of PIPS included two SOGAT, two NGA and four BPIF members. These parties appointed for the scheme a chairperson on a rotating basis.

The level of contributions allocated for standard benefits under the scheme was 7 per cent per annum of pensionable earnings, defined as all earnings, except overtime, earned in 52 weeks before 1 June each year. The 7 per cent contribution was split 2:1 in favour of the employee, whilst just short of 2 per cent of contributions was to pay for administrative costs, death in service payments for widows and widowers and early retirement pensions for those retiring on ill-health grounds. Employees could, if they wished, make additional voluntary contributions to improve the level of retirement benefits above the standard level. Benefits were determined in direct relationship to the combined employer and employee contributions made on behalf of each individual member and were dependent upon when contributions were paid and the age at which the pension started. The scheme allowed for the option to take part of the pension as a tax-free lump sum on the date of retirement and for the option to take early retirement at any time after 50. Employees took their pension with them when they moved to another printing company participating in the scheme, whilst those who transfered to a non-participating company left their retirement pension invested in the scheme allowing the pension account to continue to grow and become available to be drawn upon at any time after the employee reached 50 in the same way as for early retirement.

PIPS was more than just another pension scheme. It was specifically designed for the printing industry, was easy to understand, was value for money, could be taken from job to job and had tailor-made benefit packages. When SOGAT members retired they could choose the retirement benefits best suited to the needs of themselves and their spouses. This could be a tax-free cash sum up to the maximum allowed by Government regulations with the balance providing a pension for the rest of their life. On death after retirement the spouse received a pension equivalent to half that of the contributing member. If a SOGAT member died before reaching retirement age the pension was paid as a lump sum, but if they were married then their spouse received a pension together with a reduced lump sum. Because PIPS was industry-wide it could be taken from job to job without penalties and the economies of scale meant lower administrative charges and consequently more of the contributors' income was actually invested in the fund. Manual workers in the general printing industry were the first group of such workers to gain a voluntary industry-wide, transferable, money purchase pension scheme.

THE SINGLE EUROPEAN MARKET

In 1986 the British Government signed the European Communities Act which committed the 12 member states of the European Community to remove by 31 January 1992 all barriers to the Community becoming a genuine free trade area. The 1986 Act enabled a free movement of capital and labour within the Community. SOGAT, concerned about the likely impact of the creation of a Single European Market on its members, requested at the 1989 annual BPIF wage negotiations that a Committee be established to deal with the challenges and opportunities offered by the Single Market.

In the spring of 1989, the BPIF established a European Action Group consisting of representatives of the BPIF, SOGAT and the NGA to help the general printing industry prepare for the establishment of the Single Market by examining its implications for the industry in general, its individual product sectors and its employees. The European Action Group would evaluate the major commercial opportunities for the industry and its employees and assess the possible economic, social and environmental changes that might occur as a consequence of the Single European Market in order to develop an action plan to obtain the maximum benefits from the Single Market for the printing industry and its employees. The BPIF and SOGAT heightened the awareness of their respective memberships of the likely impact, at the workplace level, of the Single European Market by a programme of communication.

In 1990 the Action Group undertook research into the likely impact of the Single Market on the carton and magazine sector. Joint SOGAT/BPIF presentations took place with SOGAT branch secretaries. The NEC in the light of the Single Market reviewed its links with its counterparts in the European printing industry. It decided to strengthen these to gain access to the exchange of information and to start bilateral discussions covering multinational company activities. SOGAT applied to rejoin the IGF but its application had not been determined by the time SOGAT merged with the NGA.

WOMEN AND EQUALITY

Participation in the Union's Decision-making Bodies

In 1955 62,988 (44 per cent) of the NUPB&PWs 142,520 members were women. There were no women amongst the five national full-time officers and the nine regional group secretaries. Five of the 32 member NEC were women, as were two of the 11 regional organisers and nine of its 229 branch secretaries. In London, all women members were organised in the London Women's Branch. Furthermore, throughout the industrial sectors in which the union organised, all women – irrespective of their actual skill levels – were grouped under the 'women's rate' at the bottom of the grading structures, and separate chapels based on gender were commonplace.

In 1968 the SOGAT (Division A) Delegate Council accepted a Newton-Le-Willows Branch motion that an elected Women's Advisory Committee be established to advise the NEC on all issues affecting women workers, and to make recommendations and representations where necessary. The mover, Betty Tebbs, argued that the trade union movement had had little success in tackling the problems of women in industry. SOGAT, with one-third of its membership women, had only two on a 24-strong NEC. Opponents of the Committee argued that it was the fault of women themselves that they were not in more influential positions as they did not come forward but still complained about underrepresentation. The NEC argued that the matter be referred to the forthcoming SOGAT-wide Conference, that a Women's Advisory Committee would be 'a union within a union' and stated that the NEC clearly had women on sub-committees as co-opted members where necessary. By 317 votes to 108 the Delegate Council carried the Newton-Le-Willows motion. When elections to the Advisory Committee took place only 30 per cent of the ballot papers were returned, with 42 branches failing to return any. The Women's Advisory Committee met five times before being disbanded in 1972. Its members described the Committee as being tokenistic and restricted in its activity.

By 1981 women constituted 34 per cent of SOGAT membership whilst the merger with NATSOPA increased the absolute number of women members in SOGAT to 75,000. Since 1978, Sue Ledwith had edited a women's page in the *NATSOPA Journal*. This policy continued in SOGAT, which also devoted more space in the *SOGAT Journal* to women's issues.[5] Another notable development took place in the summer of 1983 when the NEC established a Positive Action Committee as a step towards adopting the TUC Charter, *Equality for Women Within Trade Unions*. SOGAT became committed to involve women at every level in the union, to examining decision-making structures to ensure women's views were heard and to setting up advisory committees at every level. The Charter also committed SOGAT to negotiate paid attendance at union meetings held during working hours, to provide child-care facilities for union meetings, training courses and conferences and to present the content of all union publications in non-sexist terms.

The 1986 Delegate Council considered a number of proposals regarding the position of women within the union, within the workplace and within society. Much of the discussion was framed around the publication *Women in SOGAT (82)*, a report commissioned by the NEC.[6] The report found women underrepresented in the union's decision-making structures. Of a total membership of 184,775, 31 per cent were women, but only one of ten national officers was a women and there were no women national organisers (of 18) and no women group area secretaries. There were two women on the 36-strong NEC, four out of 93 branch officials and 38 out of 417 BDC delegates. On chapel committees women were more strongly represented, accounting of 26 per cent of officials in chapels with 50 plus members and 21 per cent in chapels with less then 50 members. Although nearly two-thirds of branches had a female membership of at least 25 per cent, this was reflected in the gender distribution of committees in only a quarter of branches. In 70 per cent of branches there were no women officers and the London Women's Branch accounted for three out of six women branch full-timers. There were six women branch treasurers and seven trustees but only one branch secretary and one president.

The report found potential barriers to women reaching decision-making positions in the union. Women fared less well in the provision of trade union facilities whilst child-care was a particular concern. In general, branches, chapels and activists favoured policies encouraging women by positive measures. *Women in SOGAT (82)* recommended the establishment of Equality Working Parties at every level in the union and the appointment of Education and Training Officers and of Equality Officers at every level as well as reserved seats on all committees. Before the 1986 Delegate Council met, the NEC expressed its opposition to these recommendations. At the Conference the report was accepted and noted whilst a motion from the Greater London Branch called unsuccessfully for the replacement of the existing NEC Equality Committee by a National Equality Committee elected from the membership plus the General President and two NEC members. The Committee would advise the NEC on policies and activities relating to women's equality and rights at work and in the union. The delegates, however, carried an amended Glasgow Branch motion advocating positive discrimination for women at every level of the union. Branches and districts would submit a report on their progress which would be monitored by the NEC.

The 1988 BDC devoted more time to women's issues than any previous SOGAT/NUPB&PW Conference. Nevertheless, a motion from the London Clerical Branch calling for the establishment of a National Women's Advisory Committee was defeated. The mover referred to the underrepresentation of women in SOGAT and argued that the Committee would provide women with a strong voice. It was not proposed automatically to give women more representation but for action to be initiated which would encourage the greater participation of women. The opponents of the motion emphasised that the NEC was sympathetic to improving the position of women in the union, but that there already existed an NEC Positive Action Sub-committee consisting of six women and three men drawn from the NEC and National Officers and which operated well. The NEC used the delegate meeting to stress that single-gender chapels broke anti-discrimination laws, jeopardised equal pay claims and served to perpetuate unacceptable barriers to women's advancement towards equality in the union. Such chapels were contrary to SOGAT rules and BDC policy which required chapels to provide in their decision-making structures measured equality and, if necessary, reserved seats for women on such bodies. However, single-gender chapels continued and some remained at the point when SOGAT merged with the NGA despite an Industrial Tribunal finding, in the case of Thomas De La Rue in Gateshead, that single-gender representation was *prima facie* unlawful and must be remedied wherever it remained. Chapels were told to establish single negotiating units in which all members were properly represented.

The 1990 BDC saw many motions which gave a strong lead on equal opportunities and positive action. One motion called upon branches to support the TUC positive action programme by ensuring places were allocated to women on all bodies and to publicise child-care facilities to make it easier for women to participate in union affairs. In terms of SOGAT's internal policies, the delegates agreed to extend Delegate Meetings crèche facilities to enable women to attend fringe meetings and rallies, etc. Delegates also carried a motion, moved by Herts and Essex Branch, proposing an annual one-day Women's Conference to be held in working hours, funded by the national union and with a report presented to subsequent BDCs. The Conference would promote and encourage activity and the participation of women within SOGAT. The four main topics for discussion at annual Women's Conference would be equal pay, equal opportunities at work, positive action in the union and women's rights. The General Secretary would make a keynote address and workshop discussions would report back to open sessions for debate. Delegates to the Conference would be elected by the branches. The first annual Women's Conference, chaired by the General President, took place in Manchester on 18/19 November 1990 with more than 100 delegates in attendance.

Equal Pay

The 1956 NUPB&PW Delegate Council adopted a London Women's Branch motion which called upon the NEC to negotiate at the earliest possible date 75 per cent of the London Warehousemen's Branch rate for women members. Delegates were reminded that although this had been the union's policy since 1942 the gap between the warehousemen's rate and the women's rate had widened. For too long women had been paid according to their gender and not their contribution to the industry. In 1960 the union adopted a policy that women (the lowest grade) receive the same increase as general assistants (Class

4, the lowest male grade). This was to be a step towards greater equality and a reminder that the achievement of equal pay was proving protracted but that women would not give up the fight until they achieved it.

The 1966 SOGAT (Division A) Delegate Council had before it a London Central Branch motion stating that 'Conference accepts the principle of equal pay for equal work for women and calls upon the TUC to exert vigorous pressure throughout its affiliated organisations to force the Labour Government to achieve this by legislation.'[7] The objective was not equal pay for equal work but equal pay for work of equal value. The motion was passed unanimously. The 1968 Delegate Council accepted a Glasgow Branch motion instructing the NEC to press for the implementation of the principle of equal pay in the industries covered by SOGAT.

The Labour Government published its Equal Pay Bill in January 1970 and it received Royal Assent just before the June 1970 General Election, which was won by the Conservative Party. The Equal Pay Act became fully operative from 29 December 1975. SOGAT was disappointed that the Act left unanswered what was to happen to much of 'traditional women's work' if men were not engaged in the same or broadly similar work. In other words, jobs which women performed might require as much effort, skill and responsibility as those performed by men but fall outwith the description of 'the same or broadly similar work' as required by the Equal Pay Act. SOGAT pressed for the Act to be fully operative by December 1972 and remained concerned that women would be shunted into specially created areas where their jobs would be perceived as being of low value.

The theme of equal pay and its relationship to equal opportunities and training was continued at the 1972 BDC. The mover of a Manchester Branch motion pointed out that the lowest (Class 4) male rate in general print was £20.93 and that for women £17.41 per week. The NEC pointed to seven Equal Pay Agreements signed with employers' organisation but acknowledged that the greatest problem was male prejudice on the part of SOGAT members. Nevertheless, the BDC confirmed the union's aim to establish a unisex position in all its agreements with complete freedom of access to jobs for the women members of SOGAT. By the end of 1972 SOGAT was party to eight National Agreements in which women's work had been evaluated and slotted into the male grading structure. In addition, differentials between grades had been reduced. In 1975 SOGAT and the BPIF agreed that from 4 August 1975 women receive the classification rate in which they were employed or Class 3 rate, whichever was the higher. In 1977 SOGAT recorded a notable success in the field of equal pay when an Industrial Tribunal found in favour of women binding machine operatives employed at HMSO, Gateshead. Grade B women were being paid £66.96 per week whilst the lowest men's rate (Grade D) was £72.13. The tribunal backdated the award to December 1975. SOGAT was able to use this victory to gain increases for women members at HMSO's Harrow plant.

In 1982 the European Court ruled that UK equal pay legislation failed to comply with the European Community's Directive on equal pay for work of equal value. The UK government amended the Equal Pay Act (1970) with effect from 1 January 1984, to bring it into line with Community law. However, SOGAT was unhappy that the government had taken the least possible action to comply with the Community Directive and an opportunity had been lost to benefit the maximum number of women workers and to put equal pay into practice. The complex way in which the equal pay for work of equal value clause would operate would, SOGAT feared, lead to legal and practical difficulties. The Government's action was not in the spirit of the European Court's judgement. The amended Equal Pay Act did not deal with the problems of job evaluation criteria being loaded against women, that independent witnesses could not be compelled to appear or answer questions, that paying men more than women for work of equal value because of skill shortages would not be discriminatory and that no back pay could be claimed prior to January 1984.

The extent of the difficulties involved under the new procedure was underlined when SOGAT took the first steps on the long road towards success in an equal pay for work of equal value claim at J. & C. Moore's in Liverpool. The union advised members to be ambitious when choosing a comparator (i.e. the person with whom they were claiming equal pay) and the Moore's claim was taken to a Tribunal on behalf of three Class 3 tablehands and two clerical workers. The tablehands had served five-year learnerships and operated collating, numbering and folding machines as well as carrying out skilled operations by hand. They claimed their work was of equal value to that of skilled male Class 1 bindery cutters and Class 2 semi-skilled boxmen. The clerical workers' claim was on behalf of a woman supervisor and a secretary who typed all the orders to customers and suppliers. They compared their skills with NGA craftsmen and with SOGAT craft and semi-skilled operators. The tribunal referred the claim to 'independent experts' for their evaluation of the five women's work whilst SOGAT obtained the services of another job evaluation expert to compare findings and recommendations. The procedure in the Moore's case was long and onerous and it was 1990 before an out-of-court settlement was reached just before yet another hearing. The company claimed the differences in pay were due to reasons other than gender. They put forward a material factor defence to indicate they were merely complying with the national and local agreements to which SOGAT was a party. After days of legal arguments and evidence the Tribunal decided the agreements were not the reasons for the variations in pay. The eventual outcome was estimated to be worth some £22 per week for the production workers, backdated to when the claim was lodged, with bigger increases for those employed in the offices. All other women's work was then subject to job evaluation free from discriminatory factors with SOGAT involvement in the management of the scheme. The J. & C. Moore's case was the most significant equal value claim in terms of its implications for women and men covered by the BPIF agreement.

After taking industrial action in pursuit of their equal pay claim, 500 women at De La Rue security printers in Newcastle gained increases of up to £100 per week. In provincial newspapers equal pay successes were recorded by canvassers at Thames Valley Newspapers and the *Derby Evening Telegraph*. Telesales executives were also successful at the *Worcester Evening News*, whilst copy inputters pursued successful equal pay claims at the *Oxford Mail* Group and the *Coventry Evening Telegraph*. At Hazell, Watson & Viney's in Aylesbury two women machinists gained increases of £6 per week, supported by an overtime ban which lasted 1½ years and was imposed by the separate male chapel. On the other hand, the *Financial Times* announced cuts in the pay of male employees who had been used as 'comparators' in a successful equal pay claim. This action was condemned by SOGAT as an attack as yet unknown in Britain.[8]

Equal Opportunities

The 1974 Delegate Council approved a motion from the North Western Group which called on the government to legislate a comprehensive policy to guarantee social, educational and economic rights to women to be enforced by a commission with legal powers to impose decisions and award compensation in case of non-compliance. SOGAT welcomed the Sex Discrimination Act (1975) which outlawed discrimination in employment, education and in the provision of goods, facilities and services. The Act established the Equal Opportunities Commission to monitor and enforce progress towards equality. The union felt strongly that it could not go round mouthing platitudes about equality but denying it at workshop level or in the union itself.

In 1983 a major breakthrough in equal opportunities was made in national newspapers when three members of the London Machine Branch became the first women to work in a national newspaper machine room in London. Under this Branch's 'call system' for casual employment men had been sent to jobs in 'Fleet Street' but eligible women were paid by the Branch. When policy changed, five women were sent by the Branch to work on the *Daily Mail* but were turned away by management on the grounds there were no facilities for them and that it was illegal for women to work night shift. Two weeks later management at the *Observer* used similar arguments but the machine chapel FOC allocated jobs to three women sent by the Branch and the chapel set aside toilet facilities and a rest room. Although some argument took place at the next London Machine Branch meeting, the members accepted the position that women were full, contributing members of the Branch and therefore entitled to the same rights as male members including the opportunity to work in 'Fleet Street', something which had been denied to them in the past by the employers.

The Employment Appeal Tribunal ordered the *Daily Record* production chapel to pay £4,000 compensation for unlawful discrimination against a woman by allocating a job to a man with much less service. The chapel discussed the matter with the Equal Opportunities Commission to ensure it did not recur. At the *Daily Mirror*, a settlement was reached out-of-court when a women suffered harassment after moving into a traditional male area. Another breakthrough in equal opportunities occurred for SOGAT women members when Samuel Jones plc relocated and re-equipped their St Neot's factory. The chapel resisted management plans to select the highest grade machine operators purely on the basis of existing skills as this would have resulted in those jobs going only to men. The chapel successfully argued for a seniority system, resulting in 75 per cent of the jobs being filled by women. In addition, three women became fork-lift truck drivers. However, in reality, the attitudes towards SOGAT women members at the workplace and in the union continued for the most part unchanged.

At the 1990 Delegate Council the NEC again gave a strong lead on equal opportunities and positive action. Noting with concern continuing discrimination by the employers, one NEC motion proposed:

Chapels and branches are directed to translate SOGAT equal opportunities policies and agreements into positive action by ensuring that jobs and training are offered to women as well as men to black workers as well as white workers.[9]

To eliminate sex and race discrimination, branches and chapels were to examine their internal procedures, using the Equal Opportunities Commission and the Commission on Racial Equality codes of practices as well as TUC guidelines. Discrimination was viewed as being perpetuated by employers who profited from women's average earnings in general print being only 64 per cent of those of men, and as being exemplified by the fact that only 6 per cent of women were employed in skilled grades although 40 per cent of all employees in the industry were women. There were few women amongst the 31,000 SOGAT members in Class 1 jobs, but they accounted for the overwhelming majority of the 13,200 Class 2 members and the 10,200 in Class 3.

November 1988 saw, following an initiative by the Joint Training Council (see below), the launch of 'Achieving a Balance' to provide equal opportunities in the printing industry. 'Achieving a Balance' was a statement by the BPIF, SOGAT and the NGA that it was morally wrong to exclude women and ethnic minorities by concentrating on recruiting white men. The statement provided standards against which company practice could be judged and individual managers and workers performance assessed. The statement was to be incorporated into company manuals, rules and regulations or conditions of employment where appropriate. It gave practical advice on planning job descriptions, on recruitment and selection, introduction to work and induction training, job reviews and chapel practices. The statement re-affirmed the equal opportunities clause in the national wage basis agreement (see below) but in addition it committed the three parties to promote actively equal opportunities for all applicants and employees in the industry irrespective of race, religion or gender. Managements and chapels were urged to promote and encourage applications from all groups but in particular women and ethnic minorities, to provide equal opportunities to all applicants for jobs in recognised skilled occupations in the industry.

'Achieving a Balance' was a response to the expected decline in the number of school leavers in the mid-1990s. SOGAT saw the printing industry had either to broaden the area from which it recruited or to accept that work would be lost to the Single European Market in 1992. For SOGAT 'Achieving a Balance' provided the opportunity to take advantage of labour market trends favourable to women by negotiating further benefits for them in terms of the access to training and to lift them from the lower grades. Without equal access to training SOGAT women members would never achieve fully equal pay.

SOGAT sought to incorporate its equal opportunities policies into collective agreements. In 1983, a BPIF/SOGAT/NGA working party was established to consider whether existing clauses in the National Agreements relating to equal opportunities were sufficient or whether they could usefully be extended and to report back on the issue no later than 30 September 1983. As a result of this, the 1984 National Wage Basis Agreement replaced existing clauses on equal opportunities with a new one which committed the BPIF and SOGAT to developing positive policies to promote equal opportunity in employment regardless of a worker's sex, marital status, creed, colour, race or ethnic origins. The clause, which was applicable to all conditions of work, also committed the unions to draw opportunities for training and promotion to the attention of all eligible employees, to inform all employees of the BPIF/ SOGAT agreement on equal opportunities, to resolve at local level (and if this failed then via the dispute procedure provisions) any complaints by employees that they had suffered from unequal treatment on the grounds of sex, marital status, creed, colour or ethnic origins and to revise from time to time the operation of the equal opportunities clause in the Agreement. The 1984 Agreement also contained a clause covering a code of practice on race relations under which the BPIF brought to the attention of its member firms the Commission on Racial Equality's code of practice for the elimination of racial discrimination and the promotion of equality of opportunity in employment. The Equal Opportunities and Race Relations Code of Practice were also included in the 1984 Newspaper Society/SOGAT National Agreement.

SOGAT was also keen to promote equal opportunities for disabled people. The revision in 1989 of the National Agreement with the BPIF contained for the first time a clause on this issue. The BPIF and SOGAT committed themselves to develop positive policies to promote equal opportunities in employment for disabled people as recommended in the code of good practice on the employment of disabled people. BPIF member companies were encouraged to adopt a policy of commitment to equal opportunities for disabled employees and to consult employees and their representatives in the formulation and implementation of such policies. Particular attention was given to the training and promotion, recruitment and special needs of disabled people. Such employees were to have equal access to training, promotion and career development opportunities based on their individual aptitudes and abilities rather than their disabilities. BPIF member firms were to adopt recruitment practices and procedures which did not discriminate directly or indirectly against disabled people. BPIF member firms were to take all reasonable steps to meet the special needs of new or existing disabled employees in relation to access, toilet and welfare facilities and safety and health at work.

SOGAT also took a number of initiatives on the question of child-care provision, the lack of which discriminated against women and restricted severely their employment opportunities. The existence of child-care provision would have given women the confidence to put themselves forward for training and employers the confidence to select them, since the costs of training would not subsequently be lost by women remaining at home to care for children. Any career break for maternity would be followed subsequently by a return to work. The 1988 Delegate Meeting accepted a Greater Manchester Branch motion which deploring the lack of child-care and nursery facilities which it claimed should be freely available to all, and looked to a future Labour Government to redress this imbalance. A second successful motion from the Branch advocated tax relief for child-care. Although a nursery in 'Fleet Street' had been in existence since 1986, it faced problems due to the unwillingness of most employers to support it financially. Although some companies, for example IPC and Penguin, made payment of child-care expenses to their employees, these companies were very much the exception.

In 1989 the BPIF and SOGAT established a working party to consider child-care facilities. It examined existing provision from research, from BPIF member firms and other relevant organisations to study the most feasible ways of providing assistance. As a result of the working party's report, the BPIF and SOGAT agreed 'guidance notes' for the provision of childcare facilities in BPIF houses. These encouraged employers to consider their future labour needs in the face of demographic trends and the options available given the shortfall of local child-care provision. Such options, it was suggested, might include in-house arrangements provision of allowances, the use of childminding and recognition of out-of-school hours. The guide also contained practical advice on gathering local information and how to use it to the best advantage. It referred to the need to establish where local nursery provision was available or planned, the registered private nurseries in the area, the ages of the children for which they catered and other essential factors such as community nurseries and play groups. Chapels were to discuss with their employer what was needed in terms of child-care provision.

Sexual Harassment

SOGAT was amongst the first unions to tackle the issue of sexual harassment at the workplace. It defined harassment as 'looks, remarks and other uninvited attention being persistently directed at a woman or women'. It did not regard such behaviour as a joke if it continued after the victim had made it clear it was unwanted. However, sometimes women who complained of sexual harassment were 'sent to Coventry' by their work colleagues, abused, threatened and labelled as 'troublemakers'. Although the union was concerned that some chapel officials were reluctant to take up sexual harassment claims, its policy was clear in that any sexual harassment by SOGAT members was detrimental to the interests of SOGAT and should be dealt with accordingly.

In 1991 BPIF/SOGAT National Agreement contained for the first time, joint guidelines on sexual harassment in the workplace. Sexual harassment was defined as unwanted conduct of a sexual nature or other conduct based on sex affecting the dignity of women and men at work, as distinguishable from mutually acceptable friendly or social behaviour which occurs during contact between people at work. Sexual harassment was not condonable or tolerated at any workplace and was to be dealt with as a disciplinary offence. The grievance procedure could deal with complaints of sexual harassment, but employees who considered they were suffering from such behaviour were advised to make it clear to the alleged harasser that such behaviour was unwanted and unwelcome. The guidelines recommended employees complaining of sexual harassment seek advice, support and counselling in total confidence without any obligation to take a complaint further. Counselling was to assist the complainant to seek a solution without recourse to the formal disciplinary or grievance procedure. Where the grievance procedure was used, an opportunity was to be afforded to the employee complaining of sexual harassment to bring along, if desired, a friend employed at the work-place together with normal representation. Investigations of complaints required sensitive handling and any disciplinary action needed to be carried out quickly, confidentially and carefully. The guidelines stressed that if a complaint of sexual harassment was valid, prompt action should be taken to stop the harassment immediately and to prevent its recur-rence. Persons complaining or assisting in an investigation were to be protected from victimisation.

Health Issues

Women's health issues also received increasing attention within SOGAT in the 1980s. The demand for women to have the opportu-nity of cervical and breast cancer screening at work or having paid time off to attend a clinic was re-affirmed in a Glasgow Branch motion passed at the 1982 Delegate Council. A major breakthrough was achieved by SOGAT in 1988 when the BPIF and the Newspaper Society recognised the value of early detection in reducing the special dangers to women from cervical and breast cancer. The employers' associations' member firms were to encourage all women to undergo cervical smear tests and breast cancer screening at the frequency recommended by the medical profession. Member firms were recom-mended to provide on-site screening facilities where justified by the number of employees. Where this was impossible, they were advised to encourage individuals to make their own arrangements for screening and, provided mutually acceptable arrangements were made and evidence of attendance given, employees should have reasonable time off with pay for this purpose.

Maternity and Paternity Leave

SOGAT supported the minimum standards of maternity leave and benefit contained in the Employment Protection Act (1975) but sought to advance these by collective bargaining. In 1986 the union became committed by conference decision to extend the period for the right of women taking maternity leave to return to work any time before the end of a 52-week period after the natal confinement instead of the 29 provided for by legislation. This policy was justified on the grounds that it would improve the chances of women returning to work after the birth of a baby, that the union always sought to improve on statutory benefits and that for companies there would be no costs as far as wages were concerned. However, in the 1987 annual negotiations with the BPIF, the employers told SOGAT they were unable to accept an extension of the statutory maternity provision. This remained the position at the time of SOGAT's merger with the NGA.

SOGAT in 1988 adopted the policy that, when a woman took maternity leave and returned to work, paid holiday entitlement should be affected because of the employment break for the birth of a baby. In the 1989 wage negotiations with the BPIF SOGAT made progress in this area when the employers agreed that where an employee had returned to work under the existing statutory maternity provisions there would be no deduction from annual holiday entitlement for the first thirteen consecutive weeks of maternity absence. For each subsequent period of four complete weeks of maternity absence beyond thirteen weeks the deduction was five-thirteenths of the weekly wage ordinarily received.

In 1988 the SOGAT Delegate Council, against the advice of the NEC, committed the union to a policy of maternity benefit be paid at average earnings. The NEC opposition was based on three factors. First, only 2 per cent of the total SOGAT membership covered by the BPIF agreement had maternity pay levels over and above that provided by statute. Priority should be given to increasing this rather than increasing the level for those that already received benefit above the statutory level. Second, the BPIF was not prepared to grant the claim. In the 1988 wage negotiations with the BPIF SOGAT put forward a maternity/paternity claim that employees with six months service be paid 18 weeks maternity benefit with the right to return to the job within a period of up to 52 weeks. The maternity/paternity benefit demand was a week's pay plus any unconsolidated payments normally made. This was rejected by the BPIF. Third, that only industrial action or some other form of pressure from the shop floor might make the BPIF reconsider its view, but even if the members were prepared to take action it was unlikely the employers would change their attitude. As far as the NEC was concerned little progress would be made.

The 1983 wage claim to the BPIF and the NS included a demand that a Working Party be established to examine all facets of parental responsibility. Both employers' organisations' agreed to this request.

SOGAT's 1986 claim to the BPIF included a claim for comprehensive paternity leave arrangements as did its 1987 claim to the NS. Little progress was made in the 1986 negotiations but in the 1987 wage negotiations it was agreed a set of 'guidelines' be issued to BPIF members concerning paternity/maternity leave, bereavement arrangements and women's health issues. No progress was made with the NS, with whom not even a 'set of guidelines' could be agreed. The 1990 Delegate Council carried a Midland Counties Branch motion calling for a minimum of five days off with pay at the time of birth and homecoming of his child for the father to be negotiated in all national agreements to which SOGAT was a party, and where no provision already existed. The previous Delegate Council had requested SOGAT negotiators at all levels to raise with employers a revision of their maternity/paternity arrangements with the objective of achieving full maternity/paternity paid leave for parents adopting a child. Although SOGAT made little progress with these policies at the national level, it had some success in 'house agreements' with individual companies. However, as with enhanced maternity benefit so with paternity leave arrangements, only a small minority of the membership were benefiting.

TRAINING

Pre-1975

Traditionally the printing industry relied on a time-served apprenticeship system to meet its skill requirements. The system was based on the assumption that skills acquired during formative years would last a lifetime in the industry. Until 1985 the skill grades of the NUPB&PW and SOGAT were time-served apprentices whose training usually lasted five years. Apprenticeships covered bookbinding (hand and mechanised), print finishing and warehousing, and mechanical composition and machine managing in London. These apprenticeships were only available to young people and were not based on training to standards but on time served. In the 1950s and the 1960s the NUPB&PW traded wages and conditions of employment improvements in return for allowing the BFMP and the NS to have more craft apprentices (see Chapter 15). The apprenticeship system did not operate in national newspapers, where skilled labour was poached from general printing and provincial newspaper employers.[10]

The 1975 National Apprenticeship Agreement

By the early 1970s, however, technological developments in the industry were challenging whether the apprenticeship system was appropriate any longer. Following the 1972 BMPF & NS/SOGAT wages negotiation a Working Party was established to examine the operation of the apprenticeship system. The outcome was the 1975 National Apprenticeship Agreement which provided for normal qualification after four years' apprenticeship, early qualification for quick learners after 3½ years and late qualification for slow learners up to five years.[11] The agreement established the Joint Apprenticeship Panel – consisting of five BPIF members and five SOGAT members – to regulate the recruitment and training of SOGAT apprentices. The emphasis was placed on trade testing, which gave incentives to apprentices to apply for early qualification by awarding 95 per cent of the craft rate after 3½ years if they passed the trade test. Training was given in a systematic manner with the object of attaining craft standards within the period of apprenticeship. Apprentices attended an appropriate college-based City and Guilds Course and completed a programme of in-company training. A log book listed the training programme and provided a record of achievements throughout the apprenticeship.

However, by 1981 the 1975 Agreement was running beginning to run into trouble because of the burden of administration caused by having early, normal and late qualification, and the difficulty of the industry understanding or accepting the complexities of the scheme meant it was in danger of falling into disuse. In addition, the BPIF wished to reduce the length of the apprenticeship to 3 years. SOGAT saw little alternative but to seek changes to the 1975 apprenticeship system. It sought a new training agreement in two stages. First, a system for skilled operators would be established and then an Occupational Training Agreement for all other groups of SOGAT members employed by BPIF member firms. SOGAT needed to convince the BPIF that its main concern was an overall agreement and not just one for skilled occupations. The union circulated a consultative document to Printing and Binding Branches to obtain a consensus as to what was required in a new training agreement.[12]

The 1975 Agreement had been-negotiated when the craft apprentice intake into the industry was beginning to fall. The decline, by the early 1980s, had become more rapid due to recession and closures, particularly in the areas of bookbinding, print finishing and carton work, so that by mid-1984 the 1975 Agreement was only relevant to a tiny minority of the total entry into the industry and to a corresponding minority of SOGAT members. Companies, and chapels to some extent, had sought to 'escape' from its arrangements. SOGAT's 'consultative' document laid down four principles to underlie any new training agreement. First, it should improve opportunities for SOGAT members. Second, it should be simple to operate, and third, it should give chapels responsibility. Fourth, any new arrangements must cover all age groups and occupations and not just craft grades. The document envisaged chapel involvement and responsibility in all recruitment at company level in the areas covered by the new arrangements and including all age groups, not just young entrants. Against recruitment plans, the length of training would be determined by the skills needed for the job. For new entrants, at 16 years of age, the duration of training would be determined by the time taken to achieve agreed standards. Skilled status would not be granted until the trainee had completed the training and reached the age of 18. For adult entrants the training period would be determined by management and chapel agreement that the appropriate level of quality required for the job had been achieved. The consultative document advised that all entrants under 18 years of age be required to follow on a part-time basis for up to two years a further education course approved by the City and Guilds Institute. For entrants over 18 a written programme would be available which could be taken either in a college or in a company.

The 'consultative document' envisaged a new training structure introduced by a collective agreement with the BPIF and administered by a Joint Training Committee. The term 'trainee' would be used for entrants irrespective of age or method of entry into the industry. The rates of pay for trainees would be determined as part of the collective negotiations but would take account of age of entry and the rate for the job on completion of training and certification. The new training agreements would cover young entrants at 16 years of age, adult entrants over 18 years of age and existing employees required to train for other occupations as part of the agreed requirements of a company. It was essential that any new arrangements took on new technology issues and dealt with them to the benefit of SOGAT members. This could only be done if the union's total spread of membership and their occupations was covered in any new agreement, not just craft occupations.

The 1985 Recruitment, Training and Retraining Agreement

Early in 1985 a new agreement entitled the BPIF/SOGAT Recruitment, Training and Retraining Agreement was made to operate from August 1985. It embodied a flexible system of skills training in the areas of bookbinding, print finishing, carton converting and manufactured stationery. It would cope with the rapid technological changes occurring in the industry up to the turn of the century, improve opportunities for SOGAT members to update their skills, give chapels responsibility and match the needs of the job with the ability and aptitude of the trainee. The guiding principle behind the agreement was that training was not a once in a lifetime experience affecting only young entrants to the industry. While the new agreement offered new entrants a more relevant training package, the flexibility of the modular system could meet the retraining needs of existing skilled SOGAT members.[13] A major difference between the 1975 and the 1985 Agreements was the duration of the training. This now depended on the time needed by the trainee to achieve nationally agreed training standards. The required level of skills would be reached by a 'modular' scheme of training to standards coupled with related further education.

The aim was to provide a cost-effective and efficient system of training, retraining and related further education to suit the company, the industry and the trainee. Three principles underpinned the Agreement. First, training standards were determined by the achievement of standards of ability and performance rather than time served. Second, open-aged entry to allow adults, as well as school leavers, to train for skilled occupations and to provide companies with opportunities to operate flexible recruitment patterns suited to their own needs. Third, a nationally recognised system of awards based on the achievement of training modules determined by the industry at national level and applied to the equipment and processes of the individual company.

The key to the 1985 Agreement was a recruitment plan drawn up each year between management and the chapel and which specified the number of new entrants to be recruited and the number of existing skilled SOGAT worker to be trained or retrained during the period covered by the plan. If the recruitment plan could not be agreed by June in any year a quota system applied in each department, for example bookbinding, finishing and warehousing. The training was based on a modular system. It began with an induction module under which trainees were introduced to the way their own particular

504

company worked, its own structure and procedures. This was followed by the basic skills module. There were modules for each of the skilled SOGAT occupations within the industry and which established the standards that had to be achieved. Having completed one or more basic skills modules, the trainee undertook a skill development module which laid down the skilled production worker standards trainees should reach in the firms in which they worked. All trainees under the age of 18 were required to successfully complete an appropriate course of further education and employers required to give them at least one day a week off or the equivalent with pay for this purpose.

Towards the end of the 1980s, the general print industry experienced severe skill shortages and forecasts were being made of a sharp decline in the number of school leavers available in the early to mid-1990s. It was predicted that between 1989 and 1995 there would be 25 per cent fewer 16 year olds available for work. In 1989 the general print industry experienced a 54 per cent skill shortage and companies were accused by SOGAT of paying lip service to training but doing little in practical terms. Despite the vast amounts of money being invested in the latest technology, the employers had only invested relatively small sums in industrial training. The proportion of the work-force in printing and publishing in training in 1989 was lower than for manufacturing as a whole. Against this background the BPIF and SOGAT recognised the need to increase the intake of trainees into the industry and that trainees must be recruited from all groups, including adults, women, members of ethnic minorities and disabled people, as well as skilled and unskilled employees. In the 1990 annual wage negotiations a joint BPIF/SOGAT study on recruitment and training needs was established. Both parties accepted that the well-being, growth and development of the general print industry depended upon a well-trained, skilled and experienced work-force and that a balanced intake of new recruits to meet the short- and long-term needs of the industry was required. The BPIF recognised the necessity to offer career paths, training and promotion opportunities to maintain and improve the industry's economic performance. However, given the difficulties of predicting accurately staffing requirements, the BPIF and SOGAT agreed to conduct a joint study within the framework of the Joint Training Council to examine the industry's recruitment trends, to anticipate future staffing requirements, to establish an annual minimum trainee intake figure, to remove obstacles to recruitment and to promote and publicise jointly the employment advantages and opportunities within the industry.

Adult Training

Although SOGAT saw the number of young people undergoing training as of the vital importance, its policy towards vocational training was that it should not be confined to those under 25 years of age. Both adult unemployed members and those in employment should have access to vocational training which led to recognised qualifications at some level. In 1990 the union gave particular attention to retraining for adult workers.[14] In March 1989 SOGAT paid the expenses of trainees participating in a BPIF-funded guillotine work course at the Kitson College in Yorkshire. In Scotland, SOGAT, together with the SMPS and the Government funded an introductory course in litho printing for 12 assistants at the Glasgow College of Printing. Thirty redundant members in London underwent retraining on small offset presses, mostly at the London College of Printing, paid for by the *Daily Mail*. Most of those gained employment on completing the course. SOGAT's financial commitment of £25,000 to these schemes was matched by a similar amount from the Manpower Service Commission channelled via the BPIF. There were other local training initiatives into which SOGAT branches put money. However, SOGAT was unhappy to fund training as it regarded this a function to be carried out by Government and the employers. It was not the function of a trade union to set up training institutions. SOGAT was disappointed when in 1990 the Government channelled most of its training funds via the Training and Enterprise Councils (TECs) which were employer-dominated and weighted in favour of the very people who had shown themselves incapable of providing training.

Youth Training Schemes

In the late 1970s and early 1980s there was a significant increase in the number of unemployed young people. The Government alleviated the problem by the introduction of short-term work experience programmes. The first was the Youth Opportunities Scheme followed by the Youth Training Scheme (YTS) which combined the continuation of further education with on-the-job training. The trainee, however, did not receive the going rate for the job but a weekly training allowance. The YTS, originally for one year, was extended in 1986 to two years. However, at the end of the two years there was no guarantee of continued employment for the trainee.

The SOGAT policy to YTS was spelt out at the 1984 Biennial Council. YTS was condemned for not creating a platform for permanent employment, for undermining the concept of apprenticeships and wage scales for learners, and as an avenue for employing youngsters in unacceptable conditions and with no trade union rights. SOGAT would only accept YTS on five conditions. First, all YTS trainees in SOGAT houses were paid the going rate for the job. Second, employment continued at the end of the YTS period. Third, the full quota of apprenticeships and trainees be taken up before a YTS was adopted. Fourth, the firm had full health and safety representatives who had facilities to instruct trainees in health and safety matters. Fifth, all YTS schemes be agreed by the local SOGAT branch whether or not the section of work involved was organised. SOGAT believed this policy would achieve permanent employment for young people under trade union conditions.

In 1986, the Joint Training Council organised with the approval of the BPIF and SOGAT a Youth Training Scheme entitled *The Printing Skills Training Scheme*. It was designed to form the first two years of long-term training for young trainees and led to the award of the JTC's Certificate for Skilled Production Workers. The Scheme encouraged companies to recruit and train sufficient skilled workers to meet their long-term skill and labour requirements, to provide financial assistance to companies to offset the costs of employing and training young recruits, to support the industry's standards-based system of training and to encourage companies to deliver higher-quality training. As the Scheme was fully funded by the Training Commission, under the umbrella of the YTS, only young trainees under the age of 18 could participate. The trainees were full employees of the company and underwent training in recognised skilled occupations in bookbinding, carton manufacturing, machine printing, origination and print finishing. To attract the full two-year grant entitlement, the trainee had to be 16, to have left school at the first available opportunity and joined the company in the same year. The Scheme also accommodated 17 year olds who had stayed on at school or college for a further year, but their grant was only for one year. A deposit of £100 was required for each trainee place requested. The core of the Scheme was the standards-based training system operating in SOGAT areas in the industry and covered by the 1985 Recruitment, Training and Retraining Agreement.

Industrial Training Boards

In 1964 Parliament passed the Industrial Training Act to ensure an adequate supply of properly trained staff at all levels in industry, to secure an improvement in the quality, quantity and efficiency of industrial training and to share the cost of training more evenly between firms. The Act set up Industrial Training Boards consisting of employer, union and educationalists for the purpose of making better provision for the training of people in any activity in industry or commerce. No direct obligation was placed on employers to train. However, employers were obligated to pay a training levy which was paid back by way of a grant either less, the same or more than the amount collected in the levy depending on the amount of quality of the training undertaken. If an employer did not wish to train they could not be made to do so. However, where the size and training needs of the company made training necessary or desirable, the levy/grant system made it uneconomic for a firm to neglect the responsibility to train its own people.

SOGAT favoured the establishment of an all-embracing Industrial Training Board covering those sections of the industry covered by unions affiliated to the P&KTF. However, the Government in 1967 established two Industrial Training Boards. The Printing and Publishing Industry Training Board covered general printing and publishing and both national and local newspapers. The Paper and Paper Products Industry Training Board covered agents and merchants, conversion, paper, board, pulp and coating, stationary, wallpaper and waste paper. Ink manufacture was assigned to the Chemical Industry Training Board. SOGAT's members were thus divided amongst three Boards.

SOGAT played an active part in both Training Boards. Albert Powell, General President of SOGAT, was a respected Chairman of the Paper and Paper Products Industry Training Board whilst Brenda Dean served with distinction on the Printing and Publishing Industry Training Board – she was Chairperson of its most important committee, namely the Production Worker Training Committee. Although the two Training Boards were successful, the Conservative Government in 1981 announced its intention of removing Government financial support from all Training Boards. The Boards had enabled many SOGAT members to receive basic training in health and safety, collective bargaining and various new skills. No one employer had the ability, expertise or financial resources to carry out training of this character in their plants without a statutory approach based upon an Industrial Training Board. The printing and papermaking employers refused to impose a voluntary levy upon themselves to finance the continuation of the two Training Boards and in 1982 they were both abolished. They had been too successful and the unions had had an equal say in determining the policies of the training boards. This, the chairman of the Paper and Paper Products Industrial Training Board considered, was the real reasons why the Government abolished the statutory Industrial Training Board system.[15]

NOTES

1. Other items to be included in the 1979 wage claims were a consolidation of all supplementary payments into basic rates, a £15 increase in basic rates and a 35-hour working week.
2. After obtaining the maximum monetary increase for the membership, the first priority was to be given to the total consolidation of existing supplementary payments and the second to a reduction in working hours without loss of pay.
3. See Society of Graphical and Allied Trades (82) *Report of Biennial Delegate Council Meeting, 1988*, p. 11. It was debated at the 1976, 1978, 1980, 1982, 1984, 1986 and 1988 Biennial Delegate Council Meetings.
4. For details of the Scheme see 'June Start for General Print Pension Scheme' *SOGAT Journal*, February 1986 p2 and 'SOGAT Pips Up Your Pension' *SOGAT Journal*, December January 1990/1, p. 2.
5. The first of the monthly 'Women at Work' sections duly appeared in October 1982 and carried articles on the 'Fleet Street' crèche campaign, cancer screening for Essex and London and on the first women's course in the Solent Branch.
6. The report was carried out by researchers from North London Polytechnic and although the union co-operated with the project, the NEC stressed that its findings were independently arrived at and not binding. Responses to the research questionnaire were received from 77 per cent of branches, from a sample of 117 chapels, from 40 women's committees and a number of informal meetings. In addition, SOGAT's annual reports, journals, books, national agreements, etc. as well as TUC and other unions' literature about their women's membership were consulted.
7. See Society of Graphical and Allied Trades (Division A) *Report of the Biennial Delegate Council Meeting*, 1966, p. 227.
8. Although it was claimed that men at the *Financial Times* did not blame the women and recognised that the attack on their wages came from management, SOGAT's Organising Secretary linked the problem to the continued existence of single-gender chapels. SOGAT wished to eliminate single-gender chapels not by 'submerging' women but by encouraging reserved seats and full participation on the factory floor and in the branches.
9. See Society of Graphical and Allied Trades (82) *Report of the Biennial Delegate Council Meeting, 1990*, p. 84

10. The only apprenticeship permitted in 'Fleet Street' was photography.
11. For a description of the 1975 National Apprenticeship Agreement see 'A Guide to the BPIF–SOGAT Apprenticeship Agreement', *SOGAT Journal*, June 1989, pp. 16–18.
12. See 'New Plans for Training Agreement with BPIF', *SOGAT Journal*, May 1984, p. 5.
13. See 'Modular Training for General Print' *SOGAT Journal*, August 1985, pp. 8–9.
14. See Society of Graphical and Allied Trades' Biennial Delegate Council, (82) *Report on Training*, 1990, Scarborough, p. 1.
15. See 'Too Successful – and the Unions had an Equal Say', *SOGAT Journal*, January 1982, p. 9.

CHAPTER 17

PAPERMAKING AND PAPER CONVERSION

THE SECTORS

This chapter traces the development of industrial relations over the period 1955–91 in three subsectors of the papermaking and paper conversion industry – paper and board, cardboard box and paper bag. In paper- and board-making, industrial relations covering process workers were regulated by the National Agreement between the Employers' Federation of Papermakers and Boardmakers (subsequently the British Paper and Board Industry Federation)[1] and the NUPB&PW (subsequently SOGAT). This agreement provided minimum standards and formed the basis for a second tier of bargaining at company and/or chapel level. There was no national agreement covering minimum standards for staff employees, although in 1972 agreement was reached between the employers' federation and SOGAT setting the conditions for granting local recognition of the union for staff employees and the procedures to be observed for dealing with disputes in those mills where recognition was granted.

The second subsector was cardboard box production, covering cartons, fibreboard packaging case and rigid boxes. Until 1975 employment conditions were regulated by Orders from the Paper Box Wages Council which was abolished in that year. However, in 1965 fibreboard packaging was removed from the jurisdiction of the Wages Council and minimum wages and conditions of employment were regulated by a National Agreement between the British Fibreboard Packaging Case Employers' Association and the NUPB&PW (subsequently SOGAT). This agreement had originally been concluded in 1963 in view of the desire of both employers and employees to negotiate outside the Wages

511

Council's jurisdiction.[2] In carton production the union had in 1963 also persuaded the British Carton Association to conclude a national agreement, although carton production continued within the scope of the Wages Council. This National Agreement continued until 1978 when it was decided to follow the BPIF/SOGAT National Wages Basis Agreement.[3] Rigid box employees were represented by the British Paper Box Federation (subsequently the Box and Packaging Association),[4] and following the abolition of the Wages Council, minimum employment conditions were regulated by a national agreement between the Federation/Association and SOGAT.

The third subsector, was paper bag production. Until 1969 minimum terms and conditions of employment were determined by Orders from the Paper Bag Wages Council. However, in August 1964 a National Agreement, negotiated with the British Paper Bag Federation on the one hand and the NUPB&PW and NATSOPA on the other established employment standards in addition to those of the Wages Council.[5] Following the abolition of the Wages Council in 1969 this Agreement was the cornerstone for collective bargaining relationships. However, in 1982 SOGAT terminated the National Agreement believing its members stood to gain more from local-level negotiations. In 1963, the employers in the multi-wall sack sector of paper bag production formed the Multi-wall Sack Manufacturers' Employers' Association and in 1965 the first ever national agreement in this sector became operative.[6] It provided terms and conditions of employment far in excess of the Wages Council's Orders,[7] was the cornerstone of collective bargaining following the abolition of the Wages Council and remained in operation at the time of SOGAT's merger with the NGA.

PAPERMAKING AND BOARD-MAKING

Wage Rates

In 1955 employment conditions were governed by the No. 10 Agreement which had been signed in 1947. In the 1950s the NUPB&PW pressed for increases in the standard of living justified by increased productivity from the implementation of new machinery and to protect real wages by observing trends in the cost of living index such that when this increased by a certain amount submitting an application for a wage increase could be submitted. In 1958, when the employers rejected a claim for an increase in wages, they justified this in view of the present economic climate. NUPB&PW sought its branches' views on either giving the negotiating committee discretion to decide when the claim might be resubmitted or whether the issue be referred to the Industrial Disputes Tribunal. The majority of branches preferred the latter option but, before the matter could proceed to arbitration, the employers proposed that in future mills be divided into two groups for basic wage payments. When the NUPB&PW considered this suggestion neither fair nor practical, the employers made an improved offer which was acceptable to the union's members.

In the period 1964 to 1969, wage increase demands were complicated by the operation of the Government's productivity, prices and incomes policy. The 1967 claim to the Employers' Federation of Papermakers and Board-makers was declared by the TUC's vetting committee to be contrary to the Government's incomes policy. The 1969 pay negotiations were lengthy but the result was a comprehensive wage increase, the consolidation of bonuses into basic wages and stabilisation until December 1971. This was the industry's first long-term agreement and gave considerable benefits.

In 1965 the NUPB&PW and the Employers' Federation made an agreement, separate from the No. 10 Agreement, to cover employees working on a four-shift continuous process. The background was the UK's impending entry into the Common Market. It was felt that the present agreement affecting four-shift working needed examination as membership of the Common Market would lead ultimately to more four-shift system working. Indeed, the NUPB&PW recognised that this was the only means by which some mills would survive. In 1964 a special meeting of NUPB&PW papermill delegates accepted four-shift working only if it were outside the existing No. 10 Agreement. At the time only eight mills worked a four-shift system but no agreement covered them. The No. 10 Agreement acted as a guide regarding wages. The holidays and hours of work conditions in the eight mills were different than those in three-shift mills. An approach was made to the Federation to seek a shift premium of 33.33 per cent for four-shift working but the employers rejected the demand. However, in early 1965 a Four-Shift Agreement was concluded under which four crews each worked a 42-hour week (reduced from 44) but were paid for 51 hours.

By 1973 a booming economy gave papermaking workers full employment and the 1974 wage negotiations resulted in a substantial increase in basic rates, increased overtime, shift and holiday pay allowances plus a £4.40 per week 'threshold' payment stemming from the government's counter-inflation policy. The period of the TUC/Labour Government 'social contract' saw limitations to wage increases. In 1976 a £6 increase as a supplement for all adult workers was achieved whilst in the following year the supplement was increased in line with TUC/Government by 5 per cent or a cash increase of £2.50 minimum and £4.50 maximum. In December 1977 the 5 per cent supplement was consolidated into the new basic rates. The £6 supplement was not consolidated until November 1979, which also saw the abolition of the women's rate. The 1979 agreement established basic rates ranging from £46 per week for Class 3 employees to £70.87 for Class 1 workers employed on a four-shift basis.

In the early 1980s, wage negotiations between SOGAT and the British Paper and Board Industry Federation took place against an industry operating below capacity, mills closing and unemployment rising. This led in 1984 to the two parties accepting joint action at the mill level to reduce costs and thereby improve international competitiveness. Although the 1984 negotiations resulted in increased basic rates, a minimum earnings level of £77 for 40 hours and an increase in call-out payments to £4, it was rejected by the SOGAT membership, who objected to the conditions placed on workers wishing to take three consecutive weeks' holiday. The union balloted its members for strike action. But this course was heavily rejected.

In the 1985 annual negotiations SOGAT sought a more realistic relationship between national rates of pay and earnings in the mills with the objective of assisting lower-paid workers and resolving the problems of the percentage relationship between basic rates and shift rates.[8] Since 1985 anomalies had developed with the national minimum rate structure around differentials of classification and shift payments. The three process unions (SOGAT, T&GWU and GMBATU) proposed the problem be solved by a consolidation of the minimum earnings level difference, namely £7.32 into the day worker Class 3 rate and a pro rata adjustment in other class and shift rates. After long and protracted negotiations it was agreed that the first stage of a three-stage consolidation be implemented by consolidation from bonus from minimum earnings level payment of £2.44 to Class 3 day workers plus the agreed general increase and to implement pro rata for the other classification and shift rates to those mills affected. After this stage of consolidation the difference between minimum earnings level and Class 3 day minimum rate was reduced from £7.32 to £4.88. The implementation of the second and third stages meant the minimum Class 3 day rate became in 1987 the minimum earnings level, with the result that the provision for a minimum earnings level in the National Agreement ceased.

Improving the shift working differential over day working was a frequent issue of concern to SOGAT. By 1978, the differentials between shift and day rates had, in percentage terms (though not in cash terms), had been eroded by the restrictions of the Labour Government's 'social contract'. In 1978 SOGAT and BPBIF agreed that over a period of 12 months discussions would take place to reach an agreement on the basis for a percentage link between the agreed rates of shift workers and those of day workers. The 1979 revision of the National Agreement provided for a permanent percentage link between the increase agreed for shift workers and day workers. This revision established shift differentials of 2.8p per hour for Class 1 shift workers over Class 1 day workers. Class 1 three-shift workers achieved a differential of 2.3p per hour over day workers whilst Class 1 double day shift workers achieved a differential of 0.5p per hour over Class 1 day workers. In 1980 it was established for the first time that shift workers be recognised as such and paid accordingly and that this be reflected in the wage structure ending the situation whereby skilled staff and shift workers within the papermaking industry were tied to the lowest day rate.

SOGAT sought improvements to shift differentials in 1987, 1988, 1989 and 1990 but on each occasion the members rejected any improvements in shift differentials. They argued that comparisons with other continuous working industries showed paper and board in a favourable light. They contended the industry's wage structure provided composite rates which were subject to all the various forms of premium payments which meant shift differentials had to be compared in earnings for a basic contractual week rather than in hourly terms. Some industries which had superior shift differentials in hourly terms applied overtime and weekend premia to the grade rate only, thereby excluding the shift differential element of the rate. The employers argued that paper and board was a shift-working industry and increasingly one geared to continuous operation. The logic behind the National Agreement formula for determining shift differentials was becoming more not less relevant.

The employers also considered the base upon which the shift differentials structure rested was too low, given that National Agreement rates had increased by 35 per cent over the period 1986 to 1989 as a result of the consolidation of minimum earnings levels and general wage increases whilst maintaining all shift differentials. The formula that guaranteed general wage increases were of benefit across the pay structure and money used to improve shift differentials would reduce the amount available for general basic rate increases. For every £1 increase given to the day worker, continuous shift workers in the same grade received £1.63. The employers felt a further widening of this differential was unjustified as there had been no movement in National Agreement differentials since the existing system of shift differentials had been agreed in 1979. The employers also maintained that any concern about the issue could, and had, been dealt with through the industry's flexible arrangements for local bargaining. However, during the 1990 annual negotiations, the BPBIF agreed to hold discussions on improving shift differentials during the life of the agreement. By the time SOGAT merged with the NGA little progress had been made.

Against what SOGAT described as the best background to negotiate for several years, the union restricted its 1986 claim to three points: a substantial wage increase, a reduction in the working week and improvements in shift differentials. The employers' offer consisted only of a straight wage increase and was rejected unanimously by the union's members. They were balloted to take industrial action but voted by 8,406 to 3,682 against taking industrial action.

In the late 1980s and the early 1990s, negotiations took place against a difficult background, with the BPBIF arguing in each set of negotiations that because of rising costs, higher interest rates and an inability to achieve suitable product prices, any increases to employment conditions must be no more than the going inflation rate. However, SOGAT gained, *inter alia*, increases in basic rates and the call-out allowance which stood at £7.50 in 1991. To obtain these improvements, the process unions had accepted greater labour flexibility and give co-operation in all change necessary at the mill level to offset the cost increases flowing from revisions of National Agreements.

Job Classification

The National Agreement contained a skill grading structure for the process workers who were referred to as Class 1, Class 1A, Class 2 and Class 3. The most highly skilled Class 1 paper or board job was machine man. The 1956 Biennial Delegate Council adopted several resolutions which suggested upward reclassification of certain jobs, for example that of reel packer and leading stoker. After consultation with the T&GWU and the GMB, the NUPB&PW forwarded claims for job reclassification, to the Employers' Federation of Papermakers and Boardmakers with the suggestion that appropriate sub-committees discuss the matter.[9] Although the employers accepted this suggestion and a number of meetings took place, progress was slow. Agreement was not finally reached until mid-1958. Some jobs were upgraded but the membership was not entirely satisfied and motions to re-classify particular jobs continued to appear on the Delegate Council agenda. The 1966 Council approved four resolutions for upgrading, the 1970 Council one, the 1972 Council one and the 1974 Council four.[10] Matters were not helped in that in many cases the classification of jobs in Scottish mills was different from those in England, and throughout the country classifications varied between particular mills.

Concerns over the classification of jobs were an important factor in the North West Group successfully moving a motion to the 1974 Delegate Council that in the light of technological changes and the introduction of multi processes, the NEC establish a working party, comprised of National and Branch Officials and members working at the trade, to restructure the Papermaking and Board-making Agreement. Three reasons lay behind this. First, the union was making little progress in achieving the reclassification of jobs despite promises from the leadership in response to Delegate Council motions that they would be undertaken at the first available opportunity. The employers were adamant they would not concede reclassification. Second, the National Agreement had fallen behind the times. Technical changes and new machines had been introduced into the industry and had made some of the formerly lower-paid jobs of equal importance to some of the top-paid jobs. Third, re-classification claims should be settled outside the normal wage negotiations. If this happened, it would reduce the probability of general wage increases being traded against not pushing reclassification and would result in action on the re-classification front.

Following the Delegate Council, the NEC extended the terms of reference of the working party to embrace the procedure agreement, the existing wage structure, job classification, shift patterns, health and safety and lay-off and short-time working arrangements. In considering the problem of restructuring the present national classification the working party considered a number of factors including the confusion caused by the use of varying job titles which covered identical jobs across the industry, that other trade unions and the employers' federation had varying opinions on re-classification and that the exercise carried out by the working party could not be a job evaluation but a job comparison exercise. The working party concluded that it was impossible to bring the varying processes into one master classification and after some considerable discussion and evaluation, recommended to the 1976 Delegate Council that there be a three-grade classification structure throughout the different processes.[11] Their analysis resulted in two jobs being upgraded into Class I and 13 jobs being upgraded to Class 1A. This policy of a three-grade structure via the abolition of Grade 3 was accepted by the 1976 Delegate Council.

However, this policy did not meet with much sympathy from the BPBIF. In 1979 agreement was reached on classification of occupations within traditional plant classifications and an understanding at local level reached concerning implementation of the agreed classification structure. Class 3 jobs were defined as 'minimal skill jobs'. SOGAT continued to demand the abolition of this grade. The employers continued to refuse to concede, arguing that redundancies and re-organisation in the industry were reducing considerably the numbers employed in the Grade. By 1988, 1,200 employees (65 per cent of the process worker labour force) were classified as Class 3 workers and of these 270 were women. The Federation consistently argued that the Class still had relevance across the papermaking industry, to abolish it would compress the job and skill structure with inevitable consequence upon skills differentials and the sub-contracting of minimal skill jobs, such as cleaning, would take place. Abolition of Class 3 would inevitably mean it was illogical to expect those employees already in Class 2 jobs, who had achieved a degree of experience in order to perform their jobs would not seek restoration of their position. The Federation consistently argued that a four-class job structure in the National Agreement was realistic considering the range of skills covered and that most mills had more than four grades in their domestic structures. When in 1989 the union coupled its claim for the abolition of Class 3 with an expression of concern at the number of women in the Class, the BPBIF argued that in that year there were 840 men and 240 women in Class 3 which did not constitute a majority of women in either the Class or industry. The total number of women in Class 3 over the period 1987–9 had been reduced from 8.5 per cent to 6.5 per cent of the total process workforce. In the 1991 annual negotiations the BPBIF agreed to establish a working party to review, without any commitment to action, the grading structure which had last been revised in 1979.

In the 1987 annual negotiations, SOGAT claimed there should be no loss of grade classification due to the introduction of new technology. The employers rejected the claim, although they recognised that technological advances impacted upon traditional job functions leading to the need to acquire new or updated skills, the deskilling of some jobs and in some cases job losses. However, the employers claimed there was no evidence of any difficulties in this regard that could not be dealt with at mill level and argued that, in general, the proportion of the work-force in higher-skilled jobs had increased over time. The circumstances surrounding change could only be assessed and dealt with adequately at mill level. Many mills had successfully dealt with the problem in a variety of ways which had been acceptable to their employees. It was impossible, the employers considered, to give a blanket guarantee in the National Agreement about the impact of technical change on job content.

Holidays

A second week's paid holiday was negotiated in 1954 but was conditional on NUPB&PW members working overtime to recover any losses of production stemming from this second week's holiday. This lead to individual mills staggering holidays or running through a number of weekends. In 1955 the union sought to remove this overtime obligation. The employers were reluctant but agreed after protracted negotiations. They also conceded pro rata holiday pay, which was a considerable improvement on existing arrangements under which employees had to work for at least 12 months before being entitled to holiday pay, and to terminate the existing provision in the No. 10 Agreement under which for the first shift to cover absences only the flat time rate was paid.[12]

The 1958 Delegate Council approved, against the NEC's advice, an Aylesford Branch motion that a claim be made to the employers for three weeks' paid holiday. The NEC's opposition was based on Delegate Council policy that the highest priority be given to a demand for a 40-hour working week. To claim a 40-hour week and three weeks' holiday together when the economic state of the industry was poor, was unrealistic. The priority had been given to the 40-hour week. The NUPB&PW Papermaking Negotiating Committee decided to leave the three weeks' holiday demand in abeyance until the 40-hour week had been achieved. The 1962 Delegate Council agreed in the light of the 40-hour week having been achieved that the three week holiday claim be revived. In 1965 the Employers' Federation offered from January 1966 two additional days' holiday with pay over and above the existing two weeks on condition these holidays did not cause a loss of production. In 1969 the employers conceded the principle of the third week's paid holiday to be implemented by two additional days in 1969 and a complete third week from 1 January 1970.

In 1973, SOGAT submitted, successfully, a claim for a fourth week's paid holiday entitlement whilst in the 1974 negotiations an extra day's paid holiday was gained. In 1980 annual holiday entitlement increased to four weeks and two days. From 1 July 1981 entitlement became four weeks and three days, whilst from 1 July 1982 process workers were entitled to five weeks' paid holiday. It had taken five long years to get the Employers' Federation to concede a fifth week's holiday. In the 1991 annual negotiations the BPBIF rejected SOGAT's demand for six weeks' paid holiday.

As well as increasing the length of paid holiday entitlement periods, SOGAT sought to gain holiday payment based on average earnings rather than basic rates plus 16.66 per cent. In 1968 the union claimed average earnings be paid during annual holidays. The employers would not concede this demand but did increase the percentage bonus on basic rates to 20 per cent for day workers, double day shift and three-shift workers. The percentage plus for four-shift workers increased from 10 per cent to 12 per cent. In anticipation of the revision of the National Agreement in February 1973, SOGAT submitted a fresh claim for improved wages and conditions including average earnings for holidays or the basic weekly rate plus 20 per cent, whichever was the greater, and double pay for working on bank holidays. The employers granted average earnings for holidays and in 1974 they conceded the overtime rate of time and half for the five public holidays be increased to double time and New Year's day be added to the list of statutory public holidays.

Hours of Work

Papermaking is a continuous process industry thereby giving problems when changing the hours of work. It is difficult to take odd hours out of a shift pattern and make the rota balance. One consequence was that overtime working was necessary to cover labour supply problems stemming from small reductions in the working week, sickness, unauthorised absences, staff shortages and shift reliefs either not turning up or arriving late for work. The need for overtime was a bone of contention in the industry as the employees regarded it as compulsory rather than voluntary, as interfering in their social lives and keeping wage rates low. It was widely accepted that a papermaking machine man had to work an eight-hour shift, with all its social inconveniences, to earn a wage which equalled that of the carton worker, and that when overtime and bonus earnings were not taken into account, papermaking was a low-paid industry. In an attempt to resolve these problems SOGAT and the BPBIF in their 1982 annual negotiations agreed to the concept of reduced working time as opposed to a reduced working week.[13]

The Reduced Working Week

In 1954 standard hours for day workers became 45 per week spread over 5½ days and 44 per week for double day shift workers. However, under the No. 10 agreement employees were obligated to work 72 hours overtime in any six months to cover staffing shortages, so this hours reduction meant employees worked as many hours as in the past but now received extra overtime hours of pay. In 1958 the Carronvale Branch committed the NUPB&PW to secure a 40-hour week of five days without any loss of weekly wages for shift workers, but when this was rejected in the 1959 annual wages negotiations by the Employers' Federation of Papermakers and Boardmakers. However, in 1960 the union obtained a reduction of two hours in the working week, giving a 42-hour week for shift workers and a 43-hour week for day workers. Initially the employers' offer was conditional on the union agreeing to operate a four-shift system. However, this condition was dropped when a special papermill delegate meeting rejected such a system.

The 1962 the NUPB&PW decided to seek from the papermaking employers the provision that the working week be spread over five days instead of 5½. In the same year the Federation accepted that the working week of day workers be reduced from 43-hours to 42 per week but spread over 5½ days. The 1964 Delegate Council adopted the policy of obtaining a 40-hour working week of five days for all papermills and in the 1965 annual negotiations the NUPB&PW secured the introduction of a 40-hour week from 1 January 1966. The 40-hours were spread over five days but with the requirement for continuous Saturday working by day workers, with these hours paid at overtime rates. The employers claimed this condition was essential if the paper industry was to compete with the Scandinavian countries and Canada.

Although the SOGAT (Division A) members accepted this condition, there were demands by 1968 that the time had arrived to remove the overtime obligation as this denied the 40-hour week since the weekly production hours remained at 132. Members continued to work 42-hours but received overtime payments for the last two hours. The same had happened when the working week was reduced from 44-hours to 42.[14]

In 1972 SOGAT requested progress be made towards the introduction of a 35-hour working week but the employers made no serious response to the demand. The 1976 Delegate Council recommended SOGAT pursue a policy of a shorter working week with the objective of securing a 35-hour week for all members. The TUC/Labour Government's pay restraint policies complicated any moves in this regard. However, by the early 1980s both sides recognised that a reduction in the working week, increased holidays, etc. created problems relating to the running time and production hours in many mills. Tackling these by more and more overtime working was not the answer if shorter working hours were to be achieved without damaging the industry's competitiveness and if overtime, to maintain production, was to be minimised. To this end, in the 1982 annual negotiations, the employers tabled proposed guidelines for fundamental changes that could be agreed at local level to obtain consequential reductions in working time, provision for those not able or not wishing to make such major changes, and a reduction in the working year of 47-hours from 1 January 1983 subject to detailed agreement being reached by 31 March 1983. SOGAT accepted these proposals in principle, but in view of their complexity and the need to deal with the wages question promptly, both parties agreed negotiations on working time continue separately and a National Agreement covering working time be reached.

Reduced Working Time

The National Agreement of 5 February 1982, which was implemented on 1 January 1983, provided guidelines for negotiation at local level to achieve a reduction in working time using the annual hours concept coupled with the adoption of new systems of work. In principle, the annual hours concept was a method by which working time could be reduced and organised with greater efficiency. It expressed the hours to be worked on an annual basis after removing all holiday entitlements.

All working time was rostered into the system with the remainder being leisure time made up of rest days and holidays. The National Agreement was purely 'enabling', and details of how the system would operate in individual mills was to be determined at local level. Unlike the pre-1982 system, in which employee absences, holidays or overtime requirements were covered by existing employees working extra hours or by shutting down production, annual hours specified the number of actual hours an employee would work. As the National Agreement explained:

> The Annual Hours System requires identification of (a) production requirements if possible for the year, and (b) the number of hours per year that the employee is available to work after taking into account the length of the normal working week and annual and public holidays. The shift system and crewing arrangements are then designed to meet these requirements.[15]

The National Agreement on Working Time aimed to reduce the actual number of hours worked by employees and to increase production time. Safeguards were built into the agreement to restrict to a minimum the need to deal with 'unforeseen events' and to ensure employees received at least one two-week break in summer. Inclusive of the move to five weeks' holiday by 1983, annual hours were reduced from 1,931 to 1,867 for those working continuous operations (i.e. 24 hours per day, seven days per week); from 2,023 to 1,958 hours on semi-continuous operations (i.e. 24 hours per day but less than seven days per week) and from, 1,839 to 1,776 hours for those on day work (usually 6.00 a.m. to 6.00 p.m.). However, the annualised hours concept was purely voluntary. No mill was compelled to adopt an annualised hours system but the SOGAT membership regardless were still entitled to the annual reduction of the 47 hours. The Working Time Agreement meant that for the first time SOGAT members employed in paper and board mills could determine in each mill, within limits, their hours of work for the future, subject to the agreement being endorsed at branch and Head Office level.

By the end of 1990, one-third of mills were operating on an annualised hours basis. Of manual process workers 46 per cent were working annualised hours. However, SOGAT was disappointed with some aspects of the operation of the Working Time Agreement.[16] First, although 25 mills had adopted annualised hours only seven had established reductions below 39 hours. The union was particularly disappointed by this since most European and Scandinavian competitors operated on basic hours well below the UK. Second, few mills had taken up the option to reduce their basic working hours. This was especially disappointing considering that the mills adopting annual hours unanimously said it was superior to their old system of working. Third, the amount of overtime worked to provide sickness, absence and holiday cover continued at high levels, reflected in the fact that whilst basic rates were about £150 per week, actual average earnings in the industry were £300 per week. Finally, in those mills where hours had been reduced, the initiative had come from management rather than the chapel.

However, perhaps the biggest disappointment to SOGAT was that although it had treated claims for a reduction in the working week as a priority, the BPBIF had always rejected them. In 1986, 1987, 1989, 1990 and 1991 SOGAT submitted a claim for a reduction in the working week without loss of pay but on each occasion the Employers Federation stated that in view of the 1982 Agreement on Working Time they were not prepared to enhance their position on a reduced working week. They considered reductions in working time should be determined at mill or local level using the Reduction in Working Time Agreement of 1982. They said that when compared with manufacturing industry generally, the paper and board industry was part of the 86 per cent which had a basic week of 39 hours or less whilst overseas comparisons with competitor countries showed that whilst some had lower hours for shift workers, others had similar basic weekly hours for day workers and, in some cases, a longer basic week. The employers contended the annual hours provision was the basis for reducing all working time – overtime and basic hours – without damaging the competitiveness of the industry, whereas across the board reductions would damage the industry's competitive position because of the need to provide cover, under traditional working arrangements, for people taking time off. They claimed mills which had moved to annual hours showed substantially lower levels of total hours, including overtime, than those which had not. SOGAT responded to these arguments by consulting and encouraging their members at local level to commence negotiations on reductions of working time under the provision of the National Agreement. The union committed itself to monitor the progress of these negotiations and, if they proved unsuccessful, to reconsider its position regarding the Annual Hours Agreement. Little progress had been made in this regard at the time SOGAT merged with the NGA.

Overtime Working

The clause in the No. 10 Agreement requiring employees to work 72 hours overtime in any six-month period was a contentious issue and there were attempts at several Delegate Councils to have this clause withdrawn or amended.[17] The opposition was from the anti-overtime lobby. Papermill workers were not against overtime and recognised that to cope with orders, meet delivery dates, etc. a certain amount of overtime working was necessary. The opposition to the obligatory overtime was based on three things: its compulsion, the power it gave to employers and the fact that the interests of the employees, as well as employers, should be taken into account.

Under the No. 10 Agreement, the obligatory overtime clause was triggered by the employer giving 48 hours' notice. The obligation was on production overtime, which meant it could only be done at weekends. Its opponents wished to make the 72 hours' obligation voluntary so the decision to work overtime was made by each individual employee. Employees should decide whether they wished to work outside normal working hours and members should not tolerate a situation where they could not chose what they did with their leisure time. No member should be asked, at 48 hours' notice, to sacrifice a weekend which they expected to spend with their family.

Obligatory overtime meant the mill ran through six weekends in six calendar months. There was, however, nothing to prevent the employer seeking a further spell of overtime providing proper notice was given. There was also an obligation to turn out on weekends in which the mill was not working in order to carry out maintenance repairs. The clause gave the employers too much power over the workers' leisure time. Employers were seen as taking a rather unbending attitude towards the employees' obligation, such that any prior commitments of the employee had to go once the notice was posted concerning overtime. A more liberal attitude on the part of employers was required.

Members opposed to the obligatory overtime clause also disliked that the voice of the employee was not heard on whether overtime should be worked. Motions to the 1964 and 1970 Delegate Councils suggested solutions to this complaint. The 1964 Council proposed production overtime be arranged in consultation with the work-force through their trade union representatives at the mill. The voice and interests of the workers would be heard through the union official, who would be consulted by management. It was envisaged that decisions as to whether, and when,

overtime be worked would be taken in the interests not only of management but also of the workers. There were many occasions when it was
in the interests of the workers that some overtime be worked, but
workers should have a say when this might be the case. The 1970 Council
proposed management ask the employees if they wished to work the
'obligatory' overtime, and if they were willing then they should be remu-
nerated at double time.

Those who supported the 'compulsory' overtime clause argued its
opponents were deluding themselves if they did not recognise that
many members liked weekend working and the extra money this
brought. Some supported the clause as an inevitable consequence of
continuous process production whilst others supported it as the only
way the industry would remain competitive in a Europe becoming
more free-trade orientated. Although the union sought to persuade
the employers to remove the clause, they were unsuccessful. In 1970,
however, the employers agreed to increase the length of notice
required to trigger the clause from 48 hours to one week.

Another bone of contention surrounding overtime working was the
need to work on after a shift had been completed in order to cover
for staffing shortages, absenteeism and the shift mate failing to turn
up or turning up late. In these circumstances, if the employee did not
work overtime the machine would have to close down, but to continue
working could mean an employee working a further 12 hours after
completing their original shift. The 1968 Delegate Council approved a
resolution from the Barrow Branch that if a shift cover failed to materialise then the employer must find a relief within one hour or the
employee would not work on. In 1969 the Employers' Federation of
Papermakers and Boardmakers agreed to make 'reasonable efforts' to
avert shift mates having to cover for absence. Any question of abuse
would be raised at Federation level. However, although a survey by
the union on cover for shift mates absence showed most mills had
arrangements between chapels and branches for dealing with the issue,
the problem never disappeared completely. Even in the late 1980s the
issue was still raised at the Delegate Council. The 1986 Delegate
Council Meeting, for example, approved a motion from the Wales and
the West branch 'that under the terms and conditions of the BPBIF
Agreement, all reference to staying on at your place of work having
completed your shift be deleted from the said agreement'.[18]

It was argued that with employment declining in the industry, it was
absurd for members who had already worked eight to 12 hours being

compelled to wait around whilst managers decided what they would do to cover the absence. SOGAT considered the argument that such a situation was sometimes inevitable in a continuous production process to be an excuse, and that in reality management was not interested in addressing the problem.

Dispute Activity

The National Agreement contained a procedure for avoiding disputes. By the mid-1960s there was mounting discontent amongst NUPB&PW members over the time being taken to resolve matters under the procedure. In some cases this was taking up to 14 months. There was also a feeling the procedure was only worth using if there was no alternative, as it was biased in favour of the employers' interests. These concerns led delegates to accept the 1966 Delegate Council Purfleet Branch motion:

> that the present No 10 Procedure Agreement dealing with 'Provisions for Avoiding Disputes' is in our opinion undemocratic and in favour of the employer, therefore six months notice of termination of this agreement should be given and a Delegate Meeting of all Paper and Mill branches should be called to discuss a new Procedure Agreement.[19]

On 23 June 1967 a Mill Delegates Conference was held to formulate amendments to the existing disputes procedure. It decided six of the seven clauses remain unaltered but that Clause 3 be amended so that any disagreements arising in a papermill which the management and the employee or employees immediately concerned were unable to settle should be referred within ten days for consideration by a higher level of management and representatives of SOGAT (Division A). If the dispute could not be resolved at this level then the issue was to be referred to and considered within one month by a committee consisting of five members appointed by the Employers' Federation and SOGAT together with an independent chairperson acceptable to both parties. The Mill Delegates Conference agreed that at this level the local parties, whether on the management or the union side, could be called to give evidence but they should take no part in the findings.

SOGAT (Division A) and the Employers' Federation of Papermakers and Board-makers agreed in the 1968 annual negotiations that amendments to the Recognition and Procedure Agreement of the No

10 Agreement operate from 1 January 1969. Despite SOGAT (Division A) attempts to have the District Conference stage of the procedure eliminated, it remained. Of a total of 59 Conferences over the three years 1966–9, 48 had been settled at mill level, nine at district level and two at executive level. It was felt that the district stage still played an important role. At this level there was representation of four from the employers' side and four from the union side, one of which would be the Papermaking Secretary. At the District Conference Stage the Papermaking Secretary would present the union's case. The employers would then present their case and retire from the Conference room. The position which had operated in the past, whereby union officials attending the District Conference had been faced by upwards of 15 employers' representatives would cease. At the Executive Conference level stage a Conference would be held within one month of failing to resolve the issue at a District Conference level. Representative of the employers at this stage would be four people – the President of the Federation, the Director of the Federation, plus two others – with the same on the union side – the General Secretary, the Papermaking Secretary plus two others. The Chair of the Conference would be held by whichever side's behaviour was being challenged. Where the complaint was brought at the national level by the union, the Employers' Federation President would occupy the Chair. Where the complaint was by the employer, the General Secretary would occupy the Chair. SOGAT had wanted each side to have five representatives at the Executive Conference stage, and there be an independent Chair who should be a 'Birkett' type to help the parties to reach a solution but without a casting vote or having power to give a decision. It was envisaged that if there were a failure to agree, the Chair would report back to the parties who would then have decided what further action to take. Although the union had made important concessions from its ideal position, it now had a recognition and disputes procedures which was an improvement on what had operated beforehand.

The new disputes procedure worked well and most disputes were settled at Mill Conference level. There has never been a national strike in the papermaking industry. The number of mill disputes has also been low, the highest number in the last 20 years having been in 1974 when 34 strikes took place. Over the period 1980 to 1991 inclusive 46 mill-level strikes were recorded by the BPBIF, of which 33 took place between 1980 and 1984 and 13 between 1985 and 1991. Industrial relations in papermaking have been good. Relationships between the unions and the employers' association have been constructive. They had been tough but professional negotiations, with nothing conceded easily and nothing achieved easily. Both sides had had to argue their cases.

Nevertheless, there have been some bitter strikes, one of which started in December 1980 at the Roach Bridge papermill in Lancashire when, following recruitment to the union, the Father of the Chapel was dismissed and the 60 members who went on strike in support of him were sacked.[20] The crisis had developed suddenly on 19 November 1980 when the FOC, Frank Brown, was sacked in breach of normal procedures, for alleged poor timekeeping. A 24-hour picket was maintained, chemical supplies to the company blacked, the management refused to meet with SOGAT representatives, the union declared the strike official and invaluable help came from the Trades Councils of Preston, Blackburn and the Lancashire Association in the form of moral, financial, material and practical support. During the dispute some pickets were injured and others were brought before the courts on various charges. The dispute dragged on with what appeared to be little chance of resolution. Although some workers drifted away from the picket lines, a hard core remained.

On 7 August 1981 a meeting was held at the offices of ACAS in Manchester between the employer and SOGAT, and after six hours' of talks a formula was agreed which ended the dispute. The company granted SOGAT negotiating rights on behalf of its members employed by the company, the union members, including the FOC, involved in the dispute were reinstated on a phased basis starting on 8 September and concluding by the end of the year, £20 per week would be granted to all workers awaiting jobs and SOGAT would be afforded the opportunity of meeting all workers at the mill no later than the end of 1981. So ended a bitter dispute which had been described by some as the 'Grunwick of the North'. The dispute had stated on 19 December 1980 and had lasted nine months. At the time it was the longest recorded dispute in the history of the union. The company had resisted trade union recognition for 105 years.

Equality Issues

Successive Delegate Councils had declared their belief in the right of all employees to economic and political equality. The Equal Pay Act (1970) had fallen short of what SOGAT would have liked. Its policy was to establish a unisex job structure, create equal job opportunity, advance the payment of differentials and have a common adult age. Providing a unisex job structure meant taking the existing male structure and evaluating women's work then slotting their job into the male structure. The work was both long and tedious for it meant examining every single job in the papermaking industry. The result could not be said to be foolproof for the content of the same job description varied from firm to firm and in such circumstances a compromise with the employer was necessary. SOGAT settled for the cash differentials between the lowest-paid men and the women's rate to be equalised in three or four stages. An agreement with the Employers' Federation of Papermakers and Boardmakers for a staged introduction of equal pay was concluded in 1972. However, the first phased increases were stopped by the Government's counter-inflation policy. Meetings were held with the Government to have the implementation of equal pay taken out of the counter-inflation policy. However, the Government would not change its position, so the first phased introduction of equal pay on 1 December 1972 was delayed. The employers were bound by the Government policy, although at the meeting with the government they had strongly supported SOGAT's case. Following the fall in early 1974 of the Government and the end of its counter-inflation policy, the staged introduction of equal pay was restored and implemented fully by the spring of 1975.

Over time other equality issues were brought within the National Agreement covering the papermaking industry. In 1988 provision was made for women members to have reasonable time off with pay for breast and cervical cancer screening. In the following year, the employers agreed there would be merit in having an agreed basis for the provision of paternity leave. The employers and SOGAT subsequently agreed such leave be two working days or a two-shift leave of absence in the 14 days prior to the anticipated date of the birth of the child or children in the case of a multiple birth or in the 14 days after the actual birth. The paid leave was at the hourly rate or its equivalent. On previous occasions the BPBIF had rejected the union's claim for paternity leave, arguing that childbirth was a predictable event which could be planned for in advance and there was no reason why part of the annual holiday entitlement could not be reserved for this purpose. Nineteen eighty-nine saw the introduction into the National Agreement a clause covering the employment of disabled persons in which SOGAT and the BPBIF acknowledged the need for disabled people to be offered meaningful employment. The Employers Federation undertook to remind its member companies of their obligations in their recruitment and employment practices with regard to disabled persons.

Industrial Training

Unlike the printing industry, the papermaking industry did not have an apprenticeship system for the training of craft employees. However, a number of mills had their own apprenticeship systems which were based mainly on the concept of time-serving. The 1972 Delegate Council approved a Manchester Branch motion urging the NEC to seek an apprenticeship scheme for the paper industry. Such a system would be based on day-release for male learners or apprentices to obtain their City and Guilds Certificates and then enter Grade 1 occupations on finishing their apprenticeship. However, the major initiatives in training came from the Paper and Paper Products Industry Training Board which had been established in 1966. In January 1973 it outlined three principles for training key production workers in paper and board mills. These were sound introductory training, a breadth of planned experience involving a variety of relevant jobs and the provision of related further education.[21] These recommendations covered the first three years of training for employees selected to undergo extensive training to occupy key production jobs.

In 1985 the paper and board industry launched its most significant education and training initiative. The initiative, entitled 'The Process Area Education and Training Scheme', was a completely new framework of education and training for process employees.[22] The rationale behind the initiative was a firm belief that competitive business performance cannot be obtained without a positive commitment to training. The scheme resulted from close collaboration between the BPBIF and SOGAT, but was conceived and managed by the industry's Education and Training Council, a tripartite committee of employers, unions and educational representatives established to formulate, initiate and develop the industry's training and educational requirements. The Process Area Education and Training Scheme was included in the National Agreement as an appendix. It aimed to improve the industry's competitiveness by raising standards of education and training. It was a national scheme to provide a recognised multi-level framework for skilled process employees. The levels of achievement required under the scheme were recognised by awarding national industry diplomas and certificates. Its content was standard-based not time-based. Other features of the initiative included delivery by distance learning to facilitate its use by employees on shift work, access to adult and young people and quality control exercised by a registration procedure managed by a tripartite Diploma Awards Committee. The scheme comprised three levels, Foundation, Advanced and Merit, with diplomas available at each level.

The Scheme was open to all process employees in occupations covering paper and board machine crew, stock preparation, finishing and converting, quality control and laboratory staff. Some 5,000 employees were within the scope of the Scheme out of a total number of 16,000 process workers in the industry. The self-instruction packages were backed up by in-mill training and trainees kept a log book which recorded skills developed and tasks performed, all of which had been supervised and monitored. Under the Scheme individuals progressed at their own pace and in their own time. However, take-up of the Scheme was disappointingly low. In terms of Foundation Course examination candidates and the number of registrations received was on a downward trend in the first five years of operating the Scheme.[23] However, the popularity of the City and Guilds Paper and Board-making examination increased markedly over the period 1986 to 1989, but process employees receiving this education and training were not registered for the Process Scheme. By 1991 SOGAT was arguing for a framework of process worker training to benefit companies and employees seeking a structured approach to training and nationally recognised qualifications. In the 1989 revision of the National Agreement the employers and SOGAT stated their commitment to the creation of a well-trained, competent and flexible work-force to meet the future needs of the industry. They agreed to encourage the widest use of the Process Area Education and Training Scheme.

The National Agreement Under Strain?

The National Agreement establishing minimum conditions for the paper-making and board-making industry was comprehensive in its coverage. It was the cornerstone of the industry's industrial relations system. In 1991, the BPBIF claimed it was a testimony to the industry's system of industrial relations that change had been achieved without conflict. In the 1970s and 1980s considerable improvements were achieved in employment conditions which by 1991 matched many of those in the general printing industry. Although papermaking was no longer such a poor relation to the printing industry, this had not been achieved without a cost. The structure of the industry was very different than in the mid-1950s. The industry was more capital-intensive, the numbers employed were less and there were pockets of low-paid workers.

There were a number of developments in the 1980s that concerned SOGAT. First, two large US-owned firms (Scott's and Kimberley Clark) withdrew from the National Agreement demanding 'single-table' bargaining, full flexibility and no demarcation. If this was unacceptable to their members, SOGAT was informed, then they could stay out on strike for months whilst the plants were modernised. The three latest mills built in Britain – at Flint, Irvine and Shotton – decided not to participate in the National Agreement. These developments undermined the authority of the BPBIF which reacted by creating a new category of membership entitled 'non-consenting membership', which enabled companies to join the Federation for trade association purposes but not for industrial relations purposes.

Second, other US-owned companies were challenging established terms and conditions of employment but tried unsuccessfully to end premium payments for holidays, overtime and weekend working on the grounds that US unions do not have such conditions. They also questioned the need to make redundancy compensation payments arguing that the money would be better spent by investing in the training and development of those employees whose services the company wished to retain.

Third, in the last three mills built in Britain SOGAT had not been recognised. At Shotton the recognised union was the EETPU. SOGAT had been in discussion with the Shotton management, most of whom came from Ellesmere Port and had had experience of dealing with SOGAT's Merseyside and District Branch. The management was prepared to grant SOGAT sole negotiating rights on the condition it did not have to deal with the Merseyside Branch. Although the SOGAT leadership agreed the Shotton Mill to be serviced by the union's Manchester Branch the NEC rejected this on the grounds that companies could not determine with which branch they would deal. The company withdrew its offer of recognition and a signed single-union/no-strike deal with EETPU. By mid-1991, of the 480 employees in Shotton only 70 had jointed the EETPU.

At Flint, Kimberley Clark was to produce medical products and argued that the processes to produce these were different for tissues and more akin to processes traditionally organised by the Transport and General Workers' Union. SOGAT accepted the employees join the T&GWU on the condition that if there were any tissue production developments then SOGAT would be invited to organise the employees concerned. However, when this happened the company denied SOGAT recognition, producing agreement with the T&GWU showing that any developments at the mill would result in the employees concerned being organised by the T&GWU. SOGAT suspected the company had done the deal with the T&GWU to get planning permission from the local authority, which had T&GWU members amongst its councillors, to build the mill.

At Irvine, SOGAT was convinced it had an agreement to allow its officials to meet new employees to persuade them to join the union. However, for reasons which SOGAT was never able to discover, this decision was reversed. It suspected the government persuaded the Finnish owners that a modern papermaking plant required a modern union, like the EETPU, rather have one that was wrongly seen as 'Luddite'.

Although the industrial relations record of the paper- and board-making industry was good, the same could not be said of its safety record. In the early 1980s the industry was the 12th most hazardous in the UK. By 1987 it was the fifth most dangerous. The annual Joint Safety Conference no longer took place and SOGAT protested strongly to the BPBIF in 1991 when no managers from the industry attended the Paper and Board Advisory Committee which dealt with health and safety matters in the industry.

Rigid Box Production

The Wages Council and Its Abolition[24]

The paper box industry became regulated by a Wages Council (then called a Trade Board) in 1910. In the same year some employers combined to form the British Paper Box Federation, later known as the British Paper Box Association (BPBA). It provided the employers' representatives to the Wages Council and did not negotiate directly with trade unions. The workers were largely unorganised and represented by a variety of unions. Gradually the NUPB&PW emerged as the major union, although the GMWU retained representation on the

Council. The Paper Box Wages Council covered the production of three types of packaging: rigid boxes, cartons and fibreboard cases. In the 1960s collective agreements were negotiated covering large firms in the carton and fibreboard sectors. Firms producing fibreboard were removed from the Council in 1965 but, because of the difficulties of distinguishing clearly between boxes and cartons, rigid box and carton production remained within its jurisdiction.

The NUPB&PW had long favoured abolishing the Paper Box Wages Council. However, there was nothing to prevent companies within its scope from paying terms and conditions in excess of the Wages Council's Orders. The union was able to conclude 'house agreements' with the larger carton producers which provided parity with rates and conditions in the general printing industry. The same was achieved by 'house agreements' in the large fibreboard packaging case companies. The NUPB&PW policy towards the Wages Council was to use it to the maximum possible extent but to replace it with direct negotiations with the employers.

Although in the late 1950s the Paper Box Federation met with NUPB&PW to discuss voluntary negotiating machinery, little progress was made as the employers remained convinced that the retention of the Wages Council was of paramount importance, and that any agreements made would need endorsement by the Wages Council. However, the emergence of voluntary collective agreements for the British Carton Association and the Fibreboard Packaging Case Employers' Organisation led in 1965 to the Department of Employment raising with the employers the abolition of the Wages Council. The employers remained opposed to abolition but in 1971 the Department again initiated moves for abolition. The Department considered the paper box industry was a 'classic' case of a Wages Council kept in existence because the employers had impeded progress towards abolition. SOGAT supported abolition on the grounds that the Council acted as a barrier both to improving the workers' employment conditions and to the growth of trade union organisation. However, SOGAT supported the TUC policy of non-co-operation with the government in protest at the Industrial Relations Act (1971), and could not openly assist the government in ending the Paper Box Wages Council. The Department of Employment, on its own initiative, gave notice to abolish the Council. However, there were objections from one employer and from the BPBA and these were referred to the Commission on Industrial Relations (CIR) for investigation. Again, because of the policy of non-co-operation with the Industrial

Relations Act and its institutions, SOGAT could not assist in its investigations.[25]

The CIR investigation revealed substantial numbers of establishments had no trade union members and were not federated to any employers' organisation. Its survey of wages showed a marked difference between workers who were and who were not covered by voluntary collective bargaining. Two per cent of workers covered by collective bargaining and 27 per cent of those not covered were paid no more than 10 per cent above the Wages Council minimal. The CIR was so concerned about the level of wages in unorganised firms that it considered recommending retention of the Council. However, motivated by the belief that the only way to overcome the employers' opposition to collective bargaining was to remove the Wages Council, and assured by SOGAT that major recruitment campaigns amongst the smaller firms would be undertaken, the CIR recommended abolition.[26] The government accepted the CIR Report and the Wages Council was abolished in June 1975. Its abolition was not based on the grounds that wages were in practice much higher than the legal minimum or that an adequate alternative system of voluntary collective bargaining existed. Instead, it was based on the belief that the BPBA used the Paper Box Wage Council as an excuse for not entering into direct collective bargaining. SOGAT welcomed the Council's abolition stating that 'we now have a springboard to bring the converting industry into line in the same philosophy format that we have seen with the BFMP agreement.'[27]

Collective Bargaining under the Wages Council

Negotiations in the Wages Council were generally hostile and frequently ended in deadlock. Over the period 1947–74 the Wages Council met 60 times to make 24 Wages Regulation Orders. Meetings were called on 19 occasions to consider objections to new Wages Regulation Orders. Only four out of 25 proposals to increase wages did not lead to objections. The remaining 15 meetings produced no changes and were either adjourned because of failure to agree or brought to a close by the independent members of the Council voting with the employers against any change. The uneasy relations between the two sides required the independent members to take an active part in negotiations. Agreement between the employers and NUPB&PW (subsequently SOGAT) on wage increases was reached on only 13 occasions and even these required considerable conciliation efforts by the independents. On at least 13 occasions the employers refused to consider any increase in wages at all.

The differences between SOGAT and the employers' representatives on the Wages Council were particularly acute over the implementation of the Equal Pay Act. The difference proved so intractable that no increases in wages were agreed between 1971 and 1974. Seven meetings of the Wages Council were held before agreement was reached on the equal pay issue. Before the Equal Pay Act, the Paper Box Wages Council Order set out an occupational four-point grading structure for men and one separate grade for all women workers. When the equal pay negotiations began in 1972 the lowest male grade differential over the woman's grade was £3 per week. The major disagreement between SOGAT and the employers was whether the male Grade 4 or the Women's Grade should be the lowest in the new grading structure. This issue was important to the industry because of the high proportion of women employees in the labour force. Raising women's rates to Grade 4 male rates would have involved a substantial increase in labour costs. On the other hand, SOGAT recognised that to its women members in box production the equal pay negotiations presented an opportunity for substantial increases in pay and an integrated grading structure for the industry with recognition of skill differentials between women's occupations.

The employers proposed to create a six-grade structure with two extra grades covering women's occupations. In face of opposition from SOGAT, the employers modified their proposals first, by combining its proposed Grade 5 with Grades 3 and 4 whilst retaining a large unskilled grade, and then by reducing the size of the lowest grade but again creating a six-grade structure. However, throughout the negotiations the employers remained adamant that the £3 differential between Grade 4 and the Women's Grade be retained in order to avoid any general increase for unskilled women workers. SOGAT's counter-proposal was that the lowest grade become Grade 4 and the existing women's occupations be divided according to skill between Grades 3 and 4. Under this proposal all women were to receive at least £3 a week wage increase. The negotiations remained deadlocked and the issue was finally resolved by the intervention of the independents, who argued that women's rates be brought up to the minimum male rate, for although in practice men and women were engaged in different work the Grade 4 rate applied also to 'all other workers'. Furthermore, the independents felt that many women's jobs involved some skills which compensated for the lightness of the work. The compromise solution, put to the Council by the workers' representatives, to maintain the Wages Council grades but to include all female occupations in Grade 4, was passed on a vote of independents and workers. The establishment of an integrated grading structure for the industry was delayed, however until after the abolition of the Wages Council and the establishment of voluntary collective bargaining arrangements.

Wages

The Paper Box Wages Council negotiated rates for packaging workers within its scope independently of any of the packaging voluntary collective agreements. There was no evidence of the carton, fibreboard or printing agreements being used as a basis for Paper Box Wages Council settlements. The employers were unwilling to pass on improvements agreed under voluntary collective bargaining to workers still covered by the Wages Council. However, until the 1970s the voluntary arrangements failed to achieve any significant increases in minimum rates for unskilled men and women. Only skilled men in cartons and fibreboard achieved a sizeable differential above Wages Council rates, but even then the skilled rates remained below those in the general printing industry. Wage settlements in paper box followed those in the Paper Bag Wages Council until its abolition in 1969. Until then wage rates for unskilled men and women were very similar in the two industries, although the skilled male rates in the paper bag industry were relatively high. Negotiations in the two Councils took place, with NUPB&PW/SOGAT submitting the same claim. Thus the only substantial negotiations were in the Wages Council to which the claim was first submitted.

Other Conditions

In 1959, NUPB&PW gained, with support of the independents, a reduction in the working week from 45 hours to 43½ hours. In 1960 a claim for a 40-hour working week was rejected by the independents and the employers' representatives, although in the following year the standard working week was reduced to 42 hours with effect from 12 April. The 40-hour working week had been introduced into the carton and fibreboard sectors in 1965 but when in 1966 a motion to reduce weekly

538

hours to 40 was put before the Paper Box Wages Council, it was opposed by the employers although they had participated in the carton negotiations. The NUPB&PW demand was agreed with the support of the independent members and the 40-hour week became operative from 25 July 1966.

Collective Bargaining after Abolition of the Wages Council

Following the abolition of the Wages Council, the BPBA invited all firms within the scope of the Council to a meeting to discuss possible future arrangements for wage determination. The employers favoured direct negotiations with SOGAT and the GMWU and made an agreement which came into force immediately on abolition. A second agreement incorporating a new grading structure based on equal pay and raising the minimum rates to £30.50 per week became operative from 1 December 1975. The top rate became £36 per week. The new agreement was binding on all BPBA members, although neither the Association nor SOGAT established a 'policing' system. The employers insisted on two principles both of which SOGAT opposed. First, firms already paying above the new minimum rates be under no obligation to increase their rates. Second, firms be free to choose which of the Packaging Employers' Confederation employers' associations they wished to join. The BPBA insisted the new agreement was for all its members and no member be obligated to follow any other agreement, regardless of its products.

The Grading Structure

Although under the voluntary agreement, the four-grade structure was maintained, it was based on revised job descriptions. Jobs were graded on two criteria: the skill required and the complexity of the machinery. However, the wage differentials between the fourth and the first grade were widened slightly. Substantial compositional changes were also agreed. The higher skill grades were broadened to include almost all male occupations and some of the more skilled women's occupations. The overall effects of the regrading exercise were to widen differentials between the top and bottom grade, to provide a skilled pay structure for women and to introduce an almost exclusively women's grade at the bottom of a shorter grading structure.

In 1985 the Box and Packaging Association accepted that in future Grade 4 should only be used for jobs which fell within two categories. First, as a training grade for employees during their probationary period and as a rate for unskilled work requiring little physical effort, skill or training and subject to detailed direction. In the 1987 negotiations, SOGAT again pressed for the abolition of Grade 4, but the employers refused stating it was a training grade a rate for the lowest skill, so that considerable numbers of employees in the industry previously on Grade 4 jobs had moved into Grade 3 jobs. The union's claim for the abolition of Grade 4 was rejected again in 1988, but the BBPA agreed the cash increases conceded to those in Grade 3 be applied to those in Grade 4. The demand for the abolition of Grade 4 was also tabled in the 1989 annual negotiations but again the employers resisted. This time, however, they did agree to add the following clause to the National Agreement

> Each employee in a non-training job in Grade 4 should be given the opportunity to train for higher skills provided there are opportunities to move to a higher grade.[28]

Wages

The 1976 revision of the National Agreement was in conformity with the Government/TUC pay guidelines giving to adult workers a 5 per cent increase in total earnings with a cash minimum of £2.50 per week increase and an upper maximum weekly increase of £4. The 1976 National Executive Report stressed that since the abolition of the Wages Council increases in pay for Class 1 jobs had been 87 per cent, for Class 2 jobs 77 per cent, for Class 3 jobs 71 per cent, for Class 4 jobs 76 per cent, and for women 87 per cent and that these increases demonstrated the real value of direct negotiations[29]

The 1979 annual negotiations were protracted, with the employers stating they would not breach the Government guideline of 5 per cent. A number were engaged in government contracts and if the guidelines were breached these contracts would have been withdrawn with resulting unemployment. Some companies were in receipt of financial aid from the government which would again be withdrawn with adverse employment effects if the guidelines were breached. By 1984 basic weekly pay rates for Class 1 had reached £84.30 and those for Class 4 £72.40. At the time of SOGAT's amalgamation with the NGA basic weekly wage rates for Class

1 stood at £133, for Class 2 £122.75, for Class 3 £117.80 and for Class 4 £114.70. These 1991 rates were not the result of negotiations but had been agreed by letter, which the employers' association assured SOGAT was unprecedented and would not be repeated in future negotiations.

Other Employment Conditions

In 1981 annual holiday entitlement in rigid box production was increased to five weeks with effect from 1 July 1983. From 1 April 1986, the standard working week was reduced from 39 hours to 38 hours on the condition there was no additional costs to the company. In the same year, paternity leave with pay was conceded by the employers who, in the following year, extended bereavement leave to outside the immediate family. 1986 saw the introduction into the National Agreement of an equal opportunities clause stating that equal opportunities be given to all employees and to applicants for employment irrespective of their sex, marital status, race or colour. Applications from disabled people were welcomed and every attempt was made to satisfy the unemployment needs of those who were disabled with a member firm of the Association and, where appropriate, training for different work was to be arranged.

In the 1987 annual negotiations, the BPA rejected SOGATs demand for a further reduction in the working week on the grounds that a major reduction had occurred from 1 August 1986 and this, combined with the annual holidays entitlement, put the paper box industry at the forefront of progress in the working week and holiday entitlement. In the following year the economic position of the industry was still one of 'recovery' and when the employers rejected the union's claim for a further reduction in the working week SOGAT agreed to withdraw it. However, in 1989 the BPA agreed the length of the working week be reduced to 37½ hours provided local agreement was reached whereby member companies could take steps to minimise the cost from the reduction of hours. In the 1987 annual negotiations a joint working party had been established to prepare a draft Enabling Agreement on Annual Hours, with a view to implementation after 1988. The working party proposed parameters within which individual companies could implement their own schemes if they wished. In 1989 an Annual Hours Enabling Agreement was agreed. It related to seasonal fluctuations in product demand in the small firm rigid box sector rather than the need for continuous shift working as in papermaking.

In the 1987, 1988, 1989 and 1990 negotiations with the BPA SOGAT unsuccessfully sought payment of average earnings for annual and statutory holidays. The employers rejection was based on costs and that the inclusion of overtime working in the calculation was divisive as opportunities for overtime in member firms were not spread evenly amongst all employees. The 1990 negotiations saw both sides agree codes of practice on phased retirement and child care facilities. The 1987 annual negotiations resulted in agreement that although leave of absence for cancer screening was not a matter for inclusion in the National Agreement, there be a joint campaign to make employees more aware of this particular problem and to attend for regular screening. In the following year, industry-wide guidelines on the provision of time off for cancer screening were published.

FIBREBOARD PACKING CASE

In 1961 the Fibreboard Packaging Case Association (FPCA) indicated a willingness to conduct negotiations outside the Wages Council and in 1962 a separate National Agreement between the NUPB&PW and the FPCA was signed. It gave significant advances in pay and overtime, piecework and holiday rates. The standard working week was set at 42 hours for day workers and there was a London differential over the provinces. Within five months of the agreement coming into operation, increases in basic rates were secured for workers in the rigid box and carton trade through the Wages Council procedure. The NUPB&PW made an application for similar increases to the FPCEA who objected strongly and threatened to withdraw from a joint approach to the Ministry of Labour to have fibreboard packaging taken out of the Paper Box Wages Council. However, the NUPB&PW persisted with its claim and secured increased basic rates. After working with the Agreement for a year, the unions and the employers jointly approached the Ministry of Labour for the exclusion of the fibreboard industry from the Wages Council. In 1965 this finally happened.

Wages

There were annual negotiations with the FPCEA to revise basic rates laid down in the National Agreement. In larger companies these minimum rates were supplemented by negotiation at the plant or chapel level. Some progress was made in establishing parity with the general printing agreement and by mid-1971 the day rate for a 40-hour week for a Class 5 worker reached £16.50, overtime payments of 25 per cent plus had been replaced by a 50 per cent premium rate over the day rate whilst the night work extra rate had increased by 5 per cent. In 1974 the adult wage age for men and women became 18, the final stage of the 1972 Equal Pay Implementation Agreement became operative from September 1974 whilst shift rates increased to 20 per cent for double shift, 33.33 per cent for double day and 45 per cent for permanent nights.

By the mid-1970s SOGAT members in fibreboard packing considered a complete restructuring of the National Agreement was needed to facilitate an increase in plant bargaining. They were also concerned about the extent of low pay in the industry, particularly amongst women members. Rapid technological change and the increasing concentration of ownership led the 1974 Delegate Council to establish a working party to restructure the Fibreboard Packing Agreement. The working party's terms of reference also covered the procedure agreement, the wage structure, job classification, shift patterns, health and safety, and lay-off and short-time working arrangements. The Working Party successfully submitted its recommendations to the 1976 Delegate Council.[30] It had addressed two wage structure problems: how to raise substantially low pay and how to resolve the issue of shift payments. It recommended shift inconvenience payments should not be related to job or grade but to irregularities of the hours worked. This would mean national and local negotiators could argue for increases on job classification rates separately from inconvenience payment, the job classification rate could be negotiated separately and the unsocial aspects of shift working, irrespective of grade, would be equal. The working party's argument meant that day rate would be paid for a member's working responsibility and any payment made to a shift worker was for the irregularity of the hours worked. However, convincing the employer proved more difficult.

In 1975, one national rate of pay for all members working in the industry was achieved ending the practice of two basic rates, one for London and one for the provinces. By 1982 basic rates bore little relationship to earnings. The agreement laid a maximum rate for a Class 1 worker of £90.86 per week whilst earnings for such workers in most mills were £126 per week. However, attempts by SOGAT to relate basic rates more closely to earnings were hindered by the industry's economic situation of the early 1980s which led to short-time working

543

and redundancies. This led the FPCEA in 1983 to propose a wage increase offer which departed from past practice in that it would not rank for bonus. The NEC recommended the offer be rejected and industrial action take place, but the members rejected this proposal.

The issue of the application of basic rate increases to bonuses was raised by SOGAT in the 1984 negotiation. The employers would not conclude an agreement which left the bonus issue 'open-ended' since it would expose them to secondary claims at plant level. However, the union felt it essential to impact some fairness into the industry's wage structure and suggested a working party be set up to investigate the matter and report back to the Negotiating Committee by no later than April 1985. The union wanted a working party which examined the differences in the various wage structures operating in the industry, including bonus systems, and to recommend how in future basic rate increases emanating from the National Agreement should apply. As an interim measure, the employers agreed that part of the 1984 revised basic rates rank for bonus. The 1985 basic rates applied to shift and overtime payments but only part continued to count for bonus payments.

The working party's report, published in 1985, did not provide a consensus as to how the problem of bonus ranking be solved. Since 1984 the industry had applied a compromise solution of 50 per cent ranking, but there were indicators that this was no longer acceptable. The main difficulty was to find a formula which was equitable to all concerned. The problem was made worse in that the bonus systems were individual to companies and bonus rates varied from plant to plant. It was made more difficult because some plants had consolidated their bonuses, thus giving no benefits to the employees concerned from bonus ranking. Any agreement had to allow those plants which had already agreed consolidation to continue to do so and similarly for those plants which were happy with the present bonus arrangements. After many hours of difficult negotiations, a formula was agreed which provided a cash sum increase as an addition to existing bonus schemes at average performance level or a payment in lieu of bonus where no bonus schemes existed. However, this payment did not rank for overtime or shift premium.

The 1989, 1990 and 1991 negotiations resulted in changes in minimum conditions accompanied by the insertion of a productivity clause designed wherever possible for additional costs to be met by improved productivity. Both parties committed themselves to encouraging plant productivity improvements through extra production or cost savings. SOGAT accepted the obligation to co-operate actively in productivity discussions to reach mutual agreement. The self-financing of changes in employment conditions was essential for the employers if the industry was to survive the increased product market competition of the late 1980s and early 1990s. However, SOGAT emphasised its members' contribution to improved competitiveness through increased co-operation, flexibility of working hours and working practices and productivity.

Hours and Holidays

In April 1966 the basic working week was reduced from 42 hours to 40, whilst annual holiday entitlement was increased from two weeks to two weeks and two days. However, the two additional days were to be taken when they had the least effect on production. In 1968, the employers increased from 16.66 per cent to 20 per cent the payment for annual holidays and statutory holidays or average earnings for a standard week, whichever was the lesser. In addition, they conceded three weeks' paid holiday from 1 July 1970 whilst four weeks' holiday entitlement became effective in 1974. Paid holiday entitlement was increased by a further two days from 1 July 1981, whilst 12 months later five weeks' paid holiday was introduced. In 1987, the FPCEA rejected SOGAT's demand for an additional two days' holiday, believing the industry's terms and conditions compared favourably with industry at large and its own industrial sector.

The standard working week was reduced to 38 hours from 29 April 1985 subject to a number of conditions. First, plants maintained their ability to service customers effectively, and second, management retained discretion to change shift patterns and hours of attendance after consultation with the employees and/or their representatives. Third, no plant be required to reduce hours worked to less than 3,542 per week, and fourth there be agreement on measures to ensure productivity was maintained and there was no loss of output. Fifth, there was to be no increase in overtime working and there would be interchangeability of employees between machines, jobs and departments to improve plant efficiency and customer service. A further reduction in the working week became operative from 28 April 1986, when the standard working week was reduced from 38 hours to 37½ hours.

Job Classification

In 1968 SOGAT (Division A) requested a Joint Classification Committee be established to examine claims for the regrading of certain jobs and the addition of jobs not then covered by the classification of occupations. The claim arose from the 1966 Delegate Council. SOGAT argued that any wage structure should relate to adult workers only, that there be provision for advancement to Class 1 jobs, that the number of grades be based on a recruitment grade with movement through the grades based on training, experience and opportunities for promotion and that Class 5 jobs be for inexperienced recruits only. Many new processes had been introduced into the industry since the classification had been first drawn up in 1961. Such processes included flexography and glu-lock, for which *ad hoc* classifications had been agreed at the plant level. It was seen that the classification should be settled at national level to ensure uniformity. The employers accepted a working party and in September 1968 a new agreement covering alterations and extension of job classifications came into effect. In 1969 SOGAT again sought a joint working party on the classification of occupations, but the employers refused, stating that any problems relating to present classifications could be settled by existing *ad hoc* machinery for examining revisions of the classification of occupations.

In December 1977, a working party of SOGAT and employers' representatives was established to review fibreboard job classifications. The unions sought an agreement based on a four-grade structure rather than the existing five-grade structure without loss of pay. Agreement was reached that a new national classification of occupations be introduced from 1 June 1979.[31] All jobs were slotted into the classification A to E. The classification was based on machinery currently in use in the industry. When a machine was introduced for which there was no appropriate job classification the grading was determined by local discussion and agreement. There was to be local agreement on the implementation of the new grading structure in individual plants taking account of existing locally agreed job evaluation schemes. There were to be no consequential claims from employees whose jobs were not upgraded as a result of the new classification. Any disputes arising from the application of the new classification would be dealt with through the industry's disputes procedure and any technical advice or interpretation required would be obtained from the joint classification committee. The existing Class 1 to 5 structure was replaced by a new structure, E to A, with the following national basic rates of wages per week:

Class E	£51.67
Class D	£49.06
Class C	£46.97
Class B	£45.21
Class A	£42.98

The only job not classified was the central controller of the continuous running corrugator in the central control box position. A differential of £5 above the Class E rate was to be paid for this position, but the plus payments currently paid to such central controllers in a few companies was not to be increased by the nationally agreed plus payments. However, in 1987 the job was incorporated into the classification system.

SOGAT, however, continued with its policy to reduce the number of grades to four. In 1986 it successfully sought the abolition of Class A and the following year pushed hard for the abolition of Class B. The employers refused to meet this demand, arguing that it was only recently Class A had been abolished and, to remove Class B would compress differentials and represent a significant increase in the industry's cost structure. The FPCEA considered the wage structure reflected properly the different skills within the industry.

Equality Issues

In 1984 the FPCEA committed themselves to the development of positive policies to promote equal opportunities in employment regardless of a workers' sex, marital status, creed, colour, race or ethnic origin. It agreed to draw to the attention of all eligible employees opportunities for training and promotion and the existence of the agreement on equal opportunities. If individuals felt they were suffering unequal treatment on grounds of sex, marital status, creed, colour, race or ethnic origin and the matter could not be solved at the local level, it was to be dealt with by the disputes procedures. The FPCEA recommended its member firms develop employment practices and policies complying with the code of practice published by the Commission on Racial Equality for the elimination of racial discrimination and the promotion of equality of opportunity in employment. In 1989 the fibre-board packaging employers included in the National Agreement a clause which recognised the need for firms to develop policies regarding the recruitment, promotion and provision of facilities in relation to the employment of disabled workers.

In 1984 the guidelines of up to two days' paternity leave was replaced so that prospective fathers be entitled to three days' leave with pay on the birth of their child. Three years later, SOGAT and the FPCEA committed themselves to ensuring all women in the industry underwent cervical smear tests and breast cancer screening on a regular basis. Where the numbers justified it, individual employers would endeavour to arrange on-site screening facilities. In other circumstances, employees would make their own arrangements for screening, for which reasonable time off with pay would be allowed.

Other Conditions

Many individual companies operated sick pay schemes but there was no industry-wide minimum standard for sick pay. In 1989 the FPCEA urged companies where no sick pay schemes operated to introduce appropriate schemes. In the same year the employers' association accepted that its member firms assist individuals in adjusting for retirement by the provision of appropriate counselling and training for those approaching retirement age. In 1990 a joint FPCEA/SOGAT/GMB working party considered the phasing of retirement for employees. It examined the likely impact of phased retirement on the day-to-day operation of plants in terms of staffing levels and work flexibility. Following the working party's report, a clause covering phased retirement was included in the National Agreement designed to help employees to adjust more easily to retirement. The FPCEA encouraged its member firms to institute pension schemes for hourly-paid employees and develop local pre-retirement policies covering pre-retirement counselling and training and a progressive reduction in attended hours during the last period of working life. Advice was also offered on financial planning, pension options, health care, time utilisation, relationships, leisure chores and retirement locations. In 1990 bereavement leave was extended to include in-laws and in 1991 was extended further to cover siblings.

CARTON-MAKING

Hours and Holidays

A National Agreement between the NUPB&PW and the GMWU on the one hand and the British Carton Association on the other became operative in January 1964. During 1965 the NUPB&PW submitted a claim to the Carton Association for a wage increase, a 40-hour week and a third week's paid holiday. After several meetings, the union achieved a pay increase, a 40-hour working week from April 1966 and two days' additional paid holiday. In 1969 the employers agreed to raise holiday pay by an additional 16.66 per cent on basic wages for a week or average earnings for a week, whichever was the lesser. Three weeks' paid holiday entitlement operated from 1970 as did three weeks' paid holiday. An additional week was introduced in 1974.

Wages

In 1974 a radical alteration was made to shift differential payments. In previous years these payments were a straight cash figure with no direct relationship in percentage terms to the basic day work hourly rates. After a long and detailed set of negotiations, the method of payment for shift workers was altered to reflect percentage payments. The change was achieved in two stages. The double day shift premium was to be initially 16.66 per cent rising to 20 per cent. The night shift rate premium was first to be 25 per cent and then 33.35 per cent. The permanent night shift premium was originally to be 37.5 per cent increasing to 45 per cent.

In 1975 the provincial and London basic rates were replaced by one national rate. At the same time, a guaranteed week benefit was established. This was made to employees who were available for, capable of, and willing to perform such work as was required either on their own or on an alternative job of up to a maximum of 40 hours per quarter at the hourly rate. The benefit included shift rates but not bonus.

In 1975, SOGAT submitted a claim to the Carton Association that the National Agreement be re-structured in line with the BPIF agreement. The claim was based on a number of factors. First, there was a lack of recognition of the craftperson's skills by the British Carton Association member firms. Second, a considerable number of SOGAT members in carton firms were paid BPIF rates although they worked under the Carton Association classification. Third, some SOGAT members were working under the Carton Association Agreement which did not, in the union's view, reflected the skills of those members. Fourth, dramatic technological changes, particularly in the areas of cutting, creasing, stripping and automatic glueing had taken place in the carton industry over the past few years.

The negotiations were difficult because of the employers' resistance and the operation of the Labour Government/TUC pay policy. At one stage, SOGAT gave notice to terminate the National Agreement. However, in spite of these obstacles the union eventually achieved its objective, namely, a re-structured agreement which recognised the place and skills of the carton worker in the industry. The Agreement was on par with the BPIF Agreement and would be revised in the future in April of each year in the light of revisions to the BPIF agreement. By 1978 adult rates were on a par with BPIF rates and the occupational structure had been reduced to three grades to give parity with the occupational structure of general printing industry. From 1978 revisions to the British Carton Association Agreement followed those of the BPIF Agreement.

Industrial Disputes

Notwithstanding problems posed for SOGAT members as a result of technological changes affecting grading, wage rates, staffing and employment levels, the number of industrial disputes in the sector remained low. However, in 1982, Unilever's decision to close their Austin Packaging carton-making subsidiary on Merseyside provoked an occupation by the work-force and an impassioned debate at that year's Delegate Council. The NEC supported the SOGAT members occupying the plant and stated that the time had come to take a stand against the company through national industrial action. This included union members taking action in other Unilever establishments (for example Thames Board Mills and Thomas Case) and 'blacking' the company's products (such as Birds Eye, Wall's and Gibbs). By the time the Conference met, 2,000 Merseyside members in eight chapels were in dispute with their employers over the 'blacking' campaign and some work had been transferred to other organised plants.

SOGAT believed the company's intention was to concentrate carton production in Europe. Some delegates argued that the union could not take on Unilever, that there would be a reluctance to take part in any industrial action and a possible loss of membership if the dispute developed. However, others, including the NEC, insisted that failure to take on Unilever would have disastrous consequences for union members elsewhere and it was possible to win against multinationals. In the event, a last-minute deal was struck, resulting in the British Printing and Communications Corporation (BPCC) taking over the factory.

PAPER BAG PRODUCTION

The Paper Bag Wages Council

Attempts at abolition

In the late 1950s the NUPB&PW met several times with the British Paper Bag Federation to pursue its claim that joint negotiating machinery be established with the ultimate abolition of the Wages Council. However, the Federation was adamant that the best method of determining wages and employment conditions was the Wages Council, they had no desire to abolish it and they wanted the Council for self-protection. The Federation was also insistent that there be no voluntary negotiating machinery for work which was not the production of paper bags but was nevertheless performed in paper bag firms. The NUPB&PW regarded such work as following within the General Printing Agreement but the Federation refused to consider this.

At one time bag factories only made bags, and all printing was done in printing houses. However, bag producers began to do their own printing. Where this was the case, the companies normally had letterpress printing sections which operated under the General Printing Agreement although the majority of employees worked under the inferior Wages Council Orders. However, the employers argued that machine operators outside the letterpress section were rightly classified as working in the paper bag industry as a paper bag was their end product. In the paper bag industry NUPB&PW had members working under the General Printing Industry Agreement and others under the Paper Bag Wages Council Order.

The NUPB&PW encouraged branches and chapels to negotiate at the local level rates of pay and improved employment conditions in advance of those in Wages Council Orders. Some successes were achieved and the determination of the union to support local attempts to improve Wage Council conditions was seen in 1957 in a dispute with a Scottish company based at Markinch and engaged in the manufacture of paper bags and multi-wall sacks. The dispute also affected the firm's multi-wall sack factory in Kent. Following negotiations, a substantial increase in wages was obtained. The NUPB&PW's General Secretary described the dispute as follows:

> It should be remembered that there is no law against our members doing what was done at Markinch. Personally I still regard the strike weapon as the final one. Intelligent negotiations should always be given a full trial but the basic wages set up by the Paper Bag Wages Council and particularly the refusal to grant the men and women concerned normal trade union negotiation rights in my view should be resisted and wherever the men and women concerned are willing to take the risk involved in dispute action, quite frankly the NEC will support this.[32]

In the early 1960s, the policy had further successes. The abolition of the Wages Council was finally achieved in 1969 at the request of both the employers' organisations (the British Paper Bag Federation and the Multi-wall Sack Manufacturers' Employers' Association) and all the unions (SOGAT (Division A), T&GWU and the NUGMW). Abolition became effective on 27 October 1969, a development very much welcomed by SOGAT (Division A) as allowing its members 'to enjoy in the future free collective bargaining between employers and the union'.

Wages and Conditions up to Abolition

In 1956 and 1957, in the face of opposition from the employers, the NUPB&PW with the support from the independent members of the Council, gained wage increases for its members. In 1959 the independent members again supported the union against the employers to enable from February 1960 the standard working week to be reduced from 45-hours to 43½-hours. The NUPB&PW, in November 1960, approached the Wages Council for a 40-hour working week and substantial wage increases. The employers said there was no justification for pay increases but offered to reduce the standard working week to 43-hours and to increase basic rates by between 15p to 25p. The union rejected this offer and eventually secured a 42-hour standard working week and basic rate increases varying from 19½p to 40p.

In 1966 the union submitted a claim to the Wages Council for a 40-hour week and three weeks' paid holiday. The employers were only prepared to concede two days' extra annual holiday with a 40-hour week and were strongly opposed to a wage increase. The independent members supported an increase in wage rates but not at the level SOGAT (Division A) was requesting. In the event, the employers supported the independent members' view and agreement was reached on wage increases of between 40p and 52p per week, on the standard working week being reduced from 42 to 40-hours and on two additional days' holiday with pay. When the proposed agreement was submitted to the Minister of Labour for endorsement he considered it to be in excess of the government's income increase restraint policy and suggested the Council postpone the implementation of the agreement. At further meetings with the Minister in October 1966, all three groups on the Wages Council accepted the agreement be implemented without delay. The Minister accepted this view and the agreement operated from 1 January 1967.

The Paper Bag Federation

Hours and Holidays

In 1963, the Federation concluded an agreement with the NUPB&PW and NATSOPA to cover certain grades in the paper bag industry. This initial agreement established a basic rate for employees in London and for employees in Scotland, and a standard working week of 42-hours. In 1966 the basic week was reduced to 40-hours. In 1968 SOGAT approached the Federation for average earnings based holiday pay, a third week's annual holiday, for an increase in basic rates, the establishment of a Standing Joint Working Party to examine and review the classification of grades and to ensure that where a junior was employed on work recognised as adult they receive the adult rate for the job. The employers offered to increase from 12.5 per cent to 16.66 per cent the premia on basic weekly rate or average earnings, whichever was the lesser amount, as the basis of payment for annual holidays from 1 July 1969. They also accepted three weeks' paid holiday with effect from 1970. A Standing Joint Classification Committee was established, but it would be advisory, with its recommendations endorsed or rejected by the full negotiating committee. However, the employers would not concede the principle of juniors employed on adult work being paid the rate for that job as they considered this was best dealt with at the factory level. In 1972 the Federation conceded four weeks' paid holiday on the condition it was implemented in an orderly fashion and become fully operative from 1974. In 1978 annual holiday entitlement was increased by a further two days effective from 1 July 1980. In 1982 workers in the paper bag industry became entitled to five weeks' paid holiday.

Wages

In 1971 a joint working party discussed the implementation of the Equal Pay Act (1970). SOGAT's approach, as with other employers, was to establish a 'unisex' job structure with a common adult age, to create equal opportunities and to advance the payment of differentials. Agreement was reached to implement equal pay on a phased basis. However, the Agreement fell foul of the first phase of the government's wage freeze imposed in the autumn of 1972. From the following year women received additional increments towards equal pay and in 1975 women's rates were abolished from the agreement.

During the Heath Government's anti-inflation policy and the Labour Government/TUC pay restraint policy pay increases moved in line with the maximum permitted under these policies. In 1978 a substantial claim was submitted by SOGAT but was rejected by the British Paper Bag Federation on the grounds that it was in breach of the Government's 5 per cent guideline for increases in pay and would be harmful to the financial state of the industry. The 1979 annual wage negotiations were very protracted because the employers refused to breach the government's pay guidelines. They justified their attitude, stating they would not put at risk the financial aid which the industry was at the time receiving from government. An agreement was eventually reached in February 1979 when the employers offered a two-stage increase of £3.50 to £4 over three grades backdated to August 1978 and a further £1 increase over the grades from March 1989. The 1980 annual negotiations were also difficult due to the financial crisis stemming from economic recession. The 1981 negotiations were also difficult and in 1982 SOGAT terminated the National Agreement believing its members stood to gain more from local negotiations.

MULTI-WALL SACK MANUFACTURE

In 1963 the multi-wall sack manufacturers formed their own employers' organisation – the Multi-wall Sack Manufacturers Employers' Association (MSMEA). In July 1965 the first ever National Agreement for the multi-wall sack manufacturing industry came into operation. It covered basic rates, hours of work, overtime rates, shift rates, holiday entitlements and job classifications. The 40-hour week operated from April 1966. The NUPB&PW secured a supplementary agreement the effect of which was to ensure increases to all workers in the trade already enjoying wage rates equal to, or higher than, those laid down in the National Agreement.

Hours of Work and Holidays

In 1969 the employers agreed to pay holidays at a premium of 12.5 per cent or average earnings, whichever was the lesser for holidays taken in 1969. In the following year, holiday payment became average earnings or plus 20 per cent on basic rates, whichever was the lesser. Paid holiday entitlement was increased in 1969 by an additional two days to give two weeks and four days. In 1970 a further additional day's holiday accrued to give a total of three weeks. Four weeks' paid holiday was conceded by the MSMEA in 1972 to be operative from 1975. However, it was five years before further advances were made on paid holidays. From 1 June 1980 entitlement to holidays with pay was increased by a further two days. In the 1987 annual negotiations the employers rejected holidays be paid at average earnings. This issue was raised again in 1990 when the employers again rejected the demand, arguing that to accept it would increase the industry's costs by 2 to 3 per cent. The employers were only prepared to move from this position if SOGAT would trade it against smaller increases in basic rates. In 1985 the length of the standard working week was reduced from 39 hours to 38 hours. In the following year a further reduction of half an hour was gained on the condition of full cost recovery to the companies concerned.

Wages

In 1971 overtime rates were increased from time and a quarter to time and a half, piecework rates were raised from a premium of 20 per cent to 25 per cent whilst there was a 20 per cent increase in cash terms over the existing differential for night work. Following the report of a joint working party, equal pay was implemented on a phased basis to be completed by 1 September 1974, together with acceptance that the adult rate of pay for men and women be applicable at 18.

In the 1974 pay negotiation shift differentials were improved in two stages. The double day shift rate was increased initially to 16.66 per cent and then to 20 per cent whilst the permanent night rate was raised from 30 per cent to 37.5 per cent in the first stage and to 45 per cent in the final stage. The night rate premium increased initially from 16.66 per cent to 25 per cent and then to 33.33 per cent. By the mid-1970s SOGAT was calling for the National Agreement with the MSMEA to be re-structured.[33] Since 1961 many changes had taken place in the industry and new skills had emerged. Equal pay had been implemented but it was felt that this still did not recognise sufficiently the skills of women who were mainly confined to the lower-paid male categories. The majority of employees in multi-wall sack manufacture were women, and although their skills varied, women's jobs only covered one or two occupational classifications.

In 1975 the basic rate for London workers and for provincial workers was replaced by a national minimum rate. In 1976, 1977 and 1978 the basic wage rate was increased in conformity with the government pay policy. The 1981 and 1983 revisions to the National Agreement were initially rejected by the SOGAT members but when balloted on strike action to improve the offer they voted against such action. Negotiations in 1984 were protracted. An offer was eventually made by the employers but the NEC recommended its rejection. After members accepted this advice, further talks took place with the employers' association from which an unacceptable marginal improved offer was made. The union broke off national negotiations and pursued its claims on a firm-by-firm basis. Nevertheless, in 1985 the union returned to national negotiations to conclude a National Agreement which merged Grade 5 jobs with Grade 4 jobs, established a minimum earnings level of £86.83 per week and committed both parties to contain increases in costs by introducing productivity-raising work practices at the local level.

In the second half of the 1980s, negotiations with the MSMEA were difficult, with the employers arguing the industry was experiencing problems of overcapacity, increased costs and production levels which could not be offset by price increases. Profitability declined, plants closed and there were moves away from paper bags towards plastic bags. For example, in 1989 a high-volume industry – mail order – replaced about 50m paper sacks with plastic sacks. By 1991 orders for sacks for building materials were down by 12m, for root crop sacks by 15m, whilst orders for refuse sacks were almost non-existent.

Despite the depressed state of the industry, SOGAT gained some advances in wages and conditions for its members. The weekly minimum earnings level had risen to £119.79 by 25 August 1990. By the time of SOGAT's merger with the NGA, weekly rates for day workers (Class 1) stood at £139.71, for double day shift workers £167.65, for night shift with double day shift workers £186.28 and for permanent night workers £202.58. However, efforts to reduce the number of wage grades from four to three were unsuccessful. The employers considered four grades were still relevant, although they recognised local negotiation in some plants had resulted in various jobs being upgraded. They were only prepared to include in the National Agreement a clause encouraging negotiation on grading at the local level. The MSMEA also insisted in the late 1980s/early 1990s that improvements in the National Agreement had to be self-financing via increases in productivity achieved at individual company level by discussions between chapel representatives and local management. SOGAT members were not really happy with these improvement and in 1990 and 1991 voted to reject the employers' offer. However, in 1990 when balloted on taking industrial action to gain an improved offer, they voted by 392 votes to 288 against taking such action. In 1991 the offer was only accepted when the employers agreed it would also apply to temporary workers employed to cope with seasonal fluctuations in workload.

Equality Issues

In 1977 the National Agreement adopted the model TUC formula for equal opportunities under which the parties committed themselves to the development of positive policies to promote equal opportunities in employment regardless of the worker's sex, marital status, creed, colour, race or ethnic origin. The equal opportunities principle was to apply in respect of pay, hours of work, holiday entitlements, overtime payments, shift work, sick pay, pensions, recruitment, training, promotion and redundancy.

In 1986 bereavement leave was extended to cover the in-laws of employees. Two years later the scope of the National Agreement was extended to encourage women employees to undertake regularly cervical smear tests and breast cancer screening by the provision of reasonable time off with pay for this purpose and, if numbers justified it, by the provision of on-site facilities. In 1990 the MSMEA and SOGAT referred the provision of child-care facilities to a Working Party to report back during the lifetime of the Agreement. It was to devise guidelines or options on the issue. The matter had not been resolved when SOGAT ceased to be an independent union.

In 1989 the employment of disabled workers came within the National Agreement when SOGAT and the employers' association accepted the need to provide a policy of support for disabled workers and that such a policy cover equal opportunities, quotas, promotion and training and, wherever possible, the provision of jobs for existing employees who become disabled. The underlying philosophy for the employment of disabled workers was that recruitment of disabled employees should be based on their abilities rather than their disabilities. 1991 witnessed equal opportunities in the National Agreement being extended to the engagement of temporary staff who were, *inter alia*, not to be unreasonably excluded from training, taking into account their duties and duration of their contract. If temporary staff were employed continuously for a period of 12 months, then permanent employment was to be offered to those employees, and where temporary staff joined SOGAT they had the right to be represented by the union for collective bargaining purposes and health, safety, grievance and disciplinary matters.

NOTES

1. The title was adopted in 1974.
2. See National Union of Printing, Bookbinding and Paperworkers *Annual Report of National Executive Council, 1963*, pp. 7–8.
3. See Society of Graphical and Allied Trades *Annual Report of National Executive Council, 1978*, p. 9.
4. This organisation came into being in 1980.
5. See Society of Graphical and Allied Trades (Division A) *Annual Report of National Executive Council, 1970*, p. 6.
6. See National Union of Printing, Bookbinding and Paperworkers *Annual Report of the National Executive Council, 1964*, p. 8.
7. Op. cit., pp. 8–9.
8. See Society of Graphical and Allied Trades (82) *Annual Report of the National Executive Council, 1985*, pp. 21–3.
9. These included fork-lift truck drivers, coating machinemen, engineer store assis-

tants, papermaking machine assistants (all at the 1966 BDC), pallet makers and first machine assistants, turbine drivers and leading stokers, hydropulpmen and paper coating operators. These last four jobs were debated at the 1972 Biennial Delegate Council.

10. See Society of Graphical and Allied Trades *Report of the Biennial Delegate Council Meeting, 1974*, pp. 181–7.

11. See *Report of Trade Section 'B' Working Party* (Paper and Board Mills) to 1976 Biennial Delegate Council.

12. See National Union of Printing, Bookbinding and Paperworkers *Report of the National Executive Council, 1955*, pp. 3–5

13. See 'Wind of Change as Papermills Plan for Reduced Working Time' SOGAT Journal, November 1982, p. 3.

14. See Society of Graphical and Allied Trades (Division A) *Report of the Biennial Delegate Council Meeting, 1968*, pp. 167–70. The union accepted that a reduction in the working week would give a 40-hour week but that production hours for the week remained at 132, which meant employees would continue to work 42 hours a week but receive overtime at the rate of time and a half for the last two hours. The same had happened when the standard working week was reduced from 44 to 42 hours.

15. See National Agreement between SOGAT and the British Paper and Board Industries Association, Clause 10.

16. See Society of Graphical and Allied Trades *Report on the Papermaking Industry*, presented by the Papermaking Secretary to the Biennial Delegate Council, 1990, p. 13.

17. For example, the 1956 and 1958 BDC unsuccessfully sought its abolition whilst the 1962 unsuccessfully sought to have the provision changed so the overtime was voluntary rather than obligatory. The 1964 BDC voted to accept such overtime working could only be arranged in consultation with the work-force plus their trade union representatives. The 1968 BDC voted to make production overtime voluntary.

18. See Society of Graphical and Allied Trades (82) *Report of Biennial Delegate Council Meeting, 1986*, p. 127.

19. See Society of Graphical and Allied Trades (Division A) *Report of Biennial Delegate Council Meeting, 1966*, pp. 130–5.

20. For a more detailed coverage of this dispute see 'Roach Bridge Mill Dispute Settled' *SOGAT Journal*, October 1981, p. 2.

21. See 'Three Years in the Mill' *SOGAT Journal*, January 1973, pp. 6–7.

22. See 'A "Training Revolution" in the Paper and Board Industry' *SOGAT Journal*, June 1985, pp. 16–17 and 'Take Up the Training Challenge', *SOGAT Journal*, April 1987, p. 17.

23. See Biennial Delegate Council Meeting, 1990 *Report on the Papermaking Industry*, Papermaking Secretary, pp. 15–17.

24. For an account of collective bargaining in the box-making industry under the Wages Council and following its abolition, see C. Craig, J. Rubery, R. Tarling and F. Wilkinson *Abolition and After: The Paper Box Wages Council*, Research Paper No. 12, Department of Employment, June 1980.

25. See Society of Graphical and Allied Trades *Report of the National Executive Council, 1972*, p. 10.

26. See Commission in Industrial Relations, Report No. 83 *Paper Box Wages Council*, HMSO, 1974.
27. Society of Graphical and Allied Trades *Annual Report of the National Executive Council, 1974*, p. 15.
28. Society of Graphical and Allied Trades *Annual Report of the National Executive Committee, 1989*, p. 41.
29. See Society of Graphical and Allied Trades *Report of the National Executive Council, 1976*, p. 16.
30. See Society of Graphical and Allied Trades *Report of Trade Section 'C' Working Party* to 1976 Biennial Delegate Council, p. 8.
31. See 'Review of Fibreboard Job Classifications' SOGAT Journal, July/August 1979 pp. 16–17.
32. See National Union of Printing, Bookbinding and Paperworkers *Annual Report of the National Executive Council, 1957*, p. 7.
33. See Society of Graphical and Allied Trades *Report of the Biennial Delegate Council Meeting, 1974*, pp. 188.

CHAPTER 18

NATIONAL NEWSPAPER PUBLICATION AND DISTRIBUTION

NATIONAL NEWSPAPER PUBLICATION

The main employers' organisation for national newspaper production was the Newspaper Proprietors' Association (NPA) which changed its name in 1968 to the Newspaper Publisher's Association. It was formed in 1906 when the London Society of Compositors (LSC) threatened a 'general strike' in response to Hampton's, a London firm, becoming non-union. Concerned at the industrial consequences of a 'general strike' of compositors, a group of daily newspaper owners approached the LSC and agreed to withdraw from the London Master Printers' Association and to conduct separate negotiations, providing the union excluded daily newspapers from any general printing industry dispute. Daily newspaper publishers claimed their product was too perishable to risk a stoppage. As competition between national newspaper publishers increased in the 1960s and 1970s the NPA became less influential and in 1986 closed its Industrial Relations Department. The major employers had withdrawn from it for industrial relations purposes.

Wages, 1955–64

In 1955 the NUPB&PW, as part of a collective approach to the NPA, accepted an agreement which provided for the incorporation into the basic rate of a cost of living bonus of £1.05 and an addition of 12½ per cent on this consolidated rate. In April 1956 the NUPB&PW and six other unions approached the NPA for the balance of the 25 per cent increase on basic rates claimed when the 1951 Agreement terminated in October 1954. In May 1956 the NPA proposed the unions consider either a cost of living bonus scheme or negotiations at less frequent levels. In August 1956 the NUPB&PW accepted the NPA offer of a 5.5 per cent increase on existing basic rates backdated to July 1956, the incorporation of a cost of living bonus arrangement and a stabilisation period until 30 November 1957.

In August 1957 representatives of the NUPB&PW, NSES, SLADE, NUPT and NATSOPA agreed a common approach to the NPA to achieve the consolidation of the existing cost of living bonus into basic wages, an addition to the new basic rate of 12.5 per cent, a further stabilisation period and a new cost of living bonus. Eventually, agreement was reached on an increase of 5 per cent on basic rates, a cost of living bonus of 10p per point rise, adjustment of bonus payments to a three-monthly instead of a six-monthly basis and stabilisation until 30 November 1959. In anticipation of the expiry of this Agreement each print union decided to present separately its own claim to the NPA. The NUPB&PW claimed three weeks' paid holiday, a cost of living bonus and a wage increase of 10 per cent. Realising that the lack of a collective approach would make concluding an agreement a longer process than on previous occasions, the NPA made an interim offer of a 2.5 per cent increase on minimum rates with consolidation of the 50p cost of living bonus from 1 December 1959. The NUPB&PW accepted this and a final Agreement was reached in early 1960 to operate from April 1960 to 31 March 1964. It provided also for three weeks' holiday with pay.

The Incomes Policy Years, 1964–79

In 1963 the P&KTF sought to ascertain whether a joint approach to the NPA would be possible when the existing Wage Agreement expired on 31 March 1964. It was clear that a wide divergence of opinion existed between the unions and it was decided that individual approaches be made by each union to the NPA. On behalf of three of its branches – London Central, PMB and the Circulation Representatives' Branch – the NUPB&PW submitted a claim for a 15 per cent increase in wages, night rate of time and a quarter over the day hourly rate and pro rata holiday pay for all casual workers. However, following an invitation from the employers, the unions met the NPA on a collective basis.

In April 1964 the NPA proposed the establishment of machinery for joint consideration of problems of interest to both sides of the national newspaper industry. They envisaged a joint Board to make recommendations to the NPA and the unions. The unions would be represented by their General Secretaries and the publishers by their directors, together with an independent chairman. The joint Board would consider questions of broad general interest but would not remove any authority from the unions or the employers. The print unions, given satisfaction on the wages question, were prepared to participate in such a Board provided its constitution and terms of reference were satisfactory. Eventually agreement was reached providing for (a) the establishment of a Joint Board to advise on all matters affecting the efficiency and prosperity of the industry, (b) London basic rates be increased by 10 per cent from 1 April 1964, (c) Manchester rates be increased by the amounts necessary to maintain the existing London/Manchester differential, (d) the period of agreement be 1 April 1964 to 30 September 1967 and (e) the cost of living bonus continue on the existing basis.

In November 1964, the terms of reference for the Joint Board for the National Newspaper Industry were agreed. It would examine the publication and production of national newspapers and make recommendations to the NPA and the printing unions on measures to increase efficiency. The Board consisted of equal numbers of representatives of the NPA (director status) and the unions (general secretaries). The NUPB&PW argued, without success, that in addition to its General Secretary, there be a seat on the Board for the Secretary of its London Central Branch. The Joint Board would recommend methods by which benefits accruing from increased efficiency might be shared between management and employees. At the Board's first meeting, held in January 1965, Lord Devlin become its Chairman. In 1966, Bill Keys, London Central Branch secretary, became an observer member of the Joint Board. In return, the Branch co-operated fully in enquiries being made on behalf of the Board by the Economist Intelligence Unit into the efficiency of all departments of national newspaper production and all aspects of management.[1] Its report was published in November 1966 and concluded that about half the industry was operating at a loss. However, the Joint Board disappeared in 1967, having made no significant contribution to solving the industry's problems.

On 20 July 1966 the Labour Government announced a standstill on prices and all forms of income until the end of the year, to be followed by a six-month period of severe restraint. The Prices and Incomes Act

(1966) gave the Government statutory authority to impose the stand-still by order in Parliament.[2] The NPA asked to meet with the print unions, including SOGAT, whose members employed on national news-papers were entitled, under the 1964 Agreement, to an increase in the cost of living bonus of 10p per week from 1 September 1966. The NPA recognised a contractual obligation to pay the increased bonus but felt they must conform to the Government's wage freeze policy. SOGAT took the view that the bonus should be paid. A deputation, including the joint general secretaries of SOGAT accompanied by NPA representatives, met with Ray Gunter, Minister of Labour, and at the meeting it was argued that the cost of living bonus increase be paid. In an effort to break the impasse it was suggested the employers lodge the sum of money represented by the bonus with a trade charity if the Minister refused to agree to payment to the unions' members. The Minister rejected the proposal saying it would create a precedent and create more problems than it would solve, since the question of defer-ring payments entered into before 20 July 1966 was a general and not a specific one.[3] The NPA paid the cost of living bonus increase where-upon the Government made an Order to prohibit payment. The Order became operative on 29 October 1966 and payment of the bonus increase was discontinued from 13 November 1966.

In November 1967, three print unions – SOGAT, the NGA and SLADE – agreed a collective approach, via the P&KTF, for the rene-gotiation of the Wages Agreement that terminated on 30 September 1967. The claim was for consolidation of the current cost of living bonus of £3.60, continuation of the cost of living bonus, stabilisation for a period not more than three years and not less than two years and a 5 per cent increase per year of stabilisation. Both the unions and the NPA agreed that existing agreements should, continue pending new agreements. In replying to the unions' claim, the NPA said they were in a 'siege economy' as a consequence of the devaluation of the pound in November 1967 which it was estimated would add £6.5m to the industry's annual newsprint bill alone.[4] The NPA proposed nego-tiations proceed in three stages. The first was to be a top-level committee of union General Secretaries and NPA representatives to consider matters such as how the results of savings should be distrib-uted. The second stage was to be separate meetings between the NPA and each of the three unions, whilst the third was to be discussions between individual managements and chapels with the surveillance of union officials.

The unions accepted a three-tier structure of negotiations. However, after a preliminary meeting with the NPA, SOGAT concluded that because of its size it would be expected to provide the greater quantity of the concessions, the benefits of which would be spread over all unions and not just SOGAT. In the light of this, SOGAT withdrew from a joint approach and proceeded independently. The employers told SOGAT that if an increase in wages and conditions were conceded, it must financed by greater productivity. An interim payment of 50p was offered on the understanding that this represented the employee's share of any savings gained. They refused to increase the cost of living bonus and insisted the increase paid on 1 June 1968 would be the last. They were, however, prepared to consolidate 30p of the cost of living bonus into basic rates. SOGAT countered that if the employers wished to terminate the cost of living bonus then it required some compensation to ensure the value of wage increases granted was not eroded by price increases, particularly as the employers wanted redundancies, the savings from which would be permanent. Eventually agreement was reached providing for stabilisation until 1 July 1971, the absorption of the cost of living bonus, 4 per cent increase on basic rates and continuation of a cost of living bonus.

Prior to the expiry of the July 1971 Agreement, the NPA wrote to all print unions, including both Divisions of SOGAT, stating the need for a new wage structure and outlining the steps to achieve it, the chief of which was a 19 per cent reduction in labour to be achieved by means of early retirement and non-replacement. SOGAT (Division A) rejected these suggestions arguing the chronic ills of the industry could not be solved by attacking labour. In April 1971 all unions except SOGAT (Division 1) agreed a three-point claim be submitted to the NPA – an increase of 10 per cent on basic rates, consolidation of the cost of living bonus and a 12-month agreement. The NPA initially rejected the claim but when SOGAT (Division 1) joined the collective approach the employers made an offer of £1 per week increase as a flat payment to operate for six months whilst a working party examined the possibilities of compensating factors. When the unions rejected this, the NPA made a revised offer of consolidation of a cost of living bonus and a cash payment of 75p, which would not be consolidated, on the condition that all unions be party to the agreement, a working party examine compensating factors for additional payments to union members and all unions accept the principle of compensating economies and a policy of natural wastage. The unions rejected these proposals but submitted counter-proposals stating that the minimum they could possibly put to their members was consolidation of the cost of living bonus plus a £1 increase on the consolidated rate. The NPA rejected this proposal.

At a further meeting the NPA made their final offer of an increase of £1 per week on all basic rates from 1 July 1971, the existing cost of living bonus consolidated into basic rates in two stages (55p on 1 September and 55p on 31 December 1971) and the Agreement to run until 30 June 1972. In considering the NPA offer SOGAT (Division A) concluded that the end of the road had been reached and further improvements could only come from industrial action. SOGAT (Division A) therefore recommended acceptance. The NGA, however, rejected the offer on the grounds that it eroded differentials, whereupon SOGAT (Division 1) applied for a £2 per week increase. The NPA was prepared to recast their offer providing it did not involve additional money. SOGAT (Division A) was not prepared to see the amount offered to its members reduced to provide a differential to another union. The NPA stated that they would embark on new talks that would reflect their ability to offer a little more money but for longer period of stabilisation. No amounts of money were disclosed and SOGAT (Division A) would not give any assurances to the NPA.

The NGA submitted a separate claim for consolidation of the cost of living bonus, a 5 per cent increase on basic rates and a further 2.5 per cent as from the following March. When production was delayed on three consecutive nights the NPA issued an ultimatum that if production was interfered with again all papers would close down. The national press closed on 18 September 1971. It was apparent that there was a wide divergence of opinion between the unions. However, after two days of talks, the unions reached agreement amongst themselves and negotiations resumed with the NPA who agreed to the unions' proposals of an Agreement to run from 1 July 1971 until 30 September 1972 and a two-options pay offer with each union deciding which option it would take. Option 1 was either 5 per cent earnings or 10 per cent of basic rates, whichever was the greater. The outstanding cost of living bonus was consolidated in two stages – 55p on 1 January 1972 and 55p on 1 April 1972. Option 2 was either £1.12½ into basic rates or 10 per cent of basic, whichever was the greater. The outstanding cost of living bonus was to be consolidate in two stages as in Option 1.

The negotiations had been conducted bitterly both between the unions and internally within SOGAT. Criticism was levelled at SOGAT

(Division A) national leadership because they refused to have the London Central Branch NPA Sub Committee included in the negotiating team. The refusal was based on the long-established practice in negotiations with the NPA of each union having three representatives – namely the general secretary, general president and the secretary of the London Central Branch. On the instruction of the LCB Committee, their Secretary withdrew from the talks. As far as inter-union relationships were concerned, the negotiations had demonstrated a wide gap in policies, and SOGAT (Division A) speculated that there might never again be a collective approach. One thing was clear. any one print union could close 'Fleet Street' but it took all of them to re-open it. Nevertheless, SOGAT (Division A) members voted by 3,852 votes to 149 to accept the NPA's offer.

In seeking to revise the agreement due to terminate on 1 October 1972, SOGAT, with five other print unions, pursued the objective of a wage award tied to a threshold agreement. The NPA offered a 7 per cent increase for the first year of any agreement and a 6 per cent for a second year of any agreement. Both increases were tied to a threshold agreement. When the offer was rejected the NPA increased its offer to 8 per cent for the first year but refused to enhance its offer for the second year. This pay offer was also unacceptable and the threshold agreement was too complex and unfair. The negotiations became overshadowed by TUC/CBI/government talks over the possible imposition of an incomes policy. The unions were angered by NPA attempts to seek an adjournment to the negotiations pending the outcome of the TUC/CBI/government negotiations. Eventually the negotiations produced an Agreement, to operate for 24 months from 1 October 1972, on an 8 per cent increase on all earnings and basic rates, a further 8 per cent increase on all earnings and basic wages, from 1 October 1973 with the first and second year percentage increases related to an 11 points increase threshold in each case. When the offer was put to the ballot, it was accepted by 4,487 to 102, a majority of 4,385.

The provision in the agreement for a second increase effective from 1 October 1973, or an earlier date depending on changes in the cost of living, was denied by the Government's counter inflation policy. Despite meetings with the NPA to find ways of paying the money, including the setting up of a Trust Fund,[5] it was finally decided to let matters drift in the expectation of a change of Government and the withdrawal of the counter-inflation policy. The Government was defeated in the February 1974 General Election and the counter-infla-tion policy terminated in July 1974. An 8 per cent increase was paid in September 1974 plus 8 per cent interest.

SOGAT and four other unions presented a joint claim to the NPA for the revision of the 1972 agreement. SOGAT sought an increase that took into account declining real wages since the 1972 settlement and which would cushion its members against the effects of accelerating infla-tion. On the other hand, SOGAT accepted that the industry was facing major economic difficulties. The union gave the highest priority to improving the position of the lower-paid national newspaper members. Agreement was reached that the revised agreement run for 12 months from 1 October 1974, that there be a 5 per cent increase on all earn-ings and basic rates from 1 October 1975, that the present £2.80 threshold payment be paid from 1 October 1974 (expressed as a fixed house bonus)[6] that from 1 April 1975 there be an increase of 2 per cent on all earnings and basic rates, and house rates only be increased during the lifetime of the agreement as a result of genuine improvements in productivity and efficiency. The Agreement was accepted by 3,677 votes to 355, a majority of 3,322.

The 1975 negotiations resulted in a 5 per cent increase on all earn-ings and basic rates from 1 October 1974 with a further increase of 2 per cent with effect from 1 April 1975. The negotiations were diffi-cult. The industry was suffering from economic difficulties and was faced with the implementation of new technology and the insistence of each newspaper that they must have separate and sovereign nego-tiations with the unions, making the annual wage negotiations with the NPA a charade. Despite these pressures, SOGAT members voted by 3,677 to 355 to accept the NPA pay offer. The 1975 and 1976 nego-tiations saw SOGAT national newspaper workers gaining the maximum increases possible under the Labour government/TUC 'social contract'. These increases were paid as an earnings supplement and did not affect or enhance overtime or any other payments.

In 1978, SOGAT and five other unions made a collective approach to the NPA for consolidation of the two pay supplements and an increase of 25 per cent. The employers argued that they were under scrutiny from various Government departments and were unable to move outside the Government's pay guidelines which provided for increases in the total wage bill of not more than 10 per cent. They stressed that such an increase represented an additional £15m per annum on wage bills and was the absolute limit they could meet with respect to increased wages.

When it became clear that the NPA was unwilling to improve its offer, the unions recommended their members accept it, which SOGAT members did, by 3,483 votes to 216, despite the conditions attached. The most important conditions were that there be urgent joint discussions to provide the industry with a new uniform set of disputes procedures, that there be made a Joint Declaration that regular uninterrupted production of newspapers was essential to the viability of the industry and to survival of titles and that additional monies could only be provided during the lifetime of the agreement by way of mutually acceptable genuine productivity bargaining in-house on the basis of shared savings.

In respect of the NPA agreement due for revision on 1 October 1978, SOGAT agreed a common claim with five other unions which sought a substantial increase in wages, consolidation of the outstanding pay supplements, reduction in the working week and a fifth week's holiday. After many meetings with the NPA, the unions secured an offer which, with the exception of the NGA, they decided should be put to a ballot of their respective membership. The proposed agreement would run for not less than 15 months from 1 October 1978 and its provisions were as follows: from 1 May 1979 the weekly earnings supplements would be absorbed into guaranteed earnings and expressed as fixed house bonuses, there was to be an increase of 7.5 per cent on basic rates and all earnings from 1 October 1978, an increase of 2.5 per cent on basic rates and all earnings from 1 May 1979, from 1 May 1979 a minimum earnings guarantee of £65 per week in London and £60 per week in Manchester and additional monies only be provided during the lifetime of the Agreement by genuine in-house productivity bargaining. The NPA offer was a package, the implementation of which depended on its acceptance in its entirety by all unions. The SOGAT national newspaper membership rejected the employers' offer by 706 votes. However, the members of the four other unions – SLADE, NATSOPA, AUEW and EETPU – accepted the offer. SOGAT was faced with circumstances whereby four unions had accepted the employers' proposal and another had not gone to ballot whilst its own members had rejected the offer.

A further meeting with the NPA took place with all unions in attendance and at which the employers were pressed to improve their original offer. However, the four unions which had accepted the offer insisted the new Agreement be implemented, including the payment of new rates of pay and backpay which had accumulated from October

1978. The SOGAT Executive concluded that further negotiations would bring no improved offer and decided to conduct a ballot of its members seeking authority from them to call a total stoppage in all NPA offices. However, the ballot resulted in a majority of 1,995 against such action.

SOGAT reviewed the situation with which it was confronted. The members had rejected the NPA offer, mainly because of its clause proposing that revisions to current overtime rates be carried out as part of genuine self-financing productivity deals. However, SOGAT members had also rejected a call for a total stoppage in all NPA newspaper offices. The NEC saw no alternative but to advise both the membership and the NPA that the offer was acceptable.

The 1980s' Agreements

The 1979 Agreement fell for revision on 1 January 1980 and, following consultation at the TUC Printing Industries Committee, five unions – SLADE, NATSOPA, SOGAT, AUEW and the EEPTU – agreed to make a joint approach to the NPA for a 25 per cent increase on all earnings, one week of extra holiday, the incorporation of a cost of living factor which would relate movements in the Retail Price Index to a percentage movement in gross wages and a 12 month agreement to run to 31 December 1980. The negotiations were protracted. However, when the NGA, which had originally negotiated unilaterally, joined with the other unions the employers improved their offer to a level which the unions could recommend positively to their members. There was a general wage increase in two stages. The first, from 1 January 1980, was of 13 per cent and the second, from July 1980, was a 1 per cent increase on basic rates and all earnings. The Minimum Earnings Guarantee in Manchester and London rose to £80 per week from January 1980 and to £80.80 from July 1980. The agreement operated until 31 December 1980. SOGAT members accepted these proposals by a majority of 1,903. The negotiations had taken place against the background of the 11 months *Times* and *Sunday Times* dispute and the announcement that the *Evening News* would merge with the *Evening Standard*. The general picture in 'Fleet Street' was becoming depressing, with further closures and consequent redundancies expected.

In November 1980 SOGAT and five other unions met to consider a joint approach to the NPA and a letter from that organisation offering a maximum 5 per cent increase in wages coupled with a new disputes procedure which would introduce the principle of lay-offs without wages. The letter was rejected and a three-item claim agreed. The claim was for one week's extra holiday, a wage increase to match inflation and collective support for NATSOPA's low-paid clerical members. In the negotiations much time was spent devising a new disputes procedure which introduced additional procedures designed to give a quick resolution of disputes in NPA houses. The NPA offered an 8 per cent increase in basic rates and earnings which the unions considered inadequate, but they nevertheless agreed to put the offer to their members.[7] However, the SOGAT National Executive recommended the offer be rejected as the 8 per cent did not match the prevailing rate of inflation.

Following the rejection, the NPA increased its offer to 10 per cent on the condition that all unions recommend acceptance of this revised offer. The agreement was to run for at least 12 months from 1 January 1981, all full-time regular adult employees were guaranteed a new money increase of £10 per week and additional improvements were to come only from in-house genuine productivity bargaining. The unions accepted a '*Procedure for the Avoidance of Disputes*' which provided for no stoppages of work, including the holding of chapel meetings at times that would disrupt production, until the agreed procedure had been exhausted.

During the 1981 negotiations, Guardian Newspapers Ltd indicated that a 7 per cent increase was their limit and that they would no longer be a party to national negotiations. Prior to the start of the negotiations, the Express Newspapers met the unions and reached an agreement whereby they would implement the NPA offer for six months only and would not be party to national negotiations in the future. Against this background, the unions advised the NPA they would only negotiate a 1982 agreement if all 'Fleet Street' titles were party to the negotiations.

In October 1982 SOGAT together with three other unions submitted four main items to the NPA – a one year Agreement, a 10 per cent increase on all earnings, an extra week's holiday and a higher fall-back minimum wage for low-paid workers. In addition, the unions wished to establish a national newspaper industry pension fund for all print union members. In November 1982 the NPA advised the four unions that as the industry was suffering financial losses and the future looked bleak, they were unable to offer immediate monetary increase and they wanted to either extend the present agreement for a further six months or adjourn wage negotiations until July 1983. The unions argued that their members were not responsible for the financial position of the newspapers titles and they would continue to seek wage increases for their members. At subsequent meetings the NPA offered an increase of 2 per cent from 1 January 1983 and a further 1 per cent from July 1983 but refused to make any offer concerning an extra week's holiday. When the unions rejected this offer, the NPA made a revised offer of a 3 per cent increase from 1 January 1983. When the unions indicated they would recommend rejection to their members, the NPA offered 4 per cent, a one-year Agreement and a minimum earnings guarantee of £102.90 per week in London and Manchester. SOGAT members voted to accept the agreement. Initially Times Newspapers Limited had stated that they would not be party to the revised NPA Agreement but they reversed the decision and became a party to the 1983 Agreement.

In October 1983, SOGAT the NGA, AUEW and EEPTU acting collectively submitted a three-point claim to the NPA to replace the Wage Agreement due to terminate on 1 January 1984. The three points of the claim were a 12 month agreement, 10 per cent increase on all earnings and an additional week's holiday. The unions agreed to continue negotiations regarding pension schemes/retirement and at the same time sought maternity and paternity leave arrangements. The NPA advised the unions that unless a positive response was forthcoming on reducing, by natural wastage, the size of the work-force, it was impossible to make more than a token gesture towards meeting the unions' claim. In January 1984 the NPA stated that it was not prepared to make a wage offer unless the unions' agreed to either (1) authorisation for chapels to negotiate 'in-house' productivity agreements which could lead to reductions in staffing or (2) the right for the employer to 'lay-off' without pay all members of a union engaged in disruptive action leading to the loss of production. Both these proposals were rejected by the unions. In February the NPA submitted their 'final offer' of a 4.5 per cent increase on all earnings and a minimum earnings guarantee of £114.11 per week, coupled with a request that the effectiveness of the industry's joint disputes procedures be reviewed. This offer was also rejected, but the NPA remained adamant their offer was final. The four unions, in the circumstances, put the employers' offer to a ballot. SOGAT members voted to accept by 8,180 votes to 5,726, despite the NEC's advice that they should reject it.

In the 1985 wage negotiations SOGAT, acting collectively with NGA, AUEW and the EETPU, pressed for a 12-month agreement, a 12 per cent increase on all earnings and an extra week's holiday. The NPA offered a maximum 3 per cent wage increase unless undertakings were given concerning the industry's disputes procedure, increased efficiency and productivity performance and there be no interference with the content of the newspapers. The unions were unable to give such under- takings. The unions, in the light of the decision of both the Mirror Group and News International not be a party to the National Agreement, advised the NPA that unless there was considerable improvement in their wage offer and some commitment on additional holidays there was little merit in having the National Agreement. Subsequently, the employers improved their offer to 5 per cent on all earnings or £8 new money, whichever was the greater, to a minimum earnings guarantee of £119.82 per week and pro rata payment to part- time adult workers in London and Manchester, and to negotiate an improved holiday entitlement for those employees who only received four weeks' annual holiday.

Following the resignation of News International from NPA wage negotiations, separate meetings were arranged with that company. After a number of meetings, SOGAT secured an agreement the same as that with the NPA. However, negotiations with the Mirror Group proved more complex, with the company insisting that the 1985 wage award be conditional on all Mirror Group chapels playing a positive part in reducing costs in all areas of the company. SOGAT and its members rejected this pre-condition. Subsequent meetings took place but were inhibited by the Mirror Group locking out SOGAT members for a number of days as a result of the company being in dispute with the NGA. However, a settlement was eventually reached for a 5 per cent increase backdated to 1 January 1985.

In October 1985, SOGAT along with the NGA, AUEW and the EETPU presented a claim to the NPA for a 12-month agreement, a 10 per cent wage increase on all earnings, a substantial improvement in the min- imum fall-back wage, establishing the adult age for wages at 18. The NPA rejected any improvements in the minimum earnings guarantee and that the adult wage be established at 18. Nor was the NGA prepared to nego- tiate a programme for a Youth Employment Scheme within the industry. They advised the unions that during the lifetime of the Agreement they would discuss the Bank Holiday Agreement but any agreed increase would have to be taken as part of the 1987 Agreement. The employers offered a further 12-month agreement and a 2.5 per cent increase on all earnings, which was subsequently improved to 3.5 per cent, as its final offer. The minimum earnings guarantee was increased to £124.01 per week. When some NPA member companies[8] indicated that further sums of money would be available from house agreements, SOGAT recommended its acceptance.

In 1986, a number of NPA companies sought to negotiate their own disputes and procedures agreements in tandem with the introduction of new technology and a move of their production capacity from 'Fleet Street' to Docklands. The London *Evening Standard* negotiated with SOGAT the introduction of photocomposition and substantial voluntary redundancies. At the same time the *Observer* announced the end of their London-based printing operation. During 1986 many SOGAT members employed in national newspapers accepted voluntary redundancy and there were clear indications this would become an accelerating trend in the remainder of the 1980s.

In late 1986 the NPA announced it would discontinue the National Agreement when it terminated on 31 December 1986. The pay review of 1987 was 'in-house' for all titles. Despite the movement of titles from 'Fleet Street', SOGAT managed to negotiate agreements providing for automatic increases to rates of pay. At the same time, the union witnessed the decentralisation of production of many titles. Satellite printing centres had become more and more a part of the industry and SOGAT's problems in national newspapers were no longer related purely to wage revisions. By the end of 1988 the NPA had been disbanded. Moves towards individual contracts and away from collective bargaining were gathering pace. There was no National Agreement and those agreements which SOGAT negotiated were concerned with pay increases spanning two to three years. The move of national newspapers from 'Fleet Street' and Manchester had now virtually been completed. The *Observer* was printed on a contract basis whilst the *Guardian* and *Telegraph* were produced on the Isle of Dogs in London. National newspaper publishers had adopted aggressive, unco-operative and dictatorial attitudes towards SOGAT. Associated Newspapers was the leading company in this regard, already making moves towards employing their clerical workers and journalists on individual contracts. By 1989 in most national newspapers SOGAT still held house agreements but the role of chapel officials had greatly diminished. The high levels of redundancy payments on offer resulted in many national newspaper members accepting this option.

The early 1990s saw national newspaper managements becoming even more aggressive towards SOGAT. The imposition of personal contracts continued unabated, especially in the non-manual areas. In response, the print unions established the 'Press for Union Rights' campaign chaired by Barry Fitzpatrick, a SOGAT Father of the Chapel. However, the union remained optimistic that the balance of bargaining power would turn eventually against the employers. The 1990 NEC Report remarked:

> Whilst at the moment arrogant employers are imposing their will upon our members; reducing their wages, increasing their hours; reducing their holidays; whilst we continue to fight these retrograde steps in hard-won rights, it is our view that our members and their families support our policies and will use their political endeavours to rid ourselves of Thatcherism. Our turn will come.[9]

In the face of this employers' offensive, the CMS Branch, which by 1991 had the largest number of SOGAT members employed in national newspapers, maintained most of its negotiation rights and, despite derecognition and individual contracts, had maintained its membership. The Branch felt this bright a spot in an otherwise bleak scenario was due to the establishment of a Newspaper Advisory Sub-committee at which lay officers from each of the national titles met regularly to discuss developments and to issue newsletters to the membership. However, more typical of the treatment of SOGAT members in national newspapers in 1991 was that experienced at the *Daily Telegraph* (West Ferry), the *Guardian* and the *Financial Times*. At West Ferry, a 5 per cent increase was obtained in return for redundancies, further changes to work practices and shift changes which worked to the disadvantage of SOGAT members. At the *Guardian* a wage freeze was imposed whilst at the *Financial Times* there were wage cuts.

Employment Security

Newspaper Closures

October 1960 saw the closure of the *News Chronicle*, the *Star* and the *Empire News*. In December 1960, the *Sunday Graphic* closed whilst in June 1961 the *Sunday Dispatch* and the *Sunday Express* merged. These closures resulted in redundancies amongst national newspaper employees. For example, the *News Chronicle/Star* closure resulted in over 3,000 redundancies of which 500 involved NUPB&PW members. The management promised to pay in lieu of notice to all members of staff a minimum of two weeks' wages, a third week's holiday to each employee entitled to it, redundancy compensation of one week's basic pay for each year of completed service over the age of 21 and to set aside a sum of £½m to ensure pensions would continue in the future to all present pensioners.[10] The print unions persuaded the company to make interim compensation payments in hardship cases such as sick employees and those employees who had not been with the papers long enough to qualify for a pension but who, because of their age, would find it difficult to get another job.

What had caused this spate of newspaper closures and consequent concentration of ownership into fewer and fewer hands? One factor had been a steep increase in the price of newsprint, which represented the biggest single item in newspaper costs. In 1939 newsprint was £10 a ton. In 1960 it was nearly £60. In addition, there was a high degree of concentration of ownership of newsprint mills. One firm supplied over one-third of the newsprint used in the UK. A second factor was the influence that advertising revenue had on the survival of newspapers. National newspapers were highly dependent on advertising revenue to cover their production costs. In placing advertisements, agents were influenced by circulation figures. The higher a newspaper's circulation, the greater the amount of advertising revenue it attracted. In the future, if alternative advertising outlets developed, the viability of national newspapers would be threatened. The danger was not only that employment security would be lessened but that newspaper ownership would become concentrated in fewer and fewer hands, depriving substantial interest groups of a public voice and endangering the effective functioning of democracy. For the print unions, a further factor contributing to national newspaper closures was the inefficiency of management. In response to trade union and public concern over national newspaper closures, the Government established a Royal Commission on the Press in February 1961 to examine the economic and financial factors affecting the production and sale of newspapers, magazines and other periodicals in the UK.[11] The Commission took up the NUPB&PW's suggestion that it visit several newspaper offices. The NUPB&PW's General Secretary and London Central Branch officials joined the Commissioners on these visits.

The Commission's Report, published on 19 September 1962, concluded that employment security in national newspapers had lessened because production was 'gravely inefficient' and that savings of 34 per cent could be made on the staffing levels in the production and distribution stages. It also reported that the development of new machinery had not been employed to the best advantage. The Commission blamed both unions and management for the industry's inefficiencies. The employers were said to lack unity and to pay insufficient attention to the industry as a whole, whilst the employees were accused of being too exigent in their demands on an industry in which profits could not be taken for granted. It recommended more authority for the NPA so that when unity was essential, employers could act collectively in their common interests rather than pursuing individual advantage. It would be helpful, the Report said, if the P&KTF could be given more authority to act on behalf of the unions. The NUPB&PW rejected the charge that the industry was overstaffed and considered such a conclusion could only be based on a superficial study of the industry's problems[12] as it showed a lack of understanding of the need to maintain an adequate labour force in order to cope with edition times and unavoidable emergencies stemming from each day's newspaper being a completely new production.

The Commission saw the viability of national newspapers being improved by the establishment of more authoritative machinery for negotiation and consultation so that common standards prevailed in all national newspaper offices. It recommended such a body give attention to the removal of the causes of the industry's economic inefficiencies by a realistic and thorough-going revision of staffing requirements. The machinery was to include a joint standing body charged with overseeing the planning and development of national newspaper production. This was to give particular attention to pension and redundancy arrangements as well as to training and the intake of apprentices. The NUPB&PW fully shared the Commission's view that employees could not be expected to co-operate with management in the introduction of new machinery that would put them out of employment unless an effort was made by management to mitigate the effects of redundancy and share the benefits of improved efficiency. The Commission considered that industrial relations could be improved by trade union mergers. However, the NUPB&PW was critical of the Commission's failure to suggest concrete measures to deal with the serious situation facing the newspaper and periodical industry and was particularly disappointed with its conclusion that there was no acceptable legislative or fiscal means of regulating competitive and economic forces to ensure diversity of newspapers.

In January 1963 the P&KTF held a meeting of affiliates to consider the approach to be adopted when they met with the NPA to consider the Commission's Report. The meeting decided that although the P&KTF had neither the authority nor the competency to deal with some matters raised in the Commission's Report, for example the allegations of overstaffing, it should discuss with the NPA negotiating machinery, redundancy compensation and pensions. However, the affiliated unions, including the NUPB&PW and its London Central Branch, would not change their view that negotiations for the various sections were so complex that it was impossible for them to be handled by any body other than the union itself. The NPA was told that a central negotiating body was impractical and that the unions felt the present method of negotiation, by voluntary collective association through the P&KTF on matters of broad general application followed by separate union discussions with the NPA on 'domestic' matters affecting the individual unions, could not be improved upon. On the issue of redundancy compensation, the NPA was told that the unions were seeking 1½ weeks' wages for each year of service for employees with less than five years' service, two weeks' wages for each year of service for employees with over five years but less than 15 years' service and three weeks' wages for each year of service for employees with 15 years' service and over. On pensions, the P&KTF requested the NPA introduce a contributory industrial scheme with transferable rights to provide for a pension of up to half wages on retirement, depending on the total length of service. However, before there was an opportunity to put these requests formally the NPA submitted in 1962 to the print unions their memorandum *Efficiency of Production*, which included references to redundancy payments and pensions and which was to engage the attention to both sides of the national newspaper industry for several months.

However, immediately following the closure in autumn 1960 of some national newspapers, the P&KTF met with the NPA to discuss a collective agreement covering compensation for redundancy, the problems of finding work for staff discharged as a result of newspaper closures, the possibility of newspapers facing difficulties which might lead to closure discussing the situation with print union General Secretaries before a decision was finally taken, and the possibility of consultation with union General Secretaries even after management had taken a decision to close a newspaper. In March 1961 the P&KTF told the NPA that in the present state of the industry employees

578

needed guarantee of security and, to this end, the NPA establish a fund from which redundancy compensation payments could be made. The NPA replied that it did not see how a non-trading organisation could provide such a fund, although it might be achieved by the addition of a clause to existing collective agreements. The employers suggested a small Joint Working Party to fashion an agreement for the minimising of redundancy and for agreeing a basis for the calculation of redundancy compensation. The NUPB&PW and the other print unions agreed to set up The Working Party with the following terms of reference: 'To examine the possibility of avoiding redundancy and of providing compensation to those concerned in the event of redundancy arising'.[13]

The P&KTF proposed that if a newspaper was facing problems the management meet the unions' General Secretaries and talk over, in the strictest confidence, the situation that had arisen. This was justified on the grounds that the repercussions of closure on the livelihood of employees were such they should to be brought into the picture before any decision was taken. The print unions also proposed that when a firm decision had been made by newspaper management to close a newspaper, there should be consultation with union General Secretaries well before any public announcement was made. The NPA agreed to recommend to its members that where a paper was 'pining away' there should be consultation with the General Secretaries and that when management had made a firm decision to close the publication, the maximum practicable notice should be given of the decision to the General Secretaries. The NPA argued that there was no guaranteed definite period of notice which the unions could be given of a decision to close a paper, since circumstances varied in every case. For example, when a paper was dying it was possible that someone would make a bid for the title which could change the whole situation. However, the NPA was prepared to hold consultation at two stages. First, where a paper was facing difficulties and perhaps something could be done, and second, where a decision had been taken to close a paper and nothing could be done. This was acceptable to the print unions.

The unions also raised at the joint sub-committee the suggestion that it might be possible for NPA members to insure against the payment of compensation due to closures. The NPA, however, was advised by two insurance brokers that the likelihood of a newspaper closing down was not a risk capable of actuarial assessment and consequently no scheme of insurance could be devised against it. The NPA was sympathetic to the idea of the redeployment of redundant workers but complained of obstruction from individual chapels when seeking to find alternative employment for them. The unions, however, denied that this was the case. In connection with redundancy compensation, the NUPB&PW along with the other print unions stressed that their chief anxiety was continuity of employment for their members and they preferred redundancy should be avoided altogether rather than workers be paid compensation as a result of being displaced. They also stressed that the NPA suggestion that compensation should only be paid when redundancy arose as a result of the 'loss of title' did not meet their position. They considered compensation should be paid to employees who lost their jobs, not only as a result of the closure of newspapers, but also as a result of re-organisation, concentration of publications, new processes and the closure of departments. The NUPB&PW and its fellow trade unions felt strongly that the NPA proposals of compensation on the basis of one week's wages for each year of service was totally inadequate in the light of the P&KTF demand for one month's wages for each year of service.

At a further meeting of the joint sub-committee in December 1962, NPA representatives said they could not accede to the union's suggestion that the NPA establish a central fund for redundancy compensation and argued that the right approach was to have provision for compensation in unions' Agreements. The NPA said it was their firm intention to establish a basis for bringing into collective agreements provision for one week's pay for each year of service as compensation for redundancy. The P&KTF decided in January 1963 that a committee of union representatives should consider in detail the questions of compensation and an Industrial Pension Scheme. The Committee's proposals, which were accepted by the 1963 P&KTF Conference, were to go forward to the NPA for a contributory Industrial Pension Scheme with transferable rights to provide a pension of up to half wages on retirement depending on the total length of service and for payment of compensation for redundancy on the basis of a half week's pay for less than five years' service, two weeks' pay for more than five years but less than 15 years' service and three weeks' pay for 15 years' service and over. These compensation terms had been achieved in some NPA companies when redundancy had arisen and were seen as helping particularly those national newspaper workers who had given a considerable period of service to a firm. However, before the P&KTF had finished formulating its proposals the above matters were taken no further because they were overtaken by the NPAs Memorandum *Efficiency of Production.*

NPA Memorandum Efficiency of Production

In 1963 the NPA submitted to the print unions a memorandum entitled *Efficiency of Production* which set out what they considered should be done to improve the viability of the national newspaper industry. It expressed the view that the present staffing arrangements be subjected to the closest scrutiny and suggested a neutral approach be taken to the problem by a firm of industrial consultants briefed by a Joint P&KTF/ NPA Committee, making recommendations on issues from staffing levels to fringe benefits. The NPA felt there should be a smaller and higher-paid labour force resulting in greater productive efficiency, the savings being shared between management and employee. It also considered that there should be realistic staffing in all departments in all offices but that no regular employees should be displaced, since the agreed staffing levels were to be achieved over a period of time by death, retirement and normal leaving. The NPA envisaged a reduction in the large number of wage categories in the industry and that the basic wage be related to 'take-home money'. The basic wage was envisaged as a comprehensive payment for all services to management other than overtime working. The memorandum also proposed a reduction in the amount of casual working and stabilisation of regular staff as far as possible to handle all sizes of paper in all categories. Within the context of a reduced labour force providing a comprehensive and more efficient service there would be implemented schemes to provide benefits to those employed covering redundancy compensation, sick benefits and pensions.

The print unions including the NUPB&PW took the view that, with all the uncertainties about the future of national newspapers, a realistic view had to be taken of the situation. There was general agreement that the print unions needed to examine the questions raised by employers on staffing matters but there were differences as to an acceptable procedure to bring this about. There was complete agreement amongst the print unions that any inquiry should cover not only mechanical departments but the whole national newspaper industry. It was decided that the NPA should be informed that the unions were prepared to agree to independent management consultants providing they were controlled by a Joint P&KTF/NPA Committee which would select them, draw up their terms of reference and jointly pay for their services. The consultants, the unions envisaged, would be helped by 'assistants or advisers' drawn from management and union represen- tatives with an intimate knowledge of the particular departments investigated. The consultants would make a confidential report to the Joint Committee, which would consider it for forwarding to the NPA and the P&KTF. Finally, the report would be sent to the print unions who would take such action as they felt desirable on the sections affecting their departments.

By 17 September 1963 it was clear that whilst there was recogni- tion by all unions that an investigation into the national newspaper industry was necessary, there was a wide difference of opinion as to the methods by which it should be conducted. Four craft unions were agreeable to an investigation on the basis of the formula described above.[14] The NUPB&PW and NATSOPA along with the NSES and SLADE did not agree to the use of industrial consultants and consid- ered any inquiry should be undertaken by each union individually with the NPA. In these circumstances, the P&KTF informed the NPA that an independent investigation into all departments was impossible, but that the unions were prepared to participate in collective talks on the future of the national newspaper industry and to examine the possi- bility of sick pay, redundancy payments and pension schemes. In October 1963 the NPA expressed regret that after eight months the print unions had been unable to agree on a collective approach to the memorandum submitted in February 1963. However, the unions, including the NUPB&PW, continued to point out that they were prepared in various ways to look at the problem and to do something about it, they simply differed as to the method.

In November the NPA elaborated on their memorandum, explaining its objectives were to inject into the industry a degree of productive efficiency as near to the optimum as possible. They felt it necessary that outside consultants review the situation under joint control and establish what was needed to achieve a maximum possible efficiency for the industry. This, the NPA felt, was a question of fact and not of opinion, and although the way the information was obtained was grounds for negotiation, they considered that expert opinion was needed on the productive arrangements. It was time to have a re-appraisal and to move away from the difficulties of the past in order to gear the industry to modern requirements. The NPA envisaged the investigation taking five years and hoped eventually that of existing collective agreements which had grown up in the past would be replaced by ones which could be written 'on the two sides of a postcard'. The NPA stressed that its intention was not to improve efficiency in the industry by imposing the burden on those employed within it and, to this end, the memorandum guaranteed there would be no redundancies. Staff reductions would be achieved by natural wastage. The objective remained the creation of a smaller work-force, working more efficiently and which would give greater employment security to those remaining in the industry than was presently the case. The NPA agreed with the unions that fringe benefits were appropriate, but the major difficulty was cost. The NPA envisaged these would be met by the re-deployment of staff and increased industrial efficiency.

The plans were so complicated that the NPA considered the proposed investigation could not be undertaken by itself or the P&KTF alone but only by a team of industrial consultants controlled by a Joint P&KTF/NPA Committee. To encourage the print unions to participate in the proposed exercise, the NPA accepted the unions' request that the quality of management in national newspapers be included in the proposed inquiry. However, despite this further elaboration of the terms of the memorandum, the print unions were still unable to agree to the method of inquiry suggested by the employers' organisation. The P&KTF informed the NPA that it could no longer proceed with the proposed inquiry but that individual unions were prepared to meet with them to discuss the memorandum. Despite further attempts by the NPA and the P&KTF to secure agreement for the implementation of the memorandum's proposed independent investigation into staffing issues in the national newspaper industry, no progress was made. In mid-January 1964 the NPA announced they would approach the print unions individually to agree ways of improving efficiency. Three months later it suggested to the unions the establishment of a joint board to advise, guide and encourage lines of inquiry in the future interests of the newspaper industry.

The Board would have no mandatory powers but the NPA hoped it would acquire such influence that no section of the industry would disregard its pronouncements without very serious consideration. The Board would be composed of union General Secretaries, NPA directors plus an independent chairman. The unions were reassured that the employers were not proposing an arbitration forum, as the Board would only deal with questions of a general nature. The print unions, including the NUPB&PW, said they would participate in the proposed Board on the condition that suitable terms of reference were agreed and there was a satisfactory settlement to the 1964 wages claim. When these two conditions were met the Board was established.

The Joint Board commissioned a research report by the Economist Intelligence Unit, and following the report established a Joint Management Committee to take the question of labour supply and demand out of the field of collective bargaining. This failed, and the stumbling block was deciding how savings from improvements in productivity should be shared – whether amongst the members of the unions or between the unions and the management. The Joint Board disappeared in 1967 having made no significant contribution to solving the problems of the national newspaper industry.

Individual Newspaper Publishers

Early in November 1966 the Chairman of the International Publishing Corporation (IPC) asked the union General Secretaries to meet him as a matter or urgency to discuss the future of the *Sun*. He explained that the original 17-year guarantee of publication of the *Daily Herald* given to the TUC terminated in January 1968. He outlined the losses which the newspaper had sustained over a considerable period, stating that the deficit was currently running at over £1¾m and stressing that the *Sun* could not allow this to continue. The Chairman nevertheless said the company wished to continue publication beyond the guarantee period, but this could only happen providing the unions agreed to the implementation of new staffing and working arrangements. To secure the future of the *Sun* for some time to come, the unions agreed to savings estimated to amount to £300,000. Of this, £220,000 was contributed by SOGAT (both Divisions) largely because of the greater number of SOGAT members, relative to the other unions, involved in publishing the *Sun* in London and Manchester.

Shortly after IPC approached the unions regarding the *Sun*, the *Guardian* notified the P&KTF that its financial position was critical and asked for a meeting with the union General Secretaries at which it was reported the paper's financial position was such that there were doubts about whether it would be able to survive unless economies could be achieved. The unions were told of the losses each year since the paper had been printed in London (1961) as well as Manchester. In the years ending March 1965 and March 1966 the losses had been £635,000 and £601,000 respectively, and during the year up to March 1967 losses were estimated to be £934,000. Management concluded that unless a substantial reduction in costs in all departments was achieved, they would be compelled to print in only one centre – Manchester or London.

The management demanded a reduction in staffing, a saving of £½m a year and that all changes be implemented from 1 January 1967. On 2 February the *Guardian* management announced that agreement had been reached with the unions to make savings in the production departments in London and Manchester. Together with other savings, these met the required £½m. The bulk of savings had come from economies in areas where the two divisions of SOGAT were predominant. The *Guardian* was confident it would continue to publish in both Manchester and London as 'a strong, viable and independent newspaper'.

The 1974 Royal Commission on the Press

In May 1974 the government established the third Royal Commission on the Press since 1945. Included in its terms of reference were management and labour practices and security of employment in the newspaper and periodical industry. The Commission in May 1975 invited ACAS to:

> examine and report to the Royal Commission on the Press in the light of the terms of reference of the Royal Commission on the Press on the present industrial relations institutions, procedures and practices in the newspaper and periodical industry with particular reference to the national newspaper industry; and on any improvement in those matters which appear necessary or desirable.[15]

This was the first time a comprehensive study of industrial relations in the national newspaper industry had been carried out. The ACAS report was submitted in October 1976.[16] It found little consensus between the employers and the unions about solutions to day-to-day industrial relations problems such as the level and conduct of industrial disputes, bargaining practices, the lack of cohesion between employers and defective consultative machinery deficiencies. The development of industrial relations had been strongly influenced by the product market for newspapers and the daily production cycle, intense competition between newspapers, the disproportionately heavy losses incurred from minor disputes, fragmented bargaining and the short-term attitudes of employers and employees to settling disputes. The report drew attention to areas for improvement, of which the most important were the casual system of employment, the 'blow-system', demarcation, payments systems, disputes and disputes procedures, consultative arrangements and communications and bargaining arrangements at house level. Union and employer sectionalism was seen as the root of many industrial relations problems. The report did not apportion blame for past failures in industrial relations but recommended that any new approach to industrial relations concentrate on the development of more comprehensive domestic procedures as well as new joint national procedures and the strengthening of unions and management to promote broader-based authoritative collective bargaining. ACAS was convinced there was widespread recognition that change was necessary and that with a jointly agreed strategy supported by all parties beneficial reforms could be achieved. It considered that the creation of joint institutions at all levels, the growth of broader-based bargaining procedures and organisational changes by the parties would diminish conflict detrimental to the long-term future of the industry and the livelihood of its employees. The ACAS report did not see change as being achieved without consistent effort and the commitment of resources by all parties.

However, given the economic plight of the national newspaper industry, the Royal Commission was asked to present an Interim Report. In March 1976, the Interim Report was published, setting out ways to assist the industry. Its brief had been to enable as many national newspapers as possible to survive by minimising production costs, by improving industrial relations, by securing stable employment and proper remuneration for permanent employees and by reducing staff numbers and changes in methods of working in a socially acceptable way.

The Interim Report accepted the Joint Standing Committee for National Newspapers approach (see next section) as the most practical way of tackling the industry's problems. It accepted that many national newspapers were in a serious financial state caused by declining sales and advertising revenue and rapidly rising costs. In the view of the Interim Report, the only significant possibility of substantial savings lay in the reduction of production costs through the introduction of new technology and, by agreement, lowering staffing levels. The report considered national newspaper plans would mean the loss of 4,500 regular jobs in the machine, publishing, clerical and ancillary areas, plus

2,000 casuals. Up to a further 2,500 jobs were estimated to disappear from composing and related areas as a result of new techniques. Such re-structuring could only be achieved by joint action at industry level on certain issues such for decasualisation of labour, and at house level on issues such as the implementation of new technology and reduction of staffing levels. It estimated that the combined cost of the new technology and severance arrangements would be £50–£60m[17] and the Report recommended financial help be made available from the private sector to pay these re-structuring costs. New technology was now seen as the saviour of employment security in the national newspaper industry.

The Royal Commission on the Press reported in July 1977, but the Report disappointed SOGAT, which felt it lacked emphasis in a number of areas, in particular in its rejection of allegations of bias against the political left and the trade union movement. SOGAT was also concerned that the Commission had rejected its views on a levy being placed on advertising to finance a national 'launch fund' and a national printing corporation aimed at promoting and assisting the entry of new newspapers into the market, thereby creating a more diverse press. The union considered that the minority report, authored by Mr David Basnett and Mr Geoffrey Goodman, should be adopted by the government. This report proposed that market processes were unsuccessful and constituted a serious impediment to existing press diversity. The report also accepted the case for a national printing corporation. For SOGAT the minority report was more realistic in its approach to the problems of the concentration of ownership of the press than the Royal Commission Report.

The Implementation of New Technology in National Newspapers[18]

In July 1975 the TUC Printing Industry Committee, in discussing new technology and the financial position of national newspapers, decided it was desirable for unions with members in the industry to agree a common policy towards staffing and technology questions. The unions recognised that the only alternative to joint action was for discussions to continue on a solely *ad hoc* basis between individual companies on the one hand and individual unions, branches and chapels on the other. The print unions considered such a piecemeal approach would be inadequate, in the face of the immense financial and technological problems facing the industry, to protect, in either the short run or the long term, the jobs of their members. There was a paramount need to develop unity and common policies in order to ensure that changes affecting employment were carried through smoothly, that there be no compulsory redundancies, that there be joint control over the introduction of new technology and its staffing implications and that the interests of all unions and groups of workers be considered when any change was proposed.

Discussions on these issues were initiated by the unions with the newspaper publishers and agreement was quickly reached that there should be no compulsory redundancy from the introduction of new technology and new methods. In February 1976 the Joint Standing Committee (JSC) for the National Newspaper Industry, consisting of trade union General Secretaries and chief executives of the newspaper publishers, was established to oversee technological and staffing changes in the industry and to draw up a framework for joint discussions at other levels. Its chairman was Bill Keys. The JSC in no way affected the collective bargaining procedures and actions of individual unions working separately or collectively nor the procedures and actions of the employers acting separately or collectively, though any agreements negotiated in this context were to be notified to the JSC.

In November 1976, the JSC produced a plan entitled *Programme for Action*, which contained provisional agreements on redundancy compensation, pensions, decasualisation, staffing, new technology, joint house committees, disputes procedures, training and education and counselling. Under these proposals all companies were required to table a manpower plan with the JSC in which they would state when they expected to submit new technology proposals, the timetable envisaged for their introduction, the date on which they envisaged implementing optimum staffing levels in areas affected by new technology and what problems had been met or could be expected. At the planning stage, management were to indicate where demarcation problems might arise and the union side would then meet separately to consider them and report to the JSC. A special disputes procedures was to deal with demarcation issues. Company proposals were to contain, *inter alia*, an explanation of why new technology and staff reductions were necessary, a summary of the company's economic prospects and a detailed retraining programme.

On redundancy compensation, the JSC recommended that any scheme be attractive to 'individuals across the spectrum of ages and length of service', as only in this way could a balanced labour force be maintained. It put forward a plan under which redundancy payments would be calculated on two bases; length of service and wages. The JSC believed its scheme provided the best incentive and the most regard for those seeking to leave the industry on a voluntary basis. Some newspapers were expected to offer only this scheme but others would have the option to compensate employees under 60 years of age on a straight four weeks' pay for each year of service. On pensions, the JSCs target was for a pension equal to 1 per cent of final pay for each year of service based on gross earnings plus two years' gross pay for a married man who died in service, payable as a lump sum or a pension or a combination of the two. Widows of retired workers who died would receive a widow's pension of 50 per cent of the employee's pension. Existing pension schemes were not expected to change to this basis but the total value of benefits payable under them would have to be at least equal to the minimum level under the proposed new scheme.

On decasualisation the JSC agreed to establish a register of bona fide casuals wholly employed on national newspapers and to determine the number of workers in each office that needed to be taken into a regular labour force. When this had been completed a comprehensive plan for decasualisation would be presented to the JSC. A new system of joint house committees to reach agreement on the more effective use of staff in all areas to develop staff and technology policies and jointly to co-operate in all steps to facilitate the smooth introduction of new technology would be established in each newspaper or in each house. A new disputes procedure was proposed and this would operate where meetings between management and national union officials could not resolve a dispute. The parties in dispute would decide whether a disputes committee would conciliate, mediate or arbitrate. The JSC would raise funds to ensure the provision of training, education and counselling facilities in relation to the implementation of new technology and to assist those leaving the industry on a voluntary basis.

Programme for Action was a comprehensive plan in the form of provisional agreements for redundancy pay, pensions, training, disputes procedures and planning the introduction of technological change. The union officials on the JSC strongly recommended *Programme for Action* to workers throughout national newspapers as representing the best means for the industry to adapt successfully to new technology in a manner effectively influenced by trade unions. It represented the best means of preventing employers from unilaterally introducing new technology into the industry. The foreword to the *Programme for Action* warned:

> If, on the other hand, the provisional agreements are rejected, there will be no agreed overall framework through which the problems facing the industry can be dealt with, and the consequences of this could well, in our view, be extremely grave and have a serious effect on the continued viability of some titles in the industry, the maintenance of employment, and the continuation of a strong and effective trade union organisation.[19]

However, when put to ballot, SOGAT London members overwhelmingly rejected the plan by more than 4 to 1 although the SOGAT Manchester national newspaper members voted in favour. Why had the national leaders been unable to deliver? First, chapels and branches having emerged from national negotiations, feared that the plan contained in *Programme for Action* was a threat to their autonomy. Chapel- and branch-level negotiations would in the future be highly influenced by the national standards established by the JSC. Chapels and branches feared national negotiations taking over their negotiation rights. Second, by late 1976/early 1977 the national newspaper publishers had became less enthusiastic about the JSC. A major motivation for them accepting the establishment of the JSC was that newsprint prices were rising steeply and advertising revenues were declining. They were facing severe cost-reduction pressures and the JSC offered an opportunity to tackle this problem by reducing, with union co-operation, the numbers employed in the industry. However, by late 1976/early 1977 newsprint prices were falling and advertising revenue was increasing again. The newspaper publishers became more complacent about the industry's problem. This was picked up on by the chapels who no longer regarded their position as one in which they must accept the JSC provisional agreements or face the fact of there being no viable industry. Members of the NGA, NATSOPA and the EEPTU also voted against *Programme for Action*. The SOGAT leadership was disappointed at the ballot result but did not consider it to mean that national newspaper workers were against new technology. They accepted that the implementation of new technology was necessary if the industry were to survive. However, they were not yet prepared to accept diminution of chapel and branch negotiating autonomy relative to national-level negotiation as the price for accepting the implementation of new technology. It was decided that the JSC remain in being but no further meetings were held. It simply faded away, as had the Joint Board before it. The chapels and branches had, however, only secured at best a short-term victory. The national newspaper industry's financial problems continued, and in the late 1980s the prediction in the Foreword to *Programme for Action* as to what would happen if its provisional agreements were rejected came home to roost with an unexpected and brutal vengeance. It was little comfort to those who were to experience it that this that the 'evil day' had been put off for ten years (see Chapter 19).

By the early 1980s, new technology had most definitely arrived in Britain's national newspaper industry. SOGAT sent a team of officials involved in newspaper production to visit the USA and Canada in order to study the impact of changes and developments on newspaper employers. After a nine-day tour the team returned to the UK shaken by what they had seen. The NEC decided their report should be made available not just to SOGAT members employed in newspaper production but to all its members. The report argued that a consequence of not concluding agreements on the implementation of new technology was likely to be large scale de-unionisation of the newspaper industry as had happened in the USA.[20] It concluded that opposing technological change was not an option for trade unions and that unscrupulous employers would use technical change to secure reductions in staffing levels and to end the demarcation of skills. It also predicted that lack of solidarity between unions would only assist this process and also that resistance to change by one union to help another would not assist either union. On a more positive note, the report saw no reason why a new proprietor could not successfully launch and distribute a national newspaper in Britain, and it also asserted that de-unionisation would lead to more women being employed, so organising them and accepting equal opportunities would make long-term sense.

Despite SOGAT's leadership's efforts to raise their members' awareness of the threats and opportunities offered by the implementation of new technology, the eye of storm hit unexpectedly in the Wapping dispute (see Chapter 19) in which management succeeded in implementing technological change unilaterally and in de-unionising the main production and distribution areas. In the late 1980s and early 1990s trade unionism in national newspaper production and wholesaling suffered terrible set-backs. The combination of new technologies, aggressive management and anti-union laws proved a tough obstacle to overcome. Thousands of SOGAT members in national newspapers lost their jobs whilst others had their union rights threatened. Despite all this, trade unionism survived, but the employers, fearing the expansion of capital expenditure coupled with the reduction in staff would give workers greater bargaining power, introduced further policies such as individual contracts, union derecognition and dismissals, aimed at dividing the work-force.

The End of 'The Street'

Although 'Fleet Street' was to some extent the ultimate in workers' control, many of the criticisms of how SOGAT and its members conducted their business were unfounded. The union's control was matched by the service they provided to the national newspaper producers by the operation of the casual labour supply system. The pattern of work varied in 'Fleet Street'. There were permanent employees engaged in Fleet Street who would have regular employment which could be one day/night or up to five days/nights or a mixture of both days and nights. An alternative regular pattern of work embraced three days/nights from Sunday to Friday with a regular Saturday night. Unemployed members of the London Central Branch who were registered as casual workers reported to their branch on a day-by-day basis and from there were directed to work in the general print industry, wholesale distribution and national newspapers. By far the bulk of casual workers were placed in 'Fleet Street'.

The quality of service SOGAT provided to national newspaper employers was best illustrated in the case of the *Sun*. Its permanent staffing level, as with all newspapers, was determined by the lowest pagination, but special events, features, etc. meant there was always a need for casual labour. The *Sun* had 500 regular employees and, on average, approached the London Central Branch for 100 casual workers each night. At weekends this would increase to 200. The tabloid newspapers were the biggest users of casual workers. The 'quality' papers' calls were limited. However, the *Sun*'s position was typical of the number of the calls made by the tabloids. This being the case, at the height of newspaper production in 'Fleet Street', SOGAT London Branches were putting into work on a night-by-night basis over 1,000 casual workers.

In addition to supplying labour before production began, SOGAT

Branches operated a back-up or follow-up call to cater for the labour demands of national newspaper employers after production had started. Calls for additional labour could be received by a branch office as late as 10.00 or 11.00 p.m. or, in the case of wholesale newspaper distribution, as late as 2.00 or 3.00 a.m. The London Central Branch, for example, opened for labour supply purposes at 7.00 a.m. in the morning and closed for such business often as late as 3.30 a.m. the following morning. SOGAT was proud of this unique service it provided free of charge to national newspaper employers with respect to their staffing requirements. There was no other industry that could have a regular work-force geared to their lowest staffing requirements and call for additional workers and get them the same day as requested to cover the volume of work that needed to be produced that day.

'Fleet Street' had many unique features. Nowhere else in the world was there such a concentration of national newspapers in one given street. Indeed, in London all national daily and Sunday newspapers were produced in a square half mile. 'Fleet Street' was something that could not be experienced anywhere else in the world. It was busy and noisy but also had a 'village' atmosphere. The public houses on Fleet Street were frequently full of employees who were on their work break and who were dressed in overalls alongside members of the public who were well dressed and having a drink before going to one of London's theatres many of which were less than half a mile away.

'Fleet Street' was a close knit family unit in which most employees knew each other. It was famous for many things but notably for its humour and private enterprise. In the *News of the World* the employees ran a jellied eels stall in the warehouse and employees came from the other newspapers on a Saturday night to have a bowl of jellied eels. The employees of the *Daily Telegraph* and *Observer* ran their own wet bar. Every national newspaper had its own canteen run by the work-force for the work-force and profits were ploughed back into the chapel funds. 'Fleet Street' employees also had their own drinking club known as the Printers' Drinking Club. It was an old pub which had been bought by printers and was run by and for printers. Access was by private membership on payment of the appropriate membership fee. It was a place full of humour, and the club remained open until 3.30 a.m. National newspaper production was also full of different characters with nicknames that characterised their behaviour, for example 'Crazy Joe', 'Harry the Hammer' and 'Dirty Bert'. A further unique feature of 'Fleet Street' was that within different newspaper houses employees were running different types of shops. Anything, from a three piece suite to a packet of cigarettes, could be purchased at very competitive prices. Electrical goods were available in abundance, a complete outfit of clothing could be bought, and at Christmas time any amount of strong liquor was available at 'knock down' prices.

SOGAT members who worked in national newspaper production considered it to be a special place in which to have worked. They enjoyed going to work because of the people and the atmosphere to be found in 'Fleet Street'. Technical change came here late relative to the provincial newspaper industry but when it came it was dramatic in its impact.

NATIONAL NEWSPAPER DISTRIBUTION

In London, the main employers organisations were the Federation of London Wholesale Newspaper Distributors and the Sunday Newspaper Distribution Association. These organisations held collective agreements with the London Central Branch rather than the national union. Since this is a history of the national union, industrial relations developments in the London wholesale newspaper distribution industry are not analysed in depth, rather attention is focused on wholesale distribution of national newspapers in the provinces.

The Provincial Wholesale Newspaper Distributor's Association (PWNDA) represented the interests of wholesale daily newspaper distribution in England (other than London) and Wales. It held an agreement with the national union. The National Society of Provincial Wholesale Sunday Newspaper Distributors (NSPWSND) represented the interests of Sunday national newspaper wholesalers in England (other than London), Scotland and Wales. The number of union members working in firms affiliated to this organisation was low. Like its London equivalent, in 1988 due to the franchising arrangements introduced by the national newspaper publishers, it collapsed. In 1988, PWNDA helped to create the Association of Newspaper and Magazine Wholesalers (ANMW).

Wages

In 1955, the NUPB&PW accepted pay increases of 37½p for Grade 1 towns plus a further 25p from September 1955 with increases of 32½p and 22½p for Grade 2 town members. The members were dissatisfied

594

with the settlement and the union requested a further increase. The PWNDA protested strongly, only met reluctantly with the NUPB&PW and little progress was made. In 1957, the union gained further increases which it regarded as an important step towards its objective of establishing provincial wholesale newspaper distribution that was national in character. With the new increases its wage rates should be based on London rates with a differential of 37½p for Grade 1 towns and 62½p for Grade 2 towns. The employers opposed this objective arguing that the commission terms received, particularly from the NPA, were less favourable then those obtained by the London wholesalers. Although the NUPB&PW accepted this, they felt the responsibility for improved margins from the NPA lay with PWNDA members. The union was adamant that it would not accept any further widening of the differential between London and the provinces, and in the 1960 pay negotiations it achieved parity of provincial and London rates.

Having established the London rate as the basis, the NUPB&PW now began to seek the abolition of Grade 2 towns. In 1963, Grade 1 towns were redefined as towns with populations of 100,000 or over and Grade 2 towns as those with populations of under 100,000. However, the union continued to claim a sample grade for the provinces. In 1970 the definition of Grade 1 towns was altered to a town with a population of 90,000 or over. This was further reduced to 75,000 in 1972 when the cash differential between Grade 1 and Grade 2 towns was reduced from 45p to 30p. However, the Grade 2 classification was finally eliminated on 1 April 1974.

Until 1968, the PWNDA Agreement contained a cost of living bonus. The NUPB&PW, however, disliked the big difference between the bonus paid to men and that paid to women but the employers in the late 1950s opposed any narrowing of this difference. However, in 1962 they agreed to raise the payment per point increase for women from 5p to 6p whilst retaining 10p for men. In wage negotiations over the period 1958 to 1968, some consolidation of this cost of living bonus into basic rates was achieved.

By 1962, the basic rate for Grade 1 town night workers and early morning workers was £11.55 per week, and £11.07½ for day workers. The weekly rate for women in Grade 1 towns was £6.80 compared with £6.50 in Grade 2 towns, where the weekly rate for night and early morning workers was £11.12½. The rate for day workers was £11.65. In 1971, the PWNDA agreed to attend talks on equal pay, and this was implemented in 1975, which was also the year when the age for the payment of the adult rate was reduced to 19 years and then to 18 years from 1 April 1976. The weekly rate for night workers became £90 in 1983, and this year also saw the first moves towards equalisation of the clerical and counter rate with the day rate. However, it was not until the 1991 pay negotiations that equalisation of the clerical rate with basic manual rate was achieved, and only then on a phase basis to be completed by October 1992. The 1987 Delegate Council committed SOGAT negotiators to achieving a minimum rate of not less than £120 per week for night and early morning workers, but this had not happened by the time SOGAT merged with the NGA. By 1989 negotiations between the PWDNA and SOGAT were taking place against a background of traumatic changes. The complete structure of wholesale newspaper distribution had altered. Some wholesalers had closed down and national newspapers were operating a franchise system which had extremely tight deadlines. This changed environment made it impossible for SOGAT to give effect to the 1985 Delegate Council instruction to reduce the differential between PWNDA and NPA earnings.

Hours of Work

A long-standing objective of NUPB&PW members in provincial whole-sale newspaper distribution was the five day and five night week. There had been a delay in the early 1950s in pushing this claim as the priority on the collective bargaining agenda was wage increases. However, in 1955 the union decided to make no further wage applications until the five day and five night question had been resolved. Previously, when-ever the union had applied for a wage increase the PWNDA made their offers conditional on the union delaying its application for the five day and five night week. In February 1955 the employers again rejected the NUPB&PW demand for a five day and five night week. The matter was referred to arbitration. The arbitrator rejected the union's claim but did award a five-shift week for full night shift workers and for those starting work between 4.00 a.m. and 6.00 a.m.

In 1962 the union achieved a reduction of the 84-hour fortnight for day workers to 82 hours and a reduction of the 42-hour week for early morning workers to 41. In the following year the standard working week for early morning workers was reduced to 40 hours. In 1964 hours of work for night and early morning staff became 40-hours over five nights and for day workers commencing at 6.00 a.m. or after 82-hours per fortnight. Two years later these 82-hours per fortnight for day workers were reduced to 80. In 1972 the night workers' standard working week was reduced to 38-hours whilst six years later there was a further reduction of one hour for all grades of staff to give a standard working week of 39-hours for day and clerical workers and 37 hours for night and early morning workers. In 1979 SOGAT claimed a 35-hour working week and this granted on a stage basis for night and early morning workers from 1 September 1981. Reductions in hours were also achieved for clerical and day workers. In September 1979 for these latter workers standard working hours fell to 38-hours, then to 37½ hours in September 1980 and finally to 37-hours from September 1981.

Holidays

In 1968 in PWNDA houses the qualifying period for paid annual holiday was reduced to one year whilst in October 1970 the third week's holiday became effective. It was also in this year that employers conceded holiday pay be calculated on the basis of average earnings. In 1972 came the acceptance of the fourth week's paid holiday on a stage basis to become fully effective in 1974. In 1986 holiday entitlement was increased to 22 days and then to 23 from November 1986. Two years later paid holiday entitlement increased to 24 days and from 1 October 1990 to five weeks.

Organisation

By 1971, SOGAT was becoming disturbed at the large pockets of non-union firms in the industry. The PWNDA employers, whilst not agreeing to make union membership a condition of employment, agreed to give a letter to every employee inviting them to join SOGAT. Although this brought some increased membership, there still remained a relatively large number of non-unionists. In an attempt to improve the position, the PWNDA agreed in 1972 to grant suitable facilities to SOGAT for membership recruitment meetings to be held on members' premises outside working hours. Unionisation was low in the small wholesalers who employed part-time labour and who, in some cases, operated outside the PWNDA/SOGAT Agreement. In 1974 SOGAT strengthened its organising endeavours within small PWNDA houses and sought ways and means to eradicate wholesalers not applying the minimum terms of the SOGAT/PWNDA Agreement.

In 1977 SOGAT entered successful discussions with the PWNDA

for union membership agreement covering from May 1978 all manual workers in the industry. Existing non-union members were excluded from the Agreement. In 1980, the qualification period by which new manual employees had to join SOGAT was reduced from 13 to eight weeks. In the mid-1980s the agreement ceased to operate in the light of the changing structure of wholesale newspaper distribution at that period and the Government's withdrawal of legal protection for the closed shop.

Sunday Distribution

The number of SOGAT members working under the agreement with the National Society of Provincial Wholesale Sunday Newspaper Distributors (NSPWSND) was relatively small. Unlike that forged with the PWNDA, the NSPWSND Agreement was not subject to a ballot of the membership concerned but to the approval of the NEC. Pre-1970 the minimum engagement for employees was two hours. In 1970 it was increased to three hours. In 1972 the NSPWSND accepted the principle of equal pay for work of equal value.

In 1966 two Sunday holidays were given for 50 weeks' unbroken service. This was the first time a holiday provision had been included in the Agreement. In 1970 an extra paid Sunday holiday was granted whilst two years later the employers concede holiday pay based on average earnings. A post-entry closed shop agreement, excluding existing non-members, for manual employees became operative from 1 July 1978.

In 1988 the NSPWSND, due to the new wholesaling arrangements imposed by the national newspaper publishers, disbanded itself. Its membership had been decimated by the new franchise system. The ANMU accepted current Sunday terms and conditions be incorporated into their agreement with SOGAT.

NOTES

1. The Economist Intelligence Unit undertook a comprehensive survey of the industry in relation to its capital structure, revenue, raw materials, productive and managerial efficiency and employee benefits such as pensions, sick pay schemes and redundancy arrangements. Its report, entitled *The National Newspaper Industry* was published in November 1966 and covered 559 pages (150,000 words of text and over 100 pages of graphs and tables). It described the industry's wage structure as a jungle in which basic wages had little relationship to take-home pay and

which led to continual demand for extras of all kinds and which was the basic cause of friction and unrest.

2. The powers were to lapse automatically at the end of one year – on 12 August 1967.

3. See Printing and Kindred Industries Federation *Annual Report, 1966/7*, p. 12.

4. Other estimated devaluation costs quoted by the NPA were (1) £¼ million per annum increase in maintaining correspondents abroad and (2) £125,000 per year rises in fuel costs.

5. For the details of this Fund, see Society of Graphical and Allied Trades *Report of the National Executive Council, 1973*, p. 13.

6. This meant it became a house payment as opposed to an NPA payment and could never again be the subject of national negotiations.

7. The proposed agreement was only to apply to the following titles: *Daily Mail, Sun, News of the World, Sunday Telegraph, Financial Times, Observer, New Standard, Morning Advertiser* and Thomson Whithy Grove.

8. For example, Associated Newspapers and Express Newspapers.

9. See *Report on National/Regional Newspapers and Distribution* presented to the SOGAT Biennial Delegate Council, 1990, p. 12.

10. The print unions were subsequently told that shareholders had sought to restrain the company from making the compensation payments. An injunction to this effect was granted in February 1961 but in June 1962 the High Court ruled against the company. For details see Printing and Kindred Industries Federation *Annual Report, 1962–3* pp. 25–27.

11. Its full terms of reference were

> to examine the economic and financial factors affecting the production and sale of newspapers, magazines and other periodicals in the UK including (a) manufacturing, printing, distribution and other costs, (b) efficiency of production and (c) advertising and other revenue derived from television; to consider whether these factors tend to diminish diversity of ownership and control or the number or variety of such publications, having regard to the importance, in the public interest, of the accurate presentation of news and the free expression of opinion; and to report.

The Commission's report was published on 19 September 1962.

12. The NUPB&PW expressed concern that the industrial consultants who had arrived at 'these sweeping conclusions' had not spent more than two days in any one department of a newspaper office.

13. See Printing and Kindred Trades Federation *Annual Report, 1961/2*, p. 36.

14. The ACP, the LTS, the NUPT and the TA. This was also the position of the NUJ.

15. See Royal Commission on the Press, *Industrial Relations in the Newspaper Industry*, Advisory, Conciliation and Arbitration Service, Research Series, Cmnd 6680, HMSO, London, December 1976, p. vii.

16. Op. cit.

17. Of this figure, £30 million to £35 million would be needed to meet redundancy payments and £20 million for investment in technology.

18. For an account of this up to the early 1980s see R. Martin *New Technology and Industrial Relations in Fleet Street*, Oxford University Press, 1981; see also K. Sissons *Industrial Relations in Fleet Street*, Blackwell, 1975.

19. Joint Standing Committee for National Newspapers *Programme for Action*, November 1976, p. 4.

20. See *New Technology: The American Experience*, Report of SOGAT Study Group's visit to USA and Canada newspaper industry, 1985.

CHAPTER 19

THE NEWS INTERNATIONAL DISPUTE

On Thursday 5 February 1987 'the longest, most serious and most bitter dispute SOGAT has ever faced'[1] came to an end. For more than a year, 4,745 SOGAT members sacked by Rupert Murdoch's News International had fought for *'jobs, recognition and trade union rights'*[2]. The 1980s anti-union legislation was employed against them and their union together with some of the strongest police actions against strikers witnessed in Britain. Furthermore, another union, the EETPU actively connived with News International to supply an alternative work-force to undertake jobs traditionally undertaken by SOGAT members.

However, these events represent only one aspect of the dispute. The other side of the coin was the commitment and sacrifices made during the dispute by the SOGAT members involved, by their families and by other trade unionists – they behaved with dignity whilst SOGAT was prepared to put all its resources, despite sequestration and financial hardship, towards supporting and assisting them. It is right that the dedication and courage of the strikers, their families, their supporters and their union is accorded a proper place in history.

EVENTS LEADING UP TO THE DISPUTE

In 1978 News International purchased a 13-acre site in Wapping East London and began in July 1979 construction of a new plant to print the *Sun* and *News of the World*.[3] The Wapping plant was completed in early 1984 and a few months' prior to that negotiations with the unions started over staffing levels. The company made clear their desire to reduce the existing *Sun* and *News of the World* work-force when their printing was transferred from Bouverie Street to Wapping. In the summer of 1984,

601

SOGAT chapel officials were told by management that when this transfer had taken place, production of the *Sunday Times* would be moved from Gray's Inn Road to Bouverie Street. In September 1984 News International said they were ready for the move to Wapping and proposed a reduction of 24 per cent in machine room staffing levels and cuts averaging 29 per cent in the rest of the Wapping plant. During November and December 1984, members of the Bouverie Street engineering chapel visited Wapping to view the machinery which had been installed. However, on 5 December the chapel officials were unexpectedly told by the Personnel Manager to remove themselves from the site.

An indication of progress in negotiations was a letter from News International Newspapers Assistant General Manager, Tony Britton, to *News of the World* machine chapel Imperial FOC, Tony Isaacs, on 2 January 1985, confirming an interim agreement had been reached over manning levels at Wapping.[4] However, the agreement was never to be implemented. In March 1985, the *Sun* machine chapel – the largest in 'Fleet Street' with 700 members – was '11 men away from a deal with the company for the eventual move' to Wapping but was 'furious at what he perceived as deliberate delays by the company'.[5] Suspicion had been aroused by the fact that a 12-foot fence had been erected around the plant in January 1985. Having realised that the print unions would drive a hard bargain and News International would have to negotiate seriously with them over the proposed move to Wapping, News International decided to seek an alternative work-force. The EETPU was to provide this. News International was impressed with that union's approach to gaining recognition (single-union/no-strike/right to manage agreements) and was determined that there should be no recognition of the traditional print unions. For their part, the EETPU had never forgiven SOGAT for attempting to poach its Press Branch (see Chapter 14).

In March 1985, the *Daily Telegraph* reported that News International planned to produce a new newspaper entitled the *Post*, at its Wapping Plant. The company initially confirmed that the *Post* would be a London only evening paper but, if successful, would expand to become Britain's first national 24-hour newspaper. News International appointed Christopher Pole-Carew, who had succeeded in ousting the print unions from his provincial newspapers in Nottingham in the 1970s, to head the *Post* project.[6] The company also secretly ordered an Atex computerised photosetting system which would use direct inputting of text and which would be capable of handling the printing of *all* their national newspapers.[7] This was not the latest high-tech equipment; it was a tried and tested system operated by SOGAT members in other parts of the printing industry. It was renowned for its speed. The system was shipped from the USA on 12 March 1985 in boxes which had the Atex logo painted over, and delivered to a converted warehouse in south-east London for assembly and testing.

On 9 April, Pole-Carew visited Washington DC accompanied by EETPU National Secretary, Tim Rice. They visited a number of other US cities where newspapers used computerised production systems. These visits, a News International executive later explained, were crucial to the planning of the Wapping project, and to giving the EETPU understanding of the modern printing industry. Pole-Carew and Tim Rice were to have regular meetings to discuss staffing and shift patterns needed for Wapping.[8] At a '*London Post*' planning meeting held on 8 August 1985 the recruitment of technicians and the training of staff to operate the Atex system was discussed and it was noted that the EETPU had agreed to provide the necessary individuals by the end of the month. The EETPU Southampton Area Secretary, Mick Scanlon, began sending applicants for interview with a London employment agency. One applicant later recounted how he was greeted by Scanlon at the offices of the Charles Paterson agency when he went for his interview. He was told he would be working in the publishing room of the *London Post*, would receive three months' training and that News International would provide daily coach transport from Southampton. In the second interview the questions were directed towards ascertaining the applicant's politics and willingness to continue working in the event of 'trouble'. A similar exercise took place in Glasgow, with applicants for jobs in News International's Glasgow plant sending their application forms to the home address of Mr Pat O'Hanlon, an EETPU full-time official. Applicants were interviewed in the presence of Mr O'Hanlon and were asked if they minded joining the EETPU as the plant would be single-union and if they objected to crossing picket lines. After two days' employment, one AUEW member resigned on finding he was employed on print work.

News International maintained tight security inside the Wapping plant but, nevertheless, information about what was going on soon became available from some of the people employed there. By May 1985, Tony Cappi, a health and safety representative in the SOGAT RIRMA Branch, and Terry Ellis, Deputy FOC in the Bouverie Street engineering chapel, had gathered evidence of the nature and scale of the Wapping operation.[9] They had been able to confirm that an Atex system had been installed at Wapping and was being tested and that the printing presses were being converted to take broadsheet-sized paper. All this meant not only the *Sun* and the *News of the World* (News Group Newspapers), but also *The Times* and *Sunday Times* (Times Newspapers Ltd) could be printed in the plant.

Following a poorly attended exhibition organised by Cappi and Ellis to try to expose what was happening at Wapping, SOGAT General Secretary, Brenda Dean, and Bill Miles, General Officer responsible for national newspapers, were alerted to the situation.[10] Having met Cappi and satisfied herself as to the accuracy of his claims, Dean made discreet inquiries about ink and newsprint supplies to News International, the extent of NUJ membership in each title and how many journalists had received new technology training. She also requested a meeting with Rupert Murdoch of News International. At this meeting, he reassured the SOGAT General Secretary that there was nothing happening at Wapping. Nevertheless, she called a meeting on 30 July 1985 of all News International FOCs and Branch Officials to give them information about developments at the plant.

SOGAT issued a press release expressing its desire for immediate talks with News Group Newspapers on the planned move of the *Sun* and *News of the World* to Wapping. Negotiations had been delayed for too long and the union was anxious to constructively discuss the *Post*, the move to Wapping, and production of the *Sun* in Glasgow. After considerable pressure from the union, a meeting about Wapping finally took place on 30 August at which SOGAT heard denials that any personnel were being recruited or were working in the premises and being trained in jobs traditionally done by SOGAT members. They were also told that Murdoch would meet the unions to outline his policy for the Wapping plant when he was in London at the end of September, on the condition that normal production was continued until these discussions had taken place. The EETPU confirmed their members working in Wapping were engaged on traditional electricians' work only and were not dong any work which would normally be that of SOGAT.

On 6 September 1985, a 'dummy' newspaper was printed in Wapping. SOGAT leadership was sure SOGAT's News International members would take strike action when they learned of this development. However, the members did not do so, deciding instead to await the outcome of the September meeting with Murdoch. However, the following week, the London Machine Branch discussed a proposal from their Branch Committee for a 24-hour strike on all News International titles against the company's use of non-print union in the Wapping plant despite assurances to the contrary. The debate was impassioned. Those supporting the proposal argued that, in the light of the clear evidence of 'non-union labour' running the machines, a stand had to be made to show News International the members meant business, otherwise what they had fought for would be lost. Those opposing the motion argued that the PMB members were always the first in the firing line and they should only strike alongside the rest of the union branches. The motion was lost by 520 votes to 306.

The meeting with Murdoch to discuss the proposed *London Post* finally took place on 30 September. This was the first time for almost a year that News International had involved the print unions in talks. The company listed complaints about Fleet Street's industrial relations to the union General Secretaries. However, it was agreed to issue a joint press release announcing that, in a 'fresh spirit of unity', both sides were committed to concluding an agreement for the *London Post* by Christmas. If the talks made good progress then they would be extended to include the future transfer of the *Sun* and *News of the World* to Wapping. The union leaders were, therefore, displeased to find the front page of the following day's edition of *The Times* carried an attack on the print unions, in which News International's statement at the meeting was given pride of place.

News International had announced their plans for the *London Post* in March but negotiations on staffing for this publication only finally got underway in mid-October. They were led on the company's side by Bill O'Neill. After the unions had told the company they accepted the introduction of computerised typesetting and litho printing techniques, both of which were common in the printing industry other than national newspapers, O'Neill presented a seven-page document to the unions listing the company's proposals for:

(i) no local negotiations; no recognition of chapels or branches, or of union rights to represent supervisory grades;

(ii) no strikes or any other form of industrial action, and instant dismissal for anyone taking part; union repudiation of any such action;

(iii) no closed shop; union representatives 'warned' under the disciplinary procedure to lose office;

(iv)　complete flexibility and no demarcation lines;
(v)　total acceptance of management's 'right to manage' including changes in working methods; introduction of new technology; staffing levels; the hiring, classification, transfer and promotion of employees; disciplinary, laying off or dismissing employees;
(vi)　legally binding contracts.

These conditions had to be acceptable to the union and were non-negotiable. Furthermore, SOGAT was told, the company intended to cut staffing levels in the Wapping distribution and machine rooms by 50 per cent. News International had effectively declared war. It was over these non-negotiable terms that the Wapping dispute took place; it was not due to technological change, since the litho presses to be used in Wapping were 15 years old, having been bought second hand. After SOGAT and the NGA had accused each other of considering a single-union deal, the two unions accepted such an approach could prove mutually destructive and play into the hands of the company and the EETPU.

The five unions involved in News International's operations – SOGAT, the NGA, the AUEW and EETPU and the NUJ, received a letter from TUC General Secretary, Norman Willis, urging them to adopt a 'common approach'. The five union leaders met and decided to reject the proposals put forward by the company as they represented the end of effective trade unionism. However, they made it clear they were prepared to negotiate agreements providing for flexibility, the avoidance of disruption and closer inter-union working.

The five unions met News International on 10 December and were told that so long as there was no agreement on the *London Post*, it was nothing to do with them what happened at Wapping. Management would select the staff required and current employees would not automatically transfer to Wapping. Regarding the proposals of no closed shop, a no-strike clause, legally binding agreements and the unfettered 'right to manage', the company repeated that these were not negotiable. During the adjournment the EETPU told the print unions their national executive had decided to lift their opposition to these four contentious and non-negotiable clauses. Furthermore, the union had issued a press release to this effect and avoided answering SOGAT's question of whether the EETPU now intended to seek a single-union agreement by saying that this was a matter for its executive to decide. However, what was clear, was that the unions would not agree a 'common approach' and the company was aware of this when the meeting started.

When at a meeting of the Print Industries Committee the EETPU would not support a common approach to News International, the other four unions formally registered on 17 December a complaint with the TUC against the electricians. The TUC General Secretary summoned the General Secretaries of the five unions after which he wrote to them all advising it was imperative that the five unions sought a common approach and that no union should enter into an agreement or arrangement with News International covering all or part of the operations or groups of employees at Wapping except with the agreement of the other unions concerned.[11]

By this time the talks on staffing levels for the *London Post* had broken down. It would have been illegal secondary action for the unions to embark upon industrial action since none of their members were employed by the *London Post*. On 23 December SOGAT told News International of its concern about the security of their members' employment in the existing News Group and Times Newspaper plants and that it was seeking a guarantee of jobs at Wapping if work were transferred there. Although it was not SOGAT's desire, it concluded, if the company refused to discuss its concerns there was no alternative to industrial action. The union's claim was rejected on 31 December and News International announced that negotiations with SOGAT, the NGA and AUEW were over.

On 9 January 1986 News International gave six months' notice of termination of all collective agreements, covering 5,500 members of SOGAT, the NGA, AUEW and the EETPU employed on production in Gray's Inn Road and Bouverie Street.[12] At a mass meeting of SOGAT members, held on 13 January, the chapel and branch committees sought and received a mandate to take industrial action against News International. A secret ballot of the membership was then organised with the National Executive urging a 'yes' vote. The result of the ballot was a 3,534 to 752 vote in favour of strike action. Just over 90 per cent of SOGAT members participated in the ballot, and 82.5 per cent voted in favour of strike action.

On 23 January 1986, the unions met News International. In response to the unions' claim for guarantees of employment for the existing 5,500-strong work-force, the company offered 'some hundreds' of jobs in the old plants, with conditions similar to those proposed by the company during the *London Post* negotiations. The rest of the work-force would receive only statutory redundancy payments. The unions' argued that Wapping could not be divorced from the overall situation, especially since the previous weekend the company had broken long-standing agreements and recent assurances by printing a 16-page supplement to the *Sunday Times* in the plant. In a move unprecedented in 'Fleet Street', the union leaders then offered an agreement to News International ensuring strict adherence to the disputes procedure, no unofficial action, ballots before any official action, conciliation and arbitration arrangements and flexibility between jobs. However, News International had no intention of reaching an agreement. It went through the motions and then, after two hours, rejected the unions' offer. The next day – Friday 24 January 1986 – the strike began.

THE DISPUTE

On 24 January at a meeting in the London Central branch 'call room', News International FOCs were informed by the General Secretary that the NEC was calling members out on strike as authorised by the membership ballot. Those present clapped and cheered. The total number of SOGAT members involved at the start of the dispute was 4,745. As well as the production workers directly employed in printing the newspapers, the strikers included clerical workers, tele-ad workers, accountants, typists, telephonists, maintenance assistants, cleaners, catering staff, circulation representatives, technicians, firefighters and librarians. Most of the strikers were not well-paid 'Fleet Street' printers. The 'Fleet Street' members were not the most popular group in the union and the power and influence wielded by London Central Branch was resented by some officials and activists. It was important to get the message across that the strikers were taking action over jobs, union recognition and the conditions attached to the acceptance of change. Success for News International would encourage other employers to try and copy it. If this were to happen, then the consequences for the print unions in the newspaper industry as a whole in terms of future influence would be extremely serious. Accordingly, branches instructed their members not to handle any News International titles printed during the dispute. A SOGAT Dispute Office was established at the London Central Branch, and special lines set up at Head Office.

As soon as the strike started, News International transferred production of all four titles – *The Times, Sunday Times*, the *Sun* and *News of the World* – to Wapping which was protected by barbed wire fences, floodlights and electronic surveillance equipment. By combining the dismissal threats with the carrot of large wage increases, the company persuaded the majority of journalists to work at Wapping. The production work-force was supplied by EETPU. When SOGAT members at Express Newspapers in Manchester refused to print two million copies of the contracted northern edition of the *News of the World*, the work was switched to News International's Glasgow plant with the *Sun*'s northern edition.

News International issued dismissal notices to the 5,500 strikers on the grounds they had breached their contracts of employment. The company had been advised by Sir Geoffrey Richards, a senior partner in Farrer & Co., who had suggested that the cheapest way to remove the existing work-force would be to dismiss them during a strike, since the company would avoid liability for redundancy payments to the dismissed workers. The strikers were summarily dismissed by News International on Friday 24 January, the first day of the dispute.

Farrer & Co. were utilised in other areas of News International's planning for the dispute. The 1980 Employment Act restricted lawful 'secondary action' to a first customer or first supplier of the employer directly involved in a dispute. During 1985 News International set up six new companies – News International Supply, News International Distribution, News International Advertising, Times Paper, Times Printing and Times Publishing. Faced with SOGAT's instruction to its members employed in wholesale distribution not to handle any Wapping produced titles, News International transferred the contract for deliveries to the wholesalers to the newly created News International Distribution. Since the company now became News International's 'first customer' and was not the employer of the SOGAT members in dispute, any action taken by the members in wholesale became illegal. This arrangement – whereby 'buffer' companies could be created by an employer and inserted between themselves and their first customer – was permissible even though the shareholders of both corporations are identical. On Monday 27 January, News International made the first of many visits it was to make during the dispute to the courts, where they were successful in obtaining an injunction ordering SOGAT to withdraw its instruction to wholesale distribution drivers and warehouse workers not to handle Wapping titles. This was followed up two days' later by a writ from the company seeking injunctions, damages against SOGAT and requiring pickets not to follow TNT drivers.

The TUC General Council meeting of 5 February (see Chapter 13) which had decided on the content of the directives to the EETPU in relation to complaints about its behaviour in the dispute from both SOGAT and the NGA ended just before midnight. Although News International had obtained their first injunction against SOGAT on Monday 27 January, no action had been taken to enforce this, even though the unions continued to defy the injunctions. However, on 10 February – four days after the TUC decision and 14 days after the injunction had been granted – High Court Judge, Mr Justice Davies, fined SOGAT £25,000 for contempt of court in disobeying the previous order not to disrupt distribution of News International titles. Furthermore, the court appointed sequestrators to take control of all the union's funds and assets.

News International was experiencing substantial difficulties at this time, and the unions' activities in wholesale distribution were having an effect. Indeed, the February 1986 *SOGAT Journal* highlighted wholesale distribution as 'where the struggle is being conducted'. It was claimed that in the first week of printing at Wapping, of 60 main centres in England and Wales, 71 per cent did not receive the *News of the World*, and 26 per cent did not receive the *Sunday Times*. In other areas where copies did arrive, they were too late for normal delivery. As well as round-the-clock picketing of Wapping and TNT plants, the print unions organised marches and demonstrations which converged on Wapping. These activities angered News International, which admitted in February that it was giving generous rebates to advertisers to compensate them for shortfalls in distribution across all four Wapping titles.[13] However, the TUC General Council's reluctance to take a stronger line with the EETPU only encouraged the company to use the courts to prevent SOGAT from disrupting distribution. Not only were SOGAT and then the NGA served with injunctions and fined, but the High Court also granted News International injunctions against the TGWU and Union of Communication Workers, whose members had been instructed to honour picket lines and had refused to handle the *Sun*, bingo cards.

News International was authorised by the High Court on 10 February to appoint four commissioners to effect the sequestration of SOGAT funds and assets.[14] Ernst & Whinney, the accountants, selected by News International, froze all SOGAT accounts and assets, and assumed financial control of the union at every level. They warned if any attempts were made to circumvent these measures SOGAT Head Office would be closed and further punitive measures taken under the order of sequestration. Although SOGAT agreed to pay the £25,000 fine imposed by the High Court, the sequestration remained in force because the union had not purged its contempt. This meant SOGAT was unable to meet expenses for routine administration such as upkeep of the convalescent homes, accident, funeral, unemployment and dispute benefits and benevolent grants. In addition, the expenses of delegates to the TUC, NEC and other national meetings could not be met and nor could the NEC attend Council Meetings. Furthermore, early in March, as SOGAT's campaign continued, the High Court ordered all the union's cars be impounded, and threatened to close all branch and national offices. In rejecting the London CA&EP Branch application for the release of their funds, the judge confirmed that all branch and chapel funds were included in the sequestration.

Outside the Wapping plant, the picketing, rallies and demonstrations continued and were experiencing a level and intensity of policing seldom witnessed in an industrial dispute in Britain. An area one mile around the plant was routinely sealed off by police road blocks. Local residents had to prove their identity before being allowed to pass and no buses or taxis were allowed into the area. In contrast, SOGAT believed that TNT lorries distributing newspapers from the Wapping plant were allowed to exceed speed limits and to operate in contravention of by-laws restricting the movement of heavy vehicles during the night.

From the early days of the dispute, marches to Wapping were organised by the unions every Wednesday and Saturday night. SOGAT made clear its opposition to picket-line violence, but the nature of some police actions as they cleared people from the streets around the plant inevitably led to clashes. In the first month of the strike 194 arrests were made. The police hoped, by their behaviour, to intimidate SOGAT members and their supporters into staying away from the Wapping plant and thus ease the distribution of News International's four titles printed at Wapping. However, the conduct of the police led to an increasing number of complaints from many quarters.

There was evidence that those employed in the Wapping plant were being affected by the constant picketing, the huge marches and rallies and by the fortified appearance of the plant. In addition to the minority of journalists who had given up their jobs rather than move to Wapping, a number of others – especially those on the *Sunday Times* who had only voted 68–60 in favour – felt extremely uneasy about their decision to work there.[15] Through their FOCs at Wapping, the NUJ called on the company to negotiate 'an honourable settlement'. TGWU drivers employed by TNT added their weight to calls for the reopening of negotiations. Similar sentiments were expressed by 180 EETPU members employed in the Wapping plant, who stated they had been employed to work on the *London Post* and not to replace the existing work-force. Despite the position of the EETPU leadership, many of its rank and file members expressed support for SOGAT(82).[16]

On 4 April, News International offered to give the Gray's Inn Road printing works to the unions as compensation for the members who had lost their jobs. The offer included the land, buildings, presses and a £1m a year contract to print the *Guardian* newspaper for the next two years.[17] The union estimated that only about 1,000 people could be employed at Gray's Inn Road as much of the equipment was outdated and large amounts of money would be needed for investment to launch a new newspaper. Some viewed the offer as simply an imaginative public relations initiative whilst SOGAT took the view that although offer could not be considered as a settlement of the dispute, it could form part of a wider settlement.[18] On 16 April News International set a three-week deadline on its offer of Gray's Inn Road. In rejecting the offer, the unions reiterated their intention to continue to seek recognition at Wapping, and proposed a 'News International National Joint Committee' be established to have sole negotiating rights for union members, including the responsibility for negotiating an annual wage agreement for all production workers. The unions proposed arrangements for binding arbitration and offered written agreements covering continuity of production, flexibility, consultation and single status. The only response from the company was to extend the deadline to the unions to accept its plant and compensation offer from 30 May to 7 June.

On 14 April, all SOGAT branch secretaries were called to a meeting in London to discuss the situation concerning the sequestration.[19] It was reported that a number of creditors were threatening to take the union to court for default and, if this were to happen, the union would be close to receivership. On 21 April the NEC postponed a decision on purging the union's contempt of court whilst three days later the Appeal Court upheld the CA&EP Branch appeal that branch and chapel funds should not be subject to sequestration. As a result, property and funds of 80 branches were released.

Another meeting of SOGAT branch secretaries took place on 6 May, with the NEC due to meet later that day. The meeting discussed the problems sequestration was causing the branches and the national union. The union had been prevented from dealing with 6,500 unemployment benefit claims, 2,000 accident claims, convalescent benefits, retired members' pensions, and funeral benefits.[20] Some branch offices had been closed and telephones cut off. Many speakers advocated the only way forward was for the union to purge its contempt as this would release funds and enable the union to regain control of the situation and effectively to pursue the dispute. The union was in sequestration for an industrial action instruction which was not working. The NEC voted to purge the union's contempt of court but agreed the News International dispute and boycott campaign would continue, the members on strike would receive backdated dispute benefit, SOGAT branches should apply a voluntary levy and an appeal be issued, via the TUC, to the trade union movement for financial assistance and support for a series of rallies. On 8 May 1986 after 13 weeks of sequestration, SOGAT duly purged its contempt and instructed all members to halt the blacking of News International titles.

On 3 May the biggest demonstration since the dispute began occurred. News International strikers, who had walked from Glasgow to Wapping, attended the demonstration. In all, 12,000 people attended the demonstration, but 1,770 police were on duty. Women and children allegedly were charged by mounted police. SOGAT's General Secretary attacked these tactics, accusing the police of running riot and charging without warning. SOGAT called for a public inquiry to investigate the police's behaviour and a formal protest was lodged with the Home Office.

This heightened police action against the strikers and their members led the SOGAT London branches to express 'disquiet and abhorrence' at the NEC decision to purge its contempt. At a meeting organised by the London branches on 19 May, the General Secretary faced extremely strong opposition, including some interventions which the NEC believed 'went beyond the normal manner of criticising'.[21] The complaints centred upon the exclusion of chapel representatives from talks with News International, the fact that a News International Joint Committee which would reduce the power of the chapels and that there had been no consultation over the decision to purge the union's contempt of court. Some argued that continued defiance of the courts would have escalated the dispute and gained more support from the wider labour movement. Some disliked the national leadership, and not the chapels, controlling the dispute. The General Secretary reiterated the arguments that sequestration was affecting seriously many branches' ability to function, was a threat to the very existence of the union and the NEC's blacking instruction was not working. However, the mass meeting voted 'to escalate the dispute, continue picketing throughout the country' and to step up the demonstrations at the company's London printing works.

The national union leaders agreed to take part in another round of talks on 25 May which the TUC had been instrumental in arranging. Rupert Murdoch himself conducted the final stages of the negotiations on 26 May, and insisted that if this 'final offer' was not put to a ballot of the strikers within a week, then it would be withdrawn. The company offer had five points:[22]

(i)   redundancy pay of four weeks for each year of service, subject to a ceiling of £155 per week; a minimum payment of £2,000;
(ii) any dismissed worker would not be excluded from a chance of future employment;
(iii) the union recognition question at Wapping and Glasgow would be reviewed in 12 months;
(iv) provided no existing national newspaper (other than the *Guardian*) was printed there for five years, Gray's Inn Road would be transferred to the unions;
(v)   legal actions would be withdrawn on the basis of the parties bearing their own costs.

The SOGAT NEC voted by 15–9 to put the offer to ballot[23] and a five-page letter from the General Secretary was enclosed with the ballot papers. The General Secretary's letter was seen by some strikers as misleading and one-sided, whilst for others the offer was defective in that it contained no agreement over either union recognition or jobs. Furthermore, the NEC decision to conduct a postal ballot was challenged by the London Machine Branch as contrary to the union's General Rules, which required ballots to be carried out at the workplace and through the branches. Union Rules, the Branch argued, could not be altered by an emergency resolution at the NEC. The Branch applied to the High Court for an injunction to prevent the NEC proceeding with the postal ballot. The court ruled that union Rules could not be altered by emergency motions, and a postal ballot was a breach of those rules. However, because News International had demanded a deadline for a ballot response, the judge ruled on the 'balance of convenience' that it would be improper to grant the LMB injunction.

SOGAT members rejected the News International offer by 2,081 votes to 1,415.

The tensions which had become apparent within SOGAT over the NEC decision to purge the union's contempt of court and the way in which the 'final offer' ballot had been conducted were expected to come to a head at the 1986 Delegate Council Conference. The emergency motions on the News International dispute were not to be discussed until the fifth day of the Conference. However, the dispute cast its shadow from the start. In his opening address, General President, Danny Sergeant, said SOGAT was facing 'the biggest crisis in the whole of the post-war period and, perhaps, in its history'. In her first 'state of the union' speech as General Secretary, Brenda Dean emphasised the need for debate to be conducted in a spirit of tolerance of different points of view and added that she had never envisaged that within a few months of her taking office the union would be plunged into the biggest crisis in its history. Messages of support were brought to the BDC by representatives of the Australian print unions and by the General Secretary of the ICEF, whilst in his fraternal address Labour Party leader Neil Kinnock congratulated the News International strikers on their 'steadfastness'.

The first two motions dealing with the Wapping dispute were carried without opposition. The first called upon the TUC to instruct the EETPU to stop their members from doing the traditional work of the printing unions and, if the electricians failed to comply, then they be suspended from TUC membership. An NEC motion endorsed the strikers' decision to reject News International's offer, to continue the dispute and to ensure the maintenance of SOGAT as an independent union. It was also agreed the dispute come under the direct responsibility of the NEC, and that all SOGAT branches should be involved and regularly consulted. It was agreed to seek the support of all unions, including their participation in stepping up the boycott campaign and that the TUC press for a negotiated settlement with News International. A motion from the LMB advocating escalating the dispute was defeated. It called upon SOGAT members to refuse to handle News International titles. The mover argued that although what was being advocated had the danger of sequestration, they were in a situation in which anything done can be declared illegal and the strikers were entitled to expect more support than they were receiving from some areas of SOGAT and from the TUC. Replying on behalf of the NEC, the General Secretary told the delegates that the LMB motion could well lead back into sequestration over an instruction that was not proving industrially effective, the NEC was determined not to allow the courts to remove again the union from the control of the members and that SOGAT was fighting for its life. Two further motions were carried. One called for a just and honourable settlement to the dispute based upon the reinstatement of the sacked union members, full recognition for the traditional print unions in the News International plants and return of distribution to London wholesale, and the *News Of the World* would print again in Manchester. Several speakers paid tribute to the solidarity shown by the London and Manchester wholesale distribution members in refusing to handle News International titles despite the enormous cost to themselves. The other successful motion demanded a public inquiry into the role of the police at Wapping.

On the last day of the Conference, the company issued writs against the print unions in a bid to end mass picketing at News International plants and at more than 20 TNT depots.[24] As well as being directed against SOGAT, the national union injunctions were sought against three London branch secretaries – Ted Chard (LCB), Charlie Cherrill (LMB), Chris Robbins (CA&EP Branch) – one assistant branch secretary (Mike Britton (BIRMA)) and two lay members, Bill Freeman and Mike Hicks. The company asked the High Court to stop the union organising demonstrations, obstructions of the highway, nuisance or picketing which involved unlawful acts as well as interfering with trade, business or commercial contracts of News International or its subsidiaries. The union argued against granting the injunction on the grounds that it could not be held responsible for individuals who acted unlawfully despite union disapproval and that sacked News International workers gathering daily outside the Wapping plant were to registering their protest in the only way left open to them.

On 16 July the judge absolved the print unions from condoning or organising violence or intimidation and refused to ban demonstrations. However, he ruled marches or rallies at Wapping must terminate in Wellclose Square and not in the main road outside the plant.[25] Furthermore, failure by the unions to control the conduct of demonstrators might lead to a total ban and failure to comply with all the court's rulings would leave SOGAT open to contempt proceedings. National union leaders were ordered to direct their branches accordingly within three days and SOGAT did this immediately. A similar course of events followed concerning action at TNT depots, where the number of pickets was restricted to six by the unions, and SOGAT warned that any member ignoring this instruction would be subject to disciplinary action. In mid-August, News International wrote to SOGAT and the NGA to complain that the injunctions were being defied and pickets were being abusive towards the company's employees.

On 14 September News International made what it described as 'the best, last and final offer' to the unions. However, the only substantive difference to the previous offer was that the ceiling for full-time employees upon which their redundancy pay would be based was increased from £155 per week to £205. For members who worked for other companies (i.e. casuals) as well as News International this amount would be £155 per week. The compensation package would cost the company £58 million. A 'News International Joint National Council' would be established, with seats allocated to the company, the four production unions and an *ex-officio* representative of the TUC. The body would be for the purpose of consultation and communication, to deal with individual grievances and to provide advice and consultation. None of the unions would be individually or jointly recognised to any extent for the purposes of collective bargaining. The company would give no commitment to re-employ sacked union members. In return, the unions would call off their action. If the offer proved acceptable the company would withdraw its legal actions.

On 17 September the NEC put the offer to a ballot of the News International members. Meetings with the branch secretaries and FOCs/MOCs to discuss the offer were followed by mass meetings of the strikers. At one point, News International threatened to withdraw the offer because it was unhappy with SOGAT's balloting procedures. When both the TUC and SOGAT General Secretaries declared their faith in the union's practices, the company said it would accept the outcome of the vote. On 6 October, the ballot result showed SOGAT members had voted by 2,372 to 96 to reject the offer of financial compensation – the members had put trade union principles, the right to jobs and the right to proper trade union recognition before money.[26]

News International responded to the ballot result by writing to individual members offering them compensation based on the value of the rejected offer. The company imposed a deadline for acceptance and, even after extending the deadline, found almost 4,000 strikers refused to take up their offer. However, by mid-November other pressures were mounting on the strikers to resolve the dispute. On 13 November the TUC General Secretary suggested the union make further concessions to News International to get talks re-opened.[27] He proposed SOGAT accept the EETPU members employed at Wapping remain in their current jobs, including those which had previously been performed by SOGAT members. After hearing the FOCs were firmly opposed to the TUC proposals, the SOGAT Executive rejected the suggestion. The TUC General Secretary had made this suggestion despite the General Council's support for the print unions' boycott campaign directed against News International's four titles. Since the start of the dispute, the unions had spent £400,000 on publicity, distributed over six million leaflets and 300,000 posters had produced 750,000 carrier bags.[28] All TUC-affiliated unions and many other labour movement organisations had received literature about the boycott. An advertising van had toured the country, posters had been placed on major billboard sites and adverts placed in the labour movement and regional press. Sympathetic local authorities had withdrawn advertising from News International newspapers, but, on 7 November, the High Court ruled that three London councils had acted illegally in banning News International publications from public libraries. More than 30 other councils had imposed bans.

The boycott campaign was stepped up in the aftermath of the strikers' rejection of the company offer. Branches were urged to ensure every pressure on News International and every area of activity was maintained and intensified. A number of local 'boycott days' were organised in cities throughout Britain and efforts were made to establish '*Sun*-free zones'. These activities proved extremely successful both in publicising the dispute and in gaining public support. To keep the issue in the public eye, especially in the areas where media interest had tailed off, over 60 branches of the union were allocated 'boycott days' during November and December and all members were urged to volunteer their services.

However, financial pressures were impinging on the union. In the light of its financial position the NEC decided to ballot the membership on a proposal for a levy of 58p per member per week for six months. The levy was needed to meet the additional expenses the union had incurred from the News International dispute. The bill for legal costs and sequestration amounted to £1.5 million. News International's damages claims could total between £1.5m and £2.8m, and £1m had been spent on dispute benefit. In an appeal to members to accept the levy, the General Secretary argued that the union's existence was threatened by one multinational employer simply because it was defending its members from attack. By supporting the levy SOGAT members would show News International and other employers they were not a pushover. Conscious of anti-national-newspaper feelings in the union, the General Secretary referred to her own provincial background and to the sums of money already spent by the London branches to support their striking members, viz, £500,000 by the LCB, £750,000 by RIRMA, £400,000 by the CA&EP. However, despite a high-profile and concentrated campaign in support of a 'yes' vote for the levy, the result declared on 13 January 1987 was a rejection by 51,187 votes to 44,265 in a 56.2 per cent turnout. Some interpreted this result as meaning the members had indicated they felt time had run out on the Wapping strikers. Others believed the outcome was the result of differing levels of serious campaigning carried out in some localities during the course of the dispute and in the campaign for the levy itself. On 22 January 1987 the NEC decided to continue to pay the £6 dispute benefit and to strive to continue the boycott campaign.

The first anniversary of the dispute was commemorated with a disciplined and peaceful march to the gates of Wapping lead by the strikers, trade union leaders and Labour politicians and which involved nearly 25,000 people. The occasion, ended in violence, however, in which many demonstrators were injured. The police repeatedly charged the packed crowds and later running street battles were witnessed. SOGAT called for an independent inquiry into the policing of the demonstrations. They asked for an inquiry into the use of police horses, snatch squads, attacks on photographers and the use of red dye. The Home Secretary Douglas Hurd said he viewed the clashes with serious concern but gave the police his full support for their action.

Following the SOGAT membership's rejection of the a six-month levy, News International issued new writs against both SOGAT and the NGA for contempt of court. The action was based upon the claim that the unions had breached High Court injunctions banning unlawful mass picketing. News International sought sequestration of SOGAT's assets, funds and properties. On 5 February 1987, after 54 weeks of the dispute, the NEC met in emergency session. They were informed that the legal advice was that sequestration and a substantial fine were almost inevitable[29] and they voted by 23 votes to nine to end the strike. Sequestration would have been contrary to the decision of the BDC and a further sequestration would have meant the '*demise*' of the union. News International agreed to drop all legal action against SOGAT once they received written assurance that the dispute, demonstrations and the boycott campaign were at an end. The company made available the previous redundancy package and stated there would be no discrimination against former employees in filling future vacancies. The compensation offer would remain on the table until 10 March 1987. The families of members who died during the dispute would be paid compensation at double the amount offered in September 1986. SOGAT had only 24 hours to end the dispute or face sequestration and this meant it was impossible to ballot those on strike to call off the dispute.

THE AFTERMATH

Myths of Wapping

The Wapping dispute was not about a group of workers resisting the implementation of new technology. The computerised origination system that News International was to operate at Wapping had been operating in the provincial newspaper and general printing industry for many years. The lithography printing presses that were installed in Wapping were 15 years' old, having been bought second hand. The equipment to be used in the finishing areas was basic compared to what was common elsewhere in the industry. Wapping was far from being a leading-edge technologically advanced printing establishment. Compared to many provincial newspaper houses it was a 'museum piece'. However, it represented significant change for national newspaper production as this was still dominated by old metal origination, letterpress equipment and manual effort in the finishing and warehousing areas. SOGAT members in the provincial press and the general trade had long accepted cold composition, lithographic printing techniques and mechanised distribution. SOGAT could hardly deny their introduction into national newspaper production.

The trade unions were prepared to operate the new techniques to be introduced at Wapping. The dispute was over the non-negotiable conditions the company laid down to accompany this acceptance, namely, the unfettered right to manage, the absence of a closed shop, a legally binding collective agreement, a no-strike clause and the different procedures for disciplining chapel officials as opposed to employees. News International never had any intention of negotiating an agreement with the unions. They effectively declared war on the print unions. To have accepted new technology on the company's terms would have meant accepting the elimination of effective trade unionism and the introduction of 'industrial slavery'. All the negotiations with News International were about the body of any agreement and not about the details of staffing and wage rates. The dispute was thus nothing to do with modern technology. It was about management authority and the continuation of effective trade unionism.

In the eyes of many, national newspaper workers were grossly over-paid and operated unusual working practices. For those with this view, Wapping was seen as a group of 'greedy' workers getting their long-overdue comeuppance. Of the 5,000 workers involved in the dispute, the vast majority did not fit this stereotypical picture. Most of the strikers were lower-paid workers – clerical workers, canteen staff, cleaners, porters, tele-ad sales staff, drivers, library staff, circulation representatives – with long periods of services with News International. The redundancy payments offered during, and received after, the dispute were aimed at these workers rather than the higher-paid production workers. The News International Bouverie Street estab-lishment, employed 31 cleaners, most of whom had up to 34 years' service with the company when they were dismissed in January 1986. The cleaners' chapel organised a picketing rota requiring every member to do at least two shifts of picketing each week. They also partici-pated in demonstrations and marches held every Wednesday and Saturday night. They also played a prominent role in leading the singing on the regular Wapping women's marches.

Impact on SOGAT (82)

The effects of Wapping were also sharply felt by the union itself. The process of moving national newspaper production from 'Fleet Street' was quickened by the dispute with its accompanying loss of many jobs. The total work-force in national newspapers fell from 30,000 to 15,000 between 1985 and 1990 whilst SOGAT's London membership declined from 52,000 in 1982 to 17,000 by 1990. Not only was the once powerful position of the London branches within the national union greatly dimin-ished, but the strength and importance of the chapel in negotiating national newspaper industry wages and condition was also considerably weakened. Although SOGAT had been able to gather a small nucleus of members inside the Wapping plant in the late 1980s, it was only after a soul-searching debate at the 1990 Delegate Council that the union took the formal, and for many of the strikers traumatic, decision to recruit the Wapping work-force. One of the consequences of the accel-eration of the movement of national newspaper production outside of central London together with the technological changes was the ending of the casual system of employment. This system had hidden the effects of falling unemployment in the general printing trade in London. The long-term decline of this sector in London had been hidden by the ability of London branches to place unemployed/redundant general trade workers into casual employment on the national newspapers. This often resulted in these individuals receiving higher wages for less hours relative to their previous employment. This protection was lost as newspapers moved to the Surrey Docks and the Isle of Dogs and unemployment amongst SOGAT's London membership increased sharply.

SOGAT found sequestration of its funds, assets and property a brutal experience. It also meant a freezing of the payment of benefits to the members and the denial to them of servicing from all levels of the union. When its funds and assets were sequestrated in February 1986, SOGAT, in financial terms, was no longer in control of the union at branch or national level. The sequestrators had complete control of all cash and any attempts to circumvent this would have put the union in further contempt of court. It was the duty to the court of the sequestrators to locate all SOGAT's assets, at the union's expense. They had no discretionary powers and had to apply to the court for any funds which they deemed to be necessary for a particular purpose. The sequestrators had power to take control of the union if they ascertained the union was hiving off money. They could then go back to the court who could appoint a receiver, whose task would be to ensure contributions were brought into their account. Further obstructions would have meant the appointment of a receiver/manager by the court, whereby SOGAT would effectively lose its independence.

The NEC decided not to obstruct the sequestrators nor hide anything, as they felt they did not have the right to waste the members' money, which would be used in accountants' fees to trace money hidden away. This proved to be the right decision. SOGAT sought to release funds to pay the fine of £25,000. However, on 18 February 1986 the judge said he intended to make an order for the union's Head Office to be closed, the staff to be sent home and the officers' cars to be impounded. When the sequestrator's solicitors explained that SOGAT had co-operated with them, the judge ordered that £25,000 be made available to pay the fine, no active steps be taken to impound the cars and £600 be released for the purchase of oil for the Ayr convalescent home. SOGAT had found sequestration draconian, expensive and that the price of non co-operation would be the loss of democratic control of the union. It meant no expenditure, however pressing and deserving, could be made. The union could not function effectively and had no resources to support its members in their dealings with other employees. Servicing could not be provided to the membership. Having experienced sequestration once the union was determined it should not happen again, especially if the industrial objective was not being achieved by the action that had led to the union's assets, funds and property having been sequestrated.

The dispute put tremendous strain on SOGAT's financial resources. Expenditure from the dispute reduced its total assets by 50 per cent. Sequestration costs amounted to £1.5 million. Legal costs, various legal fees and costs of brining unfair dismissal claims to industrial tribunals equalled £1 million. Responding to the financial needs of the union, SOGAT branches contributed £1.7 million to the dispute. The TUC gave £50,000 to help with legal costs. The union's General Fund took in £443,000 in donations from branches, chapels, individuals, other trade unions, a voluntary levy and from foreign unions. Many unionists in SOGAT and other unions in both the UK and abroad supported the union during the dispute. Within the union support particularly came from the members employed in the London wholesale newspaper distribution sector. Members up and down the country also rallied round. Outside the union, much support came from the National Union of Railwaymen, who were involved prior to the dispute in the transportation of News International titles, the affiliates of the ICEF and the Australian printing trade unions. There was also the courage, determination and grit of the SOGAT members directly involved in the dispute who stayed loyal to trade union principles throughout the 13 months of the dispute for jobs, recognition and union rights.

Impact on Members

In all, 4,745 SOGAT members were dismissed by News International and, after 54 weeks of trying to regain their jobs, they were left with redundancy compensation based on four weeks' pay for each year of service, to a ceiling of £205 a week for those whose work was totally that of News International, and an agreement there would be no discrimination against them if they applied for future jobs at Wapping. Apart from losing their jobs, they had suffered from the brutality of the police who frequently attacked indiscriminately. For many, the Wapping dispute 'defeat' represented a loss of sense of personal identity and security. It was the demise of a lifestyle. The nepotism of the industry had produced families in which sons had inherited a traditional way of life from their fathers. The 'prestige' of working on 'the Street' had been lost, and for some it was like the loss of an institution.

The SOGAT members directly involved in the dispute suffered severe financial hardship. Many were forced to sell their homes and possessions and to take on significant levels of debt. In an effort to relieve hardship amongst the strikers' families, the Families Central Welfare Fund was established. It received £382,743 in donations from branches and chapels of SOGAT, individuals and trade unions both within and outside the UK. Payments for families were monthly. From April to June 1986 the payment was £10. This rose of £20 for July, August, September and October. In November the payment was £30, whilst in December 1993 members each received £50. The payment for January 1987 and February 1987 was £40 and £25 respectively. In addition to financial suffering, many experienced personal tragedy. Many marriages broke up, some strikers committed suicide whilst others developed long-term illnesses. Almost all suffered levels of stress.

Employment Legislation

News International had never intended to reach an accommodation with the print unions and had undertaken extensive preparations to ensure its strategy of divesting from a relationship with the print unions was successful. Part of this careful preparation was the use at the appropriate time of the provisions of the Employment Acts of 1980 and 1982. In this regard the dispute illustrated the lack of balance in these two Acts between employers' and employees' interests. The company had been able to use legal means to restrain the unions' picketing activities because Wapping was not the workplace of the dismissed print employees. That had been Gray's Inn Road (*The Times* and *Sunday Times*) and Bouverie Street (*Sun* and *News of the World*), but the employer had closed those establishments and picketing under the 1980 Act was only legal at these empty workplaces. News International had also been able to use the legislation to restrain secondary action against it. The 1980 Act permitted secondary action against employers who were a first customer or a first supplier of the company where the primary dispute was taking place. News International recognised that newspaper wholesalers, which were 100 per cent SOGAT-organised, would be first customers of its four titles and SOGAT could legally instruct its members in the warehouses to refuse to handle News International newspapers. The company overcame the problem by creating a series of 'shadow companies' – such as News International Supply Ltd – so that the warehouses ceased to be the first customer. It was on this basis that in February 1986 News International gained an order banning SOGAT from instructing its members in newspaper distribution to 'black' its papers. When this order was ignored, SOGAT suffered a £25,000 fine and sequestration. The Wapping dispute also demonstrated that it was pointless for a union to deny the law if, by doing so, its industrial objective was not being achieved. The Employment Acts of 1980 and 1982 had restrained SOGAT but as its General Secretary remarked:

> The law is so heavily loaded against the trade unions and against working people that it is now a travesty of justice. By far my strongest impression is of the total unfairness of the loading of the present industrial relations law against ordinary working people. And that not for the first time in our history the Courts of this land are not the place for them to seek justice.[30]

National Newspaper Production and Distribution

The SOGAT 'Fleet Street' chapels did not believe News International could produce and distribute national newspapers without them. Wapping was operating with fewer than 600 production workers, many of whom were only half-trained. The production of the *Sun* and *The Times* printed at Wapping on 26 January 1986 came as a shock. Indeed, throughout the dispute, the company only lost one issue of *The Times* and the *Sun*. Although initially their production was poor and their distribution scrappy, News International had produced newspapers without the assistance of the print unions. The quality of production of the papers printed at Wapping could, and did, only get better over time. News International was the only newspaper group with sufficient resources to withstand a 12-month 'siege' from the unions. However, after Wapping, other newspapers were able to follow News International but at a much lesser cost. Wapping had shown that the print unions could be taken on, the employers had the protection of the Employment Acts, management now held the advantage of the balance of bargaining power and print trade unionism was less effective.

If the News International titles could be produced without the print unions then the key to SOGAT 'winning' the dispute lay with stopping their distribution. National newspapers had traditionally been distributed by rail, but News International switched to delivering its four Wapping-produced titles by road via the TNT road haulage company. This was T&GWU-organised, but that union was unable to persuade its members employed by TNT to take action in support of the dismissed SOGAT News International workers. The distribution of newspapers by road rather than rail had been an increasing possibility as the UK system of motorways emerged, thus avoiding the use of A roads. It also offered the possibility of delivering newspapers more quickly to the wholesalers and retailers, because once the lorry was full it could get on its way and, unlike the trains, it would not have to wait the arrival of other titles and then depart at a set time. The Wapping dispute made these possibilities into a reality. The distribution of national newspapers by road improved throughout the Wapping dispute. It showed clearly that road distribution could complete with the traditional London wholesale distribution system. Following the end of the Wapping dispute all national newspapers quickly moved to distribution by road to remove the competitive edge News International had gained by doing so. Maxwell was the first to copy News International by the creation of Newsflow, which survived despite a dispute with SOGAT over union recognition. The London wholesale section of SOGAT had given magnificent and unquestioning support to the Wapping strikers, but they lost work that never returned.

The Role of the Electrical, Electronic, Telecommunications/ Plumbing Union (EETPU)

The role of the EETPU in the Wapping dispute was crucial to the company's success, and for SOGAT members and leadership its behaviour can never be forgiven. Without EETPU support it would have been difficult, if not impossible, for News International to recruit an alternative work-force to print its papers. The union had openly collaborated with the company in recruiting this alternative work-force. The SOGAT General Secretary had presented evidence to the TUC of the EETPU having taken over the jobs of SOGAT members. The national officials of the EETPU repeatedly gave assurances that there was no question of taking over the work of the print unions. Nevertheless, SOGAT always suspected that, in a union as centrally controlled as the EETPU, it was inconceivable that no words of its recruitment activities in Southampton and Motherwell could have reached the national leadership. The narrow decision of the TUC's General Council not to instruct the EETPU to tell their members to stop doing the dismissed printers' work was significant. Had the TUC decision gone the other way, then News International may have been forced to return to serious negotiations.

The Role of the Police

Almost 1,500 people were arrested during the Wapping dispute demonstrations in December 1986. A SOGAT member, Michael Hicks, was sentenced to one year's imprisonment (with eight months suspended) plus a £1,000 fine. The print unions – and latterly the TUC – repeatedly demanded a public inquiry into policing during the dispute. In the absence of the government agreeing to such an inquiry, the print unions sponsored a Report by the Haldane Society into the events of 24 January 1987. The Report, published in September 1987, accused police of making charges on horseback, and without warning, into enclosed areas where people were seeking shelter. Accusations were also reported of the police smashing windows in the first-aid vehicles, carrying injured demonstrators and singling out photographers and journalists for attack. It was claimed that the police used truncheons randomly and with unnecessary violence, as well as utilising unauthorised weapons. The Haldane Society described police tactics as resembling military operations against an enemy rather than an exercise in public order. The internal inquiry set up by the police and headed by the Chief Superintendent of Northamptonshire was criticised for restricting its scope to complaints against individual officers rather than examining overall police strategy.

The police's own inquiry into complaints arising from the demonstration of 24 January 1987 received over 400 complaints concerning assault, grievous bodily harm, wounding and perjury. In January 1989, two years after the events occurred and as a result of the inquiry's findings, 26 Police Officers were charged with a number of offences including grievous and actual bodily harm, conspiracy to pervert the course of justice and perjury.[31] However, on the grounds of the defence plea of 'unjustifiable delay' before charges were laid, the judge acquitted the first Police Officer to come to trial in May 1989 and, following on from this judgement, every other defendant was also acquitted.

However, Pat Smith, the wife of a SOGAT striker, successfully sued the police for false imprisonment, assault and malicious prosecution. Despite refusing to admit liability and denying Ms Smith's description of the events surrounding her arrest, the Metropolitan Police nevertheless agreed to pay her £4,000 in an out-of-court settlement. Michael Delaney, a local resident, was killed by a TNT lorry some distance from the plant in January 1987 and – against the advice of the coroner – the inquest jury decided by a 10–1 vote that his death was an unlawful killing. The Director of Public Prosecutions announced that insufficient evidence existed to prosecute the lorry driver and in May 1988 the High Court quashed the inquest jury's 'unlawful killing' verdict.

NOTES

1. See *SOGAT Journal*, March 1987, p. 1.
2. See Society of Graphical and Allied Trades *Annual Report of the National Executive Council*, 1986, p. 31.
3. See L. Melvern *The End of the Street*, Methuen, 1986, Chapter 1, pp. 16–17.
4. See S.M. Littleton *The Wapping Dispute*, Avebury, 1992, Chapter 5, pp. 60–1.
5. See L. Melvern *The End of the Street*, Methuen, 1986, Chapter 2, p. 30.
6. See J. Gennard *A History of the National Graphical Association*, Unwin Hyman 1990, Chapter 14, pp. 472–5.
7. See L. Melvern *The End of the Street*, Methuen, 1986, pp. 221–48.
8. Op. cit. p. 215.
9. Op. cit., pp. 221–7.
10. Op. cit., pp. 230–7.
11. See Society of Graphical and Allied Trades (82) *Annual Report of the National Executive Council, 1986*, p. 31.
12. Op. cit. p. 32.
13. See the *Guardian*, 6 February 1986.
14. See Society of Graphical and Allied Trades (82) *Annual Report of the National Executive Council, 1986*, p. 33.
15. See L. Melvern *The End of the Street*, Methuen, 1986, Chapter 6, pp. 119–60.
16. See Society of Graphical and Allied Trades *National Circular*, 6 February 1986.
17. See Society of Graphical and Allied Trades *Annual Report of the National Executive Council, 1986*, p. 34.
18. See *SOGAT Journal*, May 1986, p. 16.
19. See Society of Graphical and Allied Trades (82) *Annual Report of the National Executive Council, 1986*, p. 34.
20. See *SOGAT Journal*, June 1986, p. 3.
21. See Society of Graphical and Allied Trades (82) *Annual Report of the National Executive Council, 1986*, p. 35.
22. Ibid.
23. See *SOGAT Journal*, July 1986, pp. 14–15.
24. See Society of Graphical and Allied Trades *Annual Report of the National*

Executive Council, 1986, p. 36.

25. See *SOGAT Journal*, November 1986, pp. 2–3.
26. See Society of Graphical and Allied Trades *Annual Report of the National Executive Council, 1986*, p. 36.
27. See Society of Graphical and Allied Trades *Annual Report of the National Executive Council, 1986*, p. 37.
28. See *SOGAT Journal*, March 1987, p. 11.
29. S.M. Littleton *The Wapping Dispute*, Avebury, 1992, Chapter 6, p. 131.
30. See *SOGAT Journal*, March 1987, p. 3.
31. Op. cit.

CHAPTER 20

RELATIONS WITH OTHER EMPLOYERS' ORGANISATIONS

In this chapter attention is focused on small sections of the printing, papermaking and paper conversion industries but which nevertheless are significant and are either directly part of the printing and paper-making industries or are inseparably linked to them – for example, ink-makers. Most groups covered in this chapter are highly skilled. They were all important sections of SOGAT membership but whose work was often taken for granted and whose achievements often passed unnoticed. Unlike the big battalions of general print, newspapers, magazines and cartons and packaging, they escaped the gaze of publicity. The work they produced was highly visible. However, some of the specialised skills and trades covered in this section have virtually gone out of existence, for example vellum and parchment makers and paper tube manufacturing, which served the cotton-making industry rather than the printing and papermaking industries.

SCOTLAND

Society of Master Printers of Scotland (SMPS)/Scottish Printing Employers' Federation (SPEF)

In 1967 the SMPS, prior to the BFMP agreement (see Chapter 14) of that year, made an offer to the unions, including SOGAT, of an 80p per week increase for craftsmen with lesser sums for other grades. This offer, made whilst the BFMP was talking of lower figure, was accepted by SOGAT members in Scotland. The 80p increase eventually was offered by the BFMP along with a second payment of 70p per week, with lesser amounts for other grades, to follow in 1968. This meant further negotiations were necessary with the SMPS to secure the 70p and consequential increase paid in England, Wales and Northern Ireland. At a meeting in Edinburgh in July 1968 the employers argued that they preferred not to follow the exact pattern set in England, Wales and Northern Ireland and that if any agreement was not to fall foul of existing incomes policy guidelines, then improved productivity would have to result from it. SOGAT argued they had already conceded productivity concessions that covered two years, although they had received a wage increase to cover one year. Ultimately, the SMPS offered a £1 increase for craftsmen, corresponding increases for SOGAT grades, and the agreement to remain in force until 31 March 1970. The offer was coupled with some productivity-enhancing measures including reference to the introduction of systems of payment by results and method study. For the first time, SOGAT counted the ballot on the SMPS 1968 offer under the supervision of Head Office, with Scottish scrutineers at the union's Edinburgh office. The return of 78 per cent was one of the highest recorded for a wages increase offer ballot for SOGAT or its constituent unions. The SMPS offer was carried by 5,773 votes.

Following the merger of SOGAT and the SGA in 1975, SOGAT's Scottish Graphical Division negotiated with the SMPS to determine the pay and conditions of craft employees in the Scottish general printing industry. SOGAT negotiated for the non-craft employees and in January 1978 the National Executive backed a call from the Scottish branches to abrogate the agreement with the SMPS in this sector.[1] This followed the employers' refusal to honour a promise given in the summer of 1977 to negotiate a new pay deal. At that time, a pay offer was made which was then put to a ballot of the members. The ballot paper clearly indicated that SOGAT would return to the negotiating table later in the year for a further increase, and it was on this basis the union had recommended acceptance of the 1977 employer offer. At the 1977 negotiations, SOGAT had been informed by the SMPS, both orally and in writing, that they would honour a commitment to increase wages by around 10 per cent, and they viewed the employers refusal to honour this commitment as a complete departure from the principles of negotiation. SOGAT therefore abrogated its SMPS Agreement.

A meeting, held on 21 January 1978, attended by the SOGAT Scottish Group, including the Scottish Graphical Division, expressed deep concern at the employers' attitude. On 23 January all SOGAT Scottish printing and binding branches imposed an immediate overtime ban, refused to work extra shifts and to staff new machines. Branches and chapels ended contact with the SMPS. Chapels were instructed to approach their managements for a 10 per cent increase and, where this was conceded, to withdraw sanctions. Where less than 10 per cent was offered, chapels and branches were to seek advice from Head Office. Over 300 firms were affected by industrial action, which resulted in a meeting between SMPS and SOGAT and at which the employers offered to negotiate on a plant-by-plant basis for increases of around 5 per cent in return for productivity concessions. These negotiations took place throughout the industry and by May 1978 the bulk of SOGAT members had settled for sums of around the stated percentage. In this industrial climate SOGAT met SMPS to conclude a wage deal for 1978. The employers argued they were bound to adhere by the Government's 10 per cent pay increase guideline. After lengthy negotiations an agreement was reached providing for a 10 per cent increase on all weekly basic wage rates and a new consolidated weekly flat-rate supplement payment.

In 1979, the SMPS and SOGAT met to review their Agreement for the first time for a number of years unrestricted by Government pay policy. On the wages front, the problem was that the Scottish print and binding industry had varying wage levels stemming from flat-rate supplement payments made during the Labour Government's pay restraint policy of 1975–79. This meant the outcome of the 1979 negotiations might not satisfy everybody. For example, consideration of the flat-rate supplements would produce considerable increases for workers working shifts or high amounts of overtime or those paid on bonus systems, but it would offer little for members on the flat rate. In the 1979 pay negotiations the objective was to 'square this circle' in a manner that would produce a reasonable increase for all members. To this end, an Agreement was concluded which provided a minimum wage increase plus the consolidation of flat-rate supplement payments awarded during the period of income restraint.

The wages of SOGAT members, including those of its Scottish Graphical Branch, continued to improve throughout the 1980s. In July 1990 the payment of the adult rate for non-craft production employees at the age of 19 was achieved. By the time SOGAT merged with the NGA the minimum earnings guarantee for craft members was £165.86 per week whilst that for non-craft employees ranged between £149.27 (Grade C) and £145.13 (Grade D). SOGAT's 1991 negotiations with employers were conducted jointly with the NGA.

In 1972 SOGAT members in Scotland employed in general print were granted four weeks' paid holiday with effect from 1 October 1973. An additional day's holiday was achieved in the 1983 negotiations and a further day from October 1985 in the 1985 wage negotiations. The following year saw the introduction of five weeks' paid holidays, with holiday pay entitlement based on weekly average earnings. February 1980 saw the standard working week in the Scottish general printing industry reduced from 40 hours to 39 hours. From 6 July 1981 the standard working week was reduced to 37½ hours. In 1982/3 the rate of sick pay in the industry for all SOGAT employees became 50 per cent of the normal weekly wage for a total of six weeks, with a limit of £63 payable in any one week. This limit had increased to £105 by the time SOGAT ceased to be an independent union. In 1988 the SMPS agreed to give SOGAT women members reasonable time off to have cervical and breast cancer screening whilst 1991 saw the right of every employee to be treated with respect and dignity and to work in an environment free from sexual harassment. Complaints of sexual harassment were dealt with through the agreed procedures for such grievances.[2]

The Scottish Daily Newspaper Society (SDNS)

The NUPB&PW, SOGAT (Division A) and SOGAT had no members working in SDNS offices, and it was only after the merger with the SGA that SOGAT had a collective bargaining relationship with this employers' association. Over the period 1975 to 1978 wage agreements between the Scottish Graphical Division and the SDNS were amended in line with the government imposed pay increase guidelines of the time. A claim from the Scottish Graphical Division that the £6 flat-rate supplementary payment permitted under the pay policy of 1 July 1975 to 30 June 1976 be applied to holiday pay was submitted to independent arbitration, but it was subsequently rejected by the arbiter. When the SDNS Agreement expired on 30 June 1980 the SDNS took the view that since new agreements on a house basis were being negotiated by Thomson Regional Newspapers in Edinburgh and George Outrams in Glasgow, there was no point in revising the National Agreement. As a consequence, future negotiations were conducted at house level in the light of the circumstances of each house.

AD-SETTING HOUSES

The Advertising, Typesetting and Foundry Employers' Federation (ATFEF) came into being in 1960. The advertising trade houses provided a service to the general printing trade and to national and provincial newspapers. Ad-setting firms were in membership of the BFMP but were concerned that when that body was in dispute with the unions they could not continue to supply national newspapers. During the 1959 dispute the BFMP would not accept a separate agreement for ad-setters, so these employers approached the London print unions and made a separate agreement for which they formed the ATFEF. Not all ad-setting houses affiliated to this body, but they paid in line with the conditions established by the ATFEF Agreement. In 1972 the print unions sought a 36-hour working week from the ad-setters. The ATFEF members were prepared to offer a 37½-hour week. However, non-federated firms were prepared to concede a 36-hour working week. These firms formed themselves into the Reproduction and Graphics Association (RAGA) and concluded an agreement with the London Central Branch, and not SOGAT nationally, to provide for the 37½-hour working week from October 1972 and a 36-hour working week from November 1974.

The Advertising, Typesetting and Foundry Employers' Federation (ATFEF)

The MCTS and the PMB held Agreements, made in 1960, with the ATFEF. When the Monotype Casters and Typefounders became a branch of the NUPB&PW they continued to be responsible for maintaining and amending the Agreement with the ATFEF. However, the London Central Branch had interests in the ad-setting houses and the NUPB&PW was anxious to enter into an agreement with the ATFEF to advance the interests of its London Central Branch members. In 1968, following prolonged negotiations affecting the PMB, Monotype Casters and Typefounders' Branch and the LCB, new terms were agreed under which the craft branches achieved a basic rate of £24.25 for day workers for a 40-hour working week. There were further increases from November 1969 to give a £25 day rate and a £32 night rate. The ATFEF Agreement with the LCB covered motor drivers and semi-skilled employees and gave rates of £20.08 for day workers for a standard working week of 40 hours and £24.07½ for night workers for a 36-hour standard working week. From November 1969 these rates were £20.67½ per week and £25.35 per week respectively. In 1971 women workers received the male rate where employed on similar duties.

In 1971 the ATFEF reduced the standard working week for day workers to 37½ hours. In 1974 a further reduction to 36 hours was granted, giving equality of working hours to day and night workers. In 1971 the ATFEF conceded four weeks' paid holiday to the PMB, LCB and the Monotype Casters' Branch. In the mid-1970s, SOGAT sought to persuade the ad-setters to introduce a sick pay scheme. Many affiliated firms already operated such schemes and in 1974 the ATFEF persuaded those affiliates without sick pay arrangements to institute a sickness scheme on similar lines to those operating in affiliated firms. If this proved unsuccessful then the union would raise the issue again in 1975. This they did, and an industry-wide sickness pay scheme was introduced in 1975. The craftsmen received £1 per week sickness pay for each complete three months of employment up to a maximum weekly payment of £6 with a maximum of six weeks' sickness payments in any one calender year. The sick pay scheme provided minimal payments.[3]

In the ad-setting houses the 1970s saw a movement from hot metal composing techniques to cold composing techniques which affected the position of SOGAT members working under both the ATFEF and RAGA agreements. SOGAT attempted to maintain the traditional position of its members in page make-up and composition and, at the same time, to establish a closer working relationship with the NGA which was seeking to control these areas of SOGAT work. In an effort to resolve these inter-union problems, a number of meetings took place under the chairmanship of Professor Thomason. Unfortunately, little progress was made due to the NGA requiring acceptance by SOGAT of certain spheres of influence. Although SOGAT sought fair and reasonable arrangements for both unions to work in the ad-setting houses, the influence of the ATFEF declined in the second half of the 1970s. It lost members in the face of competition from alternative sources for producing advertisements for newspapers and magazines.

The Reproduction and Graphics Association (RAGA)

In 1972 RAGA negotiated with the LCB a two-stage agreement for packers, despatchers and drivers. The first stage was a short-term agreement providing a day wage rate of £28 per week for a 38¾-hour standard working week and a night wage rate of £36.50 per week for a standard working week of 36 hours. The second stage, which operated from 29 October 1973 to 28 October 1974, provided a weekly day wage rate of £31.50 for 37½ hours and a weekly night wage of £41.75 for 36 hours. In 1974, SOGAT's negotiations with RAGA were of historical importance, as it was the first time RAGA had met with SOGAT to negotiate a national agreement.[4] The union secured recognition, a substantial increase in wages and a reduction in hours of work. RAGA conceded recognition to the PMB, the Monotype Casters and Typefounders' Branch and the LCB, a reduction of the day workers' standard working week to 36 hours from 7 October 1974, thus equalising the standard working week for day and night workers, and a craft rate of £46 per week for day workers and £61.45 per week for night workers. The rates established for non-craft employees were £40.10 per week for day workers and £51.90 per week for night workers. By the time SOGAT merged with the NGA, the weekly day rate for the PMB and the London Machine Branch was £218.50 and the weekly night rate £283.17. The rates for London Central/Greater London Branch members were £181.59 (day workers) and £236.38 for night workers.

In 1980, the four weeks' paid holiday entitlement was increased by two days and for those on night work by two shifts. Later in the same year it was increased by a further day and for night workers by a further shift. In October 1981 annual holiday entitlement increased to five weeks. In 1989 RAGA agreed SOGAT women members be allowed reasonable time off with pay for cervical and breast cancer screening checks at the recommended intervals.

PHOTOGRAVURE PERIODICALS

In 1960 the Photogravure Periodical Agreement covered Odham Press, Watford, Sun Printers, Watford and Eric Bemrose, Liverpool. In that year negotiations took place between the three companies on the one hand and the NUPB&PW, NATSOPA and the TA on the other. Major concessions gained from the employers included three weeks' paid holiday and a 40-hour working week. In 1965, after a failure to agree on the trade union side to a further tripartite approach, a meeting was ultimately arranged with the employers. However, they would not negotiate collectively and the claim had to be pursued individually with each firm. The three companies insisted the unions act collectively in negotiating house agreements rather than have in each company three separate sets of negotiations and three separate agreements. When the unions were unable in 1966 to persuade the three firms to continue the Photogravure Periodical Agreement, terms and conditions at Odhams, Sun Printers and Bemrose became subject to house agreements.

HER MAJESTY'S STATIONERY OFFICE (HMSO)

In 1966 SOGAT explored the possibility of negotiating a special agreement with HMSO in the light of that organisation's policy of following the pattern of agreements operated by employers' organisations catering for firms engaged on comparable work. The disadvantage to SOGAT from this policy was the difficulty of the HMSO accepting other terms than those agreed with other employers' organisations, especially the BFMP. It was not until the 1970s that SOGAT succeeded in persuading the HMSO to negotiate house agreements. One covered members employed in the presses and binderies, a second those working in warehouses and garages and the third those employed in HMSO bookshops. In 1977 SOGAT balloted its members employed by the HMSO to ascertain if they wished to continue to be regulated by house agreements. The regional bookshop chapels had already decided to continue with a house agreement. The Presses and Binderies members voted 538 to 399 to continue with a house agreement. The warehouses and garages members voted 645 to 325 against continuation of a house agreement. Six months' notice was given to the HMSO to terminate the House Agreement covering these members.

The HMSO conceded four weeks' paid holidays to its press and binderies and warehouse and garage employees from 1 July 1973. This entitlement was increased to four weeks and three days in 1988. In 1975 the three existing House Agreements were amended to provide for the implementation of equal pay as required under the Equal Pay Act (1970). The equal opportunities clause, contained in the 1975 HMSO Presses and Binderies House Agreement stated:

The parties to this agreement are committed to the development of positive policies to promote equal opportunities in employment regardless of workers' sex, marital status, creed, colour, race or ethnic origins. This principle will apply in respect of all conditions of work, including pay, hours of work, holiday entitlement, overtime, shift work, work allocation, sick pay, pensions, recruitment, training, promotion and redundancy.

If any employee considers that he or she is suffering from unequal treatment on the grounds of sex, marital status, creed, colour, race or ethnic origins he or she may make a complaint which will be dealt with through the agreed procedures for dealing with grievances.[5]

In 1990 the Presses and Binderies and Bookshop Agreements saw paid maternity leave increased to 14 weeks. In addition, two days' paternity leave to be taken at the time of the baby's birth or soon afterwards was introduced. At the same time, the long-standing arrangements whereby employees getting married for the first time were granted up to five days' special leave ceased.

In 1980, the HMSO reformed its incentive payments system. The established HMSO method of calculating payment for a standard performance in incentives – 28½ per cent of group rate – had led to difficulties in the past, whilst differing practices in the Manchester press were another anomaly. To conform with normal industry practice, bonus for standard performance was in the future based on one-third of a bonus calculator in all work-measured schemes. This system was also introduced to the Regional Bookshops' and Warehouses and Garages' Agreements. The levels of calculator in the three Agreements, however, were different. In the Press and Binderies Agreement the level was £71.04 in the provinces and £73 in London. In the Regional Bookshop Agreement it was set at £69, whilst in the Warehouses and Garages Agreements the levels varied between £64 and £71 in London and between £62 and £69 in the provinces. In 1988 the introduction in the presses and binderies of productivity schemes which reflected sales or volume and service saw the end of traditional work-measured schemes and with it the end of the bonus calculator rate.[6] The new schemes used formulae to calculate performance which was translated into bonus earnings by reference to a productivity index table.

At the time SOGAT merged with the NGA the weekly wage rate for Group 3 in regional bookshops was of £172.37. For Group 2 employees the rate was £168.49 per week. New trainees recruited at 19 or over received 80 per cent of the adult rate during their 12 weeks' training. The payment of the adult rate at 19 had been conceded by the HMSO in 1990. In the presses and binderies in 1991 the weekly rate for craft employees in London was £183.30 and in the provinces £180.00. Machine Assistants received 87.5 per cent of the basic craft rate and machine extras.

SCREEN PRINTING[7]

Silk screen printers' work is highly visible. From posters on city hoardings and supermarket advertising displays to illuminated vehicle dashboards and computer control panels, high-quality screen printing forms a background to people's everyday lives. Screen printers were originally organised by the Sign and Display Trades' Union which merged with NATSOPA in 1973. The diversity of screen printing was enormous. It was a craft trade and not, as sometimes suggested, 'the Mickey Mouse side of the printing industry'. By the late 1980s modern technology had transformed the trade. Print runs were longer and new applications were being developed.

The principle of silk screen printing was that it works as a stencil. The 'screen' itself was a fine mesh through which printing ink was squeezed. Parts were blanked out while ink passed through gaps in the other areas onto the product. While the old methods were fairly basic, silk screen experienced a period of technological change and development. There was in 1991 a range of automatic or semi-automatic machines, usually incorporating ultra-violet driers. Modern origination methods produced high-quality half tones and sophisticated four-colour work. Silk screen could print on almost any material – fabrics, wallpaper, glass, metal, wood and plastics as well as paper. It could handle solid materials such as drinking mugs and keyboards, thick card or plastic sheets, which were difficult for ordinary printing presses to accommodate. Screen printers also did specialised work for the motor car industry producing printed dashboard panels and fascia units for companies such as Ford, General Motors and Audi. They printed the touch panels for equipment like computers and microwave ovens.

Silk screen printing's low profile in SOGAT belied in its importance. In 1991 there were 2,500 screen printing companies in the UK, but most were small. The vast majority were members of the Display Producers and Screen Printers' Association which negotiated an industry-wide agreement with SOGAT. The Association became, in 1990 the Screen Printers' Association (UK) Ltd. The skills of SOGAT members employed in screen printing included camera operators, production artists and screen technicians. Some artists were known in the industry as 'cardboard' engineers because of the intricate and creative advertising displays they designed from printed card.

In 1985 in screen printing the craft grades received £89.50 per week. The highest-paid groups were production artists and camera operators, with a basic rate of £97 per week. Display showcard and ticket writers and automatic screen print technicians received a basic wage of £95.50 per week. There was an apprenticeship ratio of one apprentice or junior to every three production artists, every three display showcard and ticket writers, and every three screen process printers. In 1985 the standard working week in the industry was 38 hours and the holiday entitlement, agreed in 1976 was two weeks.

When SOGAT ceased to be an independent union, the number of grades of employees covered in the National Agreement had been reduced from six to five. The re-structuring, undertaken in 1990 was designed to reward craft operatives for taking full responsibility themselves for the quality of their work. From 1990 the holiday entitlement had been five weeks paid on the basis of average weekly earnings. The Screen Printers' Agreement provided entitlement for two days' bereavement leave and two days' paternity leave. SOGAT had requested that all overtime work be paid at double time instead of double time after the first three hours of overtime. In 1990 however, the employers agreed overtime worked on a Saturday be paid at double time after the first two hours. By late 1991 the weekly rate for production artists, camera operators, display showcard and ticket writers, computerised graphic equipment and auto screen print technicians was £147. The rate for screen print technicians, computerised lettering equipment operators and craft grades was £140 per week. Semi-skilled grades had a basic rate of £135 per week.

THE FLAT GLASS INDUSTRY

Industrial relations in the flat glass industry were regulated by a National Joint Council. A National Labour Agreement, commonly known as the 'Green Book' was the main collective agreement. Annual holiday entitlement became 22 working days from 1 March 1987 but was increased in 1991 by one extra day for employees who had completed 15 consecutive years' service with one employer. In January 1989 new job classifications were introduced as follows: craftsmen, multi-skilled craftsmen, advanced craftsmen A, B and C and special advanced craftsmen. All these grades had completed manual training to standards laid down in the National Joint Council's 1987 manual of training. Following alterations to the National Labour Agreement, in 1991 the hourly rate for special advanced craftsmen varied from £3.97 to £4.30, for advanced craftsmen A from £3.83 to £4.16, for multi-skilled craftsmen from £3.59 to £3.90 and for craftsmen from £3.42 to £3.71.

THE EXHIBITION INDUSTRY

The industrial relations of the exhibition industry were governed by a National Joint Council which oversaw the operation of the Working Rule Agreement. As from September 1990 the hourly rate for craft operatives was £5.98 per hour, for labourers £5.38, for signwriters £6.15, for production artists £6.27, for copyists or copy negative makers £6.15 and for a horizontal enlarger operator £6.27. In addition, the lodging allowance was £22.50 per night, sickness benefit per week was £79.80 whilst operatives injured at work and unable to work after 16 weeks received a sum of £50 per week for a period of 104 weeks (two years). In 1990 the Joint Council for the Exhibition Industry agreed to undertake, without prejudice, an examination of the Working Rule Agreement to produce an agreement more reflective of the industry's needs in the 1990s. The review was to be completed no later than 31 March 1991, and to ensure progress was on schedule an independent monitor was appointed.

THE PUBLISHERS' ASSOCIATION

For many years the London Central Branch held an agreement with the Book Publishers' Association. However, in the 1950s a number of the publishers relocated their operations to the Home Countries, thus moving outside the scope of the LCB agreement, which only covered a 15-mile radius from Charing Cross. In 1960 the NUPB&PW approached the Publishers' Association to discuss the possibility of an industry-wide agreement for its members employed by the Publishers' Association outside the 15-mile London radius. The Publishers' Association agreed to extend the terms of the London Agreement to 15 miles from the end of the 15-mile radius from Charing Cross. There were now two Book Publishing Agreements. One covered London, for which the LCB was responsible, and one the provinces, which was the responsibility of the NUPB&PW. To avoid two separate sets of negotiations, the LCB and the NUPB&PW negotiated together, doing their own work for their own members inside their area. The two Agreements covered packers, van drivers, checkers, dispatchers, invoicers, porters and liftmen. The first Provincial Agreement operated from 1 July 1962 until 30 June 1964 and contained minimum wages levels and a cost of living bonus.

In 1966 the Publishers' Association extended the limits of the Provincial Agreement to 100 miles from the centre of London. SOGAT (Division A) wanted to extend the limits further but the Publishers' Association was anxious to tackle the extension of the Provincial Agreement one step at a time. They refused to commit themselves to an extension beyond the 100 miles. The boundary was permissive in that firms within it could, if they wished, become parties to the Provincial Agreement. Nevertheless, the Publishers' Association strongly encouraged publishing firms in the provinces to become parties to the Provincial Agreement and a number of firms, including the Pergamon Press at Oxford, did so. In 1968 SOGAT (Division A) requested the whole country, other than London, be covered by the Publishers' Association/NUPB&PW Agreement. The Association sought the views of its members on this request and suggested the extension to a nation-wide policy should be on a voluntary basis. SOGAT accepted the suggestion as a good start to what subsequently became a nation-wide (except for London) agreement.

In 1974 SOGAT sought from the Publishers' Association a National Clerical Agreement. Strong opposition was met from the Association on the grounds that other unions were also seeking recognition as the appropriate union for clerical workers within Publishers' Association offices. SOGAT responded by starting talks with the National Union of Journalists for a joint approach to the Association for a recognition and procedural agreement covering non-manual employees in book publishing. SOGAT never achieved recognition for the clerical areas of book publishing.

In 1967 the London and provincial manual agreements saw the granting of three weeks' paid holiday for employees with at least two years' service with the same firm. In April 1969 the service qualification for paid holiday was reduced to one year and the Publishers' Association agreed to pay holiday pay at average earnings. In 1971 the Publishers' Association granted a fourth week's paid holiday entitlement implemented in two stages for employees with more than one year's service with the same employer. Three additional days were given in 1972 and a further two days in 1973. In 1980 holiday entitlement was increased to 21 working days and in 1983 to 23 working days. 1985 saw the granting of a further day's paid holiday entitlement and the following year five weeks' paid holiday was implemented in book publishing.

In 1975 the 40-hour standard working week was introduced into book publishing but its implementation was delayed in return for the £6 per week supplementary payment permitted under the Government's voluntary pay restraint introduced in July 1975. In April 1978 the standard working week was reduced to 38¾ hours and then from 1 October 1978 to 38 hours. 1989 saw the Publishers' Association grant reasonable time off with pay for attendance at breast and/or cervical cancer clinics as well as conceding three days' paid bereavement leave in the event of the death of a parent, legal guardian, spouse or child. At the same time, they also conceded paid time off for SOGAT members to attend anti-natal clinics and three days' paid paternity leave on the occasion of the birth of a child by the member's spouse. In 1990 a sick pay scheme was introduced and provided, after the satisfactory completion of 12 months' service, for each employee 10 days' paid sickness leave per annum, inclusive of statutory sick pay. In 1991, the Publishers' Association/SOGAT Agreement was revised to provide a clause providing for equal opportunities for disabled people covering training, promotion, recruitment and their special needs.

In 1970 the Publishers' Association conceded without great difficulty the principle of equal pay to those women doing jobs referred to in the male agreement. Equal pay was implemented in three stages. Initially, women received 87½ per cent of the male rate. The rate increased to 90 per cent in November 1970, to 95 per cent in November 1971 and to 100 per cent in November 1972. At the time of SOGAT's merger with the NGA, the basic weekly rate in a book publishing house was £134.78, whilst the supplementary allowance, which had been introduced in 1978 for drivers and operators of sophisticated machinery varied from £0.49 to £2.06 in the case of the former and from £2.59 to £5.19 in the case of the latter. In 1991 SOGAT and the Publishers' Association committed themselves to reducing unit costs to improve performance and to identify, discuss and implement changes necessary to achieve increased output. No redundancies were to take place as a direct result of the introduction of changes in working practices without due consultation with all parties involved.

REMPLOY[8]

Remploy, a government-supported company formed in 1946 provided full-time employment for severely disabled people. It was publicly owned with the Government providing investment capital and an operating subsidy. The Government appointed the Remploy chairman and directors, including two trade union representatives nominated by the TUC. Since its formation. Remploy had developed into a large, successful, commercial company with significant growth in sales and productivity. SOGAT, and previously the NUPB&PW, was one of an eight-union consortium which negotiated collectively a Remploy National Agreement which covered 7,500 disabled people in 1974 and nearly 9,000 in 1990. SOGAT had 600 members employed in Remploy's printing and binding division.

In 1963 SOGAT members employed by Remploy gained a reduction from 4 September in their standard working week from 42 hours to 41 hours with no reduction in weekly time rate earnings. Twelve months later the standard week was reduced to 40 hours. In March 1980 standard working week was reduced to 39 hours and then in 1983 to 38 hours. From September 1987 the standard working week became 37½ hours, giving parity between Remploy and BPIF houses. In 1968 a paid annual holiday entitlement of up to 12 working days was introduced. From April 1969, three weeks' paid annual holiday operated. Four weeks' holiday plus eight statutory days was introduced in 1978 whilst an additional day was granted in 1981. Two years later paid annual holiday entitlement rose to 22 days, but with management having discretion to close Remploy factories for two weeks between 1 May and 30 September and up to one week to cover the Christmas and New Year holiday period. 1988 saw a further enhancement of holiday entitlement when employees with more than five years' service became entitled to five weeks' paid annual holidays. For those with five years' service or less the entitlement remained unchanged at 22 days.

On 1 January 1966 a sick pay scheme was introduced for Remploy employees. Eligibility was based on continuous service and benefit paid for proven days of illness or injury after the first three working days lost. To qualify for sick pay allowance Remploy employees required a minimum of 12 months' service. For employees with more than one year's service but less than five, the allowance was paid for two weeks. For those employees with more than five years' service but less than ten, the allowance was payable for three weeks, and for those with over ten years' service for four weeks. In 1969 the condition in the scheme disqualifying employees from payment of sick pay for the first three working days of any one period of illness was amended to apply only to one illness in any period of 12 months. In 1978 improvements were made in the sick pay scheme so that it provided for five weeks' allowance for employees with more than one but less than four years' service, for eight weeks' allowance for those with more than four but less than eight years' service, and for ten weeks for those with eight years' service and over. There were further improvements in 1988. Those with over three months' service but less than four years received allowance for six weeks, those with more than four but less than eight years' service were to have the sick pay allowance for ten weeks, and those with more than eight years' service for 13 weeks. The three months' minimum service with Remploy to qualify for sick pay allowance had been introduced in 1987, having been reduced from 12 months to six months in 1984.

In 1978 a new pension scheme was negotiated for Remploy employees. The scheme provided a pension related to the state pension and the employee's final salary. At the same time, a death in-service benefit of £750 was introduced over the period 1978 to 1991. This benefit progressively improved and in 1991 it stood at £3,500. In 1981 the compassionate leave regulations were amended to include provision for paternity leave. In 1984 Remploy granted its employees three days' paternity leave upon the birth of a child to the wife of an employee. Nineteen eighty-nine saw the introduction of paid time off for employees to attend cancer screening clinics. The 1991 Remploy National Agreement provided for pre-retirement leave under which special leave with pay was granted to all employees in their final year of service prior to normal retirement age based on one day for each year of completed service.

In April 1974 the basic weekly rate for Remploy adult males in the provinces was £20.37 and £20.87 in London. The corresponding rates for adult women were £19.12 and £19.62 respectively. On 1 April 1975 equal pay became fully established in Remploy with a basic weekly adult rate of £30 in the provinces and £36 in London. Ten years later the basic weekly rate in the Provinces was £74.30 and in London £84.74. At the time of SOGAT's merger with the NGA the basic weekly rate was £115.40 and the London differential had been eliminated. In 1983 the overtime premium was increased from time and a quarter to time and one-third for the first two hours of overtime each weekday. Twelve months later the premium increased to time and a half after the first two hours of overtime each weekday.

By the late 1980s, however, SOGAT Remploy employees were

becoming dissatisfied with the size of pay increases received. The 1989 National Agreement was only narrowly accepted, reflecting their continuing resentment at the government's refusal to fund Remploy so the wage resulting from an agreed formula between the Remploy unions and management could be paid. The formula gave an average of the annual pay increases gained by workers in the industries covered by Remploy. During the 1990/1 negotiations, Remploy employees rejected the first two wage proposals made to them. A third ballot was held of the members of the consortium unions and showed an overwhelming decision in favour of industrial action short of a strike to further their claim for an improved wage offer. SOGAT Remploy members voted overwhelmingly for this action and received the full support of the NEC and branches covering Remploy plants.

Following the ballot result a meeting was held with the Parliamentary Committee for the Disabled and although only Labour MPs were in attendance there was representation made to the Minister responsible for the disabled. The point was made that the Government's action of reducing the subsidy to Remploy was the main reason for workers receiving wages below those of outside industries even though the company's sales figures for 1990 had reached the £100m target. On 30 July 1990, with the proposed industrial action due to start the next day, ACAS arranged a meeting between Remploy and the eight unions at which an acceptable improved offer was made. This was approved by a majority of the unions' membership, both of the Consortium and SOGAT. This improved offer included an increase in basic wages in two stages, to give a basic rate for 1990 of £105.91 per week for 37½ hours and one day's extra holiday for all employees. All employees, with up to five years' service, received one day's extra holiday from 1991. SOGAT and the other seven union's made it clear that although the settlement had been accepted it did not correct the injustice of the rates of pay which Remploy should be paying under the Agreement in order for employees' wages to be comparable with the rates in the industries covered by Remploy's areas of work.

OTHER PAPERMAKING EMPLOYERS

Vellum and Parchment

Vellum and parchment production existed before printing was invented. Vellum parchments were inscribed by monks, who were amongst the most educated of the community. By the late 1950s the number of NUPB&PW members involved in vellum and parchment production was comparatively few and by 1969 the number had fallen to six. Production was concentrated at William Cowley Ltd in Newport Pagnell and the wage negotiations were led by the NUPB&PW/ SOGAT (Division A) President. However, by the early 1970s vellum and parchment production had to all intents and purpose ceased to exist.

Paper Tube Manufacturing

This industry was centred around Castleton in Lancashire. The Paper Tube Manufacturers' Association consisted of companies which manufactured paper tubes mainly for the cotton industry. Its member firms made the small spools which were sold in the shops loaded with thread and also made the paper cones used for the spindles on looms. Its membership was largely centred in Castleton and collective bargaining took place between the Paper Tube Manufacturers' Association and the NUPB&PW Castleton Branch assisted by Miss Whewell, a NUPB&PW Organiser. Negotiations in the 1950s and 1960s were tough because the industry's fortune fell as the cotton industry entered terminal decline. In 1958 an application to the employers' association for an increase in wages was totally rejected but when NUPB&PW threatened to take the issue to the Industrial Disputes Tribunal negotiations re-opened. The employers then made an acceptable increase of 19p to 25p per week for men and 17½p per week for women working on machines.

In 1959 the NUPB&PW Castleton Branch made an approach to the Paper Tube Manufacturers' Association for a 40-hour week. This was rejected by the employers although they granted a 5 per cent wage increase. However, in 1961 Tom Smith, as the new NUPB&PW General Secretary, intervened and secured an invitation to lunch to which he was accompanied by the Organiser (Miss Whewell) and the Castleton Branch secretary and by a small number of employers' representatives. The Branch was seeking half an hour off the 42½-hour standard working week and this was secured at the lunch meeting. The NUPB&PW indicated that they would be seeking further reductions of hours of work at a later stage together with increases in wages. Unfortunately, redundancies soon occurred in the industry and it was 1965 before a further reduction in working hours was raised. In 1965 a wage increase was obtained together with a reduction in the standard working week to 40 hours in two stages – to 41 hours in January 1966 and to 40 hours in January 1967. In addition, an extra day's paid holiday was granted by the employers with effect from the 1965/6 holiday year. However, the introduction of the 40-hour working week was delayed by the Government statutory incomes policy introduced in July 1966. The 40-hour week became operative in 1968.

Papermould and Dandy Roll Makers

The making of dandy rolls was a highly specialised job and the Papermould and Dandy Roll Makers' Society joined NUPB&PW in 1962 as a national branch of that union. Collective bargaining was between the Association of Dandy Roll and Mould Makers and the NUPB&PW/SOGAT (Division A) Papermould and Dandy Roll Makers' Branch. In June 1963 negotiations established hourly rates for a 42-hour working week of between 28p and 30p for skilled adult males. Semi-skilled workers received a percentage which varied from 70 per cent to 80 per cent of the craft rate. Relations between the employers' association and the former Papermould and Dandy Roll Makers' Society had deteriorated to the point where they were no longer able to sit down together. However, a constructive relationship was quickly established between the NUPB&PW and the Association of Dandy Roll and Mould Makers.

At a meeting held in March 1966 the employers expressed their general satisfaction at the manner in which SOGAT (Division A) members had operated under the National Agreement, particularly in respect of improved productivity. The employers offered £1 extra per week for craft employees with consequential increases for semi-skilled employees and apprentices. The employers stressed that 50p of the £1 increase compensated for increases in the cost of living and the other 50p was intended to bring the wages of the skilled workers to a position more reflective of their skills. The employers also agreed to implement the 40-hour working week. The union, however, gave notice to raise the question of additional holidays in the 1967 wage negotiations. In the event, these negotiations took place against the background of an industry in economic difficulties and the union accepted a pay increase offer of 1p per hour for all adult males with proportionate increases for apprentices and trainees. A 1p per hour increase was also granted to skilled women workers.

In 1968 a claim was made to the Association of Dandy Roll and Mould Makers covering three weeks' paid holiday payable at average earnings, improved rates for apprentices and trainees and time and a quarter for double day shift. The 1969 Agreement provided for two additional days of paid holiday to be taken as required by arrangement with management, 43 hours' pay for a 40-hour week, apprentice and trainee rates to increase by 5 per cent and for time and a quarter to be paid for double day shift. The employers agreed to a £1 a week increase for men and women, to time and a third being paid for shift work and to three weeks' paid holiday. The Agreement operated for two years.

Drawing Office Material Manufacturers and Dealers' Association (DOMMDA)

In 1960 the DOMMDA/NUPB&PW National Agreement provided for an increase of 5 per cent in basic pay, a reduction in the length of working week to 42½ hours and absorption of part of the cost of living bonus into the new basic rate. The minimum adult rate was payable at 25 but this was reduced to 21 in 1962 which was also the date the working week was reduced to 42 hours. A further reduction to 41 hours became operative in July 1965 whilst the 40-hour week was achieved in 1966. Paid holiday entitlement was also improved by granting one day's holiday for every month of service up to one year. Employees with over 12 months' service were entitled to 12 days' paid holiday. The 1968 wage negotiations secured three weeks' paid holiday entitlement by stages in that one extra day was given in 1969, a further day in 1970 and another day in 1972. A fourth week's paid holiday was implemented in July 1974.

In 1965 the cost of living bonus was incorporated into basic rates and that bonus discontinued. In 1962 the DOMMADA/NUPB&PW National Agreement provided for a London rate, a rate for provincial centres with populations of 100,000 and another rate for centres with populations of less than 100,000. The 1970 wage negotiations saw the merging of two provincial grades into one by the abolition of the rate for provincial centres with populations of less than 100,000. Parity for workers in this category with those in the higher provincial grade was gained progressively, with full parity achieved in July 1973. Equal pay became fully effective on 1 January 1974 having been phased in over three years. In 1966 overtime premium became time and a quarter for the first two hours of overtime with time and a half for the next three hours and then double time up to eight hours. In 1971 the first two hours of overtime became payable at time and one-third.

INK MANUFACTURING[9]

In 1989 ink manufacture employed some 5,000 people in managerial, clerical, distribution, technical and production occupations. The industry spanned a range of companies from small firms to multinational corporations. The majority of these firms were affiliated to the Society of British Printing Ink Manufacturers (SBPIM) which held a National Agreement with SOGAT and had held one for many years previously with NATSOPA. The biggest ink manufacturer in Britain, and the third largest in the world, was Coates/Lorilleaux, formed by a merger between the former Coates Group and the French-based Lorilleaux International. The basis of ink-making was simple – take the pigment (a coloured powder) and grind it together with a binding agent (usually some form of varnish). The colour of ink depended on the mixing of the pigments. The finish, consistency and drying qualities depend on the varnish. This in turn varied according to the mixture of resins and oil, such as linseed oil, from which it was made. Printing inks came in either liquid (running) or 'paste' (thick) form. Special grades were required to suit different printing methods – letterpress or litho, coldset or heatset, flexographic, gravure, silk screen, etc.

In addition to production workers SOGAT also represented a wide range of other staff, including clerical and technician grades where key groups were laboratory and instrument technicians. SOGAT had 200 members in ink manufacturing whose main work was in research, development and quality control. Another specialised group, separate though closely allied to the ink-makers, was the roller-making section and those servicing the rollers on printing machines.

The main agreement regulating the production side of ink manufacture was that between SOGAT and the Society of British Printing Ink Manufacturers. In May 1983 adult rates varied from £85.99 to £88.60 per week and those for youth workers from £43.13 to £77.63 per week. By 1 May 1990 the grade rate was £133.48 per week. From 1 July 1983 basic paid holiday entitlement under the Agreement was 23 working days, but this increased to 25 working days (five weeks) from July 1985. The standard working week was reduced to 38 hours in 1985, subject to changes in operational arrangements. The 1989 negotiations between

SOGAT and the SBPIM saw the introduction of up to three days' bereavement leave for the death of a parent, legal guardian, spouse or child, subject to permission being granted by the employer (but no request would be unreasonably withheld). In addition, companies were recommended to provide proper and adequate pension arrangements for their manual employees. The 1990 review of the National Agreement saw the employers agree to the introduction of three days' paid leave of absence for paternity reasons. A national sick pay scheme was operated by SBPIM members. In 1984 the method of calculating sick pay changed to include an employee's gross average earnings during the previous quarter for the calculation of a normal week. After this calculation sick pay was paid at 90 per cent or 50 per cent of pay less income tax, national insurance contributions and pension contributions. Nineteen eighty-eight saw a further amendment to the scheme so that waiting time for the payment of SBPIM sick pay was reduced from the first three to the first two consecutive working days of each period of certified sickness. Two years later the SBPIM agreed with SOGAT that the qualifying service for eligibility for sick pay under the scheme be reduced to six months unbroken employment in the same SBPIM company and the waiting time for payment of sick pay be reduced to one day for certified sickness.

CONCLUSION

So we have reached the end or our analysis of the evolution and develpment of SOGAT and its constituent societies. It has been a history of adaption to changes in technology, economic and political factors via amalgamation and changes in working practices. But at all times a democratic structure based on membership control has been maintained.

NOTES

1. See 'Scottish Employers Break Pledge on Negotiations' *SOGAT Journal*, February 1978, p. 3 and 'The Scottish Master Printers' Dispute' *SOGAT Journal*, March 1978, p. 3.
2. See Society of Graphical and Allied Trades *Annual Report of the National Executive Council, 1990/1*, p. 14.
3. See Society of Graphical and Allied Trades *Annual Report of the National Executive Council, 1975*, p. 15.
4. See Society of Graphical and Allied Trades *Annual Report of the National Executive*

Council, 1974, p. 8.

5. See Society of Graphical and Allied Trades, *Annual Report of the National Executive Council, 1975*, pp. 31–2.

6. The bonus calculator rate continued with the Bookshops Agreement. In 1991 it stood at £102.47 in London bookshops and between £77.77 and £86.48 in the provinces.

7. See 'Recognise the Skills of Silk Screen' *SOGAT Journal*, May 1989, pp. 6–8.

8. For detailed information on Remploy see 'Remploy – It's Time to Fight for a Living Wage' *SOGAT Journal*, March 1974, p. 5 and 'Jobs and Skills for Disabled People' *SOGAT Journal*, February 1990, pp. 14 and 15.

9. For background information on SOGAT's ink-makers see 'Meet the Ink Makers' *SOGAT Journal*, September 1989, pp. 12–14.

APPENDIX I

NATIONAL OFFICIALS OF NUPB&PW AND SOGAT (1955–91)

GENERAL SECRETARY

Bill Morrison (1947–60)
Tom Smith (1960–70)
Vincent Flynn (1970–4)
Bill Keys (1974–85)
Owen O'Brien (1982–3)
   (Joint Gen. Sec.)
Brenda Dean (1985–91)

GENERAL PRESIDENT

John McKenzie (–1967)
Vincent Flynn (1967–70)
Bill Keys (1970–4)
Albert Powell (1974–83)
Brenda Dean (1983–5)
Danny Sergeant (1985–91)

ORGANISING SECRETARY

Frank Axtell (–1962)
Vincent Flynn (1962–7)
Albert Powell (1967–74)
Hugh Finlay (1974–86)
John Mitchell (1986–91)

PAPERMAKING SECRETARY

Eddie White (–1968)
John O'Leary (1968–85)
George Beattie (1985–91)

GENERAL OFFICERS

Bill Miles (1972–87)
John Moakes (1982–6)
Teddie O'Brien (1982–4)
John Pointing (1982–4)
John Selby (1982–4)

DIVISIONAL OFFICERS

Danny Sergeant (1975–9)
Fred Smith (1975–84)
John Pointing (1975–9)

Danny Sergeant (1982–5)
Fred Smith (1984–91)
Ted Chard (1986–91)
Bob Gillespie (1988–91)

NATIONAL OFFICERS

Danny Sergeant (1980–2)
John Pointing (1980–2)

APPENDIX II

THE SOGAT FAMILY TREE, 1955–91

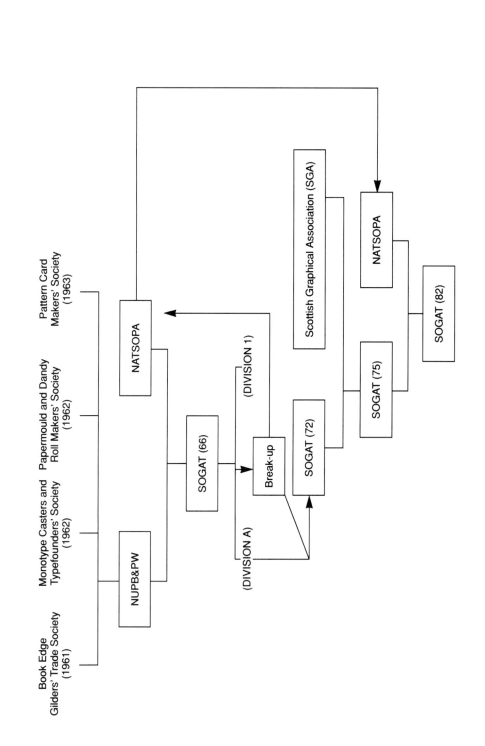

INDEX

657

INDEX

INDEX